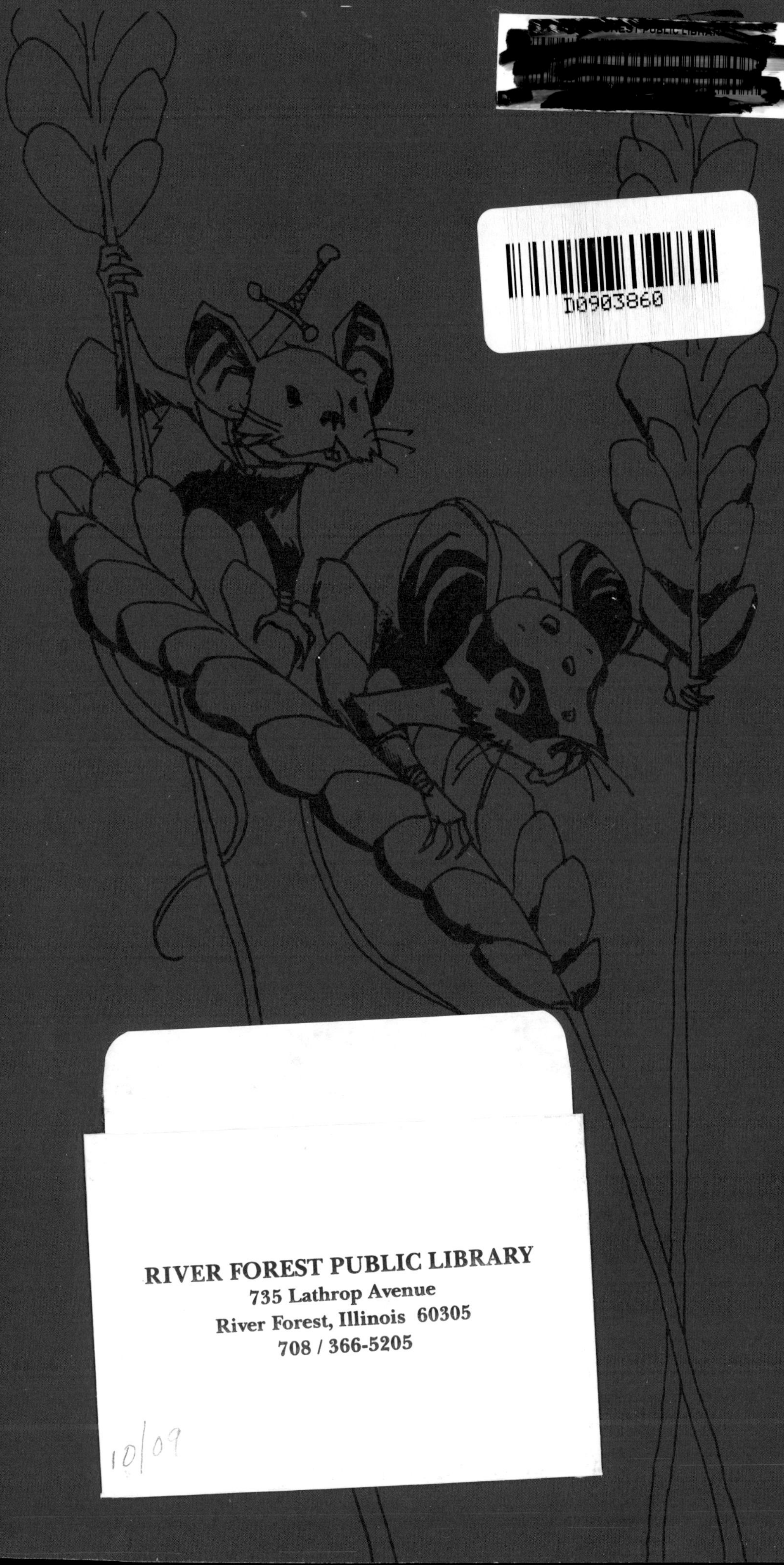

THE
PROPHECY

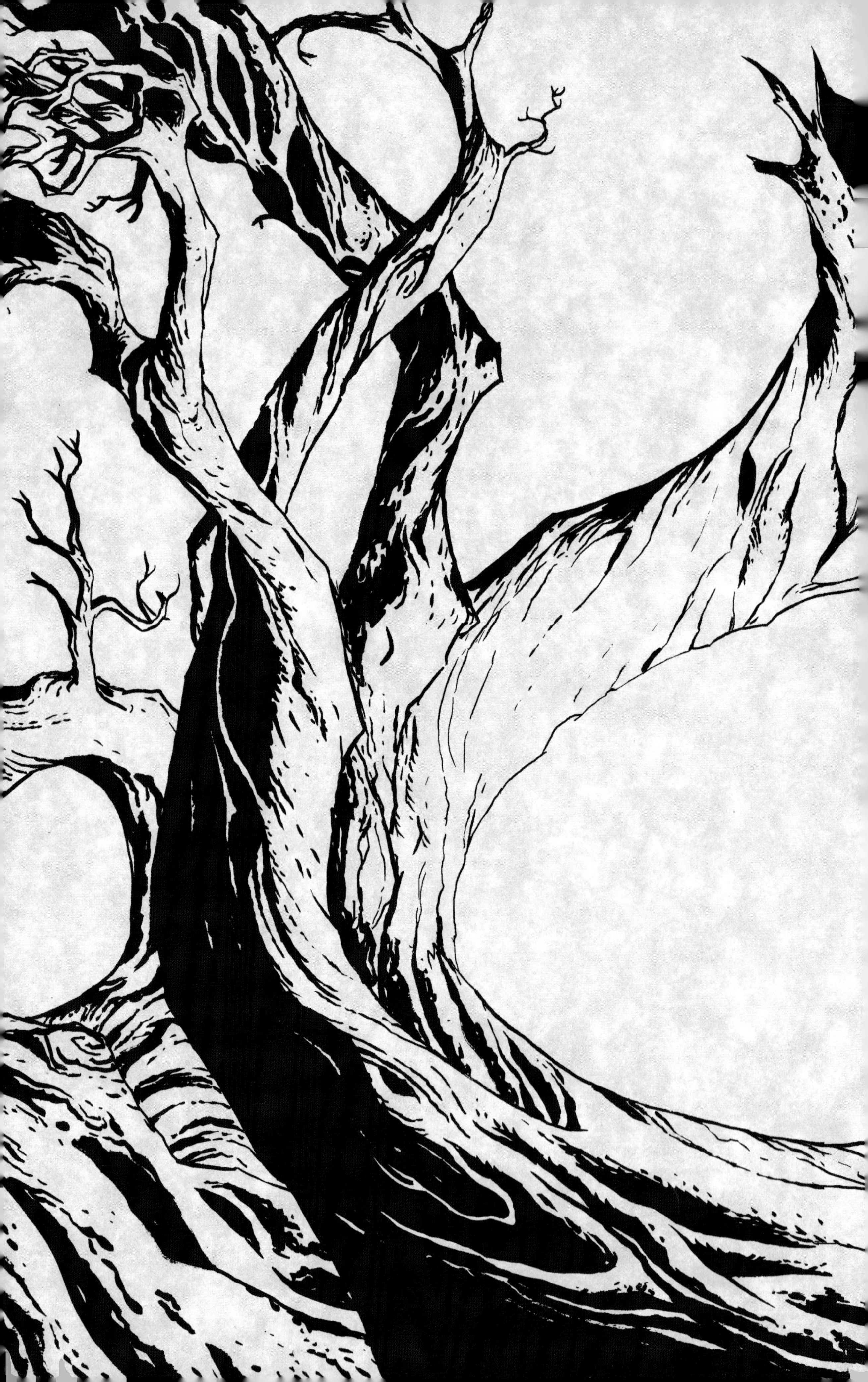

VOLUME ONE

THE
PROPHECY

CREATED BY
BRYAN J.L. GLASS &
MICHAEL AVON OEMING

STORY BY
Glass & Oeming

WRITTEN BY
Bryan J.L. Glass

ART BY
Michael Avon Oeming

COLORS BY
Wil Quintana

LETTERING BY
James H. Glass

EDITING BY
Judy Glass

EDITORIAL ASSISTANCE BY
Will Swyer

INTERIOR PRODUCTION BY
Harry Lee

BOOK DESIGN BY
James H. Glass

PRODUCTION ASSISTANCE BY
Tim Daniel

ART ASSISTS BY
Taki Soma & John Broglia

COVER PAINTED BY
Michael Avon Oeming

LOGO BY
Oeming, Kristyn Ferretti & Daniel

RUNE TRANSLATIONS BY
Elizabeth Grasso

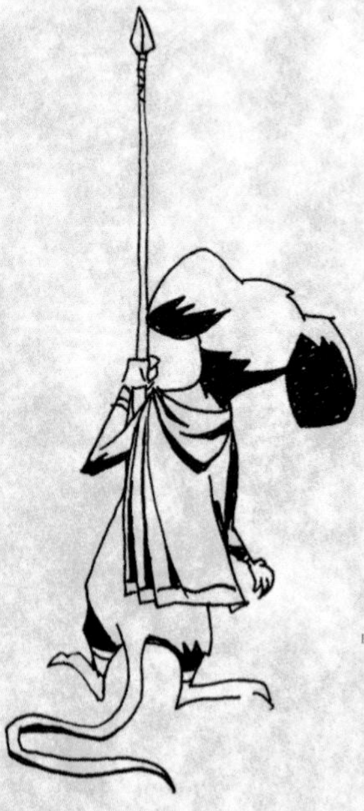

IMAGE COMICS, INC.

Robert Kirkman - Chief Operating Officer • Erik Larsen - Chief Financial Officer • Todd McFarlane - President
Marc Silvestri - Chief Executive Officer • Jim Valentino - Vice President

ericstephenson - Publisher • Joe Keatinge - PR & Marketing Coordinator • Branwyn Bigglestone - Accounts Manager
Tyler Shainline - Administrative Assistant • Traci Hui - Traffic Manager • Allen Hui - Production Manager
Drew Gill, Jonathan Chan, Monica Garcia - Production Artists

THE MICE TEMPLAR, VOL. 1: THE PROPHECY
ISBN: 978-1-58240-871-2
First Printing

Published by Image Comics, Inc. Office of publication: 1942 University Avenue, Suite 305, Berkeley, California 94704.

PRINTED IN CANADA

For Patricia Glass
Whose love gave Mornae
her voice.

—Bryan

For Ethan and Taki
Both of whom taught me
how to love and live again.

—Mike

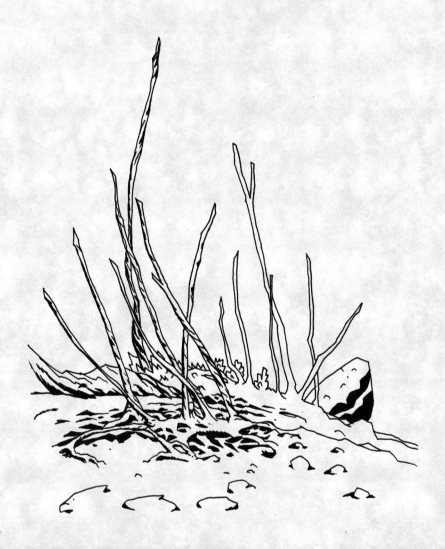

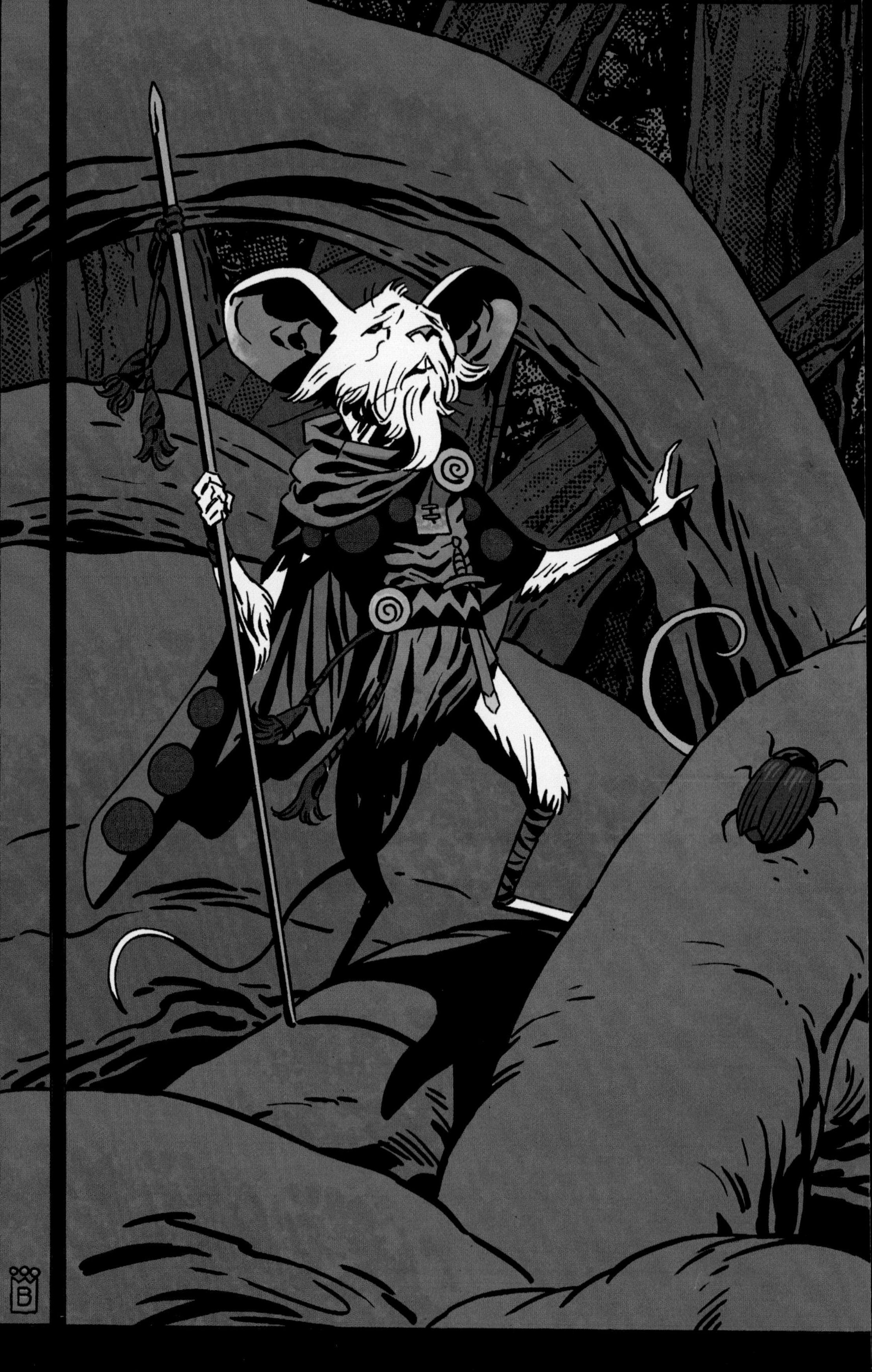

Illustration by Mark Buckingham
Colored by D'Israeli

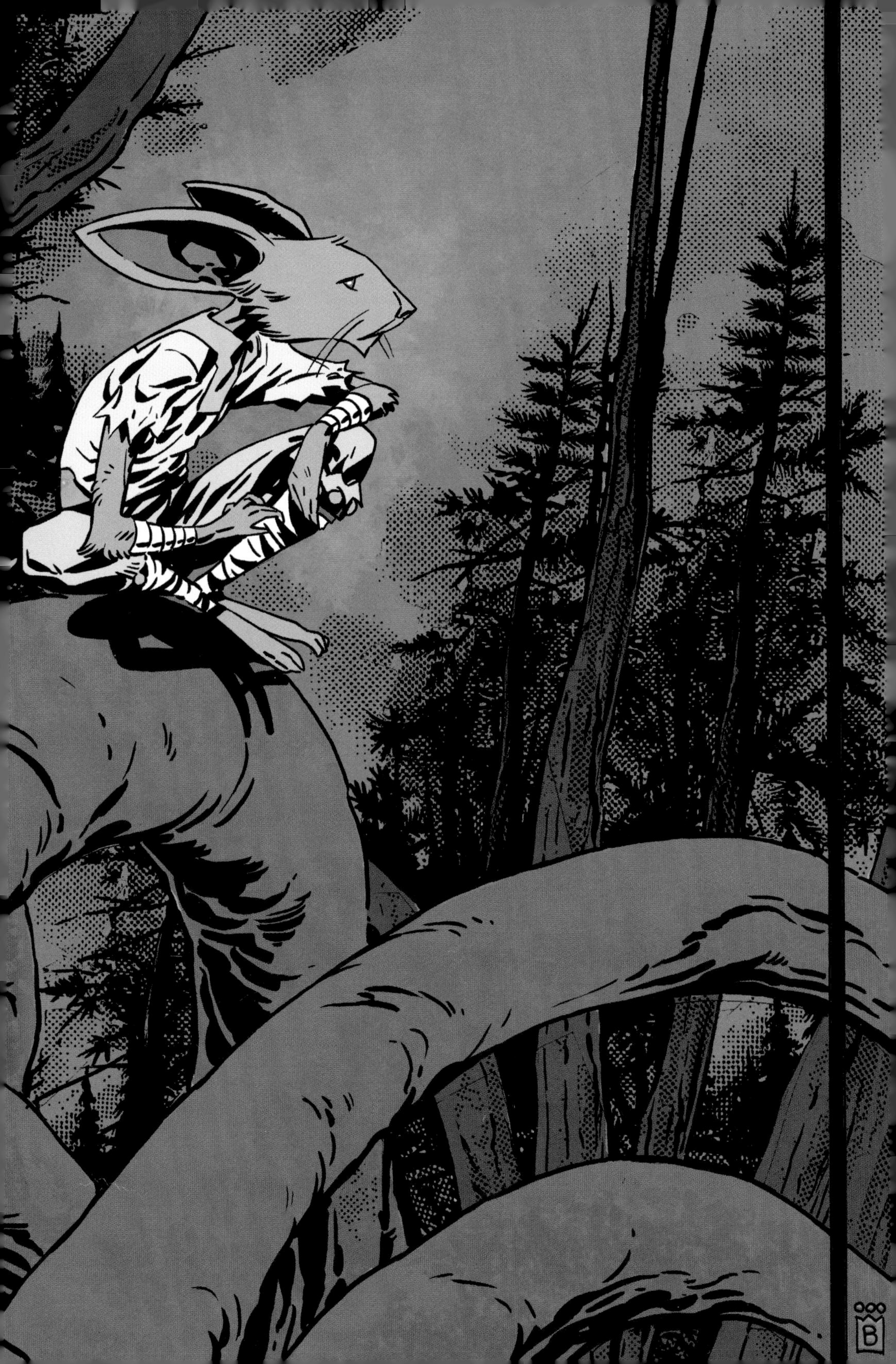

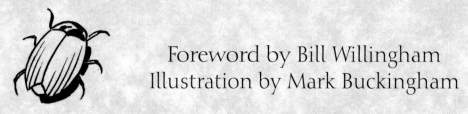

Foreword by Bill Willingham
Illustration by Mark Buckingham

The Sons of Reepicheep

I love talking animal stories, and there's plenty of evidence I'm not alone in this.

Ever read about a talking badger who exhibits bravery, feistiness and a ferocity in battle far above its stature? I have. I've even written one, a grizzled old veteran of many wars who'd often brag, "I can beat at least two of anything!" Pretty good line, huh? Perhaps my all time favorite children's book character was Rikki Tikki Tavi, Kipling's courageous mongoose who saves his adopted family by fighting off a pair of deadly vipers. It's easy to translate such animals into bold and daring fictional characters, because they really do have the qualities essential to good heroic adventure stories. In real life, a mongoose really will fight and (sometimes) kill venomous cobras (sometimes the cobra wins). Badgers actually are bold and daunting animals, who'll readily fight way above their weight class.

And sometimes one can get away with ascribing such qualities to an animal that doesn't normally possess them, as long as you can make the case that a specific member of said species was an exception to the rule. Even though the term "scaredy cat" generally fits, there are notable exceptions. My family once owned a big yellow tomcat who was the absolute terror of our neighborhood. He killed three large dogs in his lifetime (that we know of). Once he stoically came home, after winning such a battle, with his throat torn wide open. A huge flap of skin and fur hung down to the ground, revealing entirely too much torn muscle and other abused mechanics underneath. We took him to the vet, had him sewn up with far too many stitches, and in no time at all he was just fine. In fact, when the fur came back in over that wound, it was more silky smooth and glossy than ever, as if he was awarded a badge of valor celebrating his martial victory. So, it was no stretch to ennoble such a doughty creature in a talking animal adventure tale.

But this is a book about mice. What business does anyone have crafting adventure stories about mice?

Real mice aren't brave. Basically they're vermin that are usually ridden with other vermin. They breed too fast, infest too much, and should be wiped out whenever possible. (Old-fashioned mouse traps—the kind with the spring arm that breaks their spines—are still the best, by the way, but use a dab of peanut butter as bait, rather than a bit of cheese that can be too easily stolen without springing the trap.) They're the very definition of pests. They're tiny, short-lived, insignificant, timid beyond measure, and in the entire history of life on earth, there has never been so much as a single brave mouse. Not once.

So why so many stories about brave and noble talking mice? It makes no sense. It simply doesn't translate from real life.

Want to know my crackpot theory? Well, since this is my foreword, you're going to have to suffer through it anyway—unless of course you simply skip ahead to the actual story, which is always a perfectly acceptable practice for the wiser reader. Here's a dirty little secret: in the entire history of published literature, introductions have usually been boring and have never been essential or important, no matter what august personage someone corralled into writing one. Go ahead. Page forward and read the story. After all, it's what you bought this book for.

Now, for those of you still here (and why is that?), do you want to know my crackpot theory?

I think we may be paying off a debt.

Bear with me.

According to our best evidence to date, when the big cataclysm came that killed off the dinosaurs—along with vast swathes of other life on earth—tiny mammalian creatures not only survived, they flourished. They did so because they possessed all of the qualities we normally disdain and none of those we generally admire. These creatures, so much like modern mice as to qualify as same—call them proto-mice, if you will—were burrowers, and therefore escaped the worst of the climatic changes. They were small and therefore needed scant food to survive. They lived short lives, and this was a plus, because, for every generation of one of the larger dinosaurs, there were fifty or more generations of these ancestors of mice, making them fifty times more adaptable to the swift environmental changes that scourged the earth. And then, in the aftermath of that planet-wide extinction event, those mice of the ages emerged and spread out, filling empty ecological niches, growing and changing into a million new and different animals, one branch of which eventually became us.

See? We owe our very existence to the fact that we share a common ancestor with the humble and cowardly mouse.

Anyway, that's my theory. I warned you it was goofball, but yet you stayed to hear me out. Maybe we feel that debt enough to ascribe different, more humanly attractive qualities to the mice that inhabit our popular fantasy-adventure fiction. Whatever the reason, fictional mice embody everything that their factual counterparts are not.

Take Reepicheep.

He was the first example, at least in my personal voyage of discovery (and since this is, as I mentioned before, my foreword, we're going to go with my history), of the heroic mouse as swashbuckling adventurer. Reepicheep debuted, with remarkable flash and élan, in the second volume of C.S. Lewis' wonderful *Narnia Chronicles*. Reepicheep was a bold and dashing swordsmouse, with the heart of d'Artagnan, the stylish wit of Cyrano, and the cocky bravura of Robin Hood (the Errol Flynn version, if you please). And he possessed the pure martial fencing ability of the three combined. He may well have been the first hero mouse, but many others would follow.

In the funnybook world (*graphic novels* for you neophytes to the form who need to take your escapism seriously) we seem to be undergoing a bit

of a renaissance in heroic sword-wielding mouse stories. Why? Who can say? Perhaps they were all inspired by Reepicheep. Then again, in the time of steam engines, as someone once said, people build steam engines. Perhaps this is simply the time of swords-mouse comic books.

In my comic book series, *Fables*, we have the Mouse Police, who patrol distant Smalltown, keeping it safe from the outside world. David Petersen brings us the adventures of the noble *Mouse Guard*. And then there are the subjects of this volume, *The Mice Templar*.

Mice Templar is a tale of young mice with hearts that yearn for romance and adventure. It's a story of an ancient martial order of intrepid and gallant knights, brave beyond imagination, but who've fallen on hard times. Is the legendary order dead for all time, or can it thrive again, once more living up to the acme of fictional mousy qualities: duty, honor and undaunted courage in the face of overwhelming adversity?

Mice Templar was created by Bryan J.L. Glass and Michael Avon Oeming, two fellows talented beyond far their fair share. I'm not kidding. Right now there are any number of poor, bereft souls walking around, doomed to be CPAs or car wash attendants because they missed out on their ration of talent, all because these greedy guys took extra helpings. Bryan I've known for more than twenty years, first meeting him in my Philadelphia days. I was doing a series called *Elementals* back then, published by Comico. He was a young tyro, positively trembling with the desire to tell stories, but still grasping for the right outlet to do so: page ahead and you'll see he found it. Michael I met later on, when I simply had to track down the creators behind one of my favorite new funnybooks called *Hammer of the Gods*. I have no idea how Michael and Bryan eventually got together to create *Mice Templar*, but I'm glad they did. As you're about to find out for yourselves, it's a marvelous story.

The Mouse Police, the Mouse Guard, and the Mice Templar have this much in common: I believe they're all the figurative sons of Reepicheep. But that's the only way in which the word "common" applies to the characters you're about to meet. *Mice Templar* is uncommonly good. Do me and do yourself a favor. Stop reading this nonsense right now and turn the page. Start reading this wonderful tale. Enter this remarkable world. Immerse yourself in it. It's the most enjoyable way you'll ever get to pay down an outstanding debt. ◉

Bill Willingham
20 October, 2008

Bill Willingham and Mark Buckingham are the creators of the award-winning comic series *Fables*, published by DC Comics.

CONTENTS

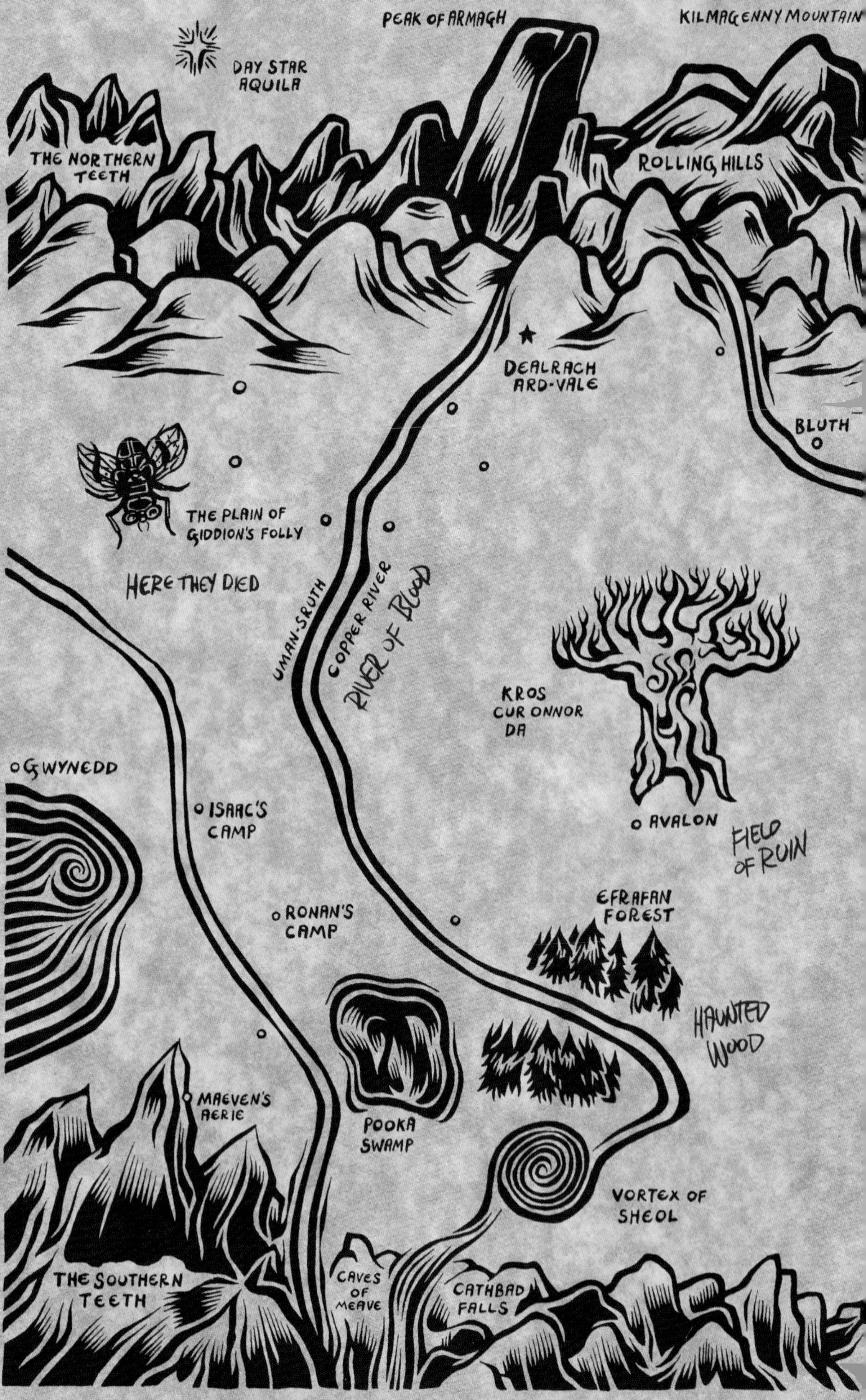

PEAK OF ARMAGH
KILMAGENNY MOUNTAIN
DAY STAR AQUILA
THE NORTHERN TEETH
ROLLING HILLS
DEALRACH ARD-VALE
BLUTH
THE PLAIN OF GIDDION'S FOLLY
HERE THEY DIED
UMAN-SRUTH
COPPER RIVER
RIVER OF BLOOD
KROS CUR ONNOR DA
GWYNEDD
ISAAC'S CAMP
AVALON
FIELD OF RUIN
EFRAFAN FOREST
RONAN'S CAMP
HAUNTED WOOD
MAEVEN'S AERIE
POOKA SWAMP
VORTEX OF SHEOL
THE SOUTHERN TEETH
CAVES OF MEAVE
CATHBAD FALLS

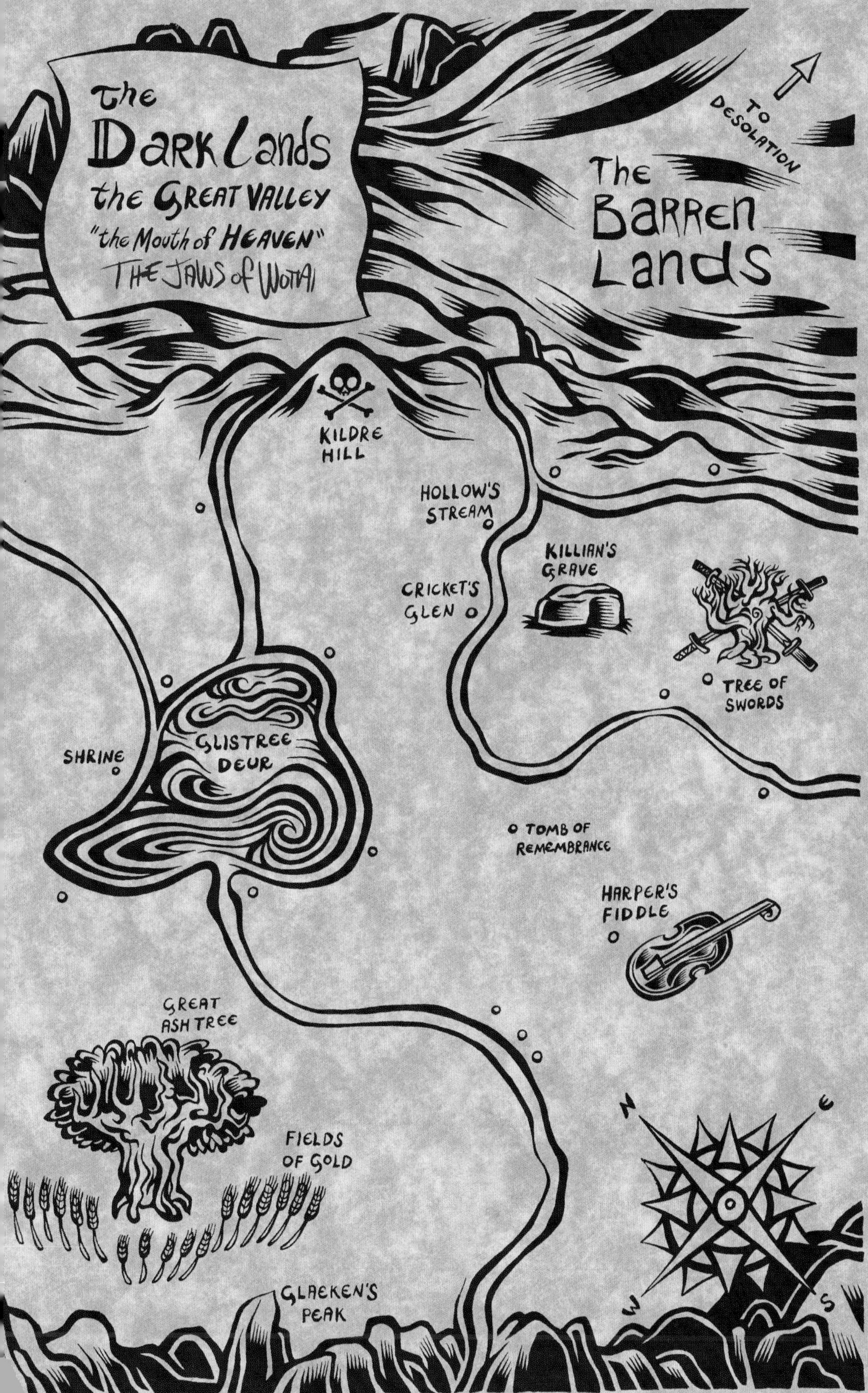
The Dark Lands
the Great Valley
"the Mouth of Heaven"
The Jaws of Wotai
To Desolation
The Barren Lands
Kildre Hill
Hollow's Stream
Killian's Grave
Cricket's Glen
Tree of Swords
Shrine
Glistree Deur
Tomb of Remembrance
Harper's Fiddle
Great Ash Tree
Fields of Gold
Glaeken's Peak
N
E
W
S

CHAPTER ONE
THE DARK LANDS

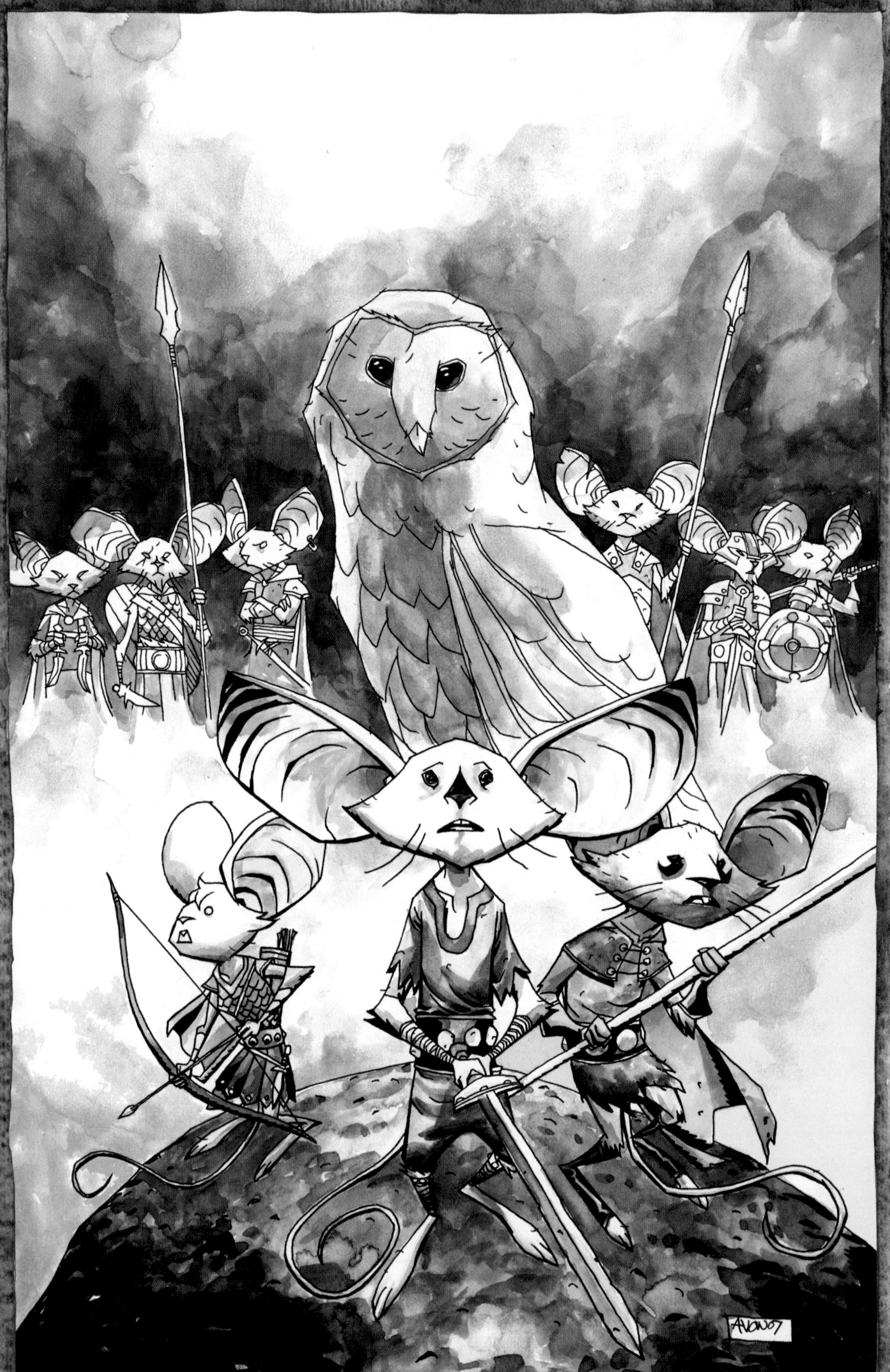

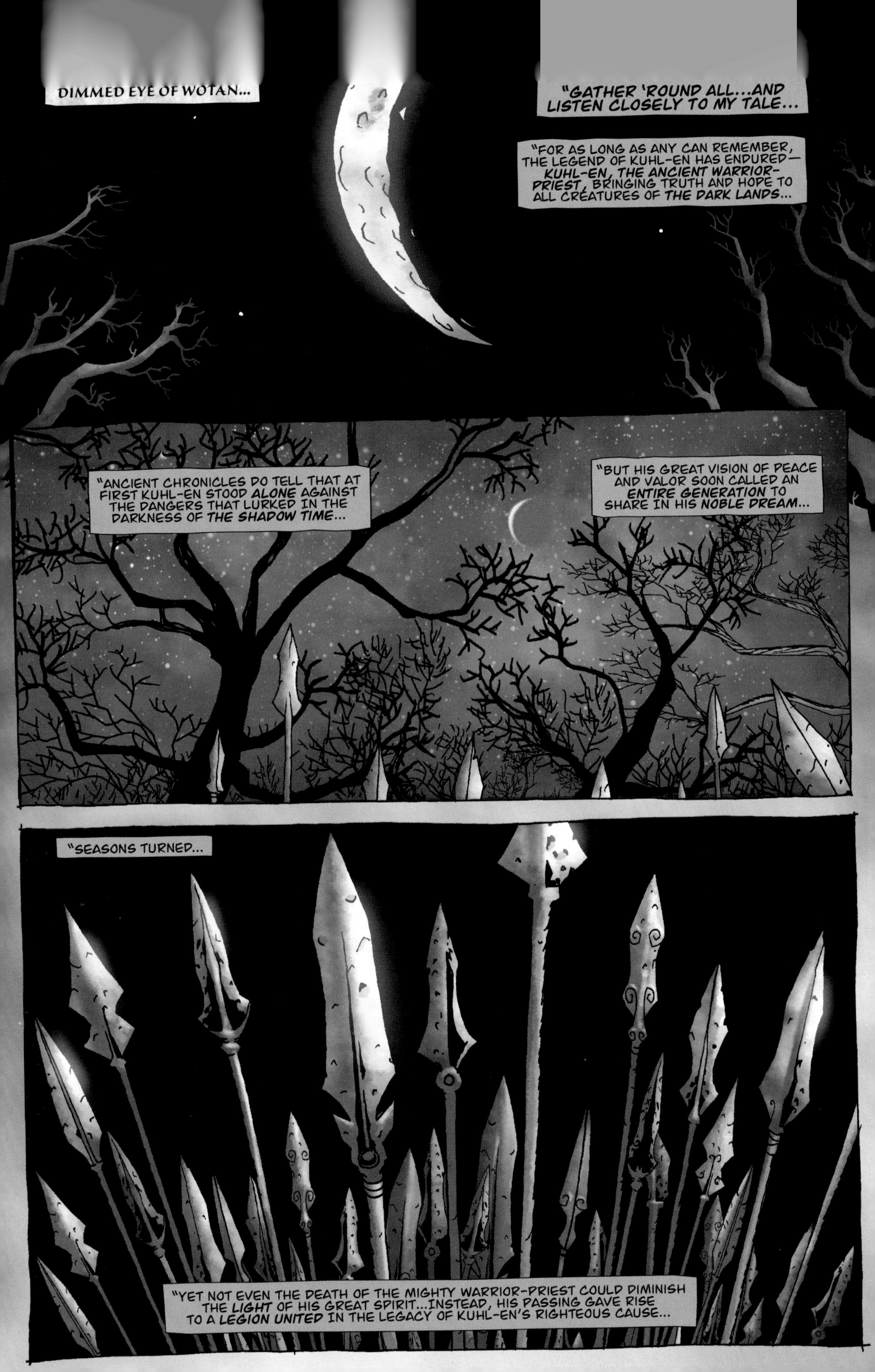
DIMMED EYE OF WOTAN...
"GATHER 'ROUND ALL...AND LISTEN CLOSELY TO MY TALE...
"FOR AS LONG AS ANY CAN REMEMBER, THE LEGEND OF KUHL-EN HAS ENDURED—KUHL-EN, THE ANCIENT WARRIOR-PRIEST, BRINGING TRUTH AND HOPE TO ALL CREATURES OF THE DARK LANDS...
"ANCIENT CHRONICLES DO TELL THAT AT FIRST KUHL-EN STOOD ALONE AGAINST THE DANGERS THAT LURKED IN THE DARKNESS OF THE SHADOW TIME...
"BUT HIS GREAT VISION OF PEACE AND VALOR SOON CALLED AN ENTIRE GENERATION TO SHARE IN HIS NOBLE DREAM...
"SEASONS TURNED...
"YET NOT EVEN THE DEATH OF THE MIGHTY WARRIOR-PRIEST COULD DIMINISH THE LIGHT OF HIS GREAT SPIRIT...INSTEAD, HIS PASSING GAVE RISE TO A LEGION UNITED IN THE LEGACY OF KUHL-EN'S RIGHTEOUS CAUSE...

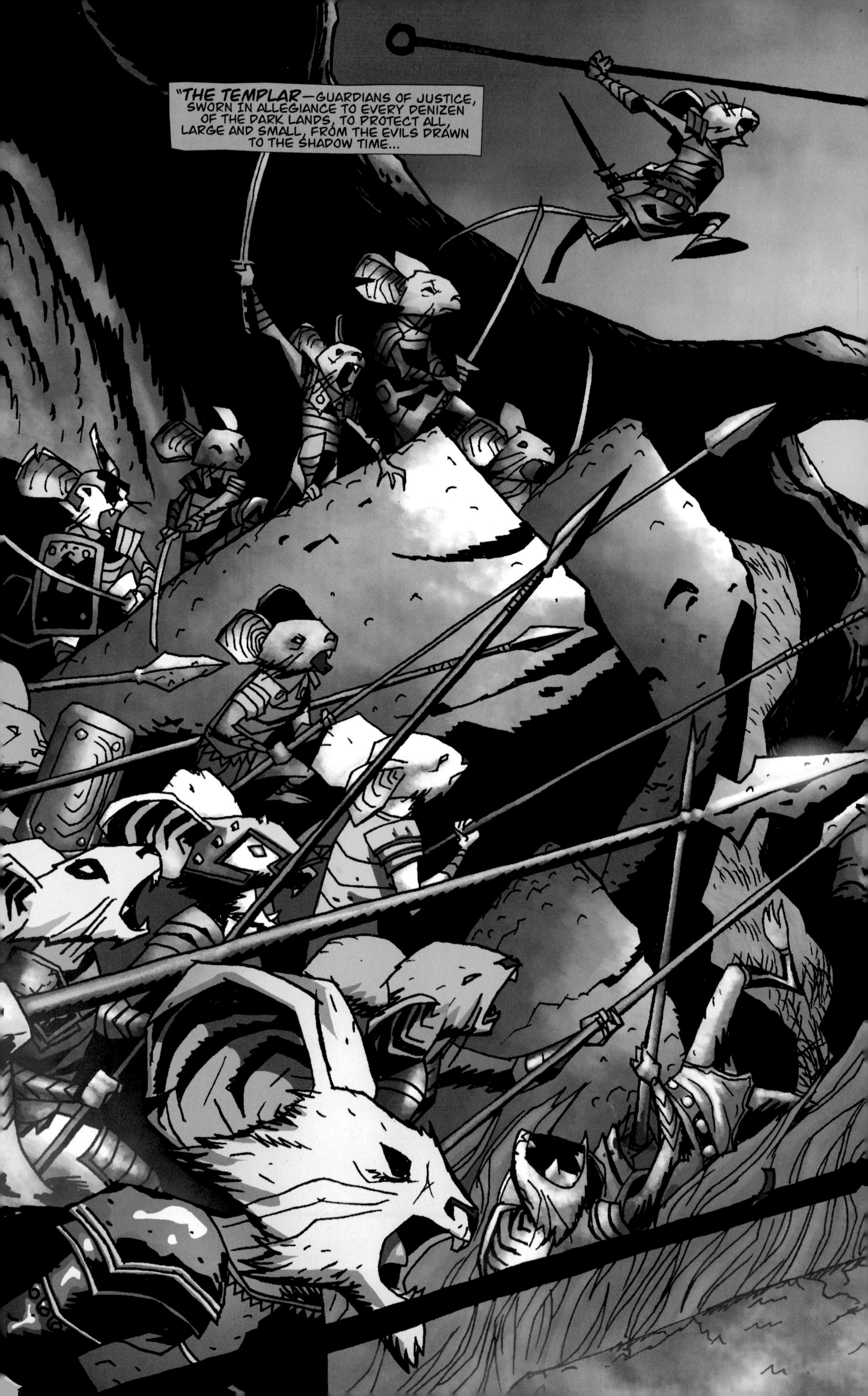
"THE TEMPLAR—GUARDIANS OF JUSTICE, SWORN IN ALLEGIANCE TO EVERY DENIZEN OF THE DARK LANDS, TO PROTECT ALL, LARGE AND SMALL, FROM THE EVILS DRAWN TO THE SHADOW TIME...

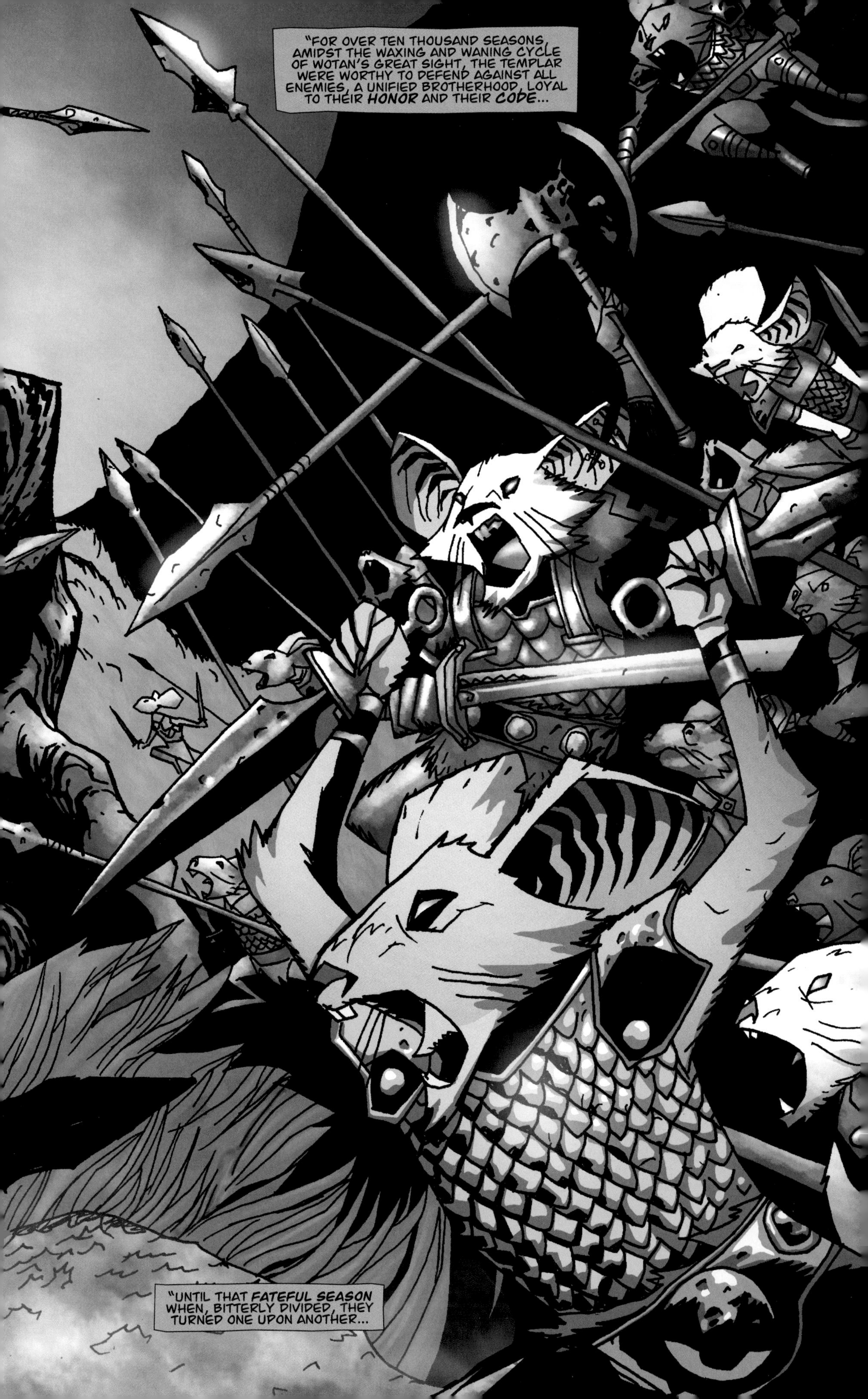
"FOR OVER TEN THOUSAND SEASONS AMIDST THE WAXING AND WANING CYCLE OF WOTAN'S GREAT SIGHT, THE TEMPLAR WERE WORTHY TO DEFEND AGAINST ALL ENEMIES, A UNIFIED BROTHERHOOD, LOYAL TO THEIR **HONOR** AND THEIR **CODE**...
"UNTIL THAT *FATEFUL SEASON* WHEN, BITTERLY DIVIDED, THEY TURNED ONE UPON ANOTHER...

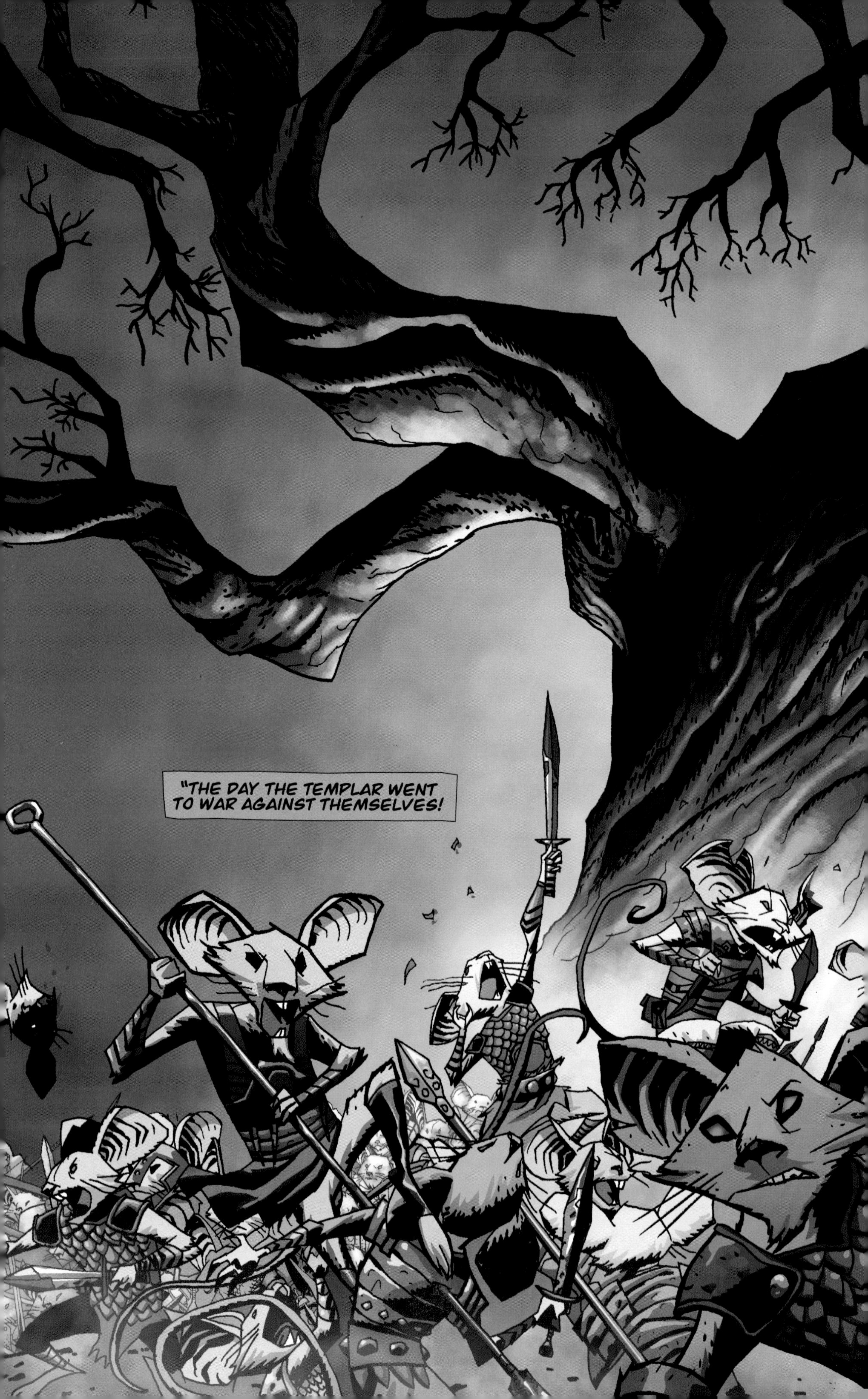
"THE DAY THE TEMPLAR WENT
TO WAR AGAINST THEMSELVES!

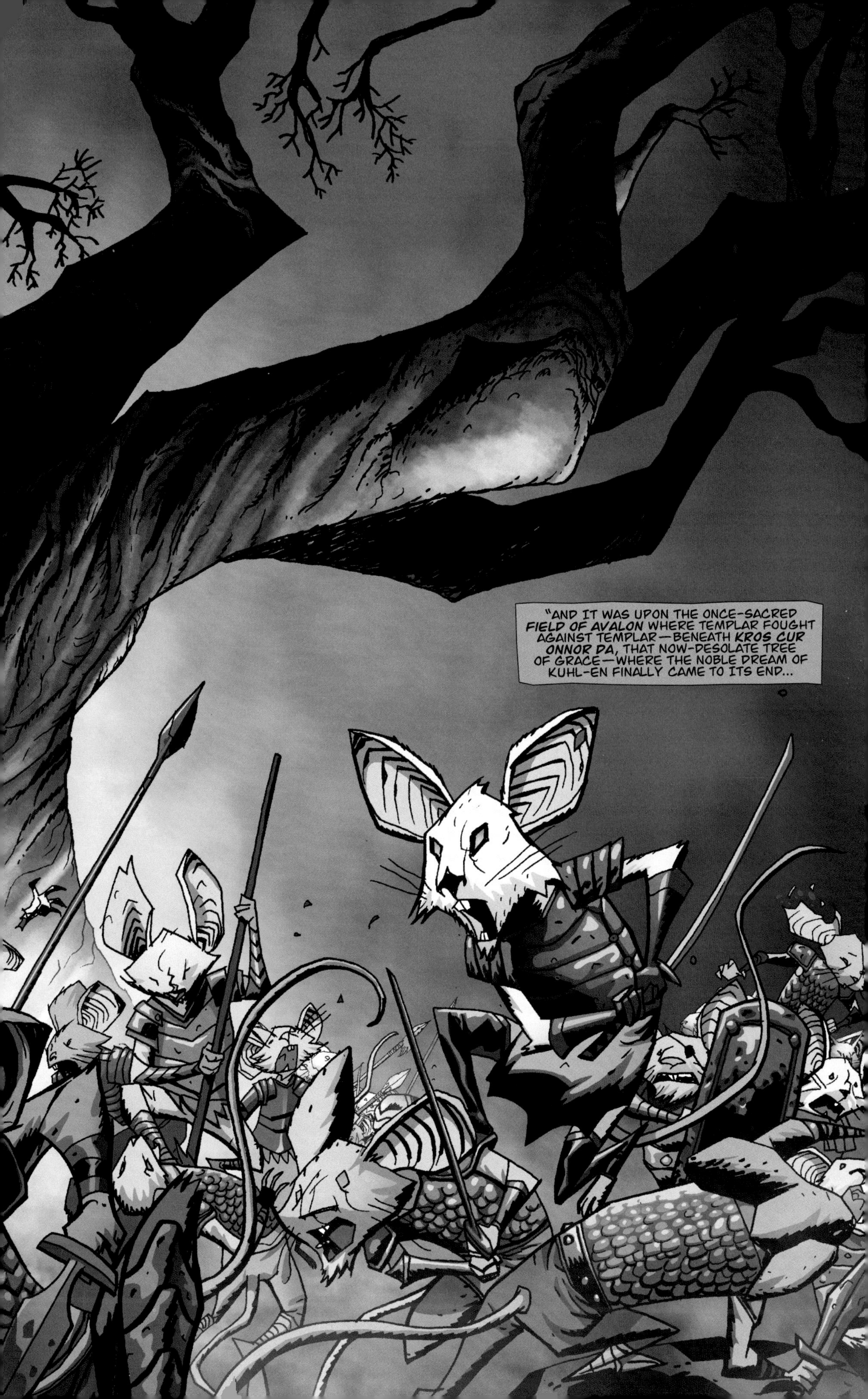
"AND IT WAS UPON THE ONCE-SACRED FIELD OF AVALON WHERE TEMPLAR FOUGHT AGAINST TEMPLAR—BENEATH KROS CUR ONNOR DA, THAT NOW-DESOLATE TREE OF GRACE—WHERE THE NOBLE DREAM OF KUHL-EN FINALLY CAME TO ITS END...

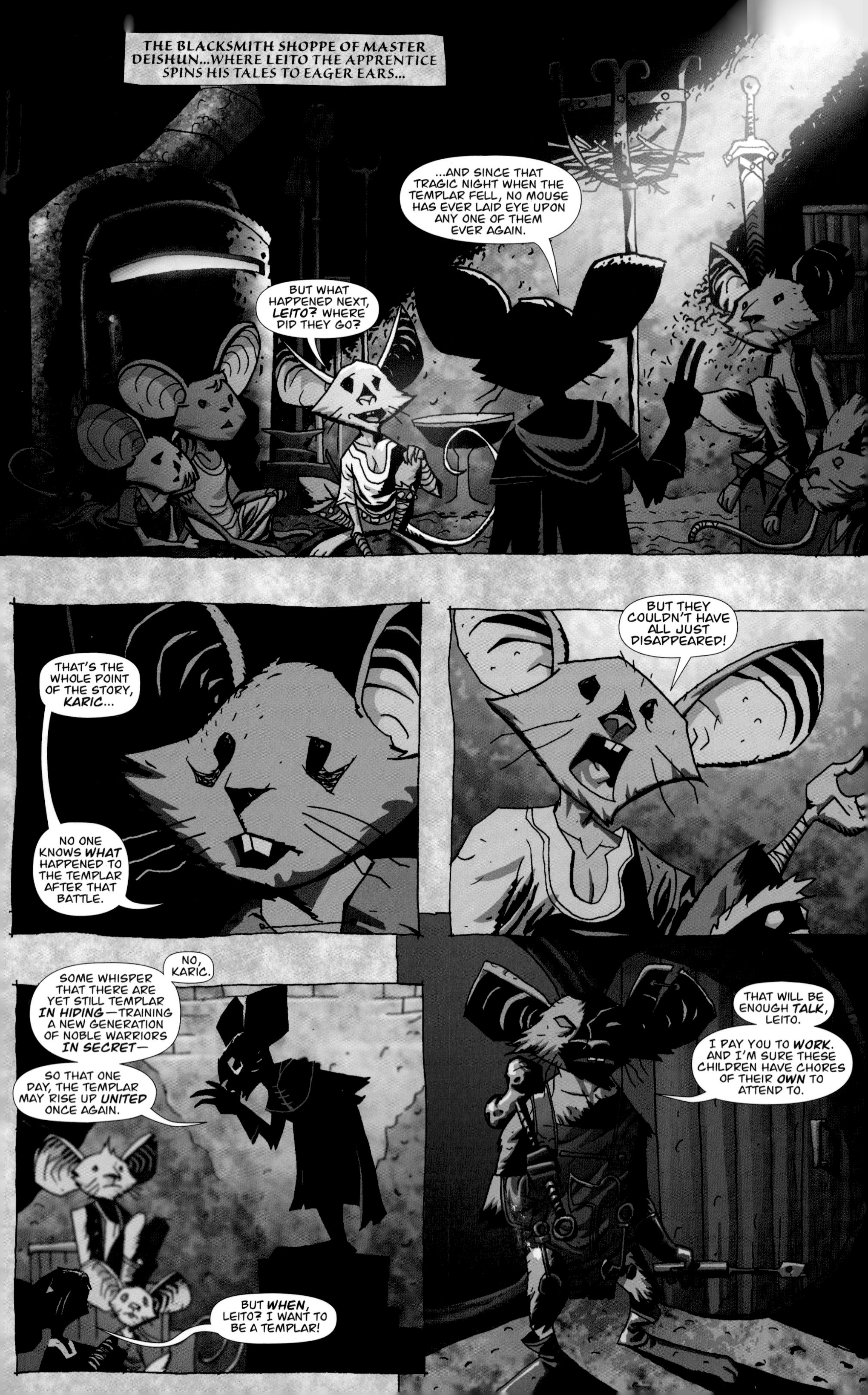
THE BLACKSMITH SHOPPE OF MASTER DEISHUN...WHERE LEITO THE APPRENTICE SPINS HIS TALES TO EAGER EARS...
...AND SINCE THAT TRAGIC NIGHT WHEN THE TEMPLAR FELL, NO MOUSE HAS EVER LAID EYE UPON ANY ONE OF THEM EVER AGAIN.
BUT WHAT HAPPENED NEXT, LEITO? WHERE DID THEY GO?
THAT'S THE WHOLE POINT OF THE STORY, KARIC...
NO ONE KNOWS WHAT HAPPENED TO THE TEMPLAR AFTER THAT BATTLE.
BUT THEY COULDN'T HAVE ALL JUST DISAPPEARED!
NO, KARIC.
SOME WHISPER THAT THERE ARE YET STILL TEMPLAR IN HIDING—TRAINING A NEW GENERATION OF NOBLE WARRIORS IN SECRET—
SO THAT ONE DAY, THE TEMPLAR MAY RISE UP UNITED ONCE AGAIN.
BUT WHEN, LEITO? I WANT TO BE A TEMPLAR!
THAT WILL BE ENOUGH TALK, LEITO.
I PAY YOU TO WORK. AND I'M SURE THESE CHILDREN HAVE CHORES OF THEIR OWN TO ATTEND TO.

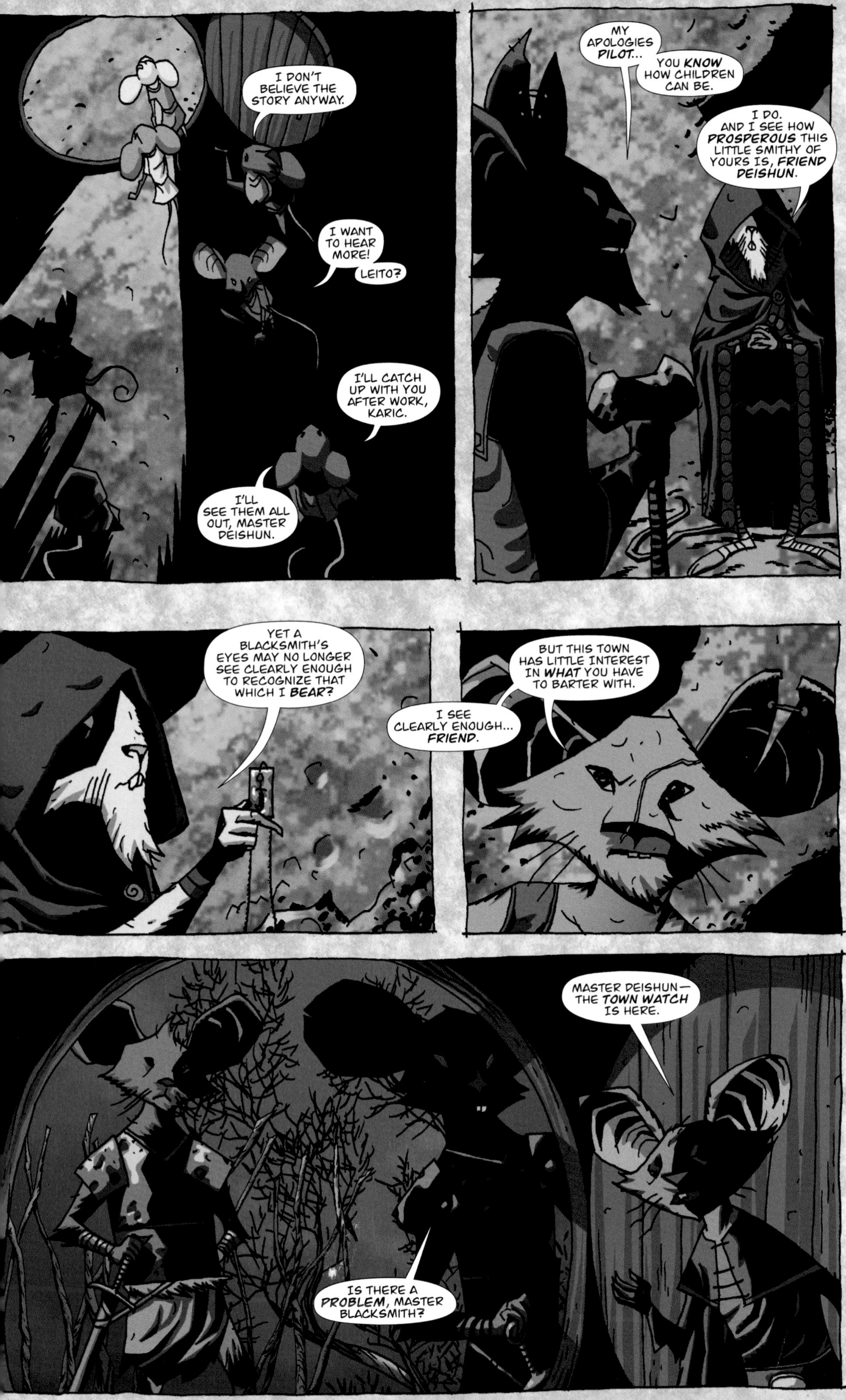

I DON'T BELIEVE THE STORY ANYWAY.
I WANT TO HEAR MORE!
LEITO?
I'LL CATCH UP WITH YOU AFTER WORK, KARIC.
I'LL SEE THEM ALL OUT, MASTER DEISHUN.
MY APOLOGIES PILOT...
YOU KNOW HOW CHILDREN CAN BE.
I DO. AND I SEE HOW PROSPEROUS THIS LITTLE SMITHY OF YOURS IS, FRIEND DEISHUN.
YET A BLACKSMITH'S EYES MAY NO LONGER SEE CLEARLY ENOUGH TO RECOGNIZE THAT WHICH I BEAR?
I SEE CLEARLY ENOUGH... FRIEND.
BUT THIS TOWN HAS LITTLE INTEREST IN WHAT YOU HAVE TO BARTER WITH.
MASTER DEISHUN— THE TOWN WATCH IS HERE.
IS THERE A PROBLEM, MASTER BLACKSMITH?

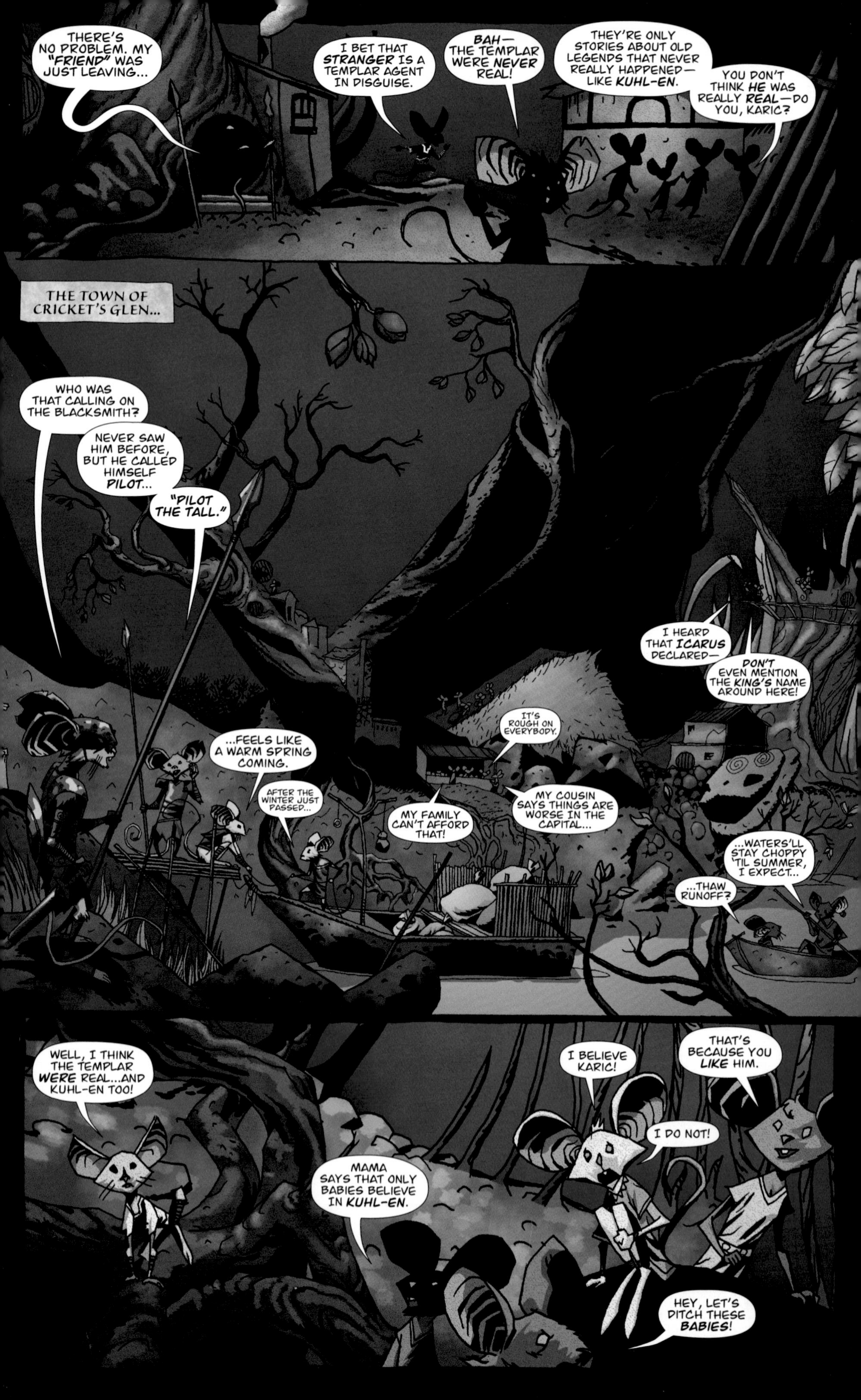

THERE'S NO PROBLEM. MY "FRIEND" WAS JUST LEAVING...
I BET THAT STRANGER IS A TEMPLAR AGENT IN DISGUISE.
BAH—THE TEMPLAR WERE NEVER REAL!
THEY'RE ONLY STORIES ABOUT OLD LEGENDS THAT NEVER REALLY HAPPENED—LIKE KUHL-EN.
YOU DON'T THINK HE WAS REALLY REAL—DO YOU, KARIC?
THE TOWN OF CRICKET'S GLEN...
WHO WAS THAT CALLING ON THE BLACKSMITH?
NEVER SAW HIM BEFORE, BUT HE CALLED HIMSELF PILOT...
"PILOT THE TALL."
I HEARD THAT ICARUS DECLARED—
DON'T EVEN MENTION THE KING'S NAME AROUND HERE!
...FEELS LIKE A WARM SPRING COMING.
AFTER THE WINTER JUST PASSED...
IT'S ROUGH ON EVERYBODY.
MY FAMILY CAN'T AFFORD THAT!
MY COUSIN SAYS THINGS ARE WORSE IN THE CAPITAL...
...WATERS'LL STAY CHOPPY 'TIL SUMMER, I EXPECT...
...THAW RUNOFF?
WELL, I THINK THE TEMPLAR WERE REAL...AND KUHL-EN TOO!
I BELIEVE KARIC!
THAT'S BECAUSE YOU LIKE HIM.
I DO NOT!
MAMA SAYS THAT ONLY BABIES BELIEVE IN KUHL-EN.
HEY, LET'S DITCH THESE BABIES!

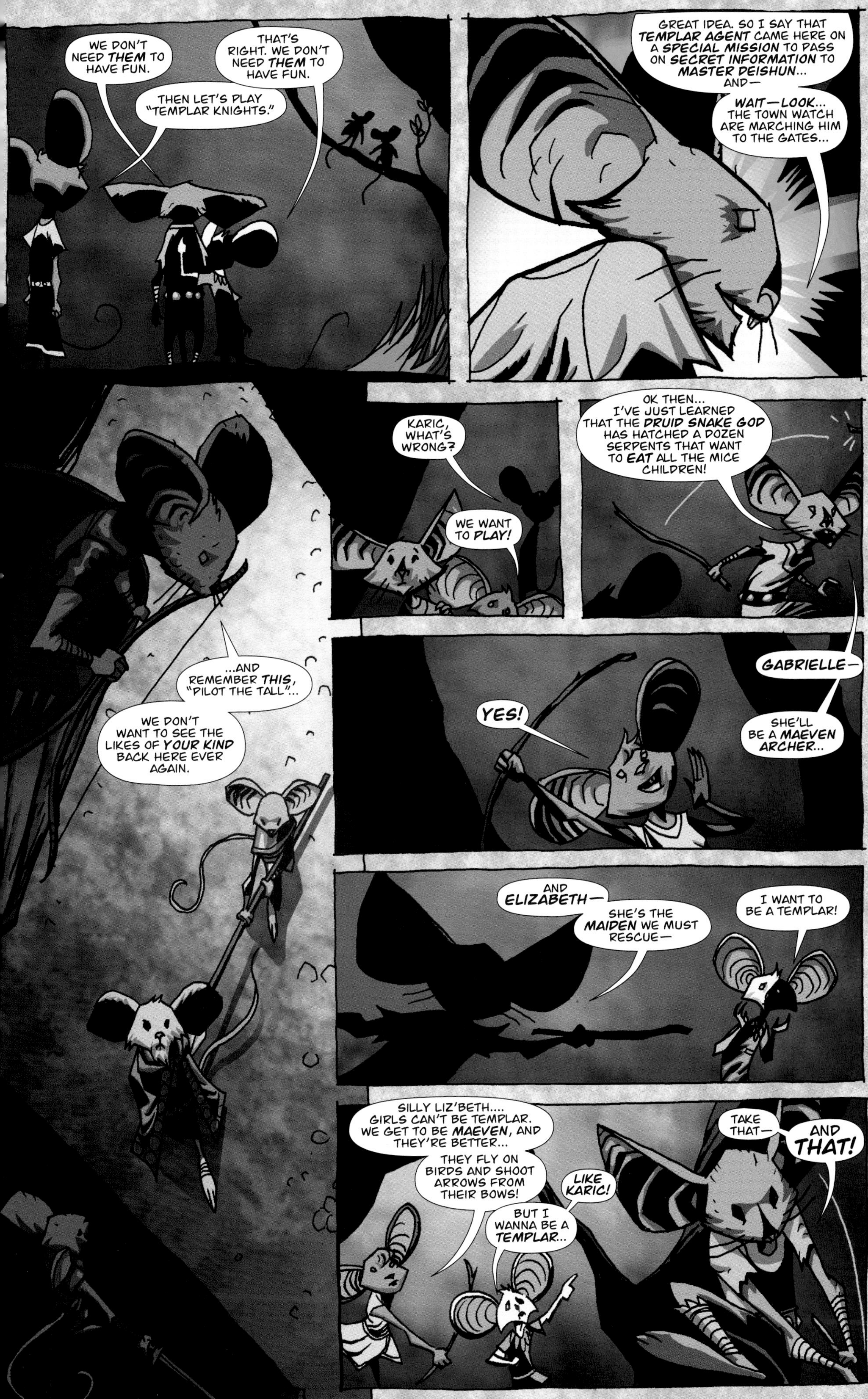
WE DON'T NEED THEM TO HAVE FUN.
THAT'S RIGHT. WE DON'T NEED THEM TO HAVE FUN.
THEN LET'S PLAY "TEMPLAR KNIGHTS."
GREAT IDEA. SO I SAY THAT TEMPLAR AGENT CAME HERE ON A SPECIAL MISSION TO PASS ON SECRET INFORMATION TO MASTER DEISHUN... AND—
WAIT—LOOK... THE TOWN WATCH ARE MARCHING HIM TO THE GATES...
...AND REMEMBER THIS, "PILOT THE TALL"...
WE DON'T WANT TO SEE THE LIKES OF YOUR KIND BACK HERE EVER AGAIN.
KARIC, WHAT'S WRONG?
WE WANT TO PLAY!
OK THEN... I'VE JUST LEARNED THAT THE DRUID SNAKE GOD HAS HATCHED A DOZEN SERPENTS THAT WANT TO EAT ALL THE MICE CHILDREN!
GABRIELLE—
SHE'LL BE A MAEVEN ARCHER...
YES!
AND ELIZABETH—
SHE'S THE MAIDEN WE MUST RESCUE—
I WANT TO BE A TEMPLAR!
SILLY LIZ'BETH.... GIRLS CAN'T BE TEMPLAR. WE GET TO BE MAEVEN, AND THEY'RE BETTER...
THEY FLY ON BIRDS AND SHOOT ARROWS FROM THEIR BOWS!
LIKE KARIC!
BUT I WANNA BE A TEMPLAR...
TAKE THAT—
AND THAT!

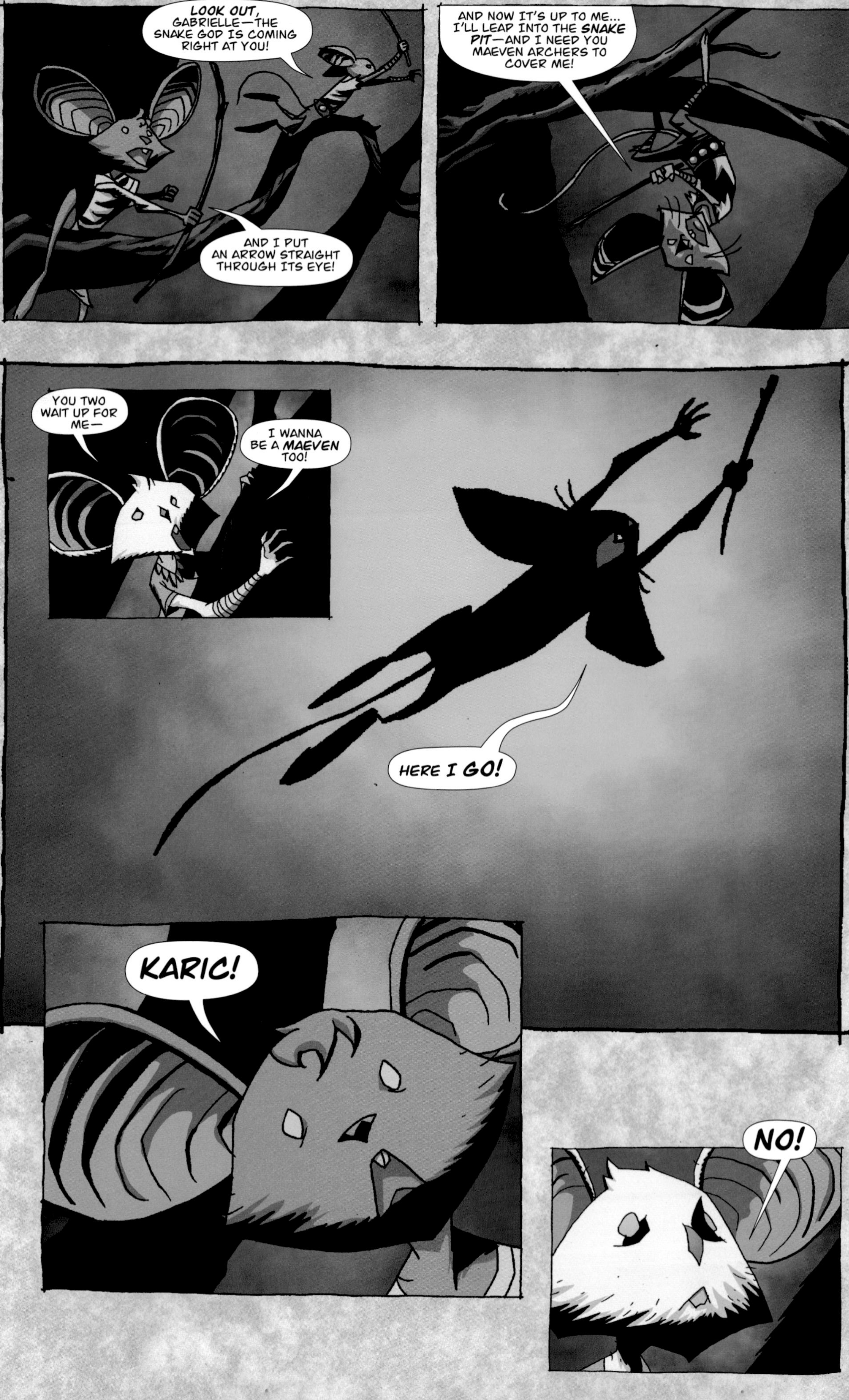
LOOK OUT, GABRIELLE—THE SNAKE GOD IS COMING RIGHT AT YOU!
AND I PUT AN ARROW STRAIGHT THROUGH ITS EYE!
AND NOW IT'S UP TO ME... I'LL LEAP INTO THE SNAKE PIT—AND I NEED YOU MAEVEN ARCHERS TO COVER ME!
YOU TWO WAIT UP FOR ME—
I WANNA BE A MAEVEN TOO!
HERE I GO!
KARIC!
NO!

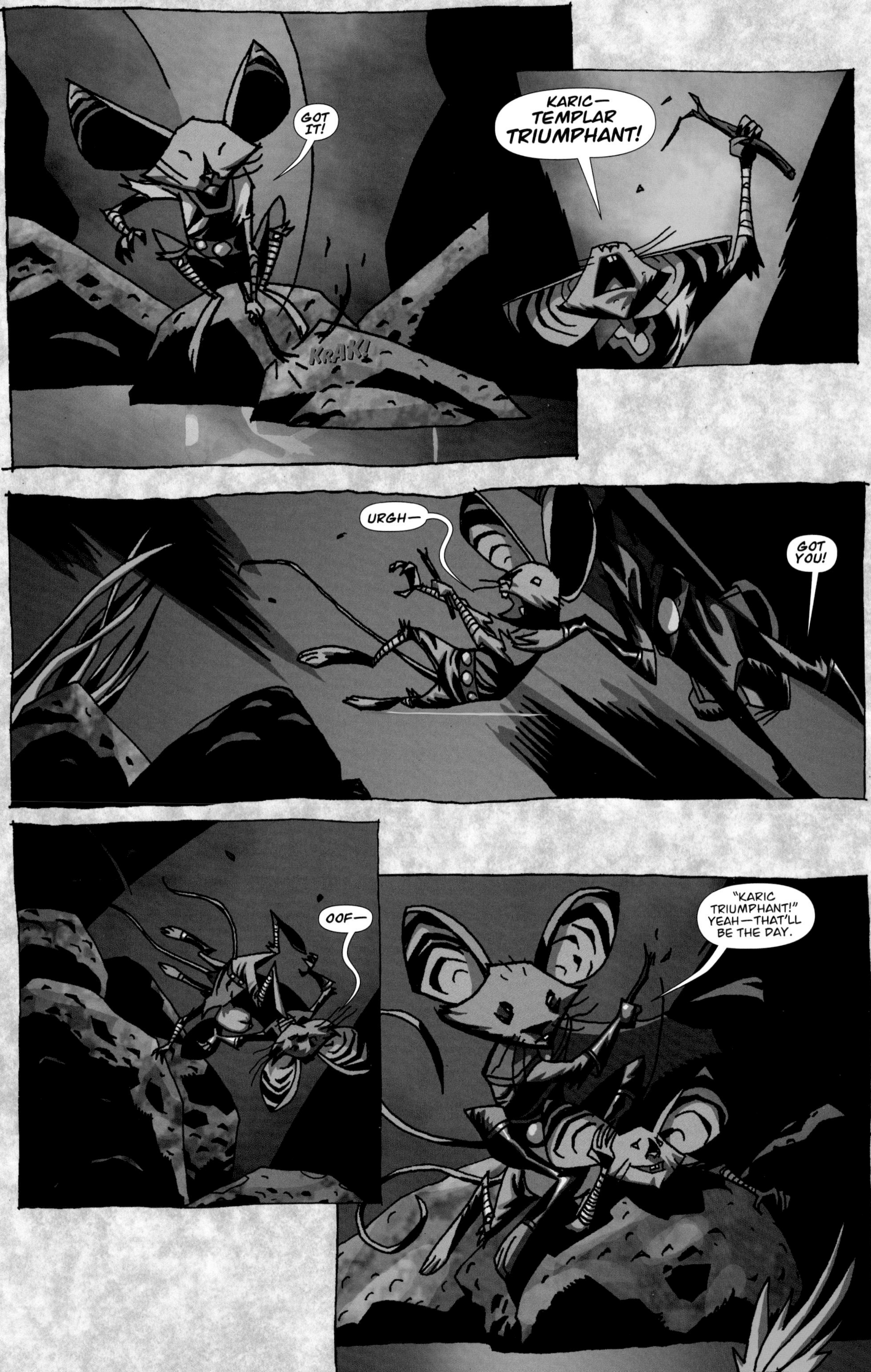
GOT IT!
KRAK!
KARIC—TEMPLAR TRIUMPHANT!
URGH—
GOT YOU!
OOF—
"KARIC TRIUMPHANT!" YEAH—THAT'LL BE THE DAY.

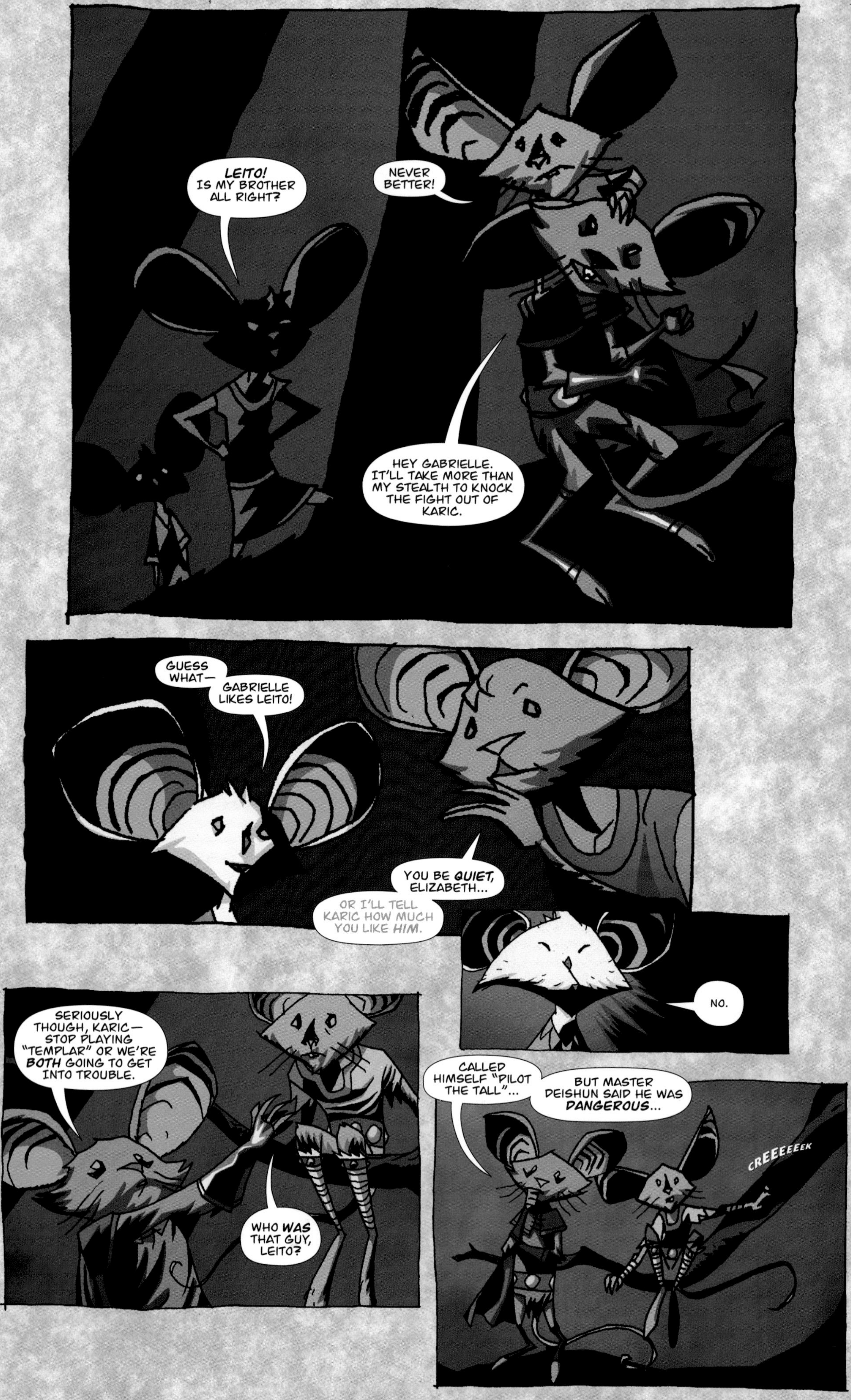
LEITO! IS MY BROTHER ALL RIGHT?
NEVER BETTER!
HEY GABRIELLE. IT'LL TAKE MORE THAN MY STEALTH TO KNOCK THE FIGHT OUT OF KARIC.
GUESS WHAT—
GABRIELLE LIKES LEITO!
YOU BE QUIET, ELIZABETH...
OR I'LL TELL KARIC HOW MUCH YOU LIKE HIM.
NO.
SERIOUSLY THOUGH, KARIC— STOP PLAYING "TEMPLAR" OR WE'RE BOTH GOING TO GET INTO TROUBLE.
WHO WAS THAT GUY, LEITO?
CALLED HIMSELF "PILOT THE TALL"...
BUT MASTER DEISHUN SAID HE WAS DANGEROUS...
CREEEEEEK

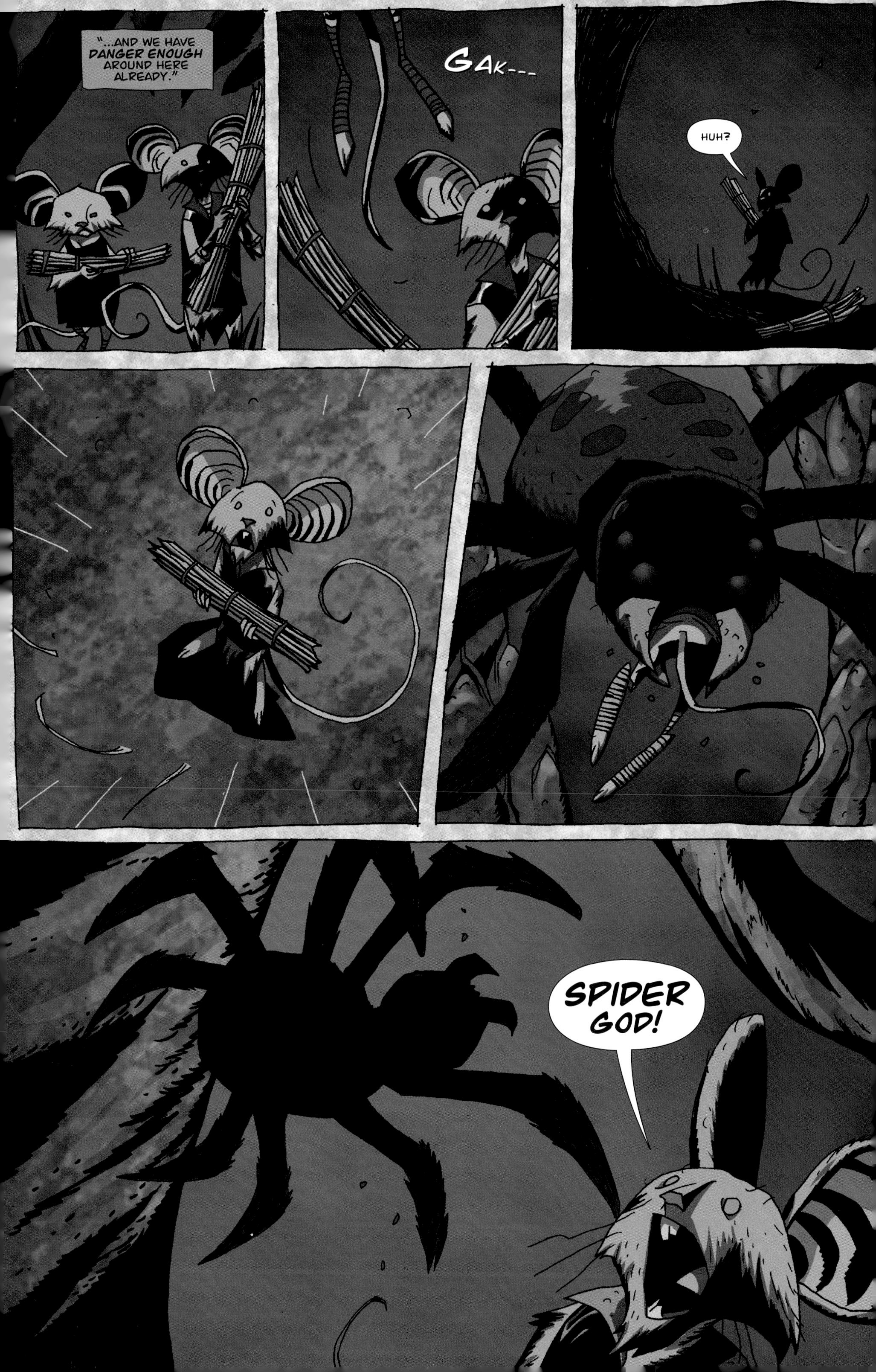
"...AND WE HAVE DANGER ENOUGH AROUND HERE ALREADY."
GAK---
HUH?
SPIDER GOD!

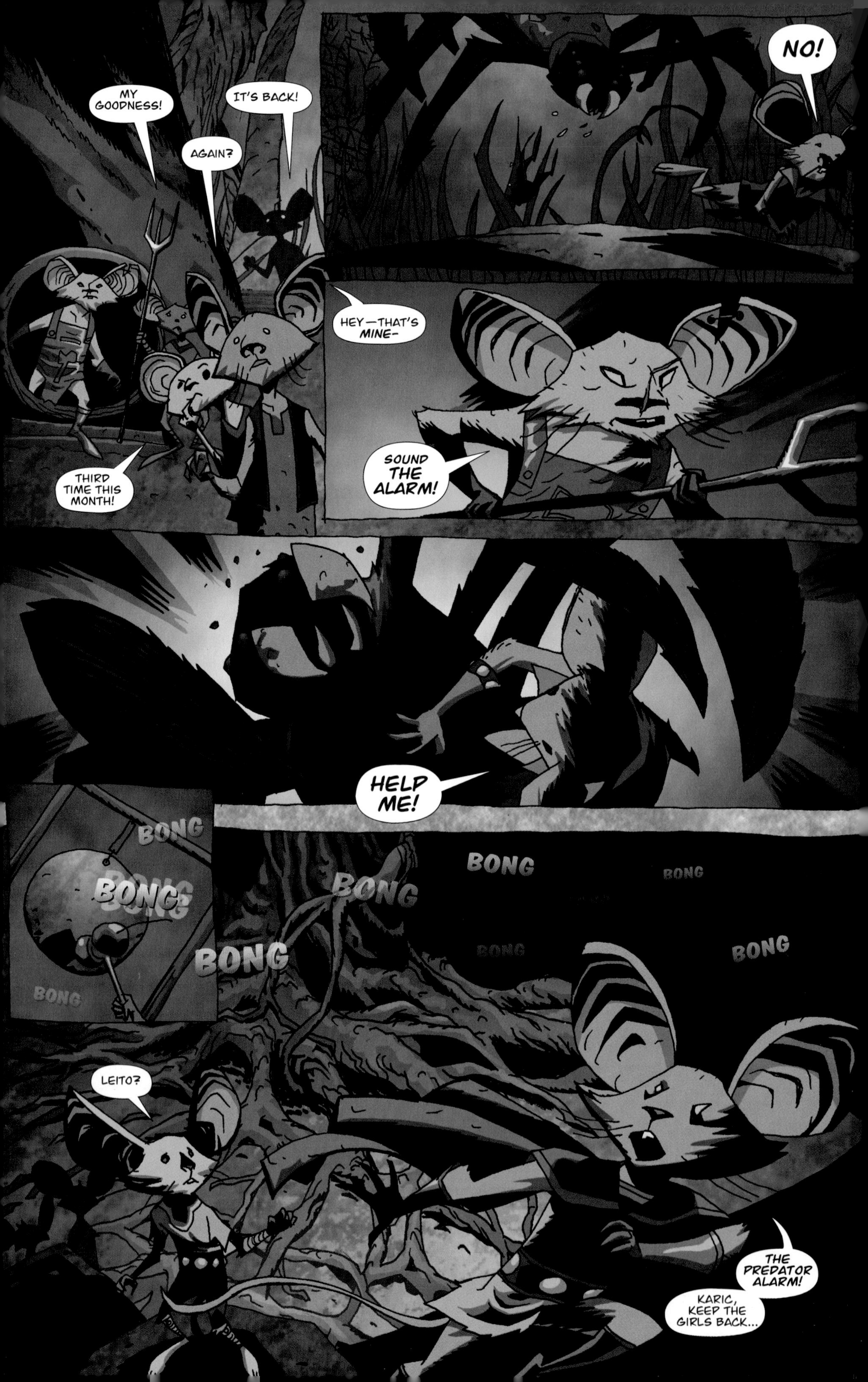
MY GOODNESS!
AGAIN?
IT'S BACK!
THIRD TIME THIS MONTH!
NO!
HEY—THAT'S MINE-
SOUND THE ALARM!
HELP ME!
BONG
BONG
BONG
BONG
BONG
BONG
BONG
BONG
BONG
BONG
LEITO?
THE PREDATOR ALARM!
KARIC, KEEP THE GIRLS BACK...

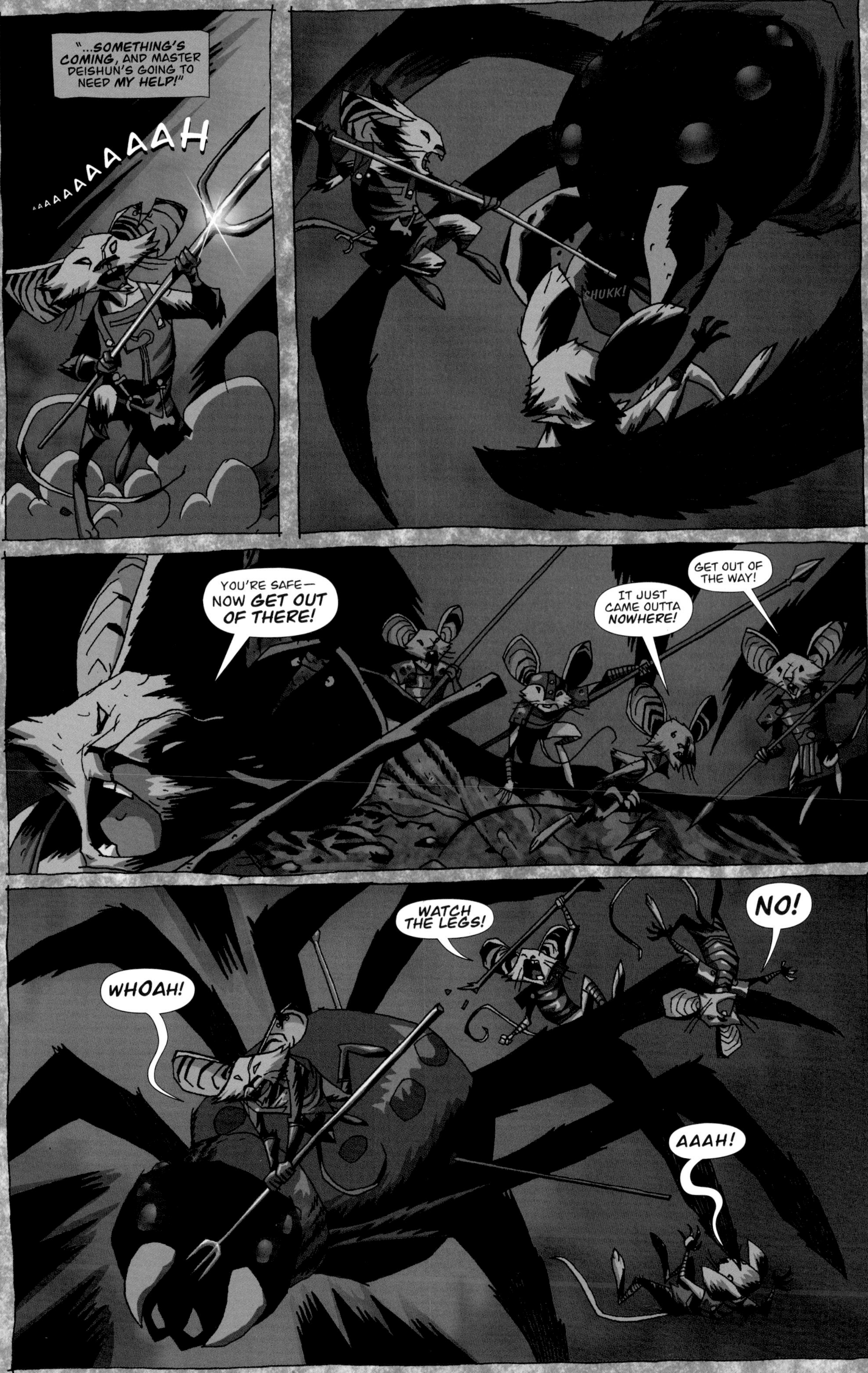
"...SOMETHING'S COMING, AND MASTER DEISHUN'S GOING TO NEED MY HELP!"
AAAAAAAAAAAAH
SHUKK!
YOU'RE SAFE— NOW GET OUT OF THERE!
IT JUST CAME OUTTA NOWHERE!
GET OUT OF THE WAY!
WATCH THE LEGS!
NO!
WHOAH!
AAAH!

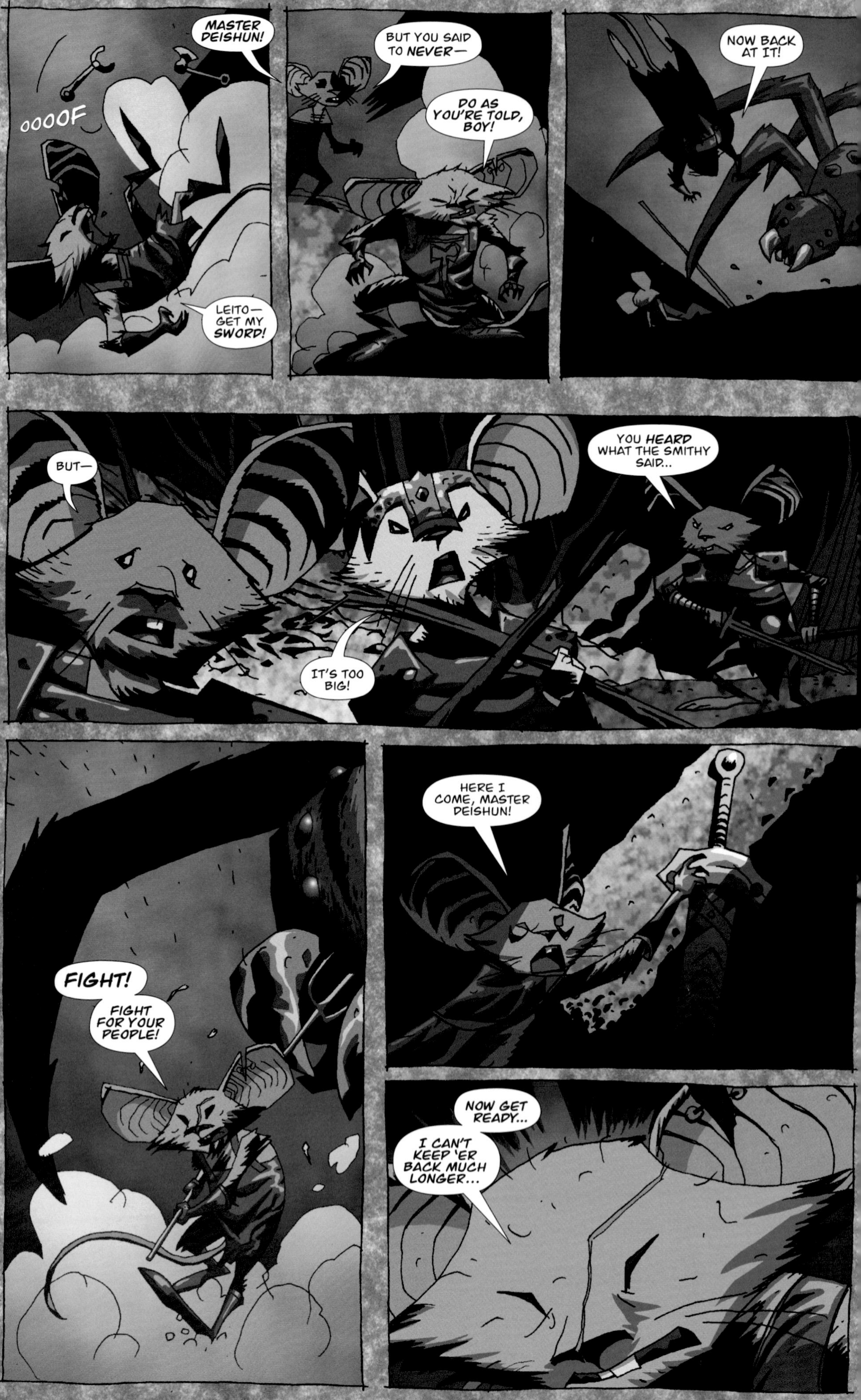
MASTER DEISHUN!
OOOOF
LEITO— GET MY SWORD!
BUT YOU SAID TO NEVER—
DO AS YOU'RE TOLD, BOY!
NOW BACK AT IT!
BUT—
YOU HEARD WHAT THE SMITHY SAID...
IT'S TOO BIG!
FIGHT!
FIGHT FOR YOUR PEOPLE!
HERE I COME, MASTER DEISHUN!
NOW GET READY...
I CAN'T KEEP 'ER BACK MUCH LONGER...

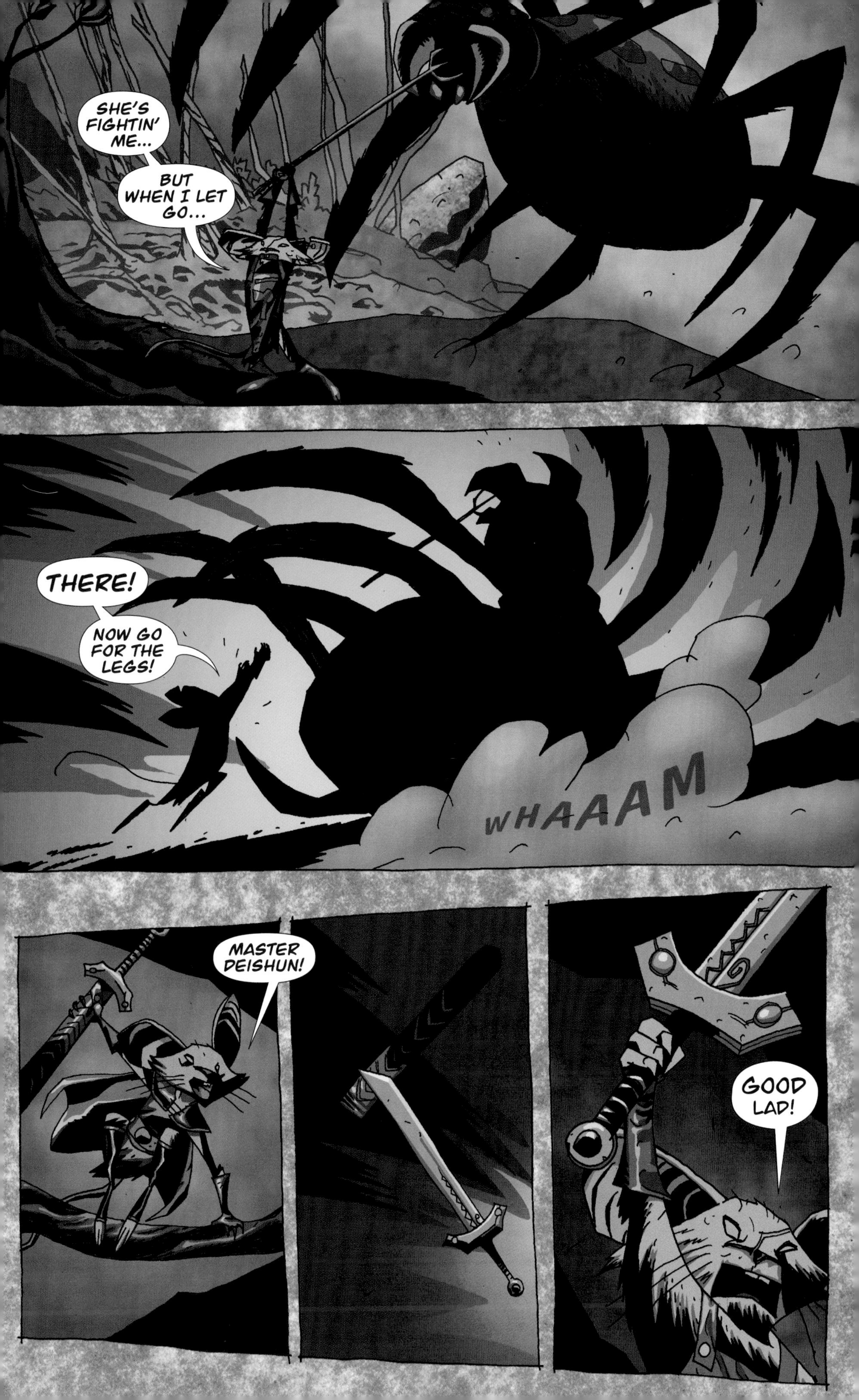
SHE'S FIGHTIN' ME...
BUT WHEN I LET GO...
THERE!
NOW GO FOR THE LEGS!
WHAAAM
MASTER DEISHUN!
GOOD LAD!

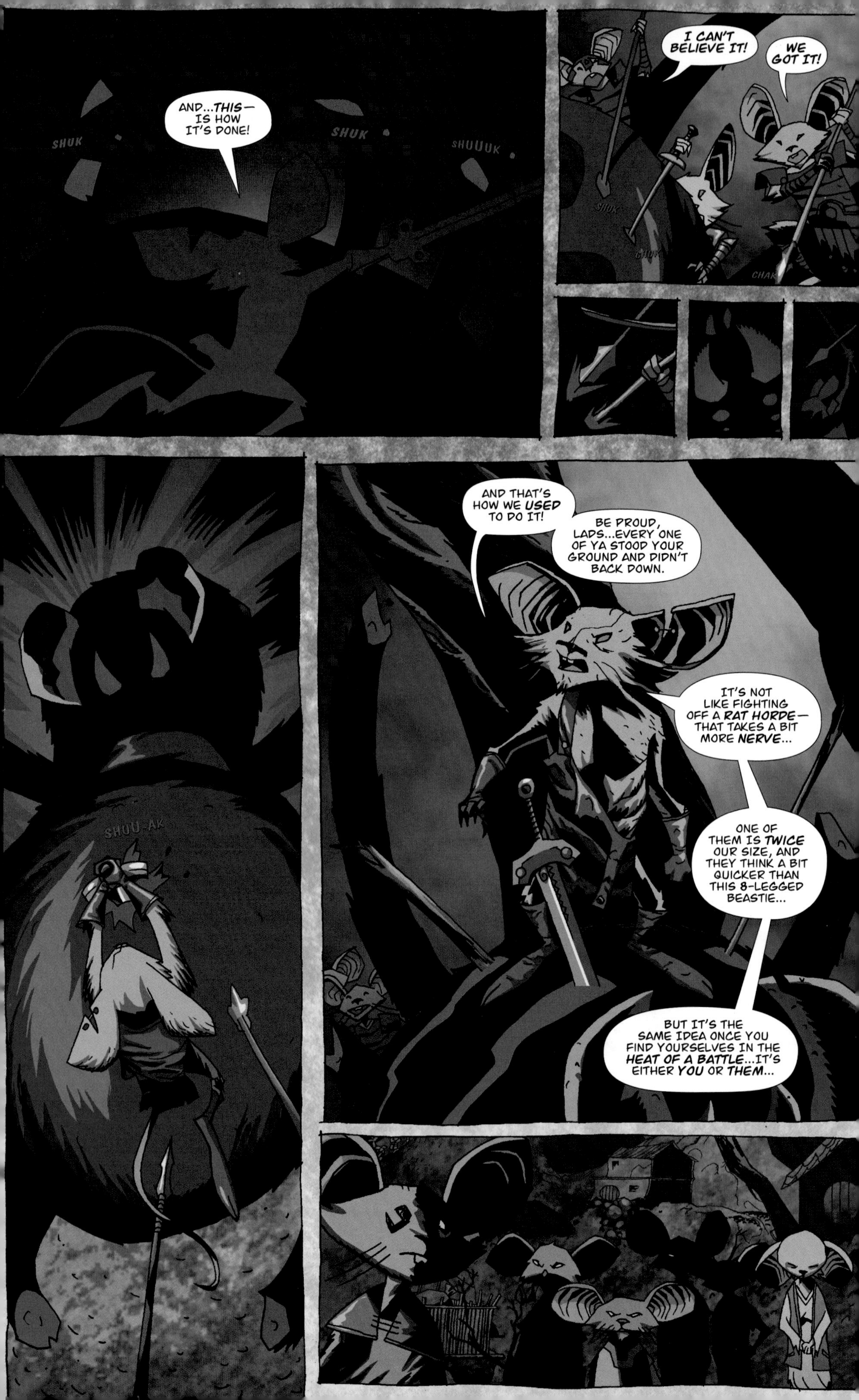
SHUK
AND...THIS—
IS HOW
IT'S DONE!
SHUK
SHUUUK
I CAN'T
BELIEVE IT!
WE
GOT IT!
SHUK
CHUK
CHAK
SHOU-AK
AND THAT'S
HOW WE USED
TO DO IT!
BE PROUD,
LADS...EVERY ONE
OF YA STOOD YOUR
GROUND AND DIDN'T
BACK DOWN.
IT'S NOT
LIKE FIGHTING
OFF A RAT HORDE—
THAT TAKES A BIT
MORE NERVE...
ONE OF
THEM IS TWICE
OUR SIZE, AND
THEY THINK A BIT
QUICKER THAN
THIS 8-LEGGED
BEASTIE...
BUT IT'S THE
SAME IDEA ONCE YOU
FIND YOURSELVES IN THE
HEAT OF A BATTLE...IT'S
EITHER YOU OR THEM...

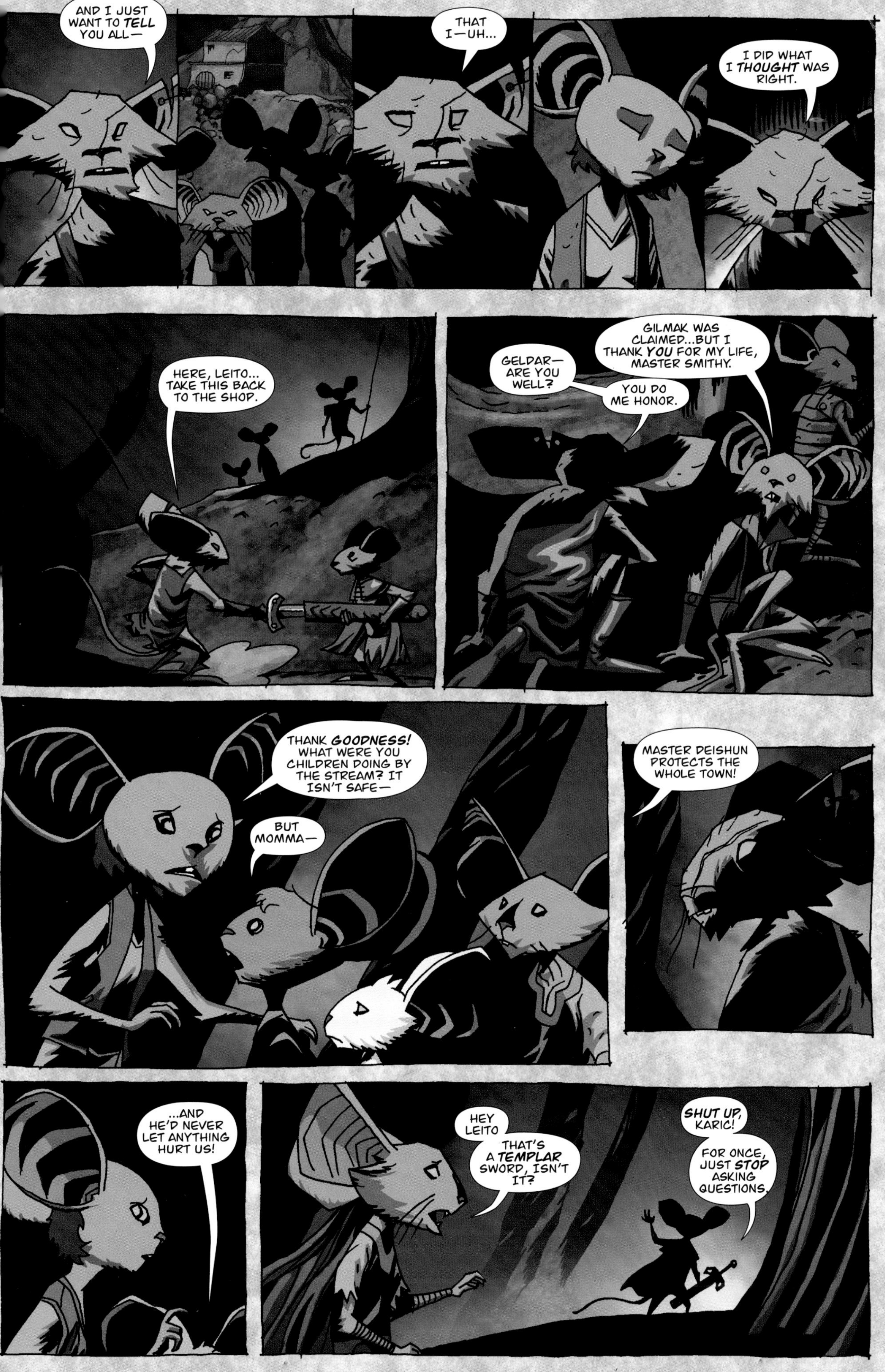
AND I JUST WANT TO TELL YOU ALL—
THAT I—UH...
I DID WHAT I THOUGHT WAS RIGHT.
HERE, LEITO... TAKE THIS BACK TO THE SHOP.
GELDAR— ARE YOU WELL?
GILMAK WAS CLAIMED...BUT I THANK YOU FOR MY LIFE, MASTER SMITHY.
YOU DO ME HONOR.
THANK GOODNESS! WHAT WERE YOU CHILDREN DOING BY THE STREAM? IT ISN'T SAFE—
BUT MOMMA—
MASTER DEISHUN PROTECTS THE WHOLE TOWN!
...AND HE'D NEVER LET ANYTHING HURT US!
HEY LEITO
THAT'S A TEMPLAR SWORD, ISN'T IT?
SHUT UP, KARIC!
FOR ONCE, JUST STOP ASKING QUESTIONS.

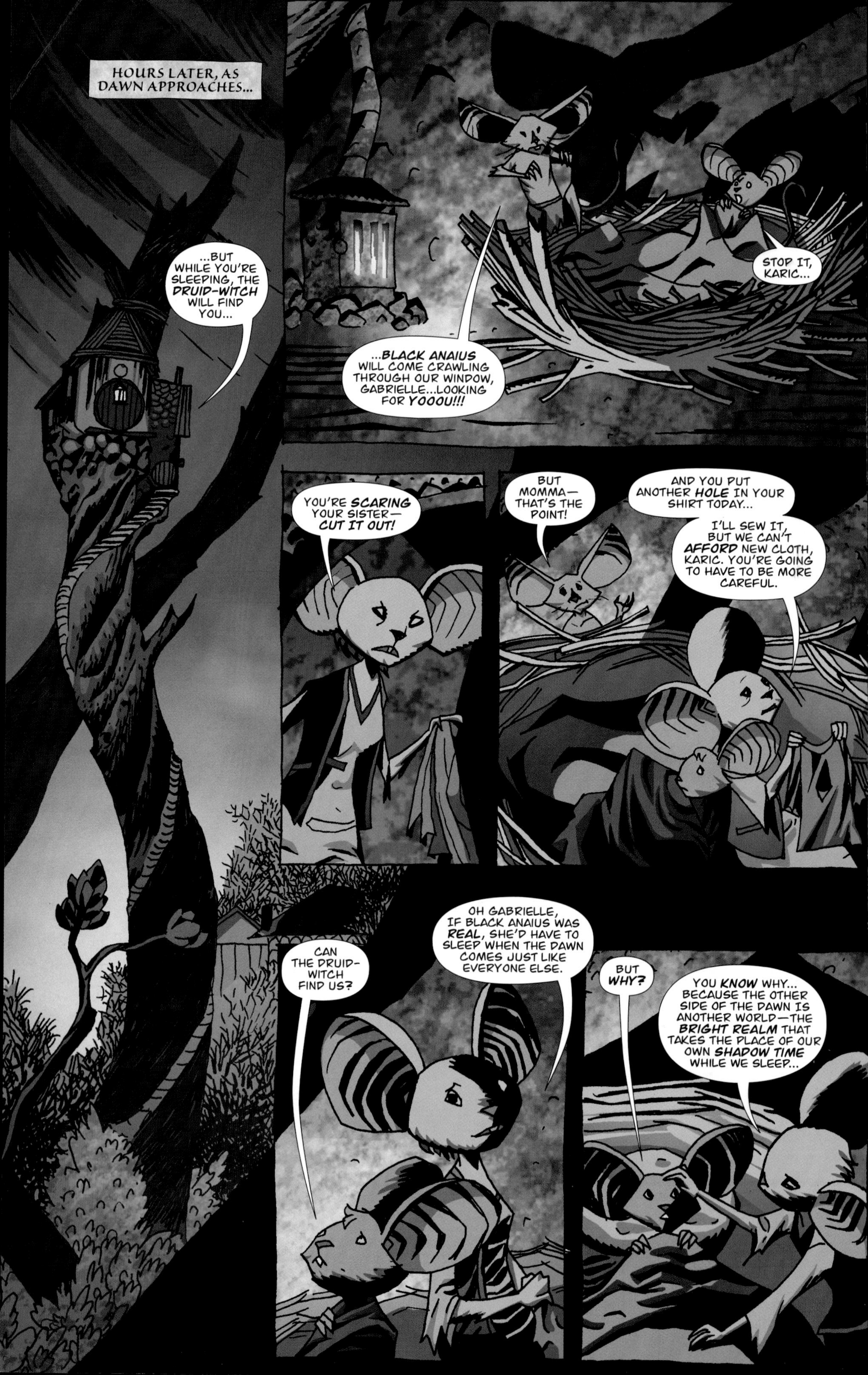
HOURS LATER, AS DAWN APPROACHES...
...BUT WHILE YOU'RE SLEEPING, THE DRUID-WITCH WILL FIND YOU...
...BLACK ANAIUS WILL COME CRAWLING THROUGH OUR WINDOW, GABRIELLE...LOOKING FOR YOOOU!!!
STOP IT, KARIC...
YOU'RE SCARING YOUR SISTER—CUT IT OUT!
BUT MOMMA—THAT'S THE POINT!
AND YOU PUT ANOTHER HOLE IN YOUR SHIRT TODAY...
I'LL SEW IT, BUT WE CAN'T AFFORD NEW CLOTH, KARIC. YOU'RE GOING TO HAVE TO BE MORE CAREFUL.
CAN THE DRUID-WITCH FIND US?
OH GABRIELLE, IF BLACK ANAIUS WAS REAL, SHE'D HAVE TO SLEEP WHEN THE DAWN COMES JUST LIKE EVERYONE ELSE.
BUT WHY?
YOU KNOW WHY... BECAUSE THE OTHER SIDE OF THE DAWN IS ANOTHER WORLD—THE BRIGHT REALM THAT TAKES THE PLACE OF OUR OWN SHADOW TIME WHILE WE SLEEP...

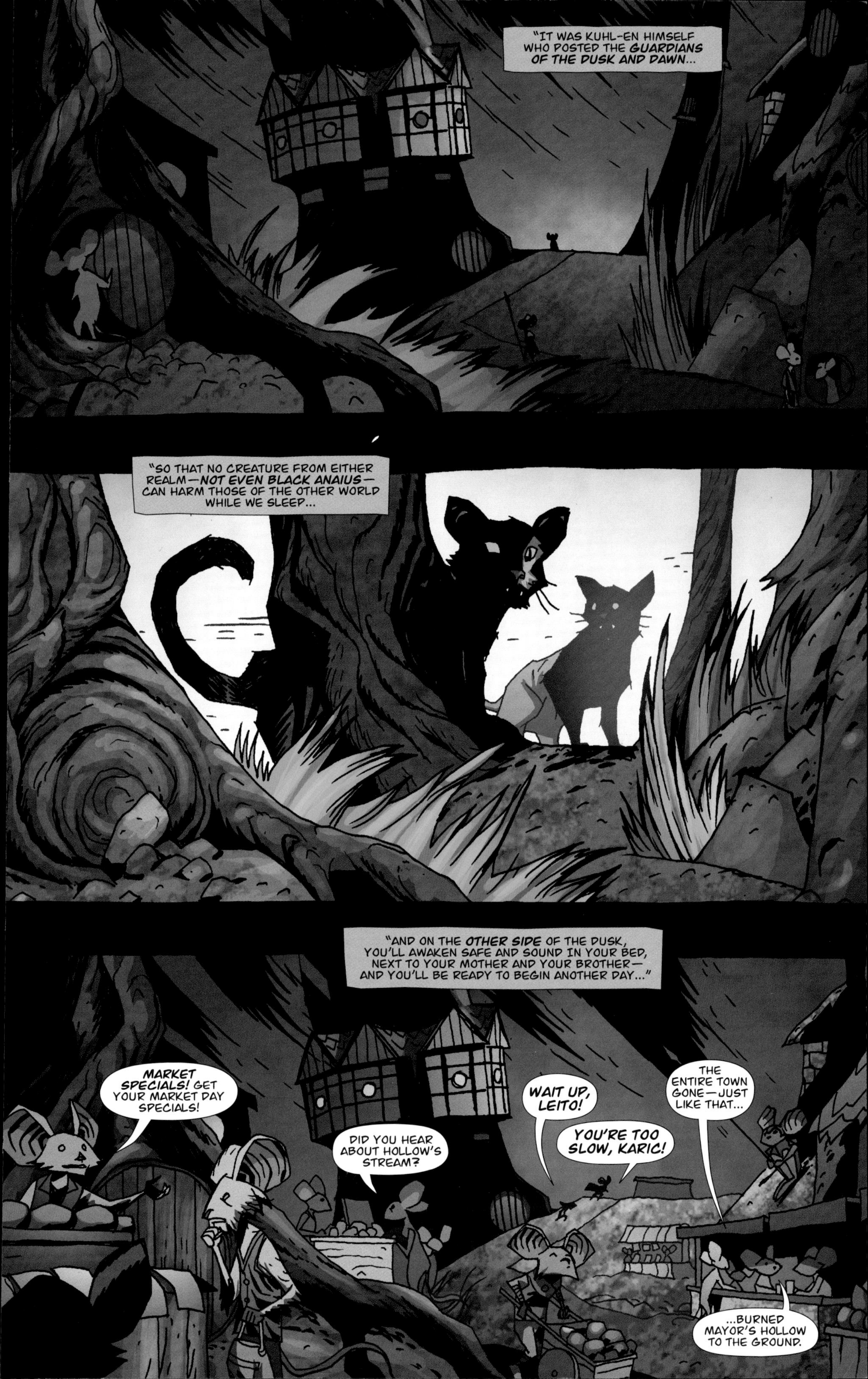
"IT WAS KUHL-EN HIMSELF WHO POSTED THE GUARDIANS OF THE DUSK AND DAWN...
"SO THAT NO CREATURE FROM EITHER REALM—NOT EVEN BLACK ANAIUS—CAN HARM THOSE OF THE OTHER WORLD WHILE WE SLEEP...
"AND ON THE OTHER SIDE OF THE DUSK, YOU'LL AWAKEN SAFE AND SOUND IN YOUR BED, NEXT TO YOUR MOTHER AND YOUR BROTHER—AND YOU'LL BE READY TO BEGIN ANOTHER DAY..."
MARKET SPECIALS! GET YOUR MARKET DAY SPECIALS!
DID YOU HEAR ABOUT HOLLOW'S STREAM?
WAIT UP, LEITO!
YOU'RE TOO SLOW, KARIC!
THE ENTIRE TOWN GONE—JUST LIKE THAT...
...BURNED MAYOR'S HOLLOW TO THE GROUND.

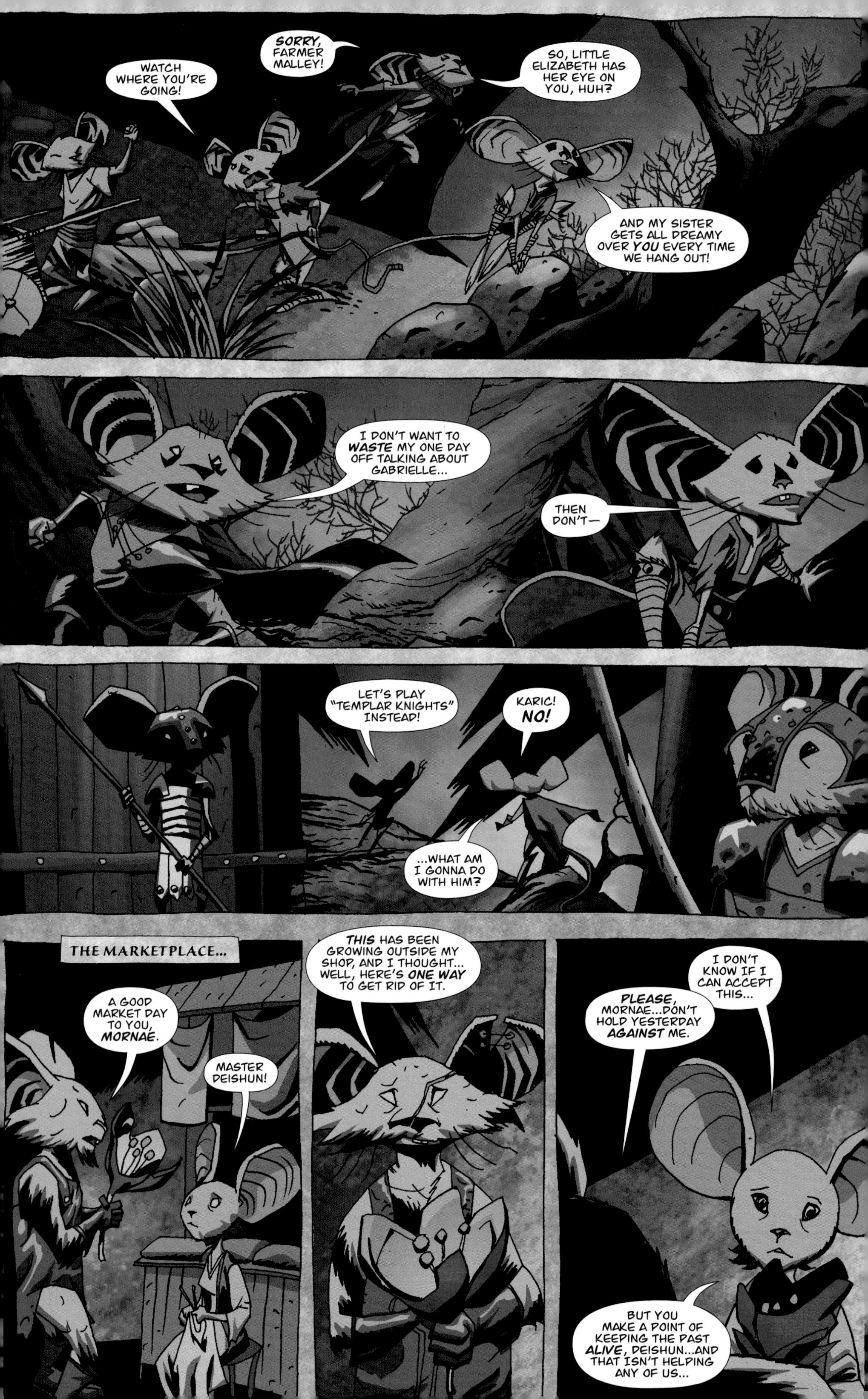
WATCH WHERE YOU'RE GOING!
SORRY, FARMER MALLEY!
SO, LITTLE ELIZABETH HAS HER EYE ON YOU, HUH?
AND MY SISTER GETS ALL DREAMY OVER YOU EVERY TIME WE HANG OUT!
I DON'T WANT TO WASTE MY ONE DAY OFF TALKING ABOUT GABRIELLE...
THEN DON'T—
LET'S PLAY "TEMPLAR KNIGHTS" INSTEAD!
KARIC! NO!
...WHAT AM I GONNA DO WITH HIM?
THE MARKETPLACE...
A GOOD MARKET DAY TO YOU, MORNAÉ.
MASTER DEISHUN!
THIS HAS BEEN GROWING OUTSIDE MY SHOP, AND I THOUGHT... WELL, HERE'S ONE WAY TO GET RID OF IT.
I DON'T KNOW IF I CAN ACCEPT THIS...
PLEASE, MORNAÉ...DON'T HOLD YESTERDAY AGAINST ME.
BUT YOU MAKE A POINT OF KEEPING THE PAST ALIVE, DEISHUN...AND THAT ISN'T HELPING ANY OF US...

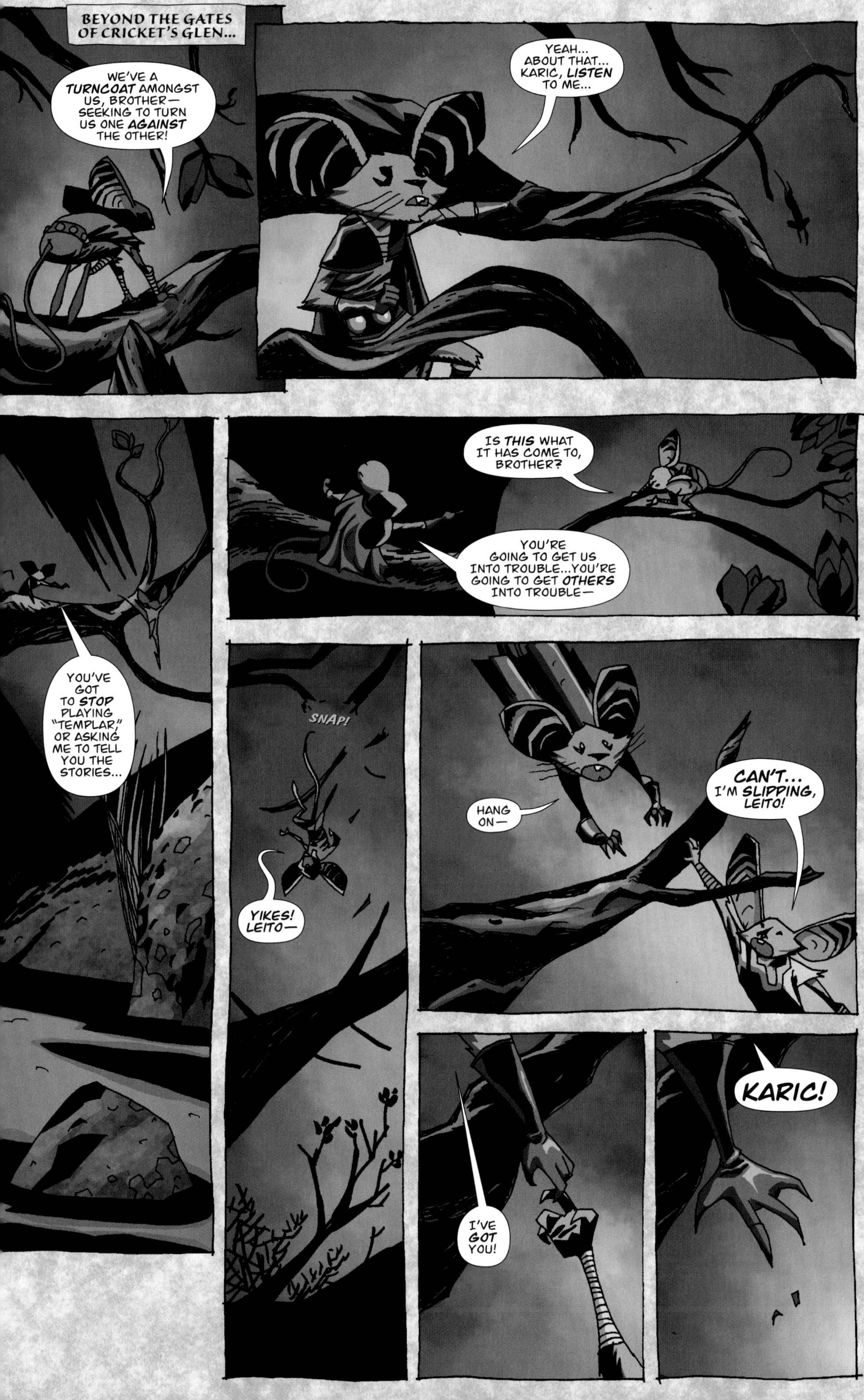
BEYOND THE GATES OF CRICKET'S GLEN...
WE'VE A TURNCOAT AMONGST US, BROTHER— SEEKING TO TURN US ONE AGAINST THE OTHER!
YEAH... ABOUT THAT... KARIC, LISTEN TO ME...
YOU'VE GOT TO STOP PLAYING "TEMPLAR," OR ASKING ME TO TELL YOU THE STORIES...
IS THIS WHAT IT HAS COME TO, BROTHER?
YOU'RE GOING TO GET US INTO TROUBLE...YOU'RE GOING TO GET OTHERS INTO TROUBLE—
SNAP!
YIKES! LEITO—
HANG ON—
CAN'T... I'M SLIPPING, LEITO!
I'VE GOT YOU!
KARIC!

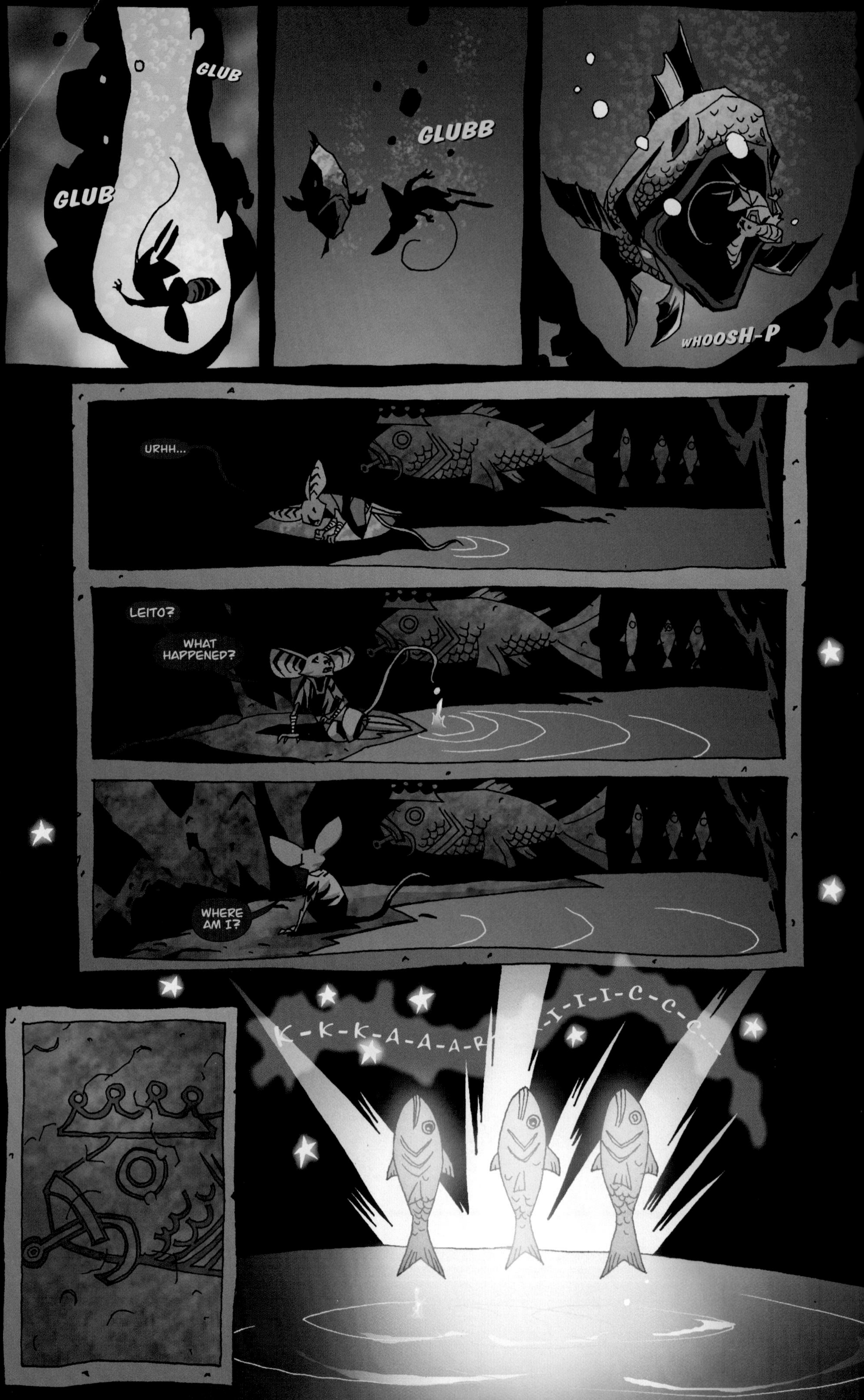

GLUB
GLUB
GLUBB
WHOOSH-P
URHH...
LEITO?
WHAT HAPPENED?
WHERE AM I?
K-K-K-A-A-A-R
-I-I-I-C-C-C

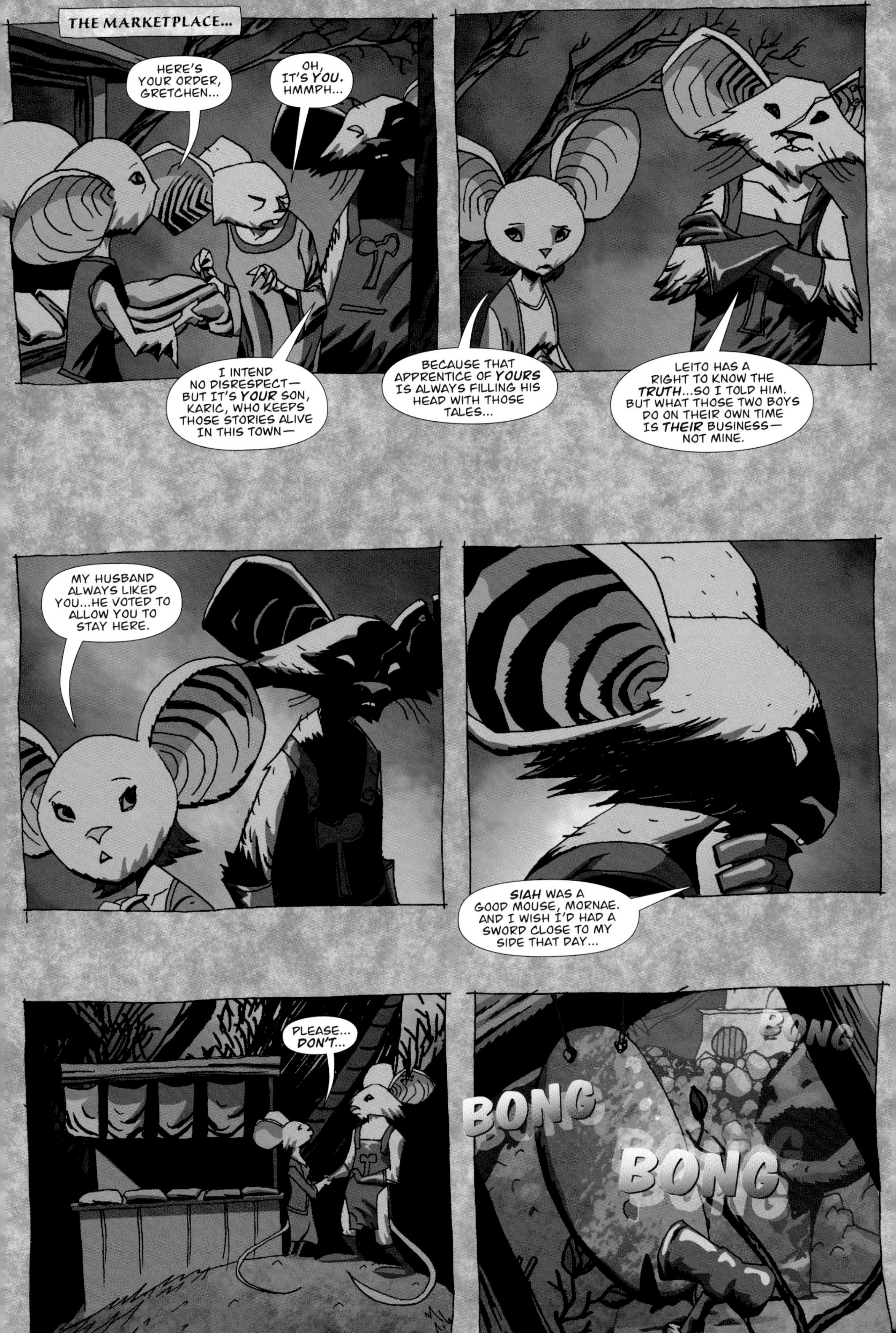
THE MARKETPLACE...
HERE'S YOUR ORDER, GRETCHEN...
OH, IT'S YOU. HMMPH...
I INTEND NO DISRESPECT— BUT IT'S YOUR SON, KARIC, WHO KEEPS THOSE STORIES ALIVE IN THIS TOWN—
BECAUSE THAT APPRENTICE OF YOURS IS ALWAYS FILLING HIS HEAD WITH THOSE TALES...
LEITO HAS A RIGHT TO KNOW THE TRUTH...SO I TOLD HIM. BUT WHAT THOSE TWO BOYS DO ON THEIR OWN TIME IS THEIR BUSINESS— NOT MINE.
MY HUSBAND ALWAYS LIKED YOU...HE VOTED TO ALLOW YOU TO STAY HERE.
SIAH WAS A GOOD MOUSE, MORNAE. AND I WISH I'D HAD A SWORD CLOSE TO MY SIDE THAT DAY...
PLEASE... DON'T...
BONG
BONG
BONG

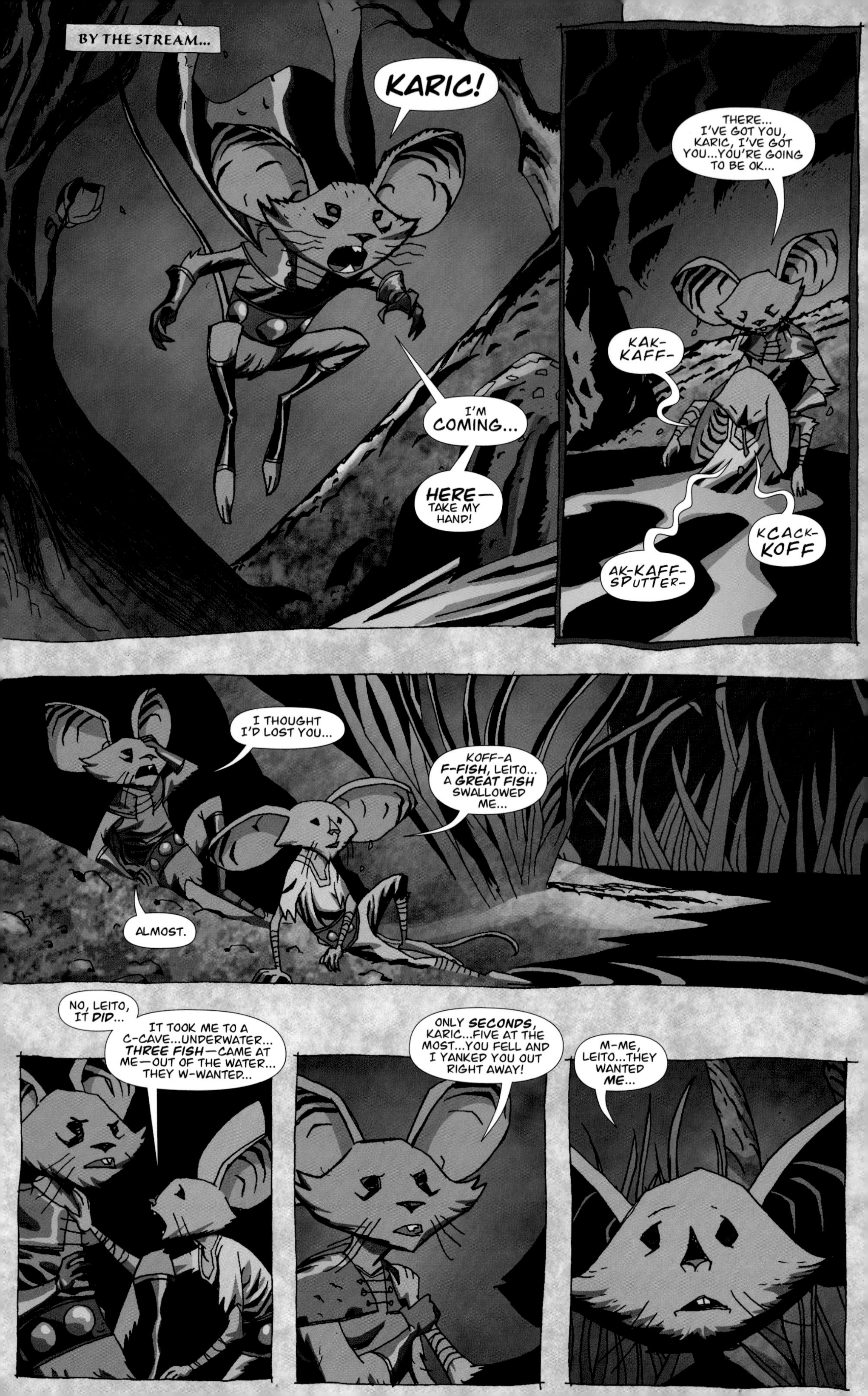
BY THE STREAM...
KARIC!
I'M COMING...
HERE— TAKE MY HAND!
THERE... I'VE GOT YOU, KARIC, I'VE GOT YOU...YOU'RE GOING TO BE OK...
KAK-KAFF-
AK-KAFF-SPUTTER-
KCACK-KOFF
I THOUGHT I'D LOST YOU...
KOFF-A F-FISH, LEITO... A GREAT FISH SWALLOWED ME...
ALMOST.
NO, LEITO, IT DID...
IT TOOK ME TO A C-CAVE...UNDERWATER... THREE FISH—CAME AT ME—OUT OF THE WATER... THEY W-WANTED...
ONLY SECONDS, KARIC...FIVE AT THE MOST...YOU FELL AND I YANKED YOU OUT RIGHT AWAY!
M-ME, LEITO...THEY WANTED ME...

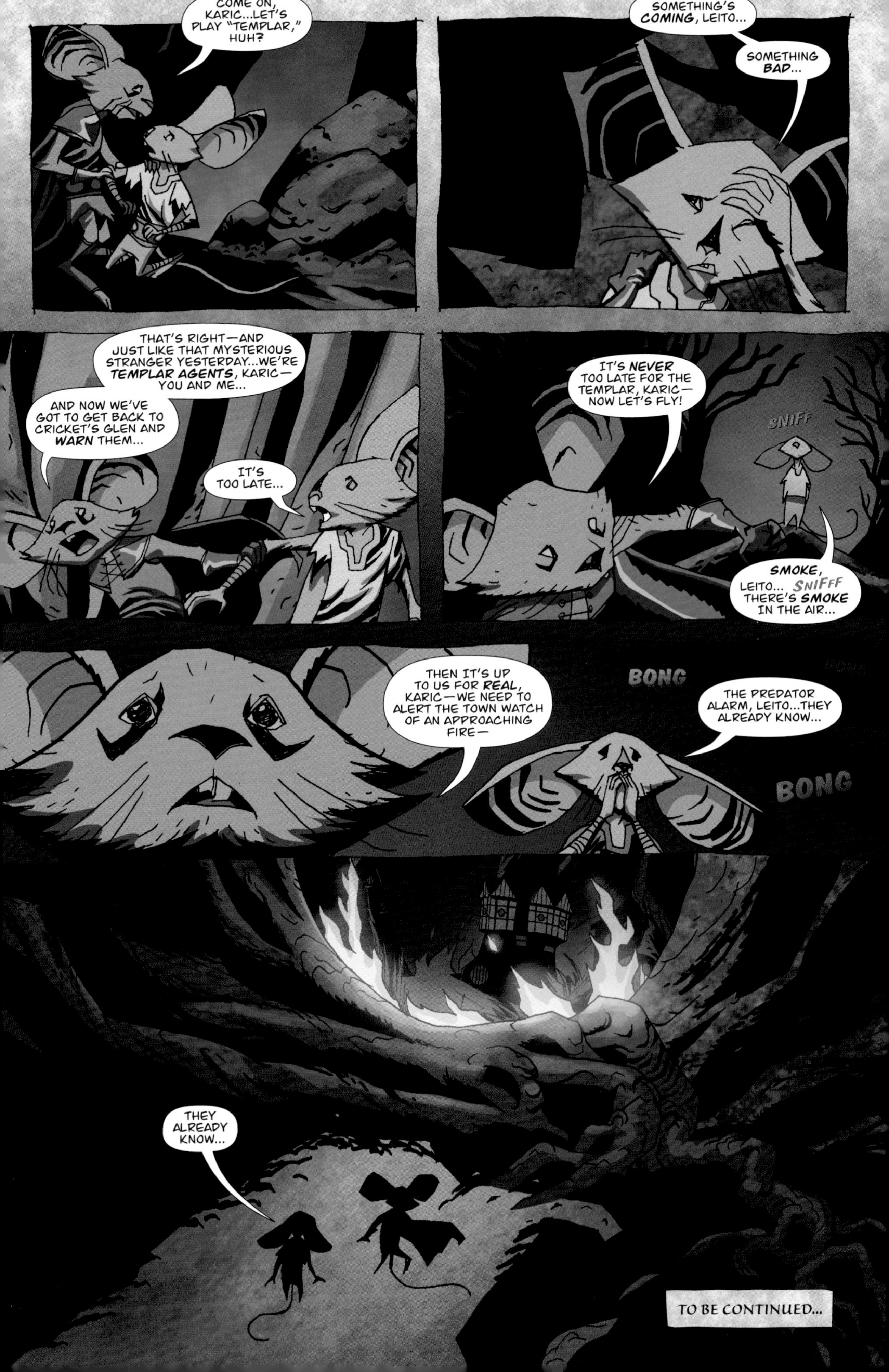
COME ON, KARIC...LET'S PLAY "TEMPLAR," HUH?
SOMETHING'S **COMING**, LEITO...
SOMETHING **BAD**...
THAT'S RIGHT—AND JUST LIKE THAT MYSTERIOUS STRANGER YESTERDAY...WE'RE **TEMPLAR AGENTS**, KARIC—YOU AND ME...
AND NOW WE'VE GOT TO GET BACK TO CRICKET'S GLEN AND **WARN** THEM...
IT'S TOO LATE...
IT'S **NEVER** TOO LATE FOR THE TEMPLAR, KARIC—NOW LET'S FLY!
SNIFF
SMOKE, LEITO... SNIFFF THERE'S **SMOKE** IN THE AIR...
THEN IT'S UP TO US FOR **REAL**, KARIC—WE NEED TO ALERT THE TOWN WATCH OF AN APPROACHING FIRE—
BONG
THE PREDATOR ALARM, LEITO...THEY ALREADY KNOW...
BONG
THEY ALREADY KNOW...
TO BE CONTINUED...

CHAPTER TWO
THE CALLING

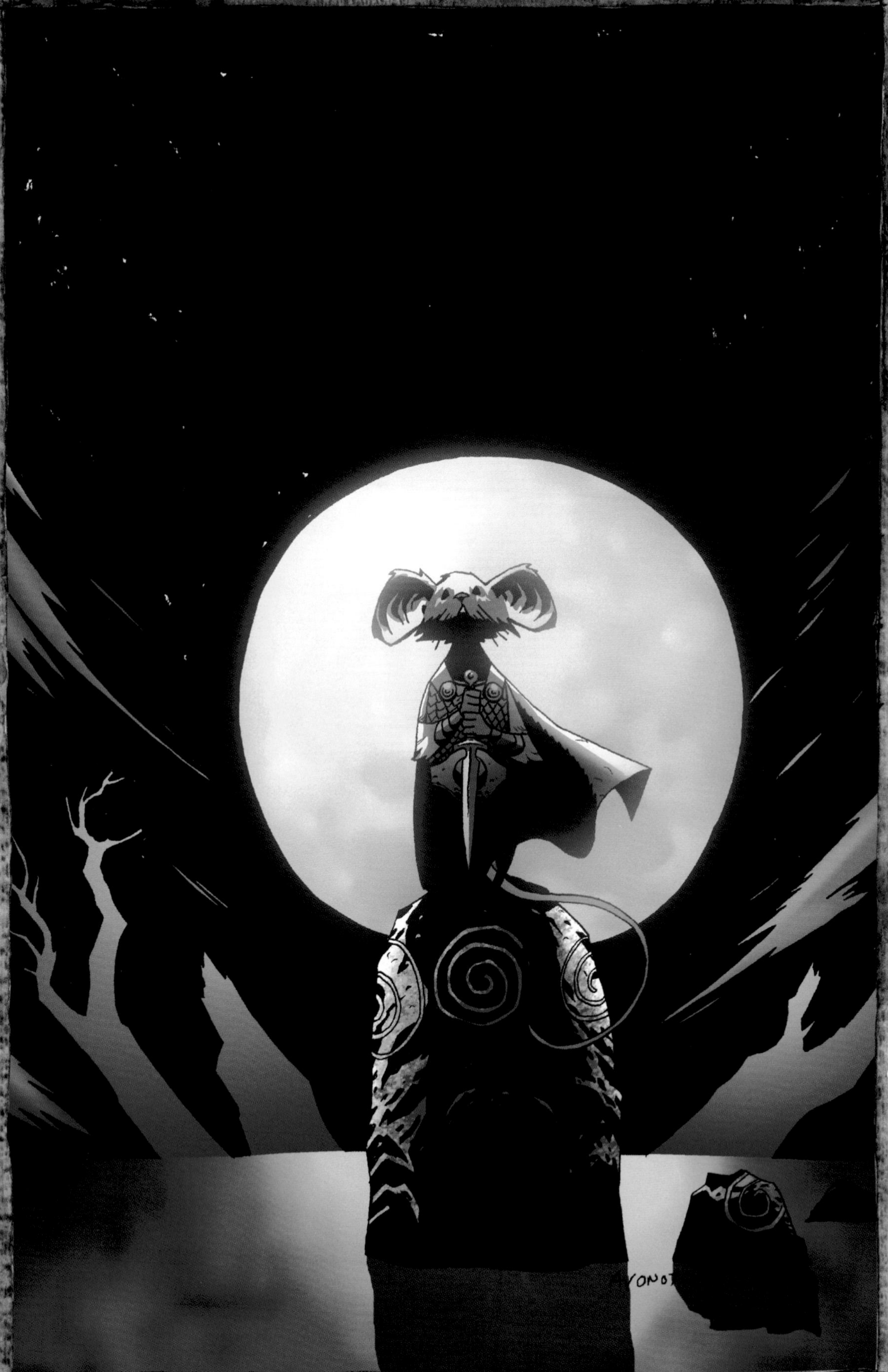

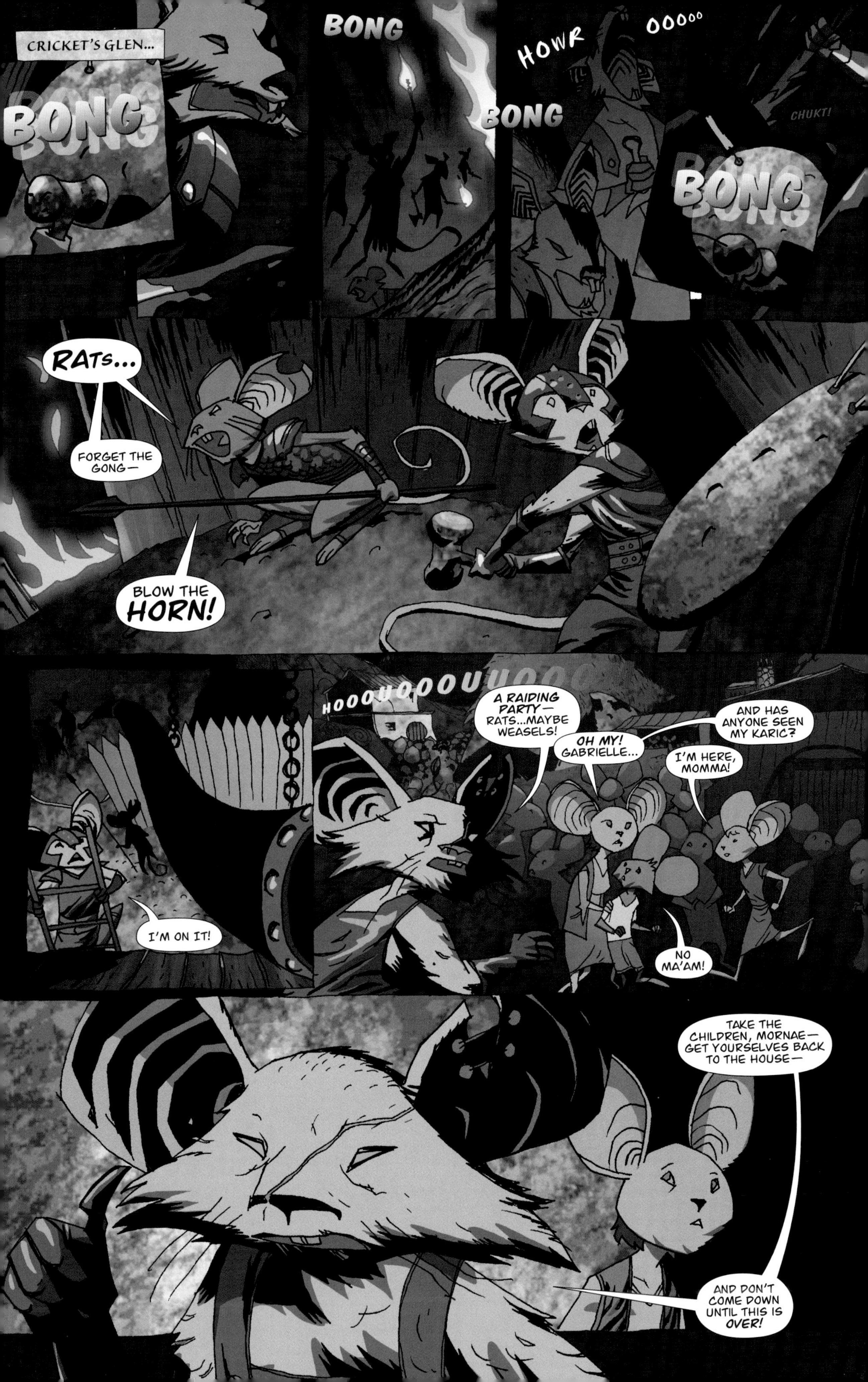
CRICKET'S GLEN...
BONG
BONG
BONG
HOWR
OOOoo
BONG
CHUKT!
BONG
RATs...
FORGET THE GONG—
BLOW THE HORN!
I'M ON IT!
HOOOUOOOUUOOO
A RAIDING PARTY— RATS...MAYBE WEASELS!
OH MY! GABRIELLE...
AND HAS ANYONE SEEN MY KARIC?
I'M HERE, MOMMA!
NO MA'AM!
TAKE THE CHILDREN, MORNAE— GET YOURSELVES BACK TO THE HOUSE—
AND DON'T COME DOWN UNTIL THIS IS OVER!

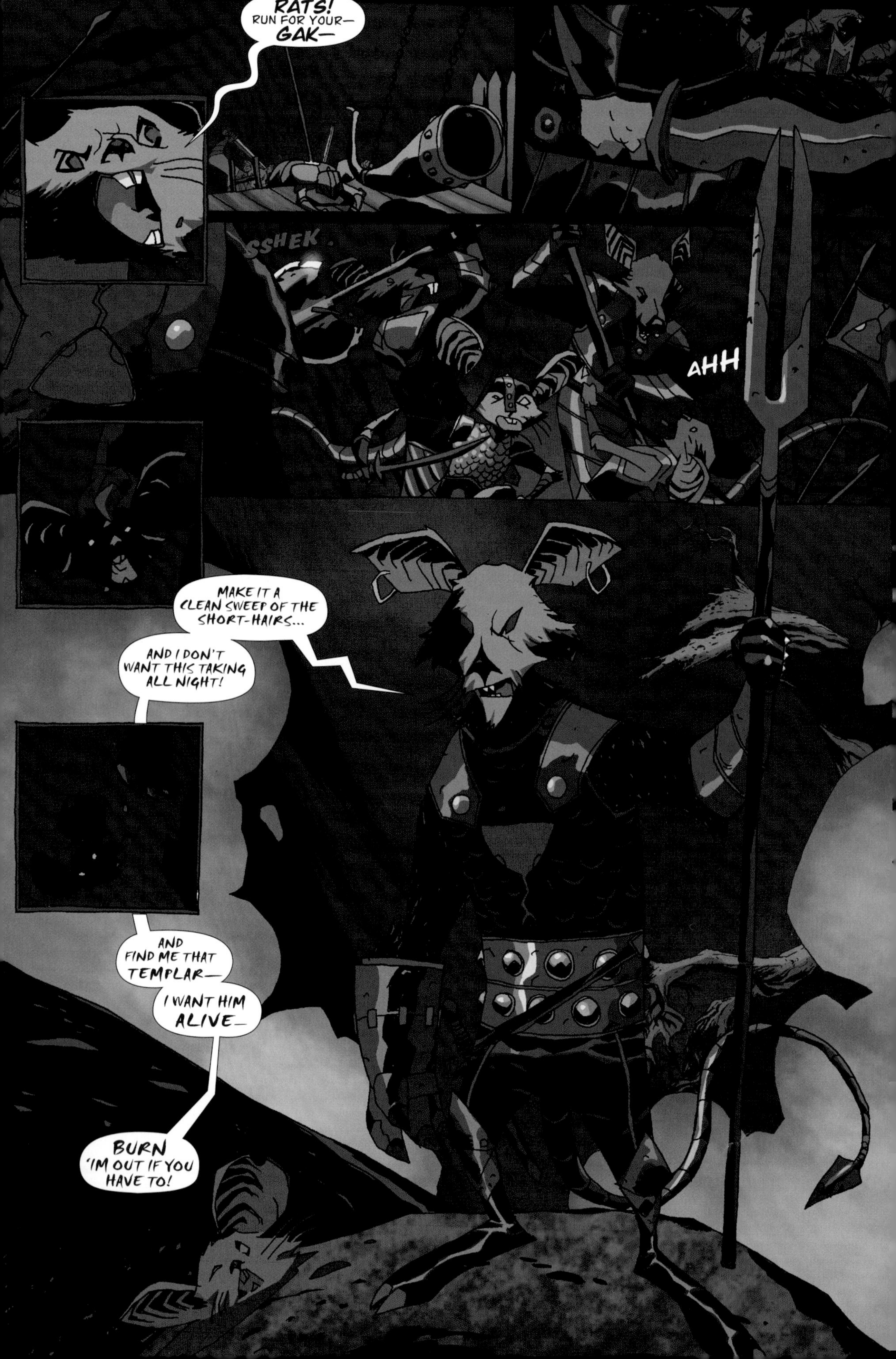
RATS! RUN FOR YOUR— GAK—
SSHEK.
AHH
MAKE IT A CLEAN SWEEP OF THE SHORT-HAIRS...
AND I DON'T WANT THIS TAKING ALL NIGHT!
AND FIND ME THAT TEMPLAR—
I WANT HIM ALIVE—
BURN 'IM OUT IF YOU HAVE TO!

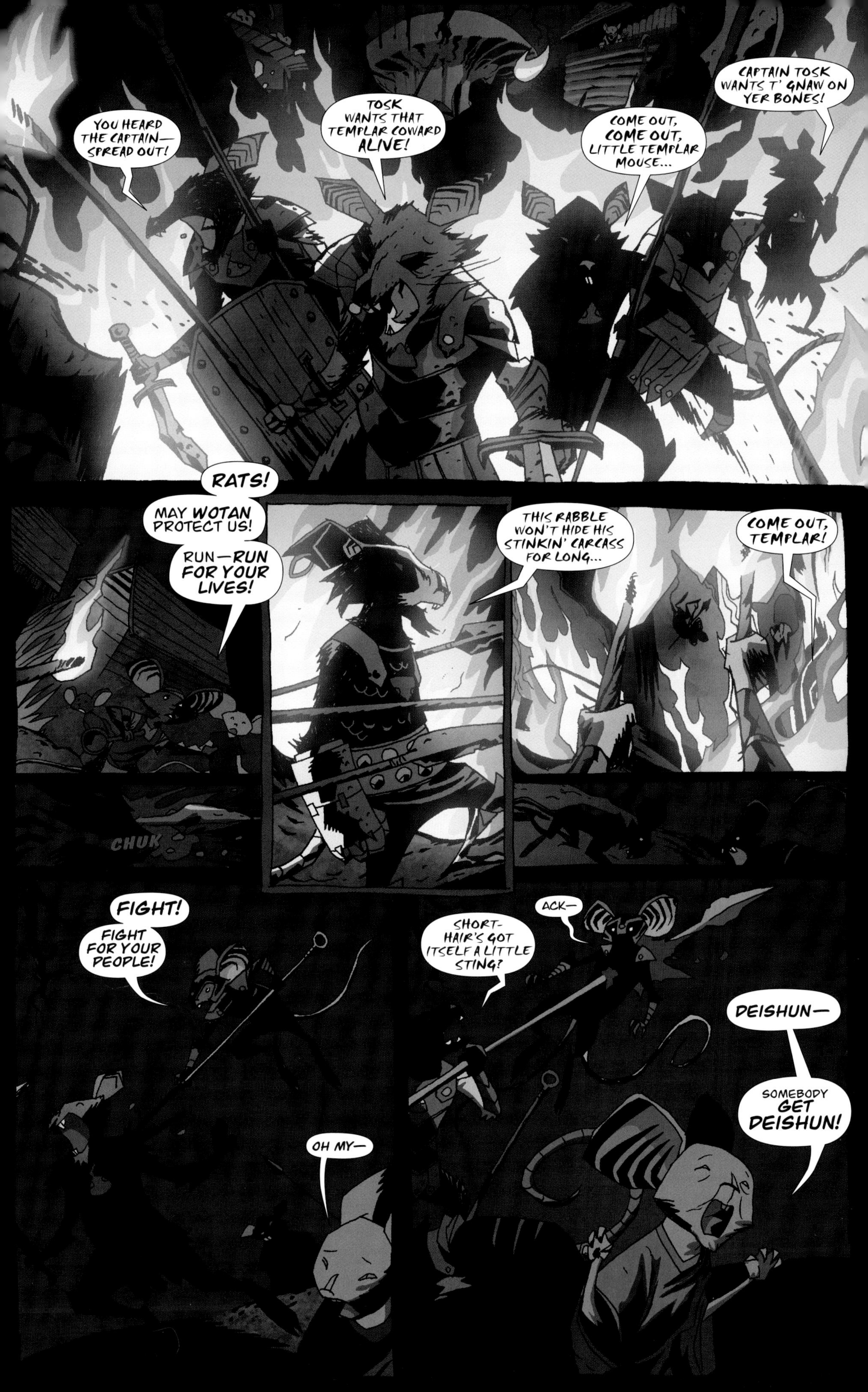

YOU HEARD THE CAPTAIN— SPREAD OUT!
TOSK WANTS THAT TEMPLAR COWARD ALIVE!
COME OUT, COME OUT, LITTLE TEMPLAR MOUSE...
CAPTAIN TOSK WANTS T' GNAW ON YER BONES!
RATS!
MAY WOTAN PROTECT US!
RUN—RUN FOR YOUR LIVES!
CHUK
THIS RABBLE WON'T HIDE HIS STINKIN' CARCASS FOR LONG...
COME OUT, TEMPLAR!
FIGHT!
FIGHT FOR YOUR PEOPLE!
SHORT-HAIR'S GOT ITSELF A LITTLE STING?
ACK—
OH MY—
DEISHUN—
SOMEBODY GET DEISHUN!

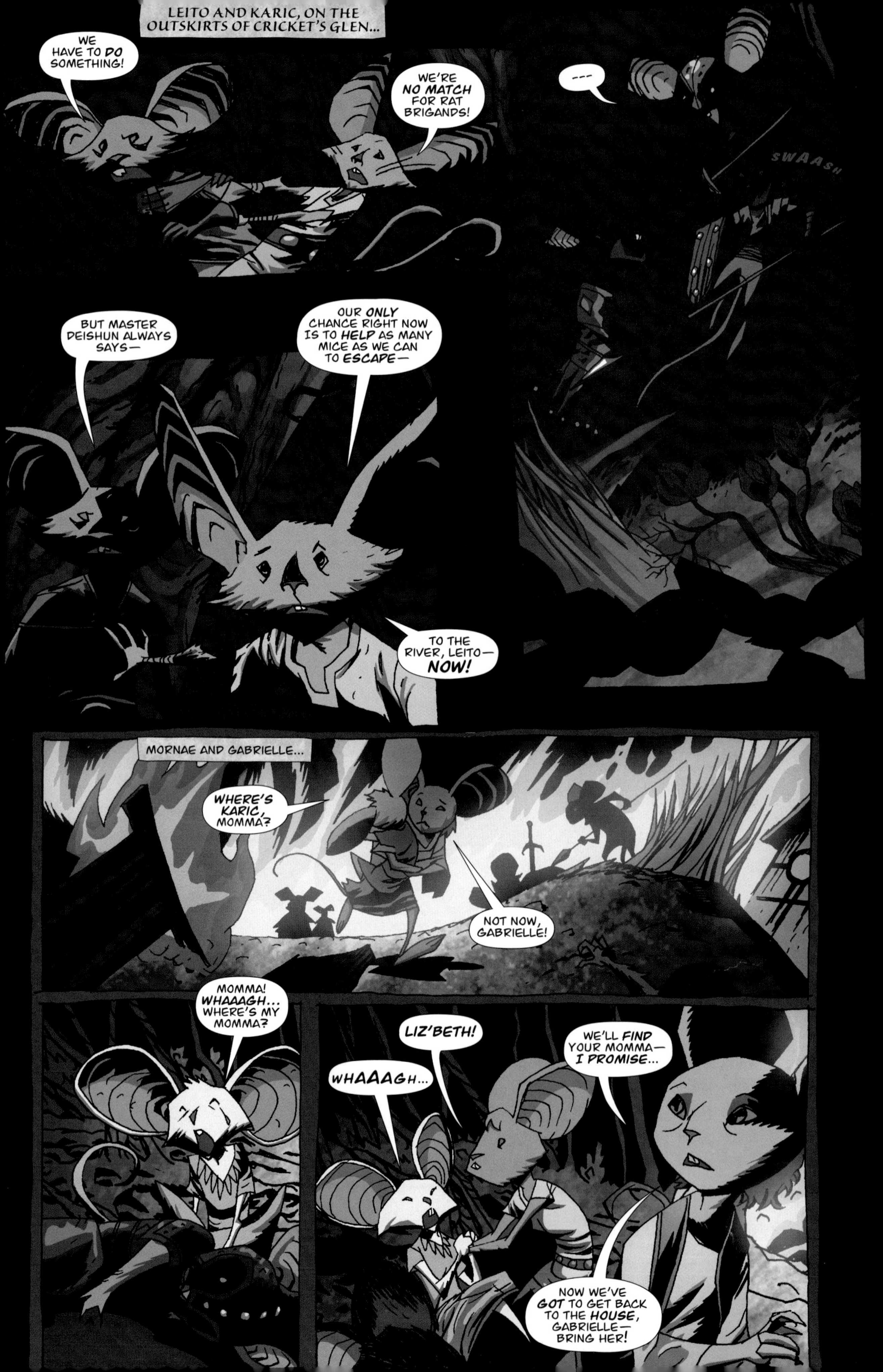
LEITO AND KARIC, ON THE OUTSKIRTS OF CRICKET'S GLEN...
WE HAVE TO DO SOMETHING!
WE'RE NO MATCH FOR RAT BRIGANDS!

SWAASH
BUT MASTER DEISHUN ALWAYS SAYS—
OUR ONLY CHANCE RIGHT NOW IS TO HELP AS MANY MICE AS WE CAN TO ESCAPE—
TO THE RIVER, LEITO— NOW!
MORNAE AND GABRIELLE...
WHERE'S KARIC, MOMMA?
NOT NOW, GABRIELLE!
MOMMA! WHAAAGH... WHERE'S MY MOMMA?
LIZ'BETH!
WHAAAGH...
WE'LL FIND YOUR MOMMA— I PROMISE...
NOW WE'VE GOT TO GET BACK TO THE HOUSE, GABRIELLE— BRING HER!

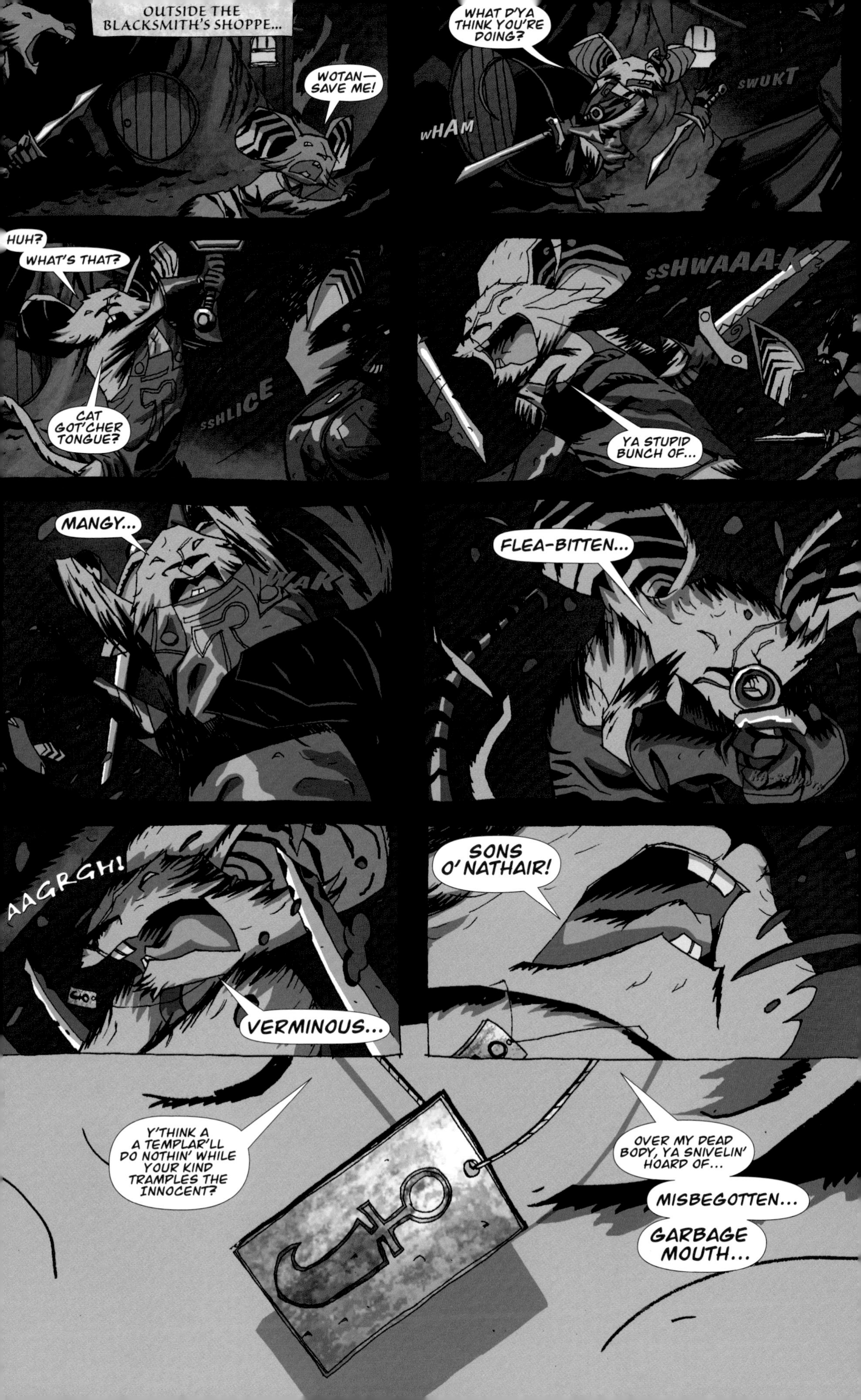

OUTSIDE THE BLACKSMITH'S SHOPPE...
WOTAN— SAVE ME!
WHAT D'YA THINK YOU'RE DOING?
WHAM
SWUKT
HUH?
WHAT'S THAT?
CAT GOT'CHER TONGUE?
SSHLICE
SSHWAAAK
YA STUPID BUNCH OF...
MANGY...
WAK
FLEA-BITTEN...
AAGRGH!
VERMINOUS...
SONS O' NATHAIR!
Y'THINK A A TEMPLAR'LL DO NOTHIN' WHILE YOUR KIND TRAMPLES THE INNOCENT?
OVER MY DEAD BODY, YA SNIVELIN' HOARD OF...
MISBEGOTTEN...
GARBAGE MOUTH...

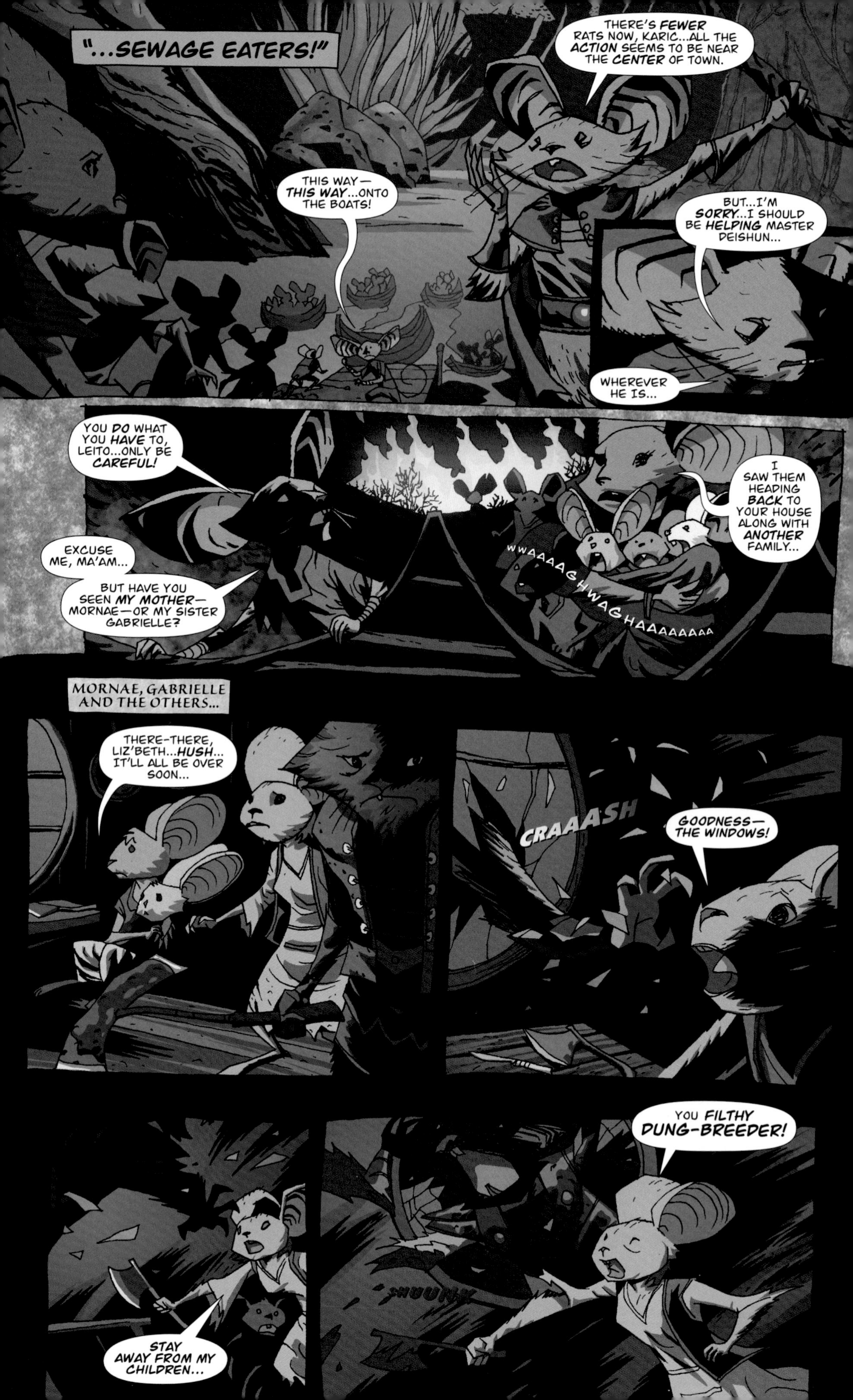
"...SEWAGE EATERS!"
THERE'S FEWER RATS NOW, KARIC...ALL THE ACTION SEEMS TO BE NEAR THE CENTER OF TOWN.
THIS WAY—THIS WAY...ONTO THE BOATS!
BUT...I'M SORRY...I SHOULD BE HELPING MASTER DEISHUN...
WHEREVER HE IS...
YOU DO WHAT YOU HAVE TO, LEITO...ONLY BE CAREFUL!
EXCUSE ME, MA'AM...
BUT HAVE YOU SEEN MY MOTHER—MORNAE—OR MY SISTER GABRIELLE?
I SAW THEM HEADING BACK TO YOUR HOUSE ALONG WITH ANOTHER FAMILY...
WWAAAAGHWAGHAAAAAAAA
MORNAE, GABRIELLE AND THE OTHERS...
THERE-THERE, LIZ'BETH...HUSH... IT'LL ALL BE OVER SOON...
CRAAASH
GOODNESS—THE WINDOWS!
STAY AWAY FROM MY CHILDREN...
YOU FILTHY DUNG-BREEDER!

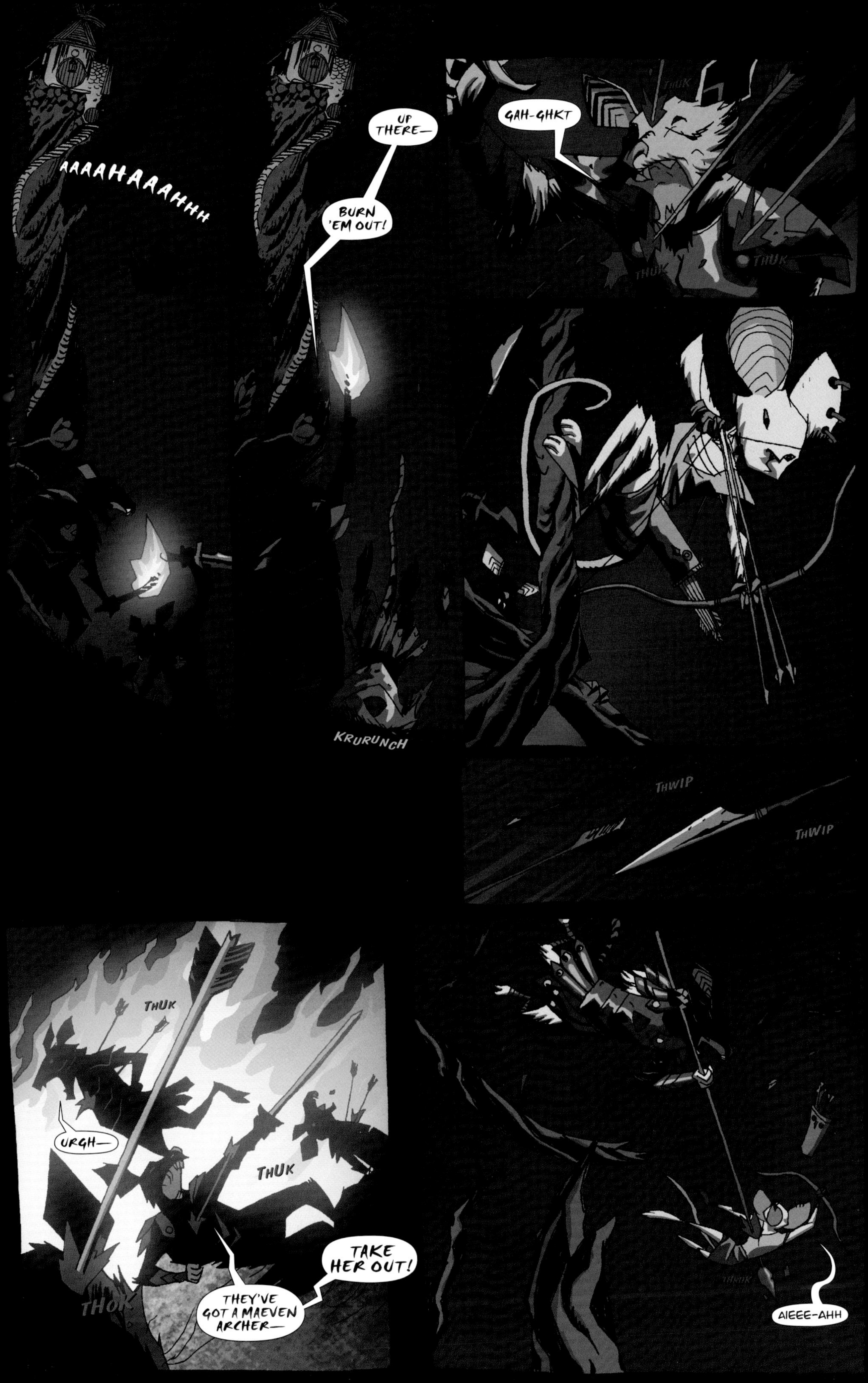
AAAAHAAAAHHH
UP THERE—
BURN 'EM OUT!
KRURUNCH
GAH-GHKT
THUK
THUK
THUK
THWIP
THWIP
THUK
URGH—
THUK
THOK
THEY'VE GOT A MAEVEN ARCHER—
TAKE HER OUT!
AIEEE-AHH

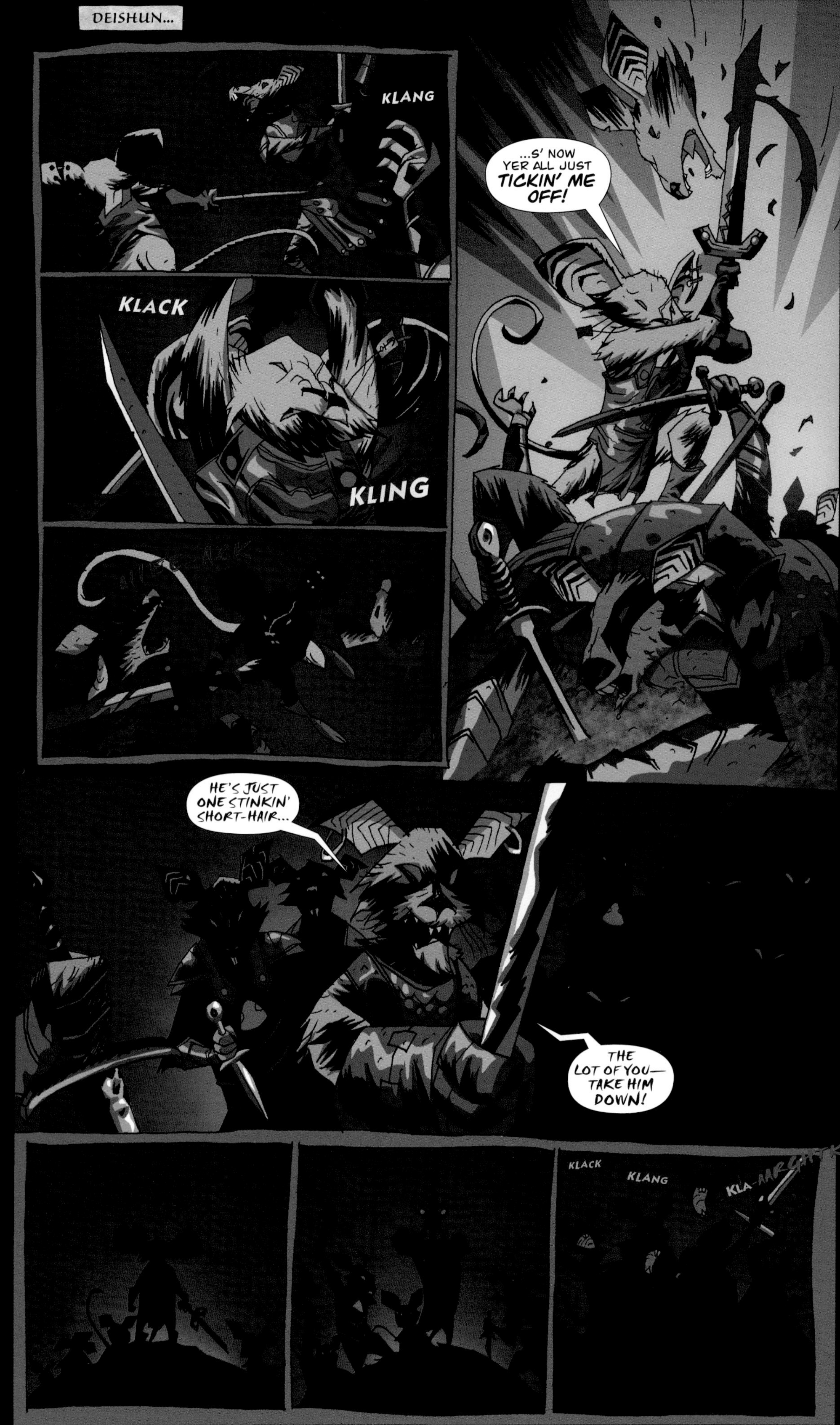
DEISHUN...
KLANG
KLACK
KLING
...S' NOW YER ALL JUST TICKIN' ME OFF!
HE'S JUST ONE STINKIN' SHORT-HAIR...
THE LOT OF YOU— TAKE HIM DOWN!
KLACK
KLANG
KLA-AARGH

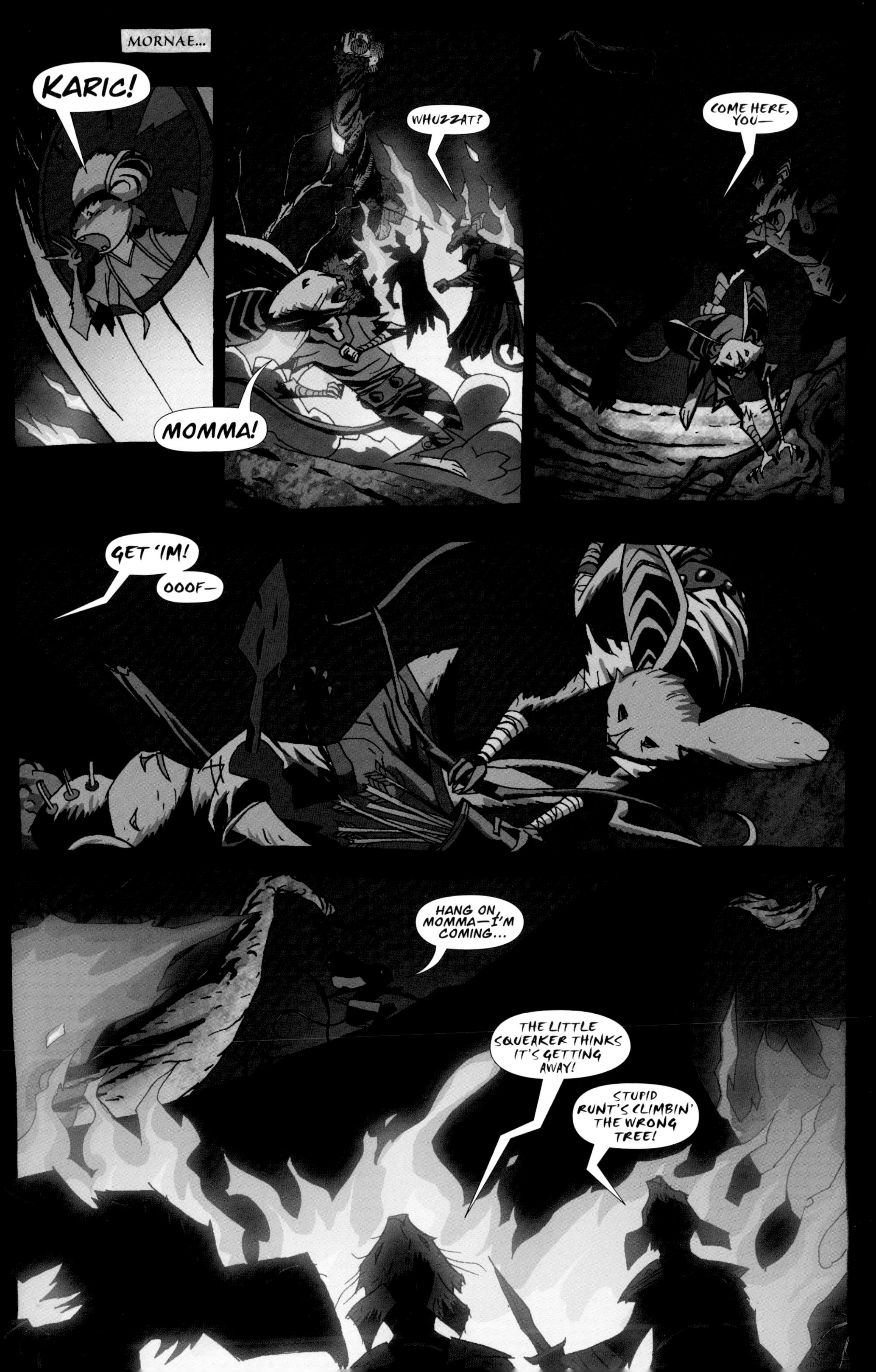

MORNAE...
KARIC!
WHUZZAT?
MOMMA!
COME HERE, YOU—
GET 'IM!
OOOF—
HANG ON, MOMMA—I'M COMING...
THE LITTLE SQUEAKER THINKS IT'S GETTING AWAY!
STUPID RUNT'S CLIMBIN' THE WRONG TREE!

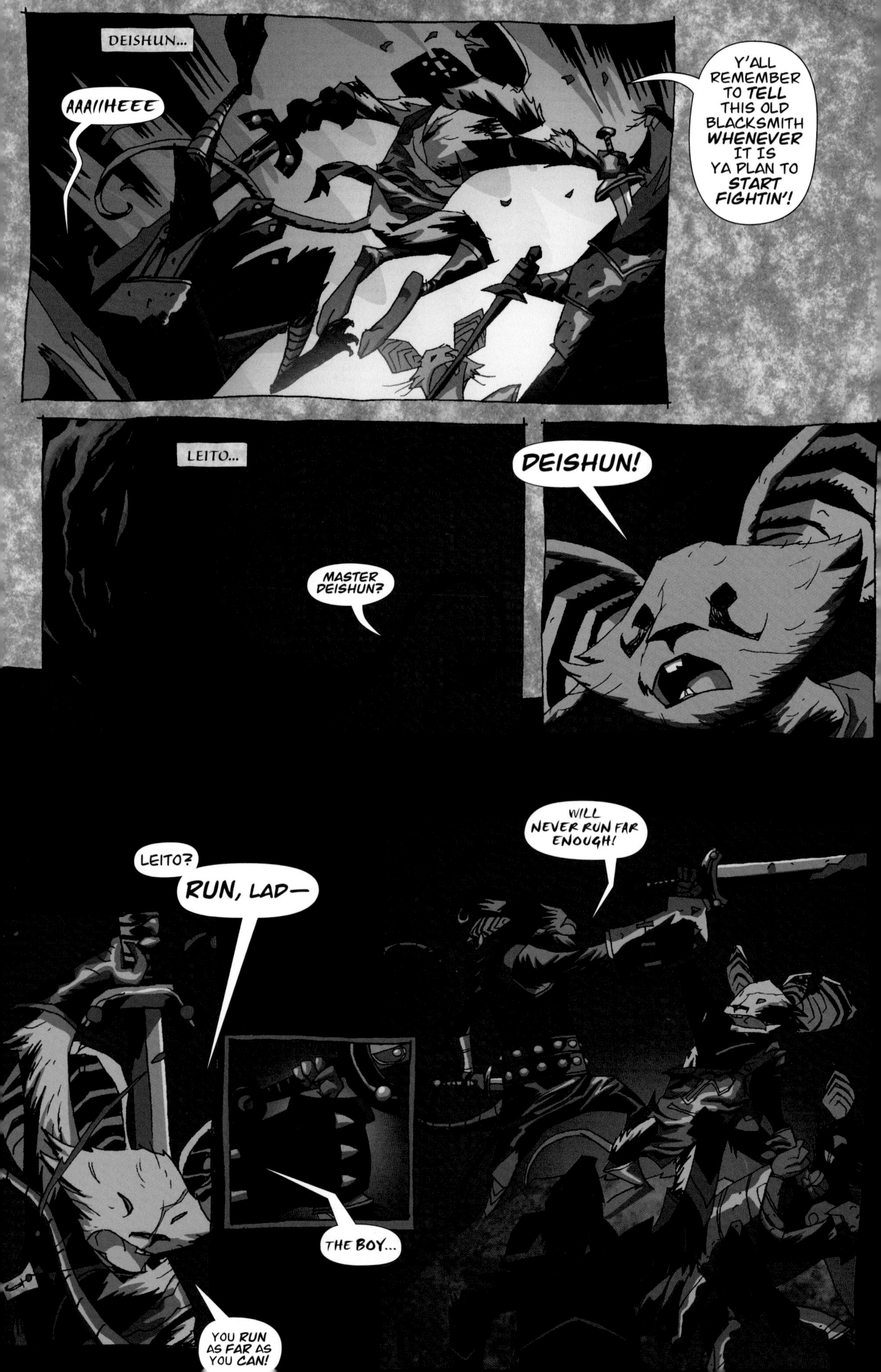
DEISHUN...
AAAIIHEEE
Y'ALL REMEMBER TO TELL THIS OLD BLACKSMITH WHENEVER IT IS YA PLAN TO START FIGHTIN'!
LEITO...
MASTER DEISHUN?
DEISHUN!
LEITO?
RUN, LAD—
WILL NEVER RUN FAR ENOUGH!
THE BOY...
YOU RUN AS FAR AS YOU CAN!

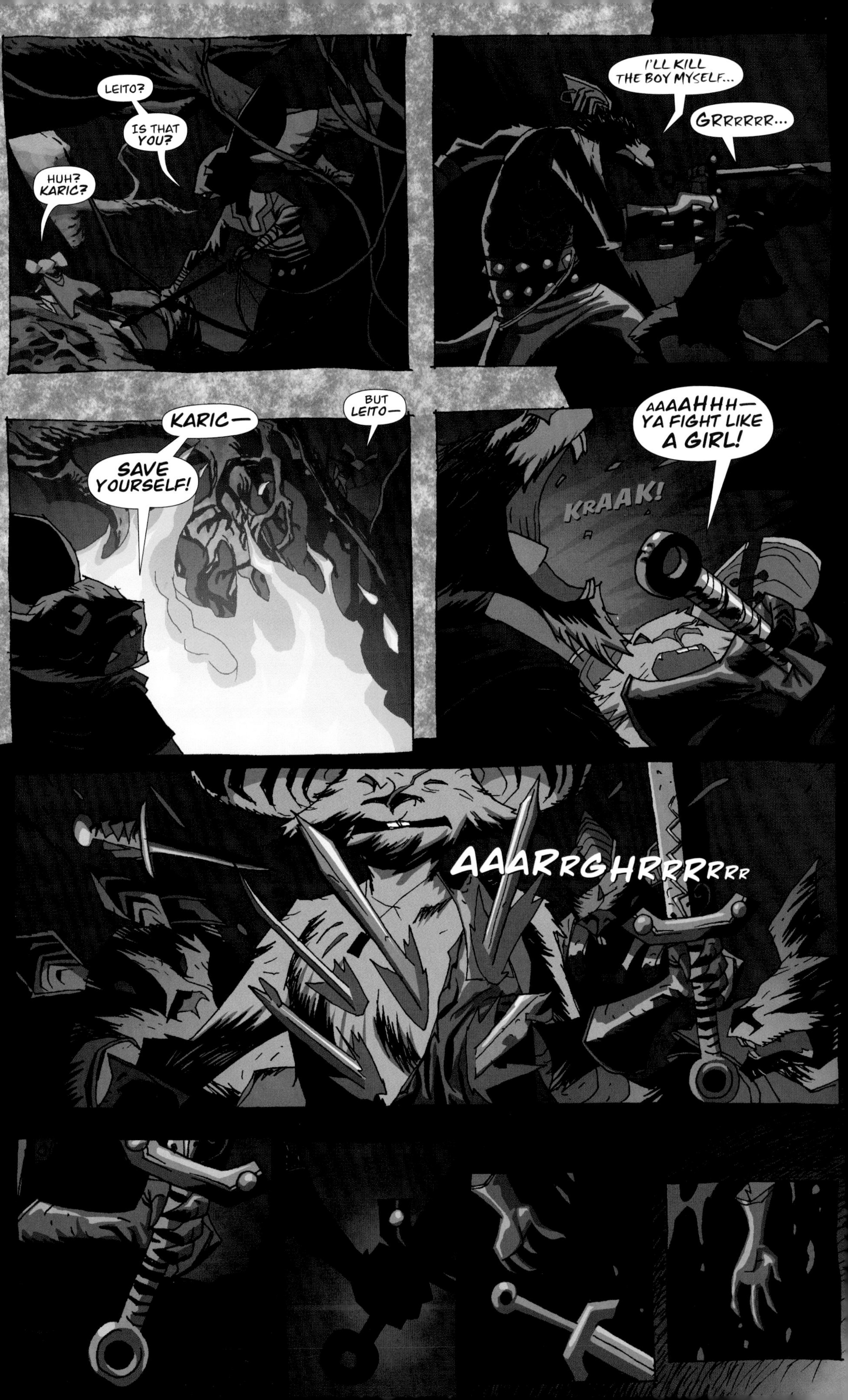
LEITO?
IS THAT YOU?
HUH? KARIC?
I'LL KILL THE BOY MYSELF...
GRRRRRR...
KARIC—
SAVE YOURSELF!
BUT LEITO—
KRAAK!
AAAAHHH— YA FIGHT LIKE A GIRL!
AAARRGHRRRRRR

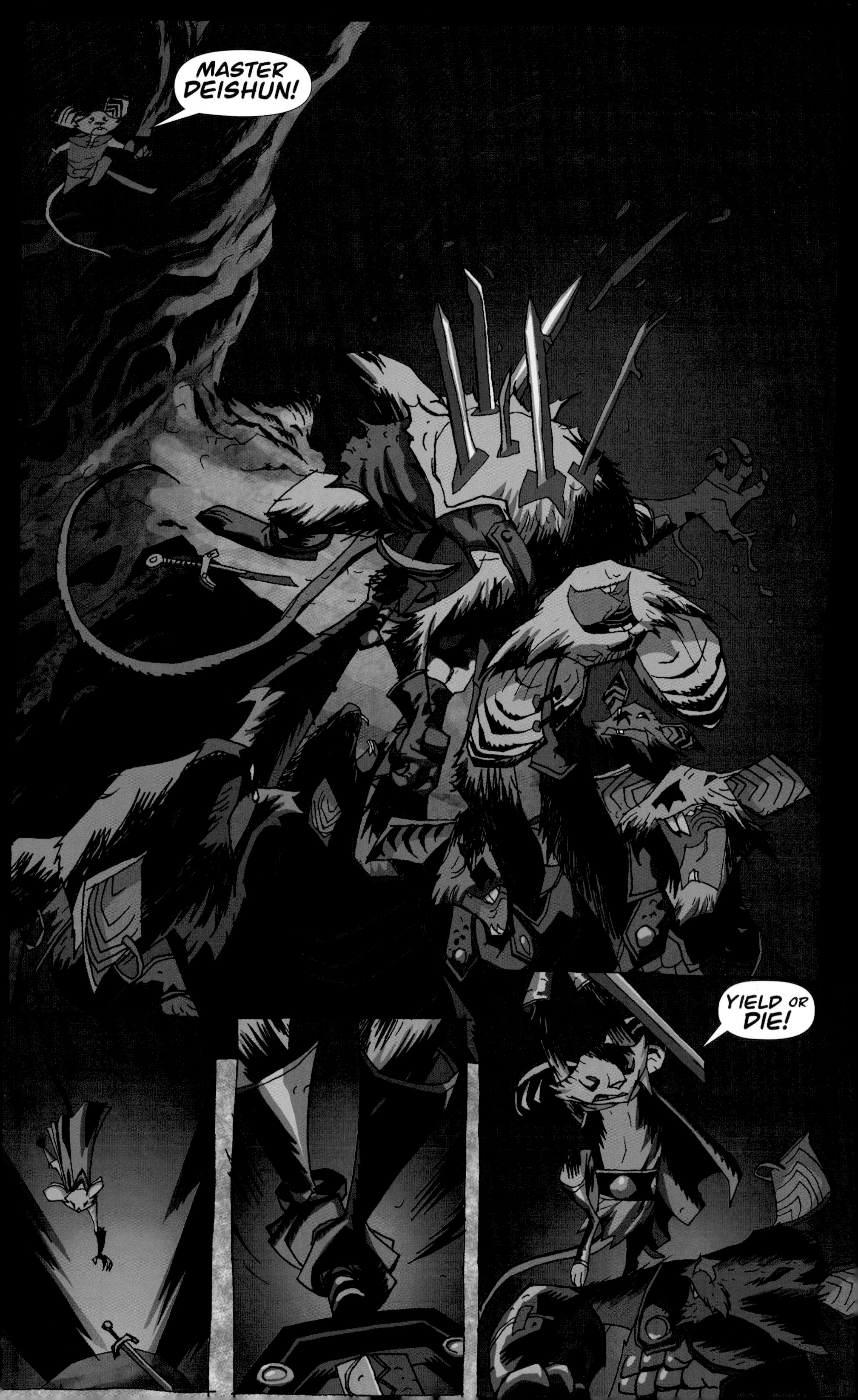
MASTER DEISHUN!
YIELD OR DIE!

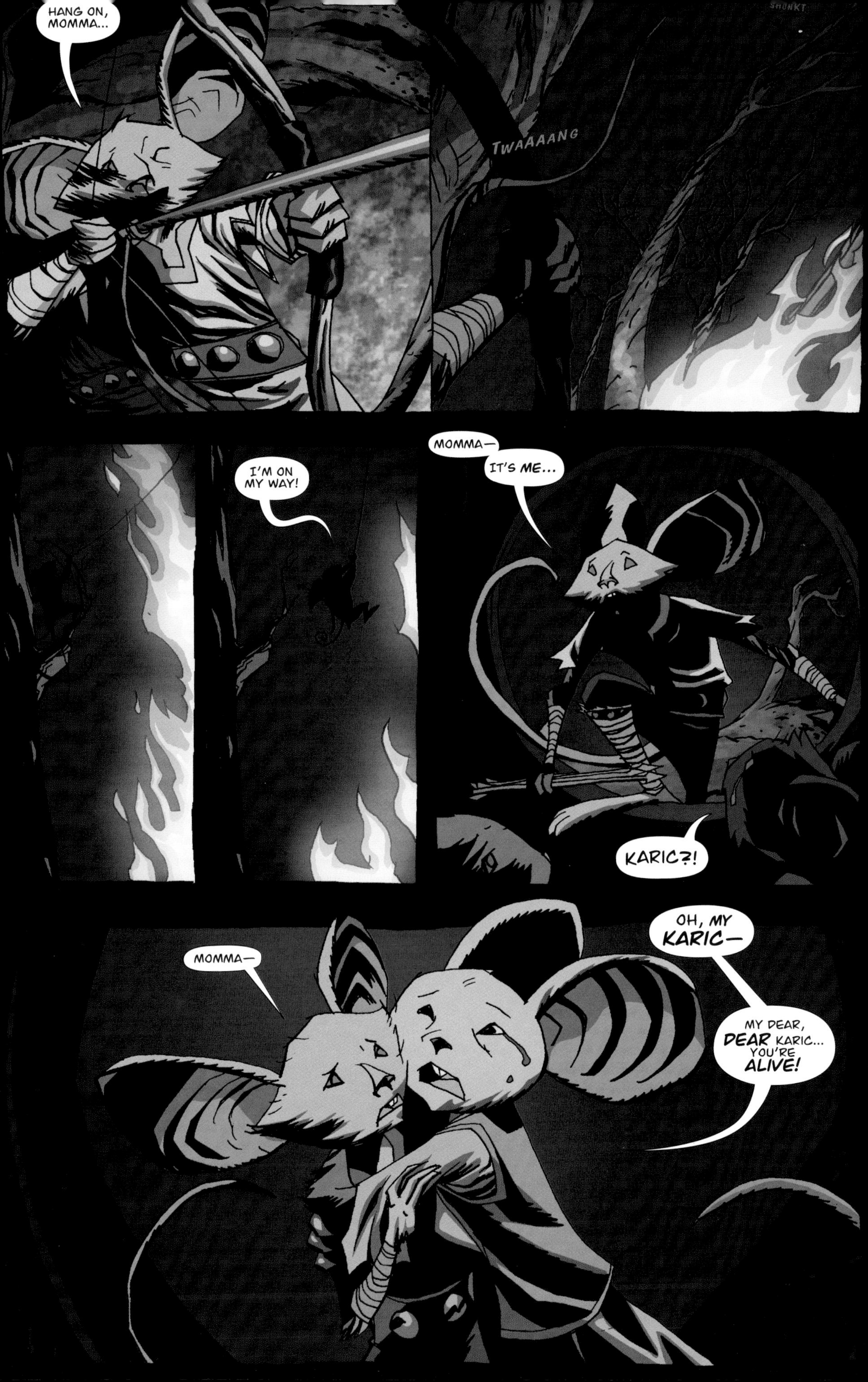
HANG ON, MOMMA...
TWAAAANG
SHONKT
I'M ON MY WAY!
MOMMA—
IT'S ME...
KARIC?!
MOMMA—
OH, MY KARIC—
MY DEAR, DEAR KARIC... YOU'RE ALIVE!

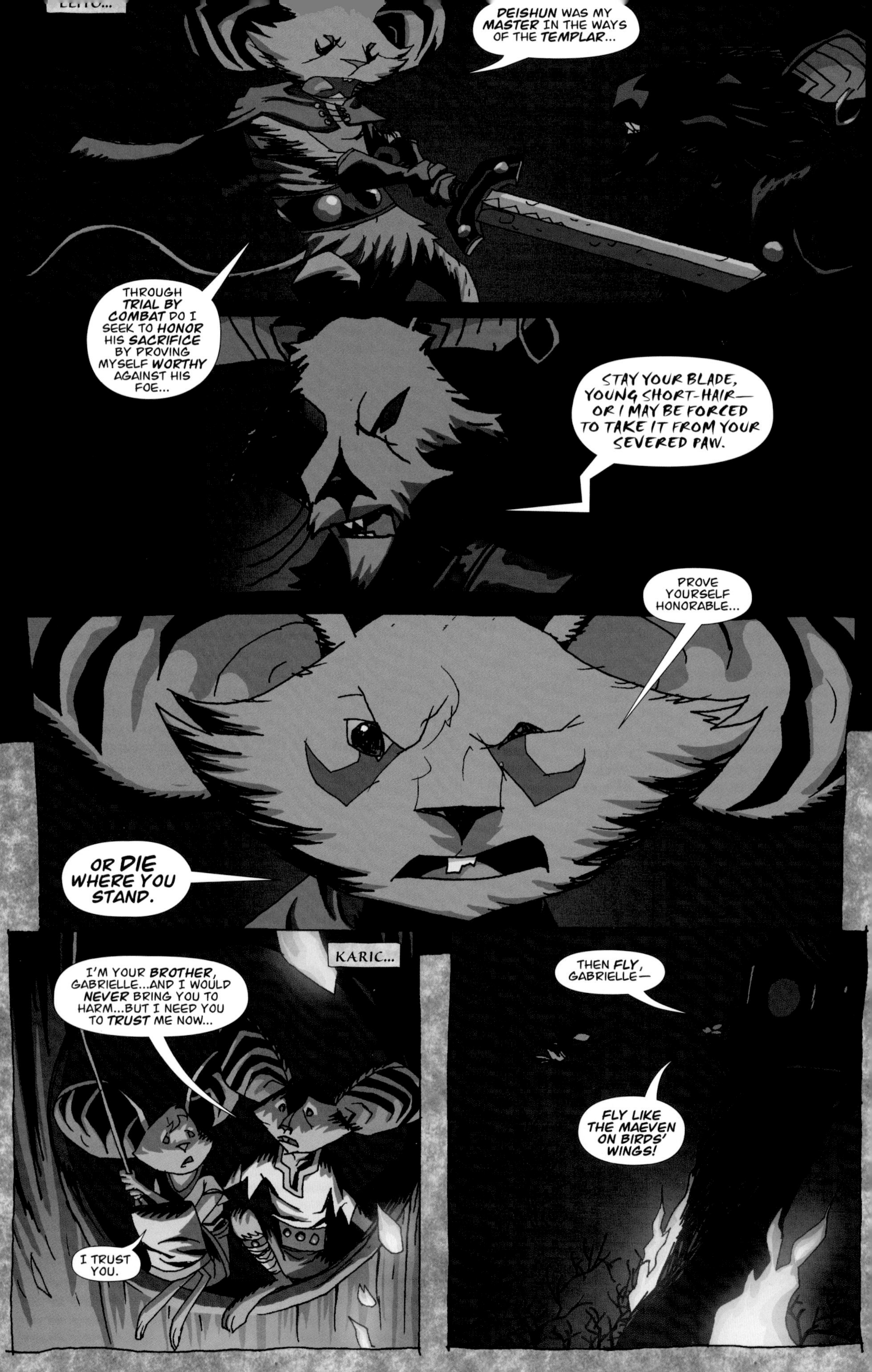
DEISHUN WAS MY MASTER IN THE WAYS OF THE TEMPLAR...
THROUGH TRIAL BY COMBAT DO I SEEK TO HONOR HIS SACRIFICE BY PROVING MYSELF WORTHY AGAINST HIS FOE...
STAY YOUR BLADE, YOUNG SHORT-HAIR— OR I MAY BE FORCED TO TAKE IT FROM YOUR SEVERED PAW.
PROVE YOURSELF HONORABLE...
OR DIE WHERE YOU STAND.
KARIC...
I'M YOUR BROTHER, GABRIELLE...AND I WOULD NEVER BRING YOU TO HARM...BUT I NEED YOU TO TRUST ME NOW...
I TRUST YOU.
THEN FLY, GABRIELLE—
FLY LIKE THE MAEVEN ON BIRDS' WINGS!

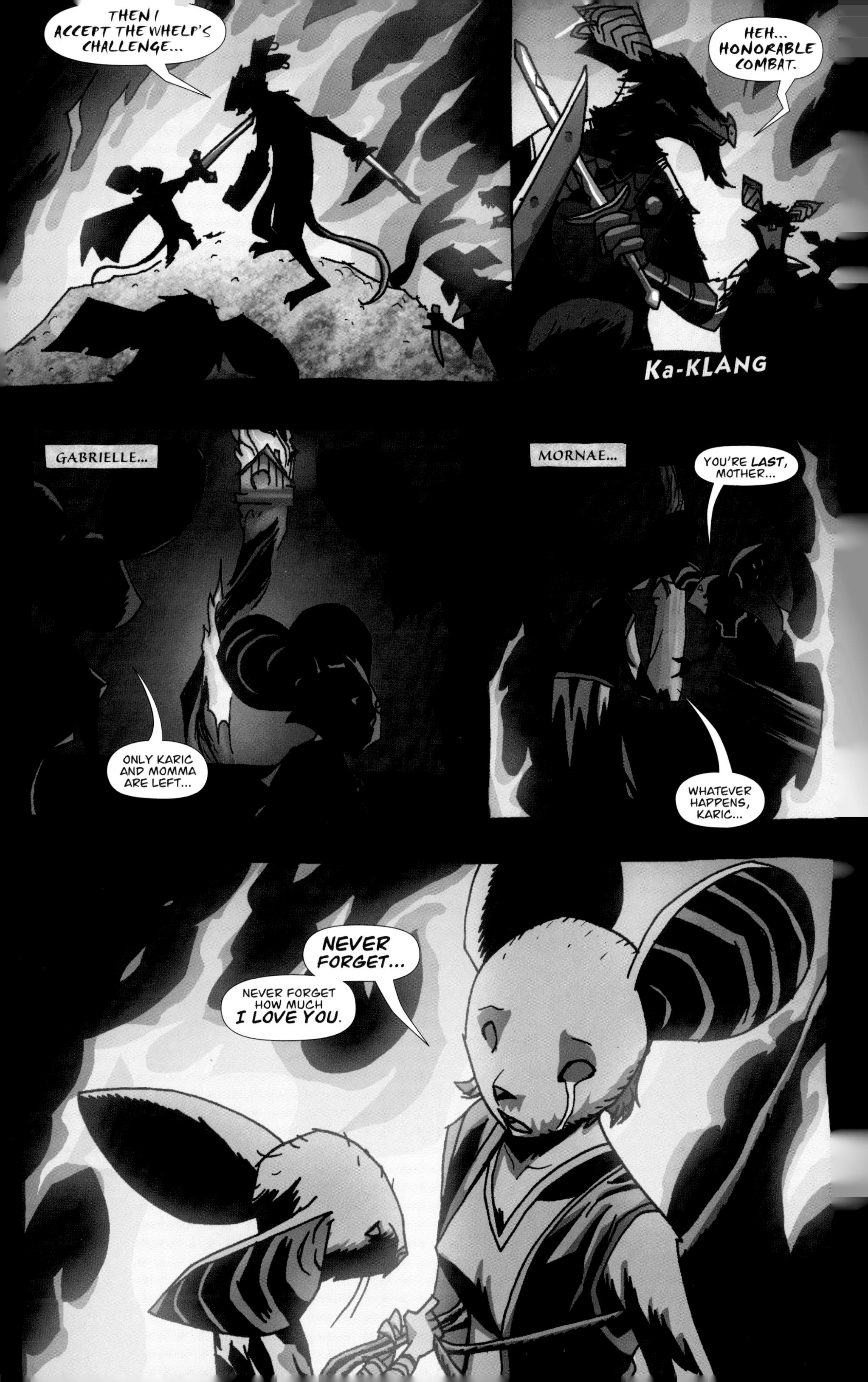
THEN I ACCEPT THE WHELP'S CHALLENGE...
HEH... HONORABLE COMBAT.
Ka-KLANG
GABRIELLE...
ONLY KARIC AND MOMMA ARE LEFT...
MORNAE...
YOU'RE LAST, MOTHER...
WHATEVER HAPPENS, KARIC...
NEVER FORGET...
NEVER FORGET HOW MUCH I LOVE YOU.

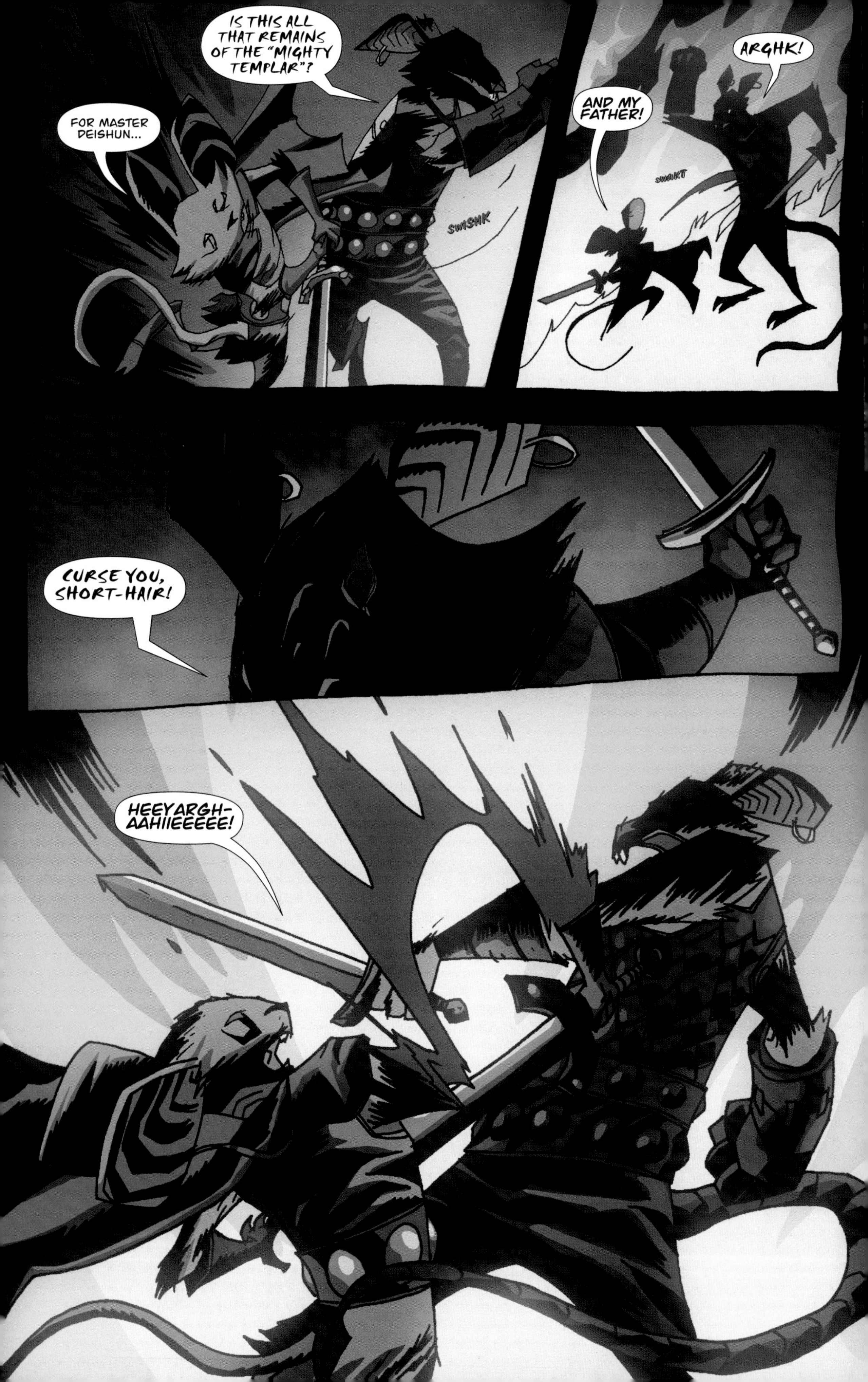
IS THIS ALL THAT REMAINS OF THE "MIGHTY TEMPLAR"?
FOR MASTER DEISHUN...
SWISHK
ARGHK!
AND MY FATHER!
SWAKT
CURSE YOU, SHORT-HAIR!
HEEYARGH-AAHIIEEEEE!

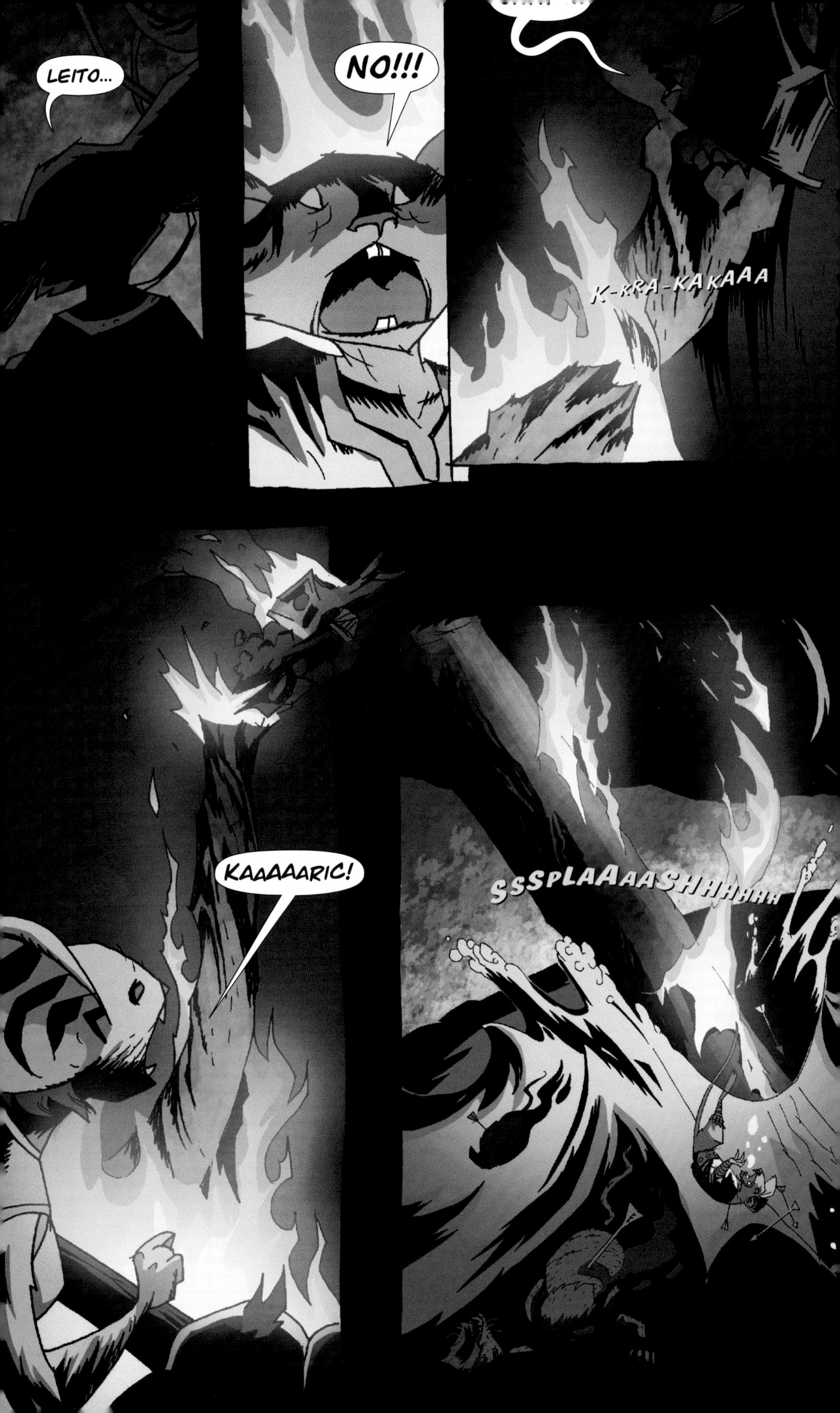
LEITO...
NO!!!
K-KRA-KAKAAA
KAAAAARIC!
SSSPLAAAASHHHHHH

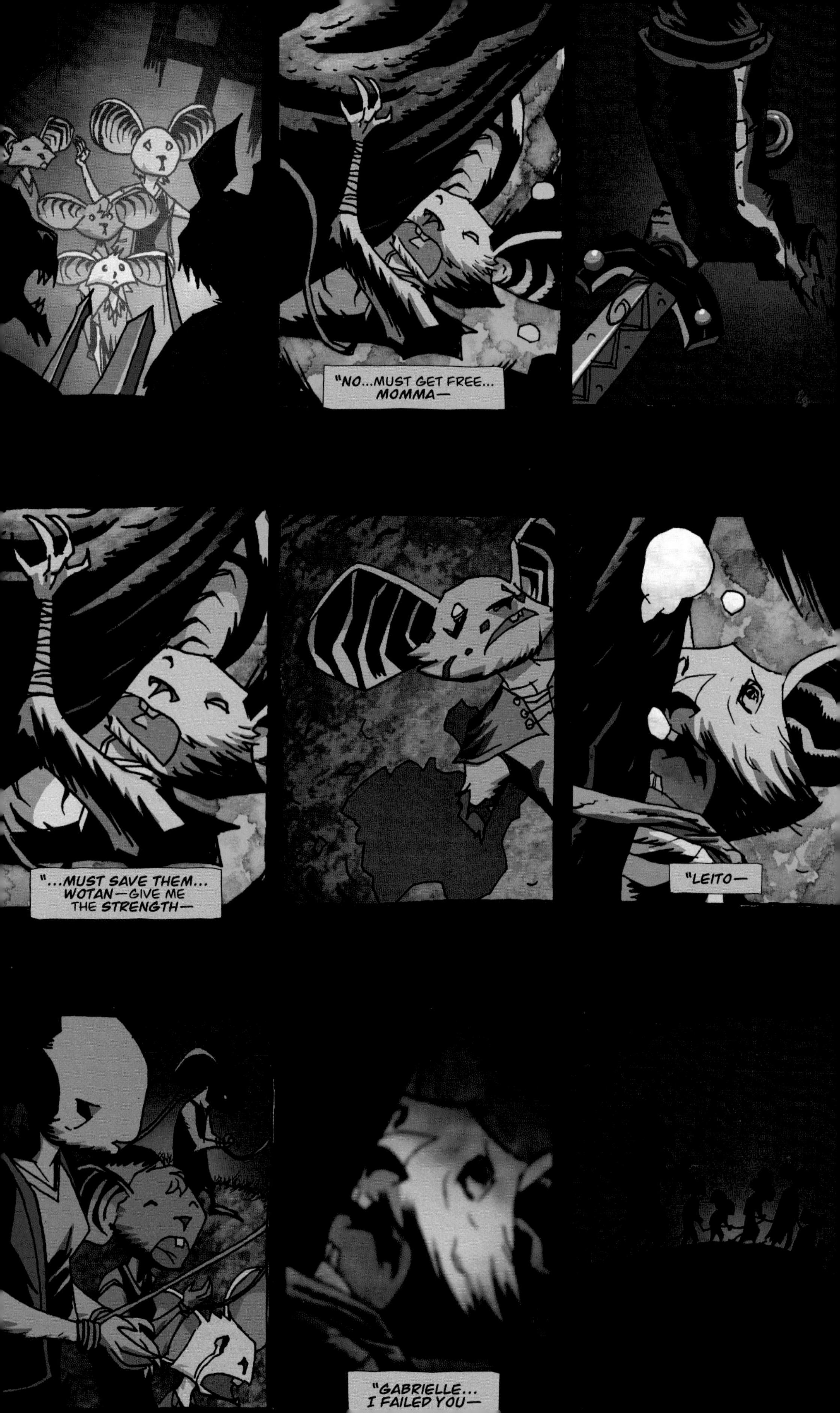
"NO...MUST GET FREE... MOMMA—
"...MUST SAVE THEM... WOTAN—GIVE ME THE STRENGTH—
"LEITO—
"GABRIELLE... I FAILED YOU—

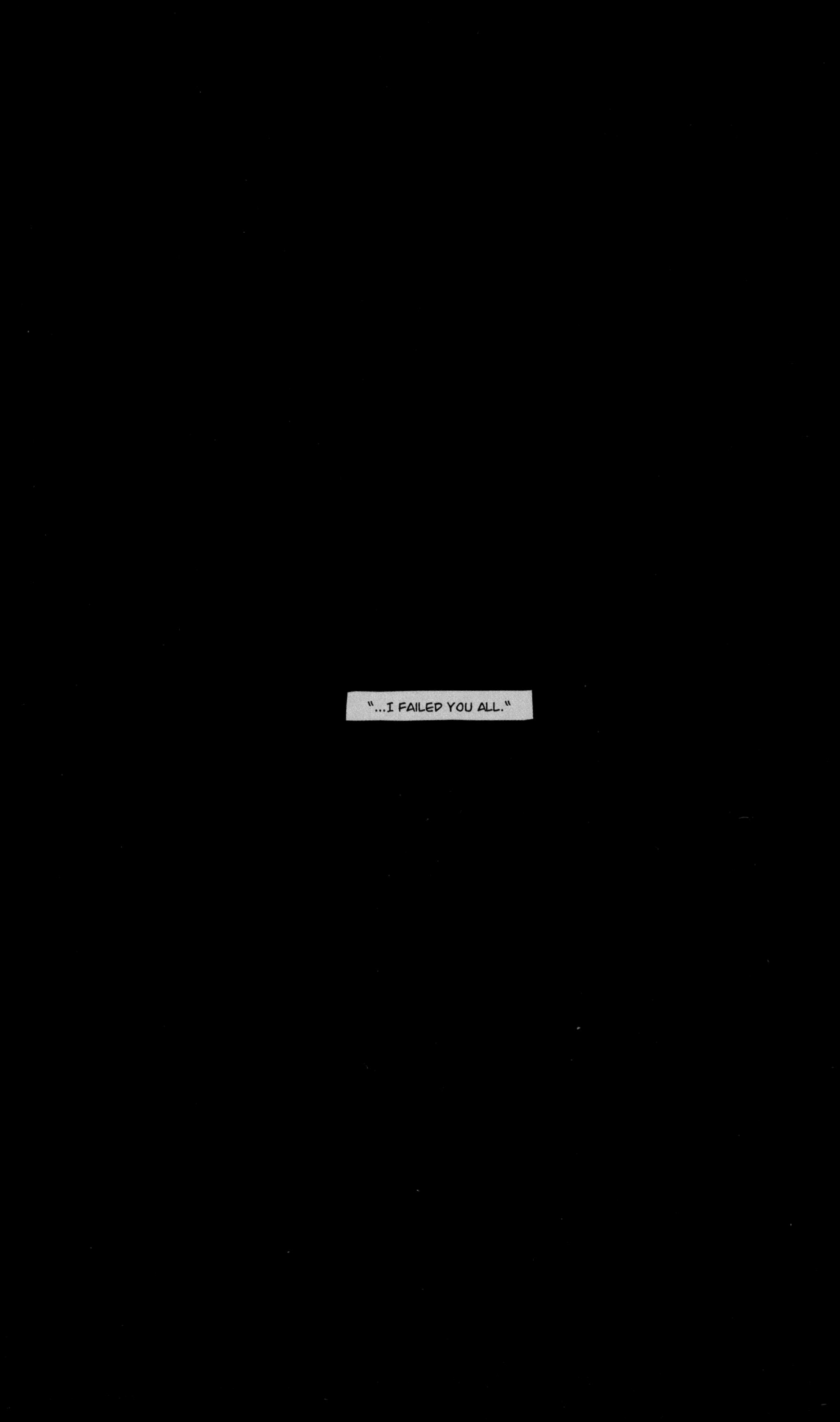
"...I FAILED YOU ALL."

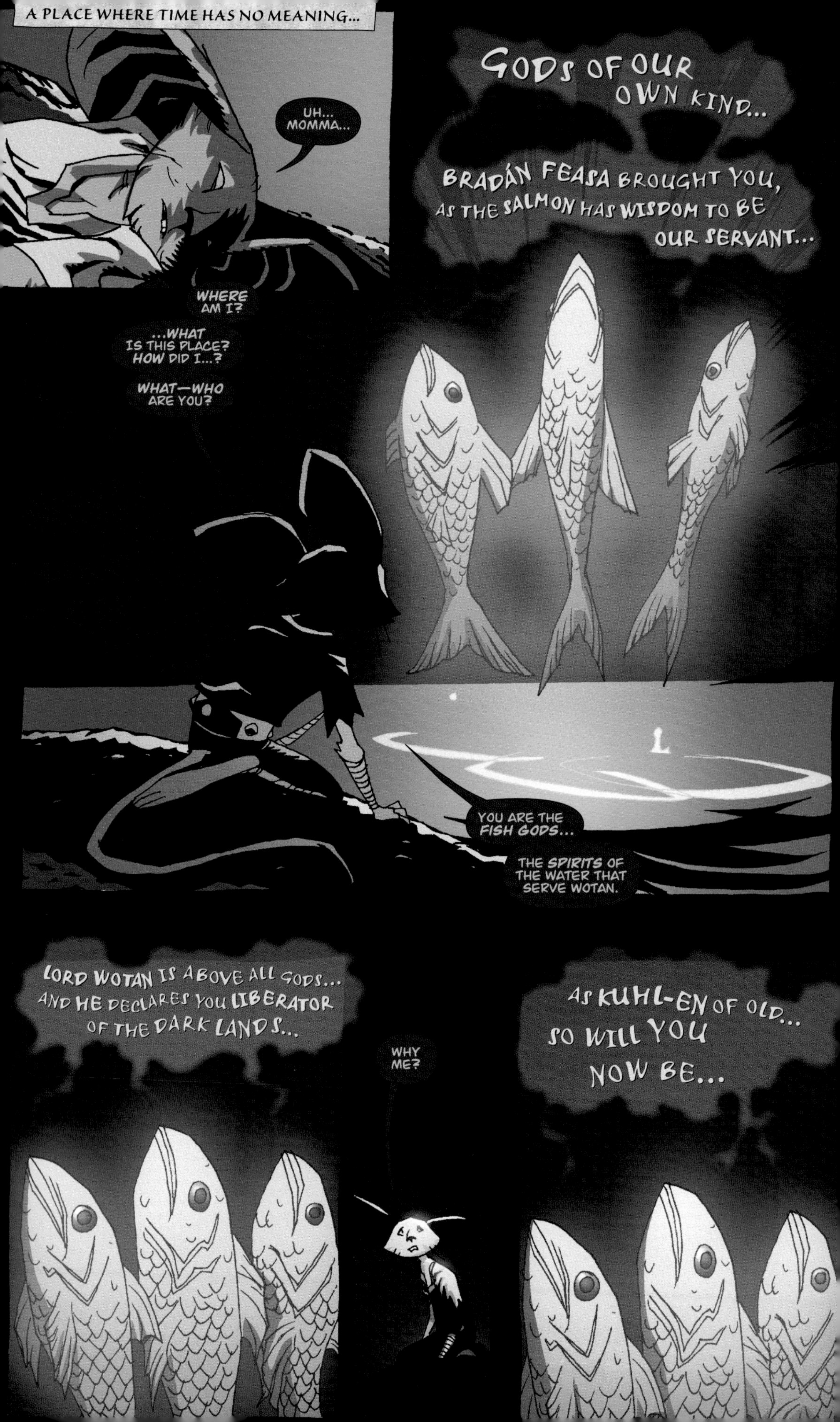

A PLACE WHERE TIME HAS NO MEANING...
UH... MOMMA...
GODS OF OUR OWN KIND...
BRADÁN FEASA BROUGHT YOU, AS THE SALMON HAS WISDOM TO BE OUR SERVANT...
WHERE AM I?
...WHAT IS THIS PLACE? HOW DID I...?
WHAT—WHO ARE YOU?
YOU ARE THE FISH GODS...
THE SPIRITS OF THE WATER THAT SERVE WOTAN.
LORD WOTAN IS ABOVE ALL GODS... AND HE DECLARES YOU LIBERATOR OF THE DARK LANDS...
WHY ME?
AS KUHL-EN OF OLD... SO WILL YOU NOW BE...

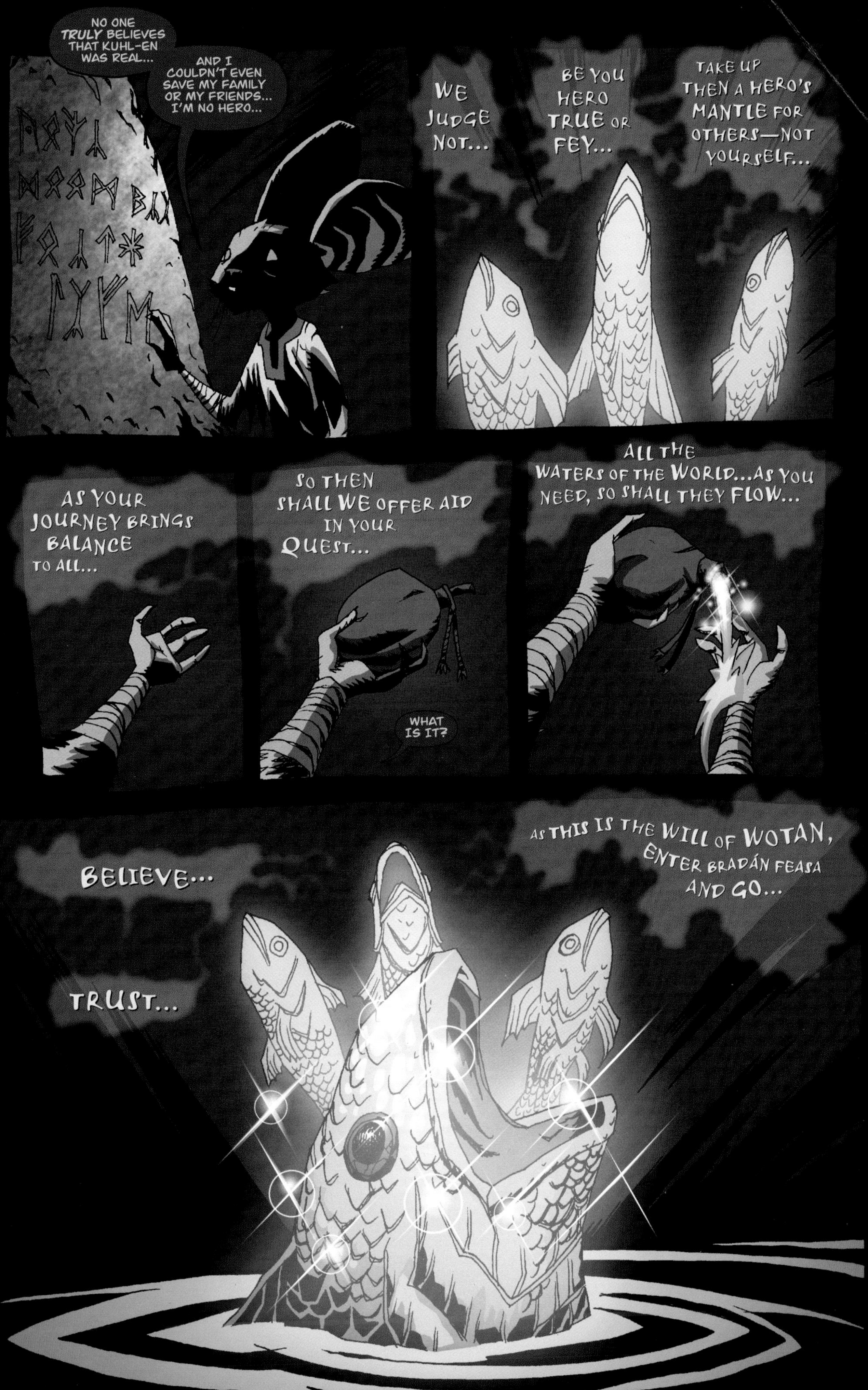
NO ONE TRULY BELIEVES THAT KUHL-EN WAS REAL...
AND I COULDN'T EVEN SAVE MY FAMILY OR MY FRIENDS... I'M NO HERO...
WE JUDGE NOT...
BE YOU HERO TRUE OR FEY...
TAKE UP THEN A HERO'S MANTLE FOR OTHERS—NOT YOURSELF...
AS YOUR JOURNEY BRINGS BALANCE TO ALL...
SO THEN SHALL WE OFFER AID IN YOUR QUEST...
WHAT IS IT?
ALL THE WATERS OF THE WORLD...AS YOU NEED, SO SHALL THEY FLOW...
BELIEVE...
TRUST...
AS THIS IS THE WILL OF WOTAN, ENTER BRADÁN FEASA AND GO...

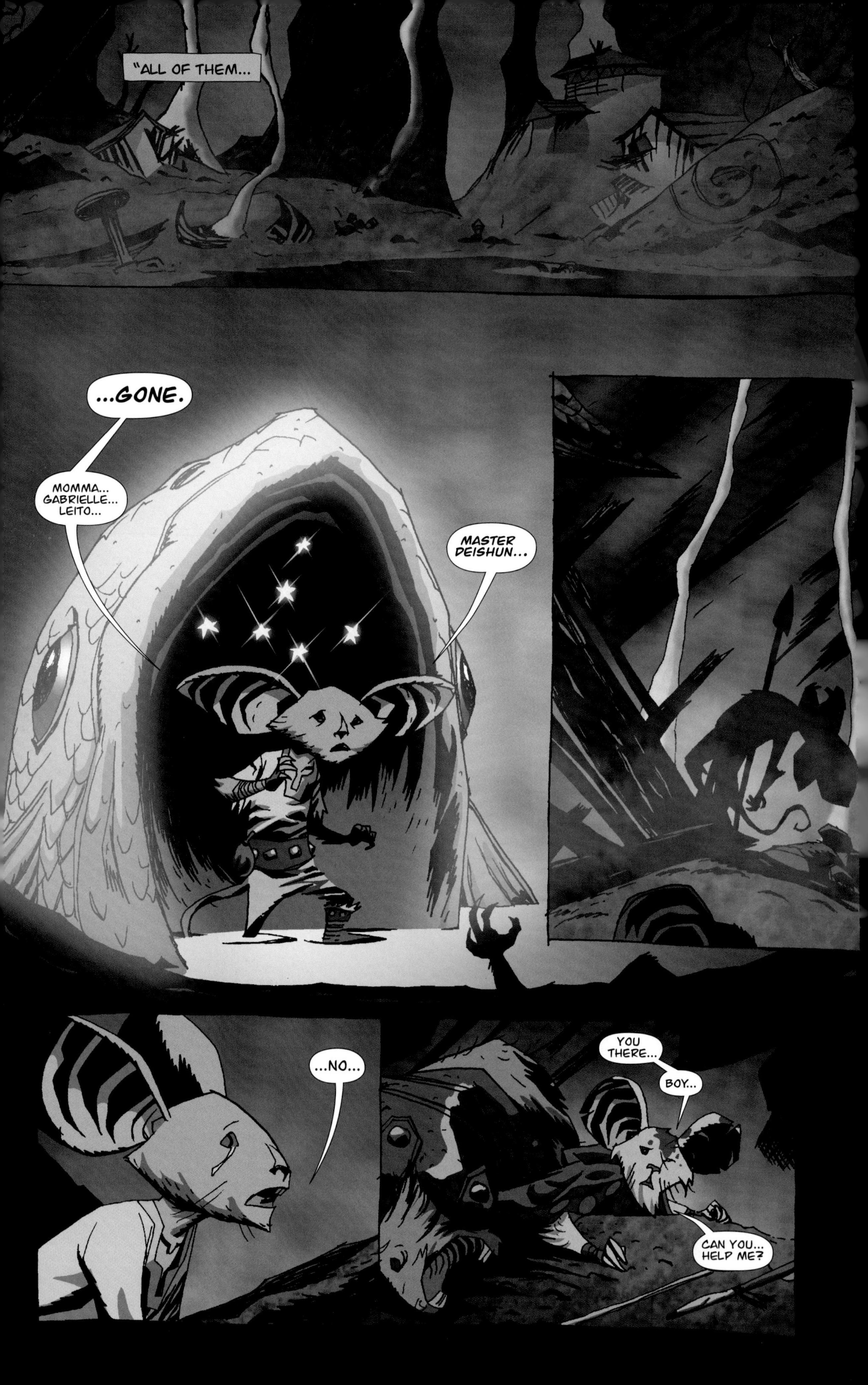
"ALL OF THEM...
...GONE.
MOMMA... GABRIELLE... LEITO...
MASTER DEISHUN...
...NO...
YOU THERE...
BOY...
CAN YOU... HELP ME?

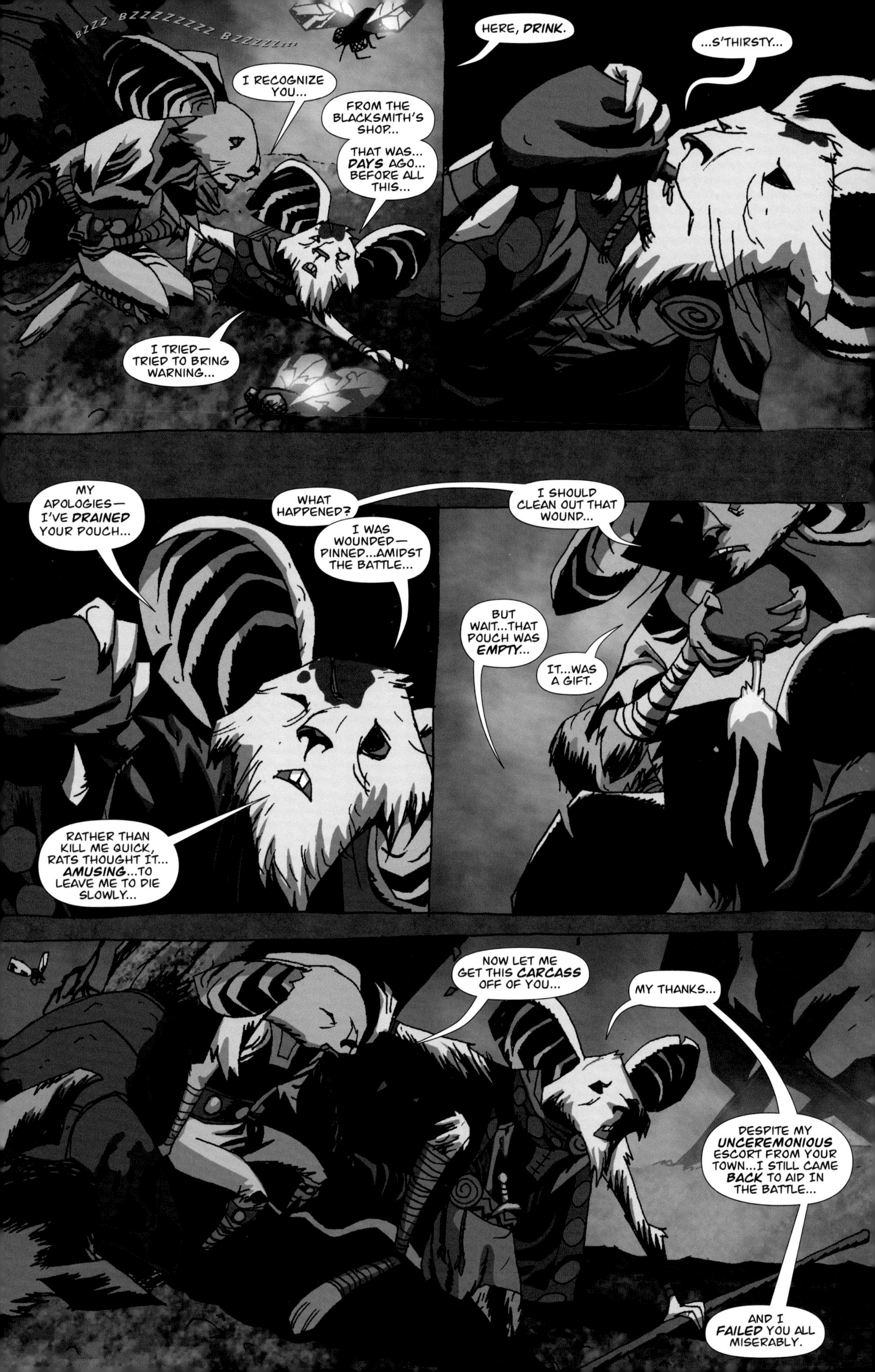
BZZZ BZZZZZZZZZ BZZZZZzzz
I RECOGNIZE YOU...
FROM THE BLACKSMITH'S SHOP...
THAT WAS... DAYS AGO... BEFORE ALL THIS...
I TRIED— TRIED TO BRING WARNING...
HERE, DRINK.
...S'THIRSTY...
MY APOLOGIES— I'VE DRAINED YOUR POUCH...
WHAT HAPPENED?
I WAS WOUNDED— PINNED...AMIDST THE BATTLE...
RATHER THAN KILL ME QUICK, RATS THOUGHT IT... AMUSING...TO LEAVE ME TO DIE SLOWLY...
I SHOULD CLEAN OUT THAT WOUND...
BUT WAIT...THAT POUCH WAS EMPTY...
IT...WAS A GIFT.
NOW LET ME GET THIS CARCASS OFF OF YOU...
MY THANKS...
DESPITE MY UNCEREMONIOUS ESCORT FROM YOUR TOWN...I STILL CAME BACK TO AID IN THE BATTLE...
AND I FAILED YOU ALL MISERABLY.

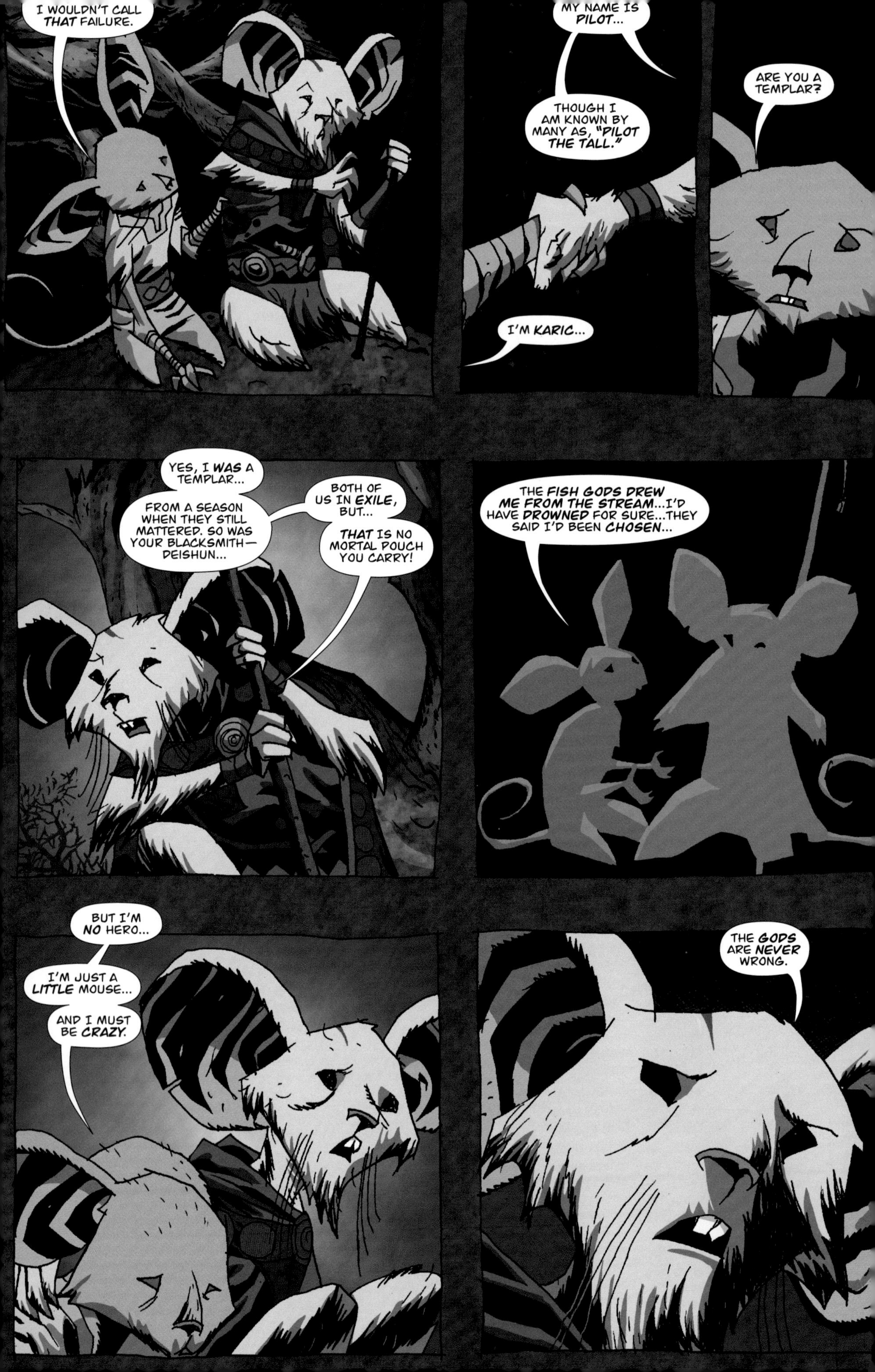
I WOULDN'T CALL *THAT* FAILURE.
MY NAME IS *PILOT*...
THOUGH I AM KNOWN BY MANY AS, *"PILOT THE TALL."*
I'M *KARIC*...
ARE YOU A TEMPLAR?
YES, I *WAS* A TEMPLAR...
FROM A SEASON WHEN THEY STILL MATTERED. SO WAS YOUR BLACKSMITH— DEISHUN...
BOTH OF US IN *EXILE*, BUT...
THAT IS NO MORTAL POUCH YOU CARRY!
THE *FISH GODS DREW ME FROM THE STREAM*...I'D HAVE *DROWNED* FOR SURE...THEY SAID I'D BEEN *CHOSEN*...
BUT I'M *NO* HERO...
I'M JUST A *LITTLE* MOUSE...
AND I MUST BE *CRAZY*.
THE *GODS* ARE *NEVER* WRONG.

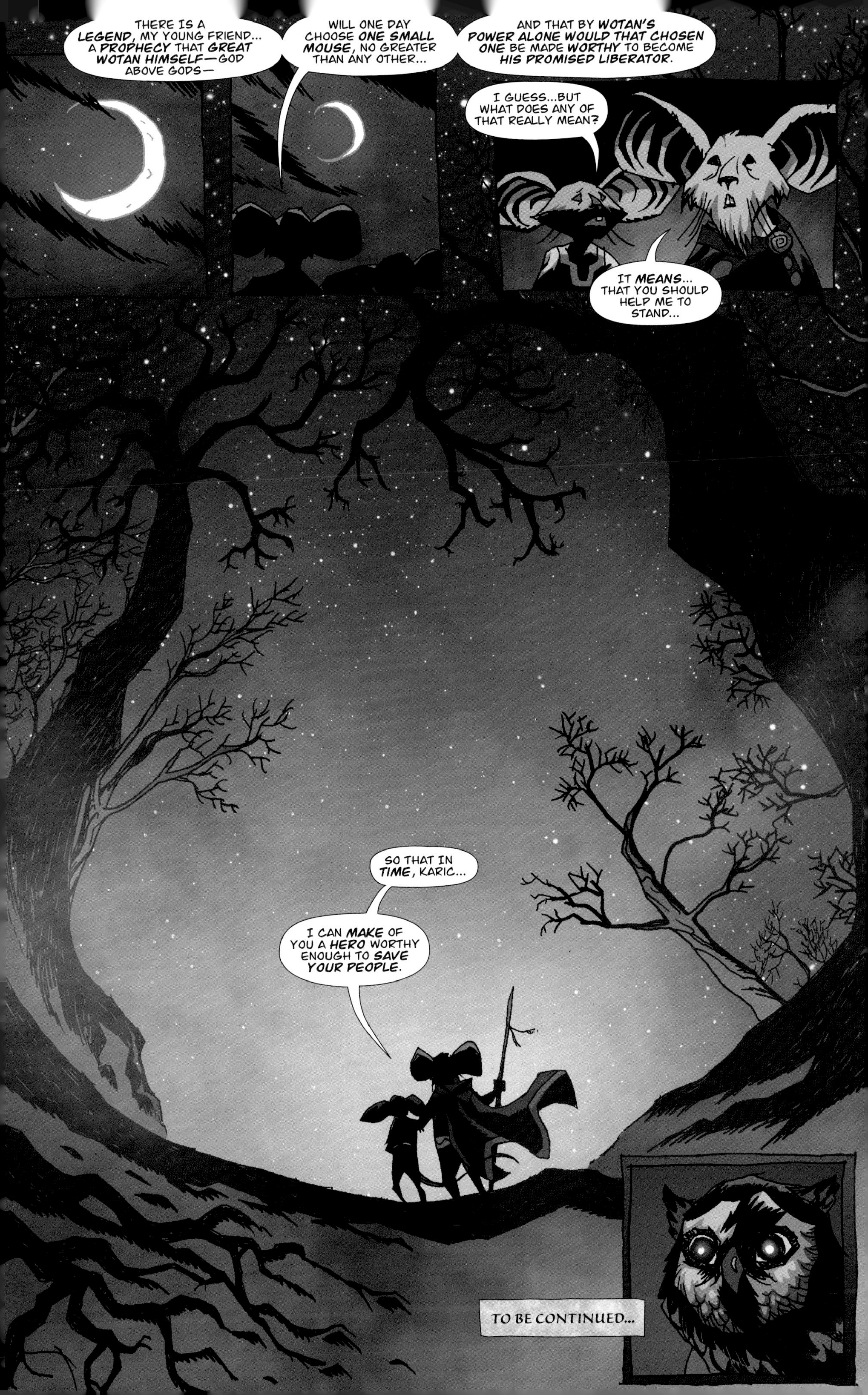
THERE IS A LEGEND, MY YOUNG FRIEND... A PROPHECY THAT GREAT WOTAN HIMSELF—GOD ABOVE GODS—
WILL ONE DAY CHOOSE ONE SMALL MOUSE, NO GREATER THAN ANY OTHER...
AND THAT BY WOTAN'S POWER ALONE WOULD THAT CHOSEN ONE BE MADE WORTHY TO BECOME HIS PROMISED LIBERATOR.
I GUESS...BUT WHAT DOES ANY OF THAT REALLY MEAN?
IT MEANS... THAT YOU SHOULD HELP ME TO STAND...
SO THAT IN TIME, KARIC...
I CAN MAKE OF YOU A HERO WORTHY ENOUGH TO SAVE YOUR PEOPLE.
TO BE CONTINUED...

CHAPTER THREE
IN THE BEGINNING

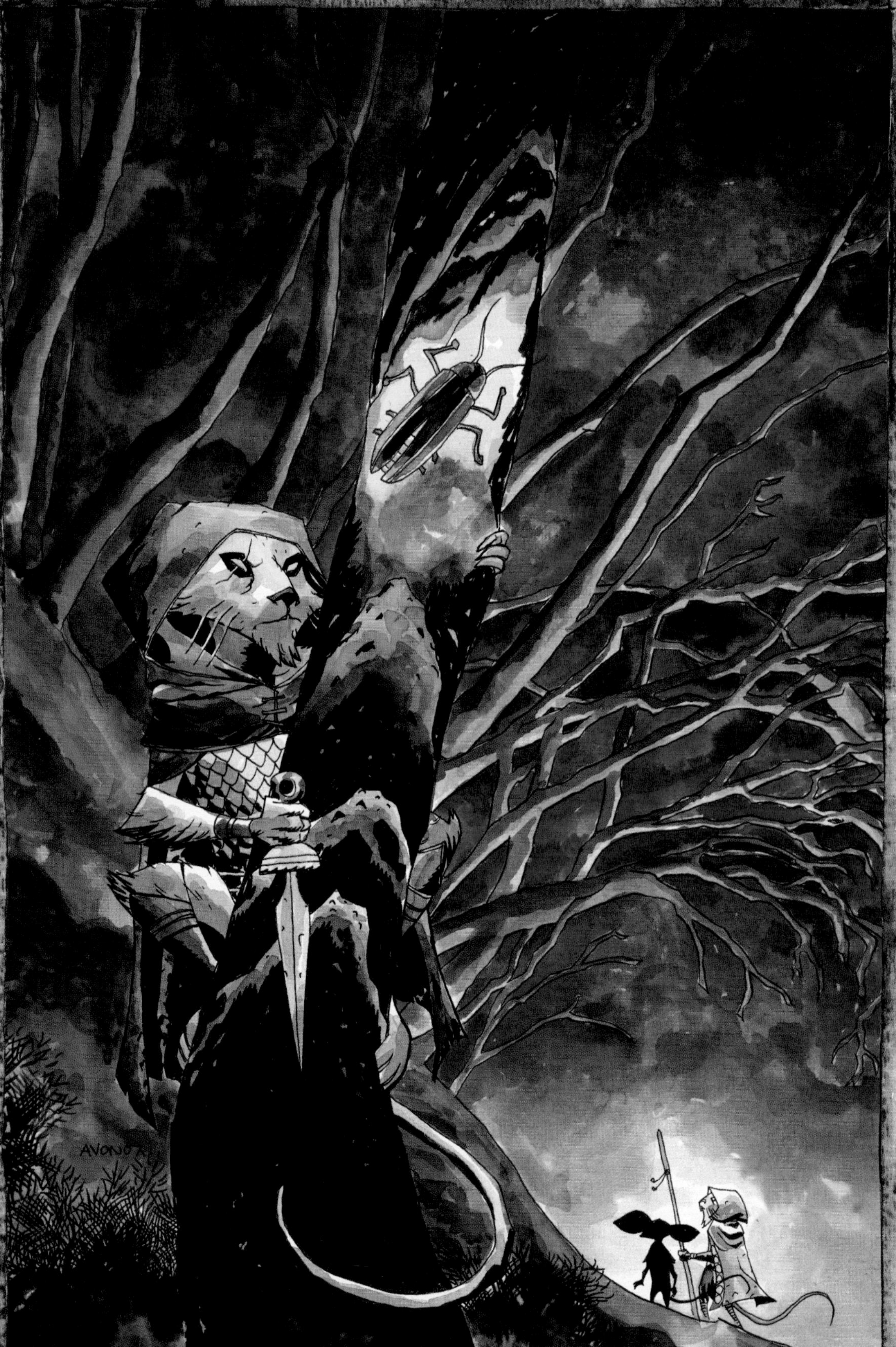
AVON07

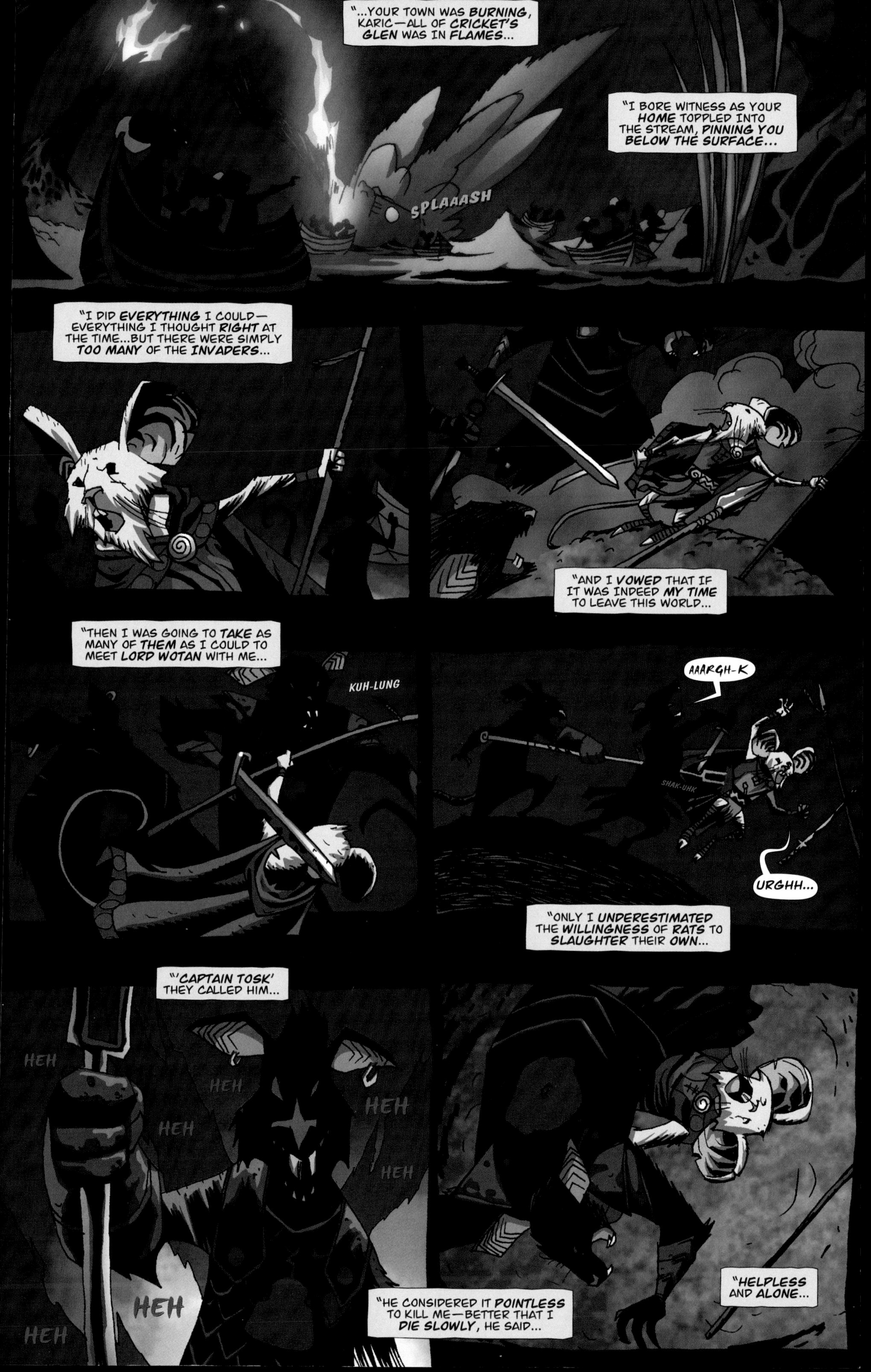
"...YOUR TOWN WAS BURNING, KARIC—ALL OF CRICKET'S GLEN WAS IN FLAMES...
"I BORE WITNESS AS YOUR HOME TOPPLED INTO THE STREAM, PINNING YOU BELOW THE SURFACE...
SPLAAASH
"I DID EVERYTHING I COULD—EVERYTHING I THOUGHT RIGHT AT THE TIME...BUT THERE WERE SIMPLY TOO MANY OF THE INVADERS...
"AND I VOWED THAT IF IT WAS INDEED MY TIME TO LEAVE THIS WORLD...
"THEN I WAS GOING TO TAKE AS MANY OF THEM AS I COULD TO MEET LORD WOTAN WITH ME...
KUH-LUNG
AAARGH-K
SHAK-UHK
URGHH...
"ONLY I UNDERESTIMATED THE WILLINGNESS OF RATS TO SLAUGHTER THEIR OWN...
"'CAPTAIN TOSK' THEY CALLED HIM...
HEH
HEH
HEH
HEH
HEH
HEH
HEH
"HE CONSIDERED IT POINTLESS TO KILL ME—BETTER THAT I DIE SLOWLY, HE SAID...
"HELPLESS AND ALONE...

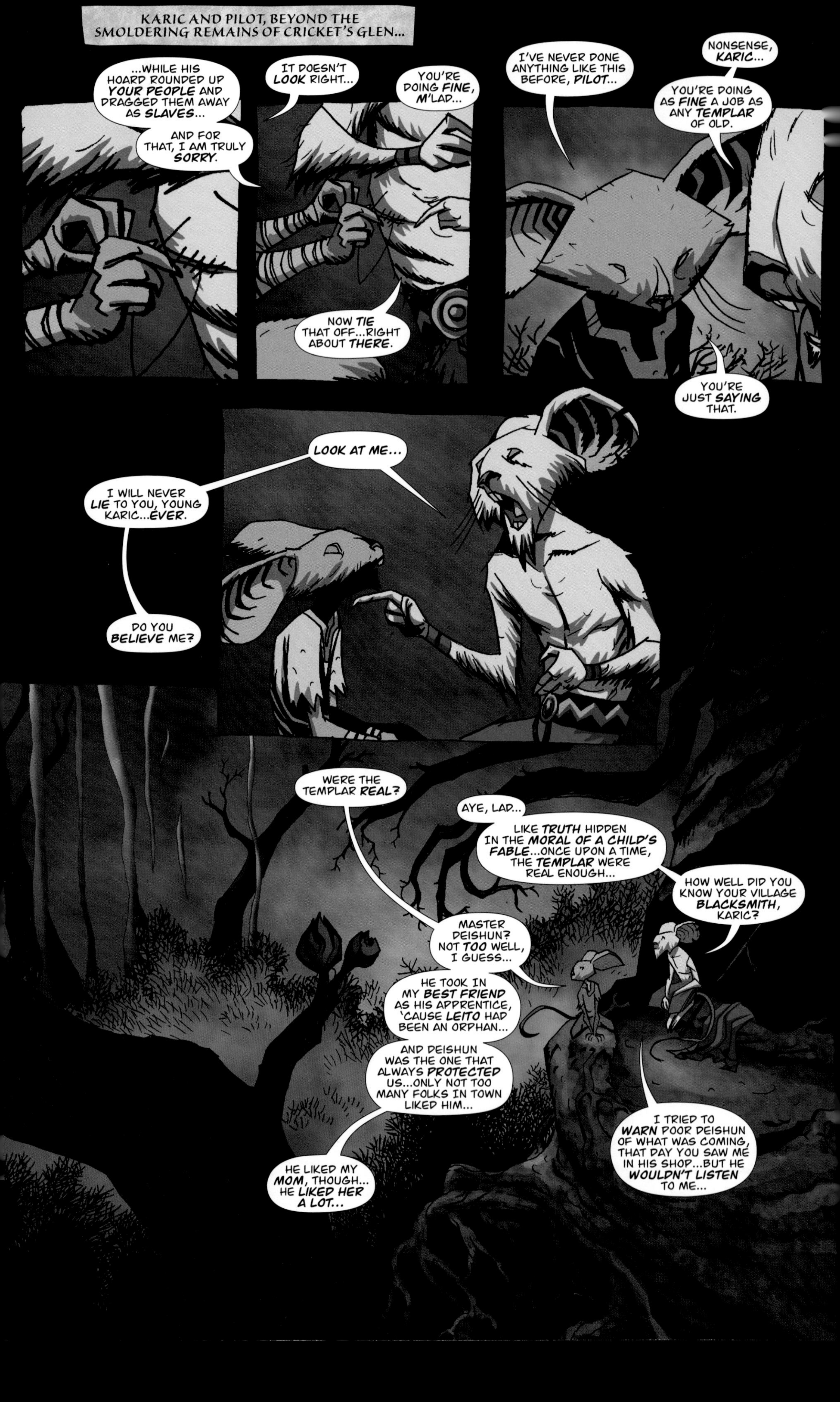
KARIC AND PILOT, BEYOND THE SMOLDERING REMAINS OF CRICKET'S GLEN...
...WHILE HIS HOARD ROUNDED UP YOUR PEOPLE AND DRAGGED THEM AWAY AS SLAVES...
AND FOR THAT, I AM TRULY SORRY.
IT DOESN'T LOOK RIGHT...
YOU'RE DOING FINE, M'LAD...
NOW TIE THAT OFF...RIGHT ABOUT THERE.
I'VE NEVER DONE ANYTHING LIKE THIS BEFORE, PILOT...
NONSENSE, KARIC...
YOU'RE DOING AS FINE A JOB AS ANY TEMPLAR OF OLD.
YOU'RE JUST SAYING THAT.
LOOK AT ME...
I WILL NEVER LIE TO YOU, YOUNG KARIC...EVER.
DO YOU BELIEVE ME?
WERE THE TEMPLAR REAL?
AYE, LAD...
LIKE TRUTH HIDDEN IN THE MORAL OF A CHILD'S FABLE...ONCE UPON A TIME, THE TEMPLAR WERE REAL ENOUGH...
HOW WELL DID YOU KNOW YOUR VILLAGE BLACKSMITH, KARIC?
MASTER DEISHUN? NOT TOO WELL, I GUESS...
HE TOOK IN MY BEST FRIEND AS HIS APPRENTICE, 'CAUSE LEITO HAD BEEN AN ORPHAN...
AND DEISHUN WAS THE ONE THAT ALWAYS PROTECTED US...ONLY NOT TOO MANY FOLKS IN TOWN LIKED HIM...
HE LIKED MY MOM, THOUGH... HE LIKED HER A LOT...
I TRIED TO WARN POOR DEISHUN OF WHAT WAS COMING, THAT DAY YOU SAW ME IN HIS SHOP...BUT HE WOULDN'T LISTEN TO ME...

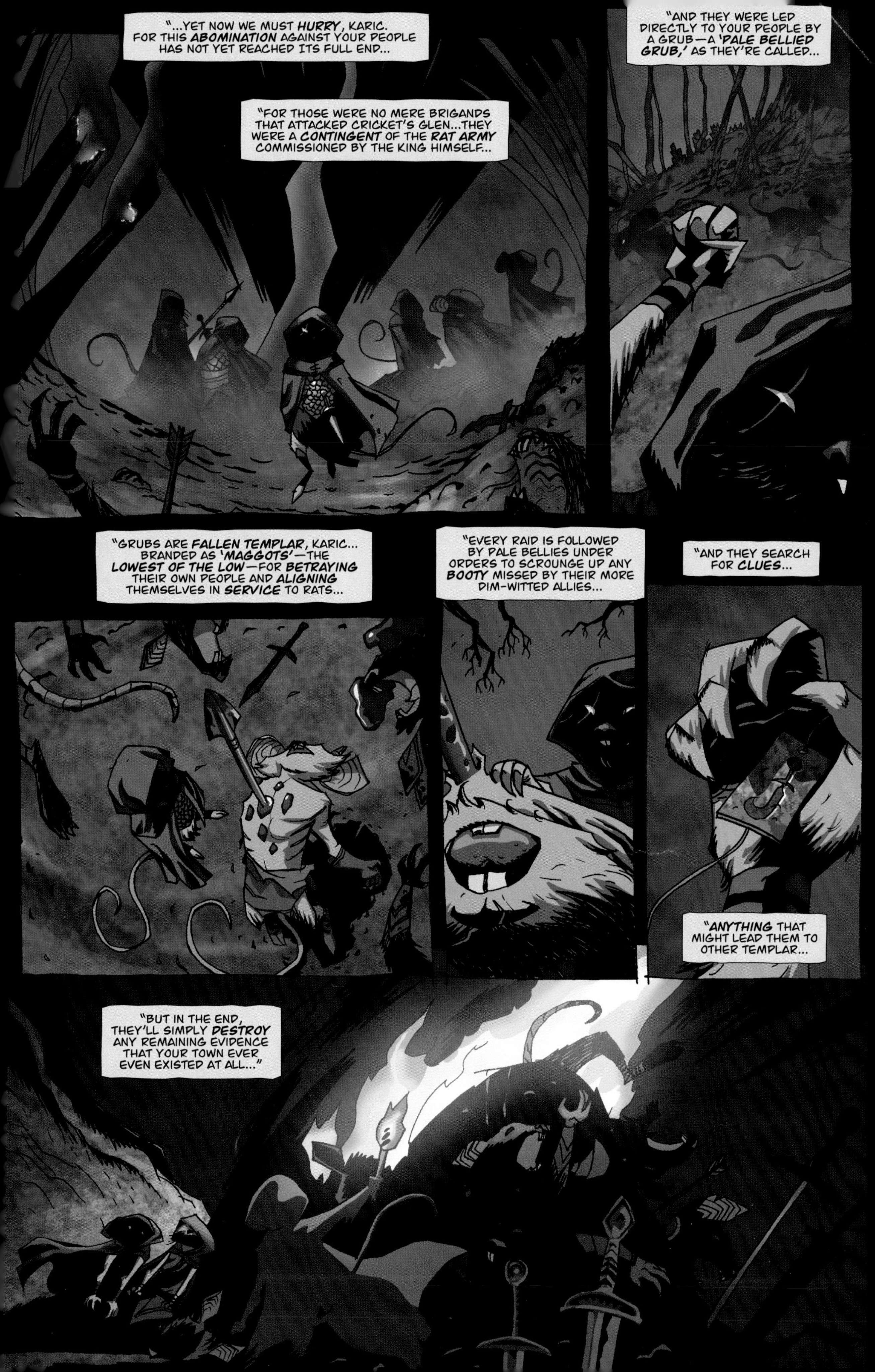
"...YET NOW WE MUST HURRY, KARIC. FOR THIS ABOMINATION AGAINST YOUR PEOPLE HAS NOT YET REACHED ITS FULL END...
"FOR THOSE WERE NO MERE BRIGANDS THAT ATTACKED CRICKET'S GLEN...THEY WERE A CONTINGENT OF THE RAT ARMY COMMISSIONED BY THE KING HIMSELF...
"AND THEY WERE LED DIRECTLY TO YOUR PEOPLE BY A GRUB—A 'PALE BELLIED GRUB,' AS THEY'RE CALLED...
"GRUBS ARE FALLEN TEMPLAR, KARIC... BRANDED AS 'MAGGOTS'—THE LOWEST OF THE LOW—FOR BETRAYING THEIR OWN PEOPLE AND ALIGNING THEMSELVES IN SERVICE TO RATS...
"EVERY RAID IS FOLLOWED BY PALE BELLIES UNDER ORDERS TO SCROUNGE UP ANY BOOTY MISSED BY THEIR MORE DIM-WITTED ALLIES...
"AND THEY SEARCH FOR CLUES...
"ANYTHING THAT MIGHT LEAD THEM TO OTHER TEMPLAR...
"BUT IN THE END, THEY'LL SIMPLY DESTROY ANY REMAINING EVIDENCE THAT YOUR TOWN EVER EVEN EXISTED AT ALL..."

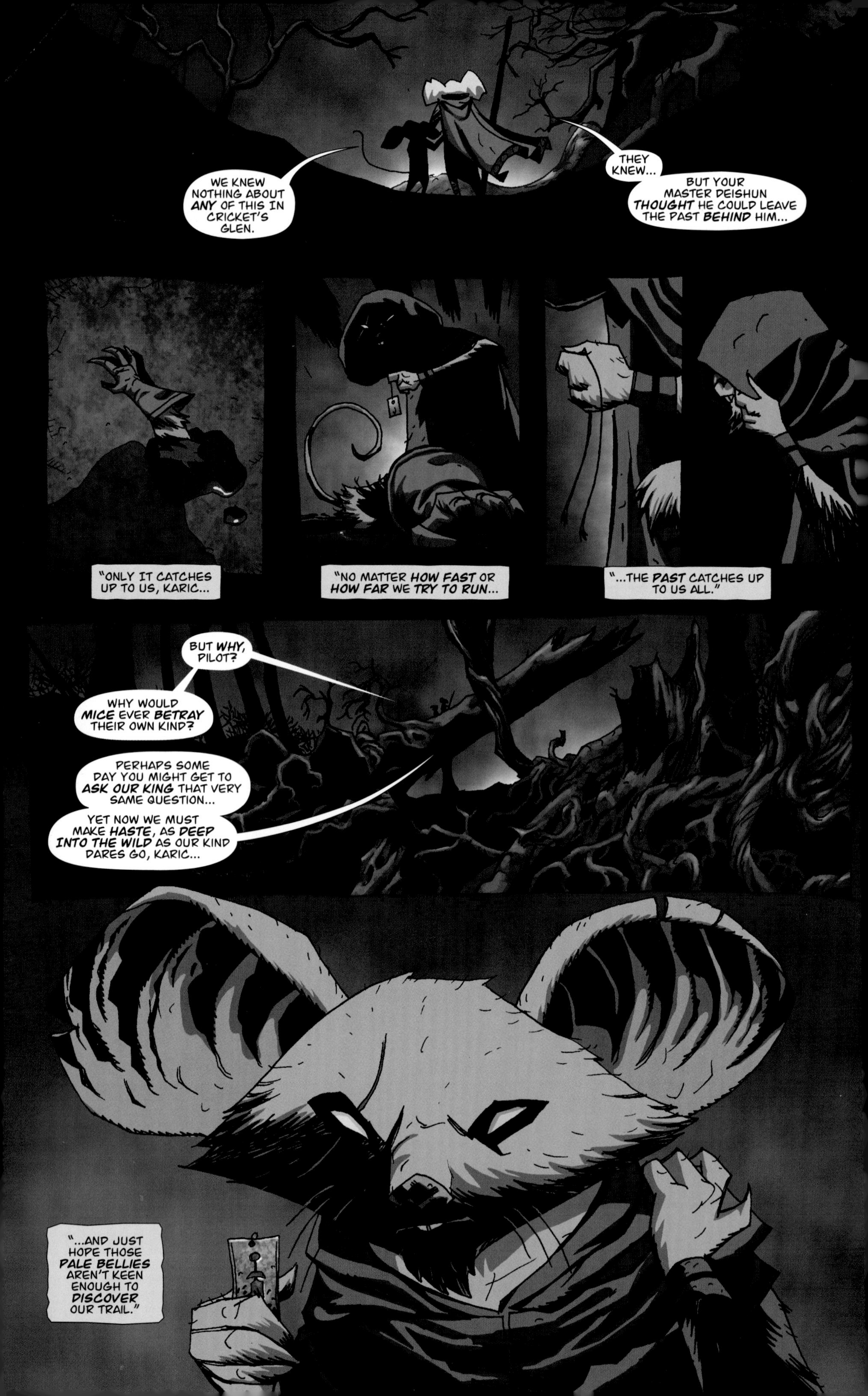
WE KNEW NOTHING ABOUT ANY OF THIS IN CRICKET'S GLEN.
THEY KNEW...
BUT YOUR MASTER DEISHUN THOUGHT HE COULD LEAVE THE PAST BEHIND HIM...
"ONLY IT CATCHES UP TO US, KARIC...
"NO MATTER HOW FAST OR HOW FAR WE TRY TO RUN...
"...THE PAST CATCHES UP TO US ALL."
BUT WHY, PILOT?
WHY WOULD MICE EVER BETRAY THEIR OWN KIND?
PERHAPS SOME DAY YOU MIGHT GET TO ASK OUR KING THAT VERY SAME QUESTION...
YET NOW WE MUST MAKE HASTE, AS DEEP INTO THE WILD AS OUR KIND DARES GO, KARIC...
"...AND JUST HOPE THOSE PALE BELLIES AREN'T KEEN ENOUGH TO DISCOVER OUR TRAIL."

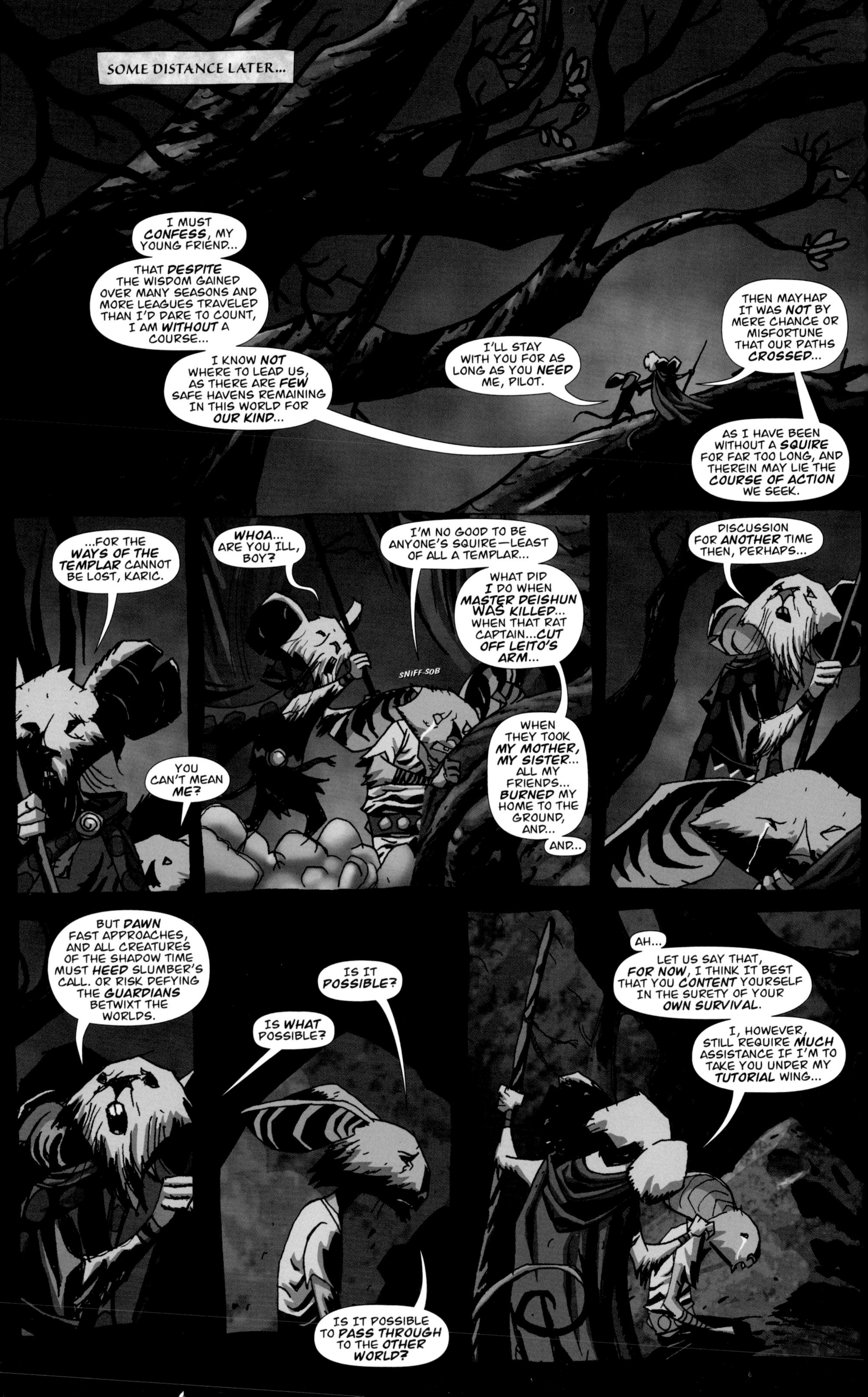
SOME DISTANCE LATER...
I MUST CONFESS, MY YOUNG FRIEND...
THAT DESPITE THE WISDOM GAINED OVER MANY SEASONS AND MORE LEAGUES TRAVELED THAN I'D DARE TO COUNT, I AM WITHOUT A COURSE...
I KNOW NOT WHERE TO LEAD US, AS THERE ARE FEW SAFE HAVENS REMAINING IN THIS WORLD FOR OUR KIND...
I'LL STAY WITH YOU FOR AS LONG AS YOU NEED ME, PILOT.
THEN MAYHAP IT WAS NOT BY MERE CHANCE OR MISFORTUNE THAT OUR PATHS CROSSED...
AS I HAVE BEEN WITHOUT A SQUIRE FOR FAR TOO LONG, AND THEREIN MAY LIE THE COURSE OF ACTION WE SEEK.
...FOR THE WAYS OF THE TEMPLAR CANNOT BE LOST, KARIC.
YOU CAN'T MEAN ME?
WHOA... ARE YOU ILL, BOY?
SNIFF-SOB
I'M NO GOOD TO BE ANYONE'S SQUIRE—LEAST OF ALL A TEMPLAR...
WHAT DID I DO WHEN MASTER DEISHUN WAS KILLED... WHEN THAT RAT CAPTAIN...CUT OFF LEITO'S ARM...
WHEN THEY TOOK MY MOTHER, MY SISTER... ALL MY FRIENDS... BURNED MY HOME TO THE GROUND, AND...
AND...
DISCUSSION FOR ANOTHER TIME THEN, PERHAPS...
BUT DAWN FAST APPROACHES, AND ALL CREATURES OF THE SHADOW TIME MUST HEED SLUMBER'S CALL. OR RISK DEFYING THE GUARDIANS BETWIXT THE WORLDS.
IS IT POSSIBLE?
IS WHAT POSSIBLE?
IS IT POSSIBLE TO PASS THROUGH TO THE OTHER WORLD?
AH...
LET US SAY THAT, FOR NOW, I THINK IT BEST THAT YOU CONTENT YOURSELF IN THE SURETY OF YOUR OWN SURVIVAL.
I, HOWEVER, STILL REQUIRE MUCH ASSISTANCE IF I'M TO TAKE YOU UNDER MY TUTORIAL WING...

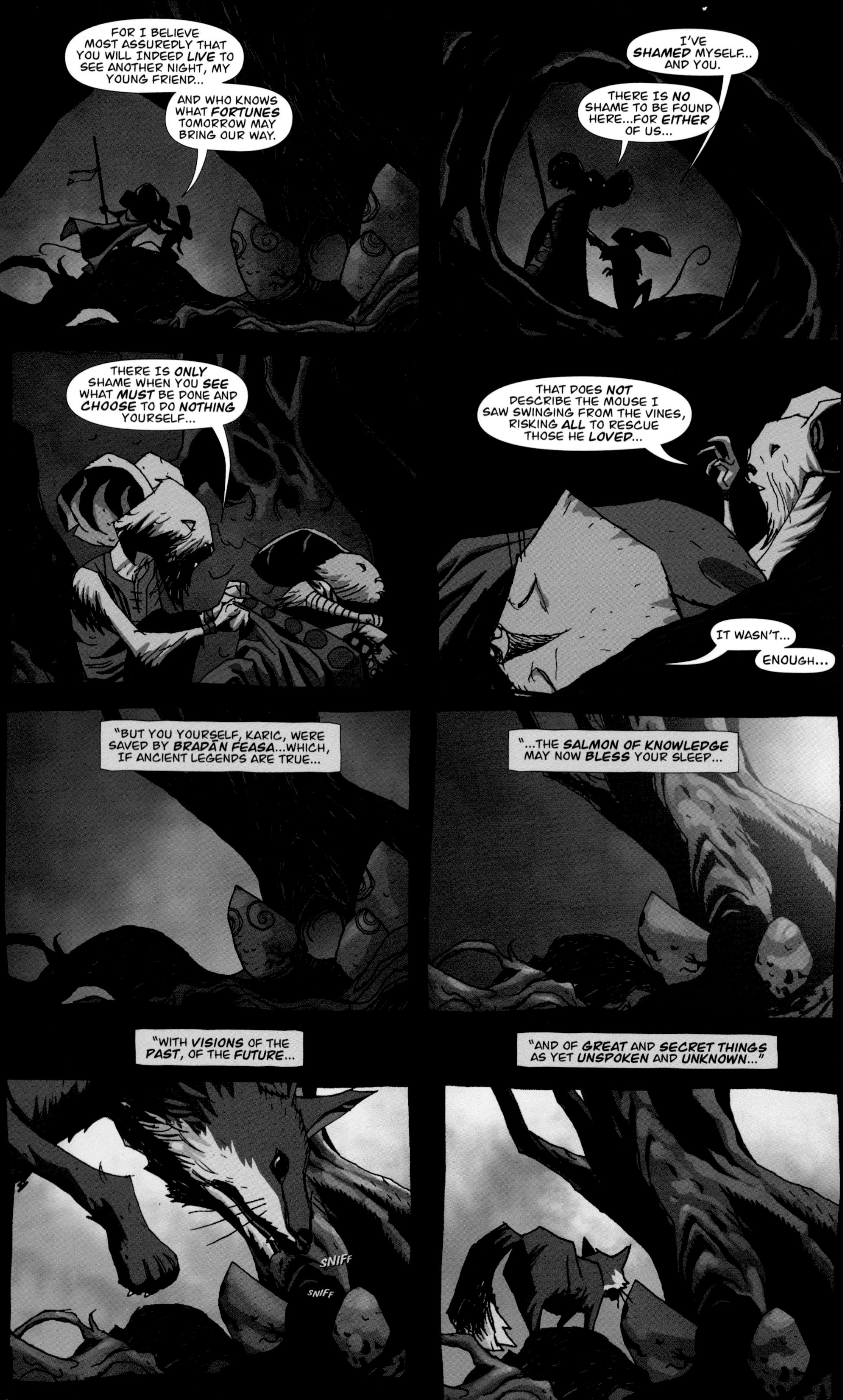
FOR I BELIEVE MOST ASSUREDLY THAT YOU WILL INDEED LIVE TO SEE ANOTHER NIGHT, MY YOUNG FRIEND...
AND WHO KNOWS WHAT FORTUNES TOMORROW MAY BRING OUR WAY.
I'VE SHAMED MYSELF... AND YOU.
THERE IS NO SHAME TO BE FOUND HERE...FOR EITHER OF US...
THERE IS ONLY SHAME WHEN YOU SEE WHAT MUST BE DONE AND CHOOSE TO DO NOTHING YOURSELF...
THAT DOES NOT DESCRIBE THE MOUSE I SAW SWINGING FROM THE VINES, RISKING ALL TO RESCUE THOSE HE LOVED...
IT WASN'T...
ENOUGH...
"BUT YOU YOURSELF, KARIC, WERE SAVED BY BRADĀN FEASA...WHICH, IF ANCIENT LEGENDS ARE TRUE...
"...THE SALMON OF KNOWLEDGE MAY NOW BLESS YOUR SLEEP...
"WITH VISIONS OF THE PAST, OF THE FUTURE...
SNIFF
SNIFF
"AND OF GREAT AND SECRET THINGS AS YET UNSPOKEN AND UNKNOWN..."

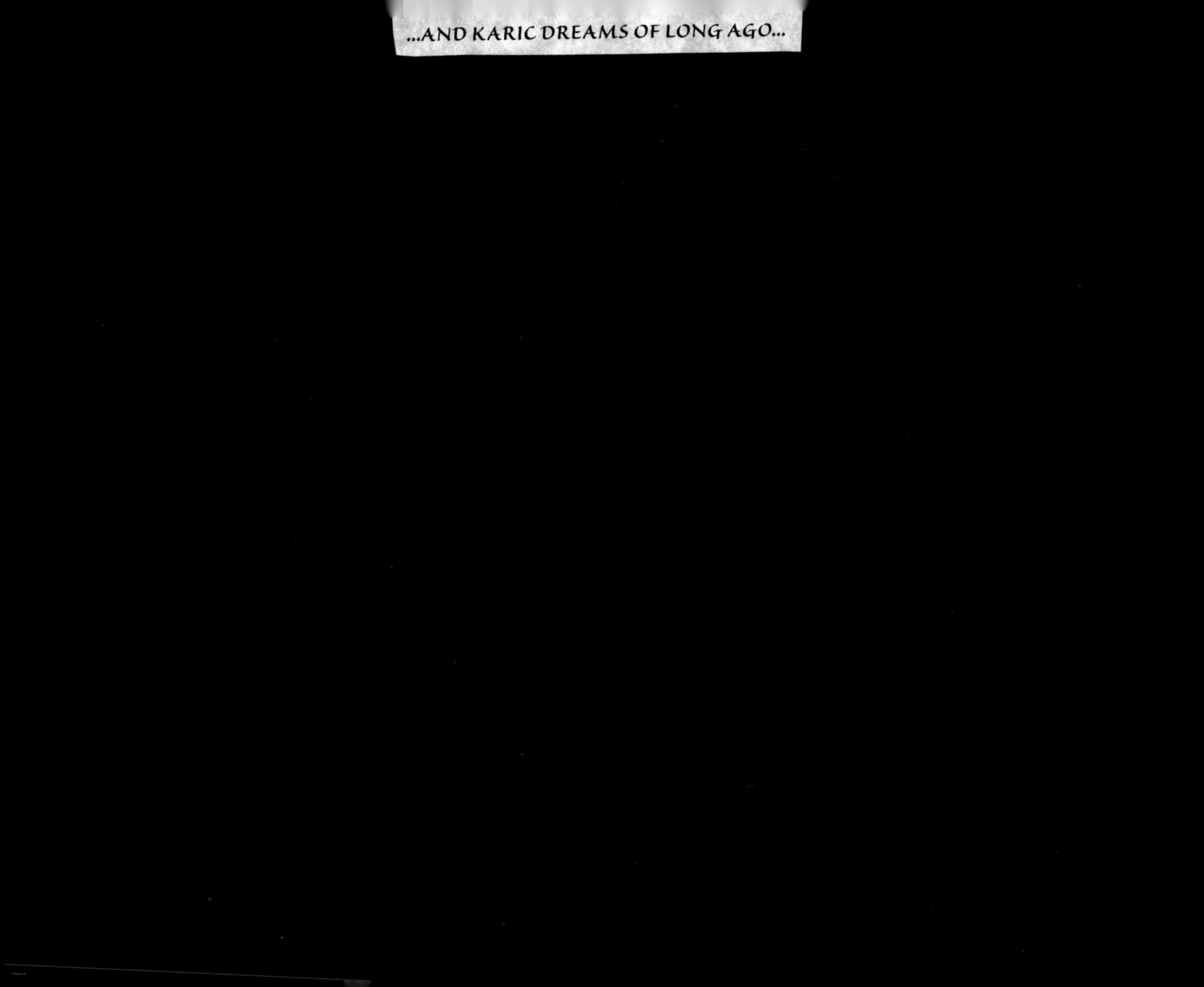
...AND KARIC DREAMS OF LONG AGO...

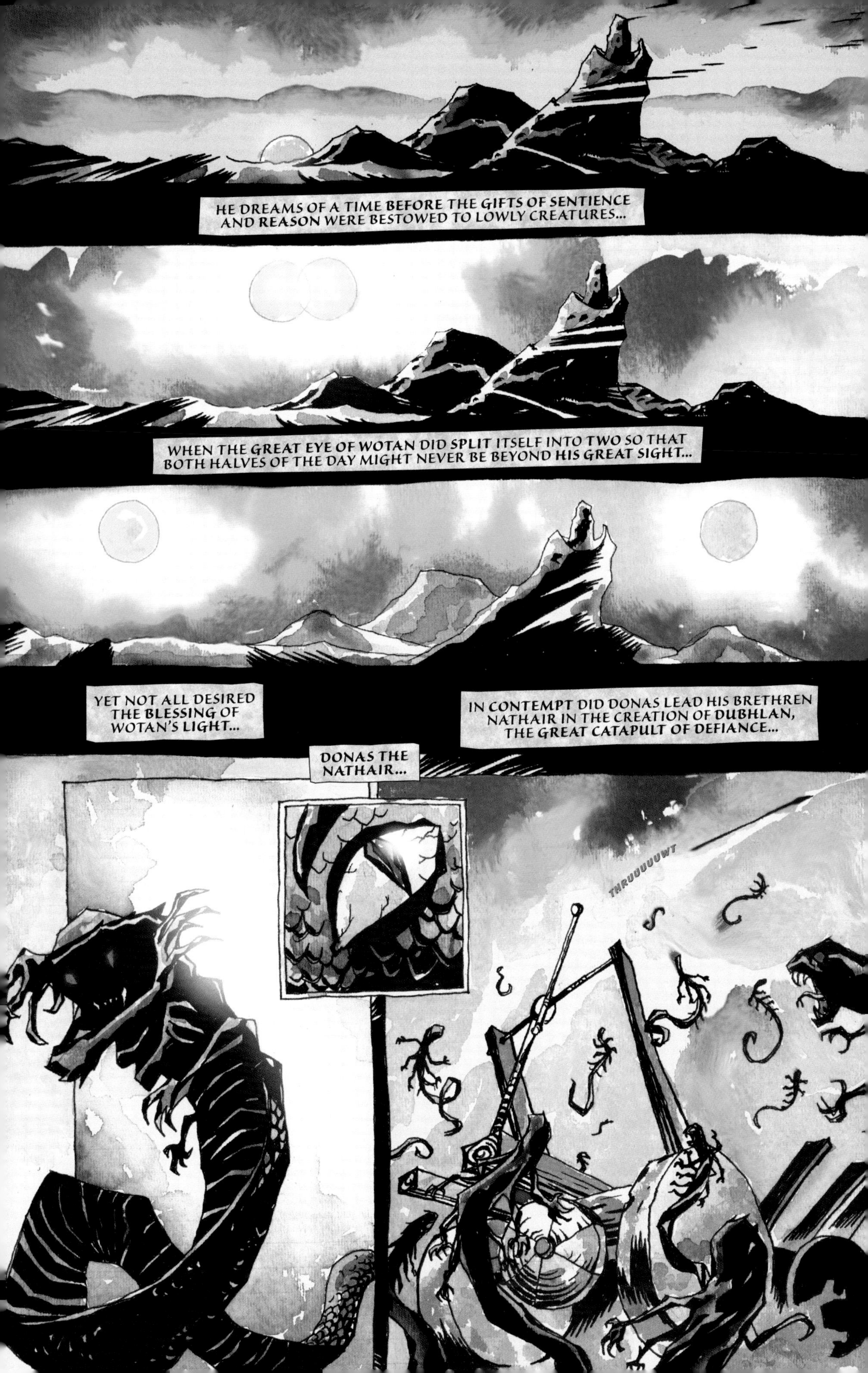
HE DREAMS OF A TIME BEFORE THE GIFTS OF SENTIENCE AND REASON WERE BESTOWED TO LOWLY CREATURES...
WHEN THE GREAT EYE OF WOTAN DID SPLIT ITSELF INTO TWO SO THAT BOTH HALVES OF THE DAY MIGHT NEVER BE BEYOND HIS GREAT SIGHT...
YET NOT ALL DESIRED THE BLESSING OF WOTAN'S LIGHT...
IN CONTEMPT DID DONAS LEAD HIS BRETHREN NATHAIR IN THE CREATION OF DUBHLAN, THE GREAT CATAPULT OF DEFIANCE...
DONAS THE NATHAIR...
THRUUUUUWT

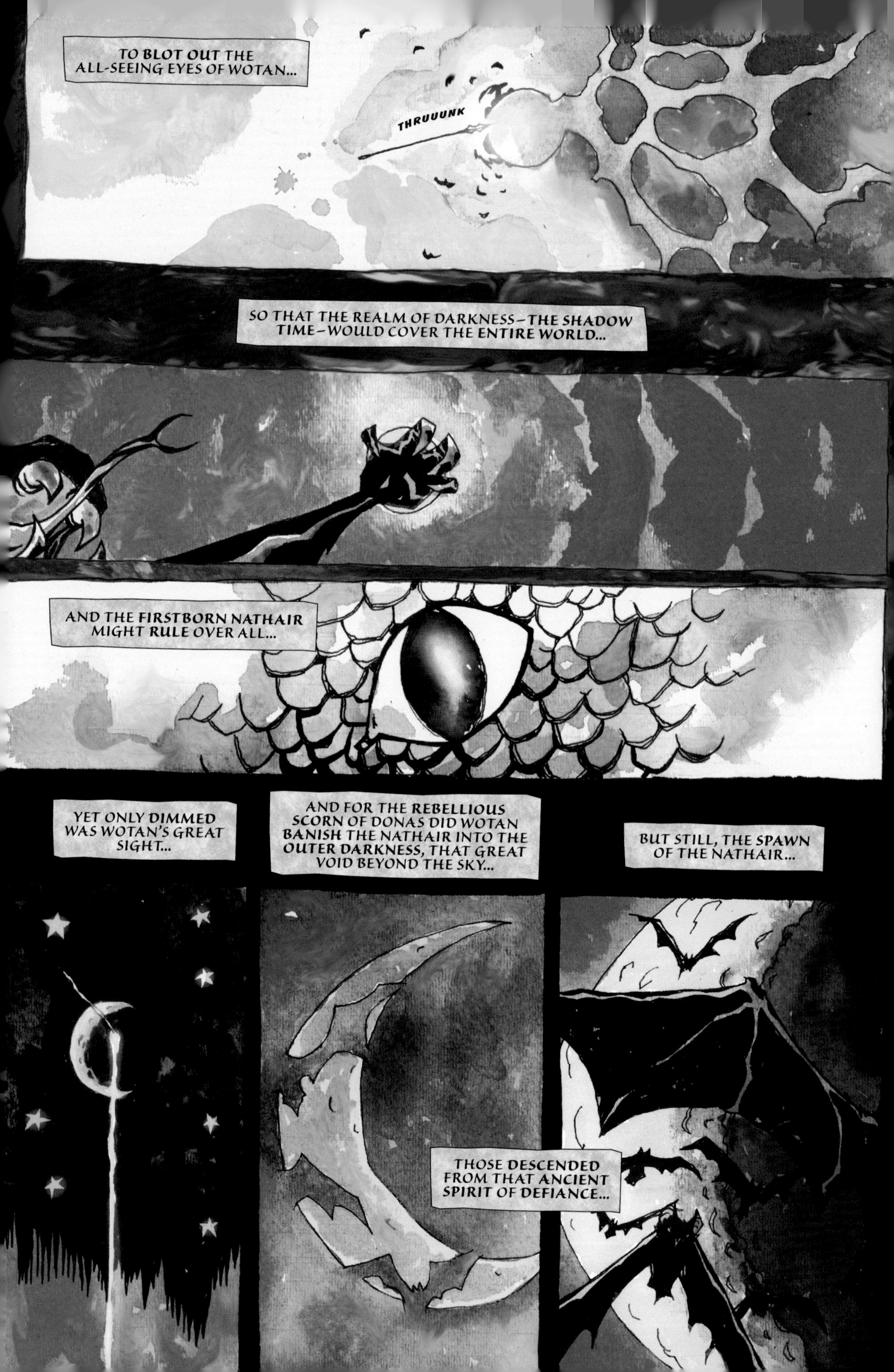
TO BLOT OUT THE ALL-SEEING EYES OF WOTAN...
THRUUUNK
SO THAT THE REALM OF DARKNESS—THE SHADOW TIME—WOULD COVER THE ENTIRE WORLD...
AND THE FIRSTBORN NATHAIR MIGHT RULE OVER ALL...
YET ONLY DIMMED WAS WOTAN'S GREAT SIGHT...
AND FOR THE REBELLIOUS SCORN OF DONAS DID WOTAN BANISH THE NATHAIR INTO THE OUTER DARKNESS, THAT GREAT VOID BEYOND THE SKY...
BUT STILL, THE SPAWN OF THE NATHAIR...
THOSE DESCENDED FROM THAT ANCIENT SPIRIT OF DEFIANCE...

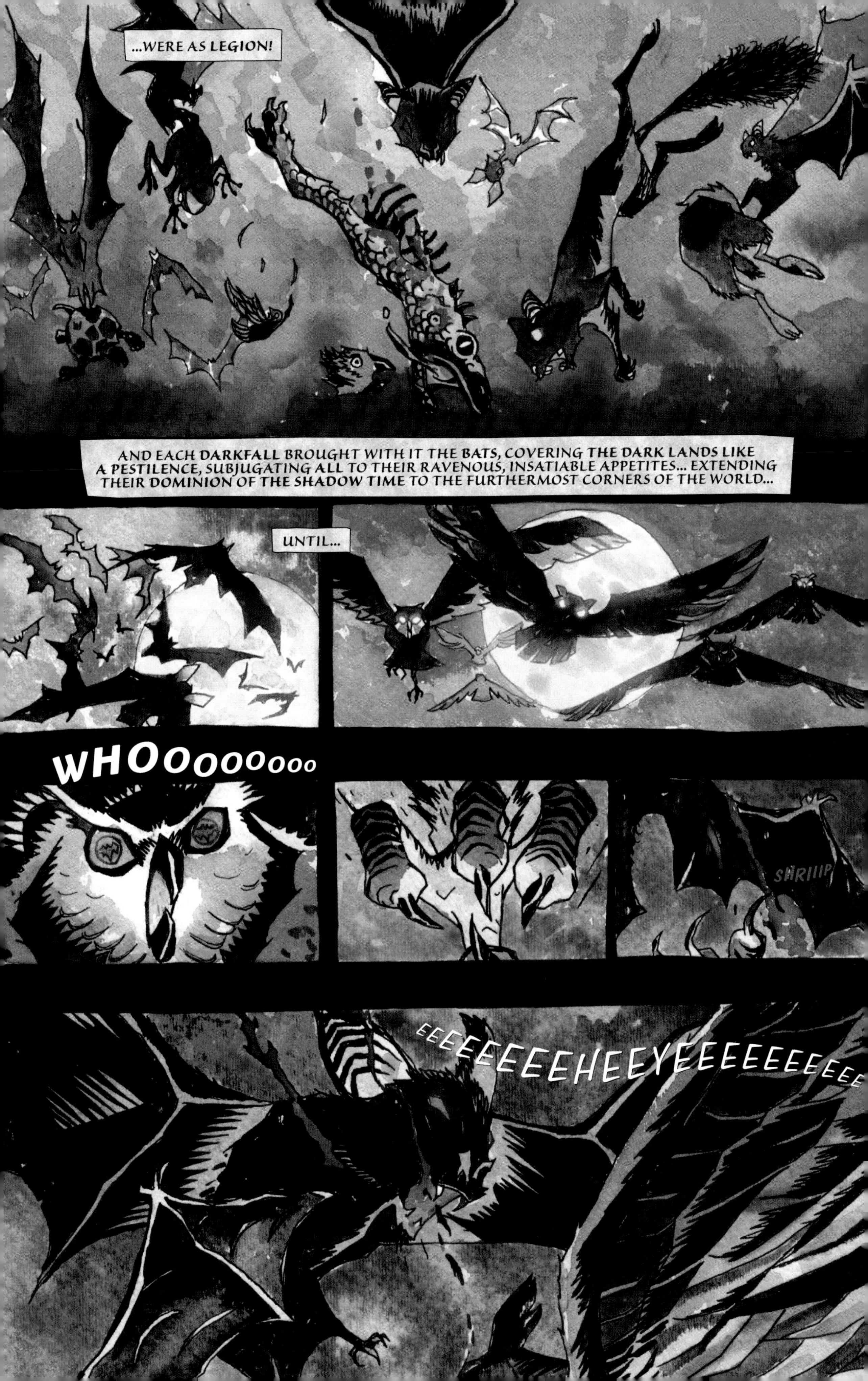

...WERE AS LEGION!
AND EACH DARKFALL BROUGHT WITH IT THE BATS, COVERING THE DARK LANDS LIKE A PESTILENCE, SUBJUGATING ALL TO THEIR RAVENOUS, INSATIABLE APPETITES... EXTENDING THEIR DOMINION OF THE SHADOW TIME TO THE FURTHERMOST CORNERS OF THE WORLD...
UNTIL...
WHOOOOOOoo
SHRIIIP
EEEEEEEEHEEYEEEEEEEEEEE

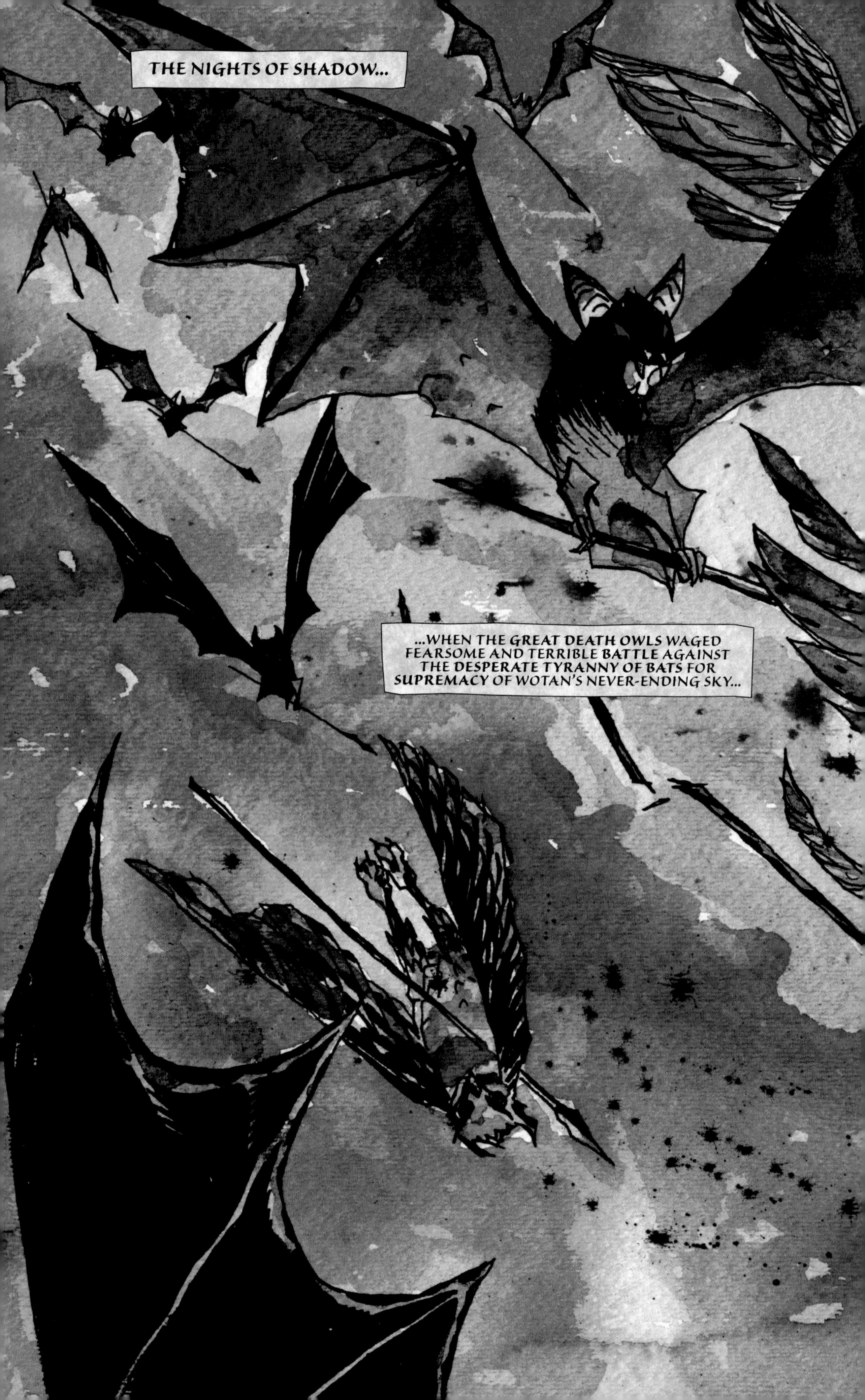
THE NIGHTS OF SHADOW...
...WHEN THE GREAT DEATH OWLS WAGED FEARSOME AND TERRIBLE BATTLE AGAINST THE DESPERATE TYRANNY OF BATS FOR SUPREMACY OF WOTAN'S NEVER-ENDING SKY...

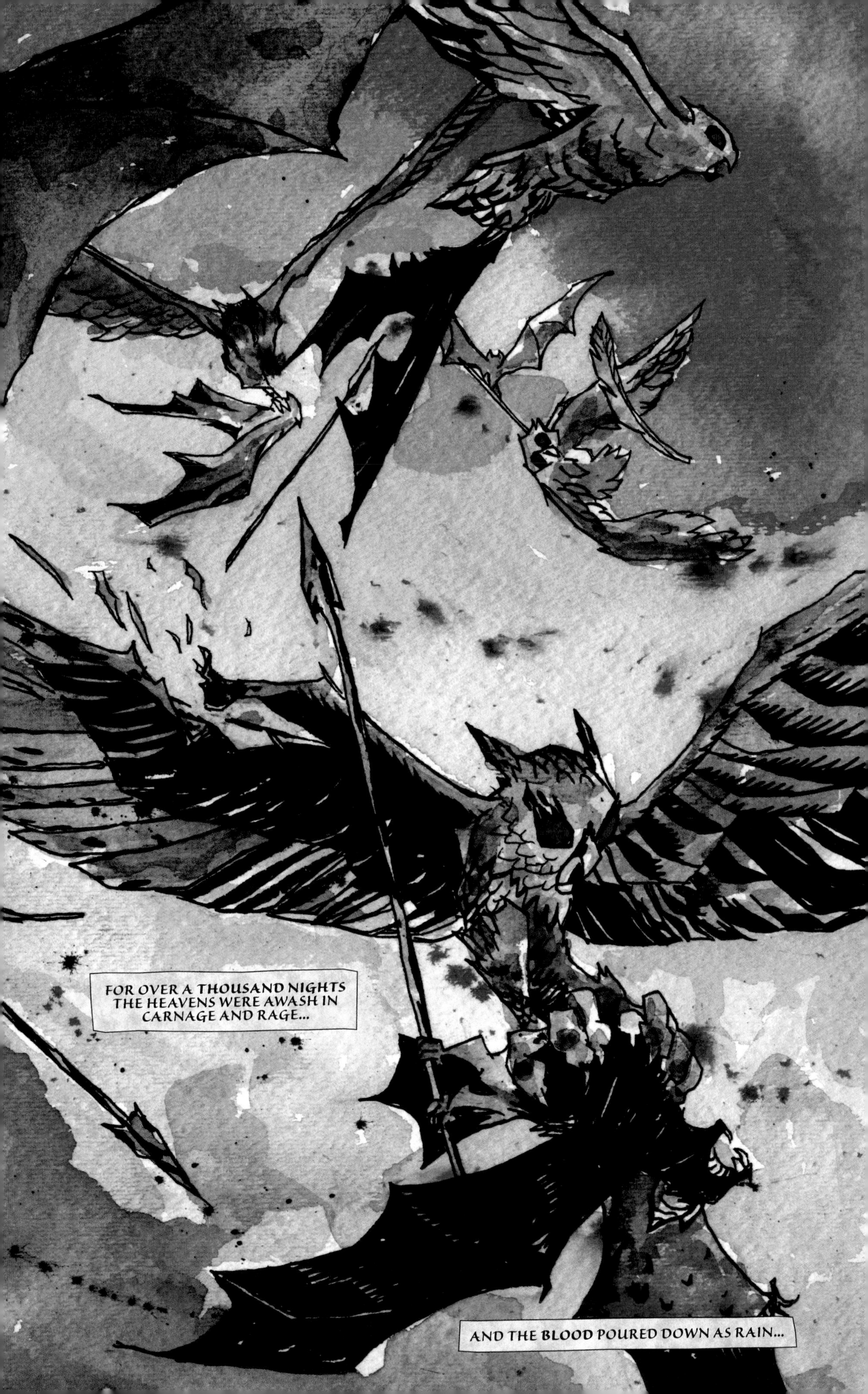
FOR OVER A THOUSAND NIGHTS THE HEAVENS WERE AWASH IN CARNAGE AND RAGE...
AND THE BLOOD POURED DOWN AS RAIN...

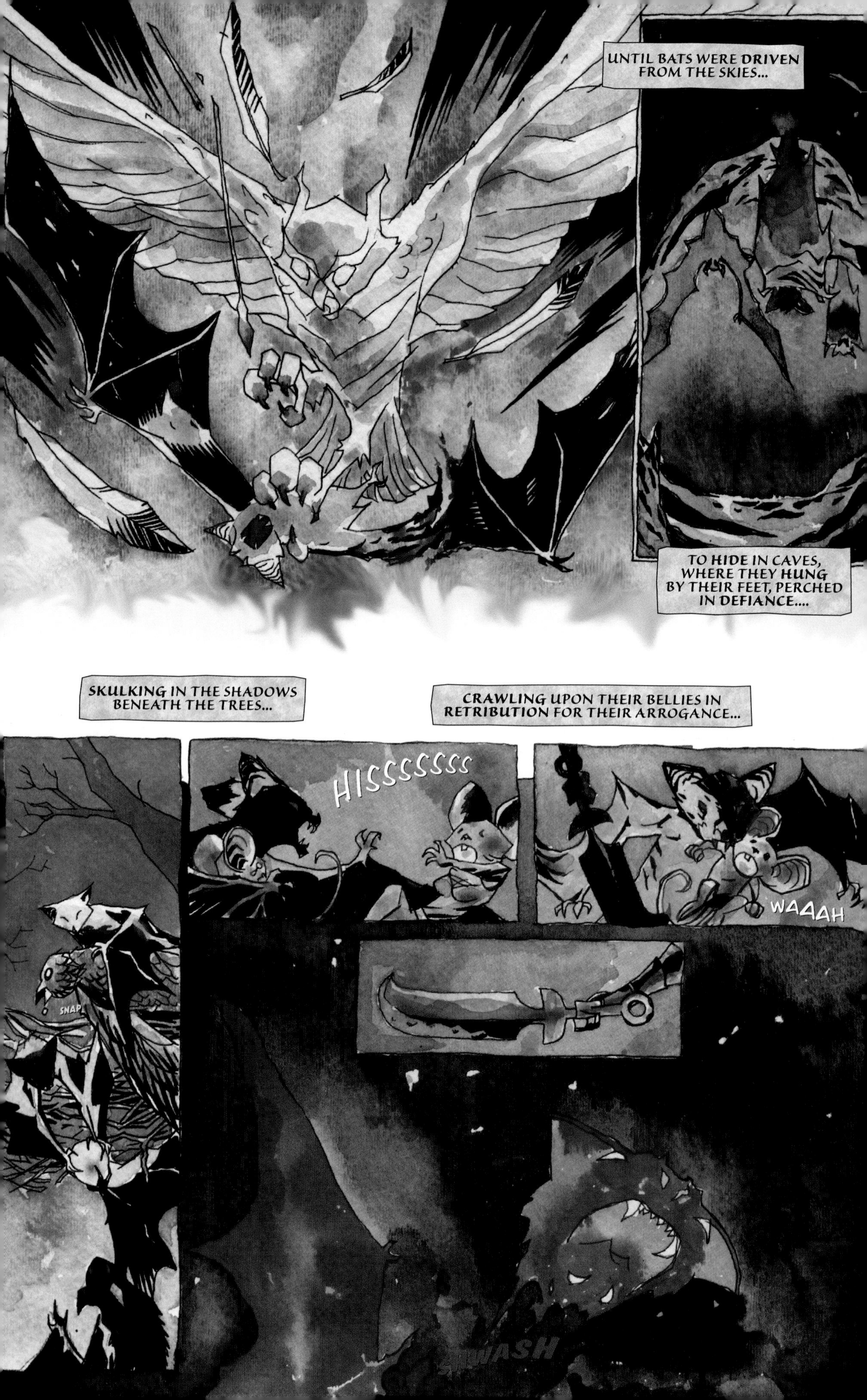
UNTIL BATS WERE DRIVEN FROM THE SKIES...
TO HIDE IN CAVES, WHERE THEY HUNG BY THEIR FEET, PERCHED IN DEFIANCE....
SKULKING IN THE SHADOWS BENEATH THE TREES...
CRAWLING UPON THEIR BELLIES IN RETRIBUTION FOR THEIR ARROGANCE...
SNAP
HISSSSSSS
WAAAH
SWASH

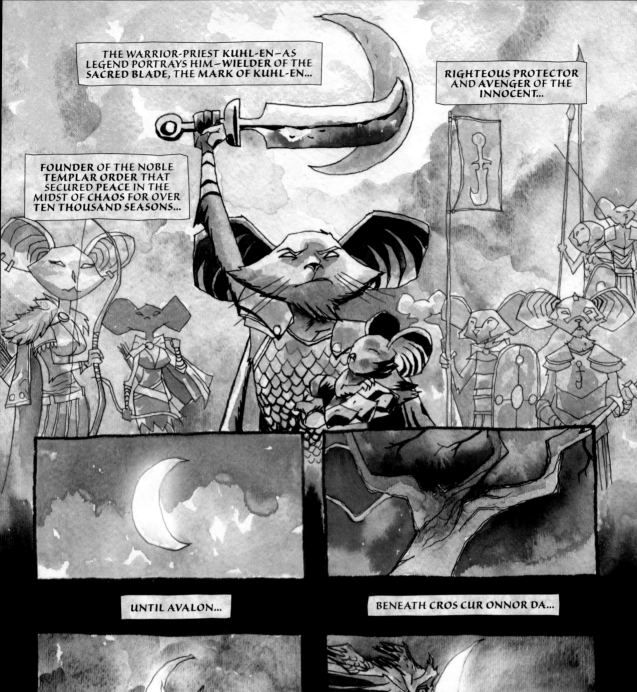

THE WARRIOR-PRIEST KUHL-EN—AS LEGEND PORTRAYS HIM—WIELDER OF THE SACRED BLADE, THE MARK OF KUHL-EN...

RIGHTEOUS PROTECTOR AND AVENGER OF THE INNOCENT...

FOUNDER OF THE NOBLE TEMPLAR ORDER THAT SECURED PEACE IN THE MIDST OF CHAOS FOR OVER TEN THOUSAND SEASONS...

UNTIL AVALON...

BENEATH CROS CUR ONNOR DA...

WHERE TEMPLAR TOOK THE BLOOD OF TEMPLAR...

WHEN THE OWLS WEPT...

AND THE GREAT DIMMED EYE OF WOTAN CLOSED...

AS THE TEMPLAR WERE AT LAST...

NO MORE...

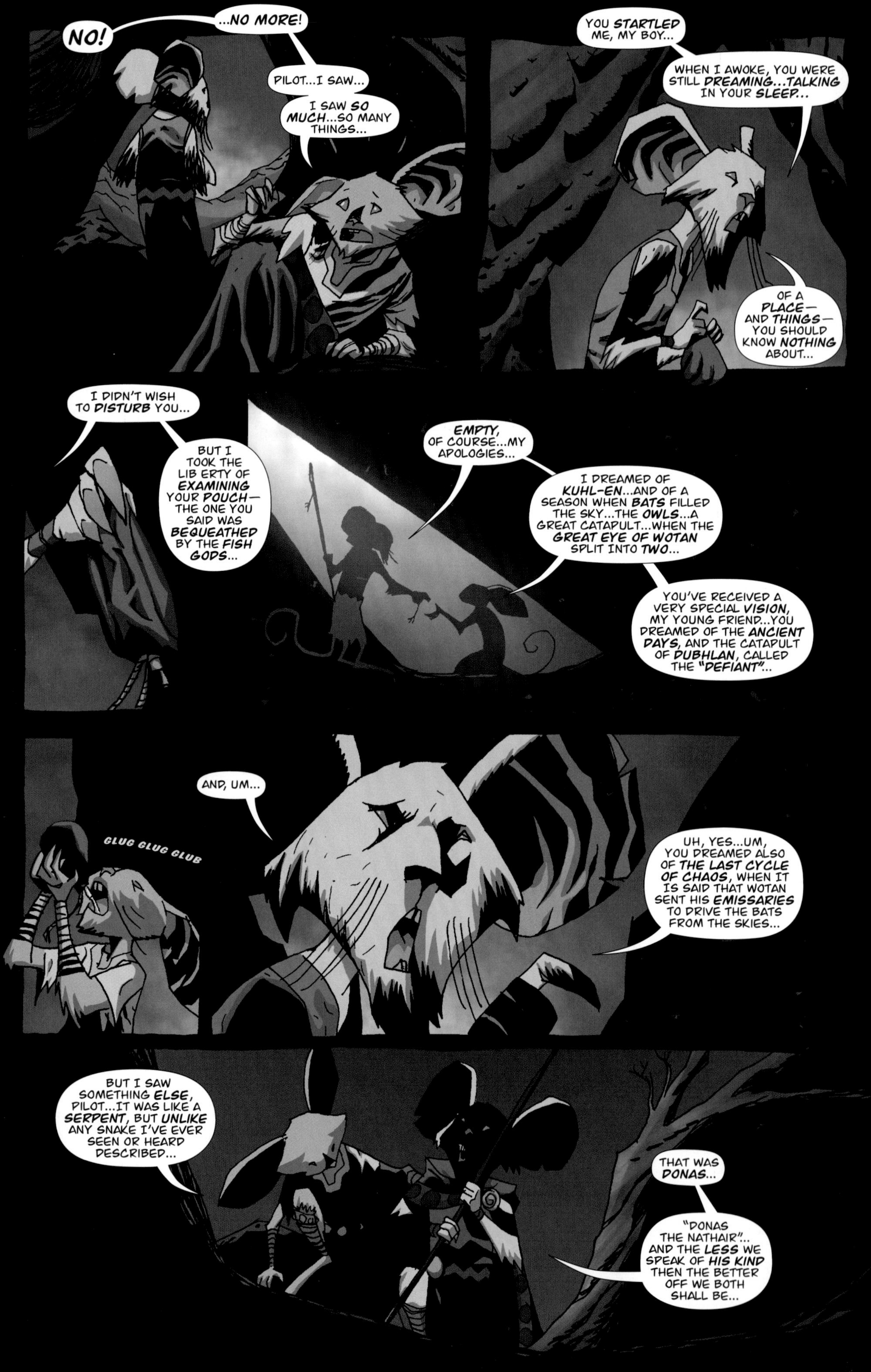
NO!
...NO MORE!
PILOT...I SAW...
I SAW SO MUCH...SO MANY THINGS...
YOU STARTLED ME, MY BOY...
WHEN I AWOKE, YOU WERE STILL DREAMING...TALKING IN YOUR SLEEP...
OF A PLACE— AND THINGS— YOU SHOULD KNOW NOTHING ABOUT...
I DIDN'T WISH TO DISTURB YOU...
BUT I TOOK THE LIB ERTY OF EXAMINING YOUR POUCH— THE ONE YOU SAID WAS BEQUEATHED BY THE FISH GODS...
EMPTY, OF COURSE...MY APOLOGIES...
I DREAMED OF KUHL-EN...AND OF A SEASON WHEN BATS FILLED THE SKY...THE OWLS...A GREAT CATAPULT...WHEN THE GREAT EYE OF WOTAN SPLIT INTO TWO...
YOU'VE RECEIVED A VERY SPECIAL VISION, MY YOUNG FRIEND...YOU DREAMED OF THE ANCIENT DAYS, AND THE CATAPULT OF DUBHLAN, CALLED THE "DEFIANT"...
AND, UM...
GLUG GLUG GLUB
UH, YES...UM, YOU DREAMED ALSO OF THE LAST CYCLE OF CHAOS, WHEN IT IS SAID THAT WOTAN SENT HIS EMISSARIES TO DRIVE THE BATS FROM THE SKIES...
BUT I SAW SOMETHING ELSE, PILOT...IT WAS LIKE A SERPENT, BUT UNLIKE ANY SNAKE I'VE EVER SEEN OR HEARD DESCRIBED...
THAT WAS DONAS...
"DONAS THE NATHAIR"... AND THE LESS WE SPEAK OF HIS KIND THEN THE BETTER OFF WE BOTH SHALL BE...

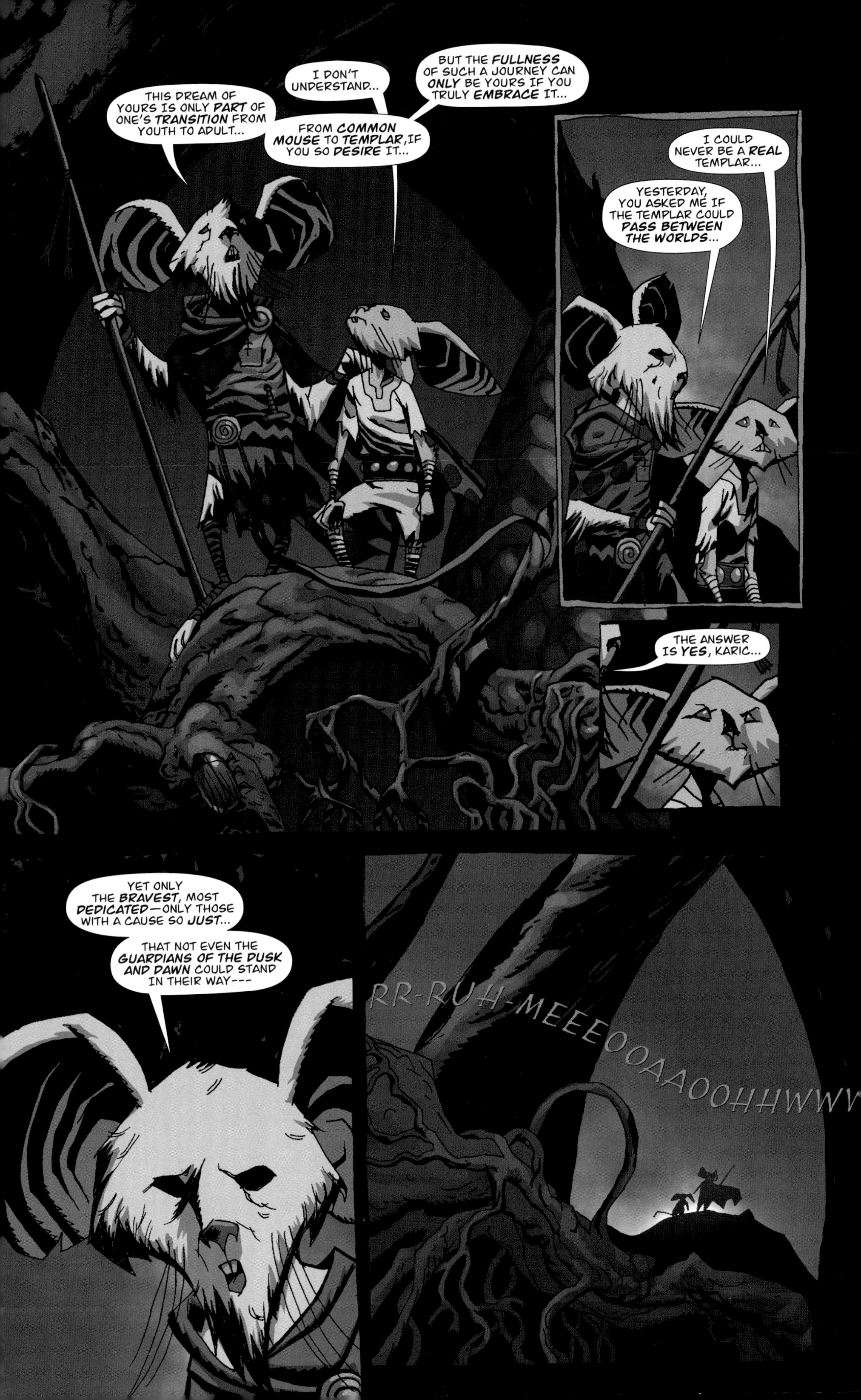
THIS DREAM OF YOURS IS ONLY PART OF ONE'S TRANSITION FROM YOUTH TO ADULT...
I DON'T UNDERSTAND...
FROM COMMON MOUSE TO TEMPLAR, IF YOU SO DESIRE IT...
BUT THE FULLNESS OF SUCH A JOURNEY CAN ONLY BE YOURS IF YOU TRULY EMBRACE IT...
I COULD NEVER BE A REAL TEMPLAR...
YESTERDAY, YOU ASKED ME IF THE TEMPLAR COULD PASS BETWEEN THE WORLDS...
THE ANSWER IS YES, KARIC...
YET ONLY THE BRAVEST, MOST DEDICATED—ONLY THOSE WITH A CAUSE SO JUST...
THAT NOT EVEN THE GUARDIANS OF THE DUSK AND DAWN COULD STAND IN THEIR WAY---
RR-RUH-MEEEOOAAOOHHWWW

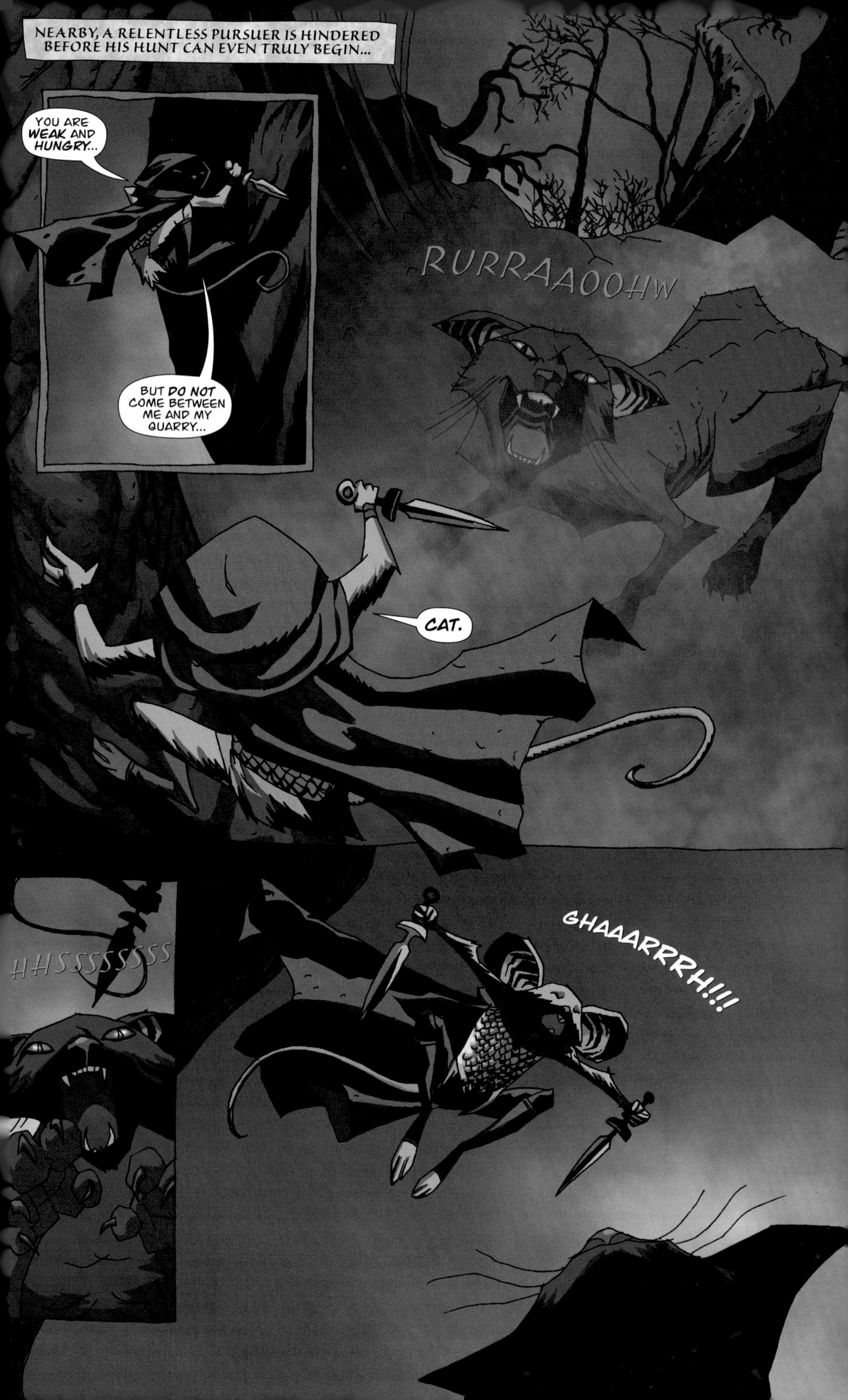
NEARBY, A RELENTLESS PURSUER IS HINDERED BEFORE HIS HUNT CAN EVEN TRULY BEGIN...
YOU ARE WEAK AND HUNGRY...
BUT DO NOT COME BETWEEN ME AND MY QUARRY...
RURRAAOOHW
CAT.
HHSSSSSSSS
GHAAARRRH!!!!

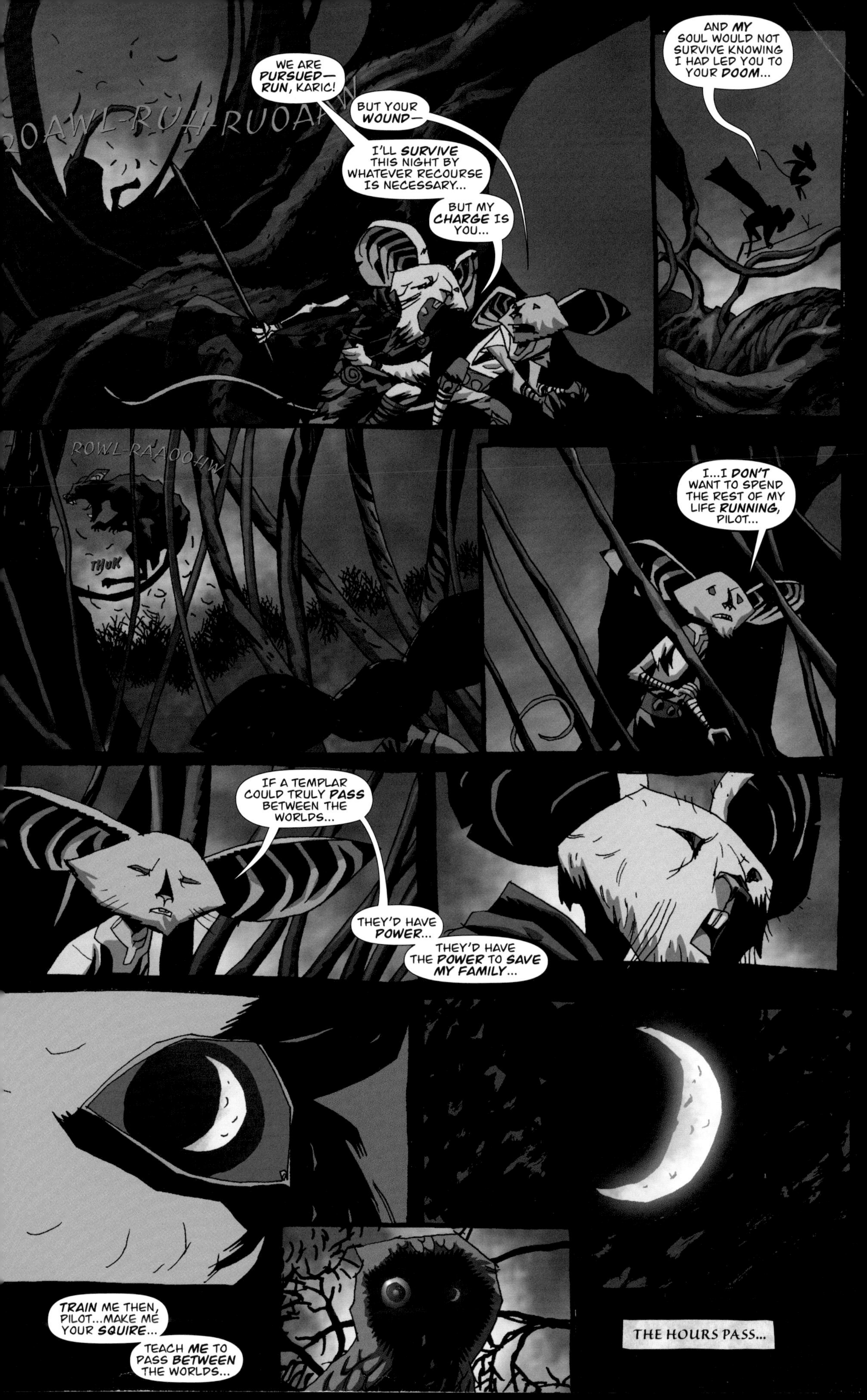
ROAWL-RUH-RUOARW
WE ARE PURSUED— RUN, KARIC!
BUT YOUR WOUND—
I'LL SURVIVE THIS NIGHT BY WHATEVER RECOURSE IS NECESSARY...
BUT MY CHARGE IS YOU...
AND MY SOUL WOULD NOT SURVIVE KNOWING I HAD LED YOU TO YOUR DOOM...
ROWL-RAAOOHW
THUK
I...I DON'T WANT TO SPEND THE REST OF MY LIFE RUNNING, PILOT...
IF A TEMPLAR COULD TRULY PASS BETWEEN THE WORLDS...
THEY'D HAVE POWER...
THEY'D HAVE THE POWER TO SAVE MY FAMILY...
TRAIN ME THEN, PILOT...MAKE ME YOUR SQUIRE...
TEACH ME TO PASS BETWEEN THE WORLDS...
THE HOURS PASS...

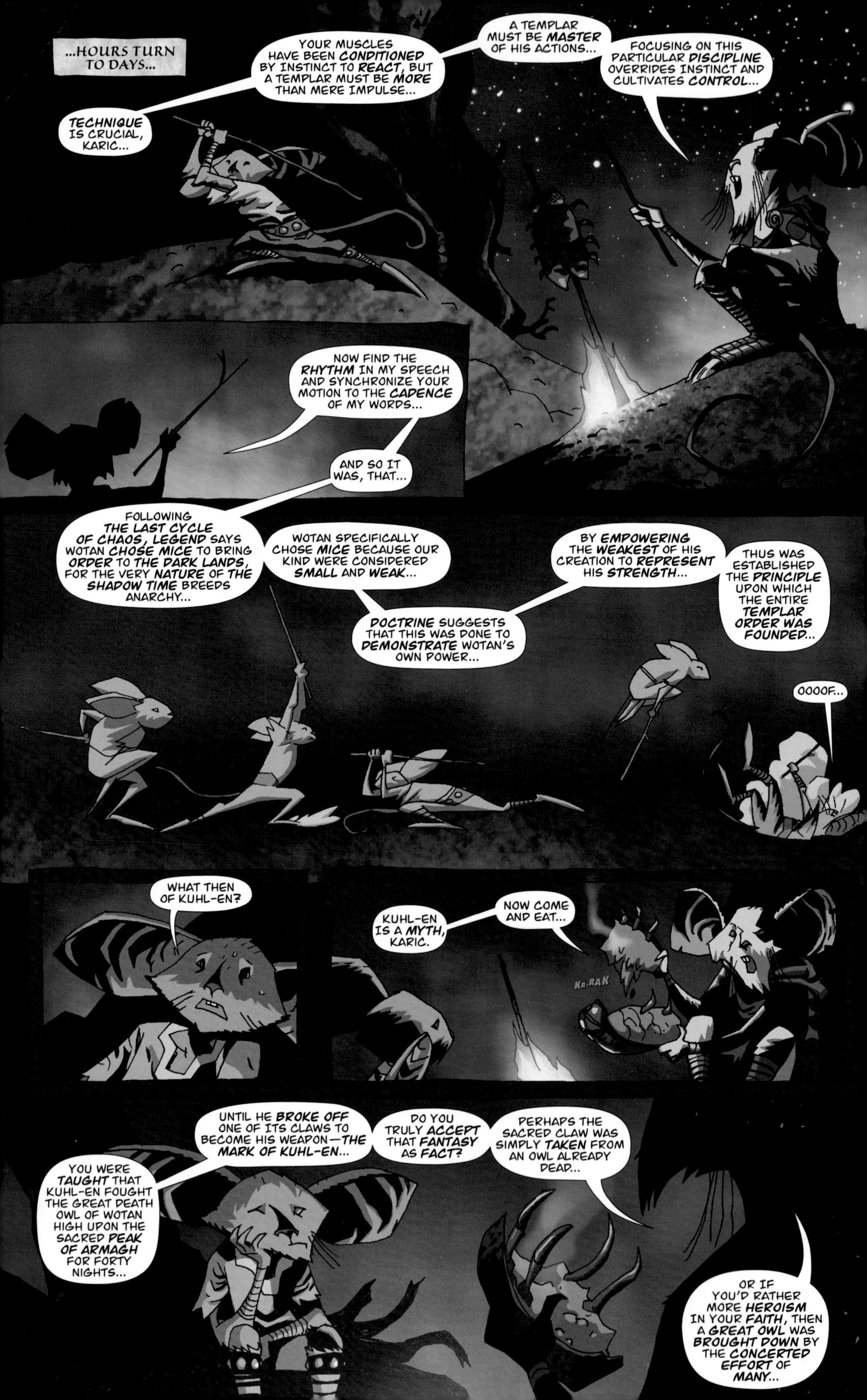

...HOURS TURN TO DAYS...
TECHNIQUE IS CRUCIAL, KARIC...
YOUR MUSCLES HAVE BEEN CONDITIONED BY INSTINCT TO REACT, BUT A TEMPLAR MUST BE MORE THAN MERE IMPULSE...
A TEMPLAR MUST BE MASTER OF HIS ACTIONS...
FOCUSING ON THIS PARTICULAR DISCIPLINE OVERRIDES INSTINCT AND CULTIVATES CONTROL...
NOW FIND THE RHYTHM IN MY SPEECH AND SYNCHRONIZE YOUR MOTION TO THE CADENCE OF MY WORDS...
AND SO IT WAS, THAT...
FOLLOWING THE LAST CYCLE OF CHAOS, LEGEND SAYS WOTAN CHOSE MICE TO BRING ORDER TO THE DARK LANDS, FOR THE VERY NATURE OF THE SHADOW TIME BREEDS ANARCHY...
WOTAN SPECIFICALLY CHOSE MICE BECAUSE OUR KIND WERE CONSIDERED SMALL AND WEAK...
DOCTRINE SUGGESTS THAT THIS WAS DONE TO DEMONSTRATE WOTAN'S OWN POWER...
BY EMPOWERING THE WEAKEST OF HIS CREATION TO REPRESENT HIS STRENGTH...
THUS WAS ESTABLISHED THE PRINCIPLE UPON WHICH THE ENTIRE TEMPLAR ORDER WAS FOUNDED...
OOOOF...
WHAT THEN OF KUHL-EN?
KUHL-EN IS A MYTH, KARIC.
NOW COME AND EAT...
KR-RAK
YOU WERE TAUGHT THAT KUHL-EN FOUGHT THE GREAT DEATH OWL OF WOTAN HIGH UPON THE SACRED PEAK OF ARMAGH FOR FORTY NIGHTS...
UNTIL HE BROKE OFF ONE OF ITS CLAWS TO BECOME HIS WEAPON—THE MARK OF KUHL-EN...
DO YOU TRULY ACCEPT THAT FANTASY AS FACT?
PERHAPS THE SACRED CLAW WAS SIMPLY TAKEN FROM AN OWL ALREADY DEAD...
OR IF YOU'D RATHER MORE HEROISM IN YOUR FAITH, THEN A GREAT OWL WAS BROUGHT DOWN BY THE CONCERTED EFFORT OF MANY...

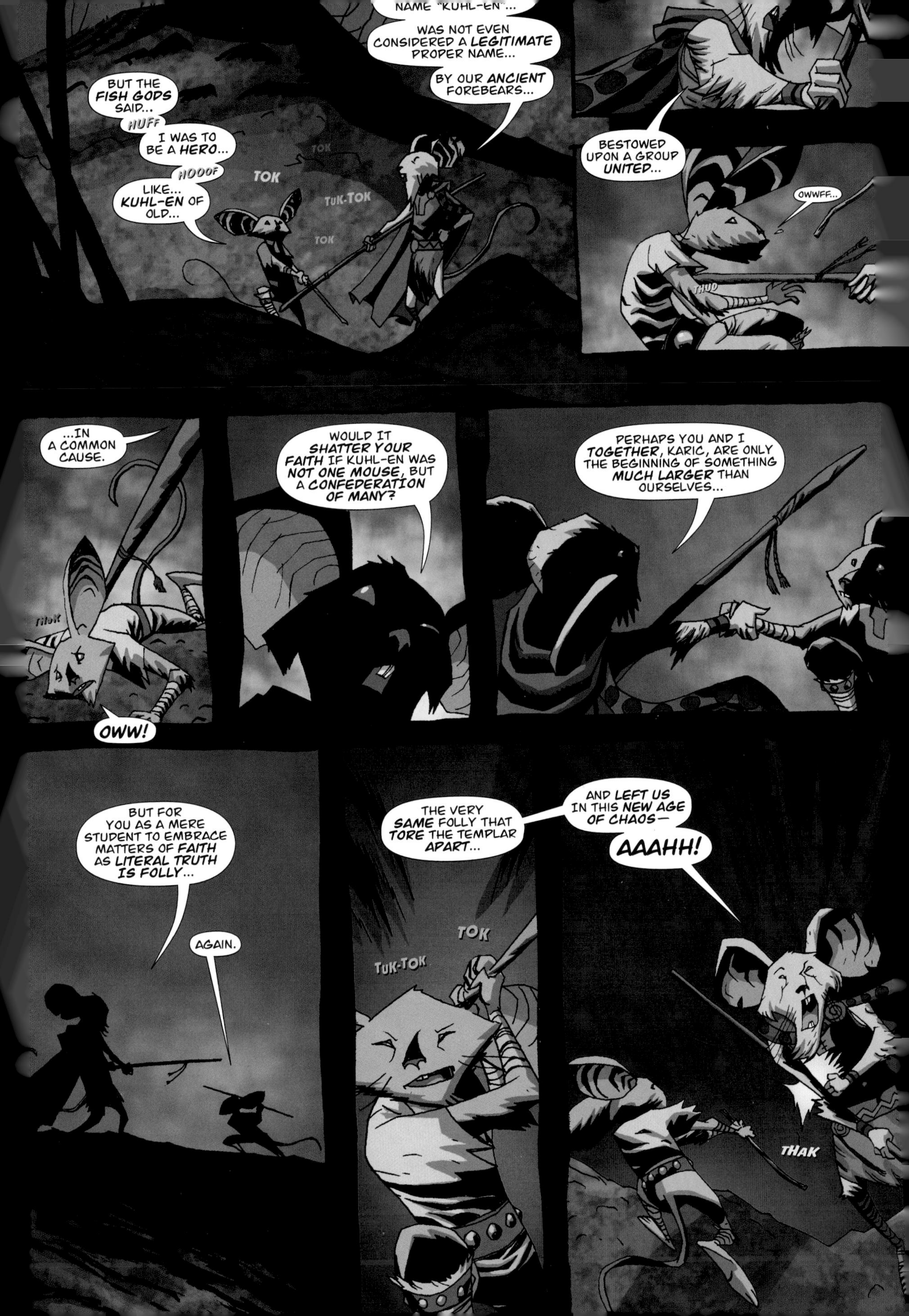

BUT THE FISH GODS SAID...
HUFF
I WAS TO BE A HERO...
HOOOF
LIKE... KUHL-EN OF OLD...
TOK
TOK
TUK-TOK
TOK
NAME "KUHL-EN"...
WAS NOT EVEN CONSIDERED A LEGITIMATE PROPER NAME...
BY OUR ANCIENT FOREBEARS...
BESTOWED UPON A GROUP UNITED...
OWWFF...
THUD
...IN A COMMON CAUSE.
OWW!
WOULD IT SHATTER YOUR FAITH IF KUHL-EN WAS NOT ONE MOUSE, BUT A CONFEDERATION OF MANY?
PERHAPS YOU AND I TOGETHER, KARIC, ARE ONLY THE BEGINNING OF SOMETHING MUCH LARGER THAN OURSELVES...
BUT FOR YOU AS A MERE STUDENT TO EMBRACE MATTERS OF FAITH AS LITERAL TRUTH IS FOLLY...
AGAIN.
THE VERY SAME FOLLY THAT TORE THE TEMPLAR APART...
TOK
TUK-TOK
AND LEFT US IN THIS NEW AGE OF CHAOS—
AAAHH!
THAK

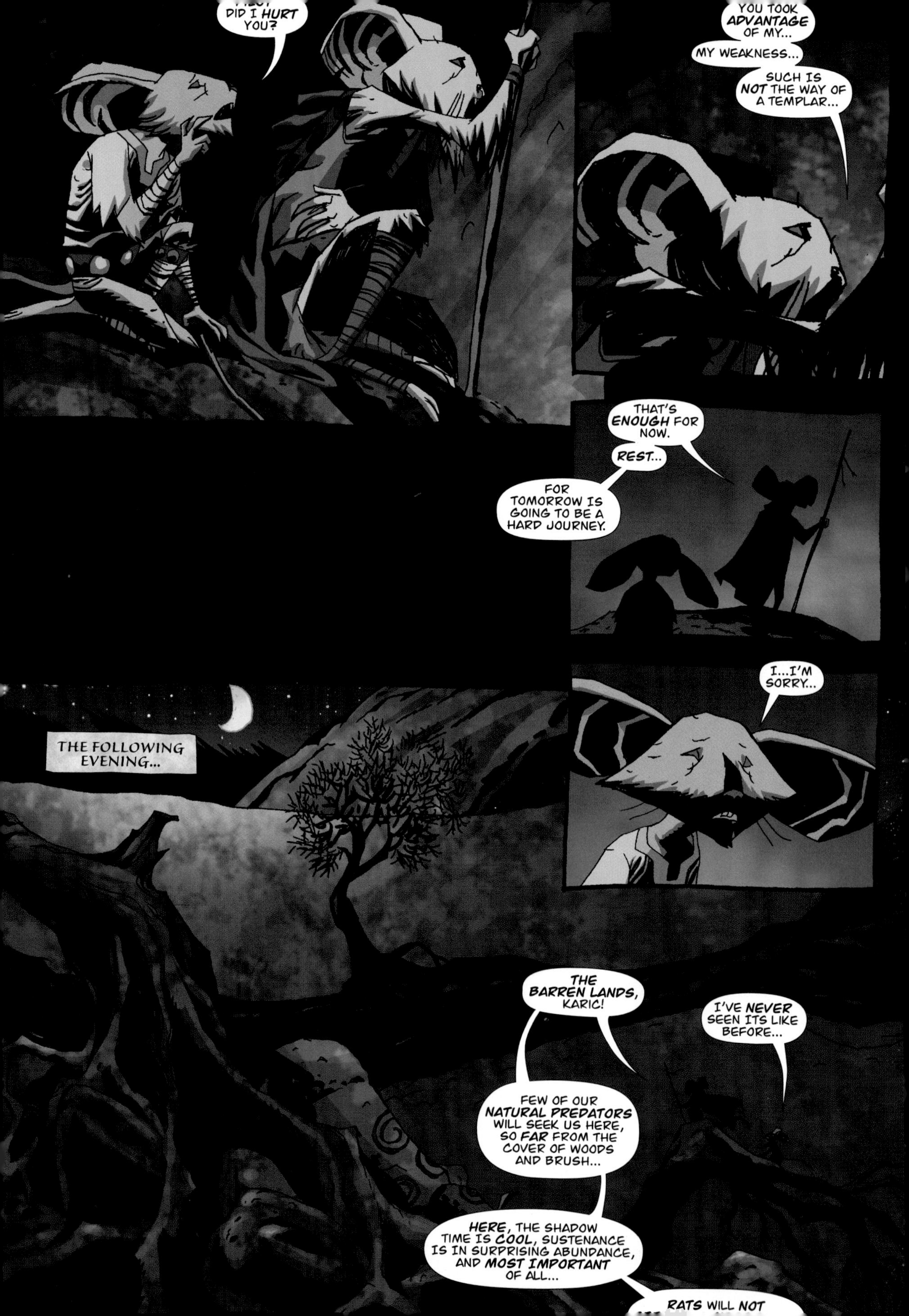
DID I HURT YOU?
YOU TOOK ADVANTAGE OF MY...
MY WEAKNESS...
SUCH IS NOT THE WAY OF A TEMPLAR...
THAT'S ENOUGH FOR NOW.
REST...
FOR TOMORROW IS GOING TO BE A HARD JOURNEY.
I...I'M SORRY...
THE FOLLOWING EVENING...
THE BARREN LANDS, KARIC!
I'VE NEVER SEEN ITS LIKE BEFORE...
FEW OF OUR NATURAL PREDATORS WILL SEEK US HERE, SO FAR FROM THE COVER OF WOODS AND BRUSH...
HERE, THE SHADOW TIME IS COOL, SUSTENANCE IS IN SURPRISING ABUNDANCE, AND MOST IMPORTANT OF ALL...
RATS WILL NOT

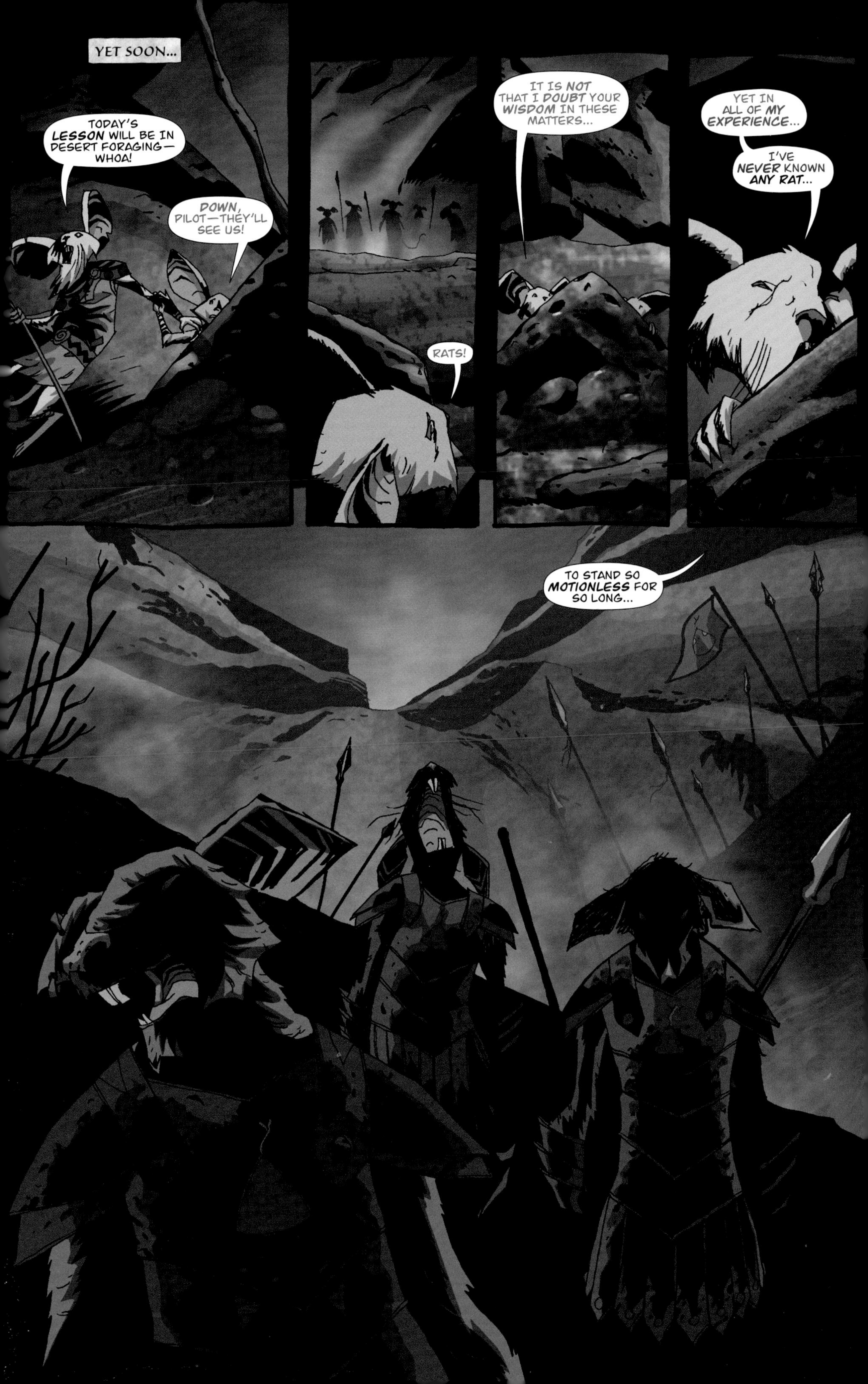
YET SOON...
TODAY'S LESSON WILL BE IN DESERT FORAGING— WHOA!
DOWN, PILOT—THEY'LL SEE US!
RATS!
IT IS NOT THAT I DOUBT YOUR WISDOM IN THESE MATTERS...
YET IN ALL OF MY EXPERIENCE...
I'VE NEVER KNOWN ANY RAT...
TO STAND SO MOTIONLESS FOR SO LONG...

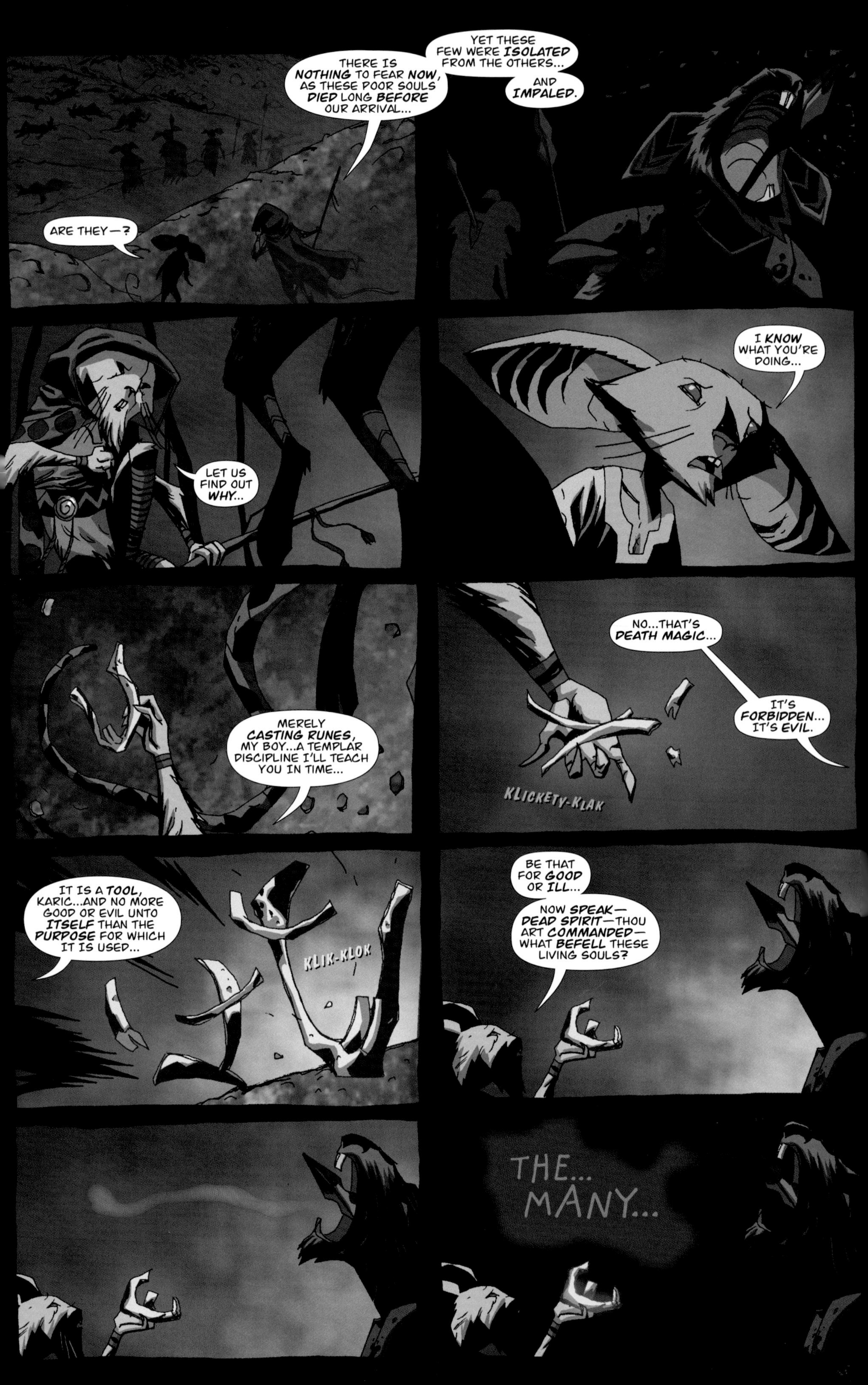

THERE IS NOTHING TO FEAR NOW, AS THESE POOR SOULS DIED LONG BEFORE OUR ARRIVAL...
ARE THEY—?
YET THESE FEW WERE ISOLATED FROM THE OTHERS...
AND IMPALED.
LET US FIND OUT WHY...
I KNOW WHAT YOU'RE DOING...
MERELY CASTING RUNES, MY BOY...A TEMPLAR DISCIPLINE I'LL TEACH YOU IN TIME...
NO...THAT'S DEATH MAGIC...
IT'S FORBIDDEN... IT'S EVIL.
KLICKETY-KLAK
IT IS A TOOL, KARIC...AND NO MORE GOOD OR EVIL UNTO ITSELF THAN THE PURPOSE FOR WHICH IT IS USED...
KLIK-KLOK
BE THAT FOR GOOD OR ILL...
NOW SPEAK—DEAD SPIRIT—THOU ART COMMANDED—WHAT BEFELL THESE LIVING SOULS?
THE... MANY...

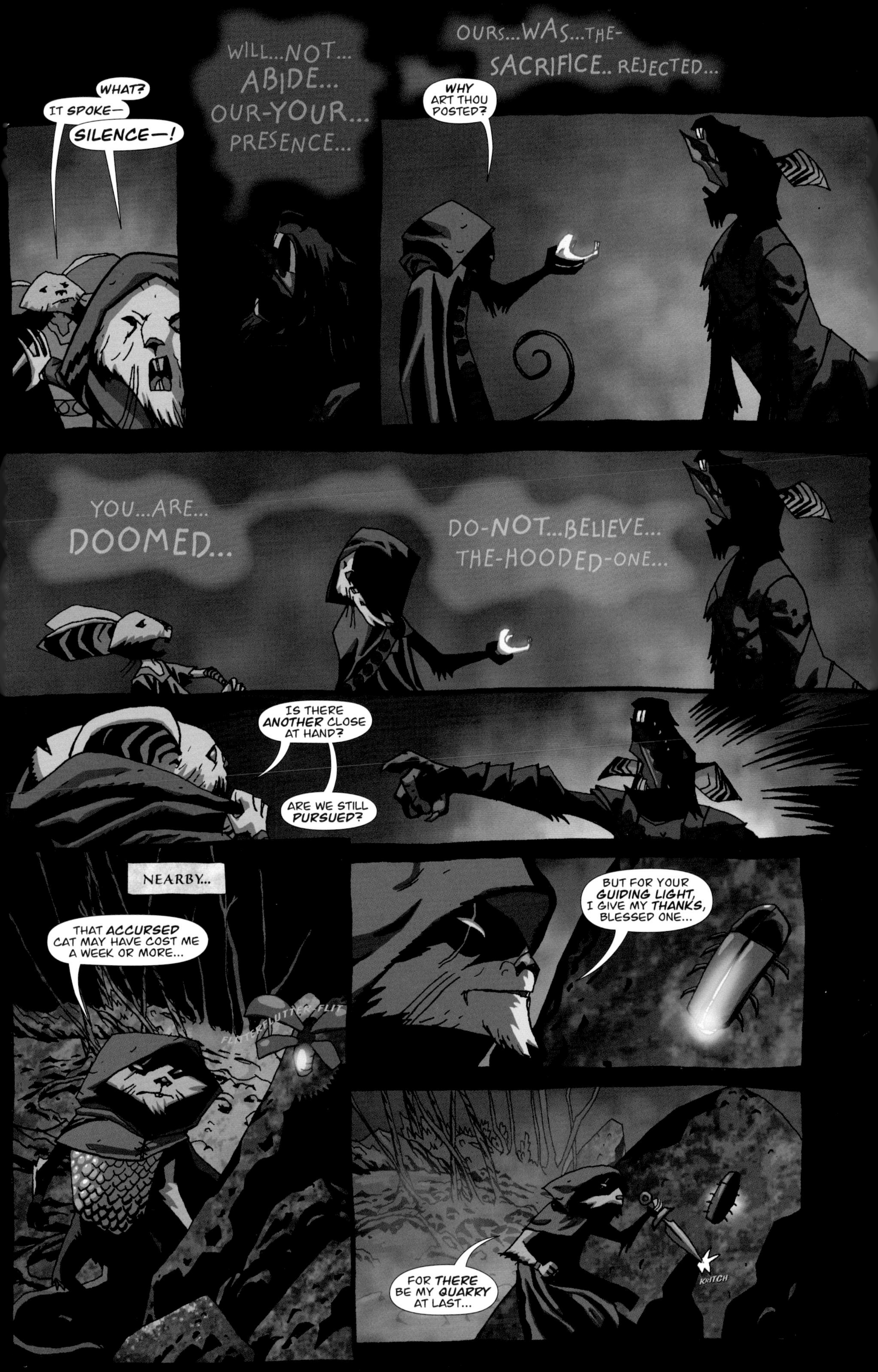
WHAT?
IT SPOKE—
SILENCE—!
WILL...NOT... ABIDE... OUR-YOUR... PRESENCE...
OURS...WAS...THE-SACRIFICE.. REJECTED...
WHY ART THOU POSTED?
YOU...ARE... DOOMED...
DO-NOT...BELIEVE... THE-HOODED-ONE...
IS THERE ANOTHER CLOSE AT HAND?
ARE WE STILL PURSUED?
NEARBY...
THAT ACCURSED CAT MAY HAVE COST ME A WEEK OR MORE...
FLUTTERFLUTTER-FLIT
BUT FOR YOUR GUIDING LIGHT, I GIVE MY THANKS, BLESSED ONE...
FOR THERE BE MY QUARRY AT LAST...
KRITCH

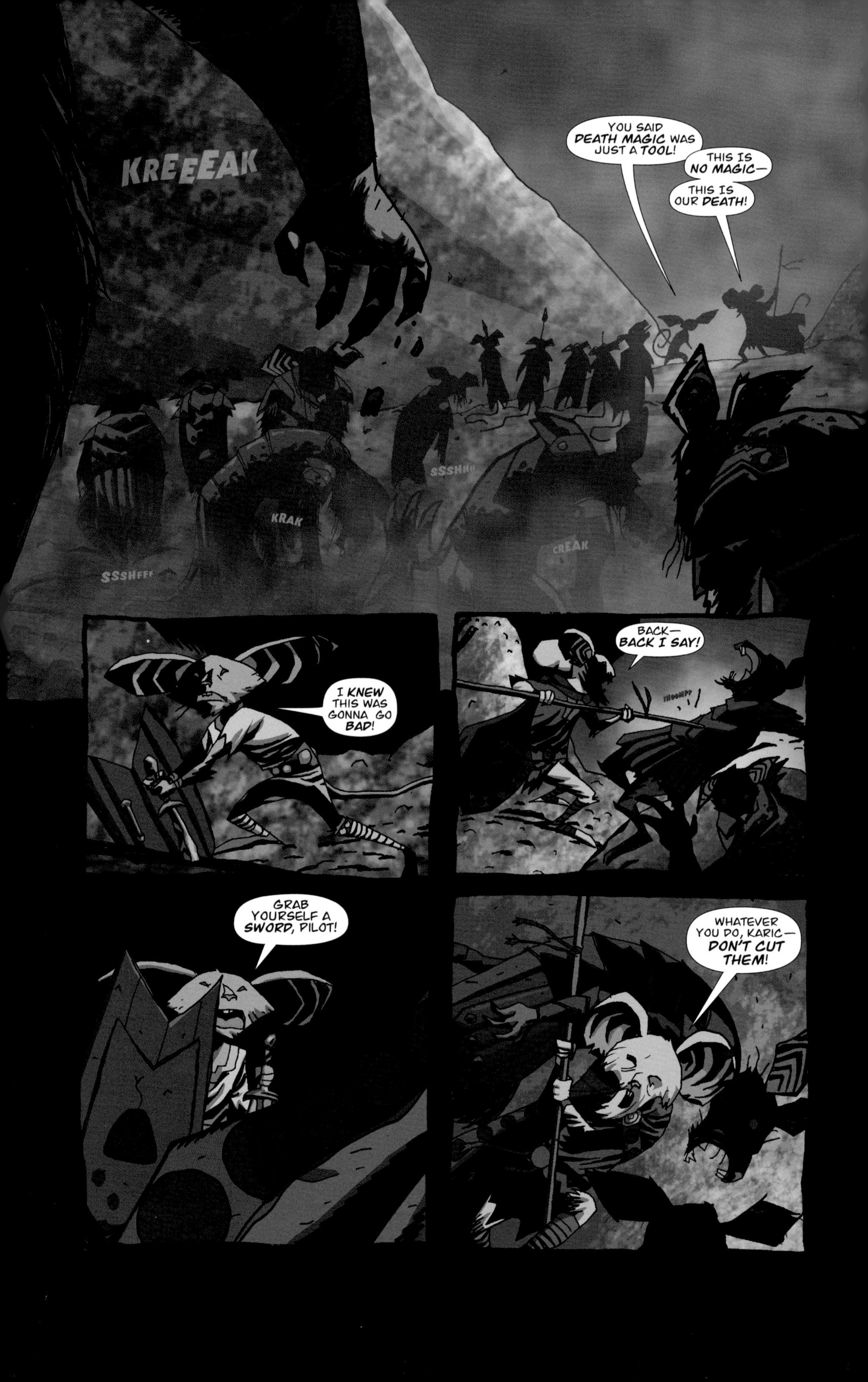
KREEEAK
YOU SAID DEATH MAGIC WAS JUST A TOOL!
THIS IS NO MAGIC—
THIS IS OUR DEATH!
SSSHH
KRAK
CREAK
SSSHFFF
I KNEW THIS WAS GONNA GO BAD!
BACK— BACK I SAY!
GRAB YOURSELF A SWORD, PILOT!
WHATEVER YOU DO, KARIC— DON'T CUT THEM!

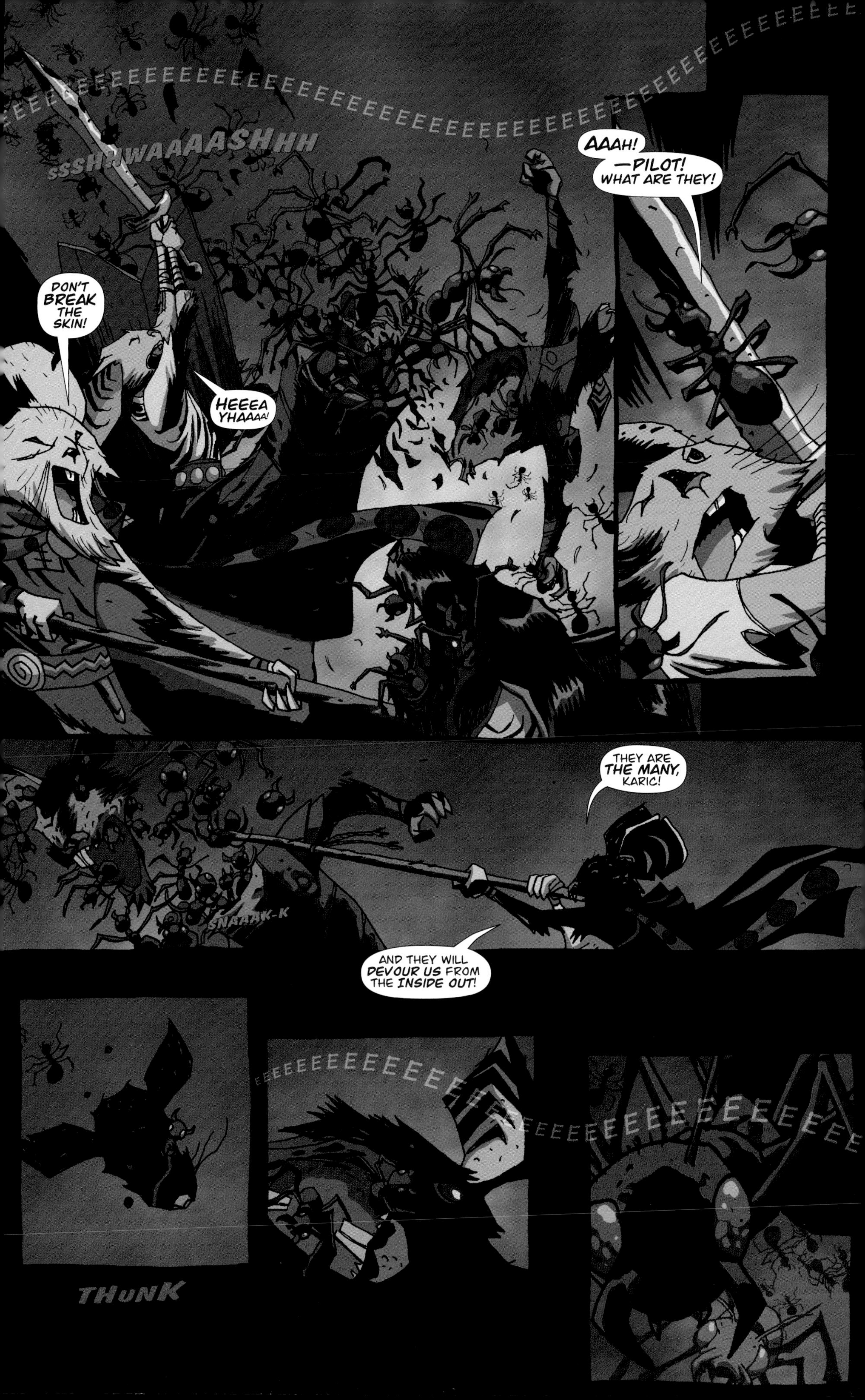
EEEEEEEEEEEEEEEEEEEEEEEEEEEEEEEEEEEEEEEEEEEE
sSSHHWAAAAASHHH
DON'T BREAK THE SKIN!
HEEEA YHAAAA!
AAAH! —PILOT! WHAT ARE THEY!
THEY ARE THE MANY, KARIC!
SNAAAK-K
AND THEY WILL DEVOUR US FROM THE INSIDE OUT!
THUNK
EEEEEEEEEEEEEEEEEEEEEEEEEEE

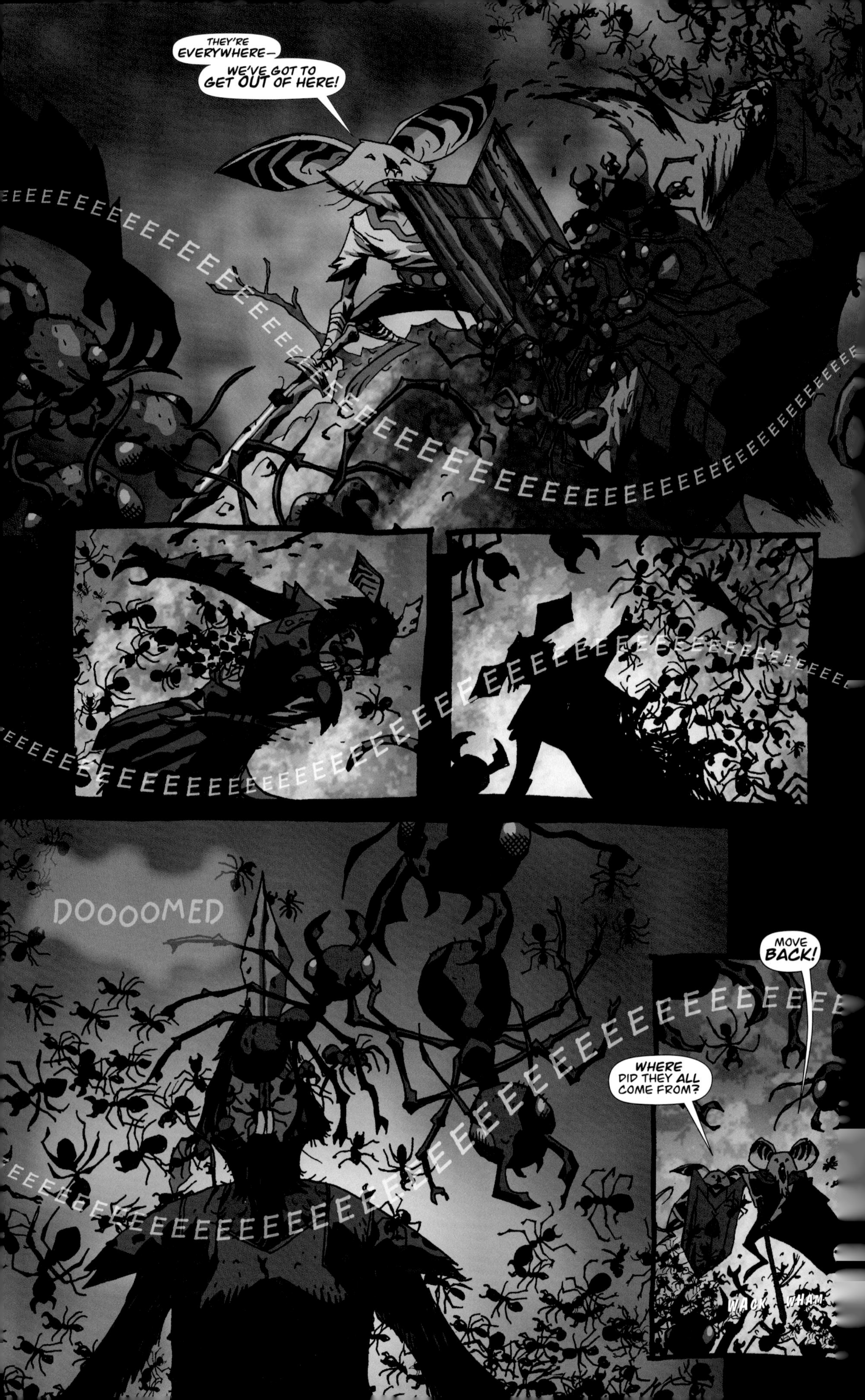
THEY'RE EVERYWHERE—
WE'VE GOT TO GET OUT OF HERE!
EEEEEEEEEEEEEEEEEEEEEEEEEEEEEEEEEEEEEEE
EEEEEEEEEEEEEEEEEEEEEEEEEEEEEEEEE
DOOOOMED
EEEEEEEEEEEEEEEEEEEEEEEEEEEEEEEEEEE
MOVE BACK!
WHERE DID THEY ALL COME FROM?
WACK
WHAM

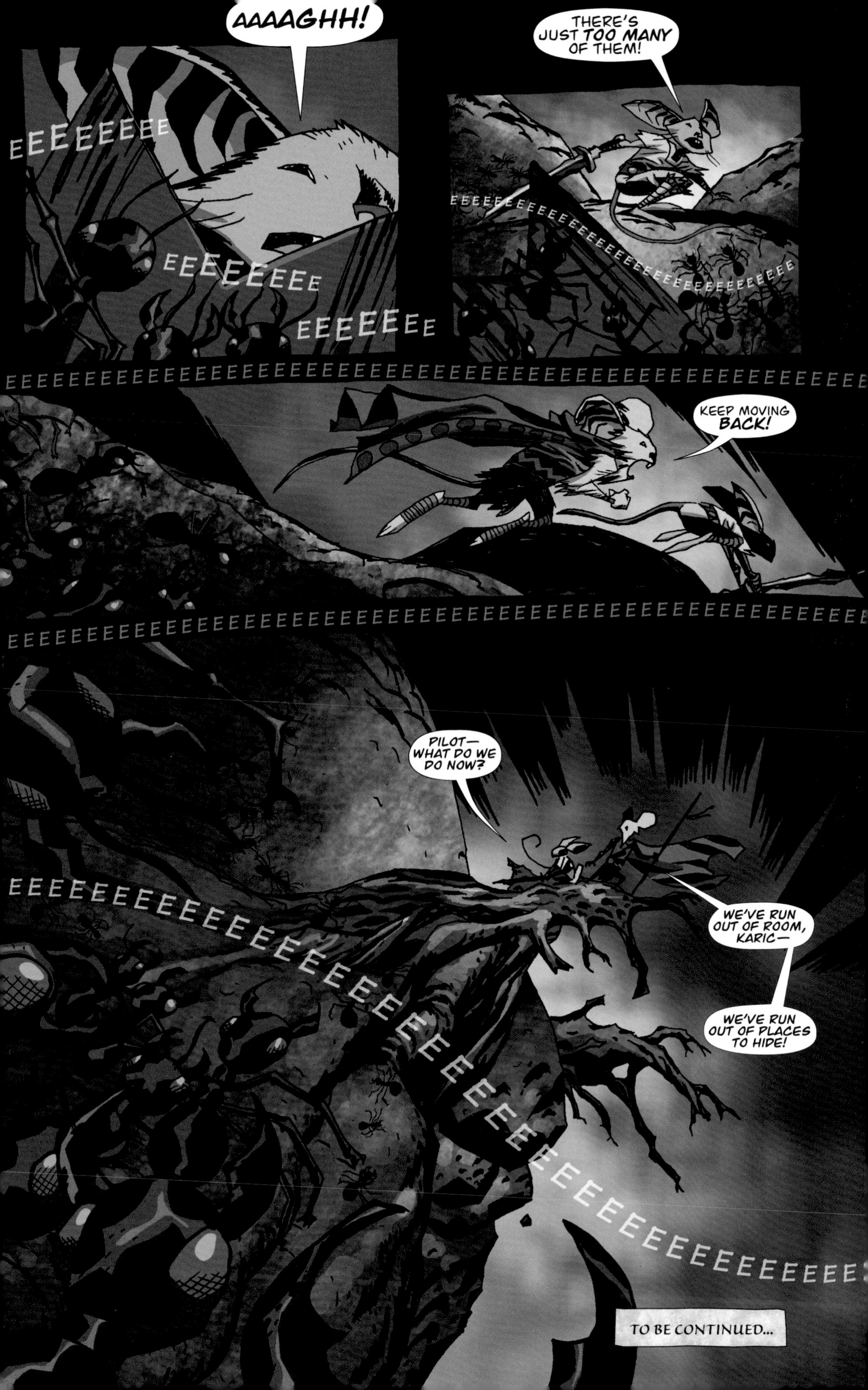
AAAAGHH!
THERE'S JUST TOO MANY OF THEM!
KEEP MOVING BACK!
PILOT— WHAT DO WE DO NOW?
WE'VE RUN OUT OF ROOM, KARIC—
WE'VE RUN OUT OF PLACES TO HIDE!
TO BE CONTINUED...

CHAPTER FOUR
BLACK ANAIUS

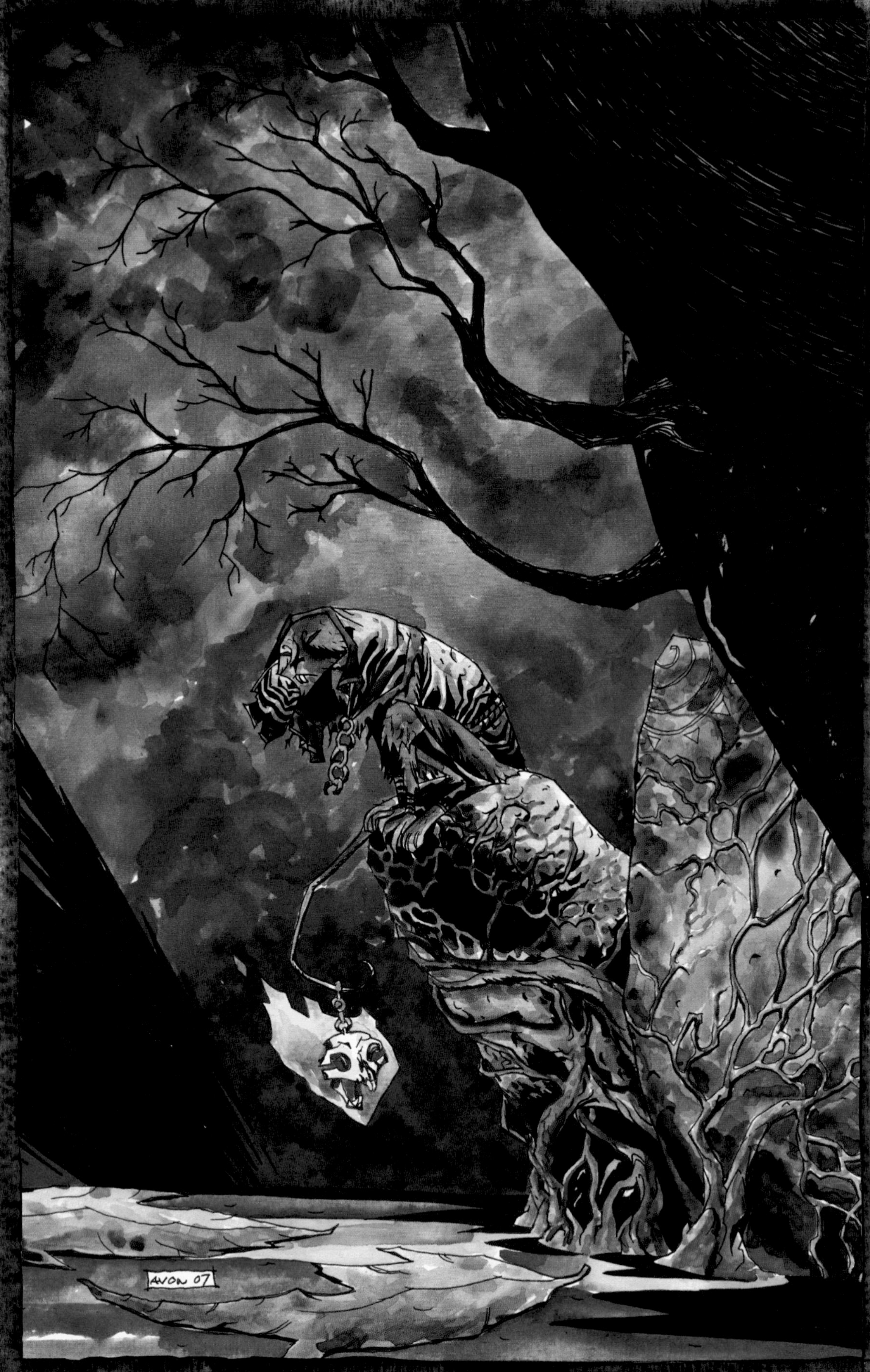
AVON 07

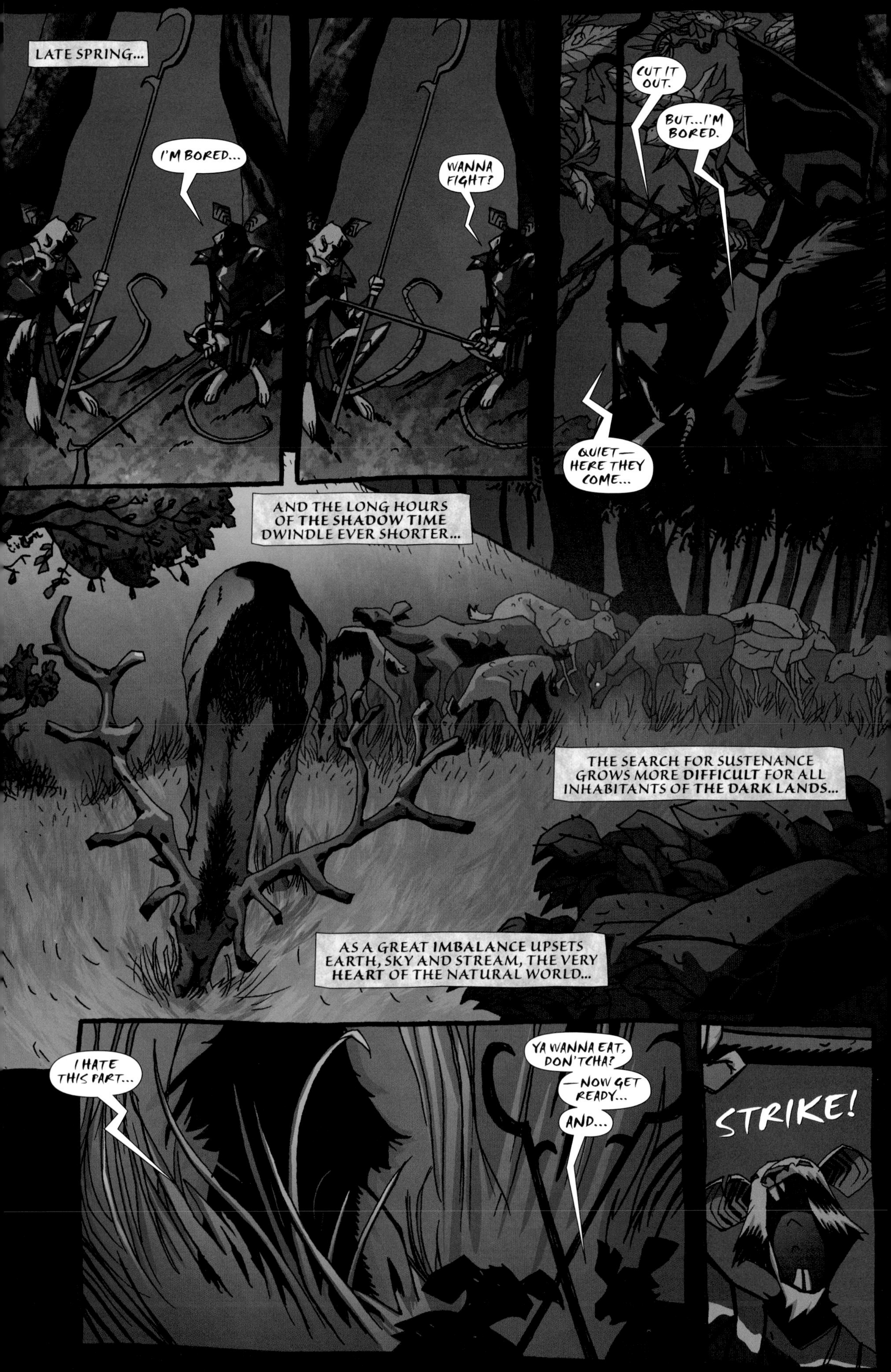

LATE SPRING...
I'M BORED...
WANNA FIGHT?
CUT IT OUT.
BUT...I'M BORED.
QUIET—HERE THEY COME...
AND THE LONG HOURS OF THE SHADOW TIME DWINDLE EVER SHORTER...
THE SEARCH FOR SUSTENANCE GROWS MORE DIFFICULT FOR ALL INHABITANTS OF THE DARK LANDS...
AS A GREAT IMBALANCE UPSETS EARTH, SKY AND STREAM, THE VERY HEART OF THE NATURAL WORLD...
I HATE THIS PART...
YA WANNA EAT, DON'TCHA?
—NOW GET READY...
AND...
STRIKE!

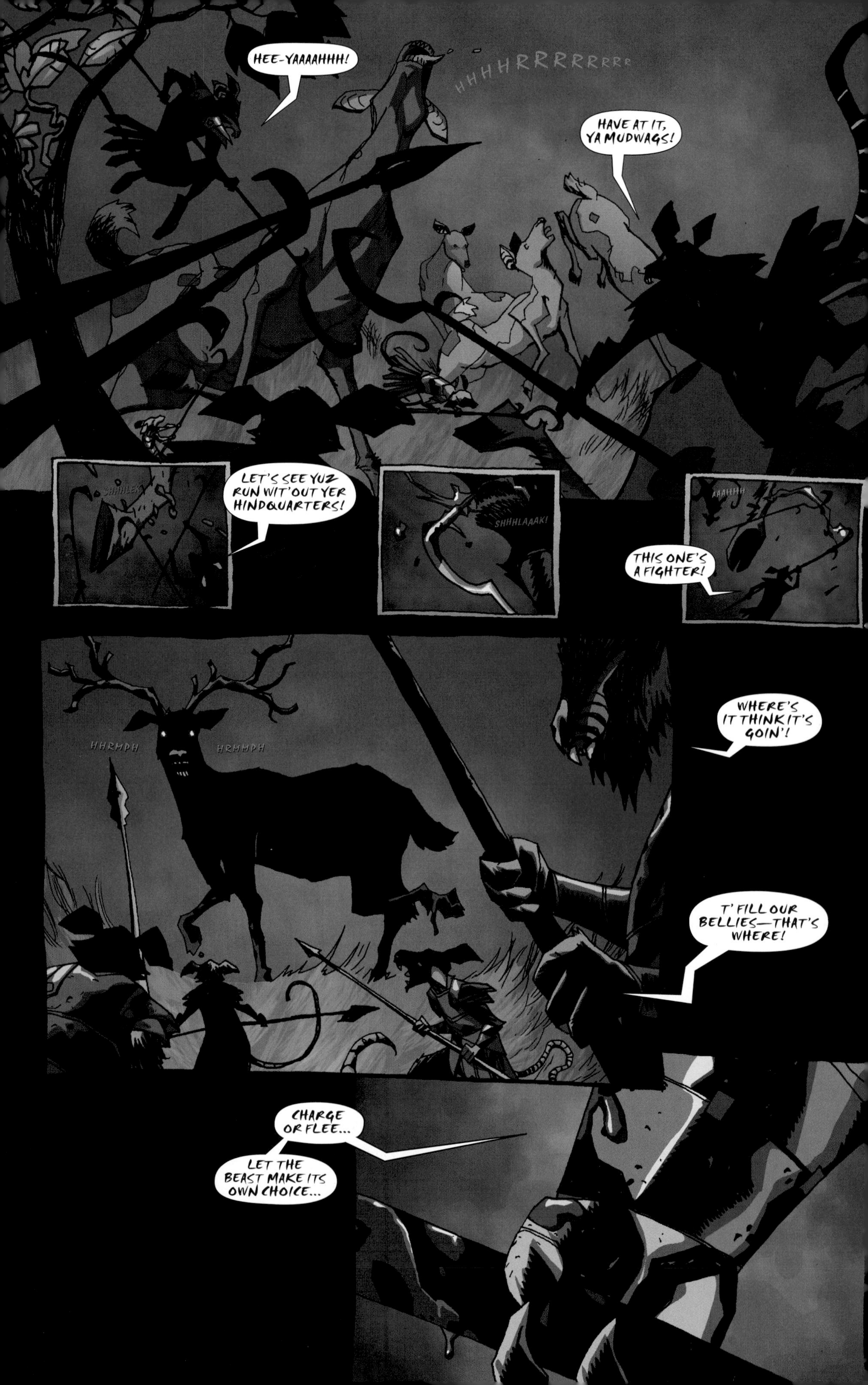
HEE-YAAAAHHH!
HHHHRRRRRRrrr
HAVE AT IT, YA MUDWAGS!
LET'S SEE YUZ RUN WIT'OUT YER HINDQUARTERS!
SHHHLAAAK!
AAAHHH
THIS ONE'S A FIGHTER!
HHRMPH
HRMMPH
WHERE'S IT THINK IT'S GOIN'!
T' FILL OUR BELLIES—THAT'S WHERE!
CHARGE OR FLEE...
LET THE BEAST MAKE ITS OWN CHOICE...

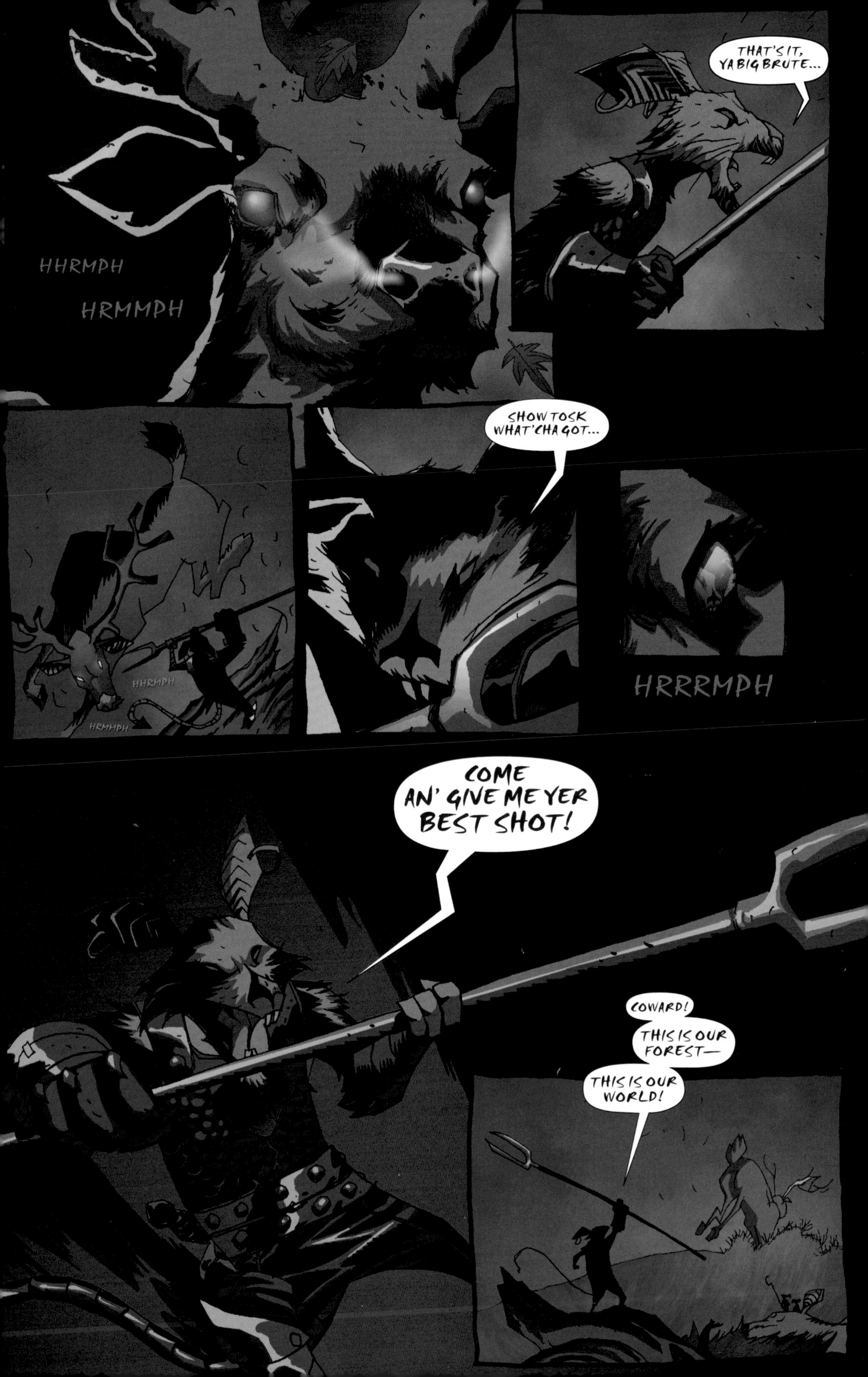
HHRMPH
HRMMPH
THAT'S IT, YA BIG BRUTE...
HHRMPH
HRMMPH
SHOW TOSK WHAT'CHA GOT...
HRRRMPH
COME AN' GIVE ME YER BEST SHOT!
COWARD!
THIS IS OUR FOREST—
THIS IS OUR WORLD!

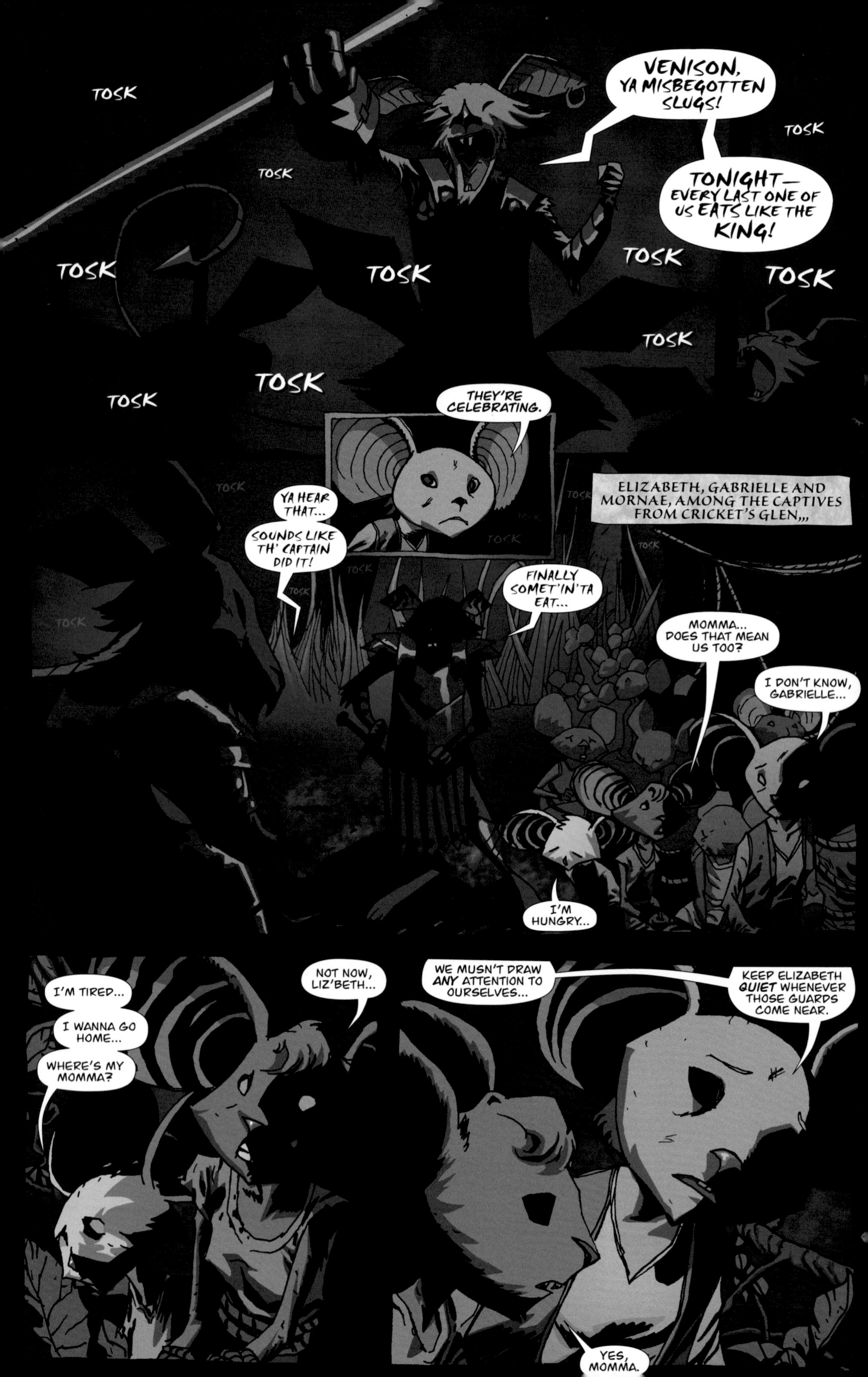
TOSK
VENISON, YA MISBEGOTTEN SLUGS!
TONIGHT— EVERY LAST ONE OF US EATS LIKE THE KING!
TOSK
TOSK
TOSK
TOSK
TOSK
TOSK
TOSK
TOSK
TOSK
THEY'RE CELEBRATING.
ELIZABETH, GABRIELLE AND MORNAE, AMONG THE CAPTIVES FROM CRICKET'S GLEN,,,
YA HEAR THAT...
SOUNDS LIKE TH' CAPTAIN DID IT!
FINALLY SOMET'IN'TA EAT...
MOMMA... DOES THAT MEAN US TOO?
I DON'T KNOW, GABRIELLE...
I'M HUNGRY...
I'M TIRED...
I WANNA GO HOME...
WHERE'S MY MOMMA?
NOT NOW, LIZ'BETH...
WE MUSN'T DRAW ANY ATTENTION TO OURSELVES...
KEEP ELIZABETH QUIET WHENEVER THOSE GUARDS COME NEAR.
YES, MOMMA.

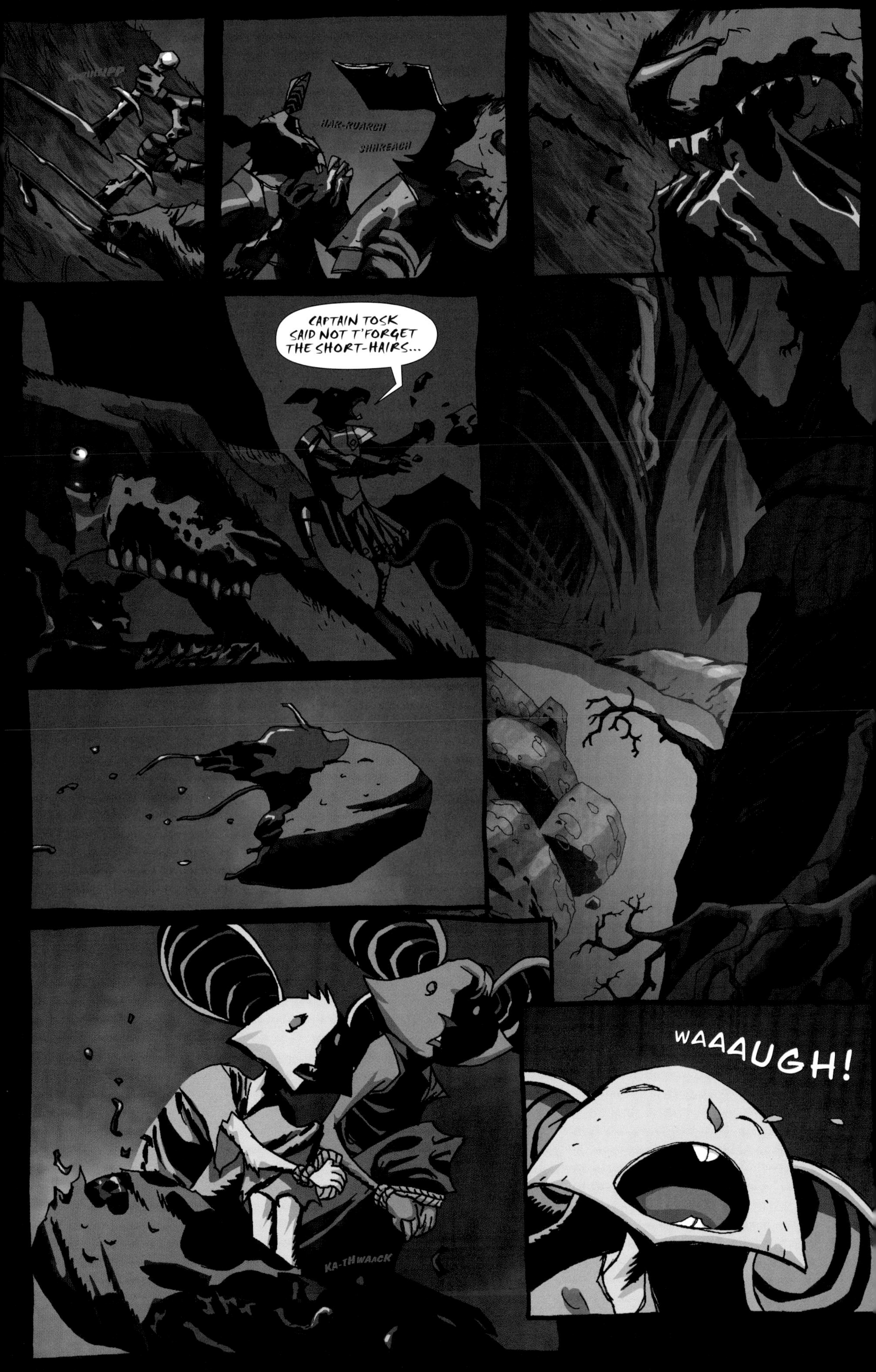
HAR-RUARCH
SHHREACH
CAPTAIN TOSK SAID NOT T'FORGET THE SHORT-HAIRS...
KA-THWAACK
WAAAUGH!

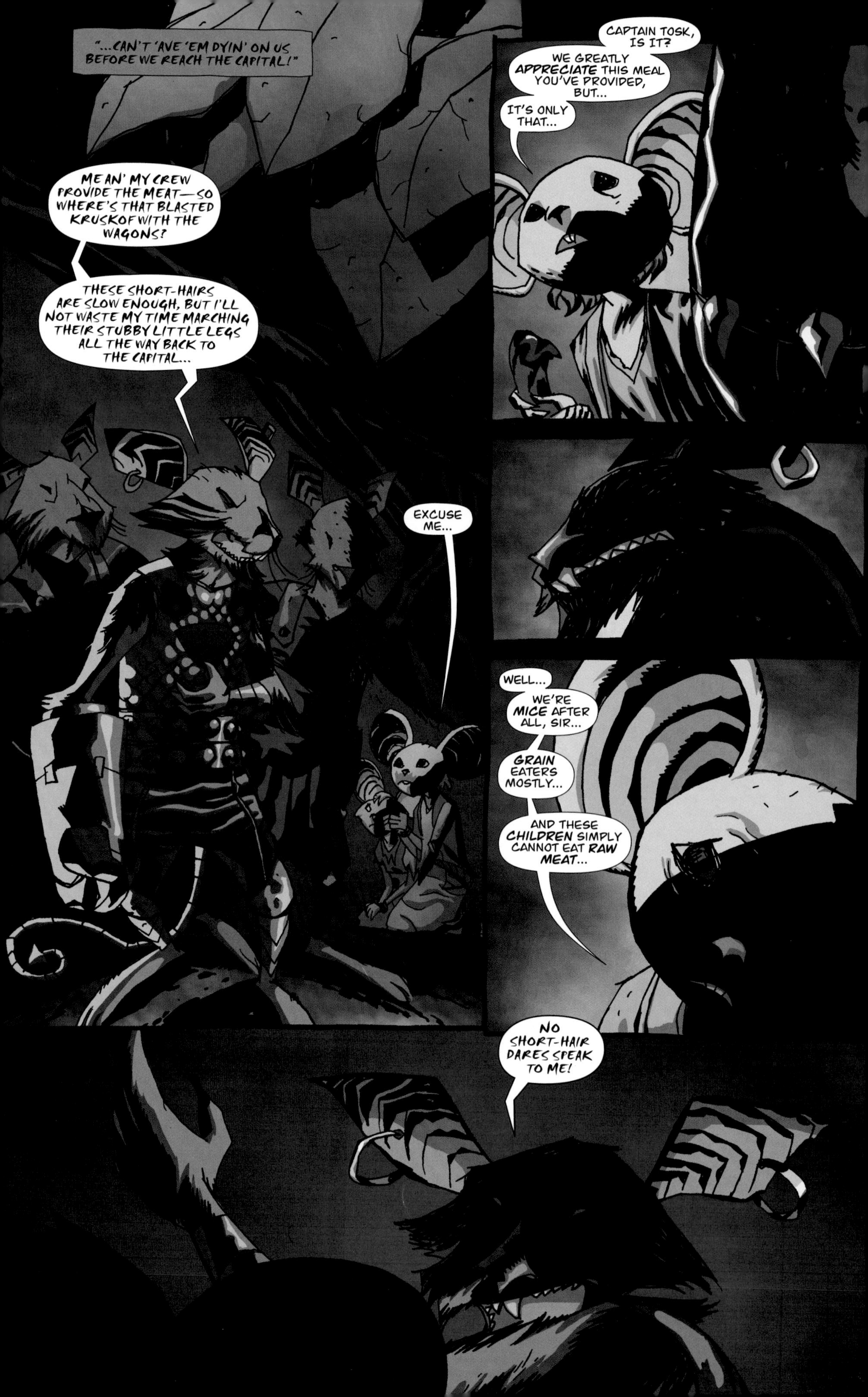
"...CAN'T 'AVE 'EM DYIN' ON US BEFORE WE REACH THE CAPITAL!"
CAPTAIN TOSK, IS IT?
WE GREATLY APPRECIATE THIS MEAL YOU'VE PROVIDED, BUT...
IT'S ONLY THAT...
ME AN' MY CREW PROVIDE THE MEAT—SO WHERE'S THAT BLASTED KRUSKOF WITH THE WAGONS?
THESE SHORT-HAIRS ARE SLOW ENOUGH, BUT I'LL NOT WASTE MY TIME MARCHING THEIR STUBBY LITTLE LEGS ALL THE WAY BACK TO THE CAPITAL...
EXCUSE ME...
WELL...
WE'RE MICE AFTER ALL, SIR...
GRAIN EATERS MOSTLY...
AND THESE CHILDREN SIMPLY CANNOT EAT RAW MEAT...
NO SHORT-HAIR DARES SPEAK TO ME!

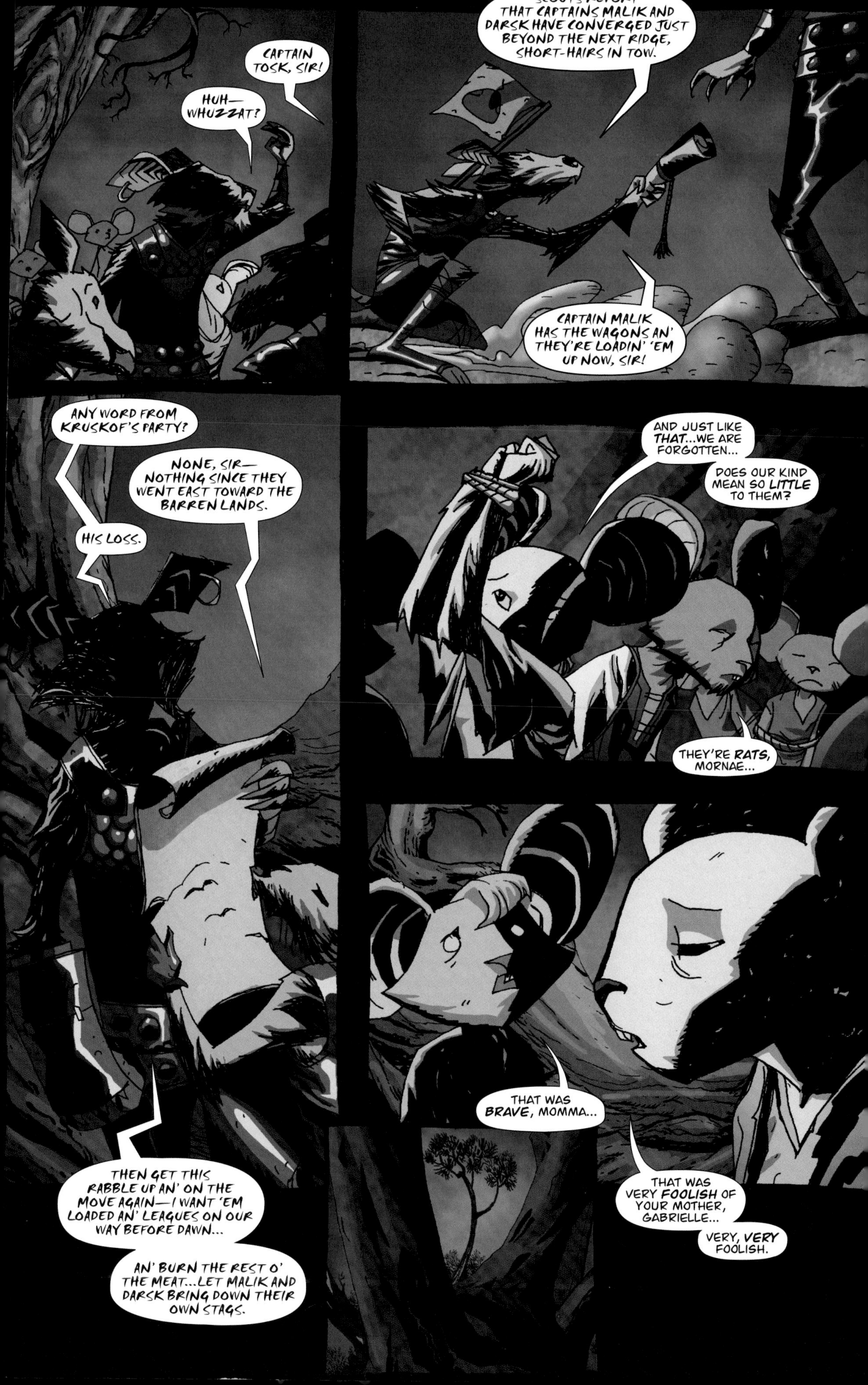
CAPTAIN TOSK, SIR!
HUH—WHUZZAT?
SCOUTS REPORT THAT CAPTAINS MALIK AND DARSK HAVE CONVERGED JUST BEYOND THE NEXT RIDGE, SHORT-HAIRS IN TOW.
CAPTAIN MALIK HAS THE WAGONS AN' THEY'RE LOADIN' 'EM UP NOW, SIR!
ANY WORD FROM KRUSKOF'S PARTY?
NONE, SIR—NOTHING SINCE THEY WENT EAST TOWARD THE BARREN LANDS.
HIS LOSS.
THEN GET THIS RABBLE UP AN' ON THE MOVE AGAIN—I WANT 'EM LOADED AN' LEAGUES ON OUR WAY BEFORE DAWN...
AN' BURN THE REST O' THE MEAT...LET MALIK AND DARSK BRING DOWN THEIR OWN STAGS.
AND JUST LIKE THAT...WE ARE FORGOTTEN...
DOES OUR KIND MEAN SO LITTLE TO THEM?
THEY'RE RATS, MORNAE...
THAT WAS BRAVE, MOMMA...
THAT WAS VERY FOOLISH OF YOUR MOTHER, GABRIELLE...
VERY, VERY FOOLISH.

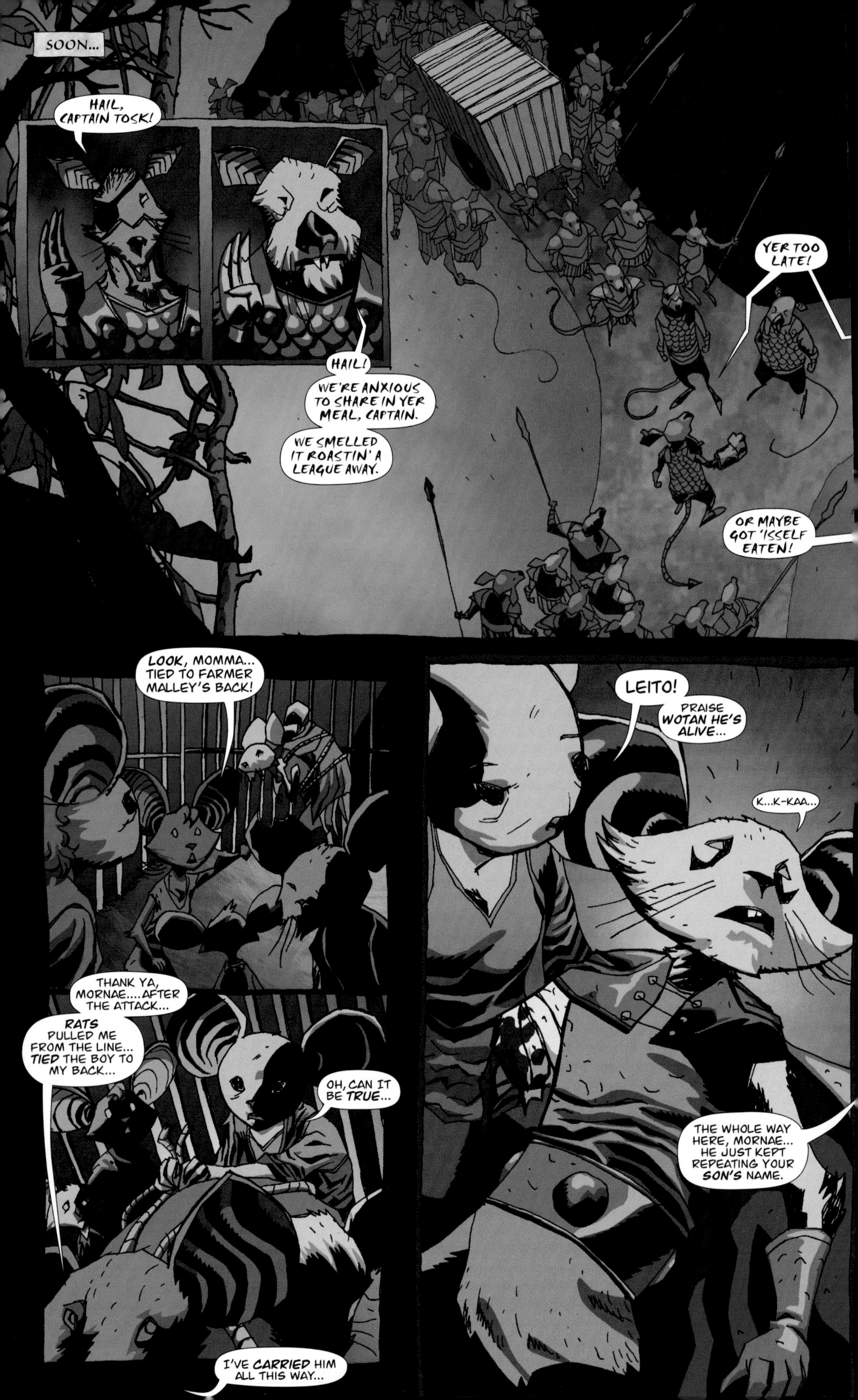
SOON...
HAIL, CAPTAIN TOSK!
HAIL!
WE'RE ANXIOUS TO SHARE IN YER MEAL, CAPTAIN.
WE SMELLED IT ROASTIN' A LEAGUE AWAY.
YER TOO LATE!
OR MAYBE GOT 'ISSELF EATEN!
LOOK, MOMMA... TIED TO FARMER MALLEY'S BACK!
THANK YA, MORNAE....AFTER THE ATTACK...
RATS PULLED ME FROM THE LINE... TIED THE BOY TO MY BACK...
OH, CAN IT BE TRUE...
I'VE CARRIED HIM ALL THIS WAY...
LEITO!
PRAISE WOTAN HE'S ALIVE...
K...K-KAA...
THE WHOLE WAY HERE, MORNAE... HE JUST KEPT REPEATING YOUR SON'S NAME.

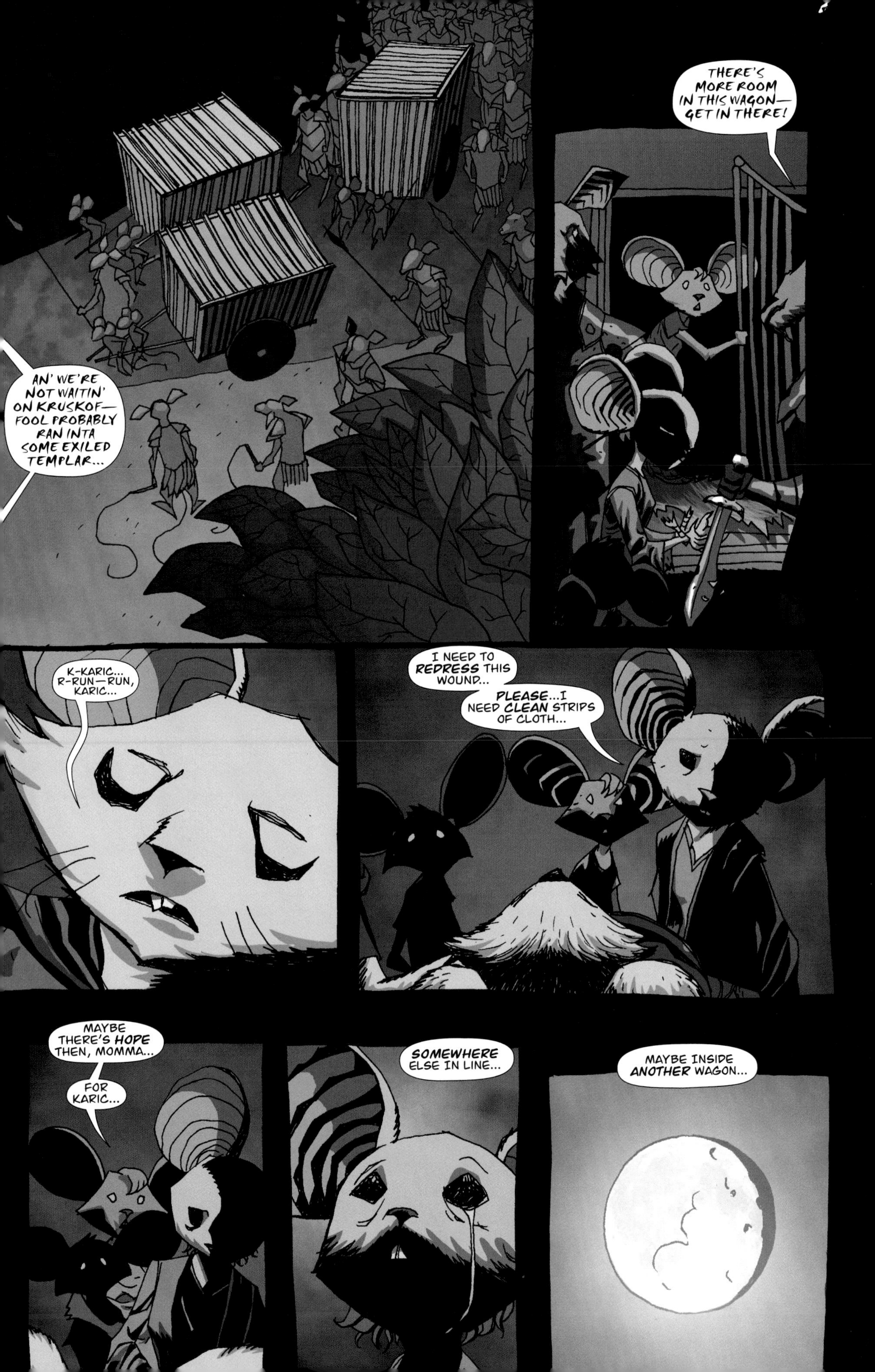

AN' WE'RE NOT WAITIN' ON KRUSKOF— FOOL PROBABLY RAN INTA SOME EXILED TEMPLAR...
THERE'S MORE ROOM IN THIS WAGON— GET IN THERE!
K-KARIC... R-RUN—RUN, KARIC...
I NEED TO REDRESS THIS WOUND...
PLEASE...I NEED CLEAN STRIPS OF CLOTH...
MAYBE THERE'S HOPE THEN, MOMMA...
FOR KARIC...
SOMEWHERE ELSE IN LINE...
MAYBE INSIDE ANOTHER WAGON...

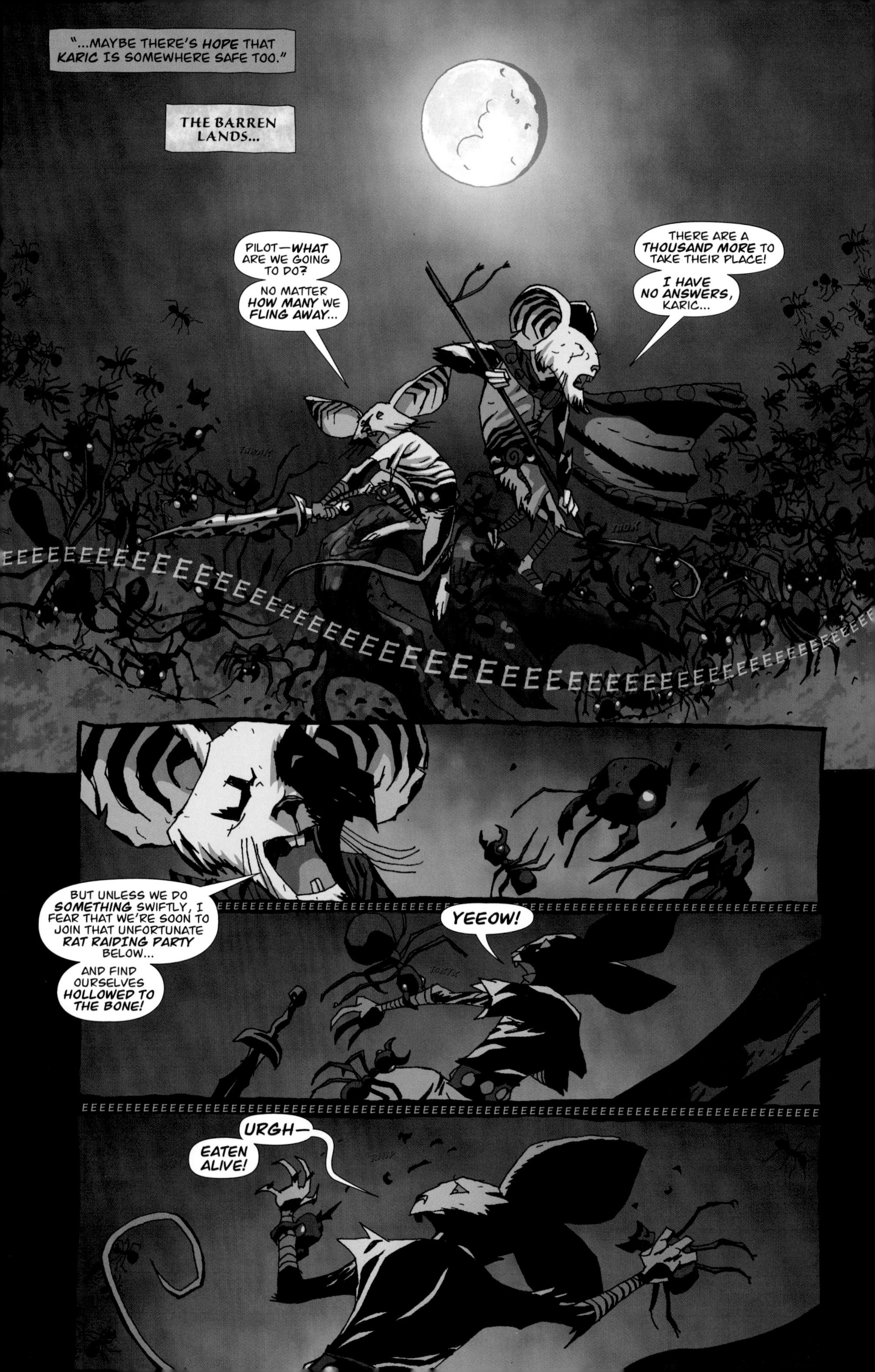
"...MAYBE THERE'S HOPE THAT KARIC IS SOMEWHERE SAFE TOO."
THE BARREN LANDS...
PILOT—WHAT ARE WE GOING TO DO?
NO MATTER HOW MANY WE FLING AWAY...
THERE ARE A THOUSAND MORE TO TAKE THEIR PLACE!
I HAVE NO ANSWERS, KARIC...
EEEEEEEEEEEEEEEEEEEEEEEEEEEEEEEEEEEEEEEEEEEEEEEEEEEEEEEE
BUT UNLESS WE DO SOMETHING SWIFTLY, I FEAR THAT WE'RE SOON TO JOIN THAT UNFORTUNATE RAT RAIDING PARTY BELOW...
AND FIND OURSELVES HOLLOWED TO THE BONE!
YEEOW!
URGH—
EATEN ALIVE!

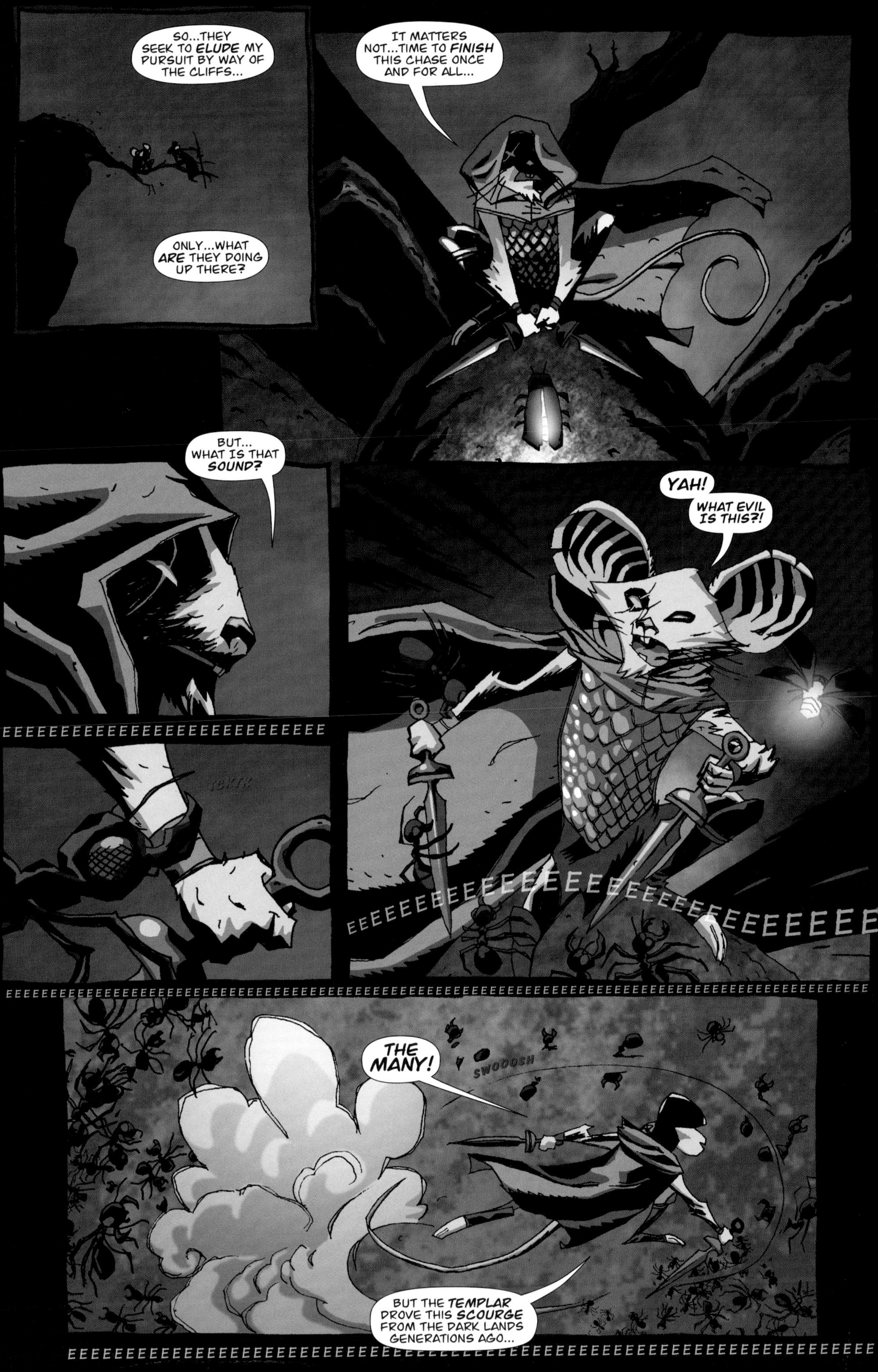
SO...THEY SEEK TO ELUDE MY PURSUIT BY WAY OF THE CLIFFS...
ONLY...WHAT ARE THEY DOING UP THERE?
IT MATTERS NOT...TIME TO FINISH THIS CHASE ONCE AND FOR ALL...
BUT... WHAT IS THAT SOUND?
EEEEEEEEEEEEEEEEEEEEEEEEEEEEEEE
YAH!
WHAT EVIL IS THIS?!
EEEEEEEEEEEEEEEEEEEEEEEEEEEEEEE
EEEEEEEEEEEEEEEEEEEEEEEEEEEEEEEEEEEEEEEEEEEEEEEEEEEEEEEEEEEEEEE
THE MANY!
SWOOOSH
BUT THE TEMPLAR DROVE THIS SCOURGE FROM THE DARK LANDS GENERATIONS AGO...
EEEEEEEEEEEEEEEEEEEEEEEEEEEEEEEEEEEEEEEEEEEEE

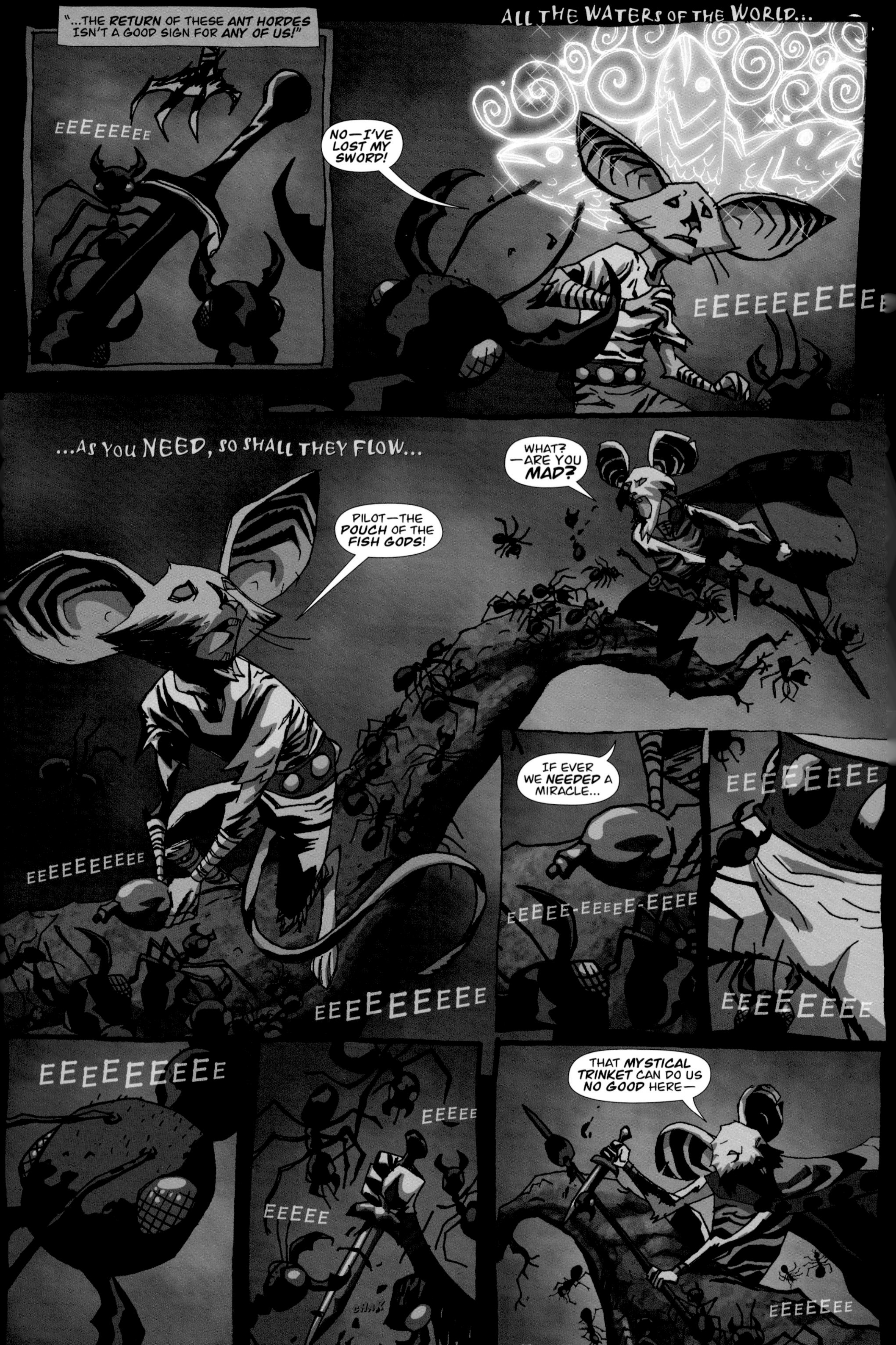
"...THE RETURN OF THESE ANT HORDES ISN'T A GOOD SIGN FOR ANY OF US!"
EEEEEEEE
ALL THE WATERS OF THE WORLD...
NO—I'VE LOST MY SWORD!
EEEEEEEEEEE
...AS YOU NEED, SO SHALL THEY FLOW...
WHAT? —ARE YOU MAD?
PILOT—THE POUCH OF THE FISH GODS!
EEEEEEEEEE
EEEEEEEEEE
IF EVER WE NEEDED A MIRACLE...
EEEEE-EEEEE-EEEE
EEEEEEEEE
EEEEEEEE
EEEEEEEEEE
EEEEE
EEEEE
THAT MYSTICAL TRINKET CAN DO US NO GOOD HERE—
EEEEEEE
EEEEEEEE

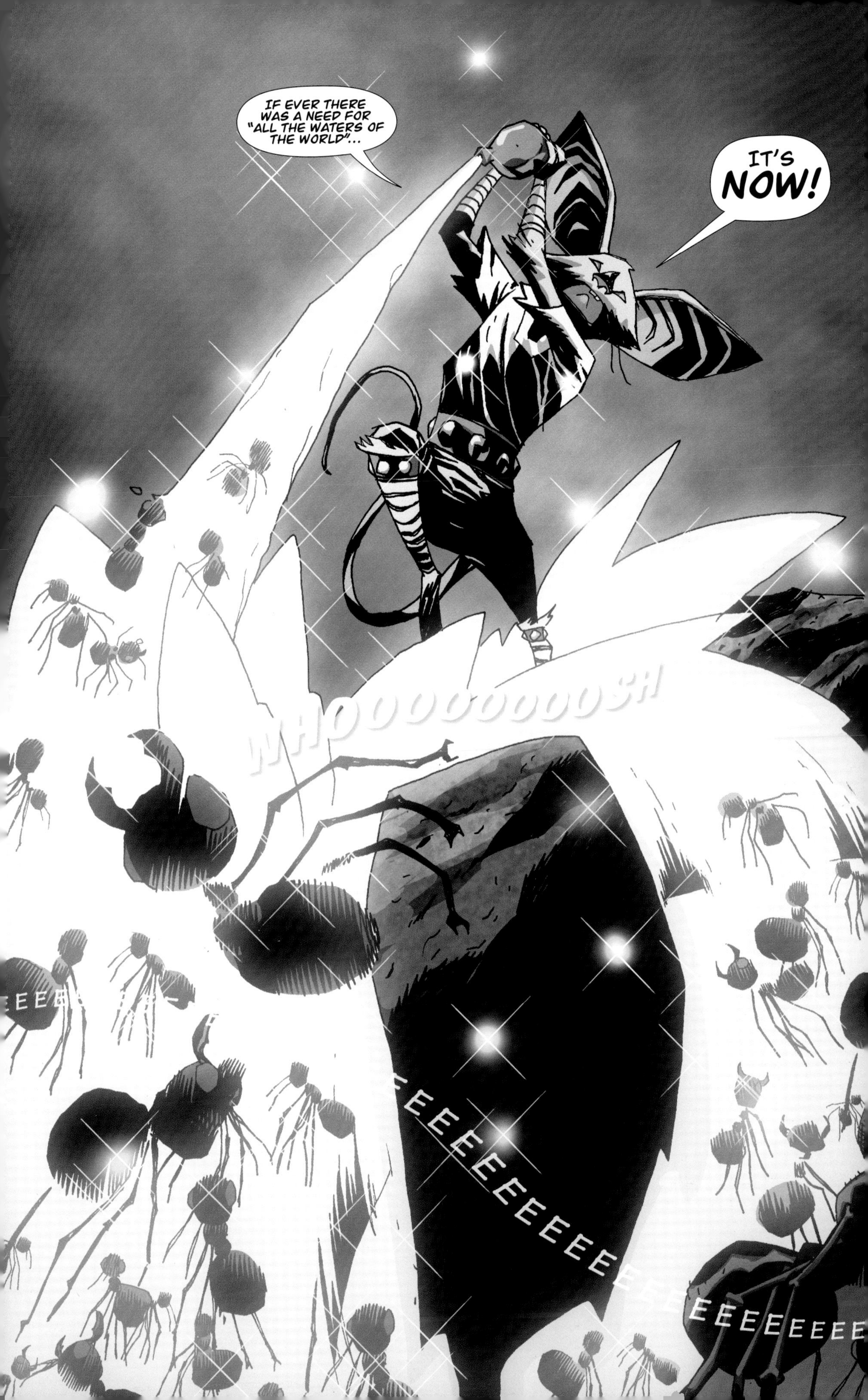
IF EVER THERE WAS A NEED FOR "ALL THE WATERS OF THE WORLD"...
IT'S NOW!
WHOOOOOOOOOOSH
EEEEEEEEEEEEEEEEEEEEEEEEE

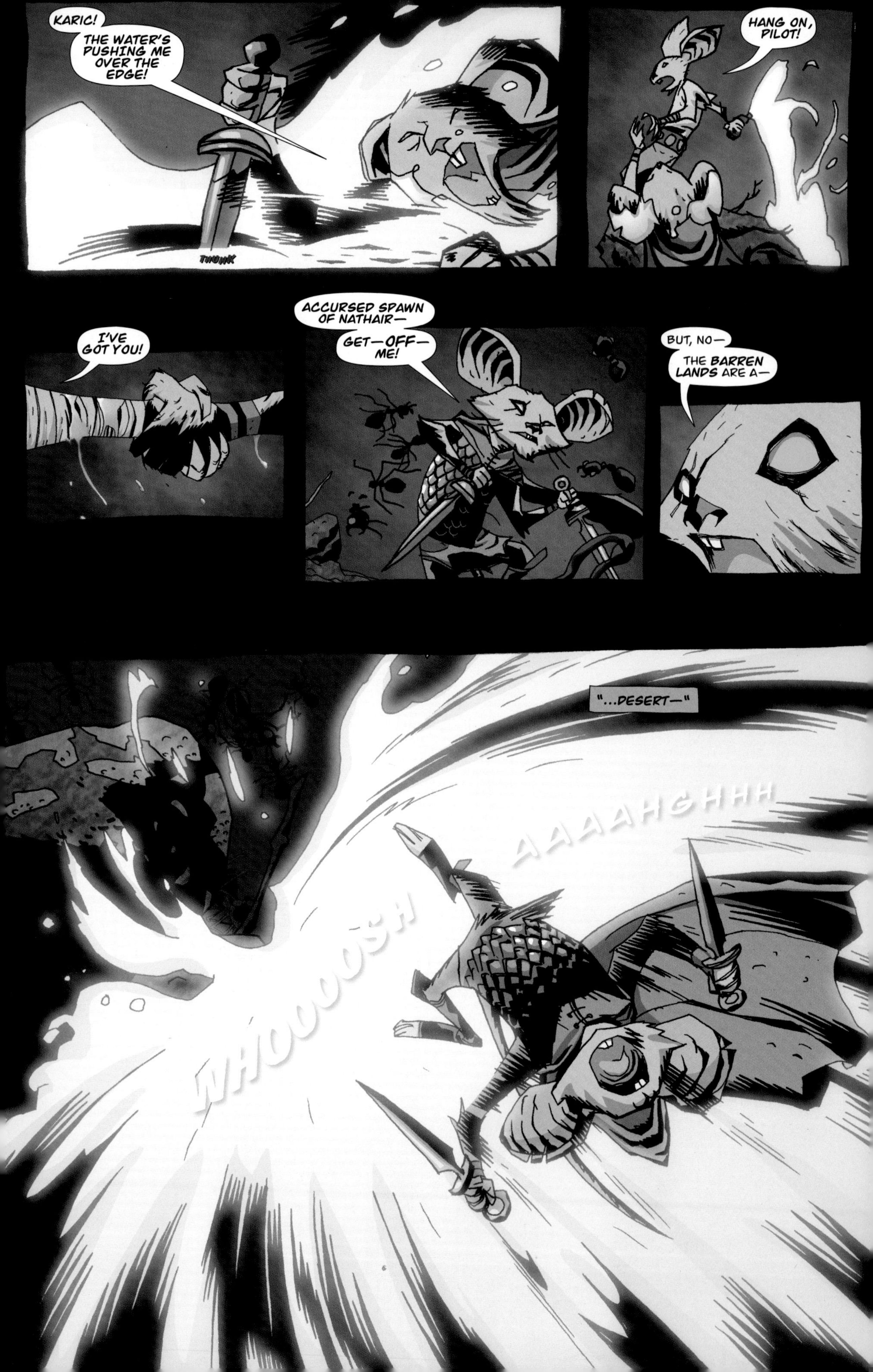
KARIC!
THE WATER'S PUSHING ME OVER THE EDGE!
THUNK
HANG ON, PILOT!
I'VE GOT YOU!
ACCURSED SPAWN OF NATHAIR—
GET—OFF—ME!
BUT, NO—
THE BARREN LANDS ARE A—
"...DESERT—"
AAAAAHGHHH
WHOOOOOSH

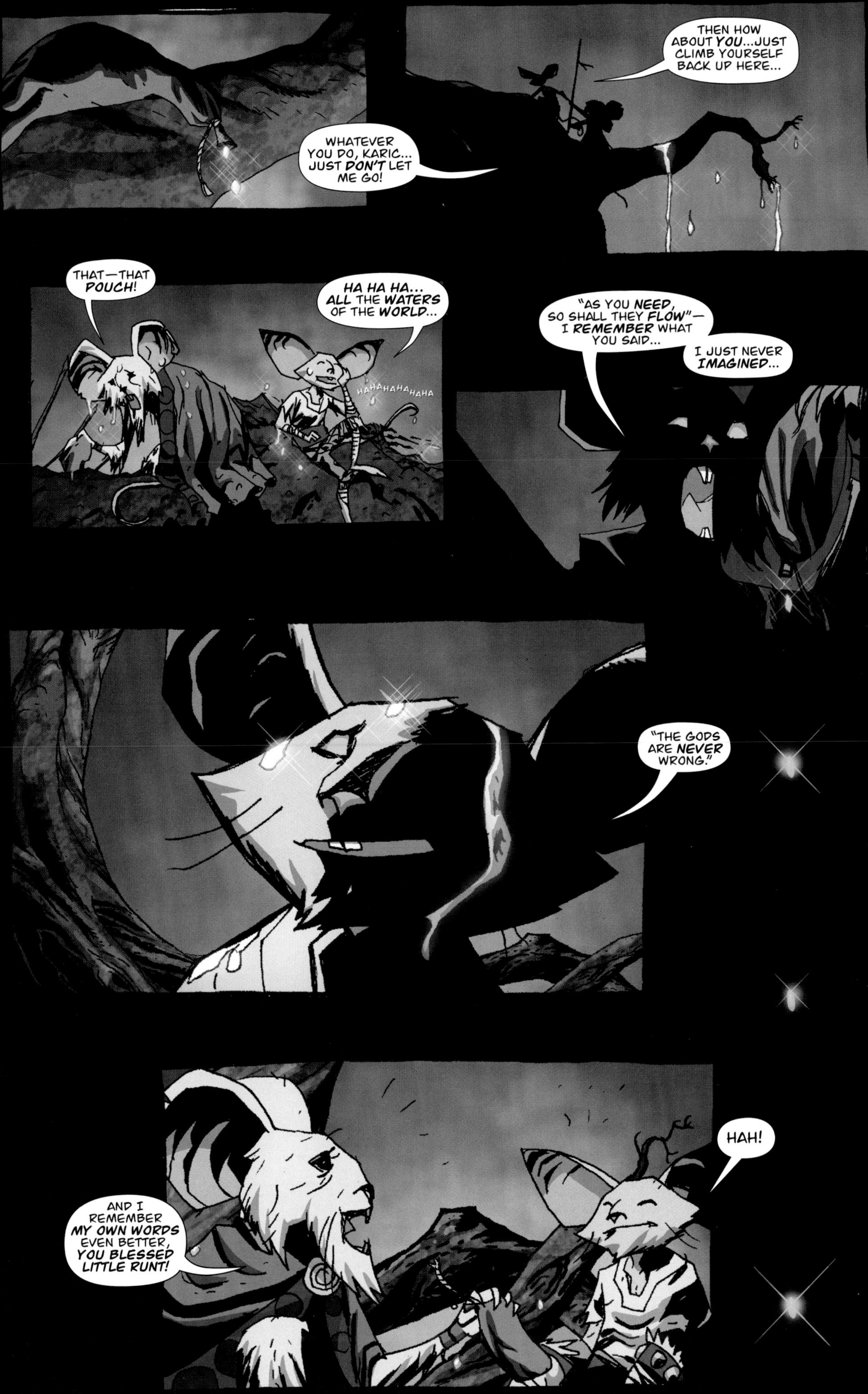
WHATEVER YOU DO, KARIC... JUST DON'T LET ME GO!
THEN HOW ABOUT YOU...JUST CLIMB YOURSELF BACK UP HERE...
THAT—THAT POUCH!
HA HA HA... ALL THE WATERS OF THE WORLD...
HAHAHAHAHAHAHA
"AS YOU NEED, SO SHALL THEY FLOW"— I REMEMBER WHAT YOU SAID...
I JUST NEVER IMAGINED...
"THE GODS ARE NEVER WRONG."
HAH!
AND I REMEMBER MY OWN WORDS EVEN BETTER, YOU BLESSED LITTLE RUNT!

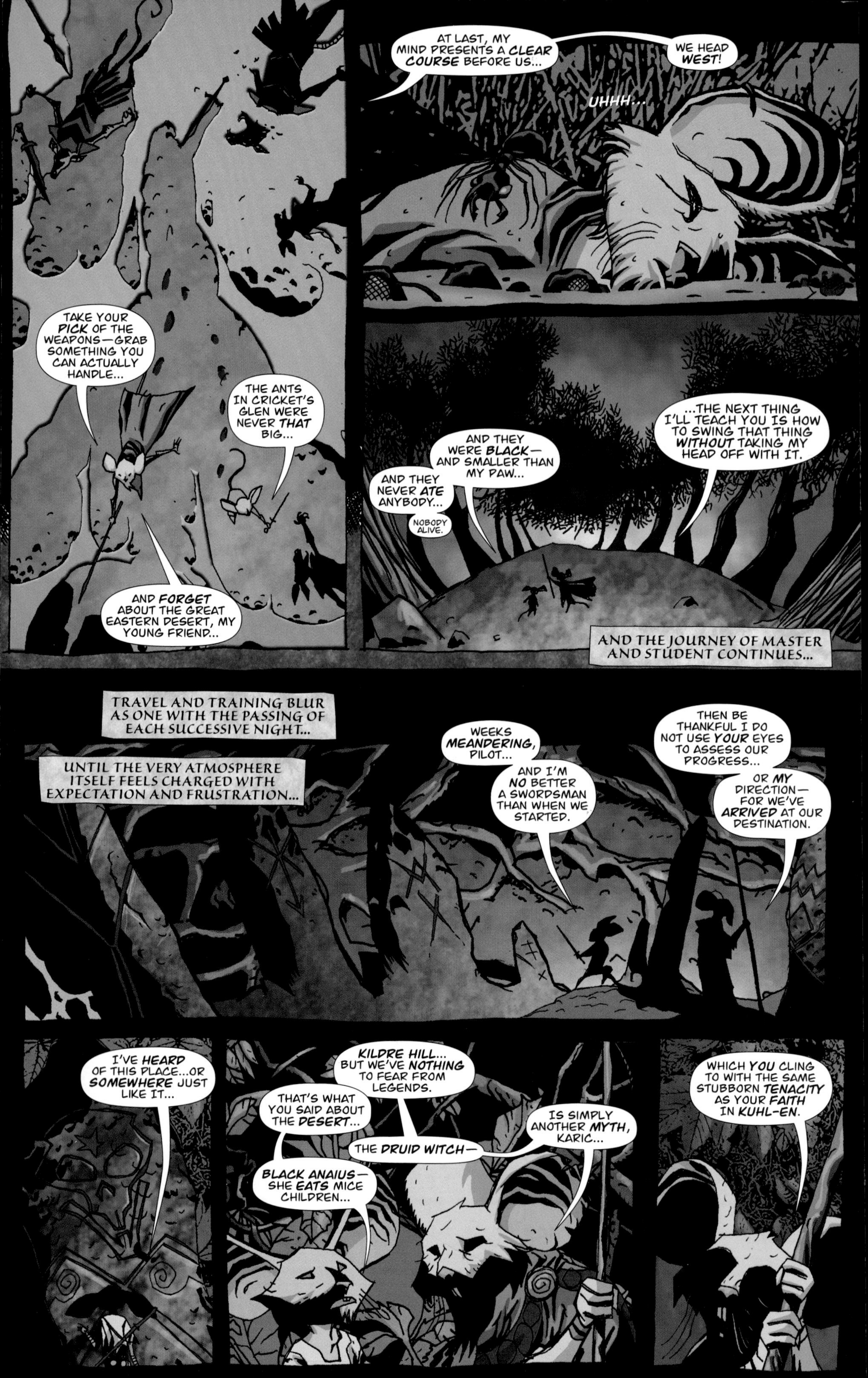
TAKE YOUR PICK OF THE WEAPONS—GRAB SOMETHING YOU CAN ACTUALLY HANDLE...
THE ANTS IN CRICKET'S GLEN WERE NEVER THAT BIG...
AND FORGET ABOUT THE GREAT EASTERN DESERT, MY YOUNG FRIEND...
AT LAST, MY MIND PRESENTS A CLEAR COURSE BEFORE US...
WE HEAD WEST!
UHHH...
AND THEY WERE BLACK—AND SMALLER THAN MY PAW...
AND THEY NEVER ATE ANYBODY...
NOBODY ALIVE.
...THE NEXT THING I'LL TEACH YOU IS HOW TO SWING THAT THING WITHOUT TAKING MY HEAD OFF WITH IT.
AND THE JOURNEY OF MASTER AND STUDENT CONTINUES...
TRAVEL AND TRAINING BLUR AS ONE WITH THE PASSING OF EACH SUCCESSIVE NIGHT...
UNTIL THE VERY ATMOSPHERE ITSELF FEELS CHARGED WITH EXPECTATION AND FRUSTRATION...
WEEKS MEANDERING, PILOT...
AND I'M NO BETTER A SWORDSMAN THAN WHEN WE STARTED.
THEN BE THANKFUL I DO NOT USE YOUR EYES TO ASSESS OUR PROGRESS...
OR MY DIRECTION—FOR WE'VE ARRIVED AT OUR DESTINATION.
I'VE HEARD OF THIS PLACE...OR SOMEWHERE JUST LIKE IT...
KILDRE HILL...
THE DRUID WITCH—
BLACK ANAIUS—SHE EATS MICE CHILDREN...
BUT WE'VE NOTHING TO FEAR FROM LEGENDS.
THAT'S WHAT YOU SAID ABOUT THE DESERT...
IS SIMPLY ANOTHER MYTH, KARIC...
WHICH YOU CLING TO WITH THE SAME STUBBORN TENACITY AS YOUR FAITH IN KUHL-EN.

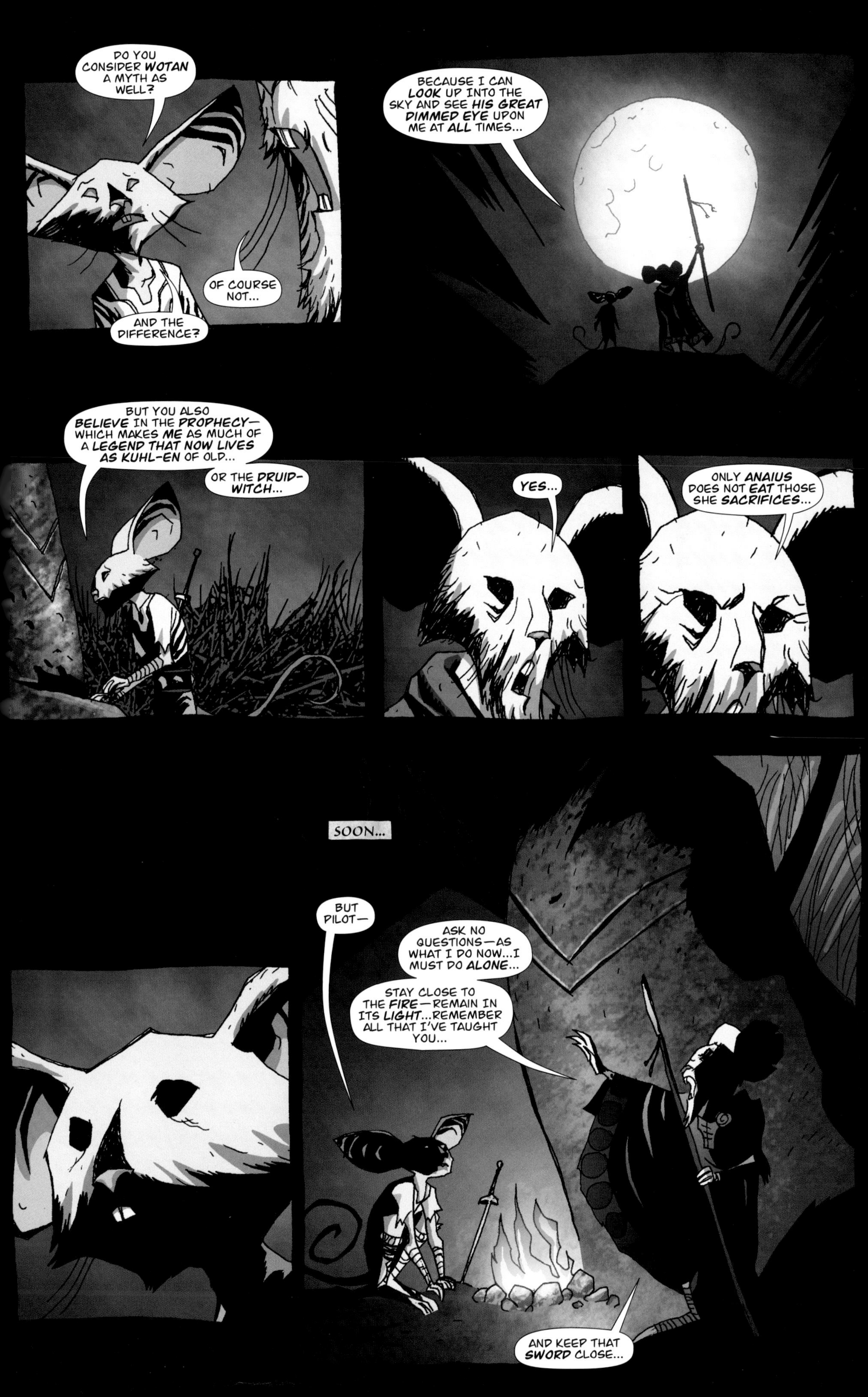
DO YOU CONSIDER WOTAN A MYTH AS WELL?
OF COURSE NOT...
AND THE DIFFERENCE?
BECAUSE I CAN LOOK UP INTO THE SKY AND SEE HIS GREAT DIMMED EYE UPON ME AT ALL TIMES...
BUT YOU ALSO BELIEVE IN THE PROPHECY— WHICH MAKES ME AS MUCH OF A LEGEND THAT NOW LIVES AS KUHL-EN OF OLD...
OR THE DRUID-WITCH...
YES...
ONLY ANAIUS DOES NOT EAT THOSE SHE SACRIFICES...
SOON...
BUT PILOT—
ASK NO QUESTIONS—AS WHAT I DO NOW...I MUST DO ALONE...
STAY CLOSE TO THE FIRE—REMAIN IN ITS LIGHT...REMEMBER ALL THAT I'VE TAUGHT YOU...
AND KEEP THAT SWORD CLOSE...

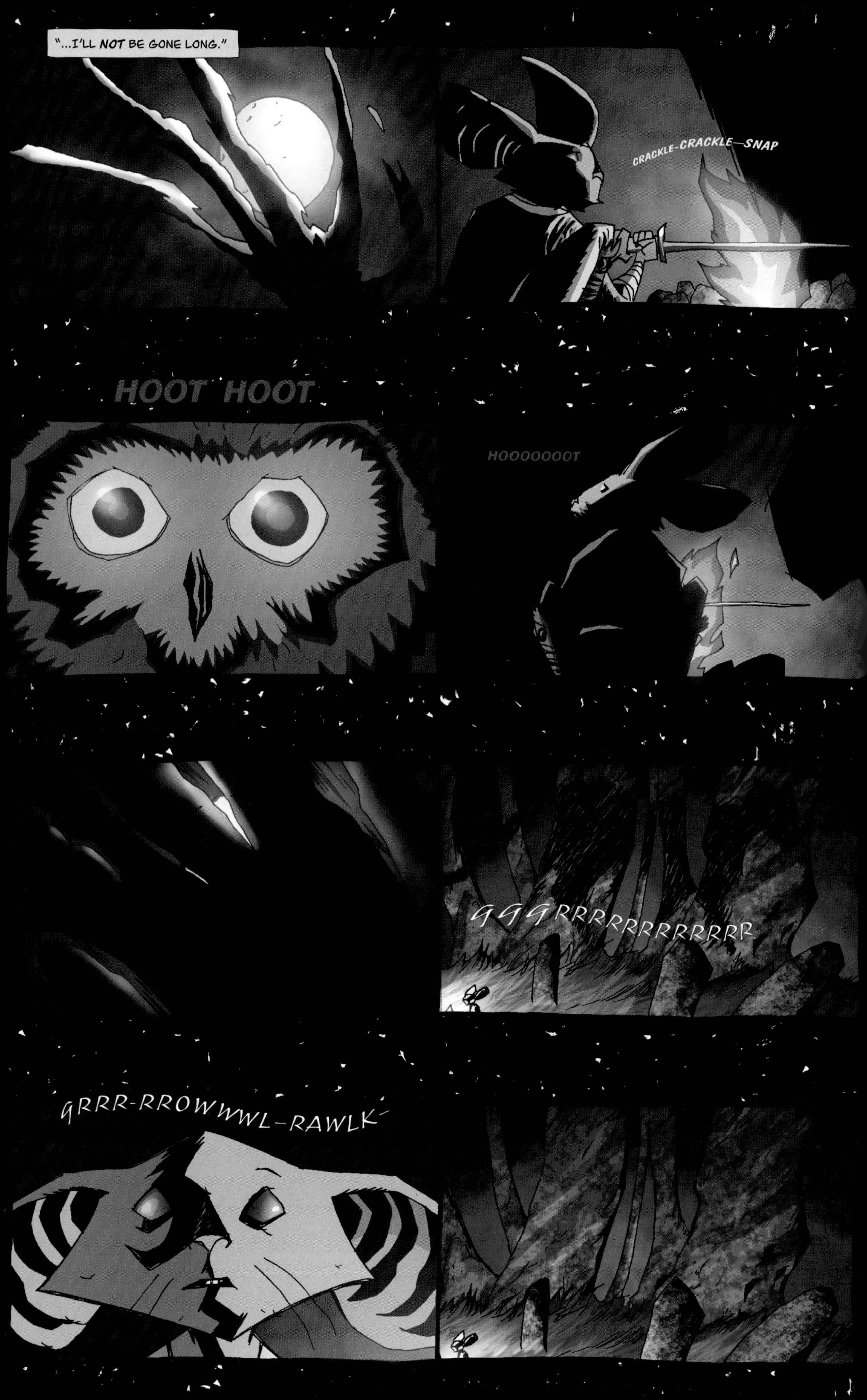
"...I'LL NOT BE GONE LONG."
CRACKLE-CRACKLE—SNAP
HOOT HOOT
HOOOOOOOT
GGGRRRRRRRRRRRRR
GRRR-RROWWWL-RAWLK

I AM NOT THE FIRST MOUSE TO STAND ALONE AGAINST THE SHADOWS...
SNAK KRAK
LIKE THE TEMPLAR OF OLD, SHALL I BE...
LIKE KUHL-EN...
DOOOOOMED...
AAAAAHHH!!!
KRAKA-KA-THOOOOOOOOOM

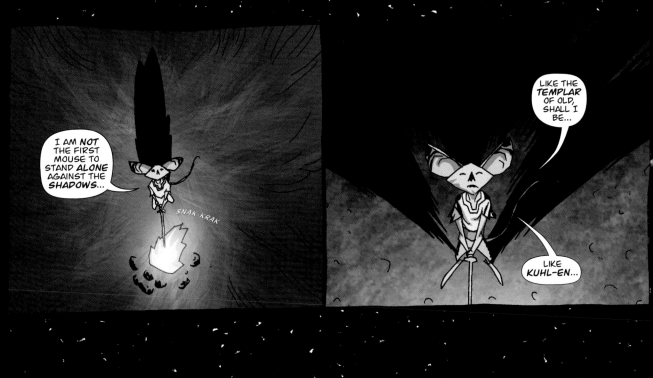

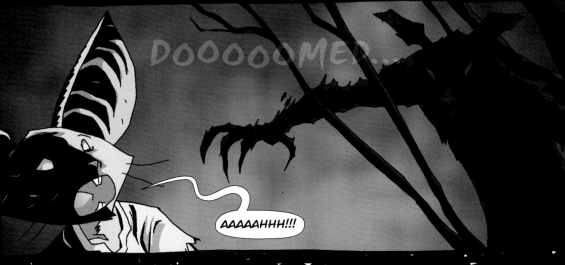

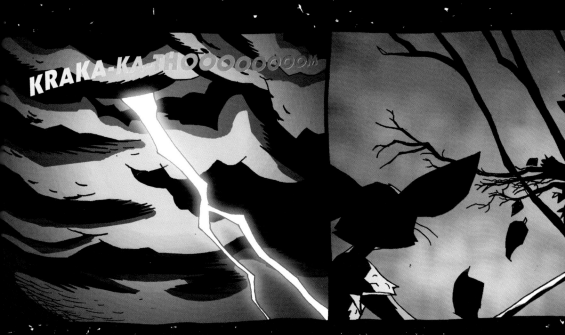

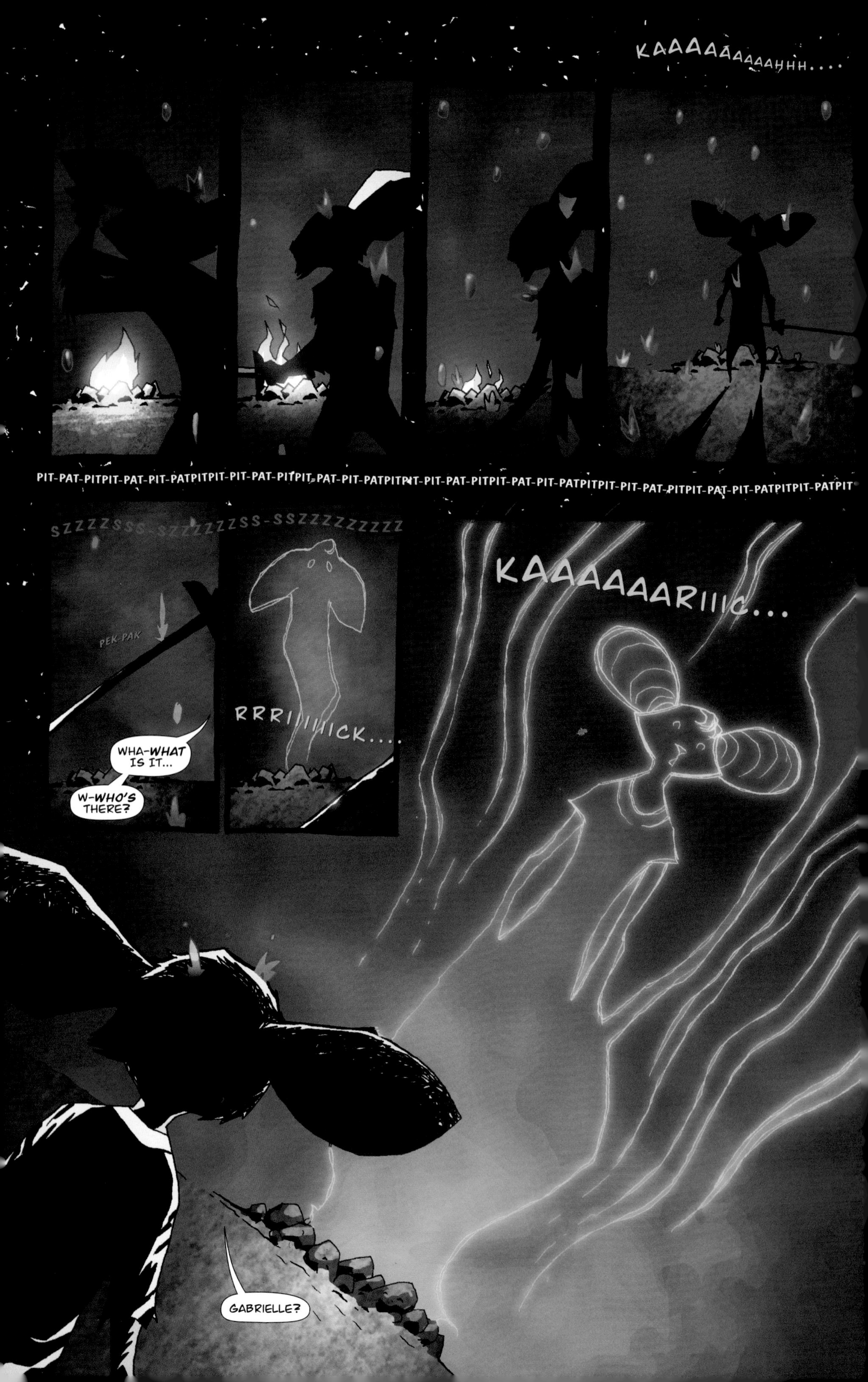
KAAAAAAAAAHHH....
PIT-PAT-PITPIT-PAT-PIT-PATPITPIT-PIT-PAT-PITPIT-PAT-PIT-PATPITPIT-PIT-PAT-PITPIT-PAT-PIT-PATPITPIT-PIT-PAT-PITPIT-PAT-PIT-PATPITPIT-PATPIT
SZZZZSSS-SZZZZZZSS-SSZZZZZZZZZ
PEK-PAK
WHA-WHAT IS IT...
W-WHO'S THERE?
RRRIIIIICK....
KAAAAAAARIIIC...
GABRIELLE?

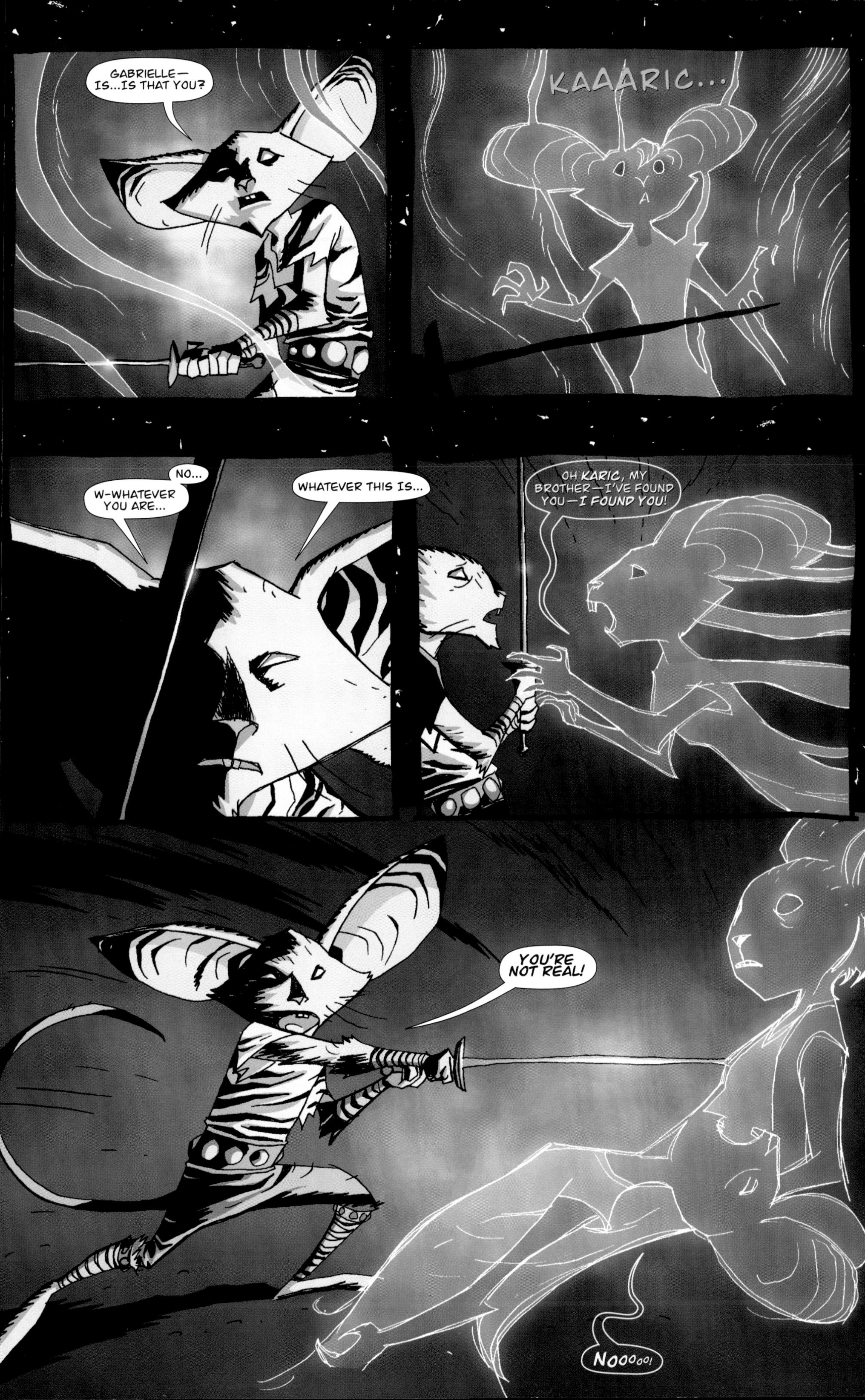
GABRIELLE—
IS...IS THAT YOU?
KAAARIC...
NO...
W-WHATEVER YOU ARE...
WHATEVER THIS IS...
OH KARIC, MY BROTHER—I'VE FOUND YOU—I FOUND YOU!
YOU'RE NOT REAL!
NOooo!

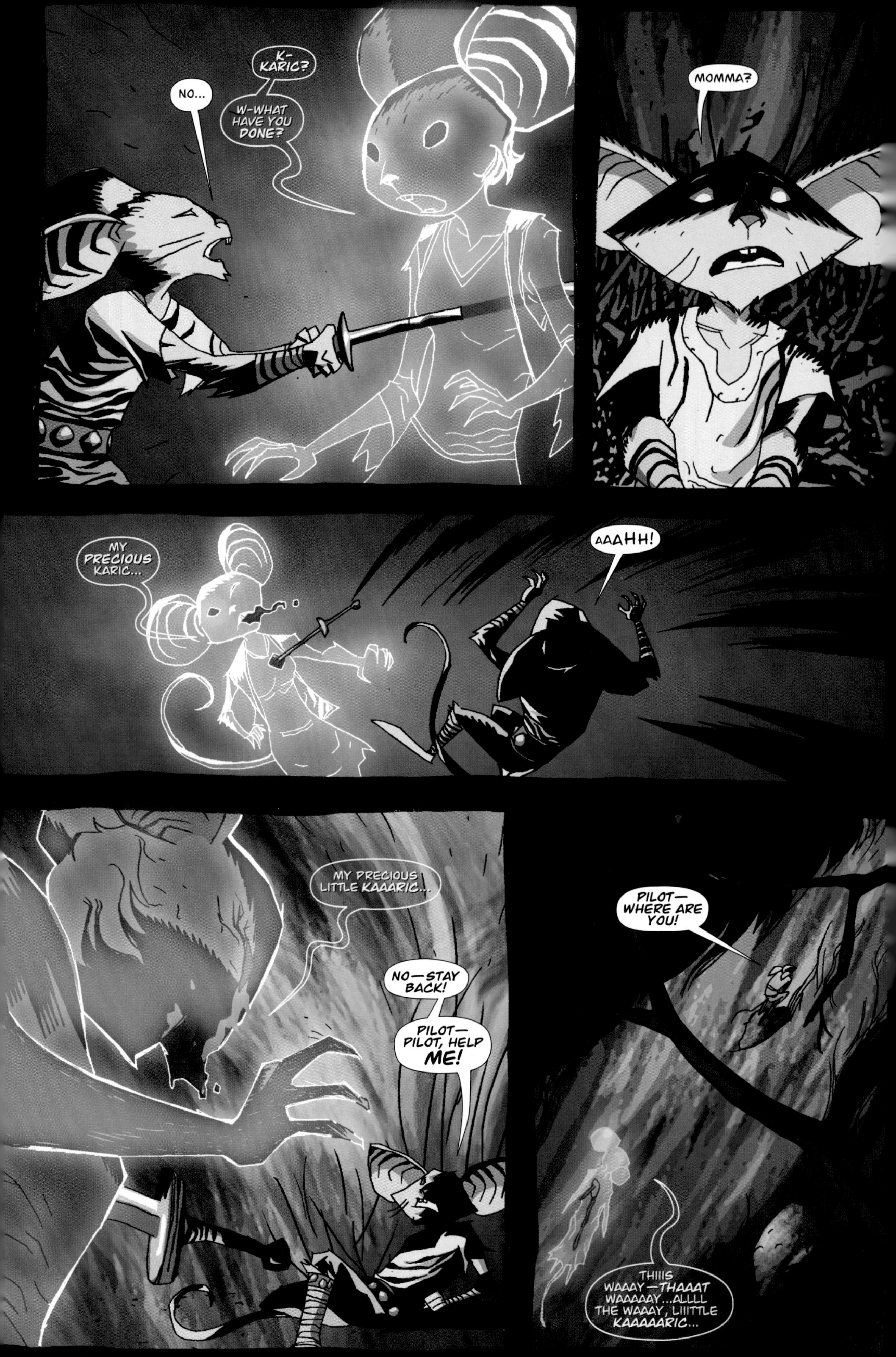
NO...
K-KARIC?
W-WHAT HAVE YOU DONE?
MOMMA?
MY PRECIOUS KARIC...
AAAHH!
MY PRECIOUS LITTLE KAAARIC...
NO—STAY BACK!
PILOT—PILOT, HELP ME!
PILOT—WHERE ARE YOU!
THIIIS WAAAY—THAAAT WAAAAAY...ALLLL THE WAAAY, LIIITTLE KAAAAARIC...

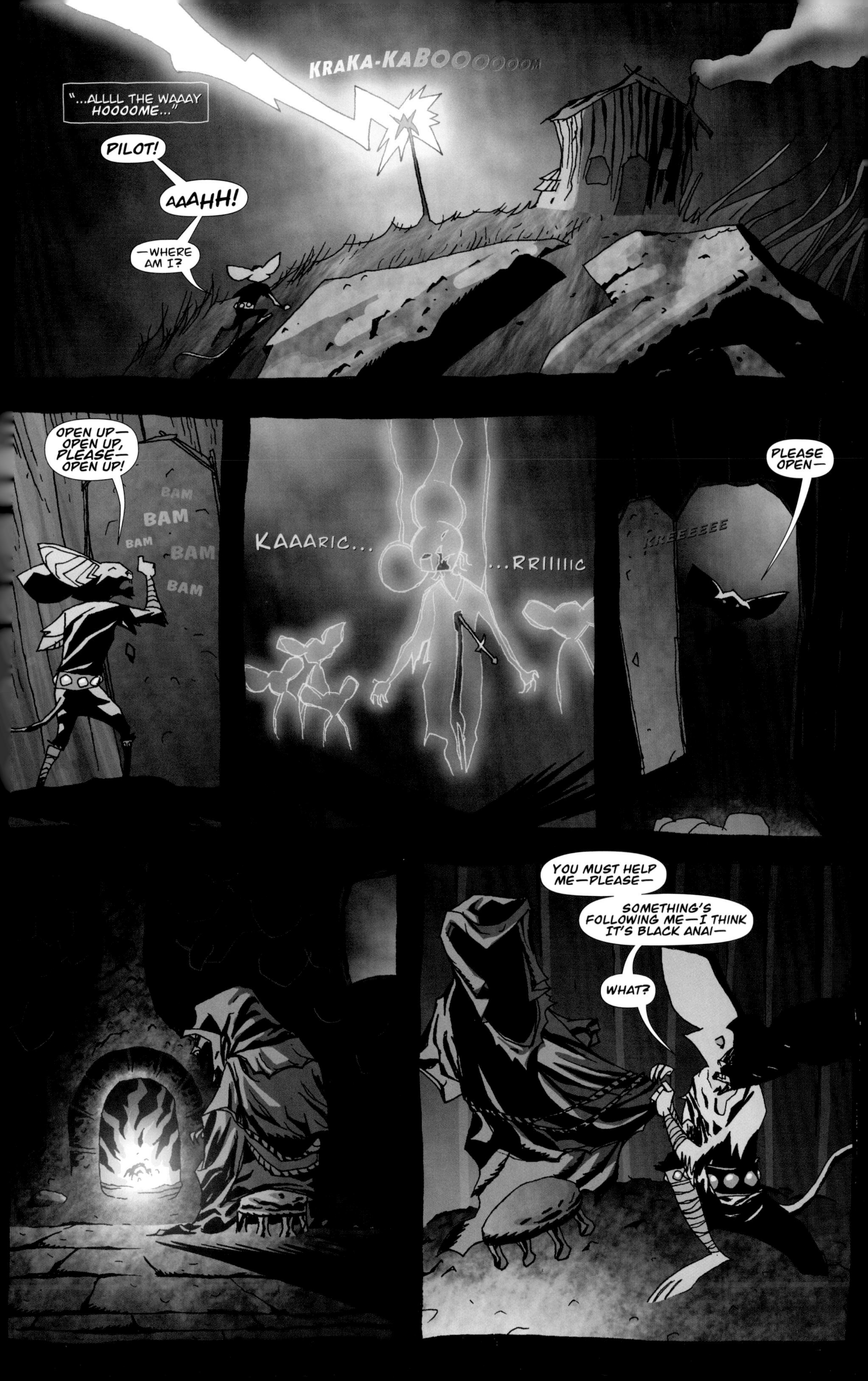

KRAKA-KABOOOOOOOM
"...ALLLL THE WAAAY HOOOOME..."
PILOT!
AAAHH!
—WHERE AM I?
OPEN UP— OPEN UP, PLEASE— OPEN UP!
BAM
BAM
BAM
BAM
BAM
KAAARIC...
...RRIIIIIC
PLEASE OPEN—
KREEEEEEE
YOU MUST HELP ME—PLEASE—
SOMETHING'S FOLLOWING ME—I THINK IT'S BLACK ANAI—
WHAT?

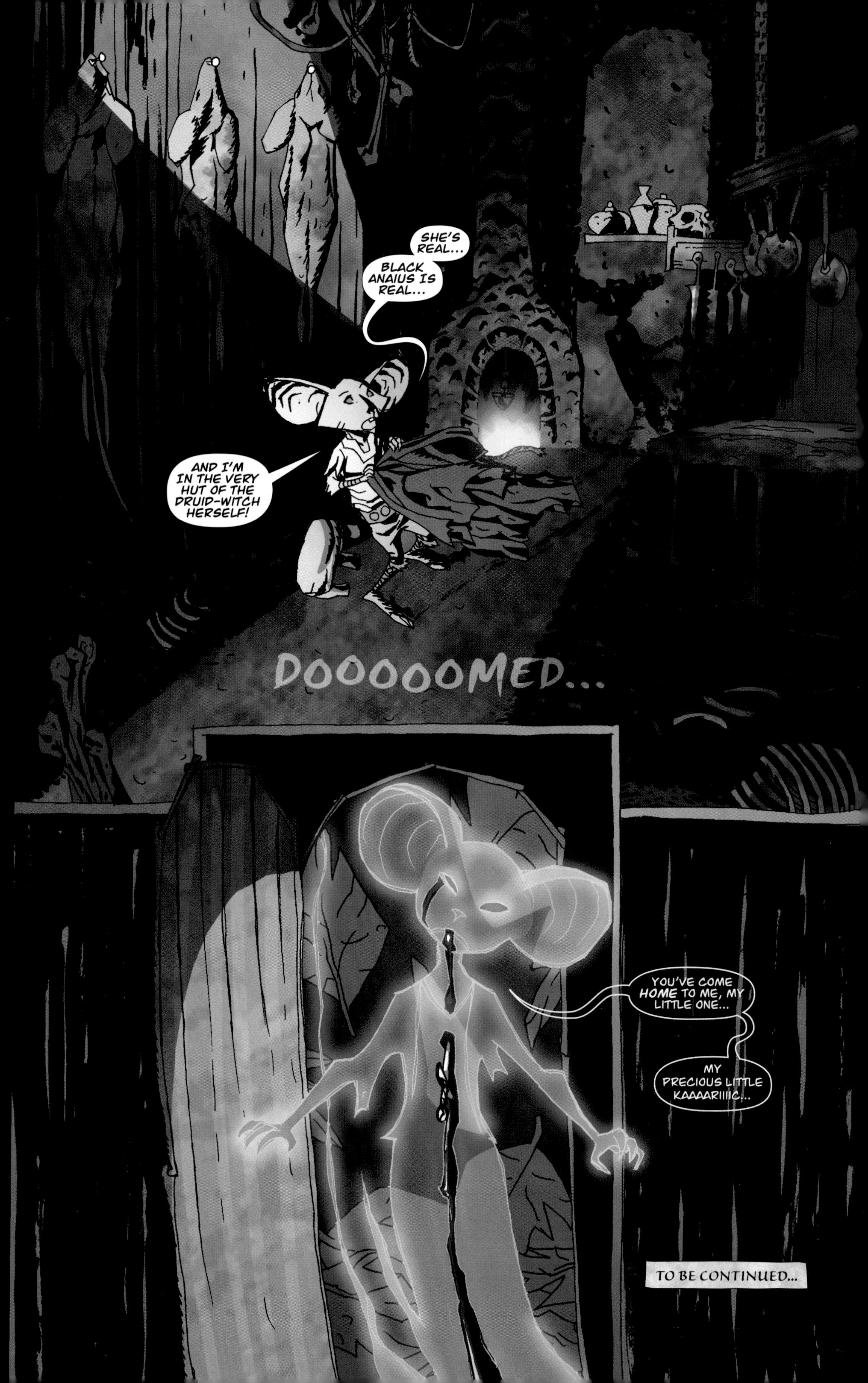
SHE'S REAL...
BLACK ANAIUS IS REAL...
AND I'M IN THE VERY HUT OF THE DRUID-WITCH HERSELF!
DOOOOOMED...
YOU'VE COME HOME TO ME, MY LITTLE ONE...
MY PRECIOUS LITTLE KAAAARIIIIC...
TO BE CONTINUED...

CHAPTER FIVE

THE READERS OF THE WHEAT

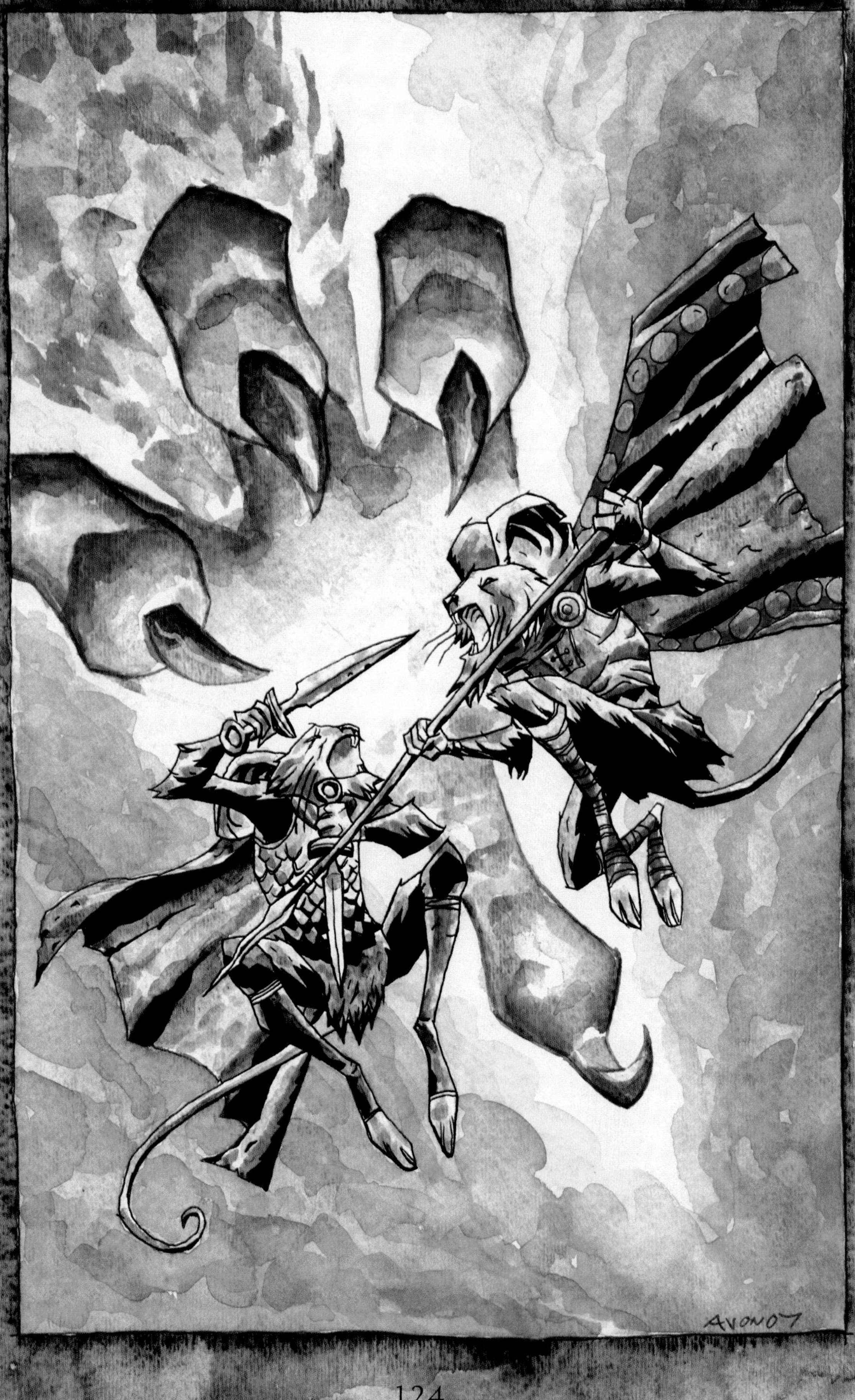

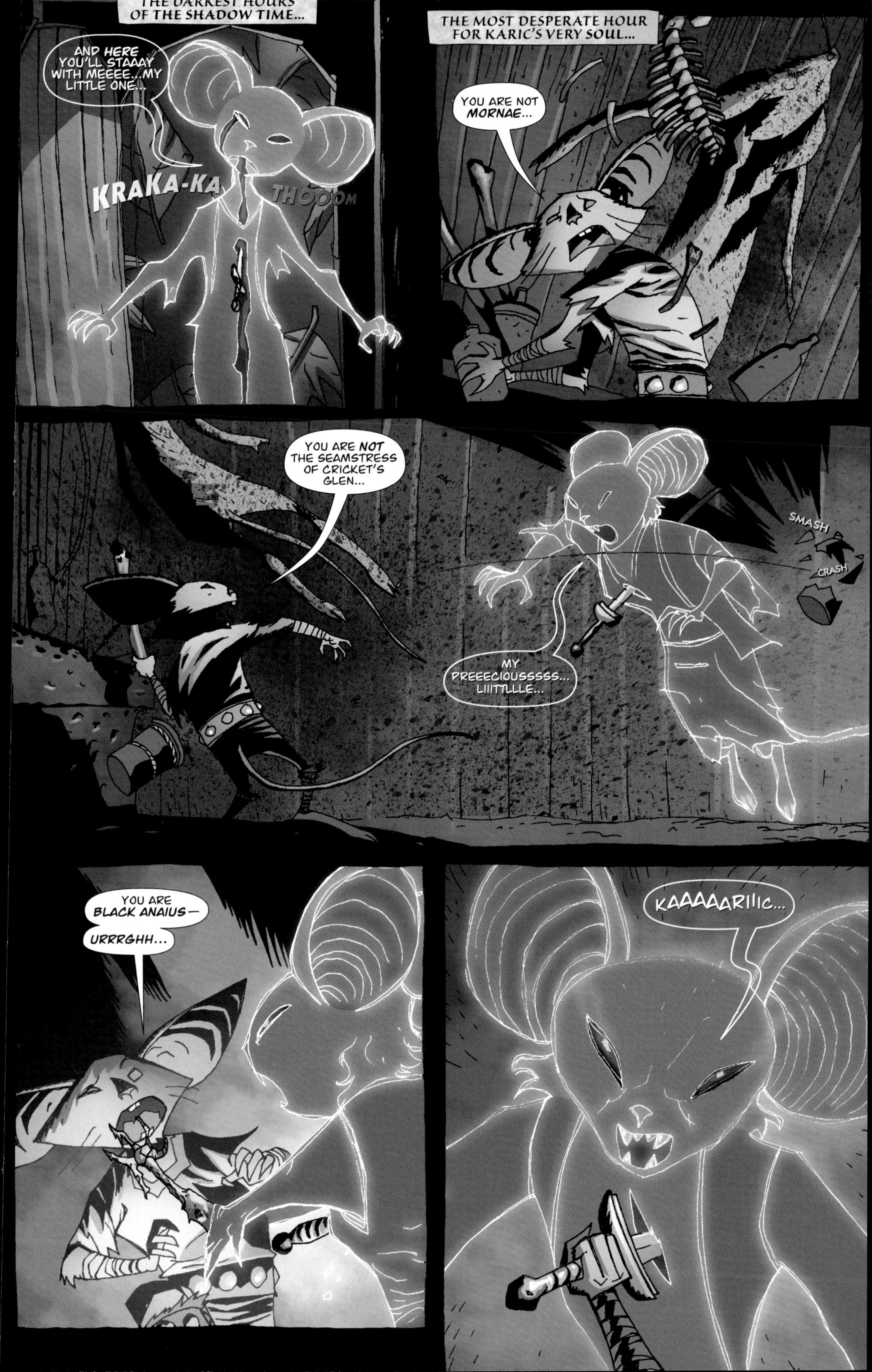
THE DARKEST HOURS OF THE SHADOW TIME...
AND HERE YOU'LL STAAAY WITH MEEEE...MY LITTLE ONE...
KRAKA-KA
THOOOM
THE MOST DESPERATE HOUR FOR KARIC'S VERY SOUL...
YOU ARE NOT MORNAE...
YOU ARE NOT THE SEAMSTRESS OF CRICKET'S GLEN...
SMASH
CRASH
MY PREEECIOUSSSSS... LIIIITLLLE...
YOU ARE BLACK ANAIUS—
URRRGHH...
KAAAAARIIIC...

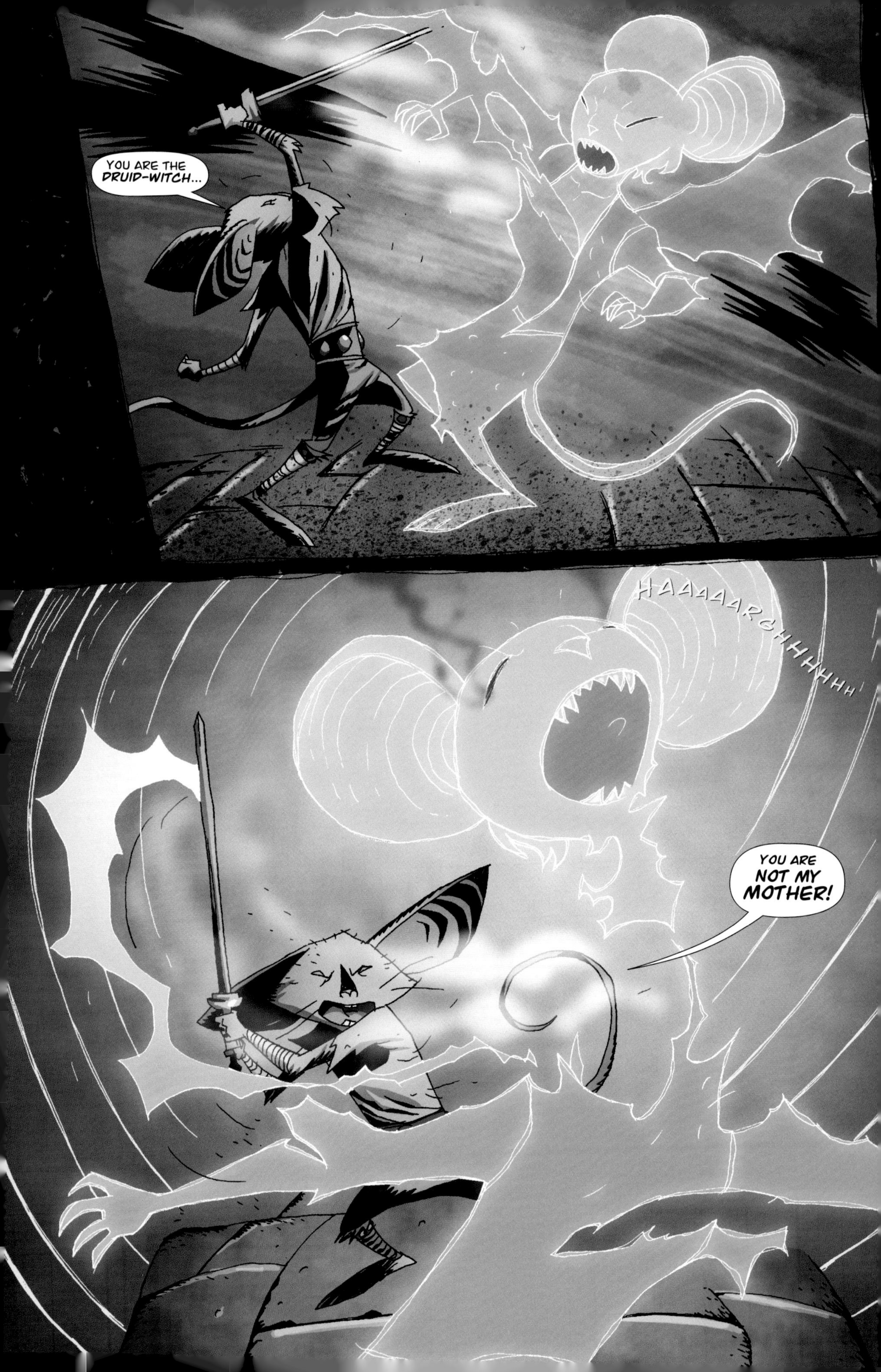
YOU ARE THE DRUID-WITCH...
HAAAAAARGHHHHHH
YOU ARE NOT MY MOTHER!

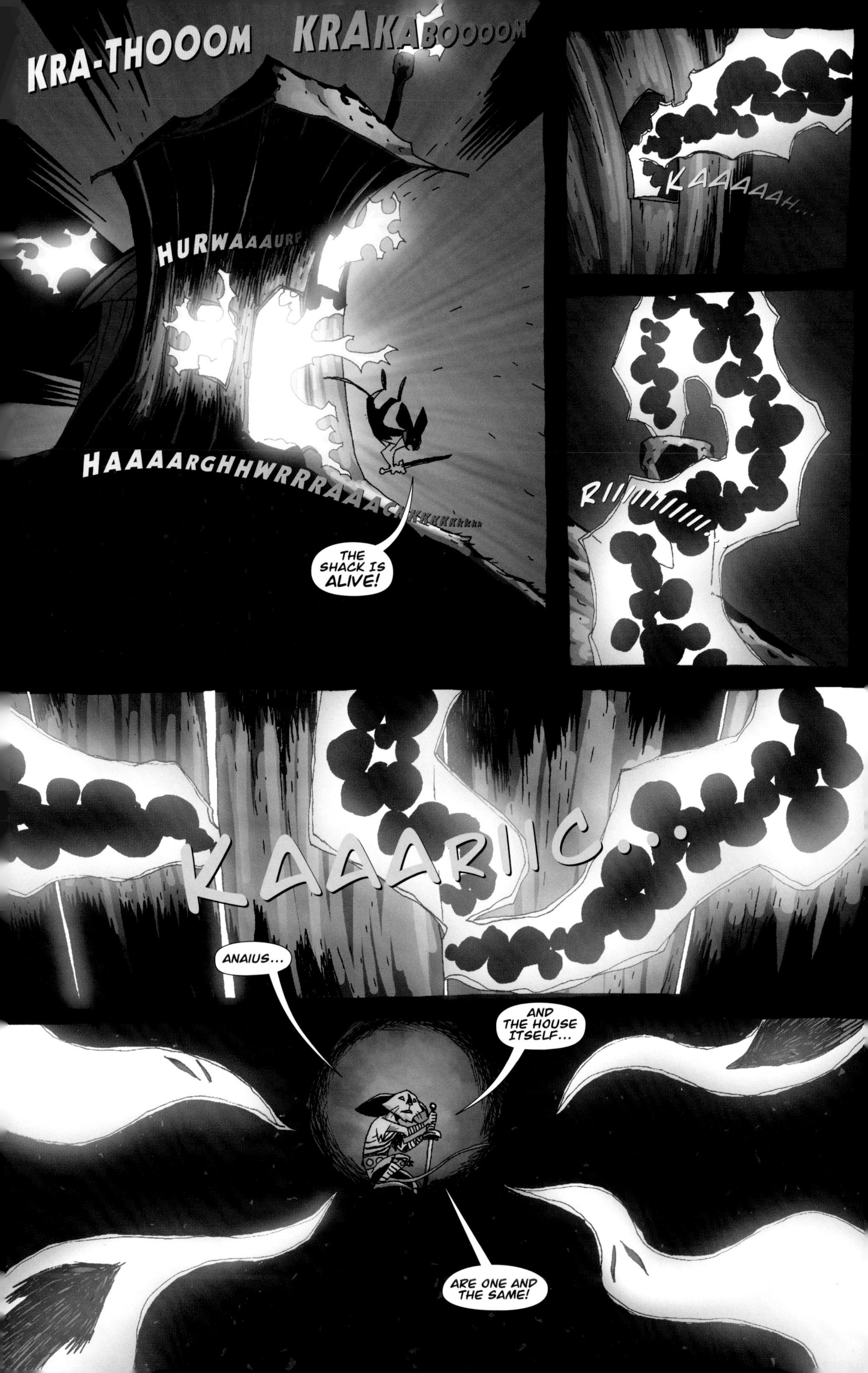
KRA-THOOOM
KRAKABOOOOOM
HURWAAAURP
HAAAARGHHWRRRRAAAACHKKKKkkkk
THE SHACK IS ALIVE!
KAAAAAH...
RIIIIIIIIIII...
KAAARIIC...
ANAIUS...
AND THE HOUSE ITSELF...
ARE ONE AND THE SAME!

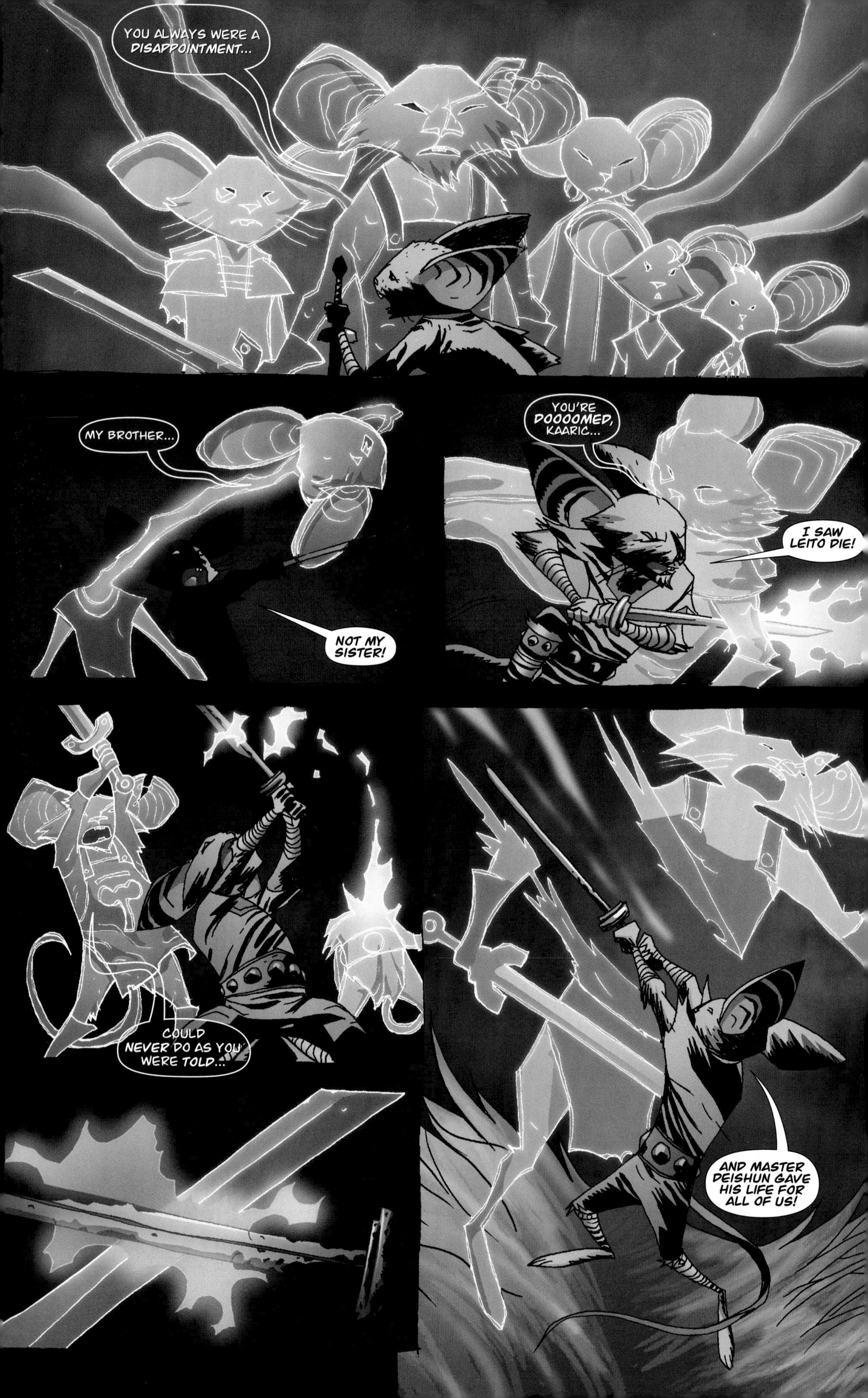
YOU ALWAYS WERE A DISAPPOINTMENT...
MY BROTHER...
NOT MY SISTER!
YOU'RE DOOOOMED, KAARIC...
I SAW LEITO DIE!
COULD NEVER DO AS YOU WERE TOLD...
AND MASTER DEISHUN GAVE HIS LIFE FOR ALL OF US!

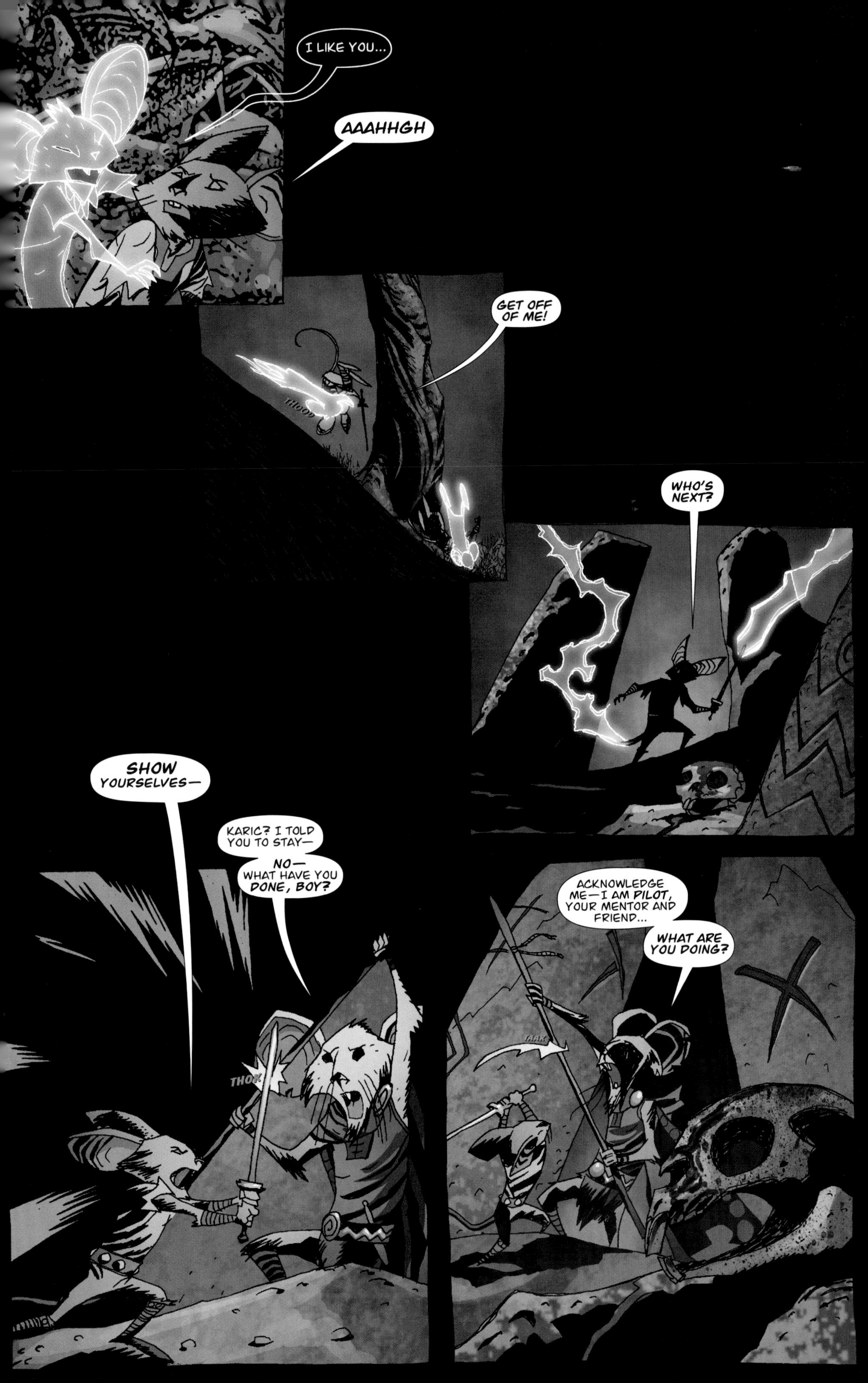

I LIKE YOU...
AAAHHGH
GET OFF OF ME!
THOOD
WHO'S NEXT?
SHOW YOURSELVES—
KARIC? I TOLD YOU TO STAY—
NO— WHAT HAVE YOU DONE, BOY?
THOK
ACKNOWLEDGE ME—I AM PILOT, YOUR MENTOR AND FRIEND...
WHAT ARE YOU DOING?
TAAK

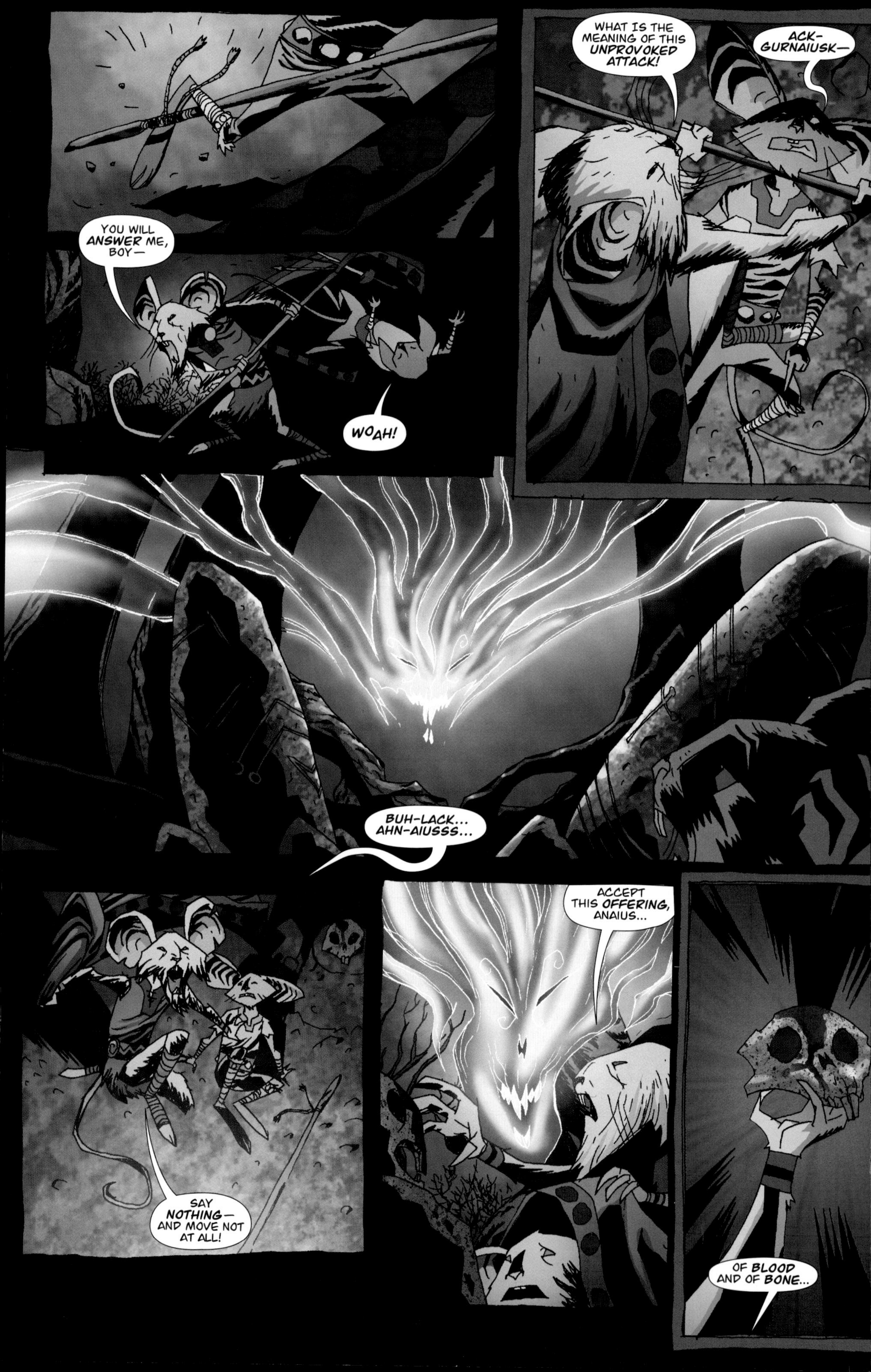
YOU WILL ANSWER ME, BOY—
WOAH!
WHAT IS THE MEANING OF THIS UNPROVOKED ATTACK!
ACK-GURNAIUSK—
BUH-LACK... AHN-AIUSSS...
SAY NOTHING— AND MOVE NOT AT ALL!
ACCEPT THIS OFFERING, ANAIUS...
OF BLOOD AND OF BONE...

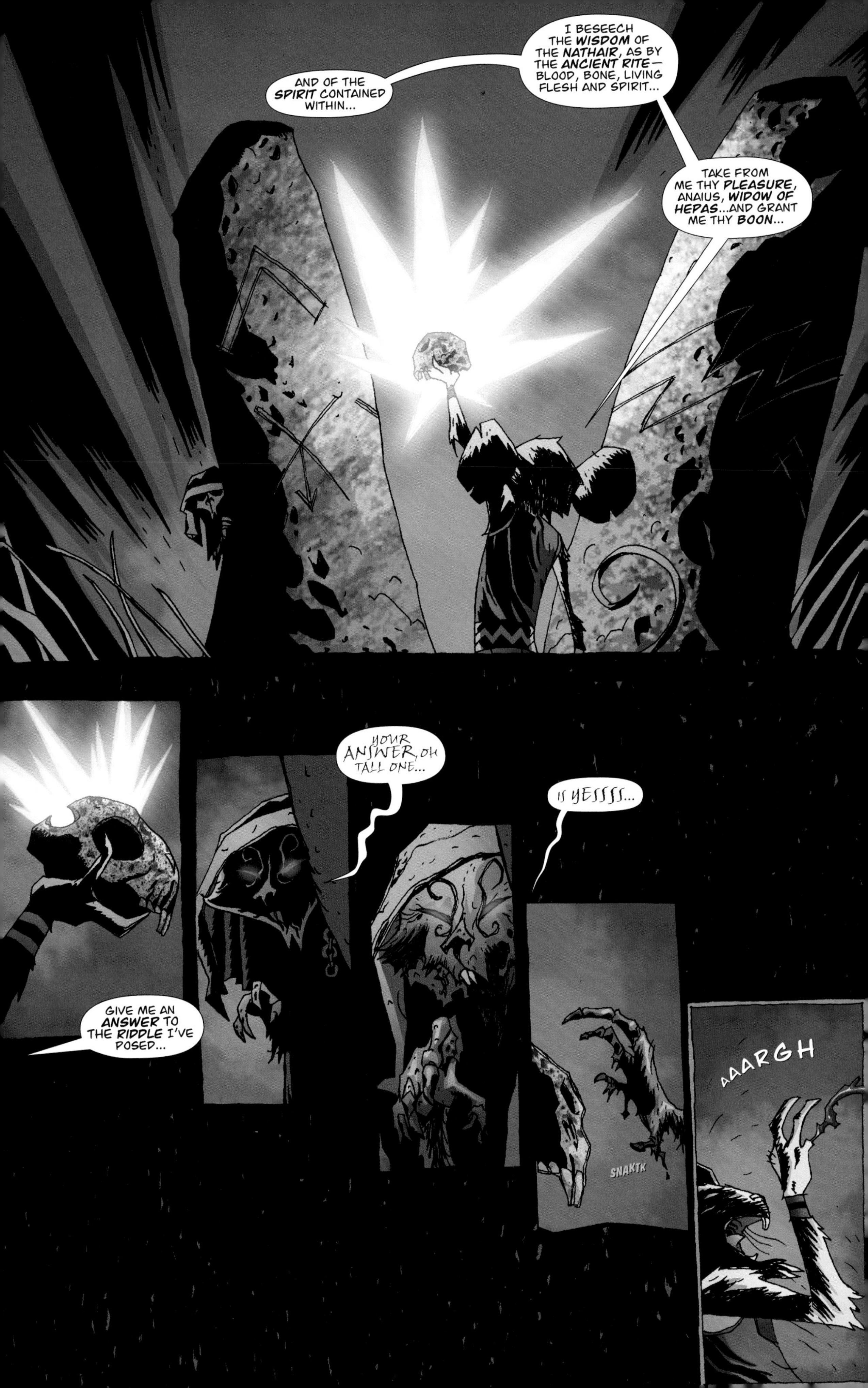
I BESEECH THE WISDOM OF THE NATHAIR, AS BY THE ANCIENT RITE— BLOOD, BONE, LIVING FLESH AND SPIRIT...
AND OF THE SPIRIT CONTAINED WITHIN...
TAKE FROM ME THY PLEASURE, ANAIUS, WIDOW OF HEPAS...AND GRANT ME THY BOON...
GIVE ME AN ANSWER TO THE RIDDLE I'VE POSED...
YOUR ANSWER, OH TALL ONE...
IS YESSSS...
SNAKTK
AAARGH

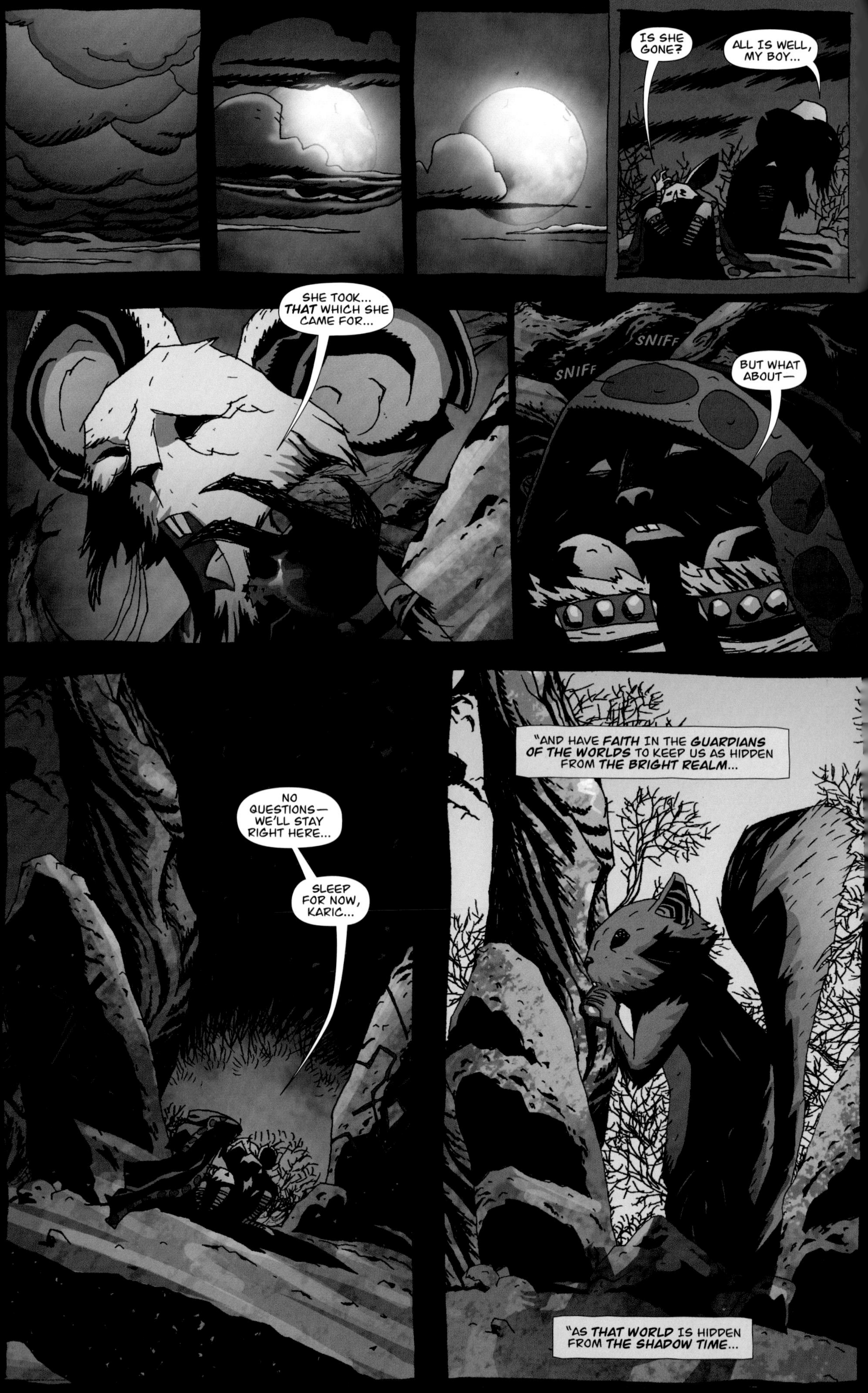
IS SHE GONE?
ALL IS WELL, MY BOY...
SHE TOOK... THAT WHICH SHE CAME FOR...
SNIFF
SNIFF
BUT WHAT ABOUT—
NO QUESTIONS— WE'LL STAY RIGHT HERE...
SLEEP FOR NOW, KARIC...
"AND HAVE FAITH IN THE GUARDIANS OF THE WORLDS TO KEEP US AS HIDDEN FROM THE BRIGHT REALM...
"AS THAT WORLD IS HIDDEN FROM THE SHADOW TIME...

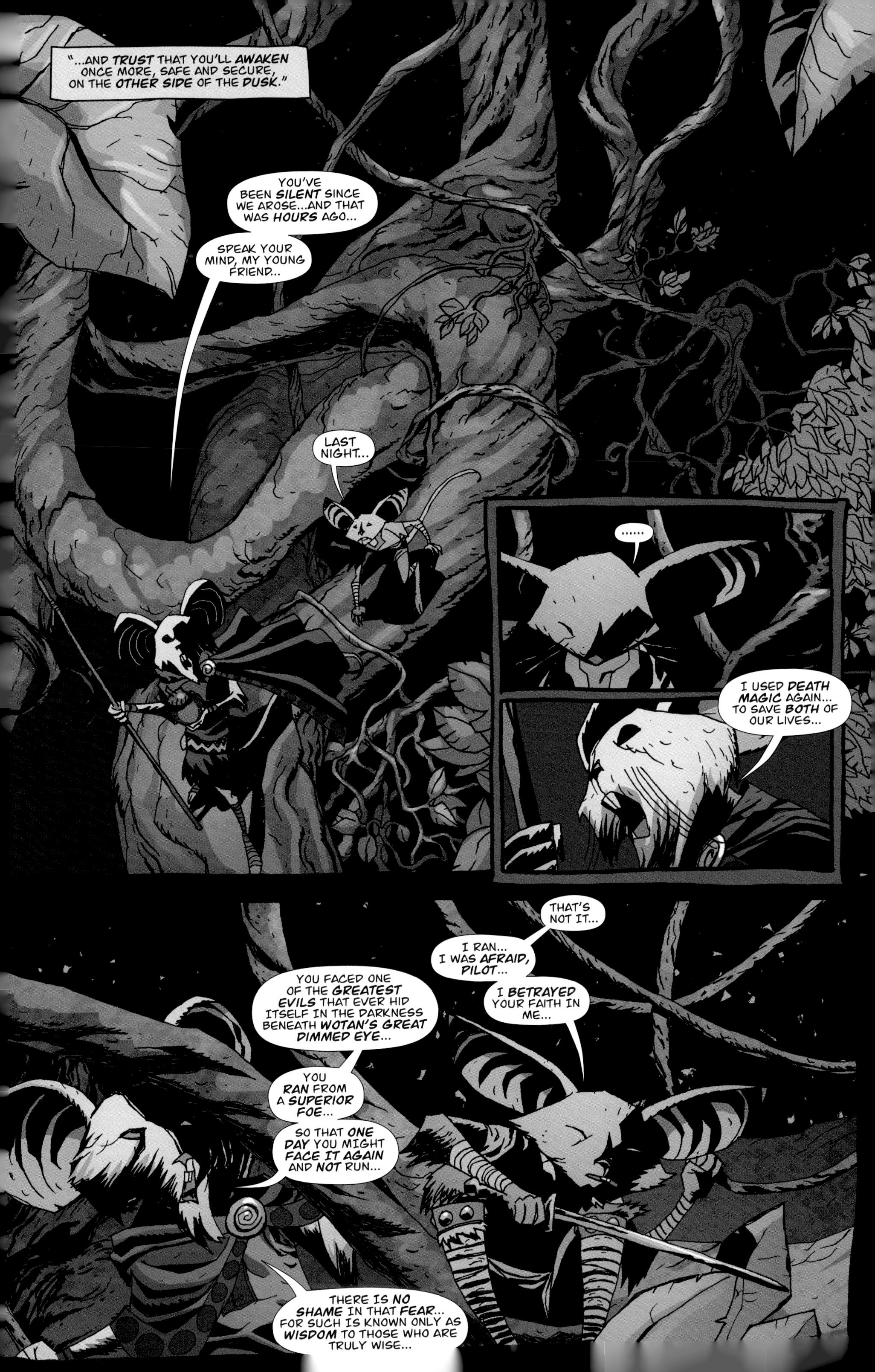
"...AND TRUST THAT YOU'LL AWAKEN ONCE MORE, SAFE AND SECURE, ON THE OTHER SIDE OF THE DUSK."
YOU'VE BEEN SILENT SINCE WE AROSE...AND THAT WAS HOURS AGO...
SPEAK YOUR MIND, MY YOUNG FRIEND...
LAST NIGHT...
......
I USED DEATH MAGIC AGAIN... TO SAVE BOTH OF OUR LIVES...
THAT'S NOT IT...
I RAN... I WAS AFRAID, PILOT...
I BETRAYED YOUR FAITH IN ME...
YOU FACED ONE OF THE GREATEST EVILS THAT EVER HID ITSELF IN THE DARKNESS BENEATH WOTAN'S GREAT DIMMED EYE...
YOU RAN FROM A SUPERIOR FOE...
SO THAT ONE DAY YOU MIGHT FACE IT AGAIN AND NOT RUN...
THERE IS NO SHAME IN THAT FEAR... FOR SUCH IS KNOWN ONLY AS WISDOM TO THOSE WHO ARE TRULY WISE...

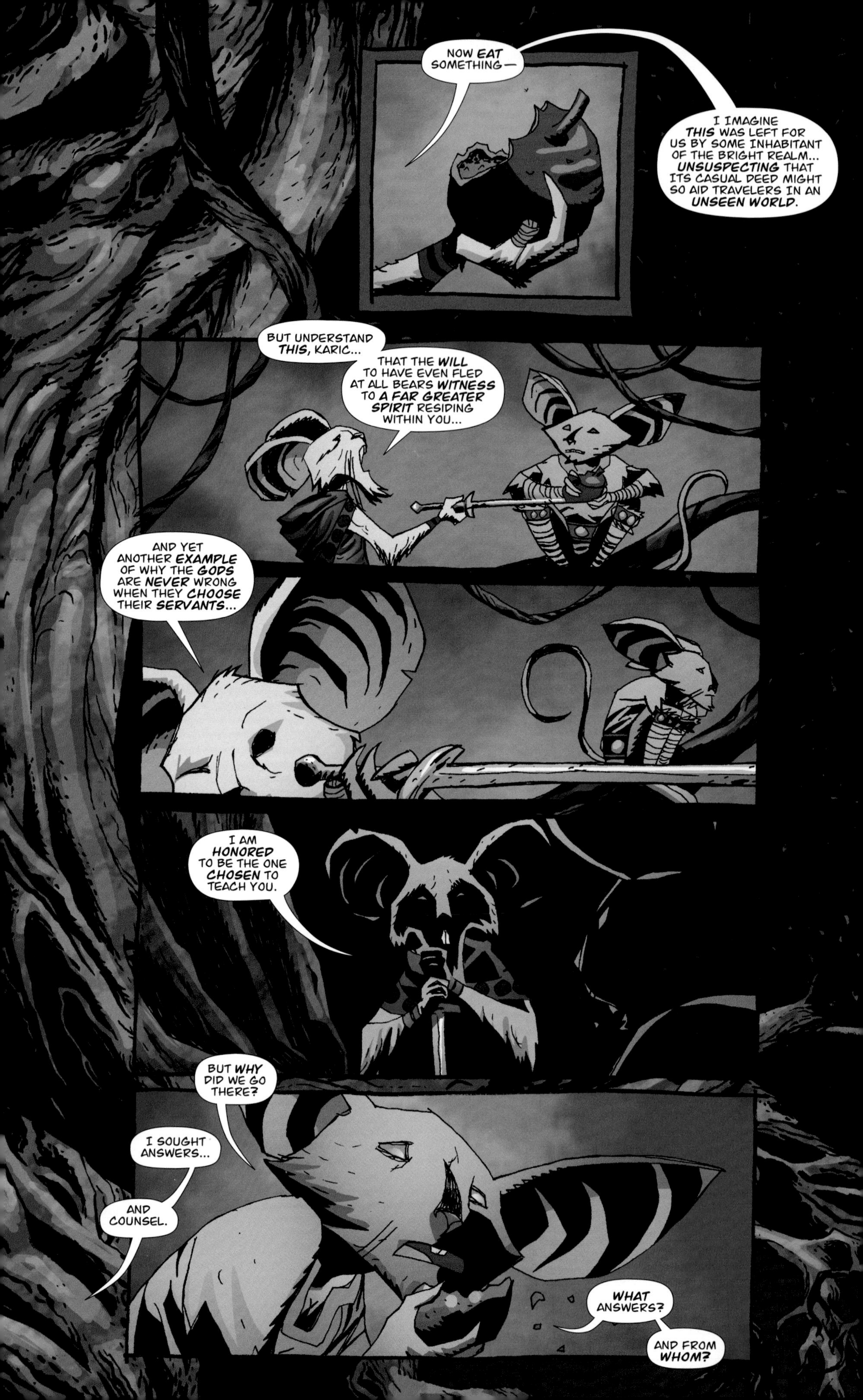
NOW EAT SOMETHING—
I IMAGINE THIS WAS LEFT FOR US BY SOME INHABITANT OF THE BRIGHT REALM... UNSUSPECTING THAT ITS CASUAL DEED MIGHT SO AID TRAVELERS IN AN UNSEEN WORLD.
BUT UNDERSTAND THIS, KARIC...
THAT THE WILL TO HAVE EVEN FLED AT ALL BEARS WITNESS TO A FAR GREATER SPIRIT RESIDING WITHIN YOU...
AND YET ANOTHER EXAMPLE OF WHY THE GODS ARE NEVER WRONG WHEN THEY CHOOSE THEIR SERVANTS...
I AM HONORED TO BE THE ONE CHOSEN TO TEACH YOU.
BUT WHY DID WE GO THERE?
I SOUGHT ANSWERS...
AND COUNSEL.
WHAT ANSWERS?
AND FROM WHOM?

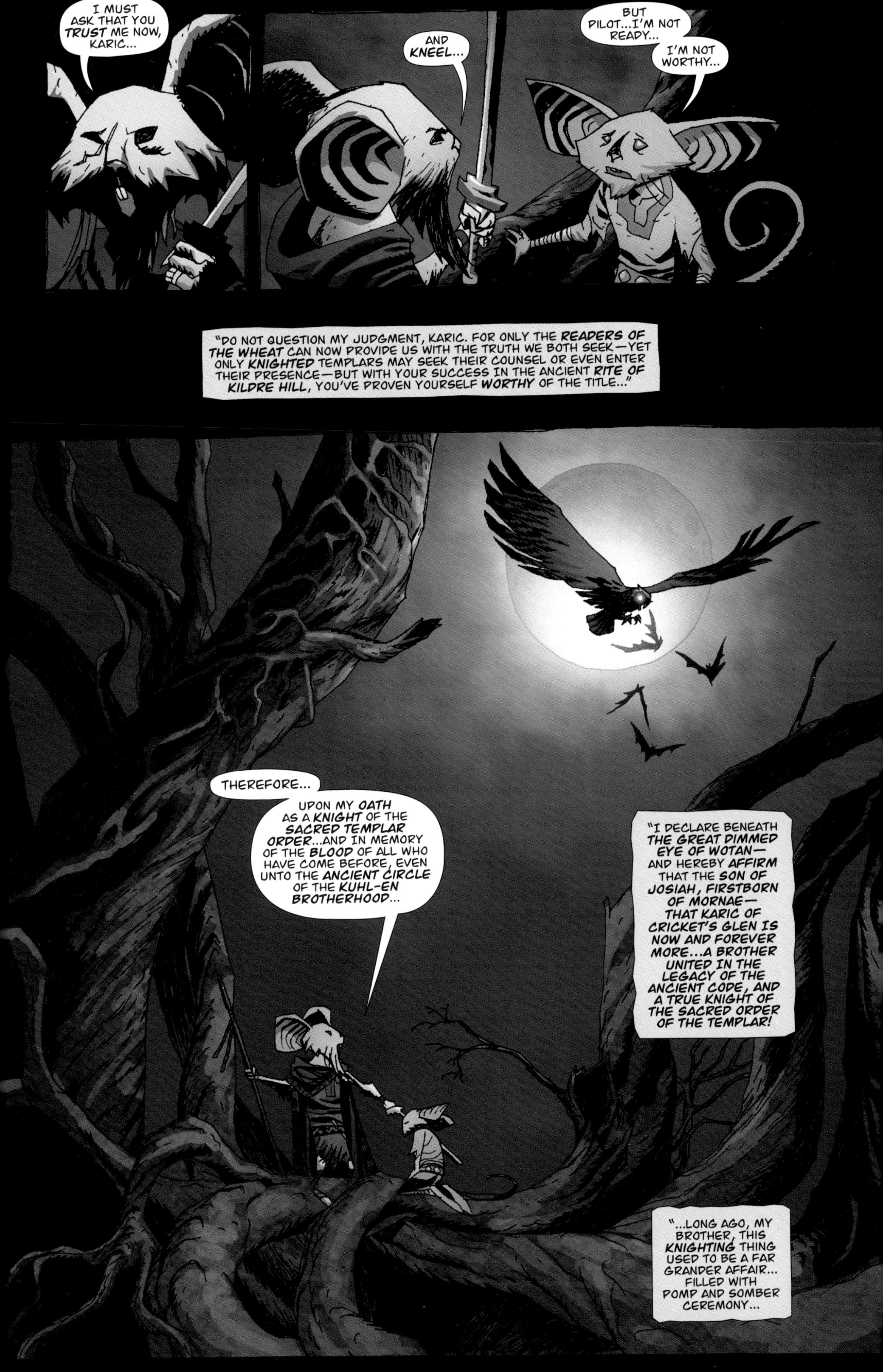

I MUST ASK THAT YOU *TRUST* ME NOW, KARIC...
AND *KNEEL*...
BUT PILOT...I'M NOT READY...
I'M NOT WORTHY...
"DO NOT QUESTION MY JUDGMENT, KARIC. FOR ONLY THE *READERS OF THE WHEAT* CAN NOW PROVIDE US WITH THE TRUTH WE BOTH SEEK—YET ONLY *KNIGHTED* TEMPLARS MAY SEEK THEIR COUNSEL OR EVEN ENTER THEIR PRESENCE—BUT WITH YOUR SUCCESS IN THE ANCIENT *RITE OF KILDRE HILL*, YOU'VE PROVEN YOURSELF *WORTHY* OF THE TITLE..."
THEREFORE...
UPON MY *OATH* AS A *KNIGHT* OF THE *SACRED TEMPLAR ORDER*...AND IN MEMORY OF THE *BLOOD* OF ALL WHO HAVE COME BEFORE, EVEN UNTO THE *ANCIENT CIRCLE* OF THE *KUHL-EN BROTHERHOOD*...
"I DECLARE BENEATH *THE GREAT DIMMED EYE OF WOTAN*—AND HEREBY *AFFIRM* THAT THE *SON OF JOSIAH, FIRSTBORN OF MORNAE*—*THAT KARIC OF CRICKET'S GLEN IS NOW AND FOREVER MORE*...*A BROTHER UNITED IN THE LEGACY OF THE ANCIENT CODE, AND A TRUE KNIGHT OF THE SACRED ORDER OF THE TEMPLAR!*
"...LONG AGO, MY BROTHER, THIS *KNIGHTING* THING USED TO BE A FAR GRANDER AFFAIR... FILLED WITH POMP AND SOMBER CEREMONY...

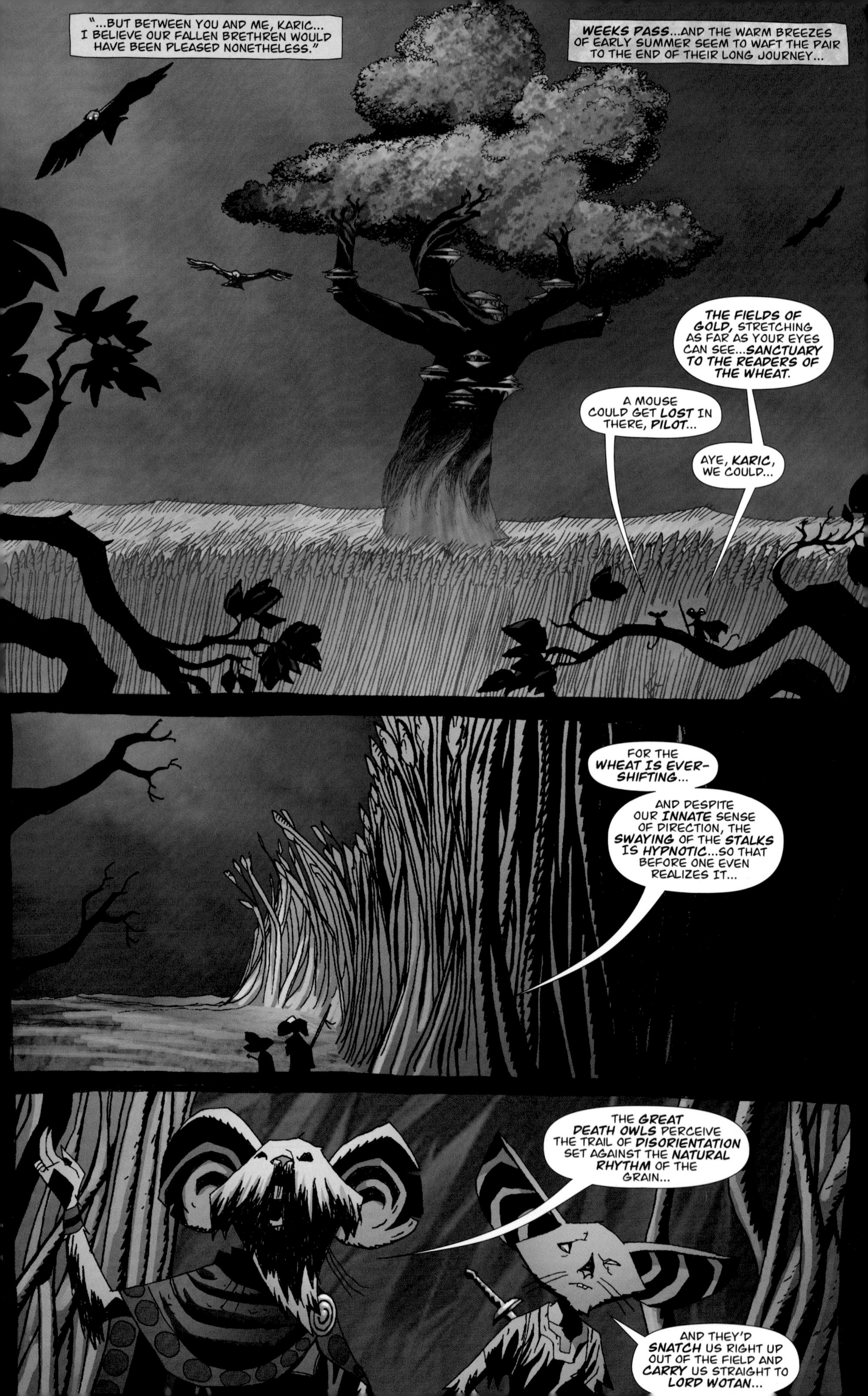

"...BUT BETWEEN YOU AND ME, KARIC... I BELIEVE OUR FALLEN BRETHREN WOULD HAVE BEEN PLEASED NONETHELESS."
WEEKS PASS...AND THE WARM BREEZES OF EARLY SUMMER SEEM TO WAFT THE PAIR TO THE END OF THEIR LONG JOURNEY...
THE FIELDS OF GOLD, STRETCHING AS FAR AS YOUR EYES CAN SEE...SANCTUARY TO THE READERS OF THE WHEAT.
A MOUSE COULD GET LOST IN THERE, PILOT...
AYE, KARIC, WE COULD...
FOR THE WHEAT IS EVER-SHIFTING...
AND DESPITE OUR INNATE SENSE OF DIRECTION, THE SWAYING OF THE STALKS IS HYPNOTIC...SO THAT BEFORE ONE EVEN REALIZES IT...
THE GREAT DEATH OWLS PERCEIVE THE TRAIL OF DISORIENTATION SET AGAINST THE NATURAL RHYTHM OF THE GRAIN...
AND THEY'D SNATCH US RIGHT UP OUT OF THE FIELD AND CARRY US STRAIGHT TO LORD WOTAN...

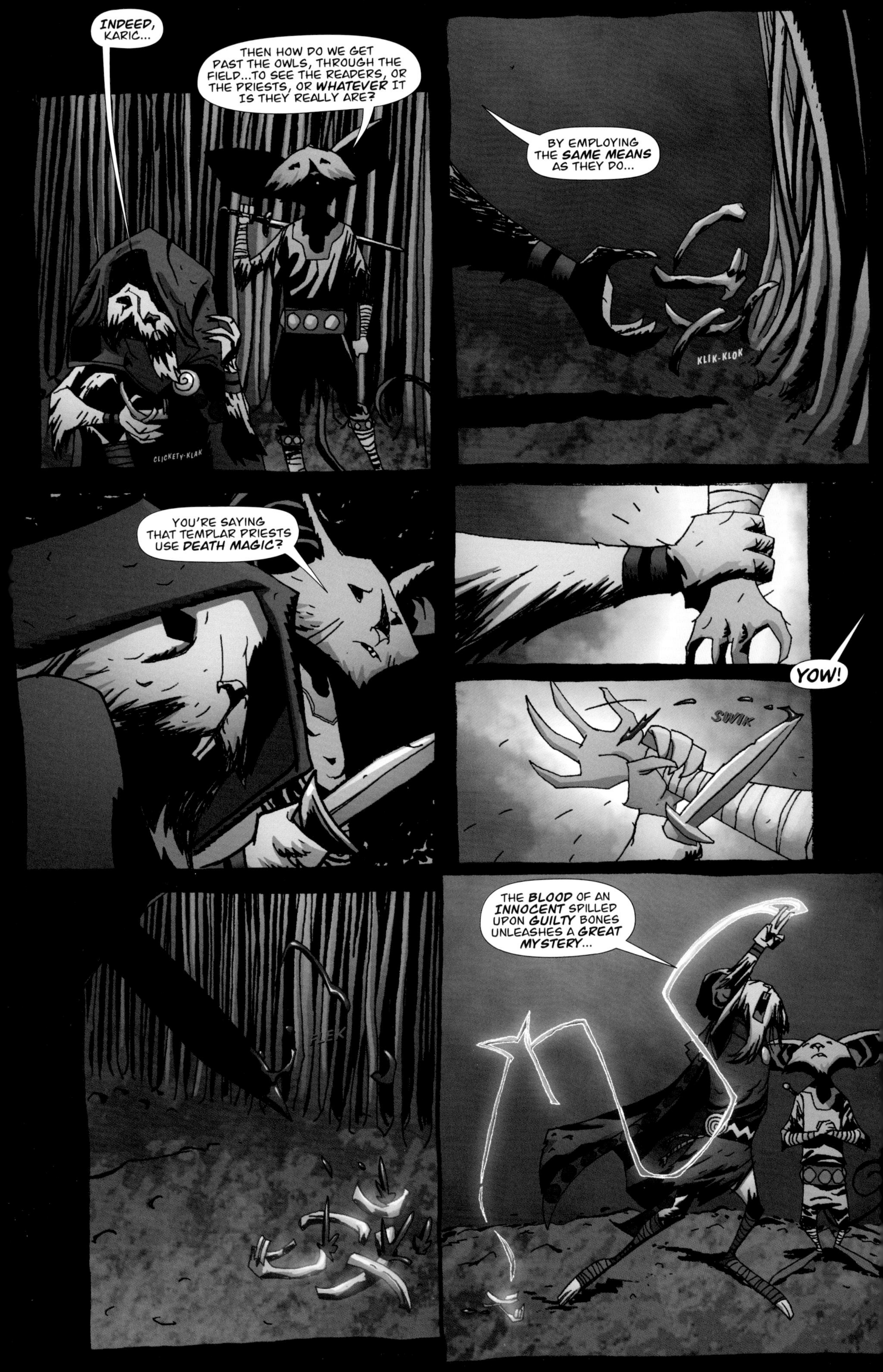
INDEED, KARIC...
THEN HOW DO WE GET PAST THE OWLS, THROUGH THE FIELD...TO SEE THE READERS, OR THE PRIESTS, OR WHATEVER IT IS THEY REALLY ARE?
CLICKETY-KLAK
BY EMPLOYING THE SAME MEANS AS THEY DO...
KLIK-KLOK
YOU'RE SAYING THAT TEMPLAR PRIESTS USE DEATH MAGIC?
YOW!
SWIK
THE BLOOD OF AN INNOCENT SPILLED UPON GUILTY BONES UNLEASHES A GREAT MYSTERY...

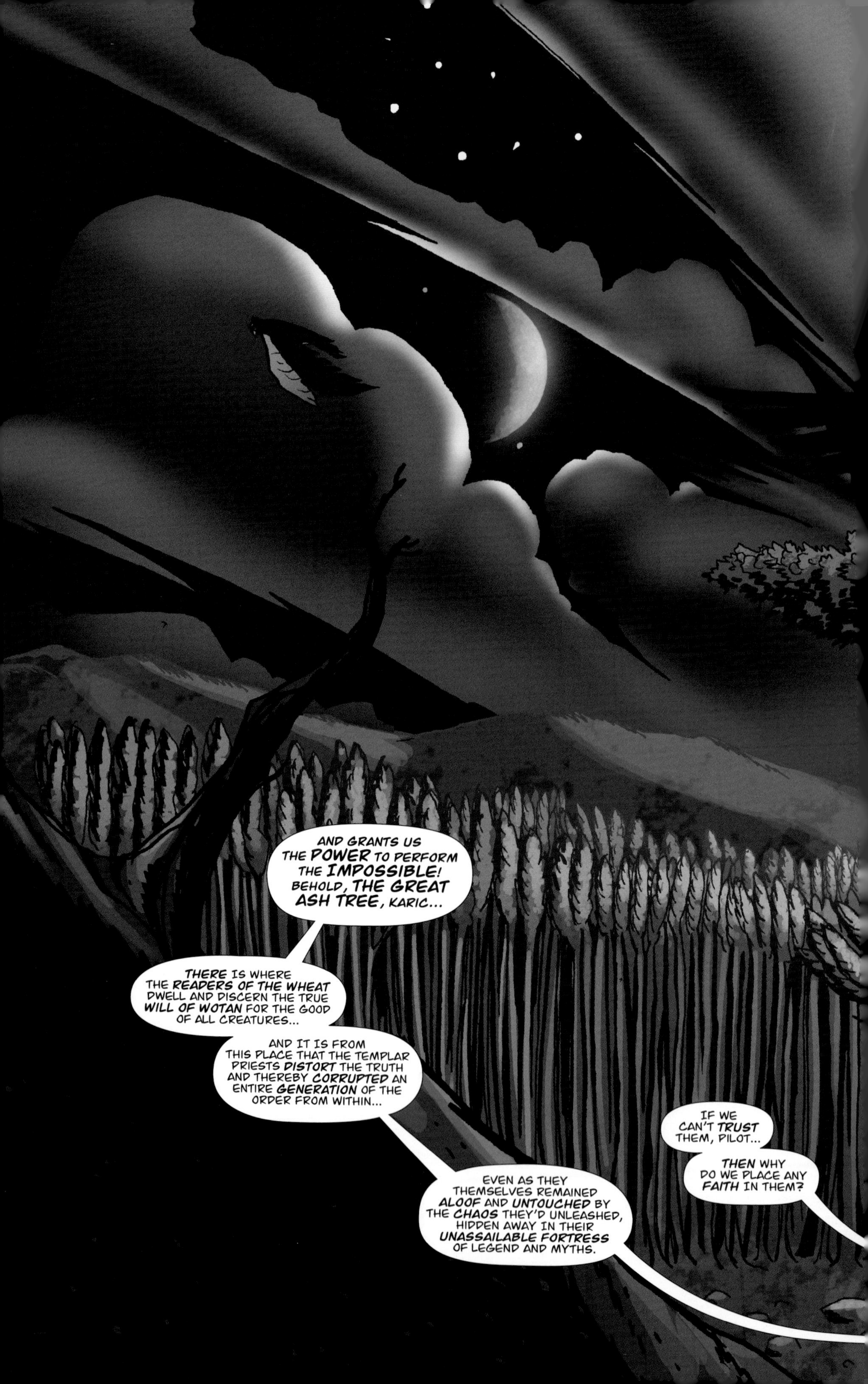
AND GRANTS US THE POWER TO PERFORM THE IMPOSSIBLE! BEHOLD, THE GREAT ASH TREE, KARIC...
THERE IS WHERE THE READERS OF THE WHEAT DWELL AND DISCERN THE TRUE WILL OF WOTAN FOR THE GOOD OF ALL CREATURES...
AND IT IS FROM THIS PLACE THAT THE TEMPLAR PRIESTS DISTORT THE TRUTH AND THEREBY CORRUPTED AN ENTIRE GENERATION OF THE ORDER FROM WITHIN...
EVEN AS THEY THEMSELVES REMAINED ALOOF AND UNTOUCHED BY THE CHAOS THEY'D UNLEASHED, HIDDEN AWAY IN THEIR UNASSAILABLE FORTRESS OF LEGEND AND MYTHS.
IF WE CAN'T TRUST THEM, PILOT...
THEN WHY DO WE PLACE ANY FAITH IN THEM?

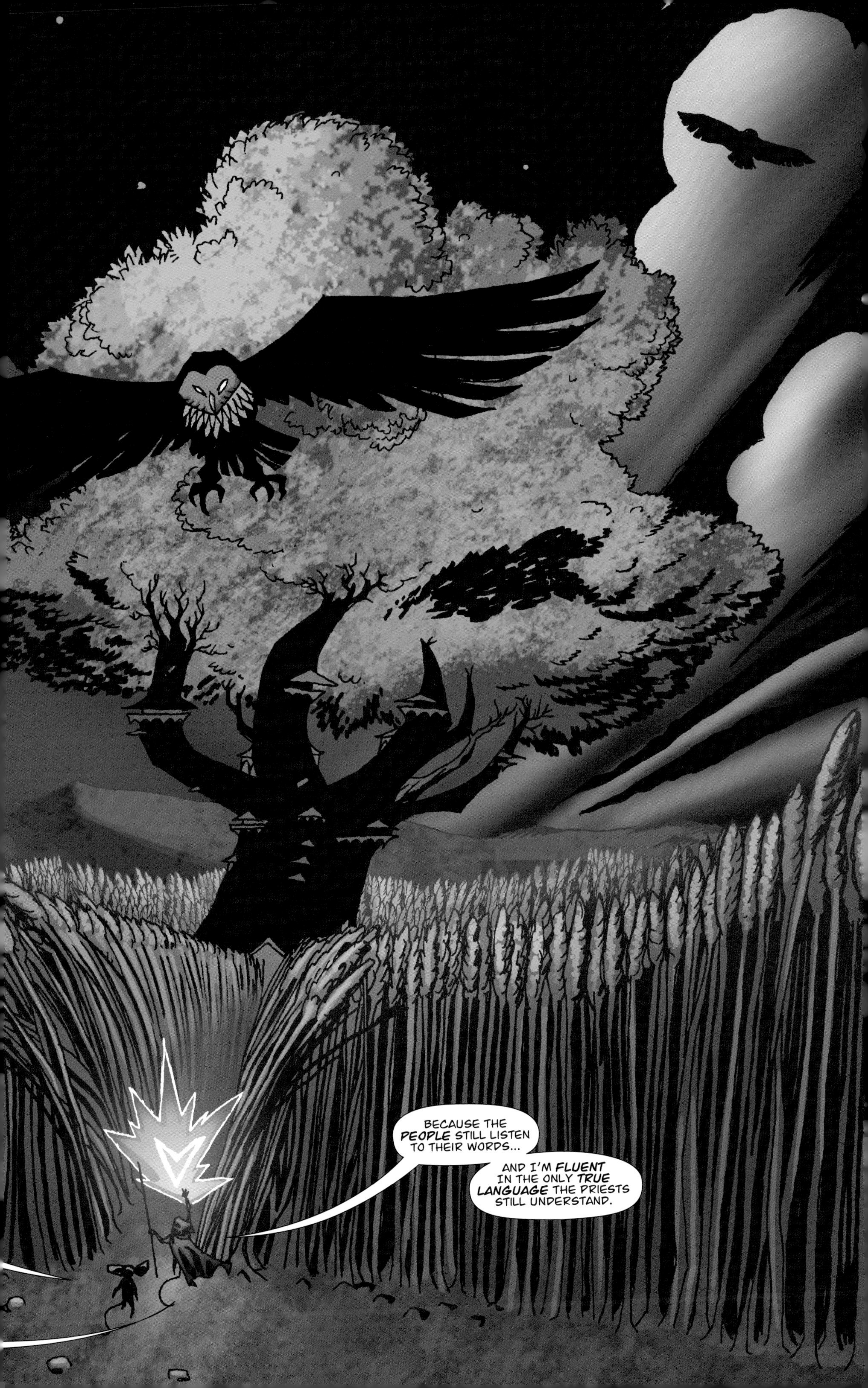
BECAUSE THE **PEOPLE** STILL LISTEN TO THEIR WORDS...
AND I'M **FLUENT** IN THE ONLY **TRUE LANGUAGE** THE PRIESTS STILL UNDERSTAND.

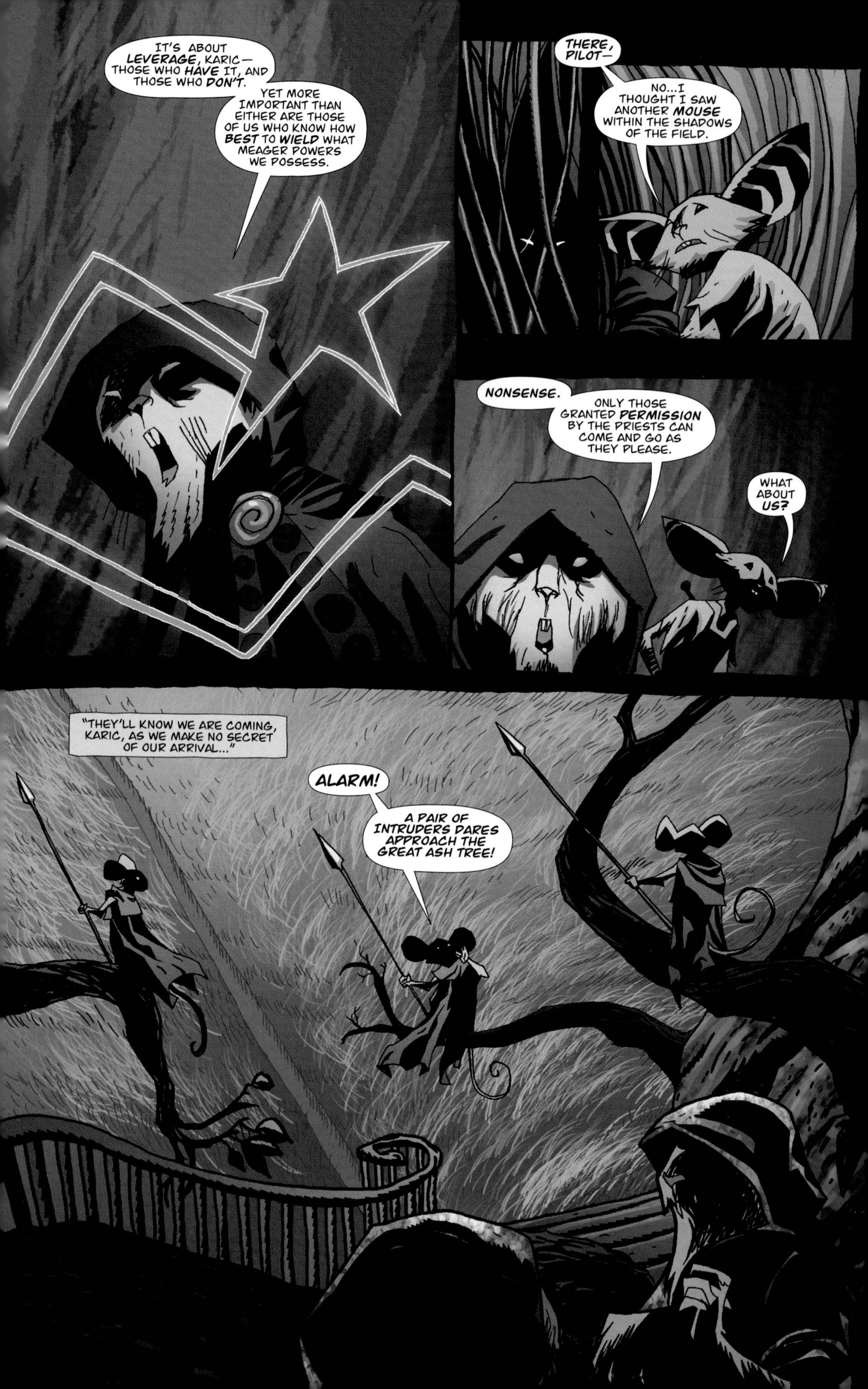
IT'S ABOUT LEVERAGE, KARIC— THOSE WHO HAVE IT, AND THOSE WHO DON'T.
YET MORE IMPORTANT THAN EITHER ARE THOSE OF US WHO KNOW HOW BEST TO WIELD WHAT MEAGER POWERS WE POSSESS.
THERE, PILOT—
NO...I THOUGHT I SAW ANOTHER MOUSE WITHIN THE SHADOWS OF THE FIELD.
NONSENSE.
ONLY THOSE GRANTED PERMISSION BY THE PRIESTS CAN COME AND GO AS THEY PLEASE.
WHAT ABOUT US?
"THEY'LL KNOW WE ARE COMING, KARIC, AS WE MAKE NO SECRET OF OUR ARRIVAL..."
ALARM!
A PAIR OF INTRUDERS DARES APPROACH THE GREAT ASH TREE!

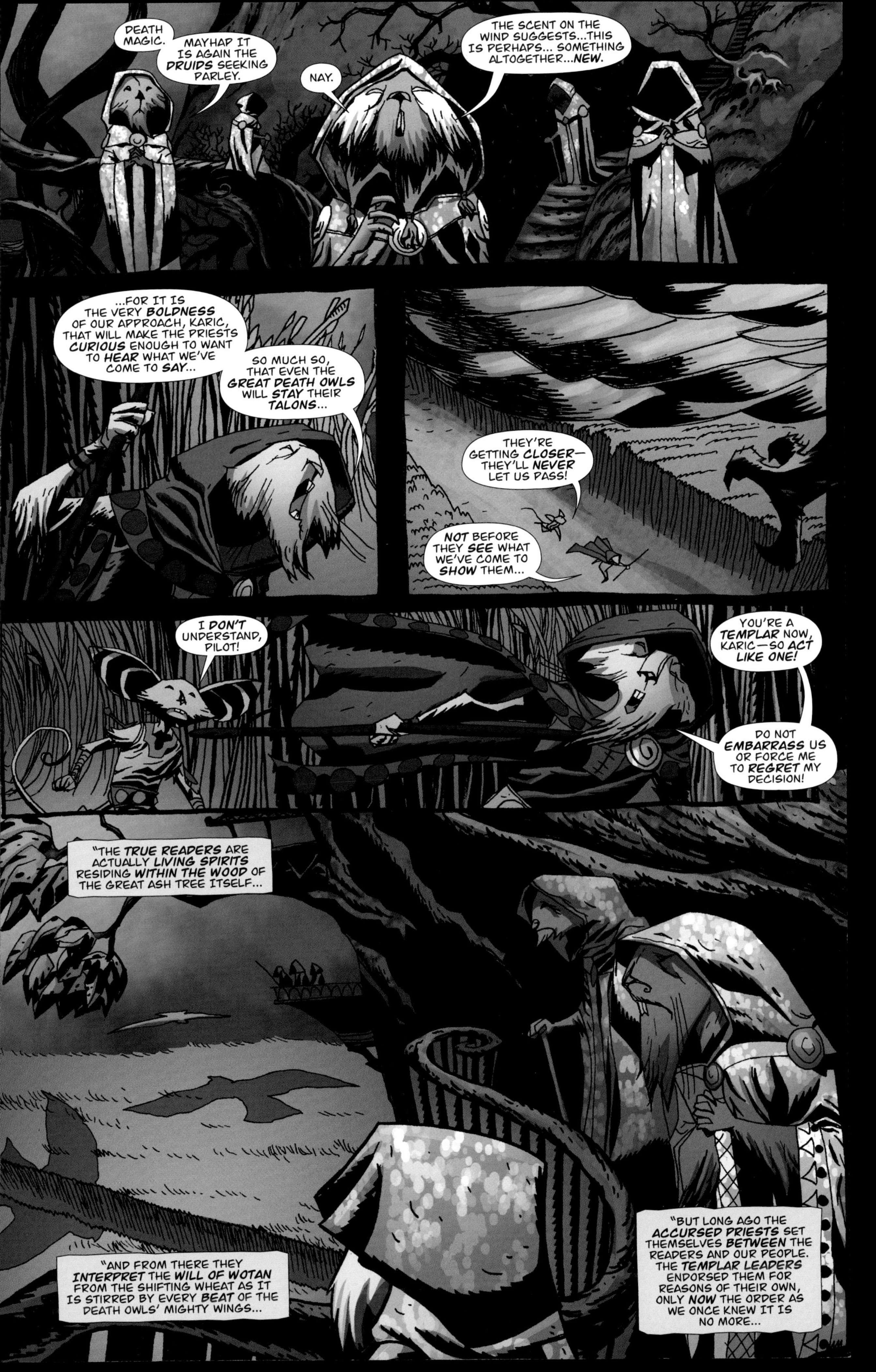
DEATH MAGIC.
MAYHAP IT IS AGAIN THE DRUIDS SEEKING PARLEY.
NAY.
THE SCENT ON THE WIND SUGGESTS...THIS IS PERHAPS... SOMETHING ALTOGETHER...NEW.
...FOR IT IS THE VERY BOLDNESS OF OUR APPROACH, KARIC, THAT WILL MAKE THE PRIESTS CURIOUS ENOUGH TO WANT TO HEAR WHAT WE'VE COME TO SAY...
SO MUCH SO, THAT EVEN THE GREAT DEATH OWLS WILL STAY THEIR TALONS...
THEY'RE GETTING CLOSER—THEY'LL NEVER LET US PASS!
NOT BEFORE THEY SEE WHAT WE'VE COME TO SHOW THEM...
I DON'T UNDERSTAND, PILOT!
YOU'RE A TEMPLAR NOW, KARIC—SO ACT LIKE ONE!
DO NOT EMBARRASS US OR FORCE ME TO REGRET MY DECISION!
"THE TRUE READERS ARE ACTUALLY LIVING SPIRITS RESIDING WITHIN THE WOOD OF THE GREAT ASH TREE ITSELF...
"AND FROM THERE THEY INTERPRET THE WILL OF WOTAN FROM THE SHIFTING WHEAT AS IT IS STIRRED BY EVERY BEAT OF THE DEATH OWLS' MIGHTY WINGS...
"BUT LONG AGO THE ACCURSED PRIESTS SET THEMSELVES BETWEEN THE READERS AND OUR PEOPLE. THE TEMPLAR LEADERS ENDORSED THEM FOR REASONS OF THEIR OWN, ONLY NOW THE ORDER AS WE ONCE KNEW IT IS NO MORE...

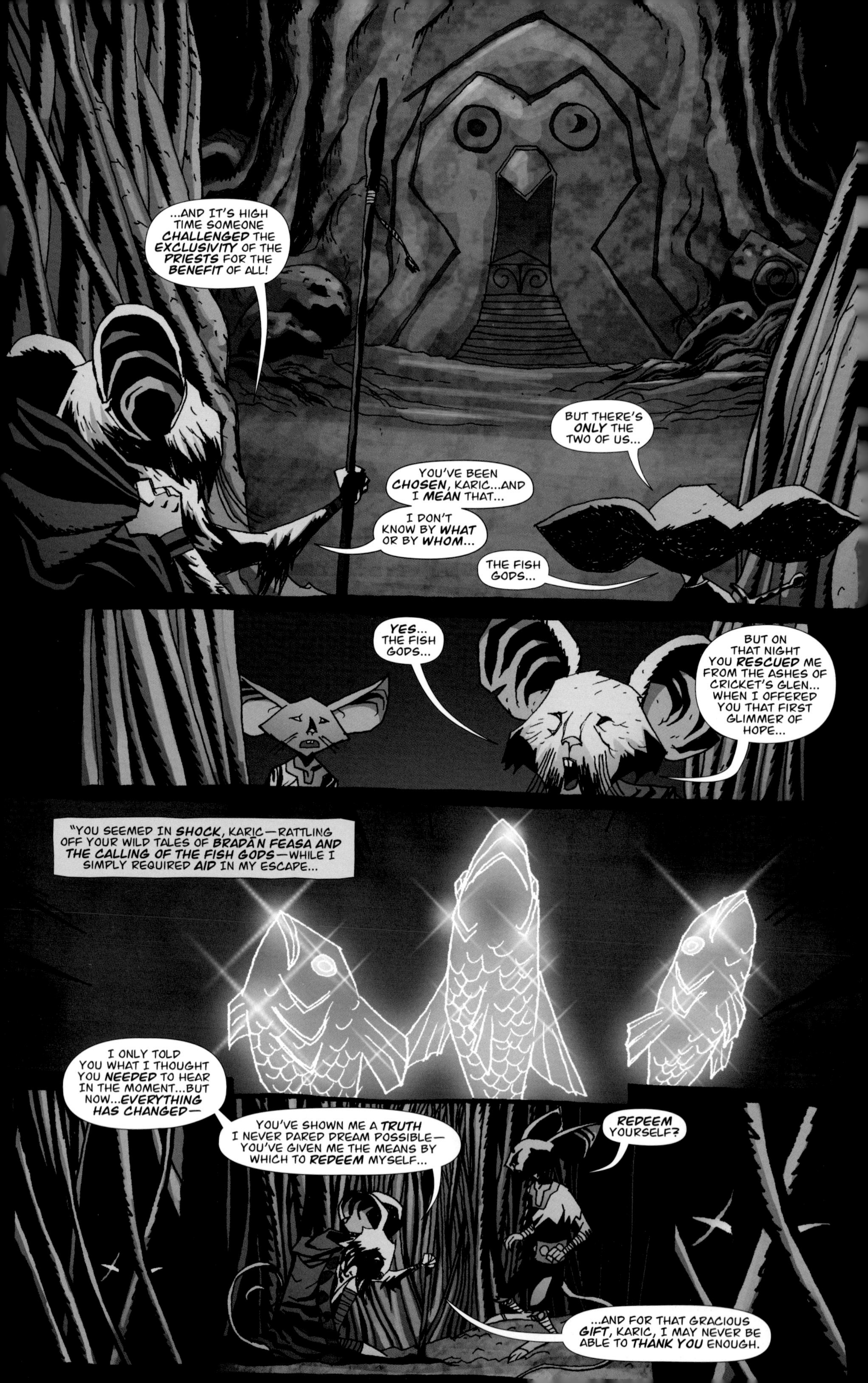
...AND IT'S HIGH TIME SOMEONE CHALLENGED THE EXCLUSIVITY OF THE PRIESTS FOR THE BENEFIT OF ALL!
BUT THERE'S ONLY THE TWO OF US...
YOU'VE BEEN CHOSEN, KARIC...AND I MEAN THAT...
I DON'T KNOW BY WHAT OR BY WHOM...
THE FISH GODS...
YES... THE FISH GODS...
BUT ON THAT NIGHT YOU RESCUED ME FROM THE ASHES OF CRICKET'S GLEN... WHEN I OFFERED YOU THAT FIRST GLIMMER OF HOPE...
"YOU SEEMED IN SHOCK, KARIC—RATTLING OFF YOUR WILD TALES OF BRADĀN FEASA AND THE CALLING OF THE FISH GODS—WHILE I SIMPLY REQUIRED AID IN MY ESCAPE...
I ONLY TOLD YOU WHAT I THOUGHT YOU NEEDED TO HEAR IN THE MOMENT...BUT NOW...EVERYTHING HAS CHANGED—
YOU'VE SHOWN ME A TRUTH I NEVER DARED DREAM POSSIBLE—YOU'VE GIVEN ME THE MEANS BY WHICH TO REDEEM MYSELF...
REDEEM YOURSELF?
...AND FOR THAT GRACIOUS GIFT, KARIC, I MAY NEVER BE ABLE TO THANK YOU ENOUGH.

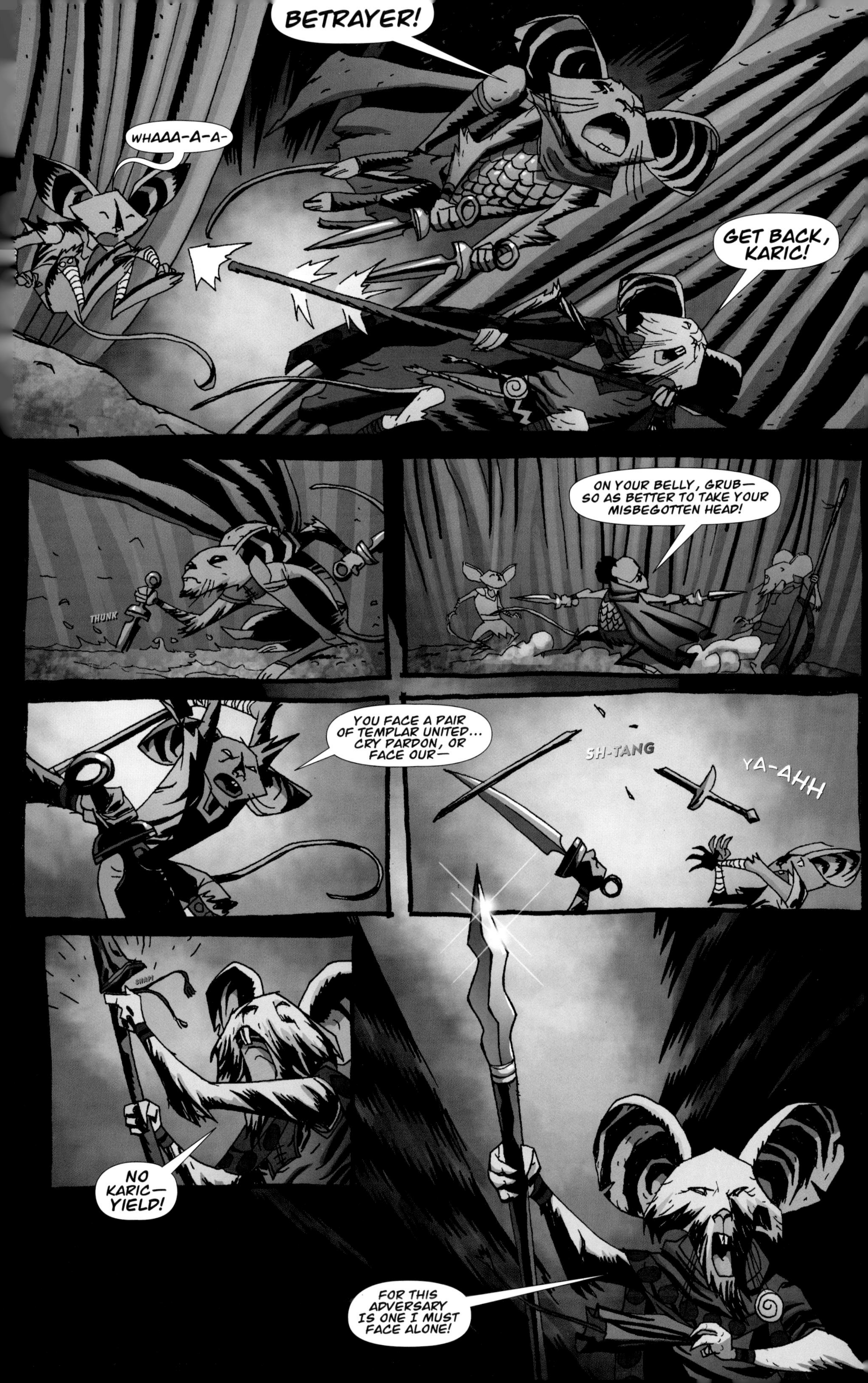
BETRAYER!
WHAAA-A-A-
GET BACK, KARIC!
THUNK
ON YOUR BELLY, GRUB— SO AS BETTER TO TAKE YOUR MISBEGOTTEN HEAD!
YOU FACE A PAIR OF TEMPLAR UNITED... CRY PARDON, OR FACE OUR—
SH-TANG
YA-AHH
SNAP!
NO KARIC— YIELD!
FOR THIS ADVERSARY IS ONE I MUST FACE ALONE!

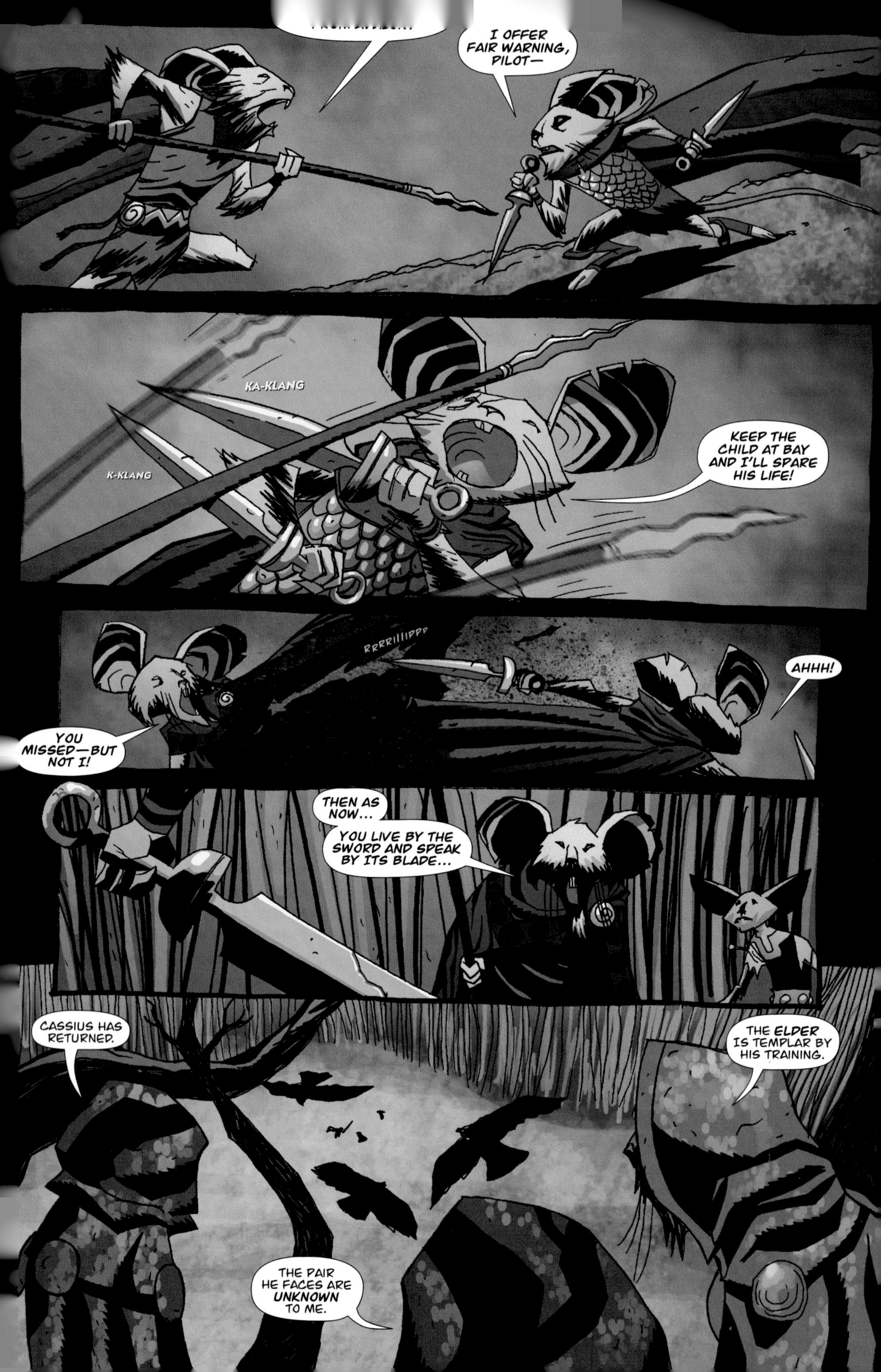

I OFFER FAIR WARNING, PILOT—
KA-KLANG
K-KLANG
KEEP THE CHILD AT BAY AND I'LL SPARE HIS LIFE!
RRRRIIIIPPP
AHHH!
YOU MISSED—BUT NOT I!
THEN AS NOW...
YOU LIVE BY THE SWORD AND SPEAK BY ITS BLADE...
CASSIUS HAS RETURNED.
THE ELDER IS TEMPLAR BY HIS TRAINING.
THE PAIR HE FACES ARE UNKNOWN TO ME.

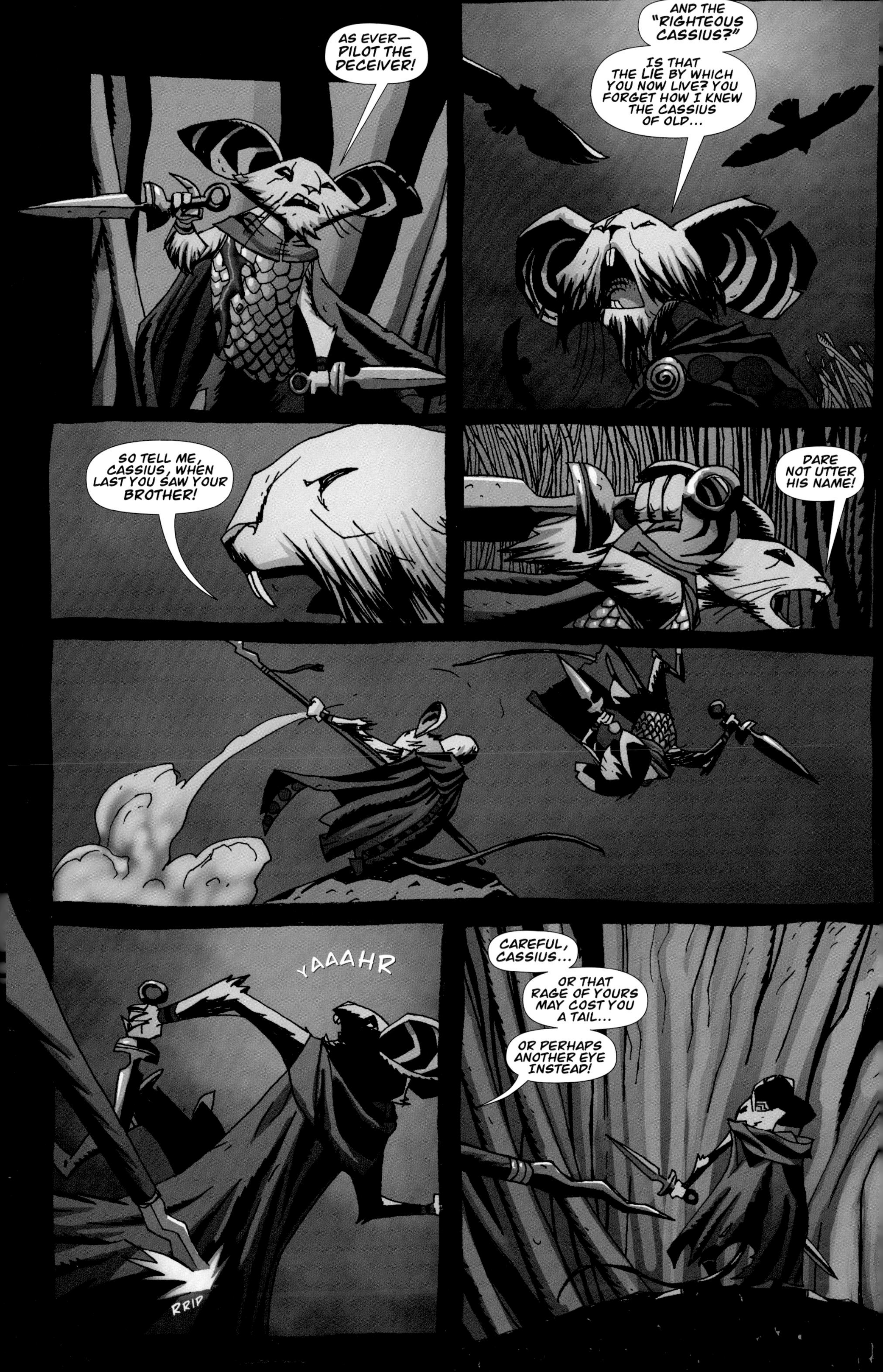
AS EVER—
PILOT THE DECEIVER!
AND THE "RIGHTEOUS CASSIUS?"
IS THAT THE LIE BY WHICH YOU NOW LIVE? YOU FORGET HOW I KNEW THE CASSIUS OF OLD...
SO TELL ME, CASSIUS, WHEN LAST YOU SAW YOUR BROTHER!
DARE NOT UTTER HIS NAME!
YAAAHR
RRIP
CAREFUL, CASSIUS...
OR THAT RAGE OF YOURS MAY COST YOU A TAIL...
OR PERHAPS ANOTHER EYE INSTEAD!

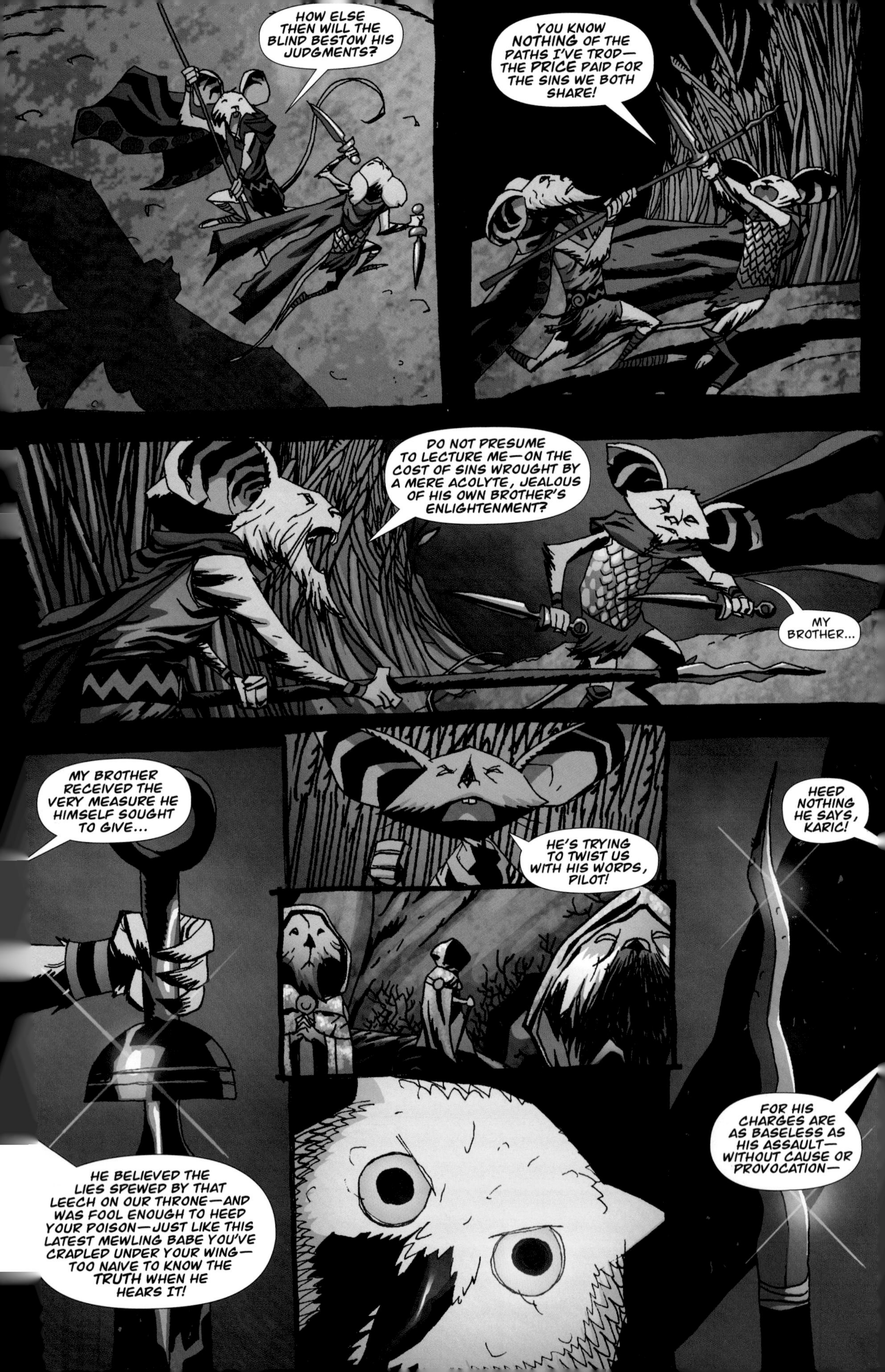
HOW ELSE THEN WILL THE BLIND BESTOW HIS JUDGMENTS?
YOU KNOW NOTHING OF THE PATHS I'VE TROD— THE PRICE PAID FOR THE SINS WE BOTH SHARE!
DO NOT PRESUME TO LECTURE ME—ON THE COST OF SINS WROUGHT BY A MERE ACOLYTE, JEALOUS OF HIS OWN BROTHER'S ENLIGHTENMENT?
MY BROTHER...
MY BROTHER RECEIVED THE VERY MEASURE HE HIMSELF SOUGHT TO GIVE...
HE'S TRYING TO TWIST US WITH HIS WORDS, PILOT!
HEED NOTHING HE SAYS, KARIC!
HE BELIEVED THE LIES SPEWED BY THAT LEECH ON OUR THRONE—AND WAS FOOL ENOUGH TO HEED YOUR POISON—JUST LIKE THIS LATEST MEWLING BABE YOU'VE CRADLED UNDER YOUR WING—TOO NAIVE TO KNOW THE TRUTH WHEN HE HEARS IT!
FOR HIS CHARGES ARE AS BASELESS AS HIS ASSAULT—WITHOUT CAUSE OR PROVOCATION—

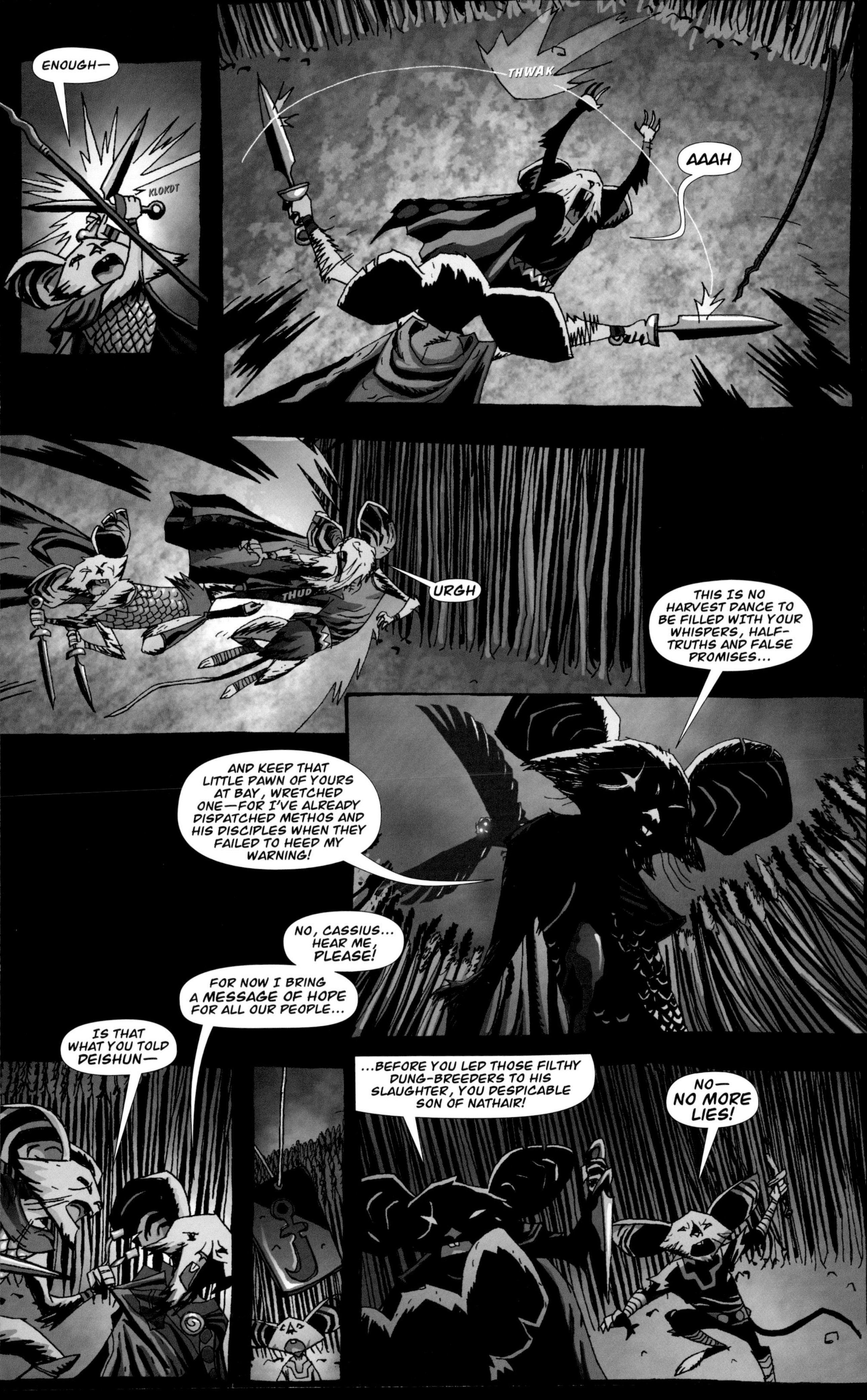
ENOUGH—
KLOKDT
THWAK
AAAH
THUD
URGH
THIS IS NO HARVEST DANCE TO BE FILLED WITH YOUR WHISPERS, HALF-TRUTHS AND FALSE PROMISES...
AND KEEP THAT LITTLE PAWN OF YOURS AT BAY, WRETCHED ONE—FOR I'VE ALREADY DISPATCHED METHOS AND HIS DISCIPLES WHEN THEY FAILED TO HEED MY WARNING!
NO, CASSIUS... HEAR ME, PLEASE!
FOR NOW I BRING A MESSAGE OF HOPE FOR ALL OUR PEOPLE...
IS THAT WHAT YOU TOLD DEISHUN—
...BEFORE YOU LED THOSE FILTHY DUNG-BREEDERS TO HIS SLAUGHTER, YOU DESPICABLE SON OF NATHAIR!
NO— NO MORE LIES!

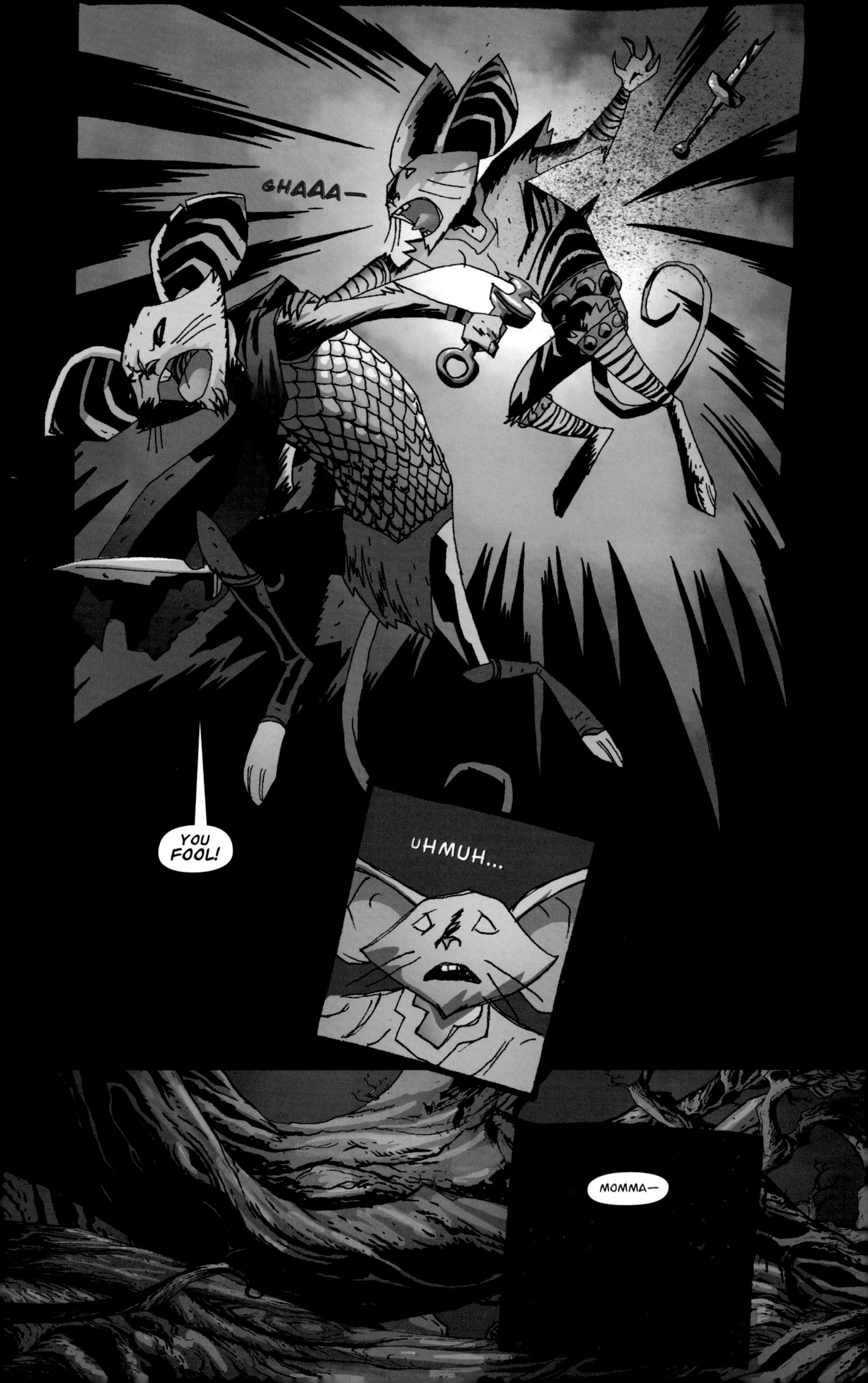
GHAAA—
YOU FOOL!
UHMUH...
MOMMA—

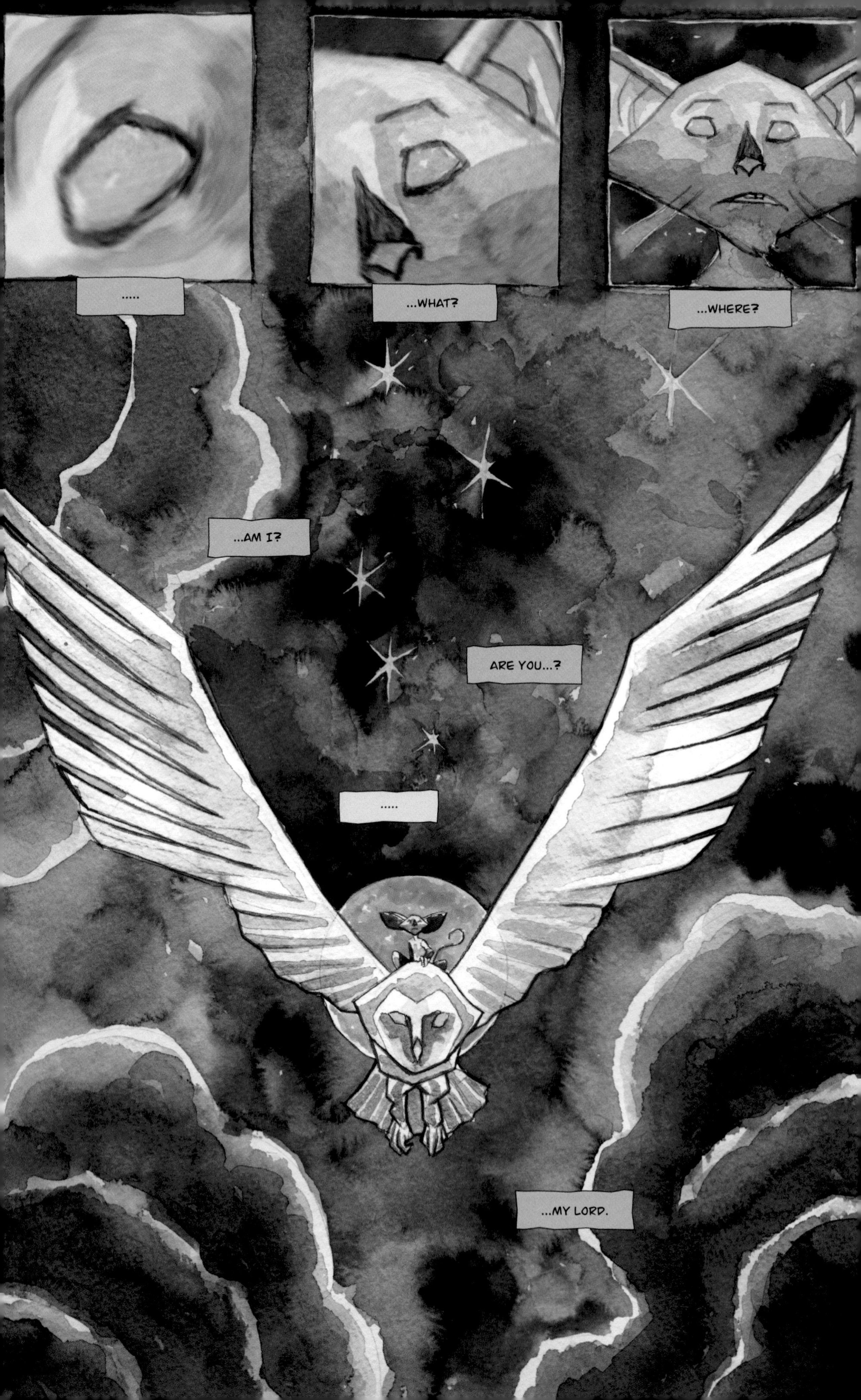
.....
...WHAT?
...WHERE?
...AM I?
ARE YOU...?
.....
...MY LORD.

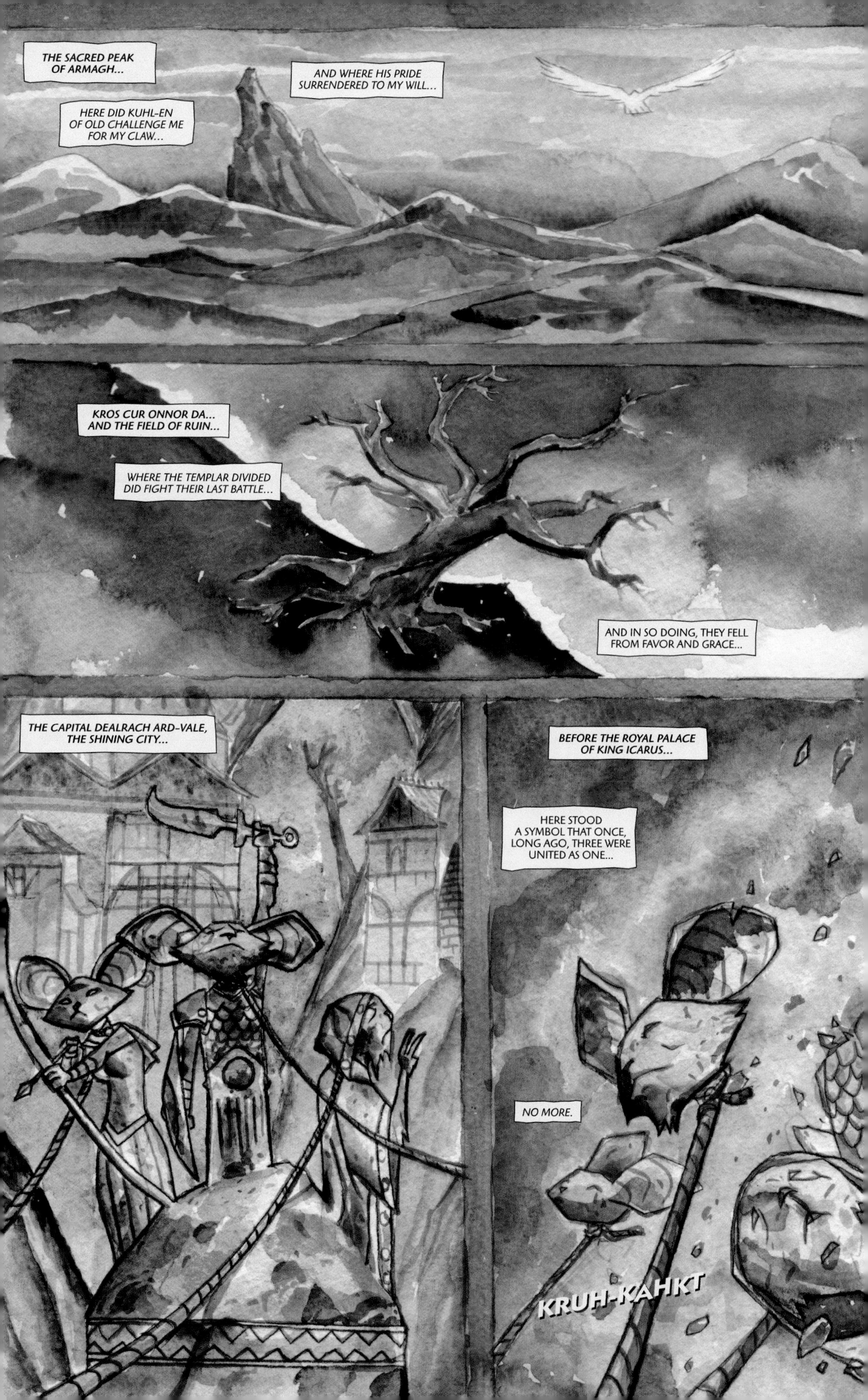
THE SACRED PEAK OF ARMAGH...
HERE DID KUHL-EN OF OLD CHALLENGE ME FOR MY CLAW...
AND WHERE HIS PRIDE SURRENDERED TO MY WILL...
KROS CUR ONNOR DA... AND THE FIELD OF RUIN...
WHERE THE TEMPLAR DIVIDED DID FIGHT THEIR LAST BATTLE...
AND IN SO DOING, THEY FELL FROM FAVOR AND GRACE...
THE CAPITAL DEALRACH ARD-VALE, THE SHINING CITY...
BEFORE THE ROYAL PALACE OF KING ICARUS...
HERE STOOD A SYMBOL THAT ONCE, LONG AGO, THREE WERE UNITED AS ONE...
NO MORE.
KRUH-KAHKT

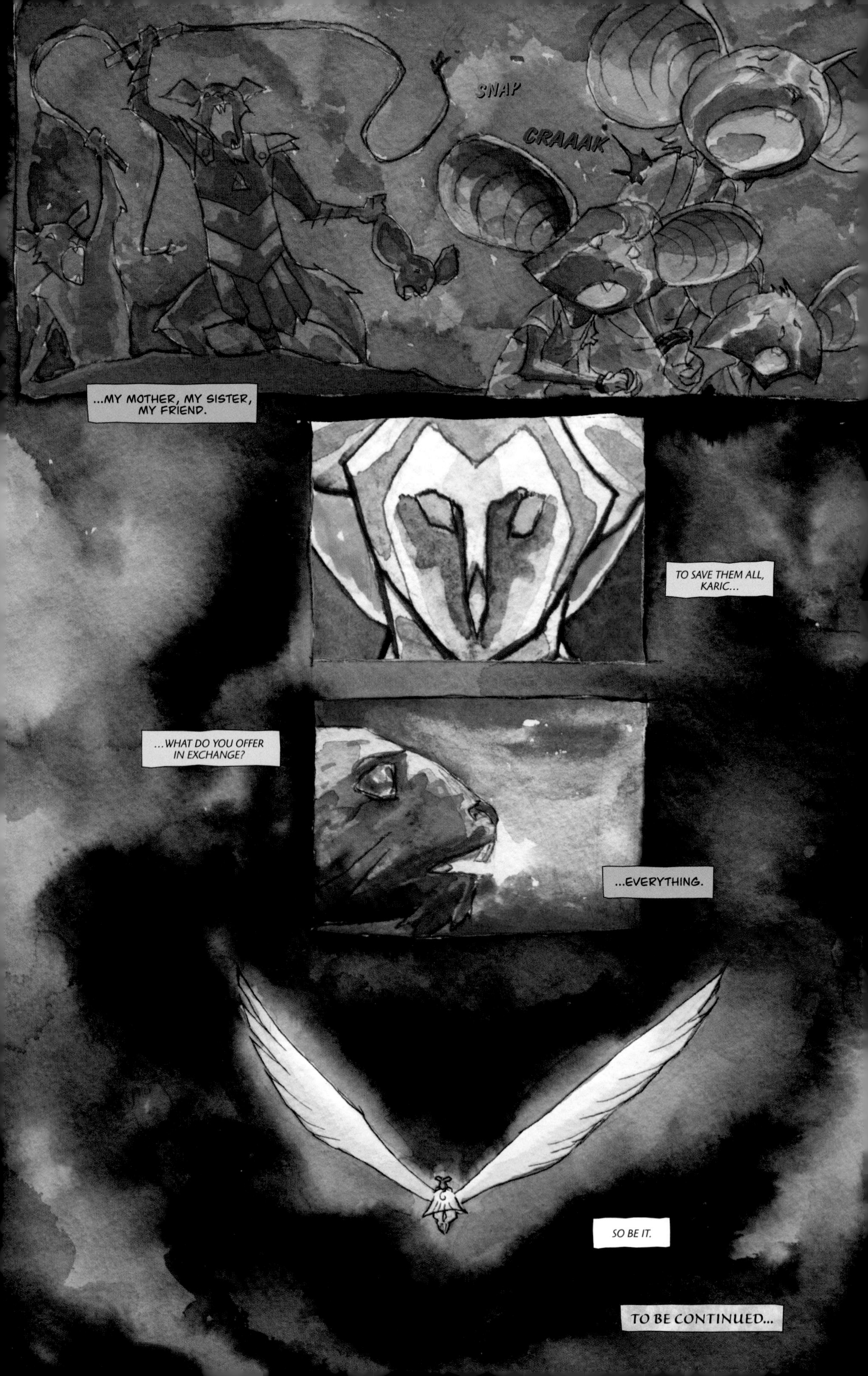
SNAP
CRAAAK
...MY MOTHER, MY SISTER, MY FRIEND.
TO SAVE THEM ALL, KARIC...
...WHAT DO YOU OFFER IN EXCHANGE?
...EVERYTHING.
SO BE IT.
TO BE CONTINUED...

CHAPTER SIX
TRUTH BEHIND THE LIES

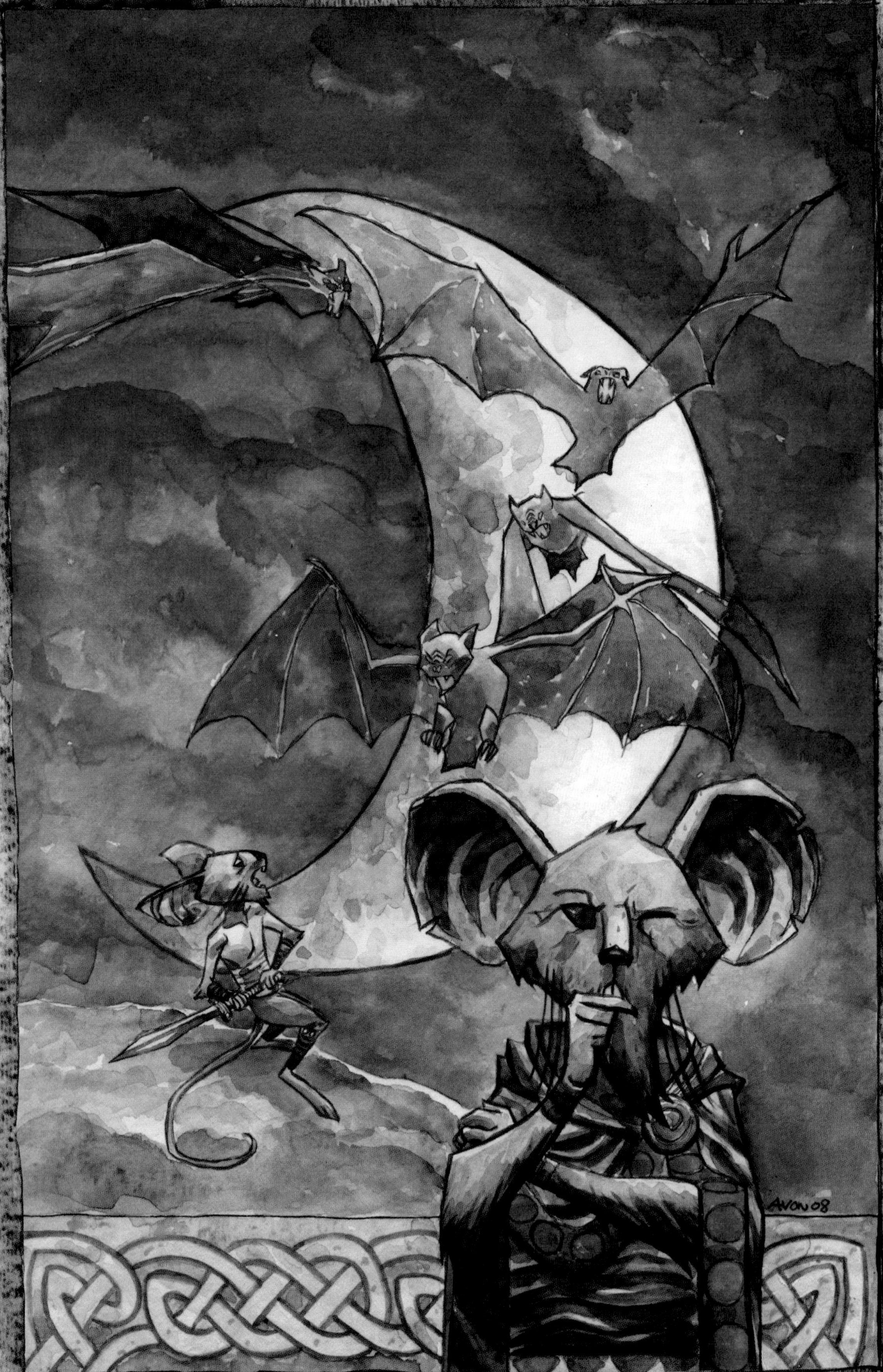
AVON 08

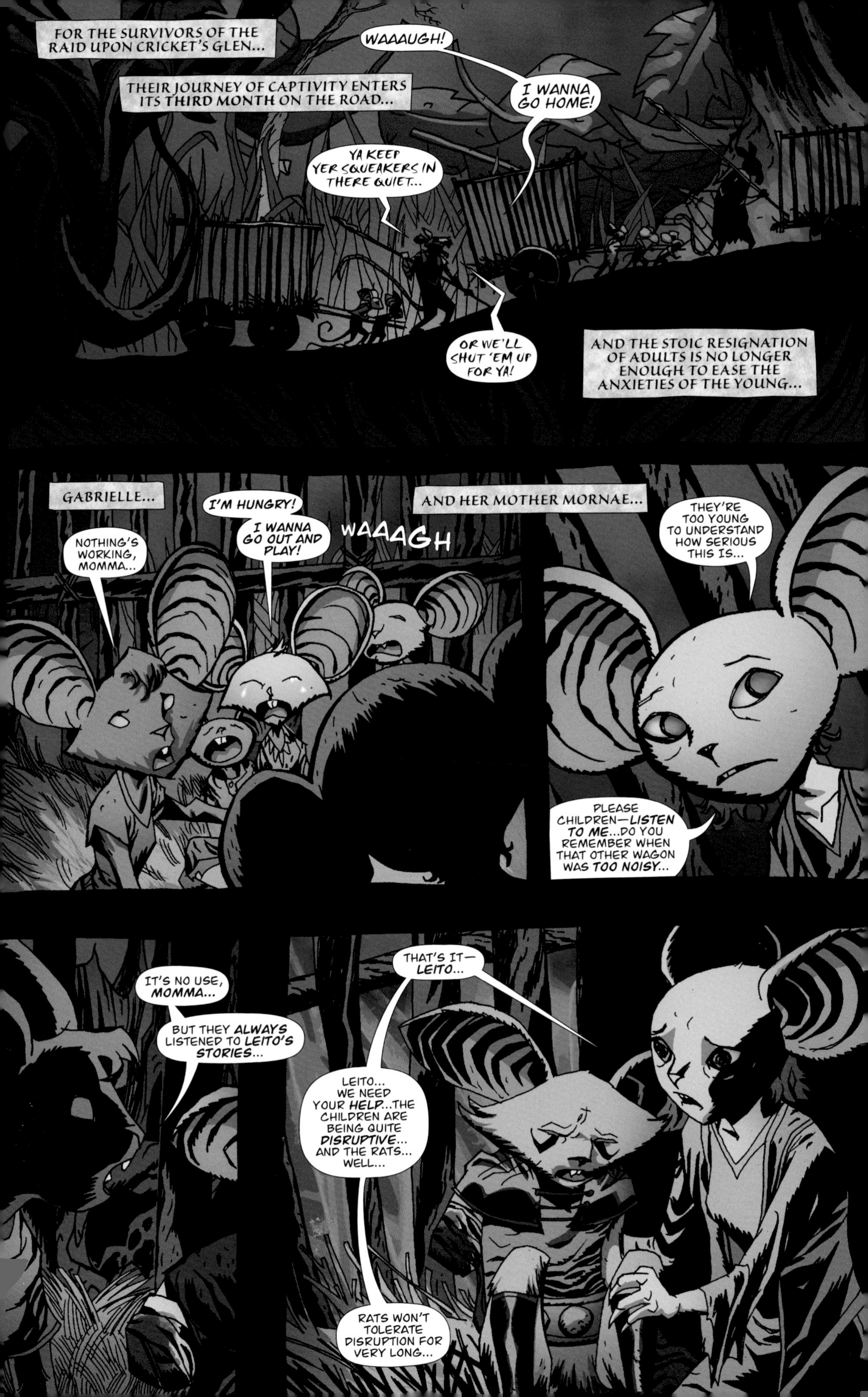
FOR THE SURVIVORS OF THE RAID UPON CRICKET'S GLEN...
THEIR JOURNEY OF CAPTIVITY ENTERS ITS THIRD MONTH ON THE ROAD...
WAAAUGH!
I WANNA GO HOME!
YA KEEP YER SQUEAKERS IN THERE QUIET...
OR WE'LL SHUT 'EM UP FOR YA!
AND THE STOIC RESIGNATION OF ADULTS IS NO LONGER ENOUGH TO EASE THE ANXIETIES OF THE YOUNG...
GABRIELLE...
NOTHING'S WORKING, MOMMA...
I'M HUNGRY!
I WANNA GO OUT AND PLAY!
WAAAGH
AND HER MOTHER MORNAE...
THEY'RE TOO YOUNG TO UNDERSTAND HOW SERIOUS THIS IS...
PLEASE CHILDREN—LISTEN TO ME...DO YOU REMEMBER WHEN THAT OTHER WAGON WAS TOO NOISY...
IT'S NO USE, MOMMA...
BUT THEY ALWAYS LISTENED TO LEITO'S STORIES...
THAT'S IT—LEITO...
LEITO... WE NEED YOUR HELP...THE CHILDREN ARE BEING QUITE DISRUPTIVE... AND THE RATS... WELL...
RATS WON'T TOLERATE DISRUPTION FOR VERY LONG...

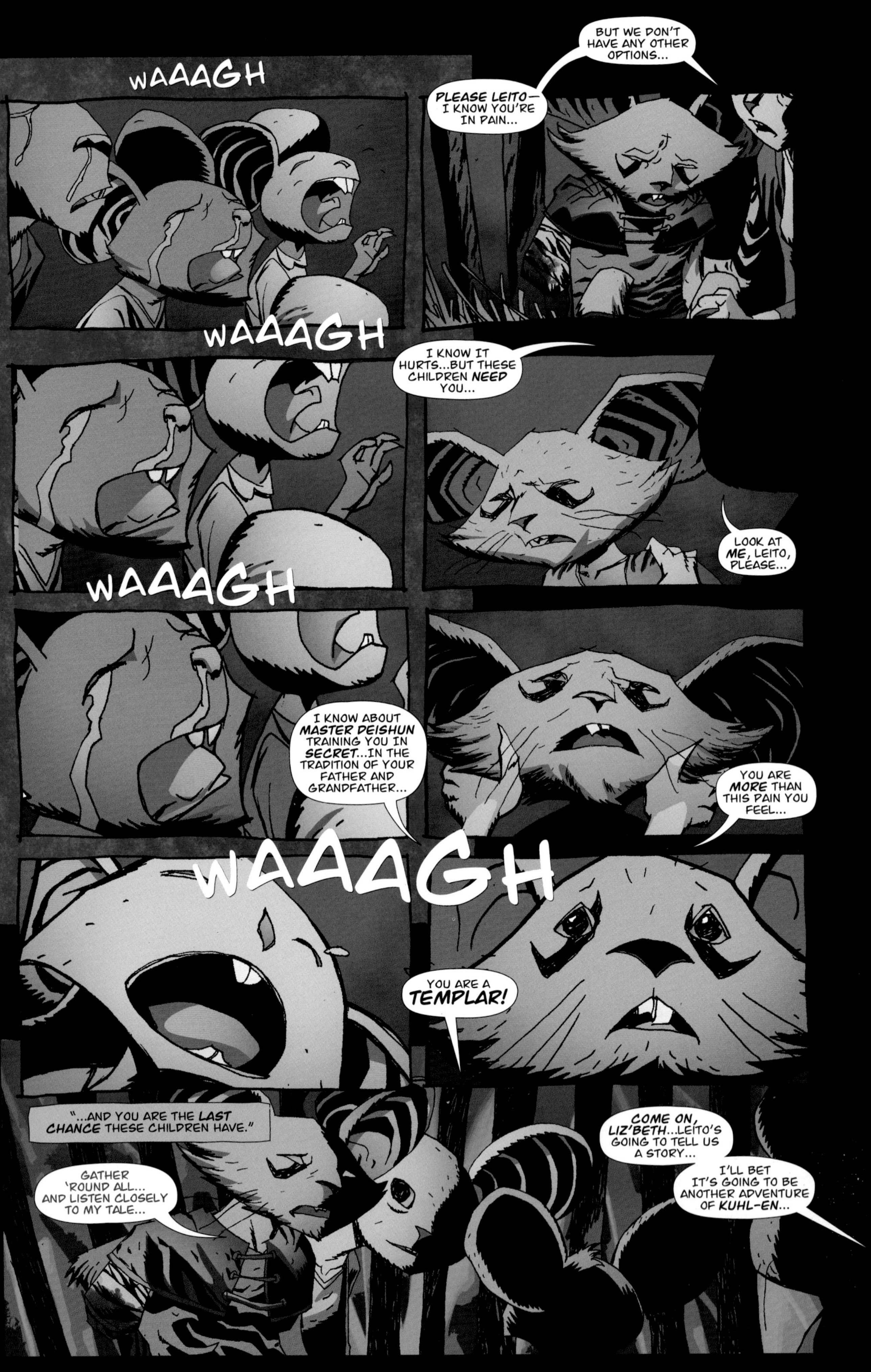
WAAAGH
PLEASE LEITO— I KNOW YOU'RE IN PAIN...
BUT WE DON'T HAVE ANY OTHER OPTIONS...
WAAAGH
I KNOW IT HURTS...BUT THESE CHILDREN NEED YOU...
LOOK AT ME, LEITO, PLEASE...
WAAAGH
I KNOW ABOUT MASTER DEISHUN TRAINING YOU IN SECRET...IN THE TRADITION OF YOUR FATHER AND GRANDFATHER...
YOU ARE MORE THAN THIS PAIN YOU FEEL...
WAAAGH
YOU ARE A TEMPLAR!
"...AND YOU ARE THE LAST CHANCE THESE CHILDREN HAVE."
GATHER 'ROUND ALL... AND LISTEN CLOSELY TO MY TALE...
COME ON, LIZ'BETH...LEITO'S GOING TO TELL US A STORY...
I'LL BET IT'S GOING TO BE ANOTHER ADVENTURE OF KUHL-EN...

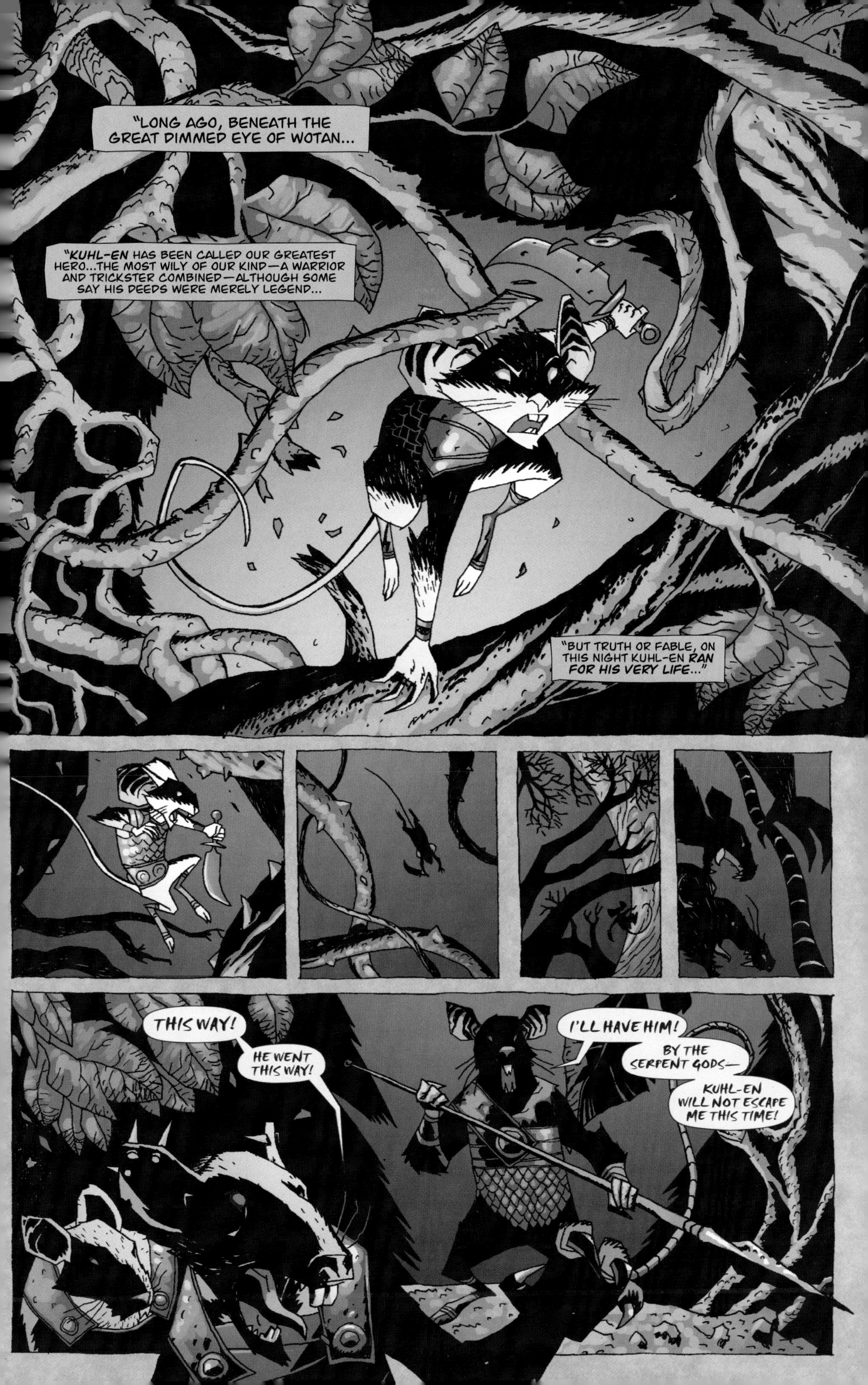
"LONG AGO, BENEATH THE GREAT DIMMED EYE OF WOTAN...
"KUHL-EN HAS BEEN CALLED OUR GREATEST HERO...THE MOST WILY OF OUR KIND—A WARRIOR AND TRICKSTER COMBINED—ALTHOUGH SOME SAY HIS DEEDS WERE MERELY LEGEND...
"BUT TRUTH OR FABLE, ON THIS NIGHT KUHL-EN RAN FOR HIS VERY LIFE..."
THIS WAY!
HE WENT THIS WAY!
I'LL HAVE HIM!
BY THE SERPENT GODS—
KUHL-EN WILL NOT ESCAPE ME THIS TIME!

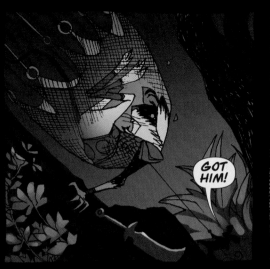

GOT HIM!
WE HAVE HIM, SIR—
KUHL-EN!
"BUT IT WAS NOT KUHL-EN'S ENEMIES THAT HAD SNARED HIM...
THE "MIGHTY KUHL-EN" RETURNS.
BUT WHERE IS THE ARMY HE PROMISED WOULD RETURN WITH HIM TO AID IN OUR STRUGGLE AGAINST THE RATS?
YOU MUST RELEASE ME!
EVEN AS WE SPEAK, A RAT RAIDING PARTY IS HARD UPON MY TRAIL, LED STRAIGHT INTO OUR TRAP, JUST AS WE'D PLANNED!
DECEIVER!
YOU COME ALONE...
AND I SAY TO ALL OF YOU THAT KUHL-EN HAS STRUCK A DEAL WITH THE RATS TO SELL US ALL INTO SLAVERY.
NO!
YOU MUST TRUST ME. WOTAN HAS NOT ABANDONED ANY OF YOU.
HAVE FAITH. THAT IS ALL HE ASKS OF US.
YOU STILL CLAIM TO SPEAK FOR WOTAN?
WELL, THE EYE OF WOTAN SLEEPS THIS NIGHT, AND OFFERS US NO FAVOR...
I HOLD THE SACRED BLADE.
I NOW SPEAK FOR WOTAN!
AND TONIGHT WE SEND A MESSAGE TO ALL OUR OPPRESSORS THAT WE WILL NOT BE DUPED INTO CAPTIVITY.
SO I SAY THAT WE SPILL THE BLOOD OF THIS SELF-PROCLAIMED SAVIOR AND LEAVE IT FOR THE RATS TO DRINK!

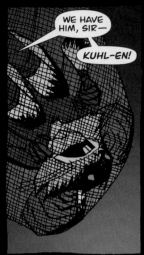

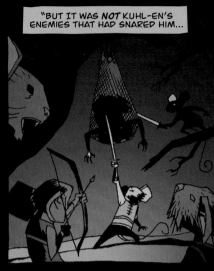

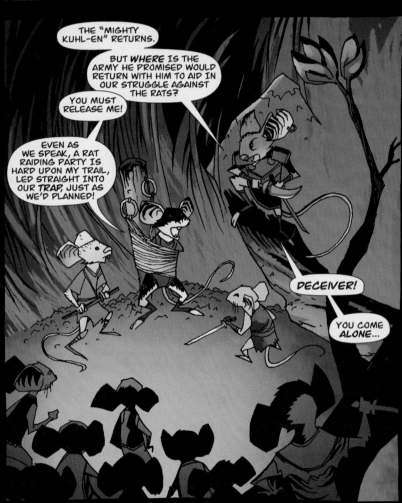

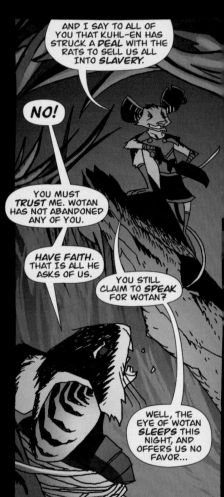

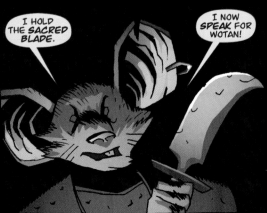

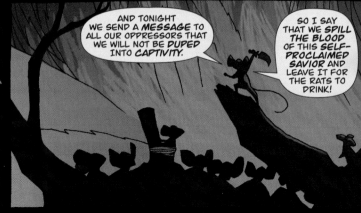

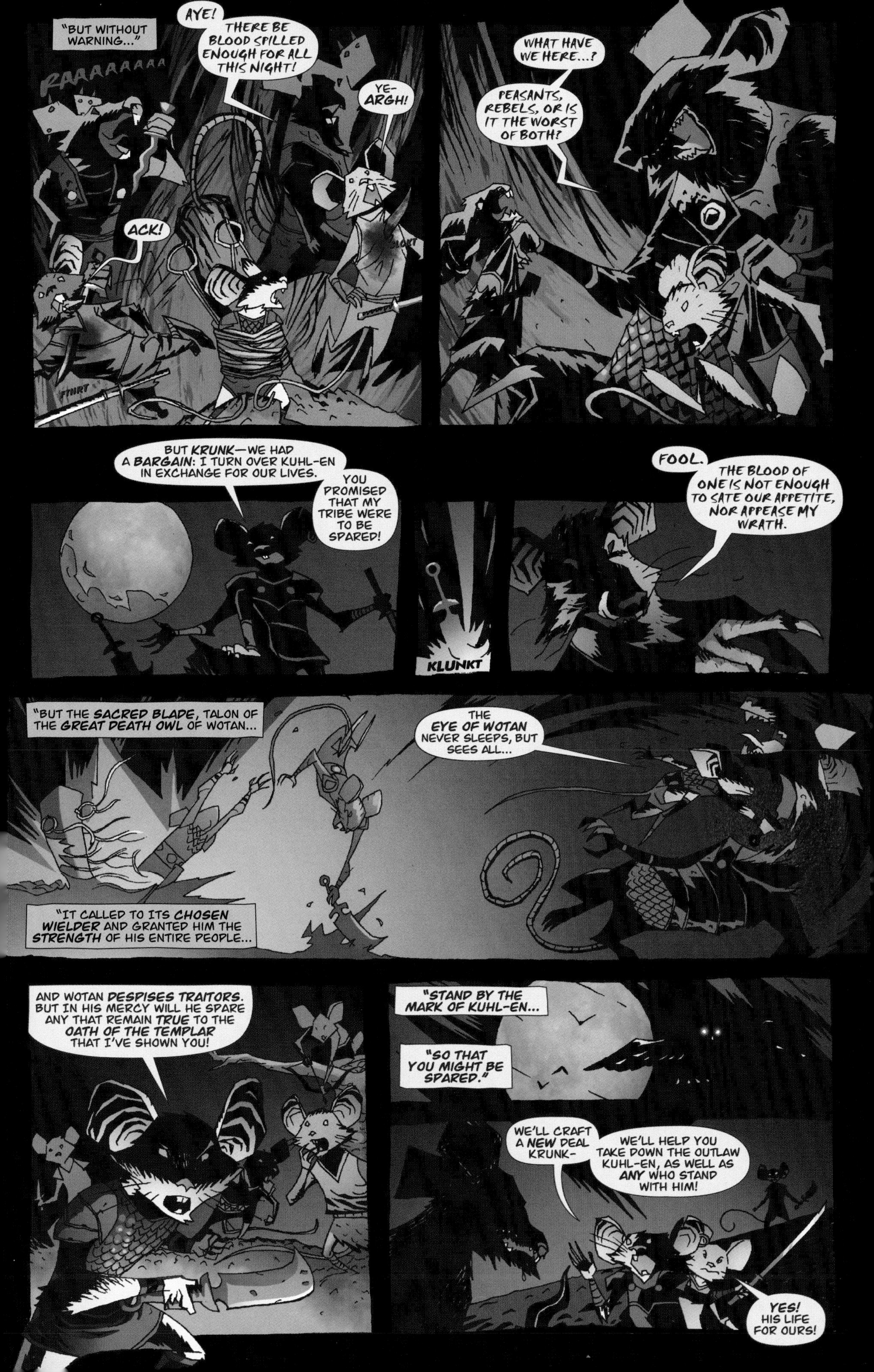
"BUT WITHOUT WARNING..."
RAAAAAAAAAA
AYE! THERE BE BLOOD SPILLED ENOUGH FOR ALL THIS NIGHT!
YE-ARGH!
ACK!
WHAT HAVE WE HERE...?
PEASANTS, REBELS, OR IS IT THE WORST OF BOTH?
BUT KRUNK—WE HAD A BARGAIN: I TURN OVER KUHL-EN IN EXCHANGE FOR OUR LIVES.
YOU PROMISED THAT MY TRIBE WERE TO BE SPARED!
KLUNKT
FOOL.
THE BLOOD OF ONE IS NOT ENOUGH TO SATE OUR APPETITE, NOR APPEASE MY WRATH.
"BUT THE SACRED BLADE, TALON OF THE GREAT DEATH OWL OF WOTAN...
THE EYE OF WOTAN NEVER SLEEPS, BUT SEES ALL...
"IT CALLED TO ITS CHOSEN WIELDER AND GRANTED HIM THE STRENGTH OF HIS ENTIRE PEOPLE...
AND WOTAN DESPISES TRAITORS. BUT IN HIS MERCY WILL HE SPARE ANY THAT REMAIN TRUE TO THE OATH OF THE TEMPLAR THAT I'VE SHOWN YOU!
"STAND BY THE MARK OF KUHL-EN...
"SO THAT YOU MIGHT BE SPARED."
WE'LL CRAFT A NEW DEAL KRUNK-
WE'LL HELP YOU TAKE DOWN THE OUTLAW KUHL-EN, AS WELL AS ANY WHO STAND WITH HIM!
YES! HIS LIFE FOR OURS!

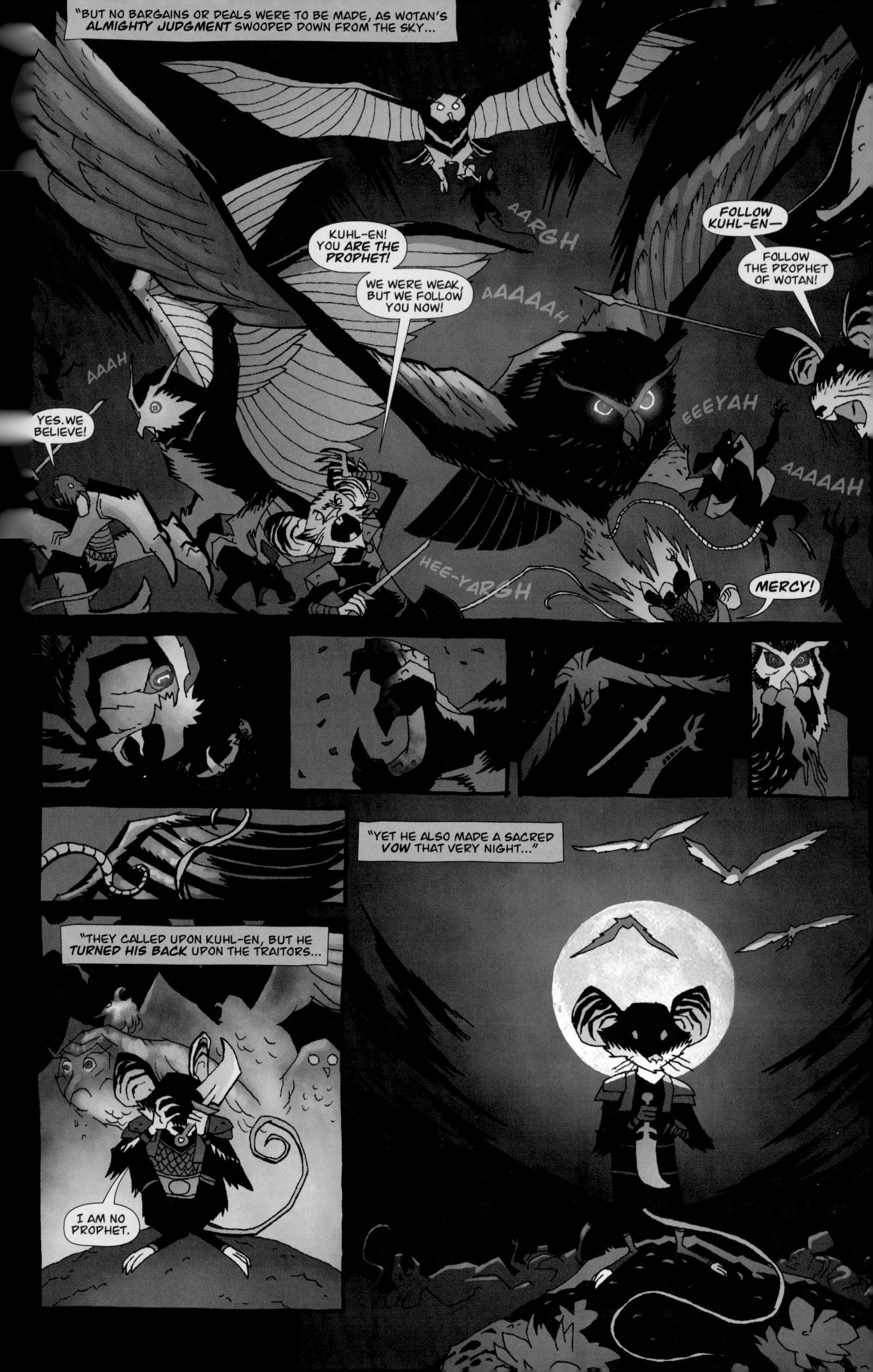
"BUT NO BARGAINS OR DEALS WERE TO BE MADE, AS WOTAN'S ALMIGHTY JUDGMENT SWOOPED DOWN FROM THE SKY...
AARGH
KUHL-EN! YOU ARE THE PROPHET!
WE WERE WEAK, BUT WE FOLLOW YOU NOW!
AAAAAH
FOLLOW KUHL-EN—
FOLLOW THE PROPHET OF WOTAN!
AAAH
YES. WE BELIEVE!
EEEYAH
AAAAAH
HEE-YARGH
MERCY!
"YET HE ALSO MADE A SACRED VOW THAT VERY NIGHT..."
"THEY CALLED UPON KUHL-EN, BUT HE TURNED HIS BACK UPON THE TRAITORS...
I AM NO PROPHET.

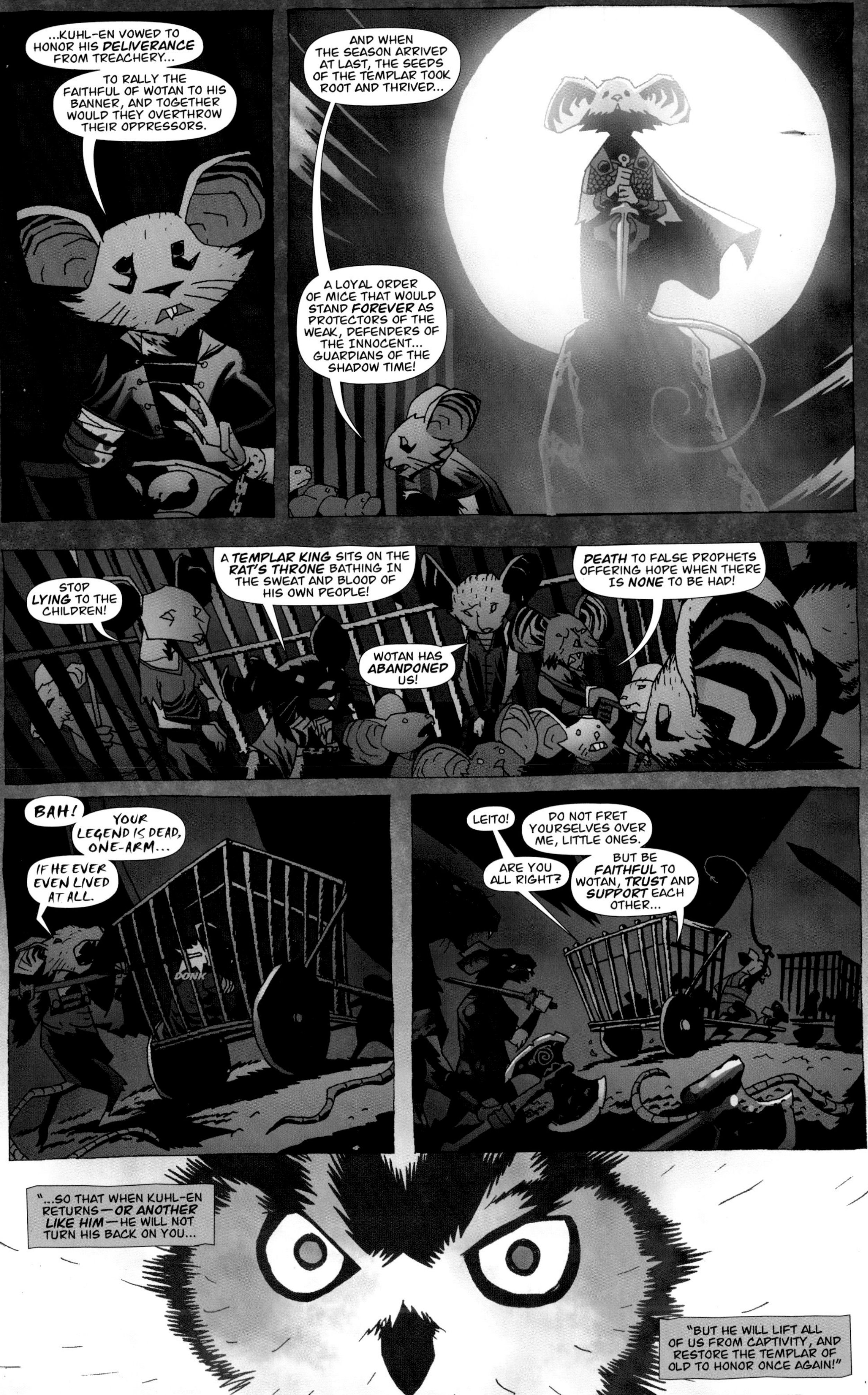

...KUHL-EN VOWED TO HONOR HIS DELIVERANCE FROM TREACHERY...
TO RALLY THE FAITHFUL OF WOTAN TO HIS BANNER, AND TOGETHER WOULD THEY OVERTHROW THEIR OPPRESSORS.
AND WHEN THE SEASON ARRIVED AT LAST, THE SEEDS OF THE TEMPLAR TOOK ROOT AND THRIVED...
A LOYAL ORDER OF MICE THAT WOULD STAND FOREVER AS PROTECTORS OF THE WEAK, DEFENDERS OF THE INNOCENT... GUARDIANS OF THE SHADOW TIME!
STOP LYING TO THE CHILDREN!
A TEMPLAR KING SITS ON THE RAT'S THRONE BATHING IN THE SWEAT AND BLOOD OF HIS OWN PEOPLE!
WOTAN HAS ABANDONED US!
DEATH TO FALSE PROPHETS OFFERING HOPE WHEN THERE IS NONE TO BE HAD!
BAH!
YOUR LEGEND IS DEAD, ONE-ARM...
IF HE EVER EVEN LIVED AT ALL.
DONK
LEITO!
ARE YOU ALL RIGHT?
DO NOT FRET YOURSELVES OVER ME, LITTLE ONES.
BUT BE FAITHFUL TO WOTAN, TRUST AND SUPPORT EACH OTHER...
"...SO THAT WHEN KUHL-EN RETURNS—OR ANOTHER LIKE HIM—HE WILL NOT TURN HIS BACK ON YOU...
"BUT HE WILL LIFT ALL OF US FROM CAPTIVITY, AND RESTORE THE TEMPLAR OF OLD TO HONOR ONCE AGAIN!"

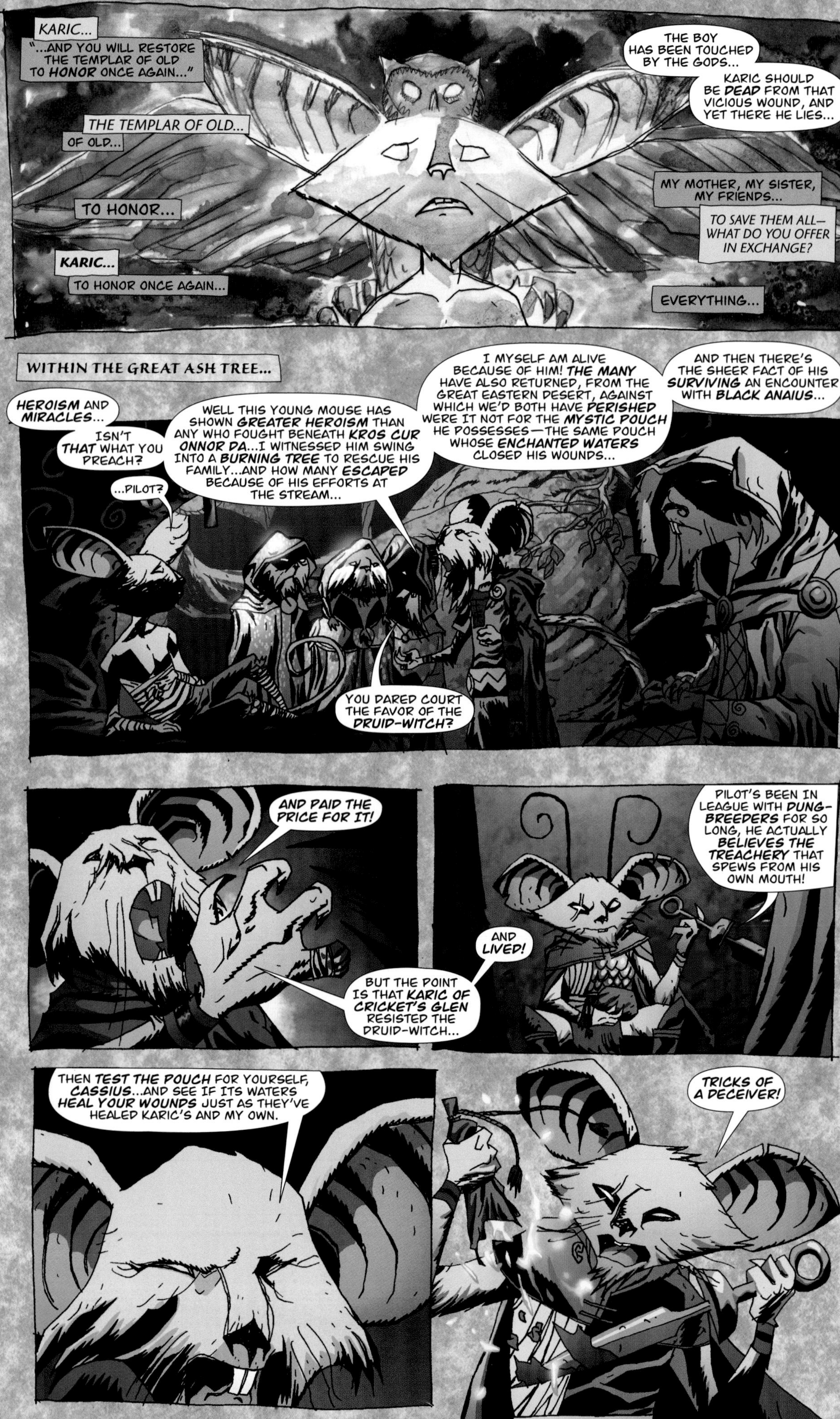
KARIC...
"...AND YOU WILL RESTORE THE TEMPLAR OF OLD TO HONOR ONCE AGAIN..."
THE TEMPLAR OF OLD...
OF OLD...
TO HONOR...
KARIC...
TO HONOR ONCE AGAIN...
THE BOY HAS BEEN TOUCHED BY THE GODS...
KARIC SHOULD BE DEAD FROM THAT VICIOUS WOUND, AND YET THERE HE LIES...
MY MOTHER, MY SISTER, MY FRIENDS...
TO SAVE THEM ALL— WHAT DO YOU OFFER IN EXCHANGE?
EVERYTHING...
WITHIN THE GREAT ASH TREE...
HEROISM AND MIRACLES...
ISN'T THAT WHAT YOU PREACH?
...PILOT?
WELL THIS YOUNG MOUSE HAS SHOWN GREATER HEROISM THAN ANY WHO FOUGHT BENEATH KROS CUR ONNOR DA...I WITNESSED HIM SWING INTO A BURNING TREE TO RESCUE HIS FAMILY...AND HOW MANY ESCAPED BECAUSE OF HIS EFFORTS AT THE STREAM...
I MYSELF AM ALIVE BECAUSE OF HIM! THE MANY HAVE ALSO RETURNED, FROM THE GREAT EASTERN DESERT, AGAINST WHICH WE'D BOTH HAVE PERISHED WERE IT NOT FOR THE MYSTIC POUCH HE POSSESSES—THE SAME POUCH WHOSE ENCHANTED WATERS CLOSED HIS WOUNDS...
AND THEN THERE'S THE SHEER FACT OF HIS SURVIVING AN ENCOUNTER WITH BLACK ANAIUS...
YOU DARED COURT THE FAVOR OF THE DRUID-WITCH?
AND PAID THE PRICE FOR IT!
AND LIVED!
BUT THE POINT IS THAT KARIC OF CRICKET'S GLEN RESISTED THE DRUID-WITCH...
PILOT'S BEEN IN LEAGUE WITH DUNG-BREEDERS FOR SO LONG, HE ACTUALLY BELIEVES THE TREACHERY THAT SPEWS FROM HIS OWN MOUTH!
THEN TEST THE POUCH FOR YOURSELF, CASSIUS...AND SEE IF ITS WATERS HEAL YOUR WOUNDS JUST AS THEY'VE HEALED KARIC'S AND MY OWN.
TRICKS OF A DECEIVER!

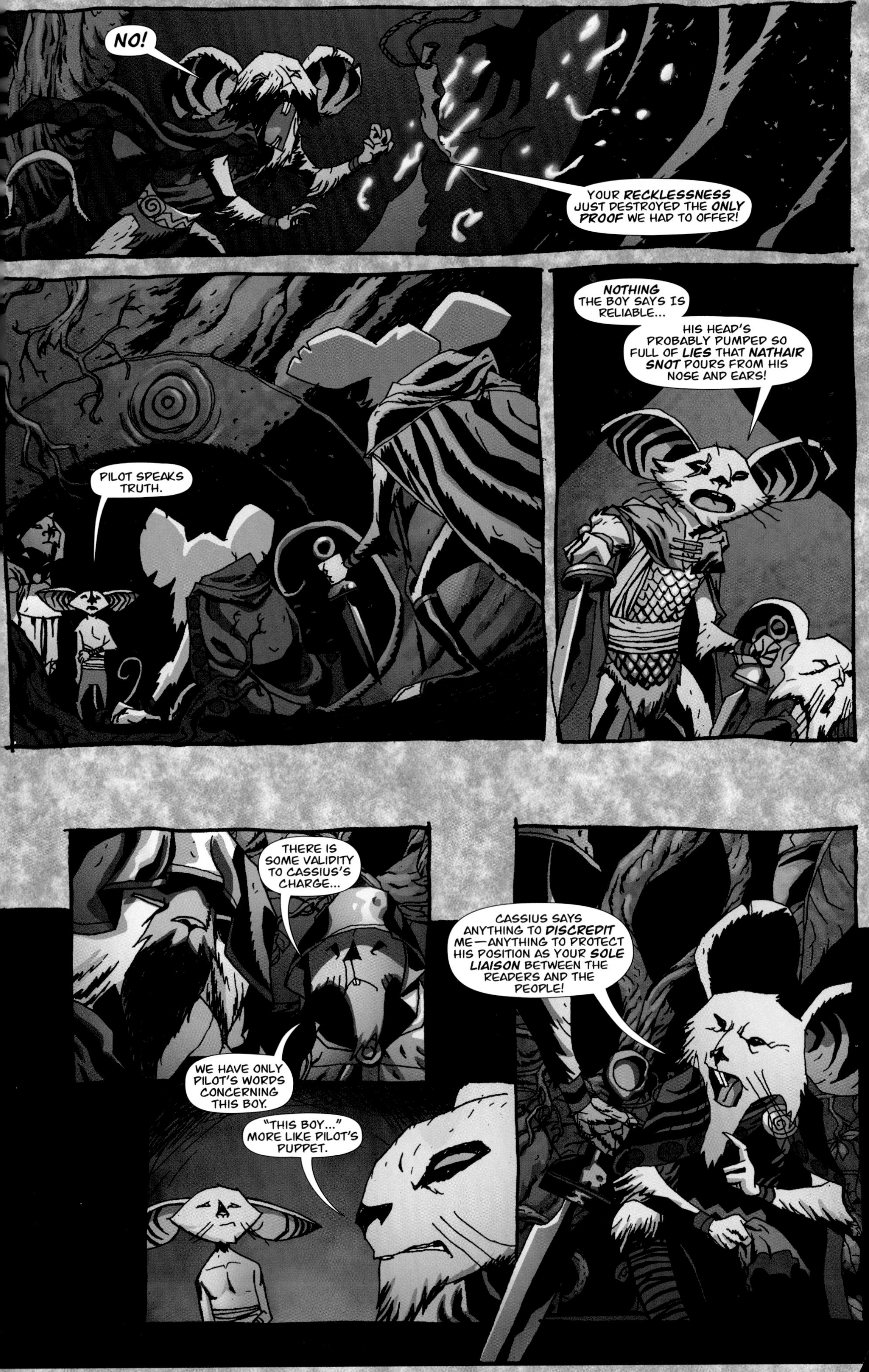

NO!
YOUR RECKLESSNESS JUST DESTROYED THE ONLY PROOF WE HAD TO OFFER!
PILOT SPEAKS TRUTH.
NOTHING THE BOY SAYS IS RELIABLE...
HIS HEAD'S PROBABLY PUMPED SO FULL OF LIES THAT NATHAIR SNOT POURS FROM HIS NOSE AND EARS!
THERE IS SOME VALIDITY TO CASSIUS'S CHARGE...
WE HAVE ONLY PILOT'S WORDS CONCERNING THIS BOY.
"THIS BOY..." MORE LIKE PILOT'S PUPPET.
CASSIUS SAYS ANYTHING TO DISCREDIT ME—ANYTHING TO PROTECT HIS POSITION AS YOUR SOLE LIAISON BETWEEN THE READERS AND THE PEOPLE!

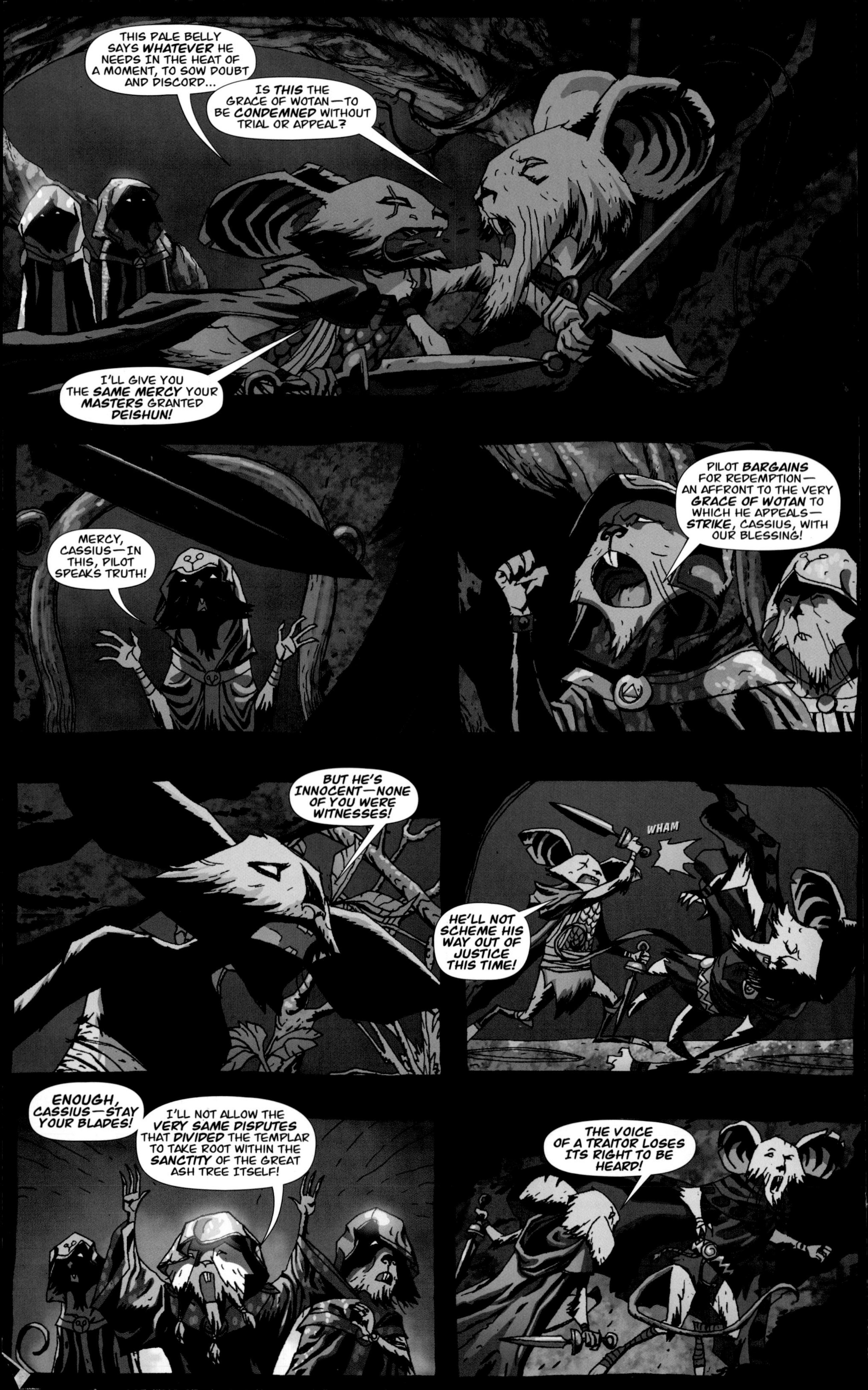
THIS PALE BELLY SAYS WHATEVER HE NEEDS IN THE HEAT OF A MOMENT, TO SOW DOUBT AND DISCORD...
IS THIS THE GRACE OF WOTAN—TO BE CONDEMNED WITHOUT TRIAL OR APPEAL?
I'LL GIVE YOU THE SAME MERCY YOUR MASTERS GRANTED DEISHUN!
MERCY, CASSIUS—IN THIS, PILOT SPEAKS TRUTH!
PILOT BARGAINS FOR REDEMPTION—AN AFFRONT TO THE VERY GRACE OF WOTAN TO WHICH HE APPEALS—STRIKE, CASSIUS, WITH OUR BLESSING!
BUT HE'S INNOCENT—NONE OF YOU WERE WITNESSES!
WHAM
HE'LL NOT SCHEME HIS WAY OUT OF JUSTICE THIS TIME!
ENOUGH, CASSIUS—STAY YOUR BLADES!
I'LL NOT ALLOW THE VERY SAME DISPUTES THAT DIVIDED THE TEMPLAR TO TAKE ROOT WITHIN THE SANCTITY OF THE GREAT ASH TREE ITSELF!
THE VOICE OF A TRAITOR LOSES ITS RIGHT TO BE HEARD!

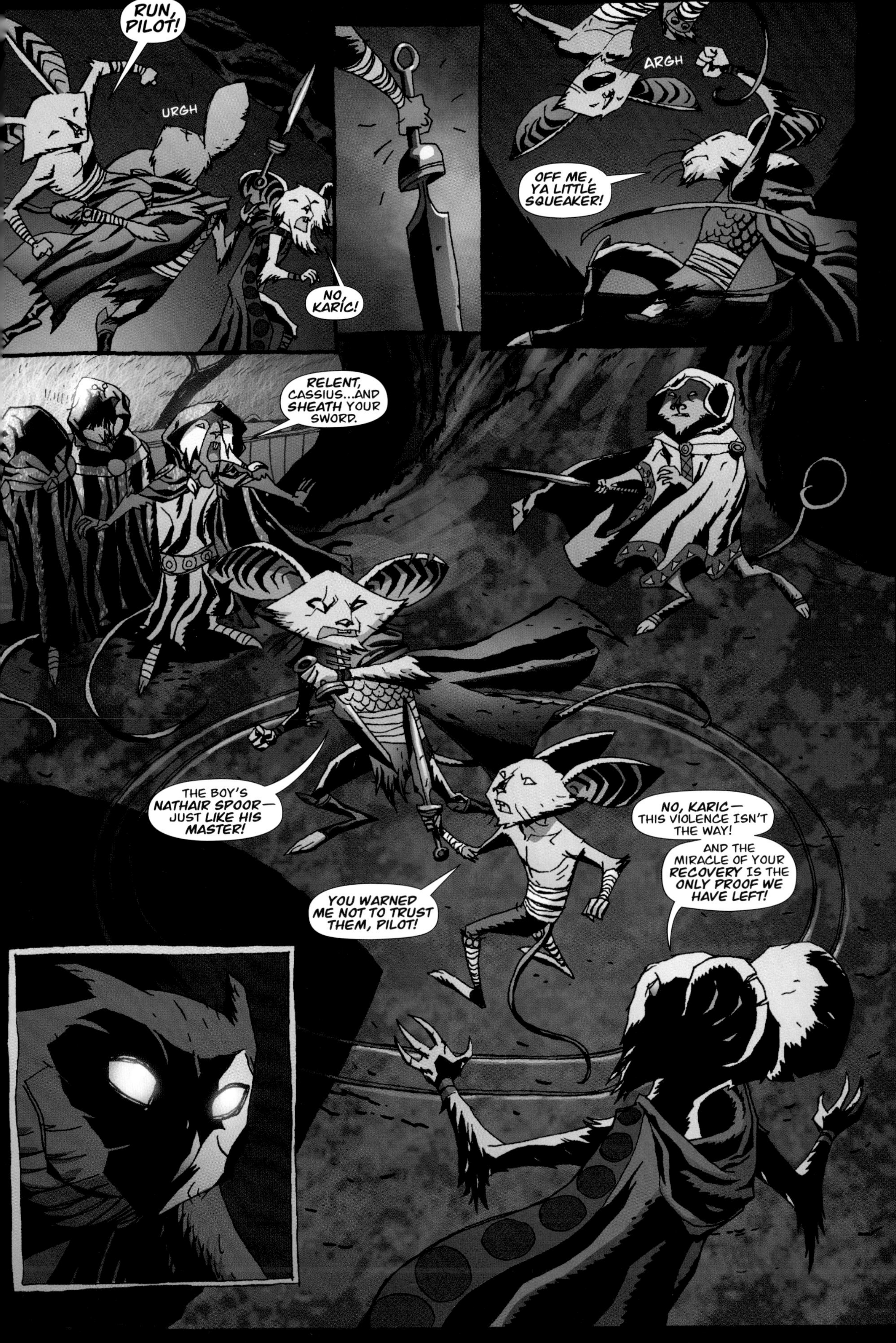
RUN, PILOT!
URGH
NO, KARIC!
ARGH
OFF ME, YA LITTLE SQUEAKER!
RELENT, CASSIUS...AND SHEATH YOUR SWORD.
THE BOY'S NATHAIR SPOOR—JUST LIKE HIS MASTER!
YOU WARNED ME NOT TO TRUST THEM, PILOT!
NO, KARIC—THIS VIOLENCE ISN'T THE WAY!
AND THE MIRACLE OF YOUR RECOVERY IS THE ONLY PROOF WE HAVE LEFT!

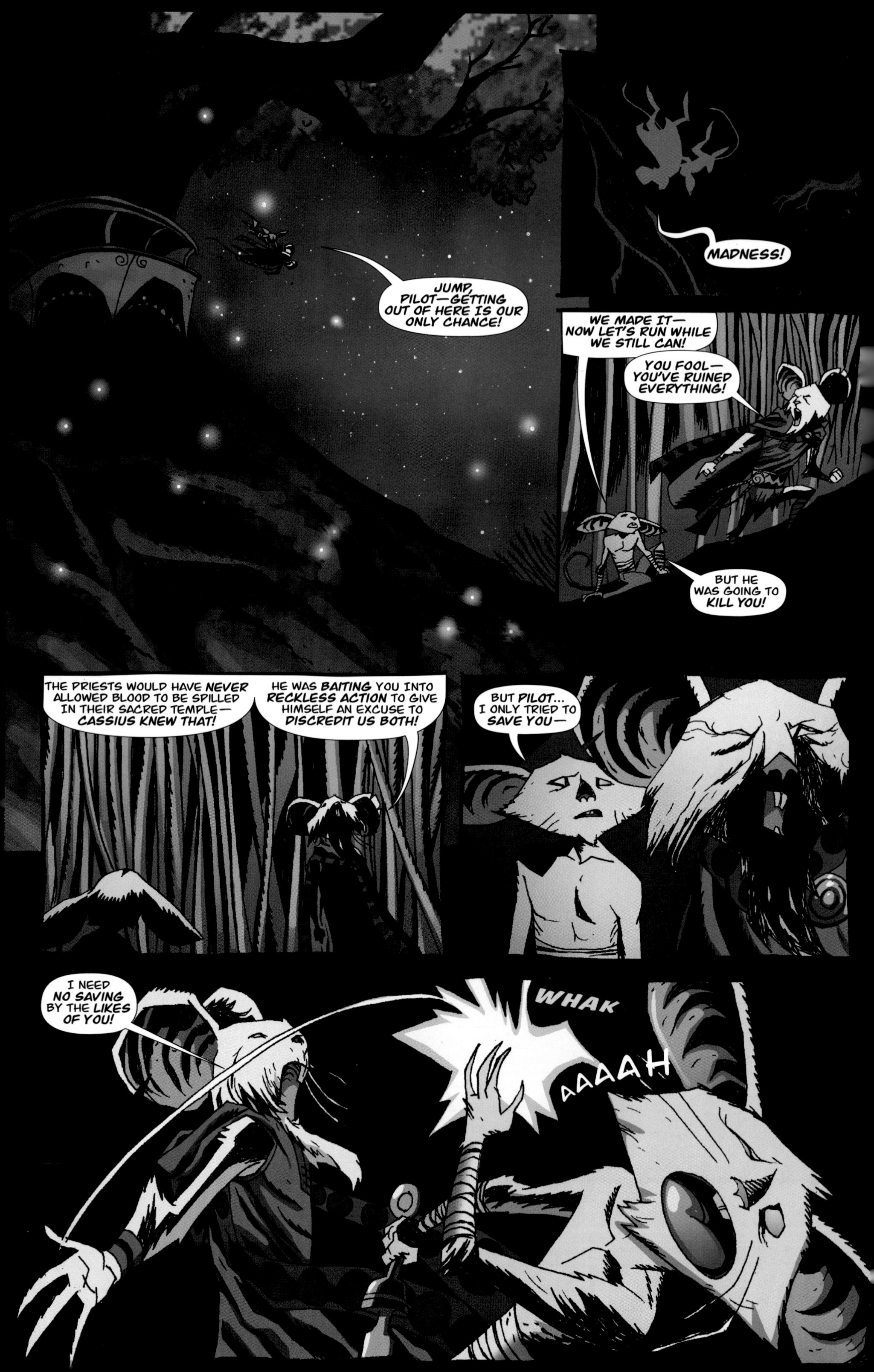
JUMP, PILOT—GETTING OUT OF HERE IS OUR ONLY CHANCE!
MADNESS!
WE MADE IT—NOW LET'S RUN WHILE WE STILL CAN!
YOU FOOL—YOU'VE RUINED EVERYTHING!
BUT HE WAS GOING TO KILL YOU!
THE PRIESTS WOULD HAVE NEVER ALLOWED BLOOD TO BE SPILLED IN THEIR SACRED TEMPLE—CASSIUS KNEW THAT!
HE WAS BAITING YOU INTO RECKLESS ACTION TO GIVE HIMSELF AN EXCUSE TO DISCREDIT US BOTH!
BUT PILOT... I ONLY TRIED TO SAVE YOU—
I NEED NO SAVING BY THE LIKES OF YOU!
WHAK
AAAAH

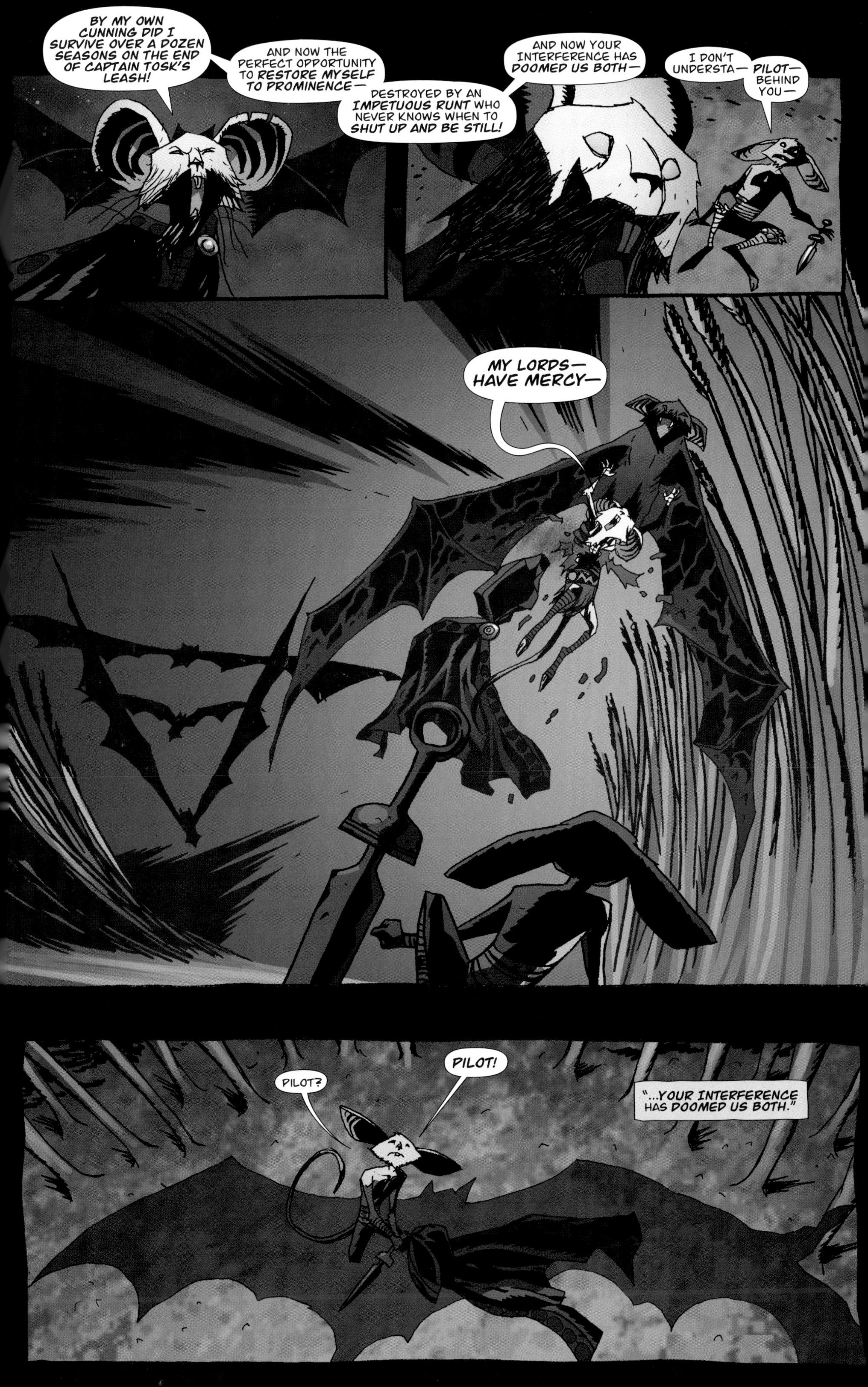
BY MY OWN CUNNING DID I SURVIVE OVER A DOZEN SEASONS ON THE END OF CAPTAIN TOSK'S LEASH!
AND NOW THE PERFECT OPPORTUNITY TO RESTORE MYSELF TO PROMINENCE—
DESTROYED BY AN IMPETUOUS RUNT WHO NEVER KNOWS WHEN TO SHUT UP AND BE STILL!
AND NOW YOUR INTERFERENCE HAS DOOMED US BOTH—
I DON'T UNDERSTA—
PILOT— BEHIND YOU—
MY LORDS— HAVE MERCY—
PILOT?
PILOT!
"...YOUR INTERFERENCE HAS DOOMED US BOTH."

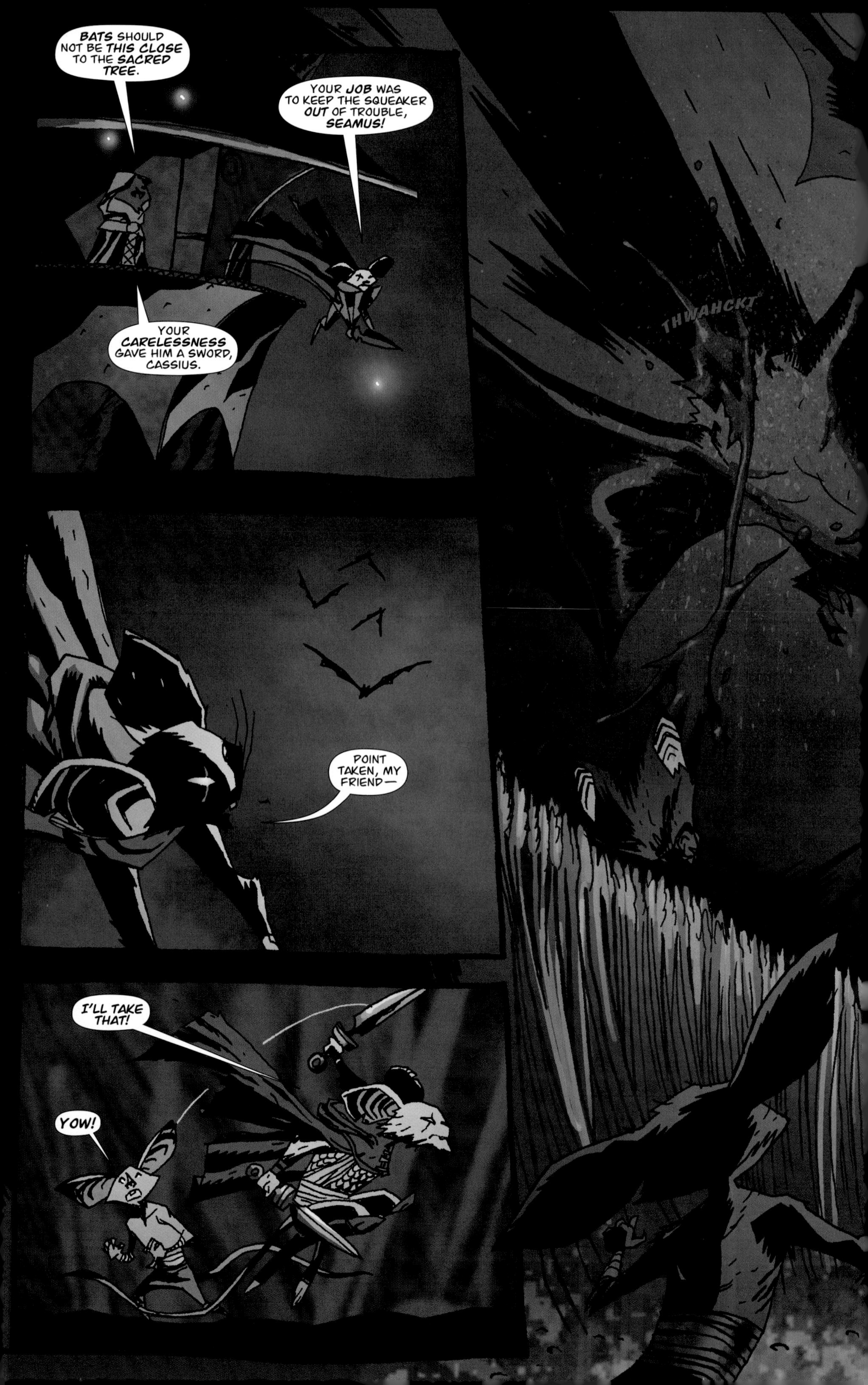
BATS SHOULD NOT BE THIS CLOSE TO THE SACRED TREE.
YOUR JOB WAS TO KEEP THE SQUEAKER OUT OF TROUBLE, SEAMUS!
YOUR CARELESSNESS GAVE HIM A SWORD, CASSIUS.
THWAHCKT
POINT TAKEN, MY FRIEND—
I'LL TAKE THAT!
YOW!

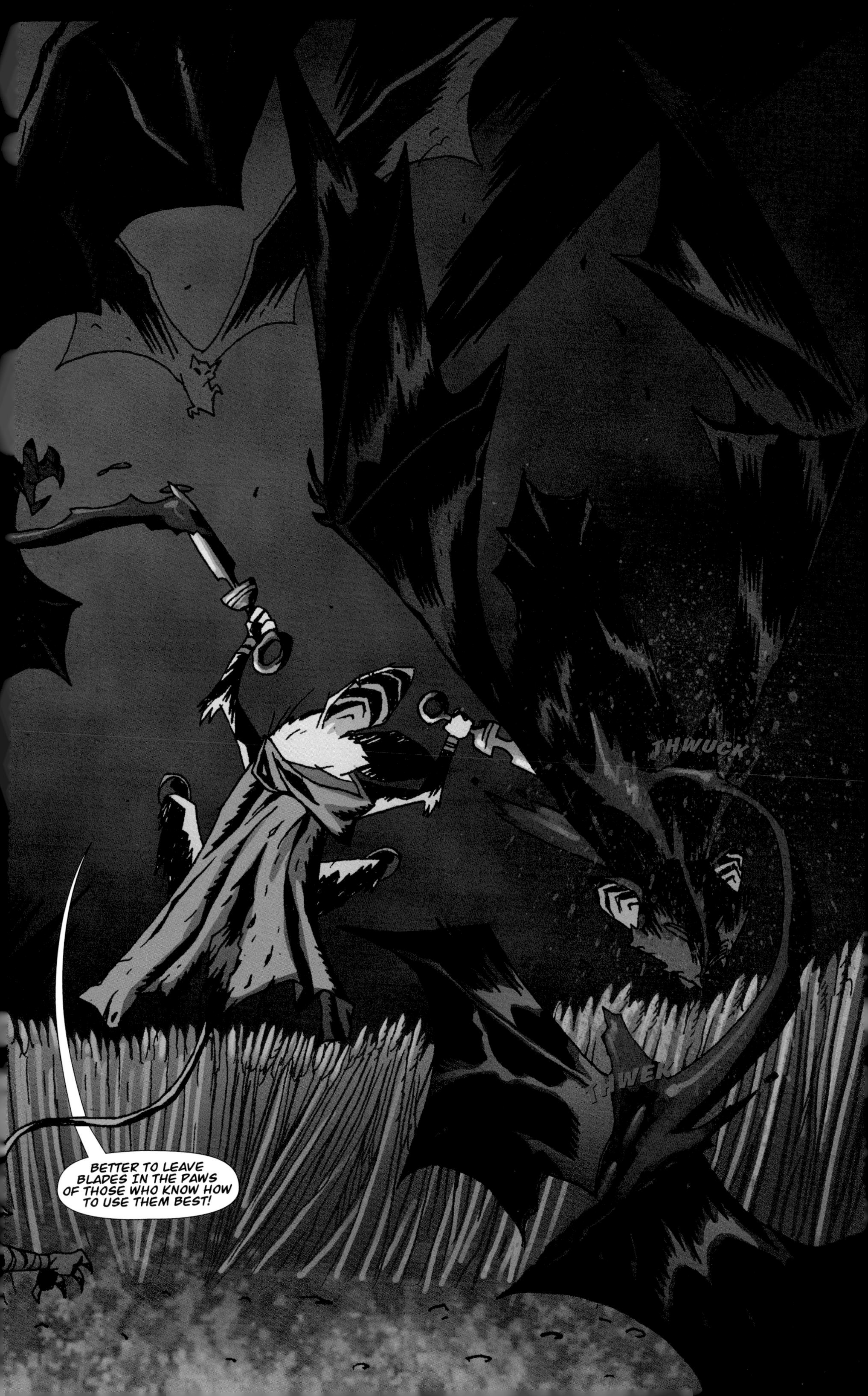
THWUCK
THWEK
BETTER TO LEAVE BLADES IN THE PAWS OF THOSE WHO KNOW HOW TO USE THEM BEST!

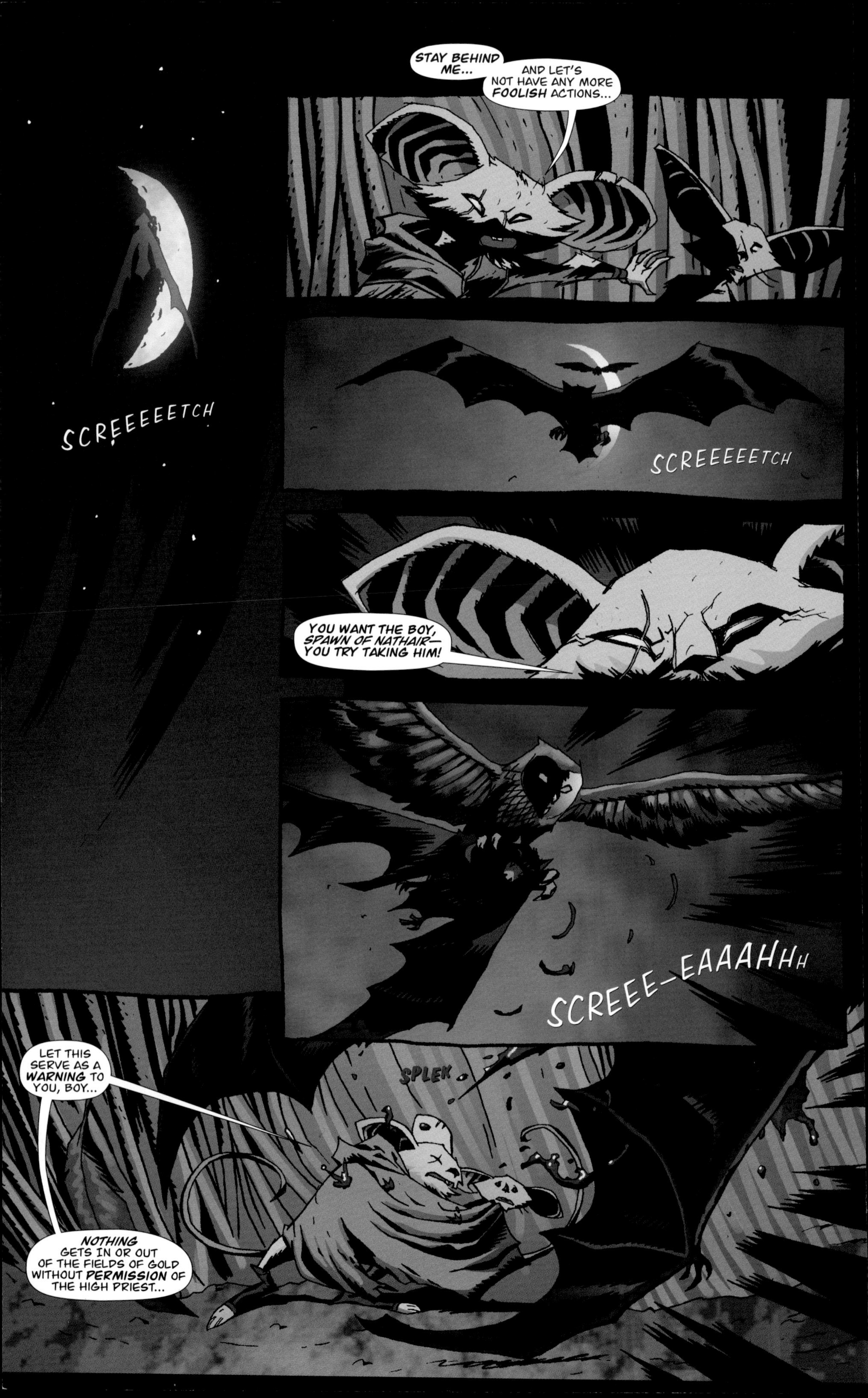

STAY BEHIND ME...
AND LET'S NOT HAVE ANY MORE FOOLISH ACTIONS...
SCREEEEETCH
SCREEEEETCH
YOU WANT THE BOY, SPAWN OF NATHAIR— YOU TRY TAKING HIM!
SCREEE-EAAAHHH
SPLEK
LET THIS SERVE AS A WARNING TO YOU, BOY...
NOTHING GETS IN OR OUT OF THE FIELDS OF GOLD WITHOUT PERMISSION OF THE HIGH PRIEST...

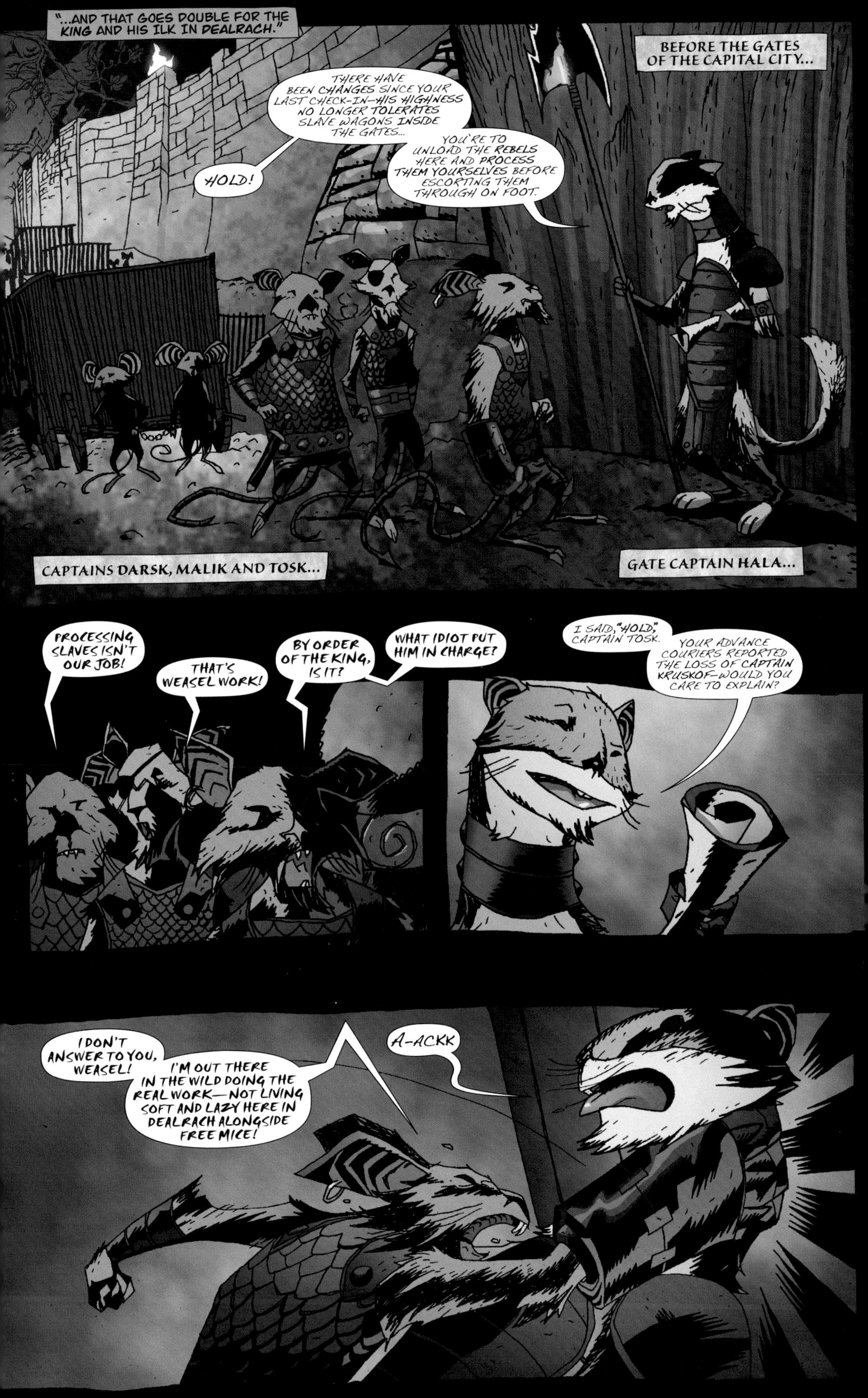
"...AND THAT GOES DOUBLE FOR THE KING AND HIS ILK IN DEALRACH."
BEFORE THE GATES OF THE CAPITAL CITY...
HOLD!
THERE HAVE BEEN CHANGES SINCE YOUR LAST CHECK-IN–HIS HIGHNESS NO LONGER TOLERATES SLAVE WAGONS INSIDE THE GATES...
YOU'RE TO UNLOAD THE REBELS HERE AND PROCESS THEM YOURSELVES BEFORE ESCORTING THEM THROUGH ON FOOT.
CAPTAINS DARSK, MALIK AND TOSK...
GATE CAPTAIN HALA...
PROCESSING SLAVES ISN'T OUR JOB!
THAT'S WEASEL WORK!
BY ORDER OF THE KING, IS IT?
WHAT IDIOT PUT HIM IN CHARGE?
I SAID, "HOLD," CAPTAIN TOSK.
YOUR ADVANCE COURIERS REPORTED THE LOSS OF CAPTAIN KRUSKOF–WOULD YOU CARE TO EXPLAIN?
I DON'T ANSWER TO YOU, WEASEL!
I'M OUT THERE IN THE WILD DOING THE REAL WORK—NOT LIVING SOFT AND LAZY HERE IN DEALRACH ALONGSIDE FREE MICE!
A-ACKK

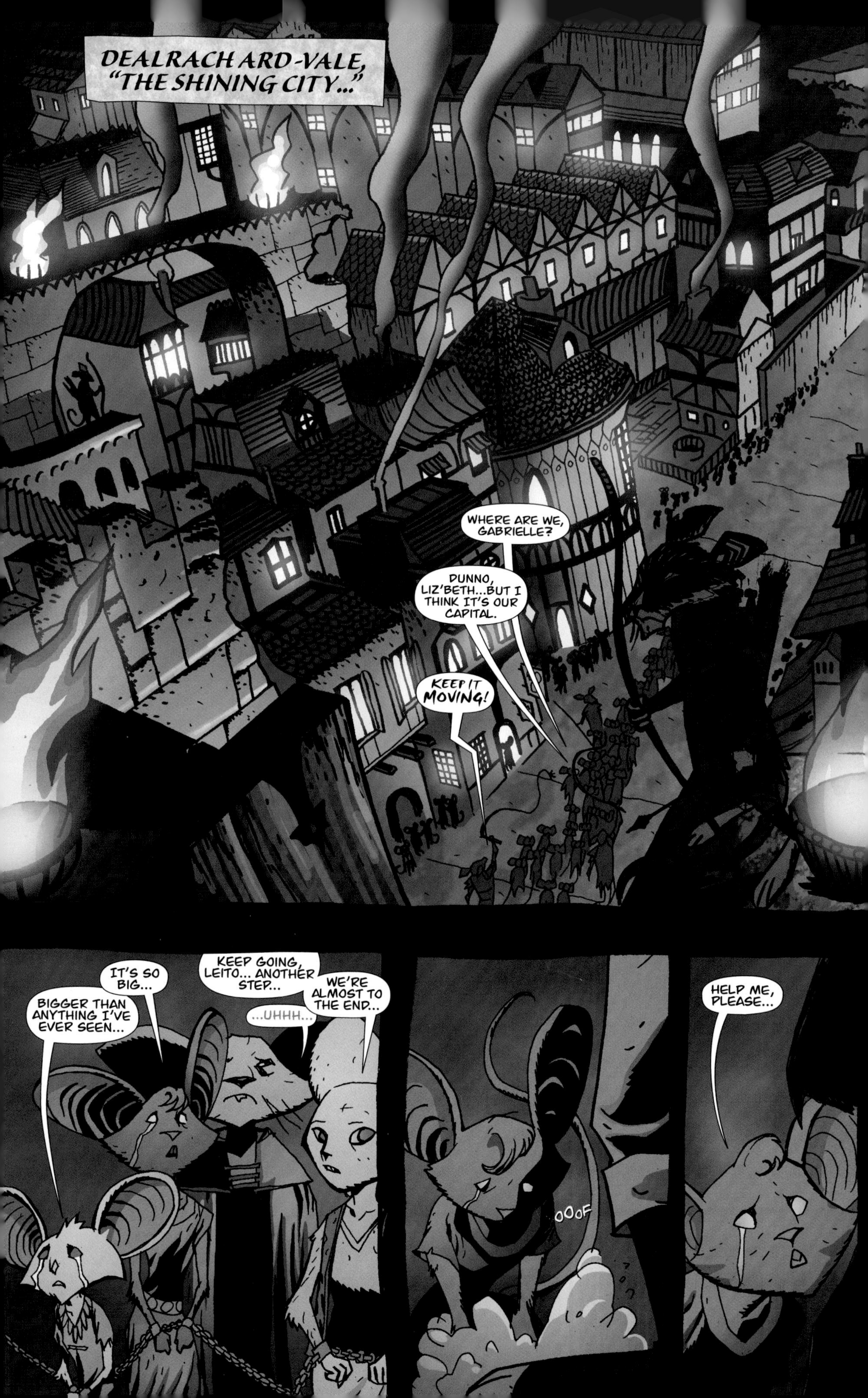

DEALRACH ARD-VALE, "THE SHINING CITY..."
WHERE ARE WE, GABRIELLE?
DUNNO, LIZ'BETH...BUT I THINK IT'S OUR CAPITAL.
KEEP IT MOVING!
IT'S SO BIG...
BIGGER THAN ANYTHING I'VE EVER SEEN...
KEEP GOING, LEITO... ANOTHER STEP...
...UHHH...
WE'RE ALMOST TO THE END...
OOOF
HELP ME, PLEASE...

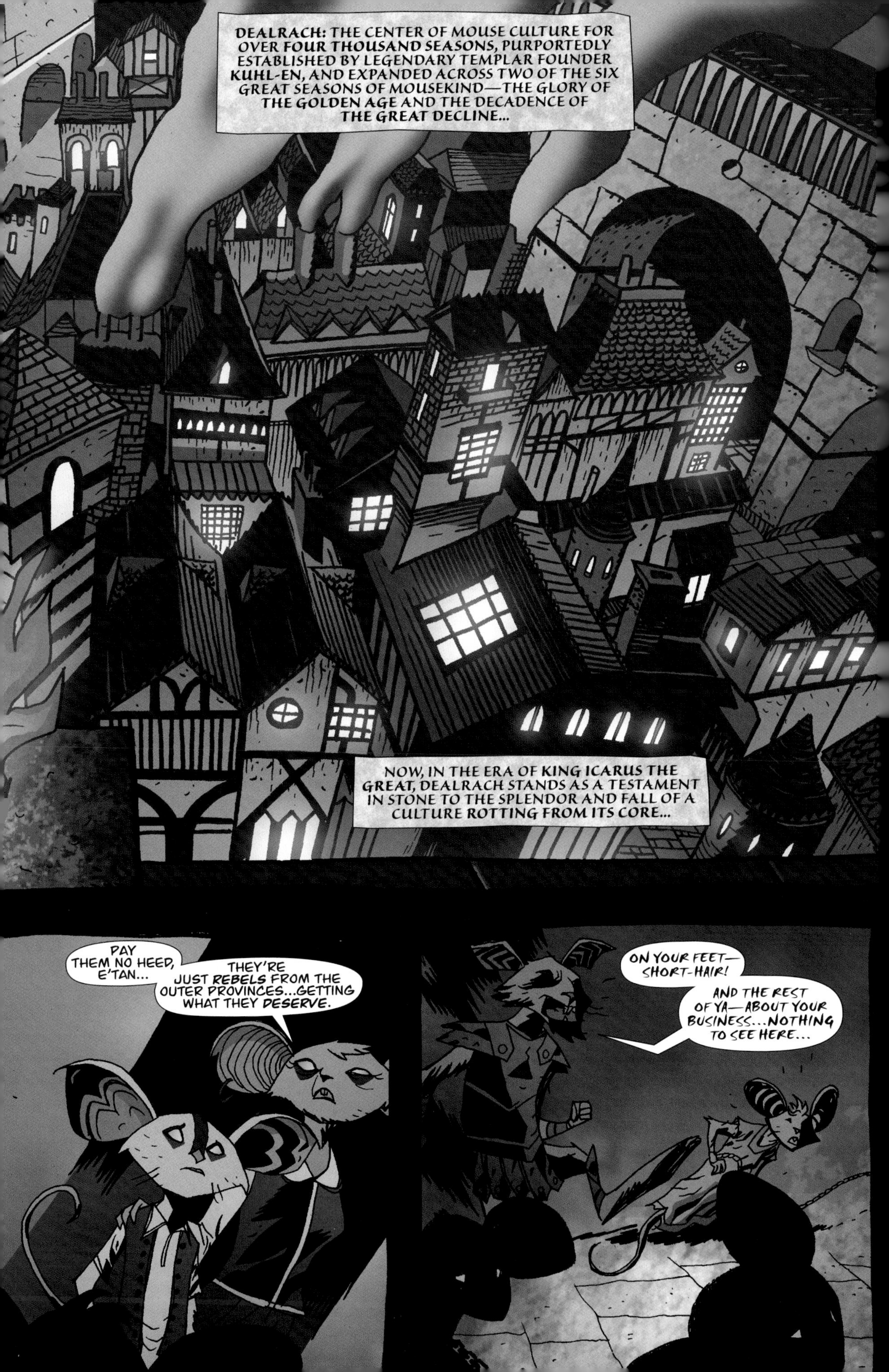
DEALRACH: THE CENTER OF MOUSE CULTURE FOR OVER FOUR THOUSAND SEASONS, PURPORTEDLY ESTABLISHED BY LEGENDARY TEMPLAR FOUNDER KUHL-EN, AND EXPANDED ACROSS TWO OF THE SIX GREAT SEASONS OF MOUSEKIND—THE GLORY OF THE GOLDEN AGE AND THE DECADENCE OF THE GREAT DECLINE...
NOW, IN THE ERA OF KING ICARUS THE GREAT, DEALRACH STANDS AS A TESTAMENT IN STONE TO THE SPLENDOR AND FALL OF A CULTURE ROTTING FROM ITS CORE...
PAY THEM NO HEED, E'TAN...
THEY'RE JUST REBELS FROM THE OUTER PROVINCES...GETTING WHAT THEY DESERVE.
ON YOUR FEET—SHORT-HAIR!
AND THE REST OF YA—ABOUT YOUR BUSINESS...NOTHING TO SEE HERE...

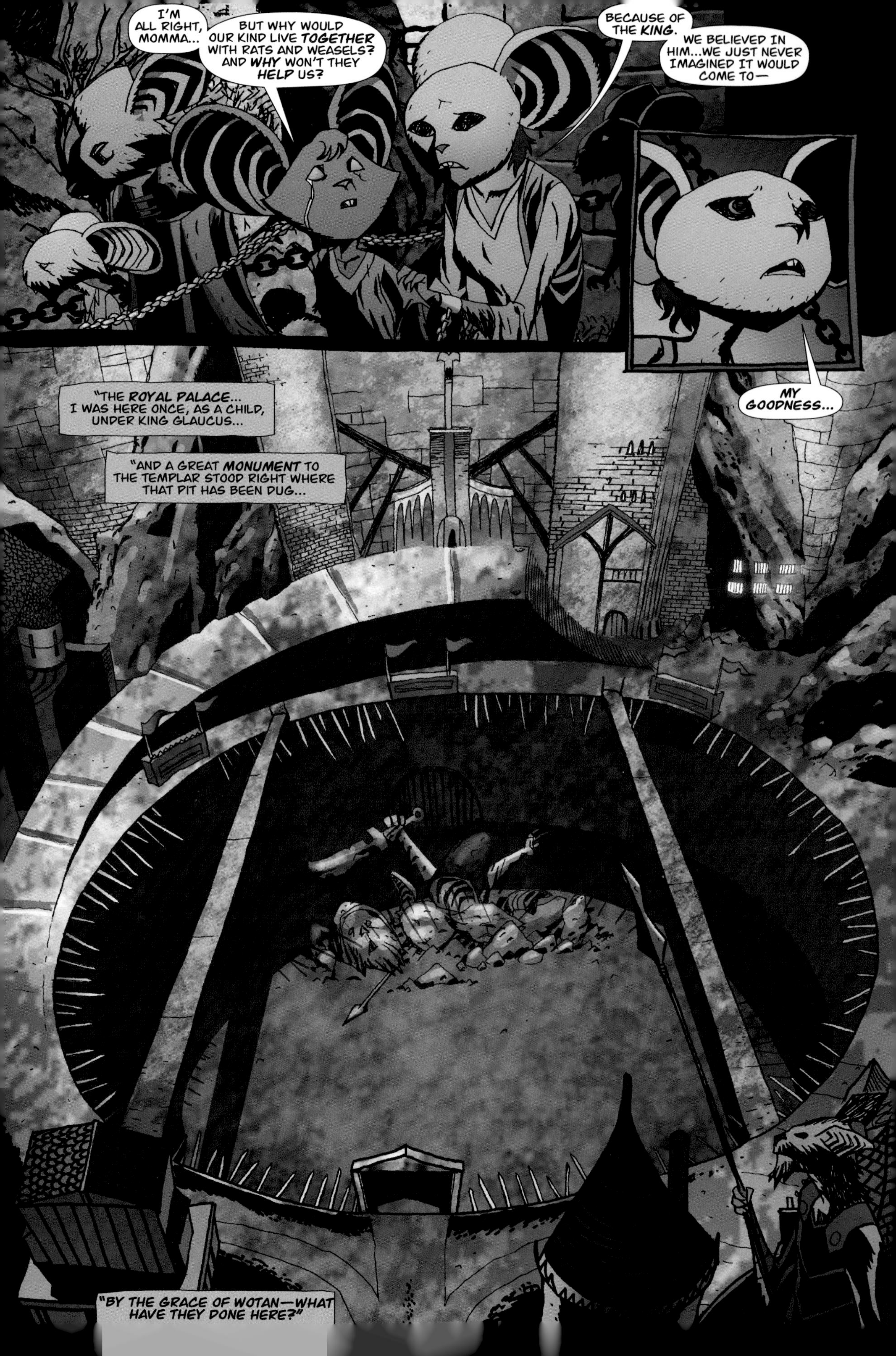
I'M ALL RIGHT, MOMMA...
BUT WHY WOULD OUR KIND LIVE TOGETHER WITH RATS AND WEASELS? AND WHY WON'T THEY HELP US?
BECAUSE OF THE KING.
WE BELIEVED IN HIM...WE JUST NEVER IMAGINED IT WOULD COME TO—
MY GOODNESS...
"THE ROYAL PALACE... I WAS HERE ONCE, AS A CHILD, UNDER KING GLAUCUS...
"AND A GREAT MONUMENT TO THE TEMPLAR STOOD RIGHT WHERE THAT PIT HAS BEEN DUG...
"BY THE GRACE OF WOTAN—WHAT HAVE THEY DONE HERE?"

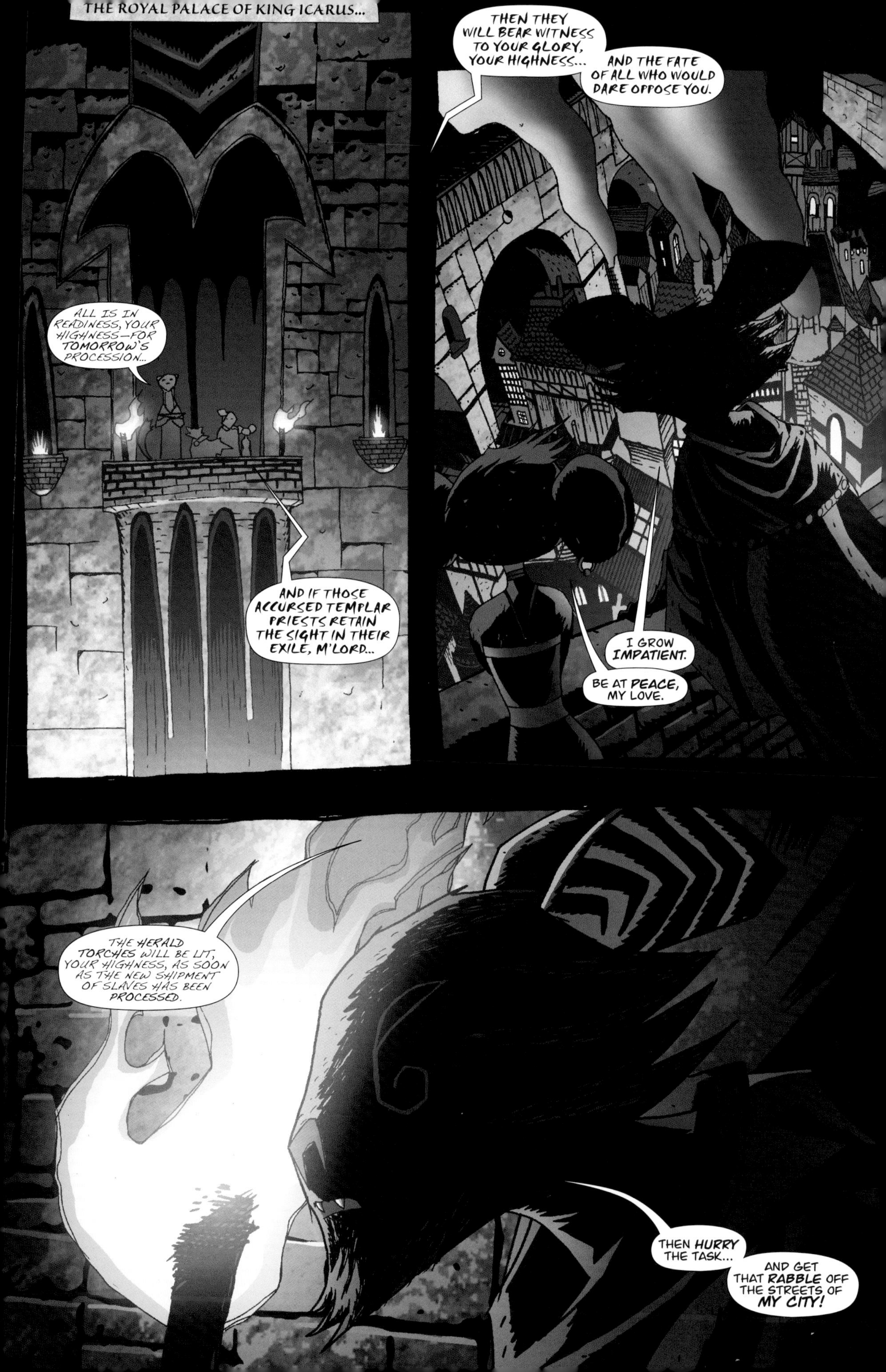
THE ROYAL PALACE OF KING ICARUS...
ALL IS IN READINESS, YOUR HIGHNESS—FOR TOMORROW'S PROCESSION...
AND IF THOSE ACCURSED TEMPLAR PRIESTS RETAIN THE SIGHT IN THEIR EXILE, M'LORD...
THEN THEY WILL BEAR WITNESS TO YOUR GLORY, YOUR HIGHNESS...
AND THE FATE OF ALL WHO WOULD DARE OPPOSE YOU.
I GROW IMPATIENT.
BE AT PEACE, MY LOVE.
THE HERALD TORCHES WILL BE LIT, YOUR HIGHNESS, AS SOON AS THE NEW SHIPMENT OF SLAVES HAS BEEN PROCESSED.
THEN HURRY THE TASK...
AND GET THAT RABBLE OFF THE STREETS OF MY CITY!

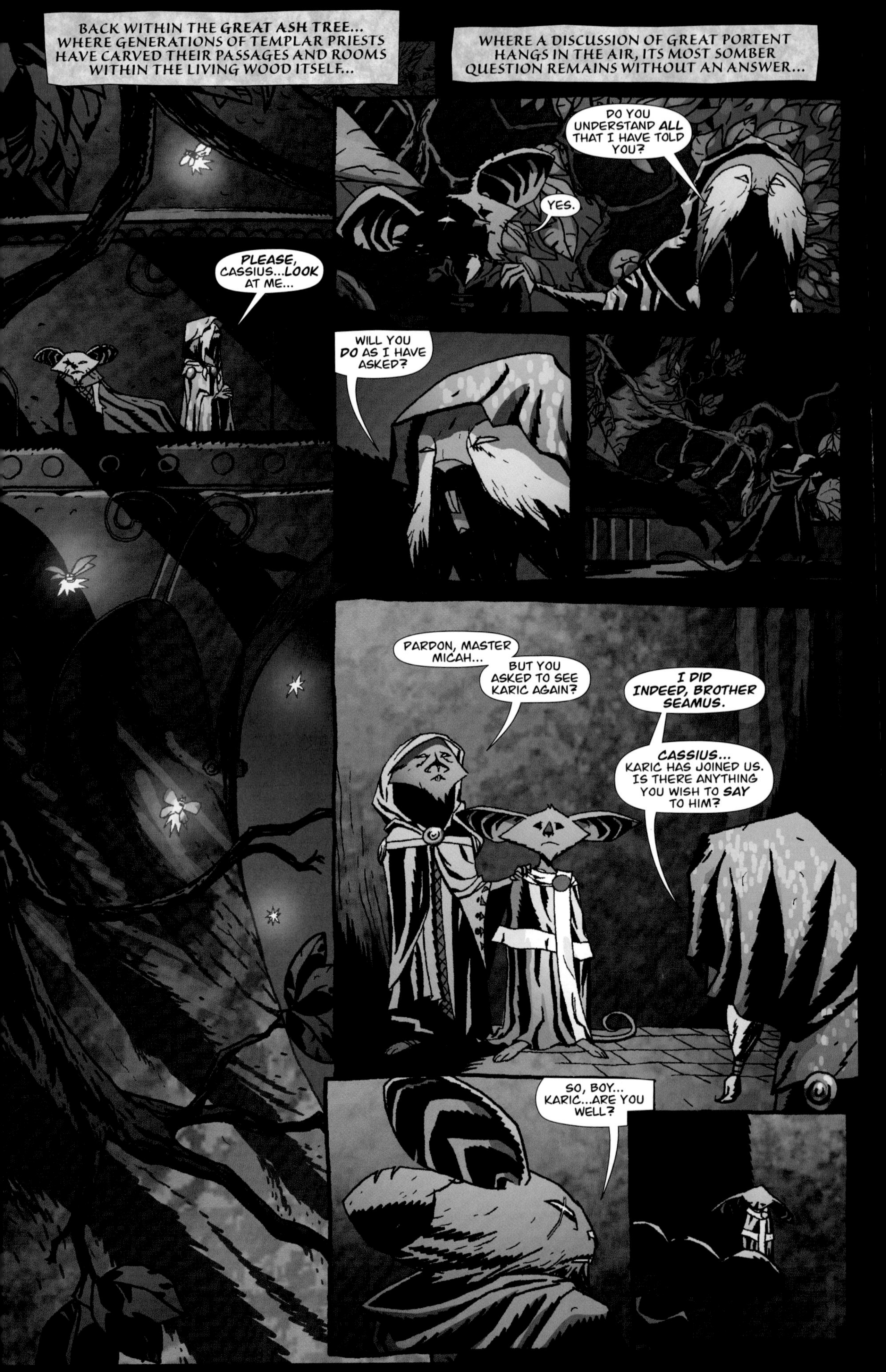
BACK WITHIN THE GREAT ASH TREE... WHERE GENERATIONS OF TEMPLAR PRIESTS HAVE CARVED THEIR PASSAGES AND ROOMS WITHIN THE LIVING WOOD ITSELF...
WHERE A DISCUSSION OF GREAT PORTENT HANGS IN THE AIR, ITS MOST SOMBER QUESTION REMAINS WITHOUT AN ANSWER...
PLEASE, CASSIUS...LOOK AT ME...
DO YOU UNDERSTAND ALL THAT I HAVE TOLD YOU?
YES.
WILL YOU DO AS I HAVE ASKED?
PARDON, MASTER MICAH...
BUT YOU ASKED TO SEE KARIC AGAIN?
I DID INDEED, BROTHER SEAMUS.
CASSIUS... KARIC HAS JOINED US. IS THERE ANYTHING YOU WISH TO SAY TO HIM?
SO, BOY... KARIC...ARE YOU WELL?

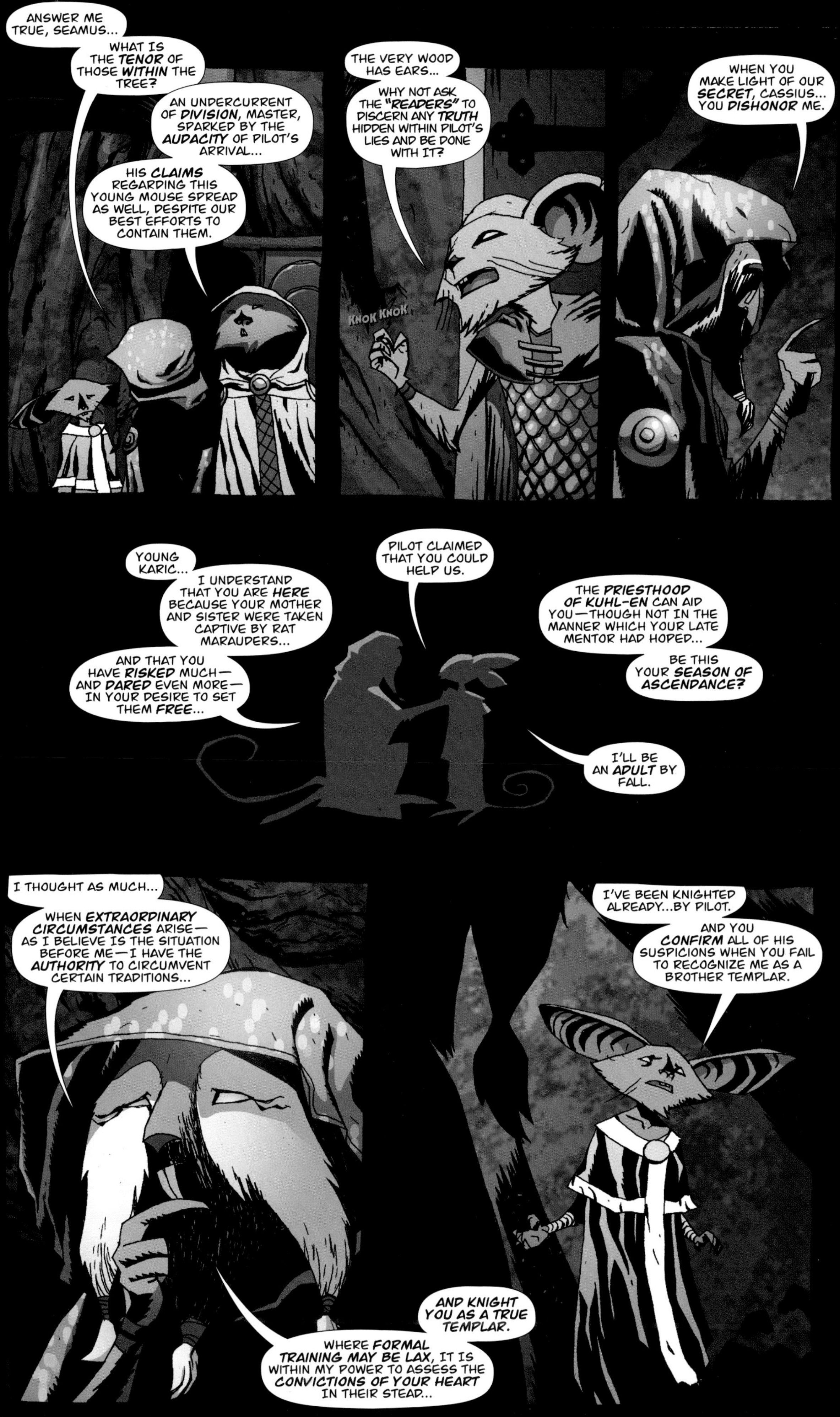

ANSWER ME TRUE, SEAMUS...
WHAT IS THE TENOR OF THOSE WITHIN THE TREE?
AN UNDERCURRENT OF DIVISION, MASTER, SPARKED BY THE AUDACITY OF PILOT'S ARRIVAL...
HIS CLAIMS REGARDING THIS YOUNG MOUSE SPREAD AS WELL, DESPITE OUR BEST EFFORTS TO CONTAIN THEM.
THE VERY WOOD HAS EARS...
WHY NOT ASK THE "READERS" TO DISCERN ANY TRUTH HIDDEN WITHIN PILOT'S LIES AND BE DONE WITH IT?
KNOK KNOK
WHEN YOU MAKE LIGHT OF OUR SECRET, CASSIUS... YOU DISHONOR ME.
YOUNG KARIC...
I UNDERSTAND THAT YOU ARE HERE BECAUSE YOUR MOTHER AND SISTER WERE TAKEN CAPTIVE BY RAT MARAUDERS...
AND THAT YOU HAVE RISKED MUCH—AND DARED EVEN MORE—IN YOUR DESIRE TO SET THEM FREE...
PILOT CLAIMED THAT YOU COULD HELP US.
THE PRIESTHOOD OF KUHL-EN CAN AID YOU—THOUGH NOT IN THE MANNER WHICH YOUR LATE MENTOR HAD HOPED...
BE THIS YOUR SEASON OF ASCENDANCE?
I'LL BE AN ADULT BY FALL.
I THOUGHT AS MUCH...
WHEN EXTRAORDINARY CIRCUMSTANCES ARISE—AS I BELIEVE IS THE SITUATION BEFORE ME—I HAVE THE AUTHORITY TO CIRCUMVENT CERTAIN TRADITIONS...
WHERE FORMAL TRAINING MAY BE LAX, IT IS WITHIN MY POWER TO ASSESS THE CONVICTIONS OF YOUR HEART IN THEIR STEAD...
AND KNIGHT YOU AS A TRUE TEMPLAR.
I'VE BEEN KNIGHTED ALREADY...BY PILOT.
AND YOU CONFIRM ALL OF HIS SUSPICIONS WHEN YOU FAIL TO RECOGNIZE ME AS A BROTHER TEMPLAR.

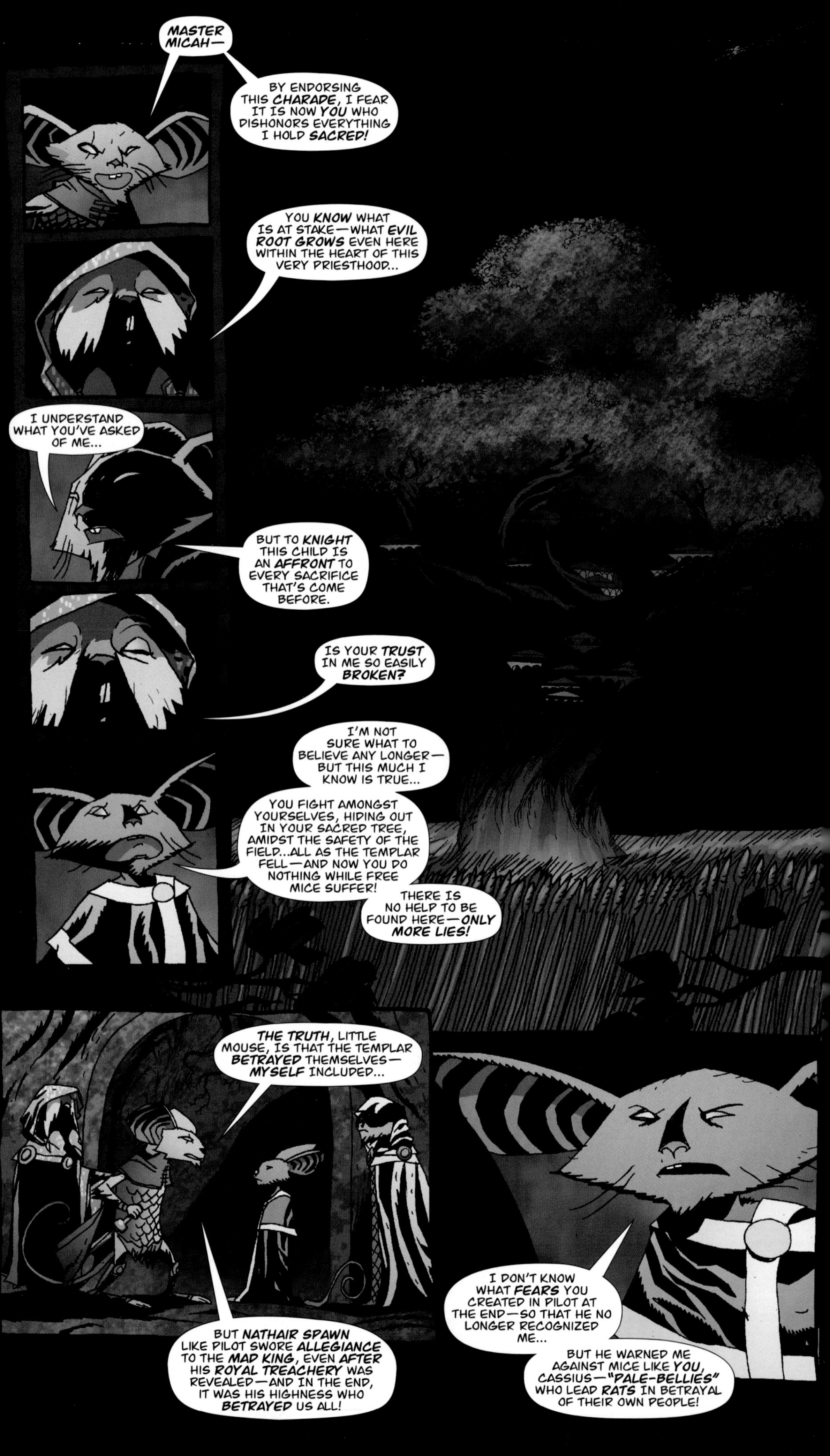

MASTER MICAH—
BY ENDORSING THIS CHARADE, I FEAR IT IS NOW YOU WHO DISHONORS EVERYTHING I HOLD SACRED!
YOU KNOW WHAT IS AT STAKE—WHAT EVIL ROOT GROWS EVEN HERE WITHIN THE HEART OF THIS VERY PRIESTHOOD...
I UNDERSTAND WHAT YOU'VE ASKED OF ME...
BUT TO KNIGHT THIS CHILD IS AN AFFRONT TO EVERY SACRIFICE THAT'S COME BEFORE.
IS YOUR TRUST IN ME SO EASILY BROKEN?
I'M NOT SURE WHAT TO BELIEVE ANY LONGER—BUT THIS MUCH I KNOW IS TRUE...
YOU FIGHT AMONGST YOURSELVES, HIDING OUT IN YOUR SACRED TREE, AMIDST THE SAFETY OF THE FIELD...ALL AS THE TEMPLAR FELL—AND NOW YOU DO NOTHING WHILE FREE MICE SUFFER!
THERE IS NO HELP TO BE FOUND HERE—ONLY MORE LIES!
THE TRUTH, LITTLE MOUSE, IS THAT THE TEMPLAR BETRAYED THEMSELVES—MYSELF INCLUDED...
BUT NATHAIR SPAWN LIKE PILOT SWORE ALLEGIANCE TO THE MAD KING, EVEN AFTER HIS ROYAL TREACHERY WAS REVEALED—AND IN THE END, IT WAS HIS HIGHNESS WHO BETRAYED US ALL!
I DON'T KNOW WHAT FEARS YOU CREATED IN PILOT AT THE END—SO THAT HE NO LONGER RECOGNIZED ME...
BUT HE WARNED ME AGAINST MICE LIKE YOU, CASSIUS—"PALE-BELLIES" WHO LEAD RATS IN BETRAYAL OF THEIR OWN PEOPLE!

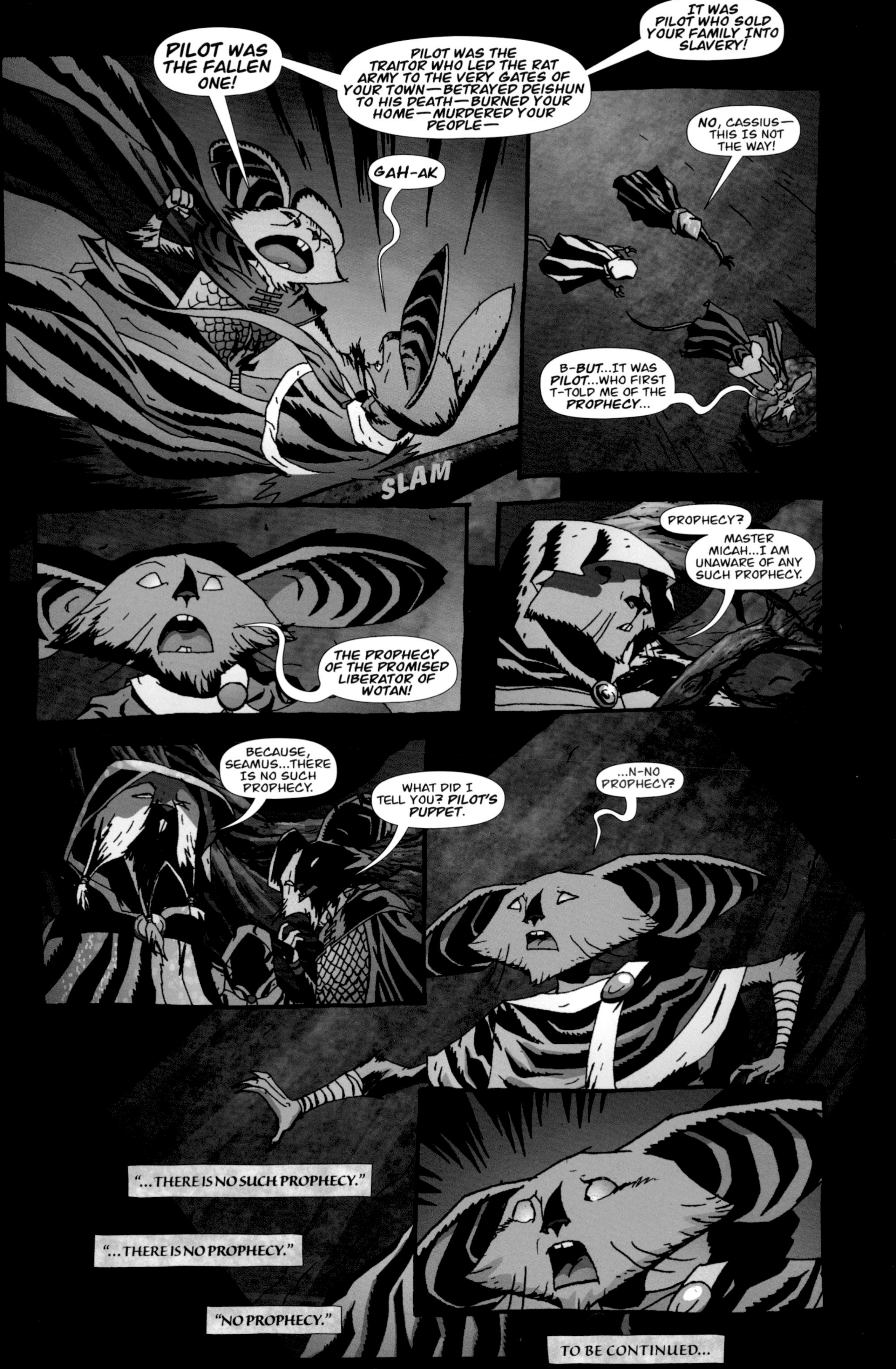
PILOT WAS THE FALLEN ONE!
PILOT WAS THE TRAITOR WHO LED THE RAT ARMY TO THE VERY GATES OF YOUR TOWN—BETRAYED DEISHUN TO HIS DEATH—BURNED YOUR HOME—MURDERED YOUR PEOPLE—
IT WAS PILOT WHO SOLD YOUR FAMILY INTO SLAVERY!
GAH-AK
SLAM
NO, CASSIUS—THIS IS NOT THE WAY!
B-BUT...IT WAS PILOT...WHO FIRST T-TOLD ME OF THE PROPHECY...
THE PROPHECY OF THE PROMISED LIBERATOR OF WOTAN!
PROPHECY?
MASTER MICAH...I AM UNAWARE OF ANY SUCH PROPHECY.
BECAUSE, SEAMUS...THERE IS NO SUCH PROPHECY.
WHAT DID I TELL YOU? PILOT'S PUPPET.
...N-NO PROPHECY?
"...THERE IS NO SUCH PROPHECY."
"...THERE IS NO PROPHECY."
"NO PROPHECY."
TO BE CONTINUED...

CHAPTER SEVEN
THE SYMBOL

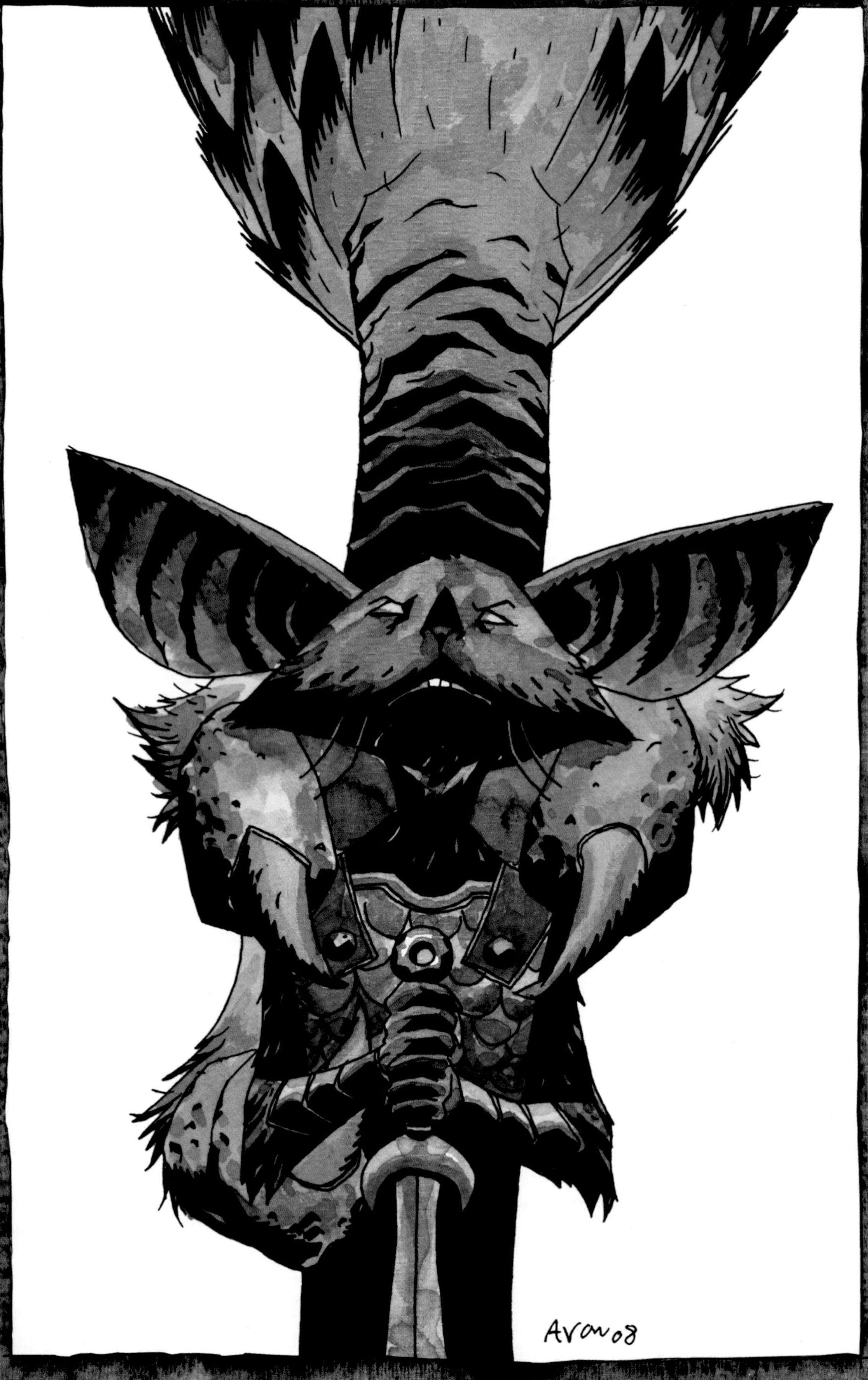
Avon08

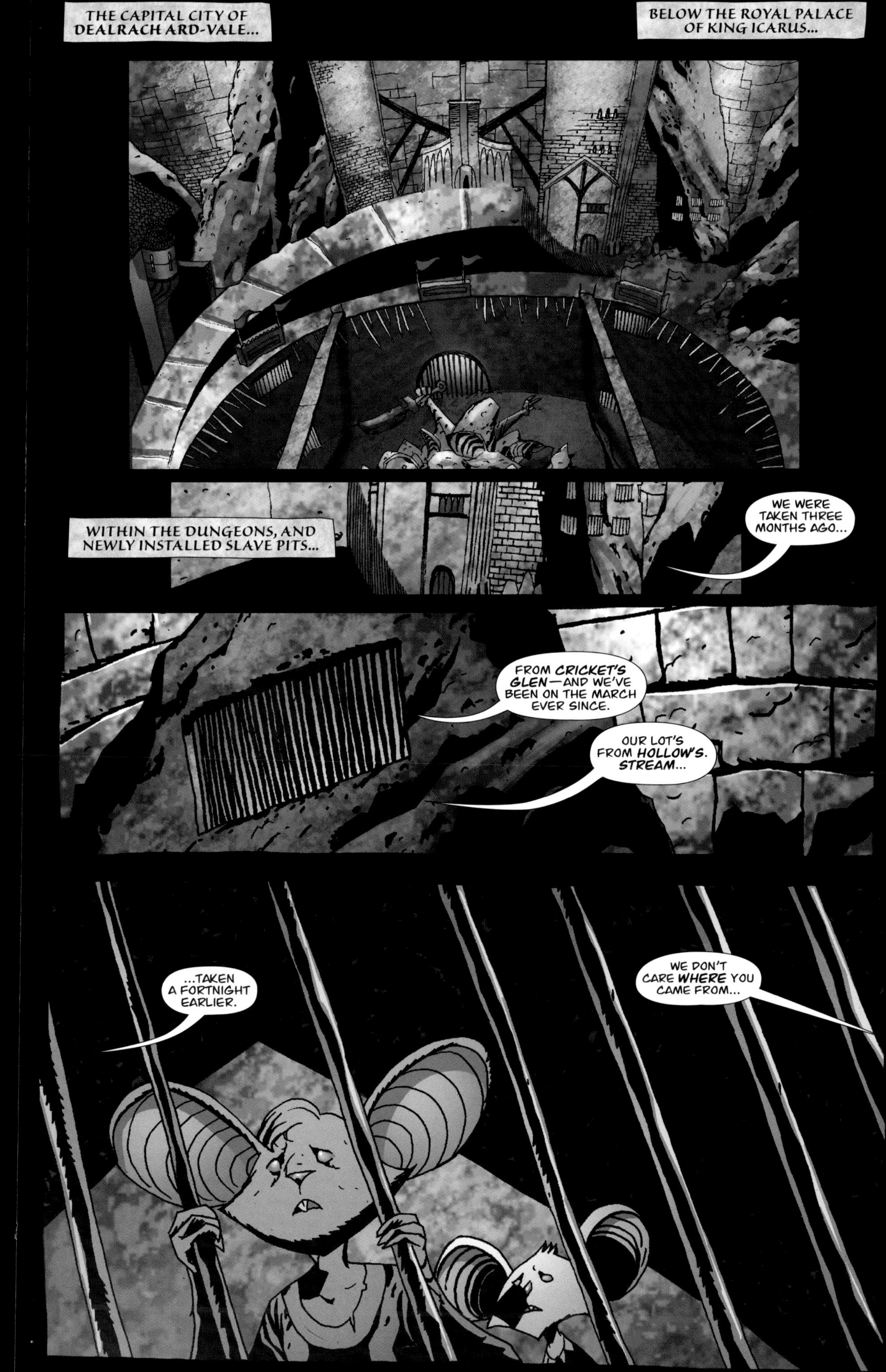
THE CAPITAL CITY OF DEALRACH ARD-VALE...
BELOW THE ROYAL PALACE OF KING ICARUS...
WITHIN THE DUNGEONS, AND NEWLY INSTALLED SLAVE PITS...
WE WERE TAKEN THREE MONTHS AGO...
FROM CRICKET'S GLEN—AND WE'VE BEEN ON THE MARCH EVER SINCE.
OUR LOT'S FROM HOLLOW'S. STREAM...
...TAKEN A FORTNIGHT EARLIER.
WE DON'T CARE WHERE YOU CAME FROM...

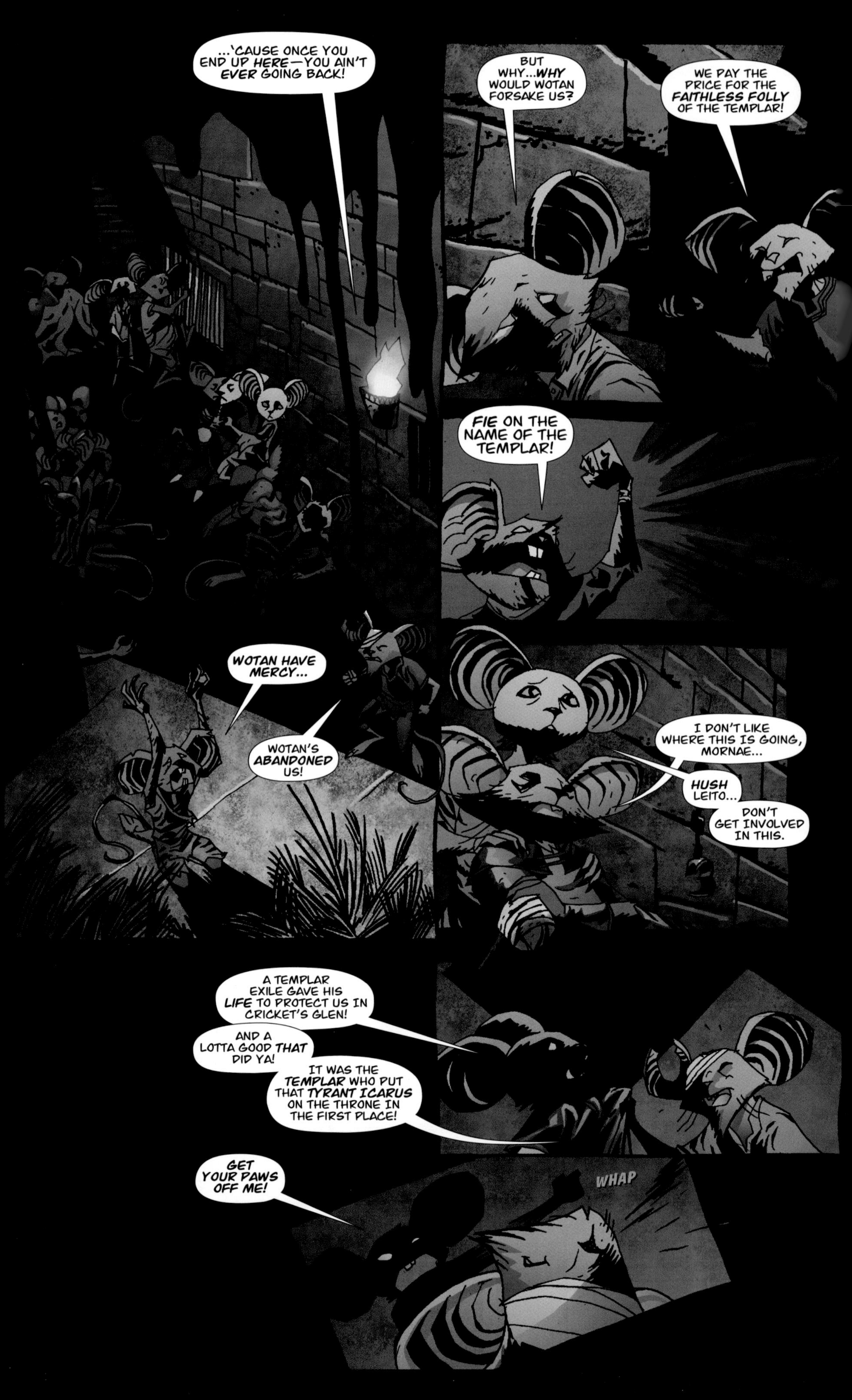
...'CAUSE ONCE YOU END UP HERE—YOU AIN'T EVER GOING BACK!
BUT WHY...WHY WOULD WOTAN FORSAKE US?
WE PAY THE PRICE FOR THE FAITHLESS FOLLY OF THE TEMPLAR!
FIE ON THE NAME OF THE TEMPLAR!
WOTAN HAVE MERCY...
WOTAN'S ABANDONED US!
I DON'T LIKE WHERE THIS IS GOING, MORNAE...
HUSH LEITO...
DON'T GET INVOLVED IN THIS.
A TEMPLAR EXILE GAVE HIS LIFE TO PROTECT US IN CRICKET'S GLEN!
AND A LOTTA GOOD THAT DID YA!
IT WAS THE TEMPLAR WHO PUT THAT TYRANT ICARUS ON THE THRONE IN THE FIRST PLACE!
GET YOUR PAWS OFF ME!
WHAP

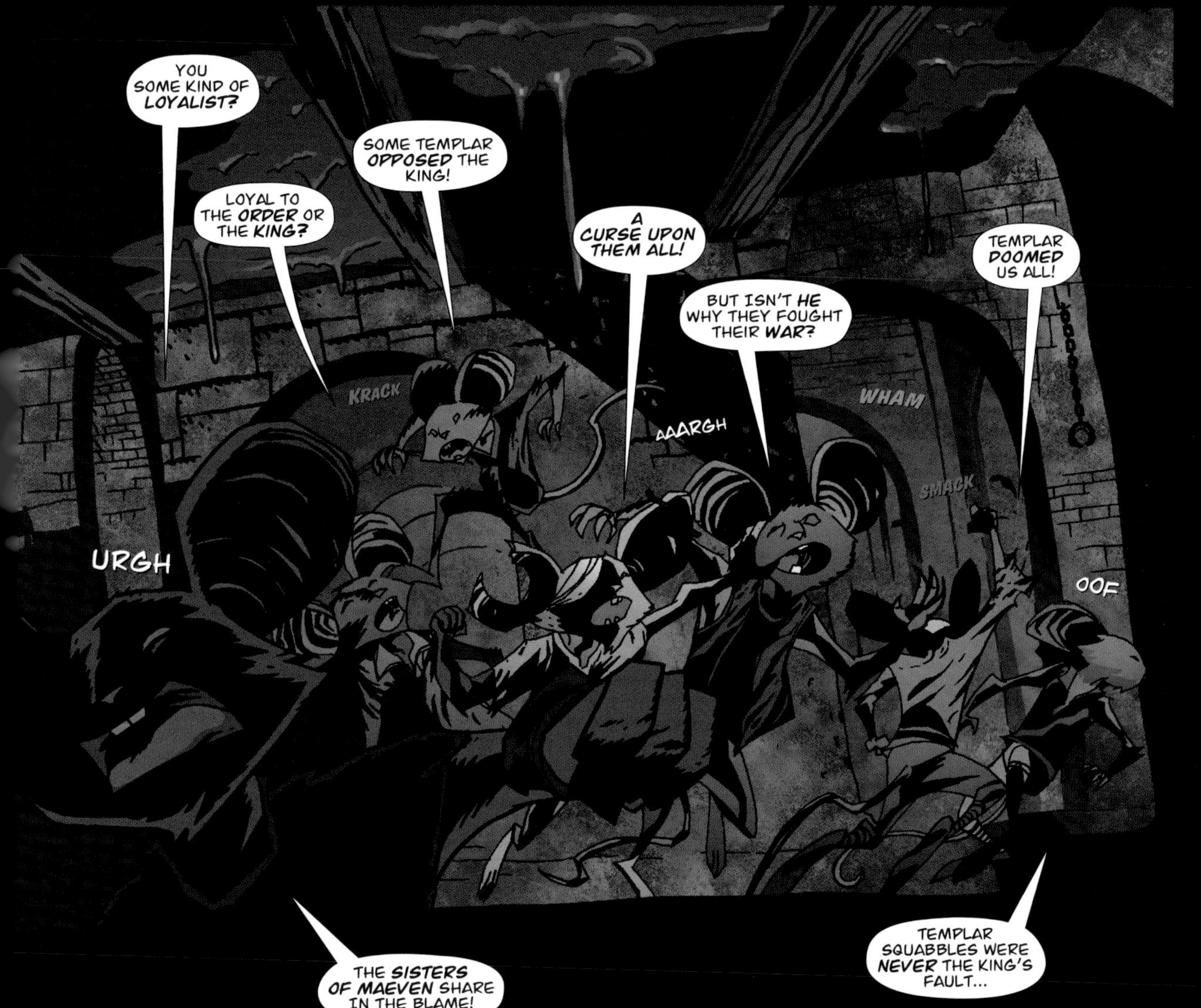
YOU SOME KIND OF LOYALIST?
LOYAL TO THE ORDER OR THE KING?
SOME TEMPLAR OPPOSED THE KING!
A CURSE UPON THEM ALL!
BUT ISN'T HE WHY THEY FOUGHT THEIR WAR?
TEMPLAR DOOMED US ALL!
KRACK
WHAM
AAARGH
SMACK
URGH
OOF
THE SISTERS OF MAEVEN SHARE IN THE BLAME!
TEMPLAR SQUABBLES WERE NEVER THE KING'S FAULT...

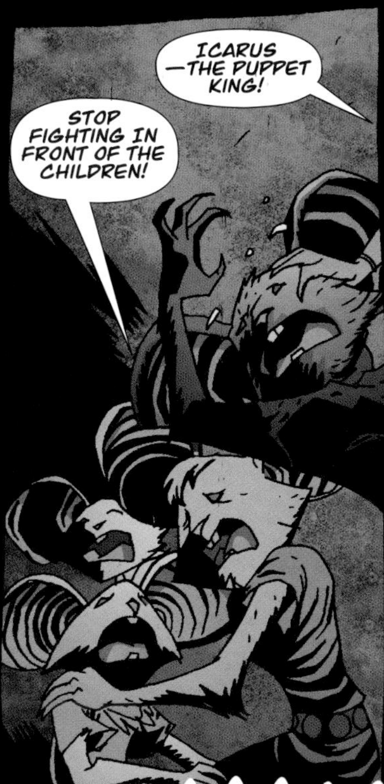
ICARUS —THE PUPPET KING!
STOP FIGHTING IN FRONT OF THE CHILDREN!
WAAAAAAAAAAGH

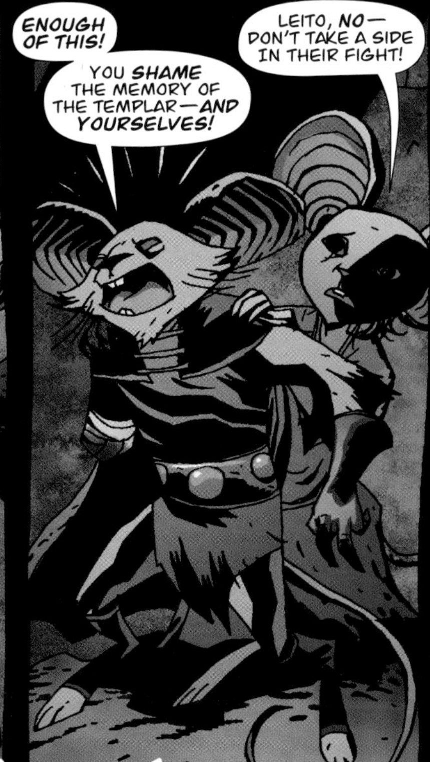
ENOUGH OF THIS!
YOU SHAME THE MEMORY OF THE TEMPLAR—AND YOURSELVES!
LEITO, NO—DON'T TAKE A SIDE IN THEIR FIGHT!

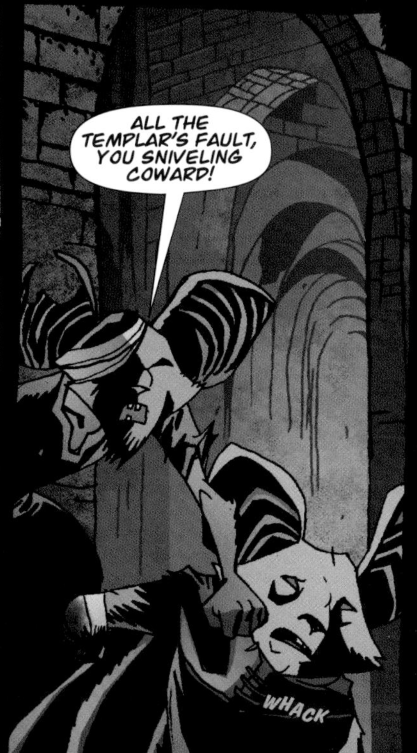
ALL THE TEMPLAR'S FAULT, YOU SNIVELING COWARD!
WHACK

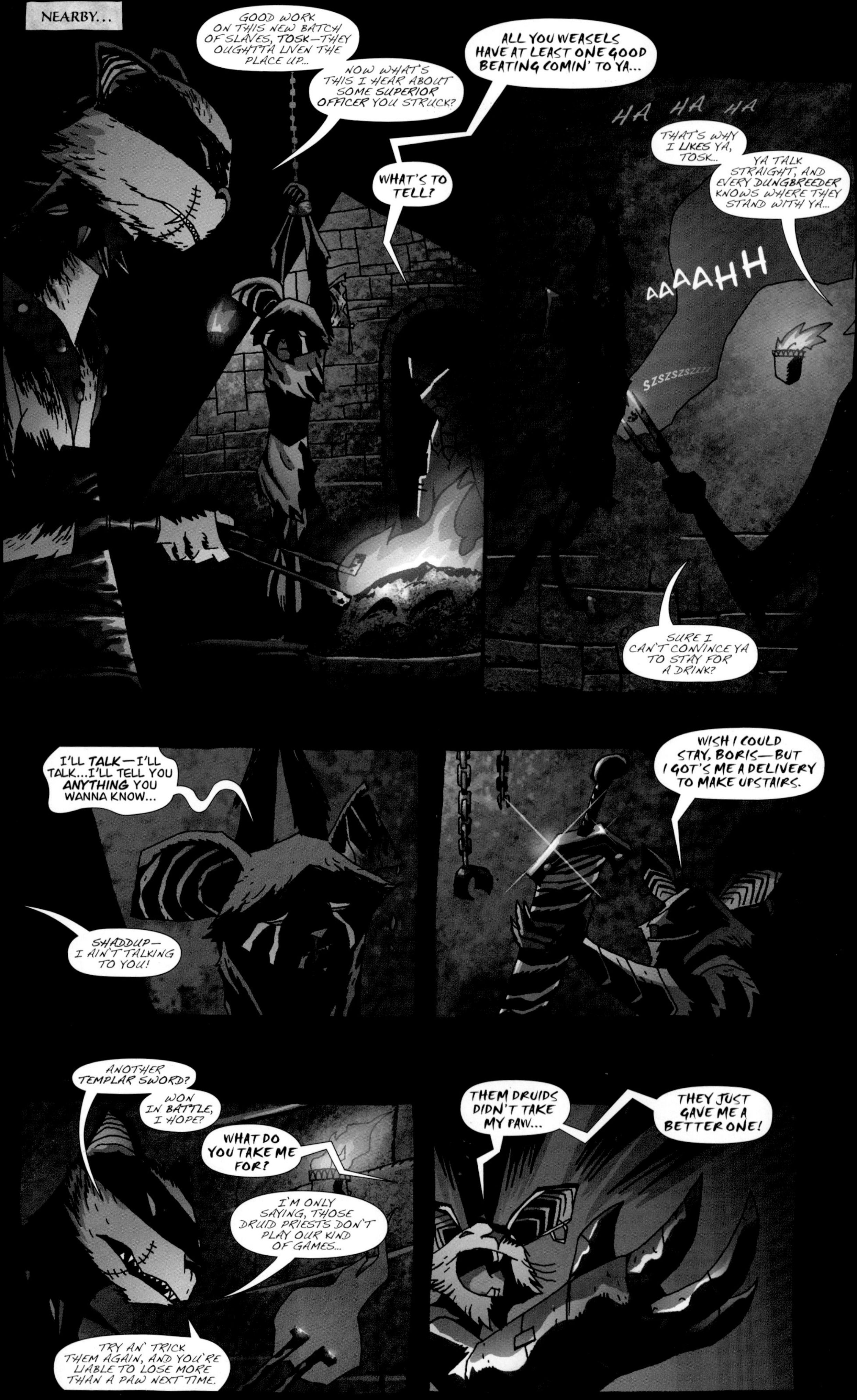
NEARBY...
GOOD WORK ON THIS NEW BATCH OF SLAVES, TOSK—THEY OUGHTTA LIVEN THE PLACE UP...
NOW WHAT'S THIS I HEAR ABOUT SOME SUPERIOR OFFICER YOU STRUCK?
WHAT'S TO TELL?
ALL YOU WEASELS HAVE AT LEAST ONE GOOD BEATING COMIN' TO YA...
HA HA HA
THAT'S WHY I LIKES YA, TOSK...
YA TALK STRAIGHT, AND EVERY DUNGBREEDER KNOWS WHERE THEY STAND WITH YA...
AAAAHH
SZSZSZSZZZZ
SURE I CAN'T CONVINCE YA TO STAY FOR A DRINK?
I'LL TALK—I'LL TALK...I'LL TELL YOU ANYTHING YOU WANNA KNOW...
SHADDUP—I AIN'T TALKING TO YOU!
WISH I COULD STAY, BORIS—BUT I GOT'S ME A DELIVERY TO MAKE UPSTAIRS.
ANOTHER TEMPLAR SWORD?
WON IN BATTLE, I HOPE?
WHAT DO YOU TAKE ME FOR?
I'M ONLY SAYING, THOSE DRUID PRIESTS DON'T PLAY OUR KIND OF GAMES...
TRY AN' TRICK THEM AGAIN, AND YOU'RE LIABLE TO LOSE MORE THAN A PAW NEXT TIME.
THEM DRUIDS DIDN'T TAKE MY PAW...
THEY JUST GAVE ME A BETTER ONE!

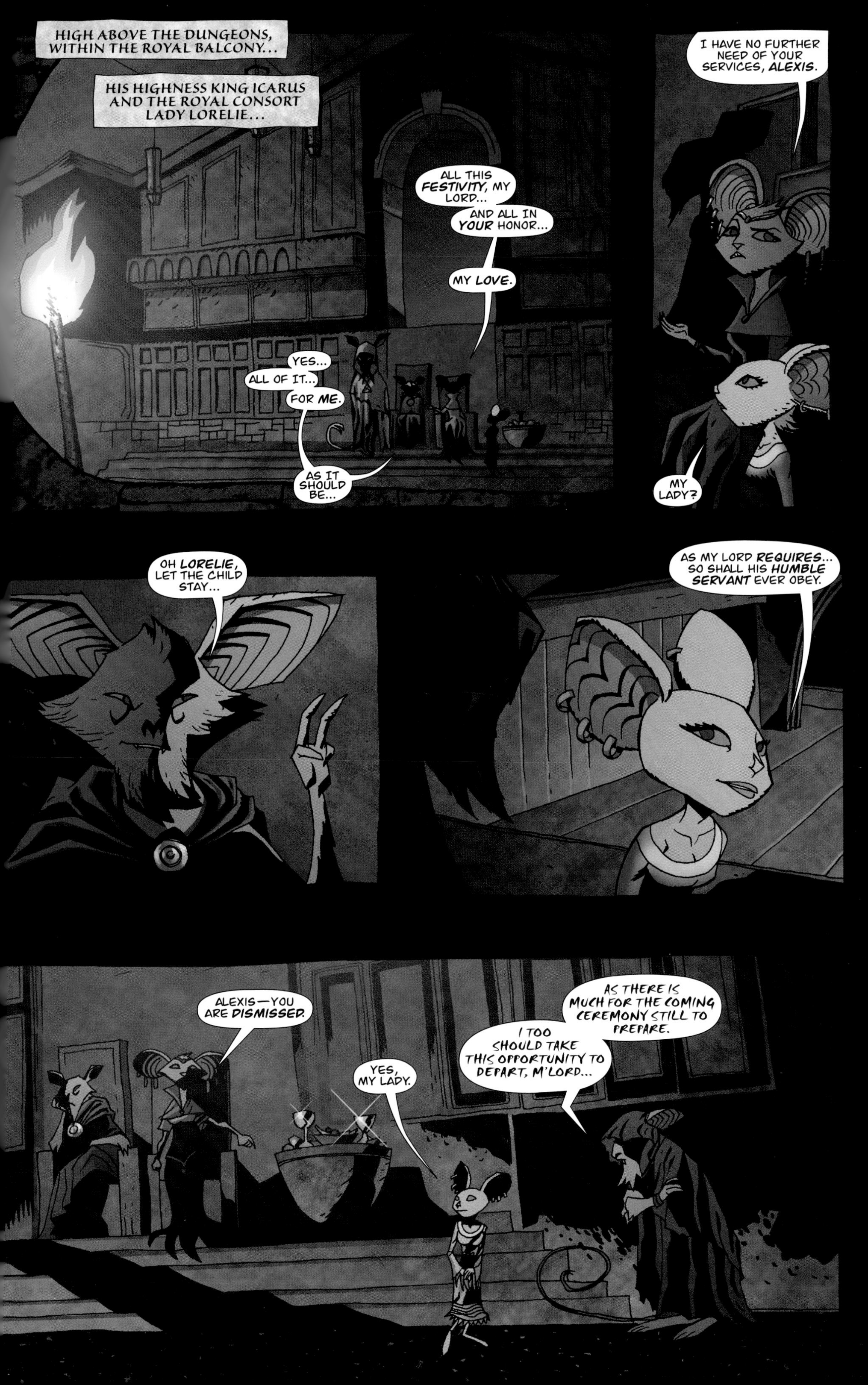
HIGH ABOVE THE DUNGEONS, WITHIN THE ROYAL BALCONY...
HIS HIGHNESS KING ICARUS AND THE ROYAL CONSORT LADY LORELIE...
ALL THIS FESTIVITY, MY LORD...
AND ALL IN YOUR HONOR...
MY LOVE.
YES...
ALL OF IT...
FOR ME.
AS IT SHOULD BE...
I HAVE NO FURTHER NEED OF YOUR SERVICES, ALEXIS.
MY LADY?
OH LORELIE, LET THE CHILD STAY...
AS MY LORD REQUIRES... SO SHALL HIS HUMBLE SERVANT EVER OBEY.
ALEXIS—YOU ARE DISMISSED.
YES, MY LADY.
I TOO SHOULD TAKE THIS OPPORTUNITY TO DEPART, M'LORD...
AS THERE IS MUCH FOR THE COMING CEREMONY STILL TO PREPARE.

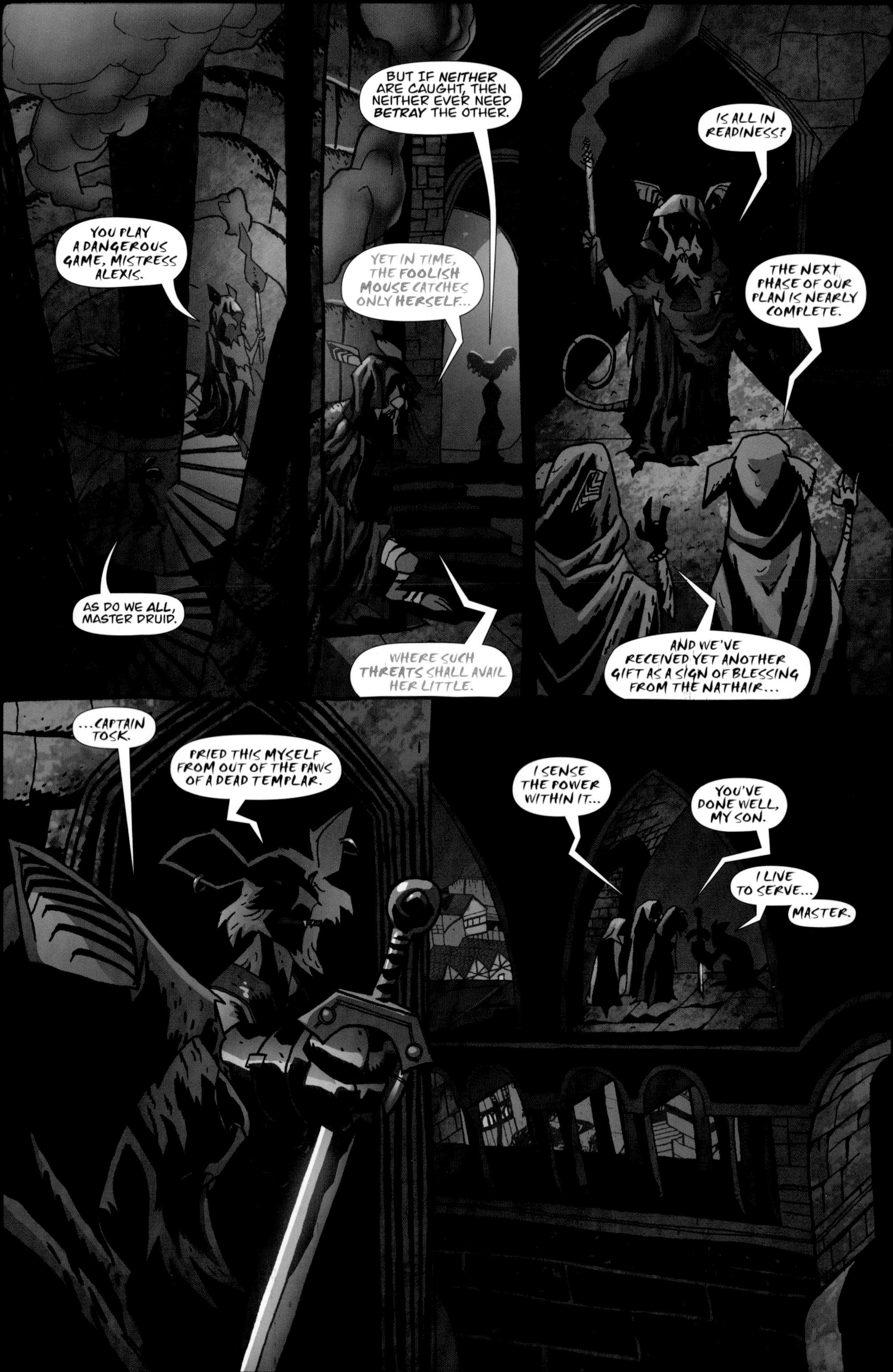

YOU PLAY A DANGEROUS GAME, MISTRESS ALEXIS.
AS DO WE ALL, MASTER DRUID.
BUT IF NEITHER ARE CAUGHT, THEN NEITHER EVER NEED BETRAY THE OTHER.
YET IN TIME, THE FOOLISH MOUSE CATCHES ONLY HERSELF...
WHERE SUCH THREATS SHALL AVAIL HER LITTLE.
IS ALL IN READINESS?
THE NEXT PHASE OF OUR PLAN IS NEARLY COMPLETE.
AND WE'VE RECEIVED YET ANOTHER GIFT AS A SIGN OF BLESSING FROM THE NATHAIR...
...CAPTAIN TOSK.
PRIED THIS MYSELF FROM OUT OF THE PAWS OF A DEAD TEMPLAR.
I SENSE THE POWER WITHIN IT...
YOU'VE DONE WELL, MY SON.
I LIVE TO SERVE...
MASTER.

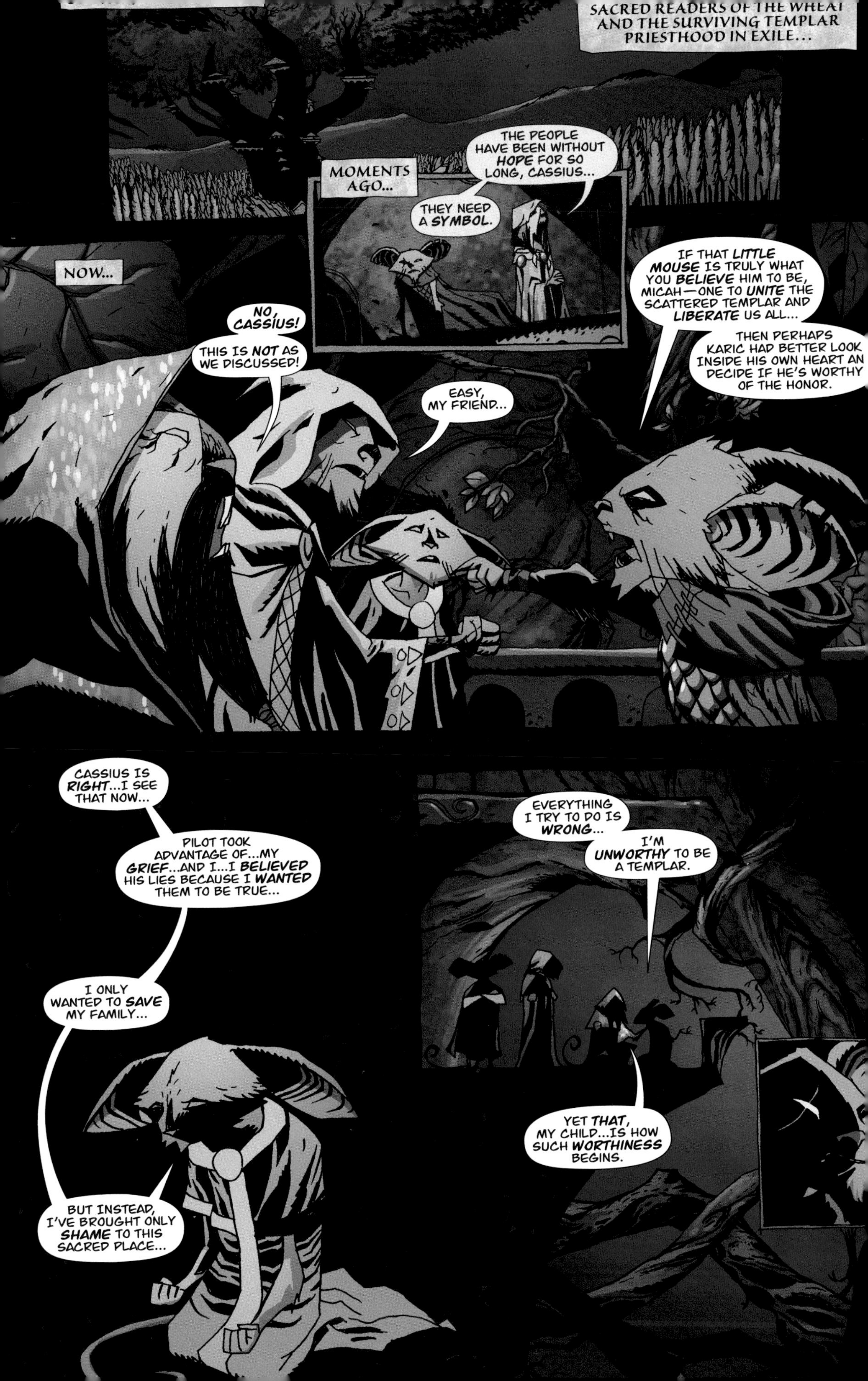
SACRED READERS OF THE WHEAT AND THE SURVIVING TEMPLAR PRIESTHOOD IN EXILE...
MOMENTS AGO...
THE PEOPLE HAVE BEEN WITHOUT HOPE FOR SO LONG, CASSIUS...
THEY NEED A SYMBOL.
NOW...
IF THAT LITTLE MOUSE IS TRULY WHAT YOU BELIEVE HIM TO BE, MICAH—ONE TO UNITE THE SCATTERED TEMPLAR AND LIBERATE US ALL...
THEN PERHAPS KARIC HAD BETTER LOOK INSIDE HIS OWN HEART AN DECIDE IF HE'S WORTHY OF THE HONOR.
NO, CASSIUS!
THIS IS NOT AS WE DISCUSSED!
EASY, MY FRIEND...
CASSIUS IS RIGHT...I SEE THAT NOW...
PILOT TOOK ADVANTAGE OF...MY GRIEF...AND I...I BELIEVED HIS LIES BECAUSE I WANTED THEM TO BE TRUE...
I ONLY WANTED TO SAVE MY FAMILY...
BUT INSTEAD, I'VE BROUGHT ONLY SHAME TO THIS SACRED PLACE...
EVERYTHING I TRY TO DO IS WRONG...
I'M UNWORTHY TO BE A TEMPLAR.
YET THAT, MY CHILD...IS HOW SUCH WORTHINESS BEGINS.

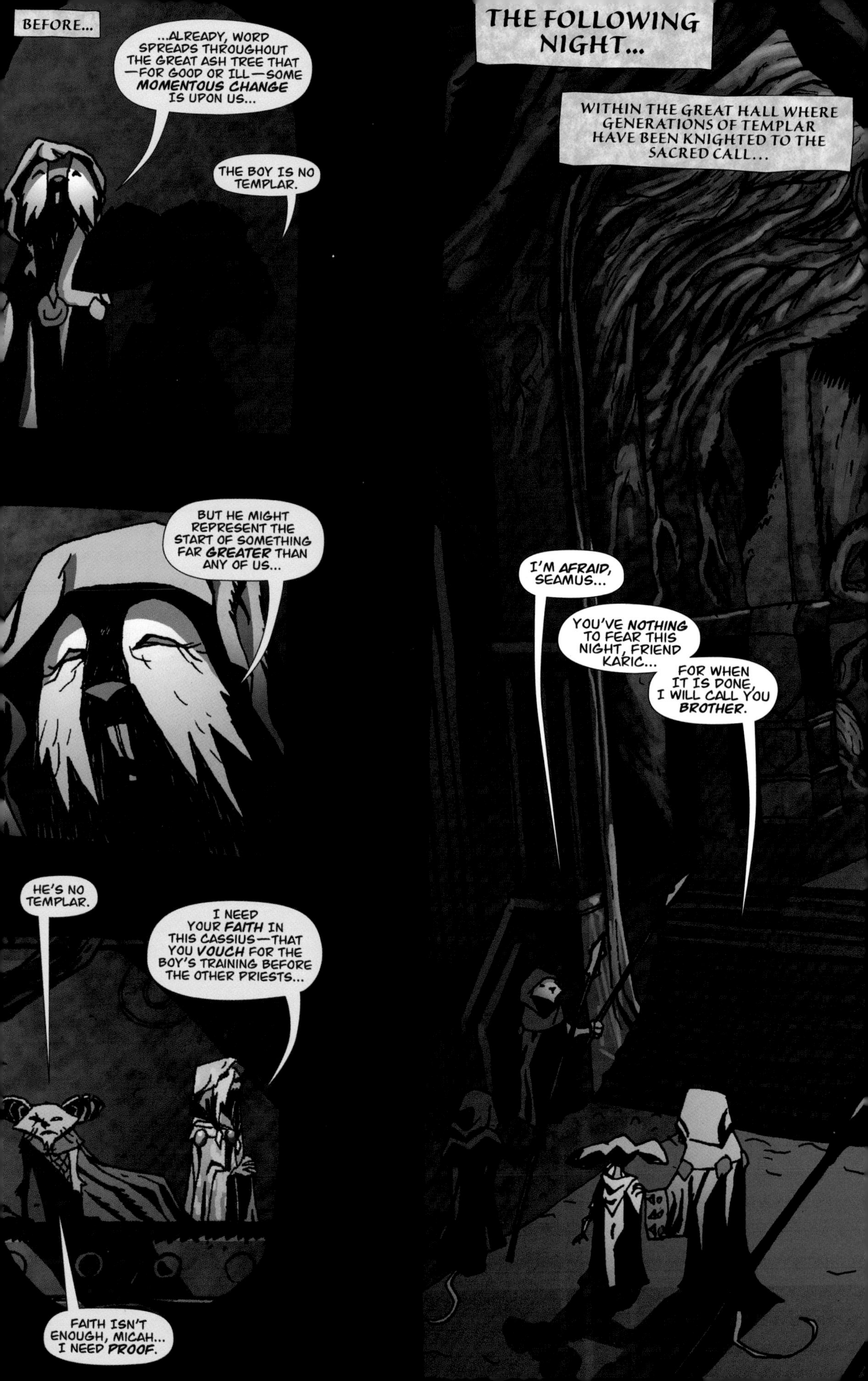
BEFORE...
...ALREADY, WORD SPREADS THROUGHOUT THE GREAT ASH TREE THAT —FOR GOOD OR ILL— SOME MOMENTOUS CHANGE IS UPON US...
THE BOY IS NO TEMPLAR.
BUT HE MIGHT REPRESENT THE START OF SOMETHING FAR GREATER THAN ANY OF US...
HE'S NO TEMPLAR.
I NEED YOUR FAITH IN THIS CASSIUS—THAT YOU VOUCH FOR THE BOY'S TRAINING BEFORE THE OTHER PRIESTS...
FAITH ISN'T ENOUGH, MICAH... I NEED PROOF.
THE FOLLOWING NIGHT...
WITHIN THE GREAT HALL WHERE GENERATIONS OF TEMPLAR HAVE BEEN KNIGHTED TO THE SACRED CALL...
I'M AFRAID, SEAMUS...
YOU'VE NOTHING TO FEAR THIS NIGHT, FRIEND KARIC...
FOR WHEN IT IS DONE, I WILL CALL YOU BROTHER.

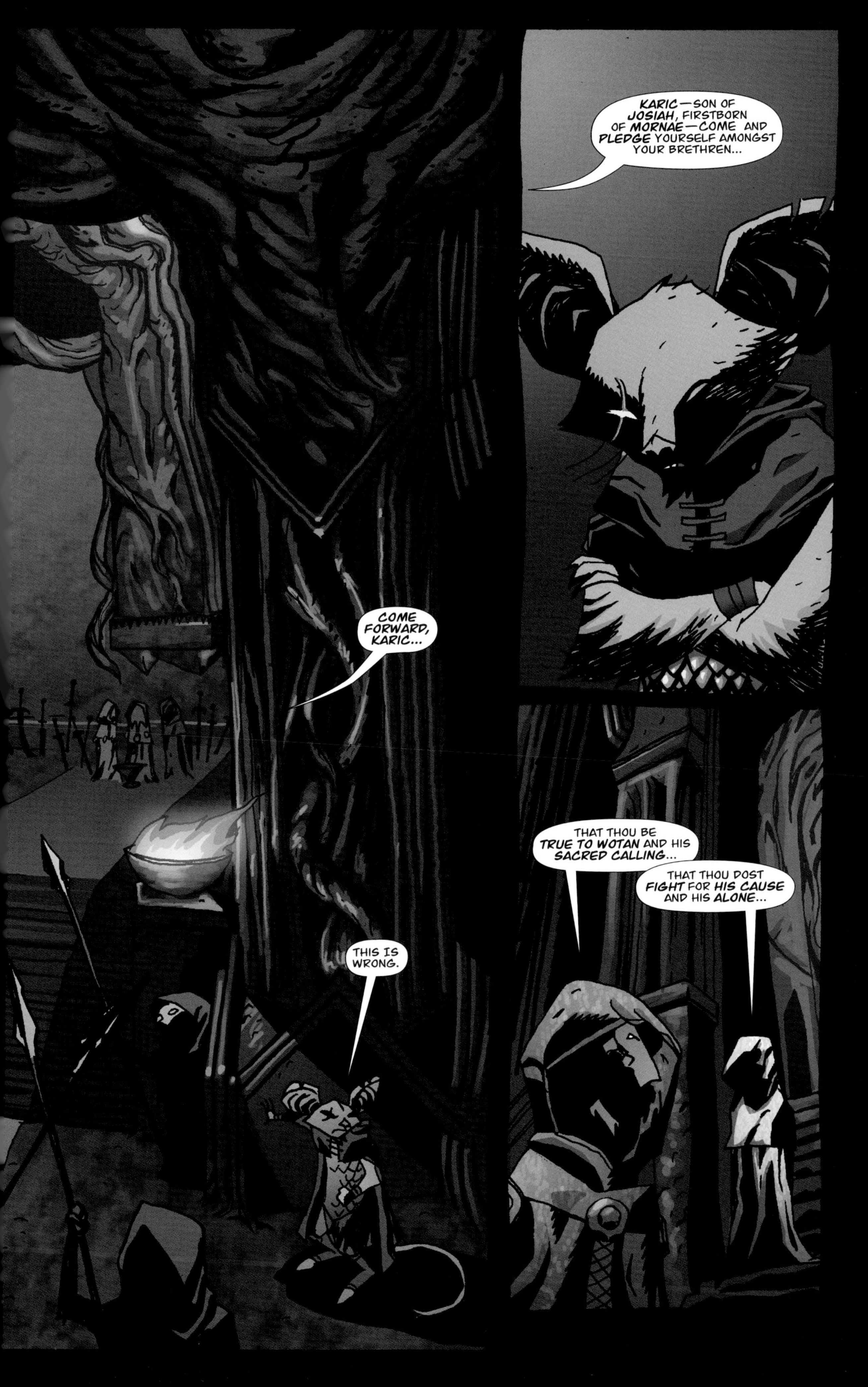
KARIC—SON OF JOSIAH, FIRSTBORN OF MORNAE—COME AND PLEDGE YOURSELF AMONGST YOUR BRETHREN...
COME FORWARD, KARIC...
THIS IS WRONG.
THAT THOU BE TRUE TO WOTAN AND HIS SACRED CALLING...
THAT THOU DOST FIGHT FOR HIS CAUSE AND HIS ALONE...

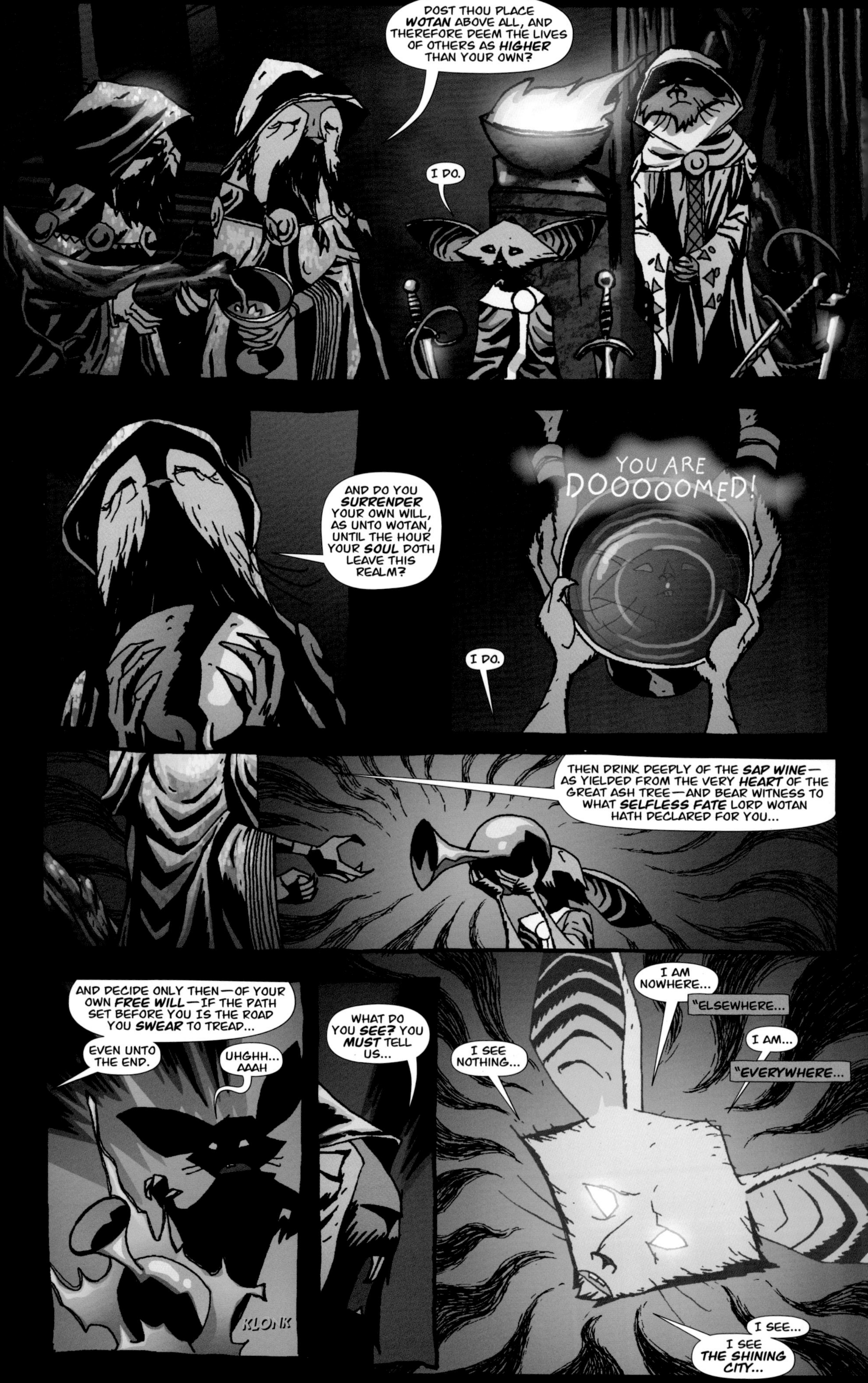

DOST THOU PLACE WOTAN ABOVE ALL, AND THEREFORE DEEM THE LIVES OF OTHERS AS HIGHER THAN YOUR OWN?
I DO.
AND DO YOU SURRENDER YOUR OWN WILL, AS UNTO WOTAN, UNTIL THE HOUR YOUR SOUL DOTH LEAVE THIS REALM?
YOU ARE DOOOOOMED!
I DO.
THEN DRINK DEEPLY OF THE SAP WINE—AS YIELDED FROM THE VERY HEART OF THE GREAT ASH TREE—AND BEAR WITNESS TO WHAT SELFLESS FATE LORD WOTAN HATH DECLARED FOR YOU...
AND DECIDE ONLY THEN—OF YOUR OWN FREE WILL—IF THE PATH SET BEFORE YOU IS THE ROAD YOU SWEAR TO TREAD...
EVEN UNTO THE END.
UHGHH... AAAH
KLONK
WHAT DO YOU SEE? YOU MUST TELL US...
I SEE NOTHING...
I AM NOWHERE...
"ELSEWHERE...
I AM...
"EVERYWHERE...
I SEE...
I SEE THE SHINING CITY...

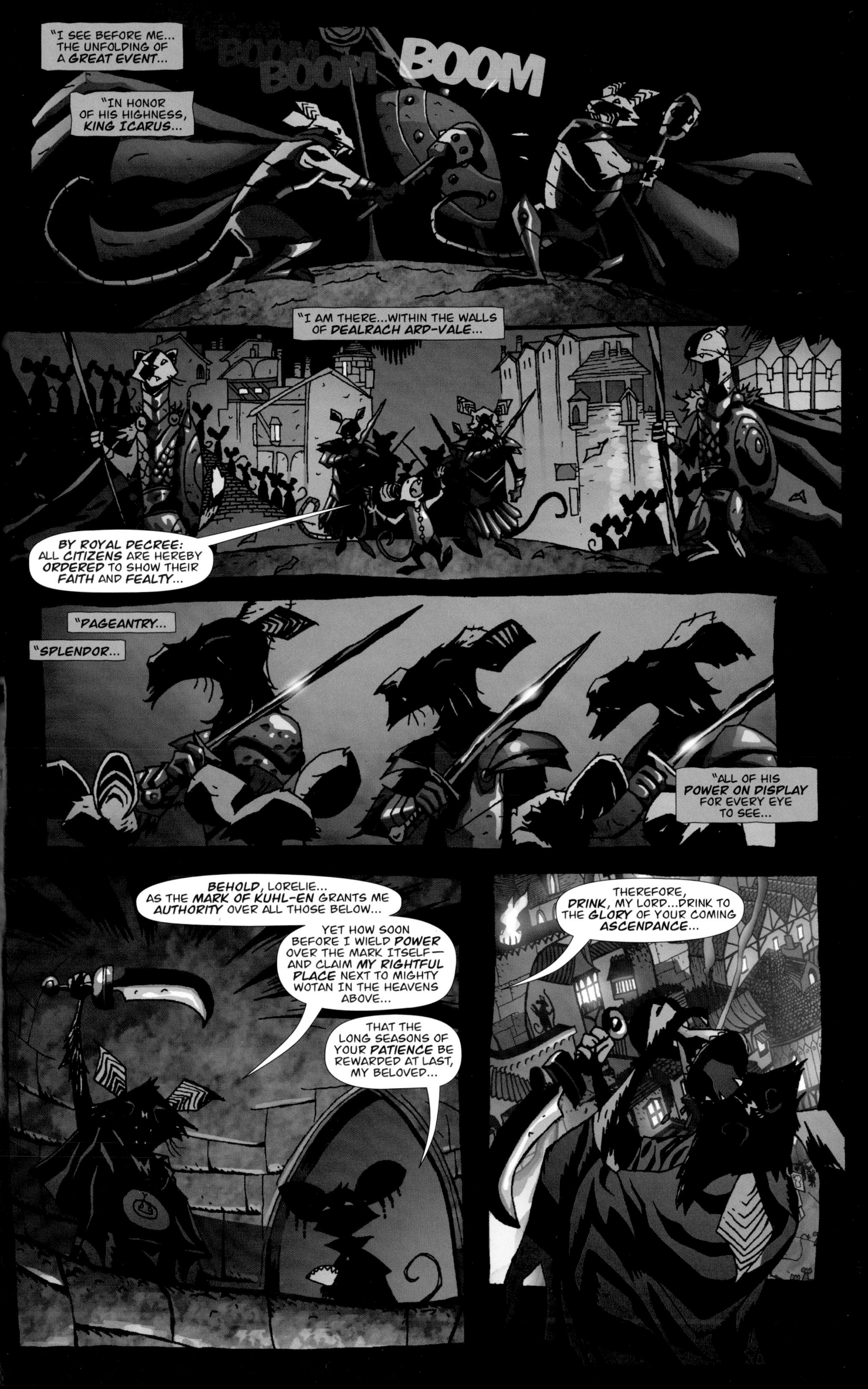
"I SEE BEFORE ME... THE UNFOLDING OF A GREAT EVENT...
BOOM BOOM BOOM
"IN HONOR OF HIS HIGHNESS, KING ICARUS...
"I AM THERE...WITHIN THE WALLS OF DEALRACH ARD-VALE...
BY ROYAL DECREE: ALL CITIZENS ARE HEREBY ORDERED TO SHOW THEIR FAITH AND FEALTY...
"PAGEANTRY...
"SPLENDOR...
"ALL OF HIS POWER ON DISPLAY FOR EVERY EYE TO SEE...
BEHOLD, LORELIE... AS THE MARK OF KUHL-EN GRANTS ME AUTHORITY OVER ALL THOSE BELOW...
YET HOW SOON BEFORE I WIELD POWER OVER THE MARK ITSELF— AND CLAIM MY RIGHTFUL PLACE NEXT TO MIGHTY WOTAN IN THE HEAVENS ABOVE...
THAT THE LONG SEASONS OF YOUR PATIENCE BE REWARDED AT LAST, MY BELOVED...
THEREFORE, DRINK, MY LORD...DRINK TO THE GLORY OF YOUR COMING ASCENDANCE...

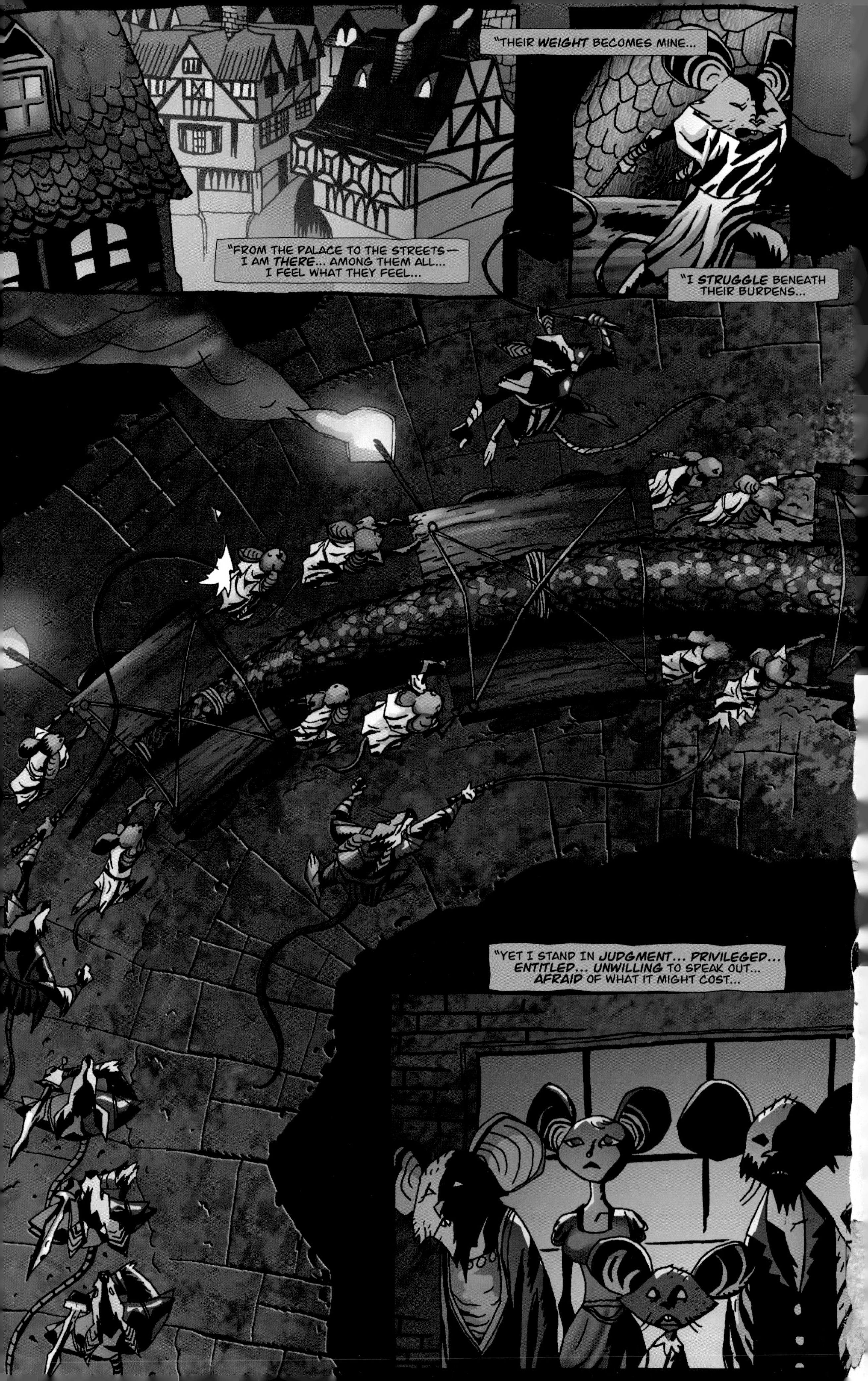
"FROM THE PALACE TO THE STREETS— I AM THERE... AMONG THEM ALL... I FEEL WHAT THEY FEEL...
"THEIR WEIGHT BECOMES MINE...
"I STRUGGLE BENEATH THEIR BURDENS...
"YET I STAND IN JUDGMENT... PRIVILEGED... ENTITLED... UNWILLING TO SPEAK OUT... AFRAID OF WHAT IT MIGHT COST...

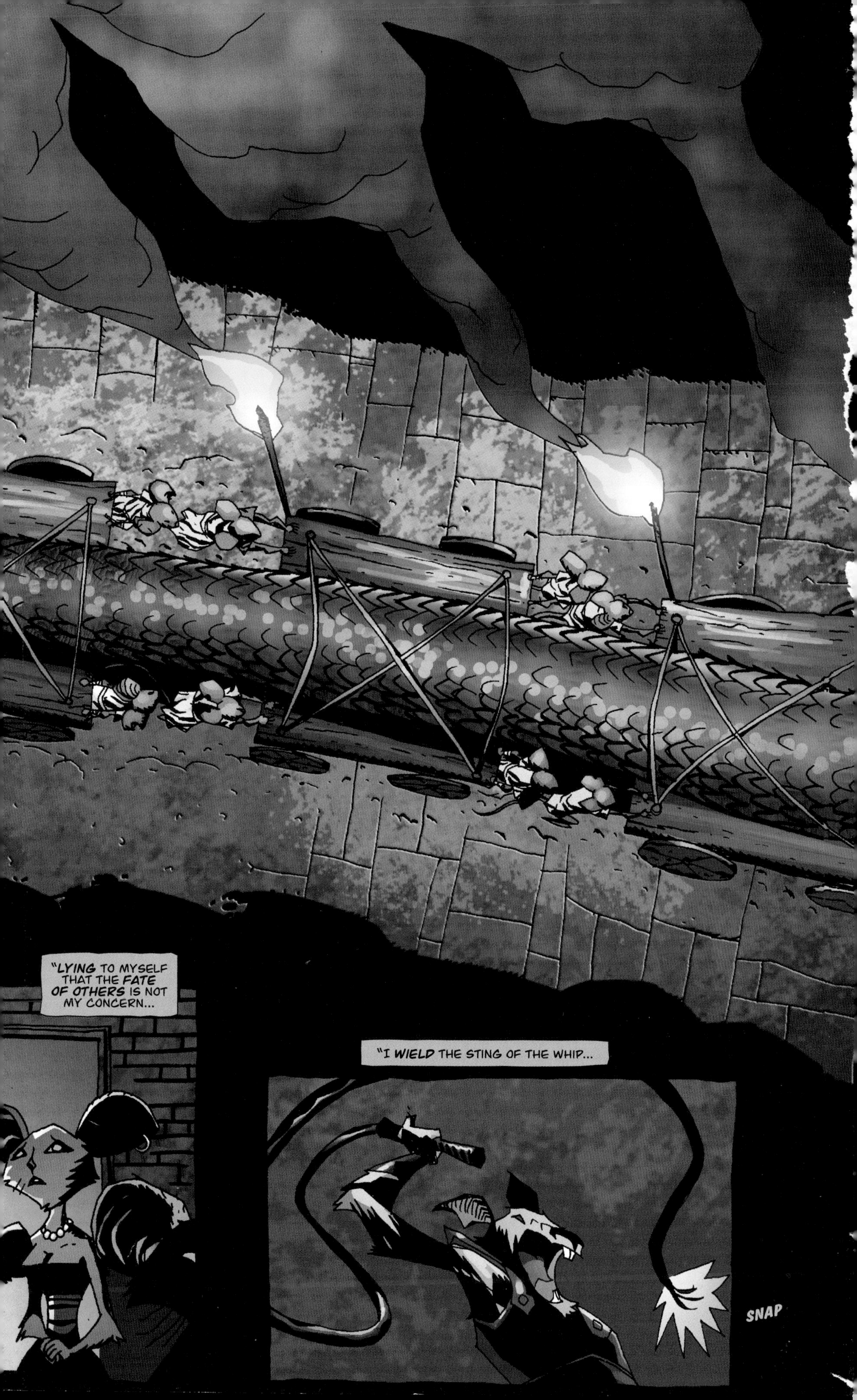
"LYING TO MYSELF THAT THE FATE OF OTHERS IS NOT MY CONCERN...
"I WIELD THE STING OF THE WHIP...
SNAP

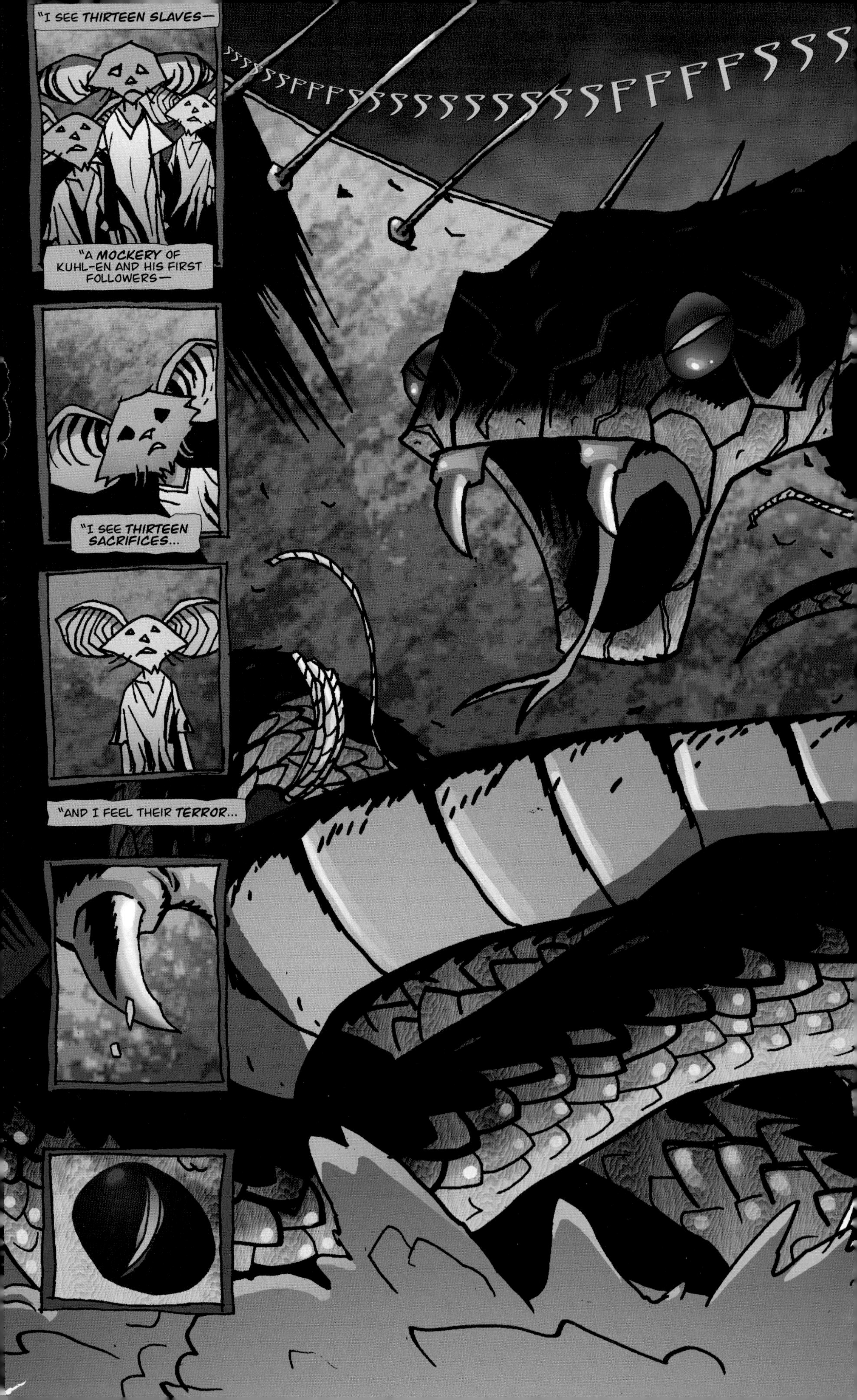
"I SEE THIRTEEN SLAVES—
"A MOCKERY OF KUHL-EN AND HIS FIRST FOLLOWERS—
"I SEE THIRTEEN SACRIFICES...
"AND I FEEL THEIR TERROR...
SSSSSSSFFFSSSSSSSSSSSSSSSSSSFFFFFSSSS

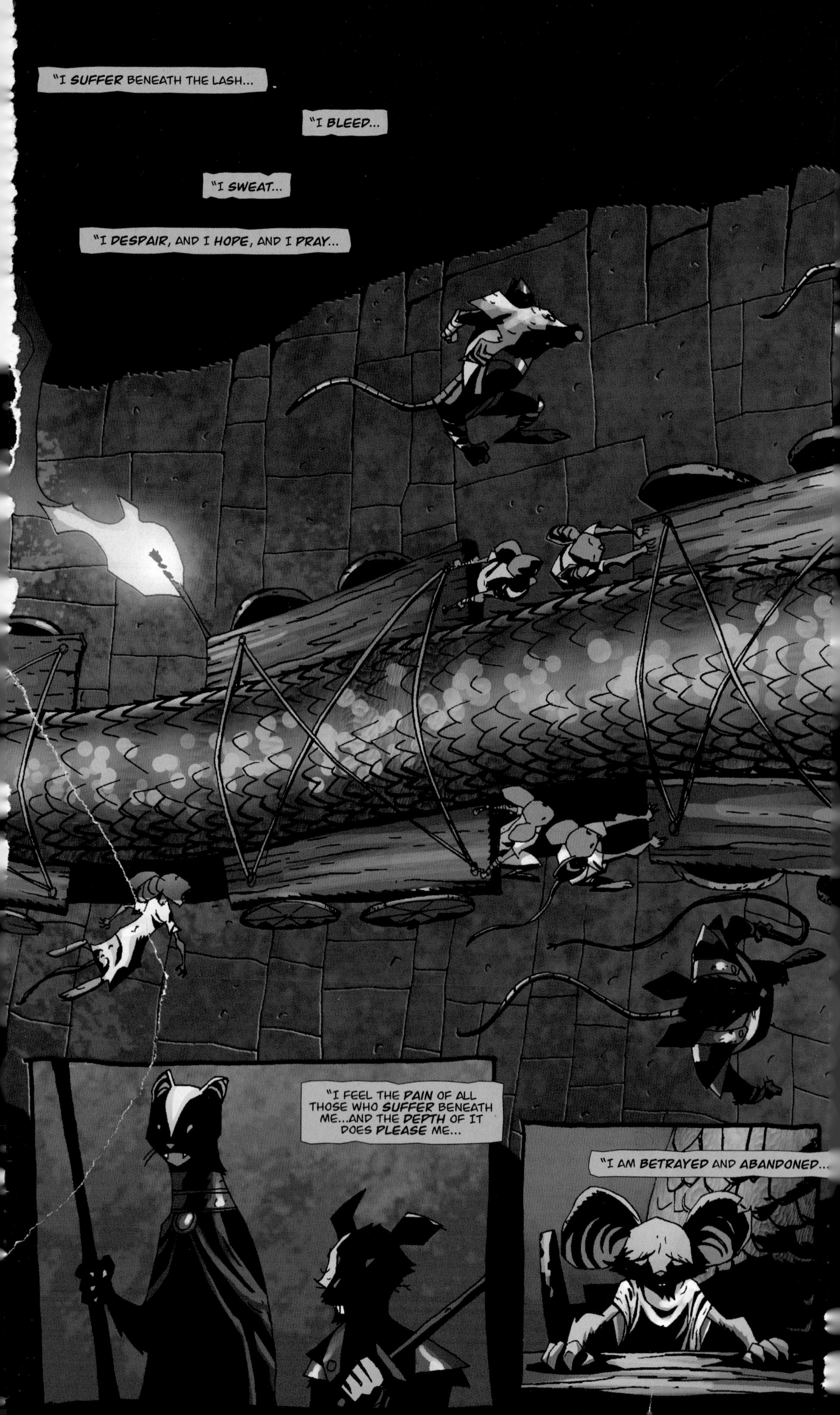
"I SUFFER BENEATH THE LASH...
"I BLEED...
"I SWEAT...
"I DESPAIR, AND I HOPE, AND I PRAY...
"I FEEL THE PAIN OF ALL THOSE WHO SUFFER BENEATH ME...AND THE DEPTH OF IT DOES PLEASE ME...
"I AM BETRAYED AND ABANDONED...

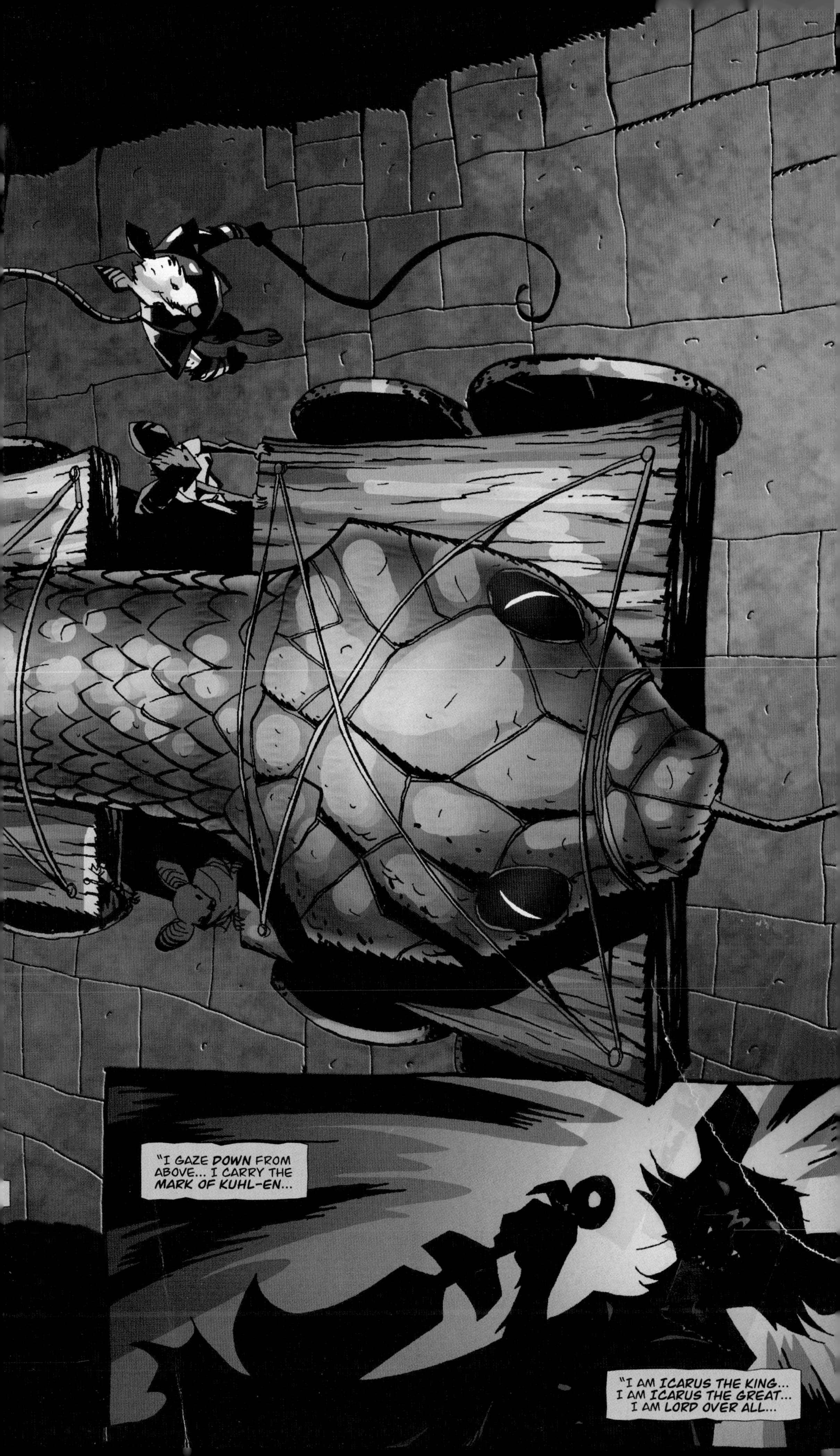
"I GAZE DOWN FROM ABOVE... I CARRY THE MARK OF KUHL-EN...
"I AM ICARUS THE KING... I AM ICARUS THE GREAT... I AM LORD OVER ALL...

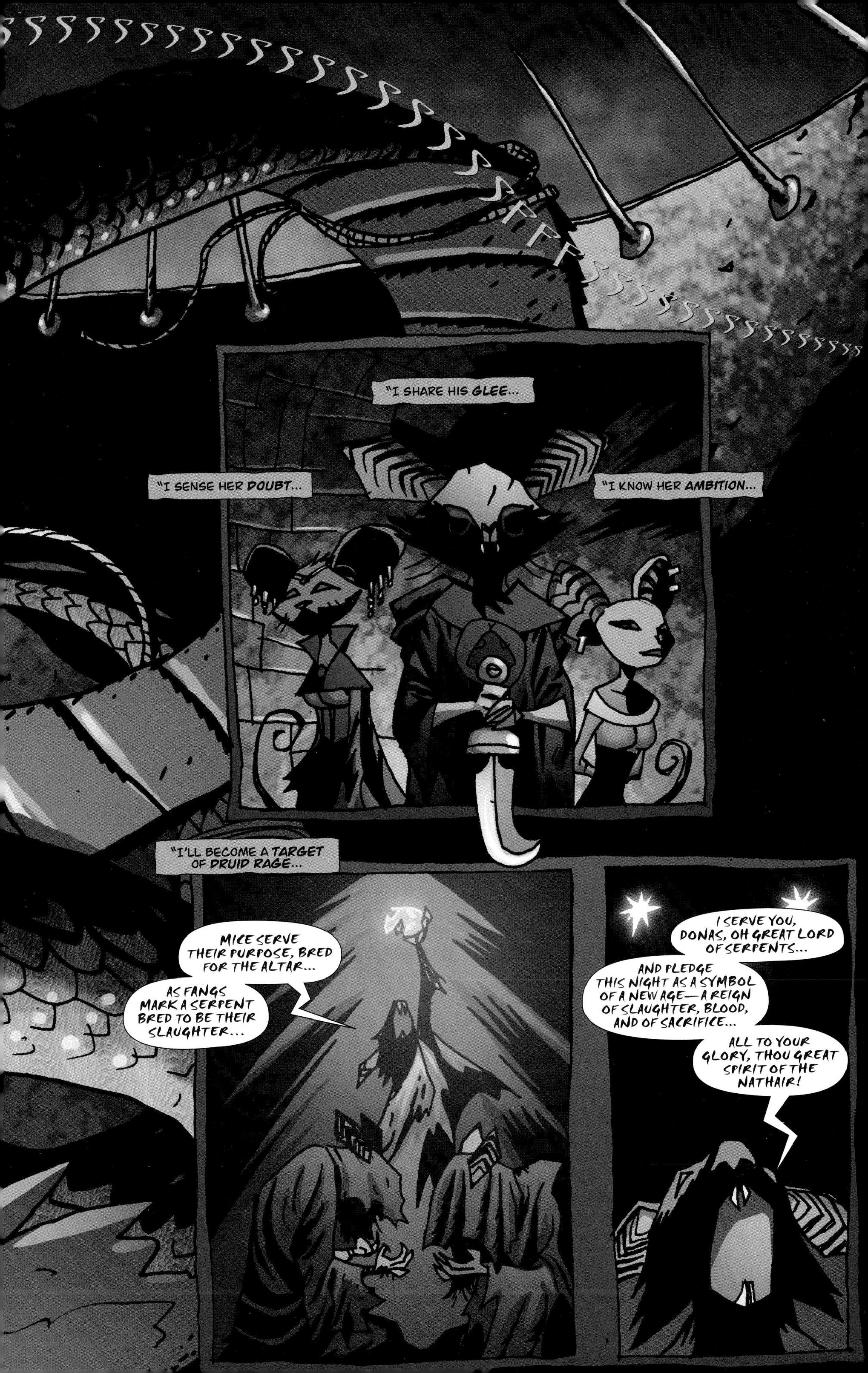
SSSSSSSSSSSSSSSSSSSSSSSSSSSSSSSSSSSSSSSSSSSSSSSSSS
"I SHARE HIS GLEE...
"I SENSE HER DOUBT...
"I KNOW HER AMBITION...
"I'LL BECOME A TARGET OF DRUID RAGE...
MICE SERVE THEIR PURPOSE, BRED FOR THE ALTAR...
AS FANGS MARK A SERPENT BRED TO BE THEIR SLAUGHTER...
I SERVE YOU, DONAS, OH GREAT LORD OF SERPENTS...
AND PLEDGE THIS NIGHT AS A SYMBOL OF A NEW AGE—A REIGN OF SLAUGHTER, BLOOD, AND OF SACRIFICE...
ALL TO YOUR GLORY, THOU GREAT SPIRIT OF THE NATHAIR!

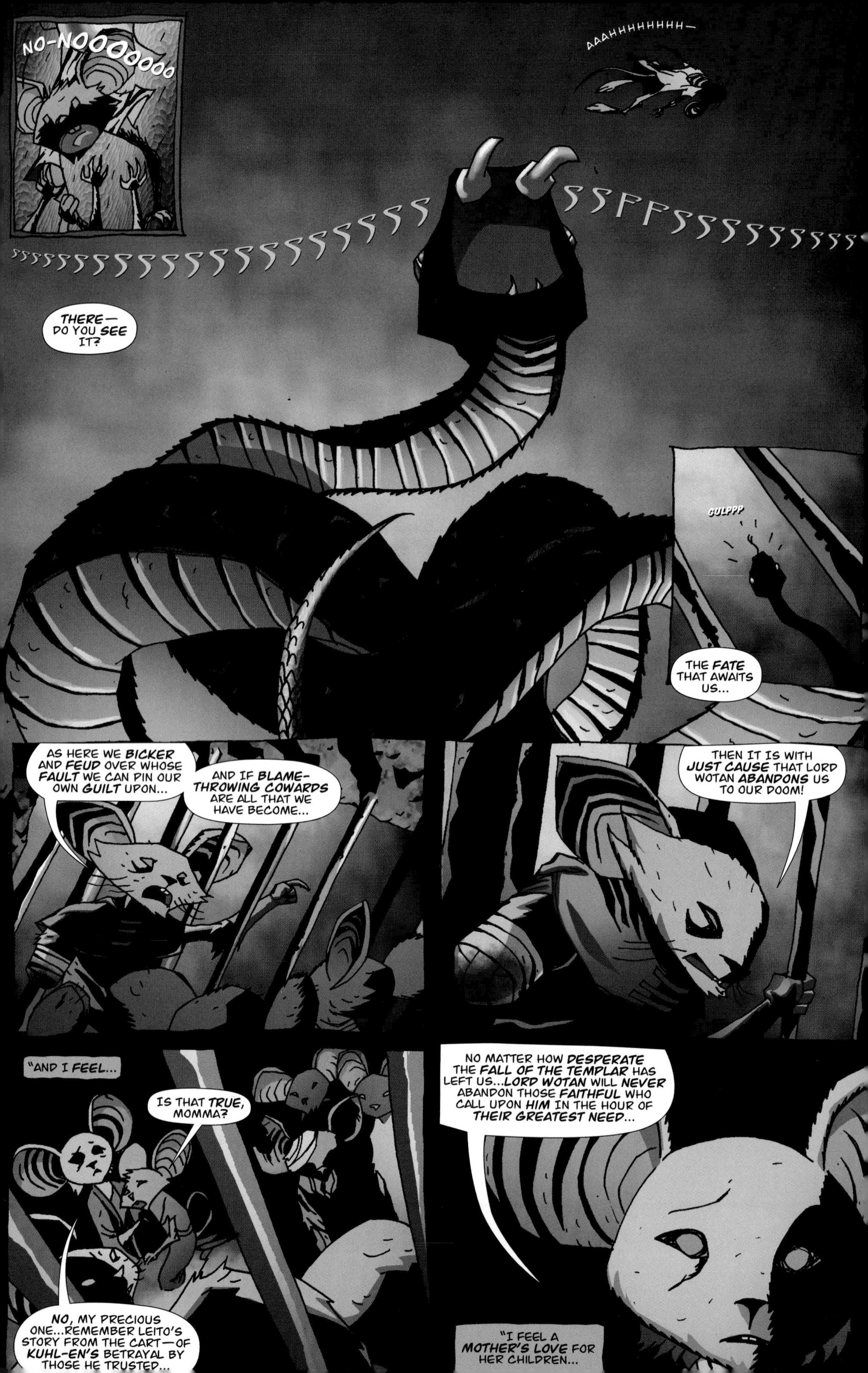
NO-NOOOOOOOO
AAAHHHHHHHH—
SSSSSSSSSSSSSSSSSSSSSSSSSSSSSSSSSSSPFFSSSSSSSSSSSSSS
THERE—DO YOU SEE IT?
GULPPP
THE FATE THAT AWAITS US...
AS HERE WE BICKER AND FEUD OVER WHOSE FAULT WE CAN PIN OUR OWN GUILT UPON...
AND IF BLAME-THROWING COWARDS ARE ALL THAT WE HAVE BECOME...
THEN IT IS WITH JUST CAUSE THAT LORD WOTAN ABANDONS US TO OUR DOOM!
"AND I FEEL...
IS THAT TRUE, MOMMA?
NO, MY PRECIOUS ONE...REMEMBER LEITO'S STORY FROM THE CART—OF KUHL-EN'S BETRAYAL BY THOSE HE TRUSTED...
NO MATTER HOW DESPERATE THE FALL OF THE TEMPLAR HAS LEFT US...LORD WOTAN WILL NEVER ABANDON THOSE FAITHFUL WHO CALL UPON HIM IN THE HOUR OF THEIR GREATEST NEED...
"I FEEL A MOTHER'S LOVE FOR HER CHILDREN...

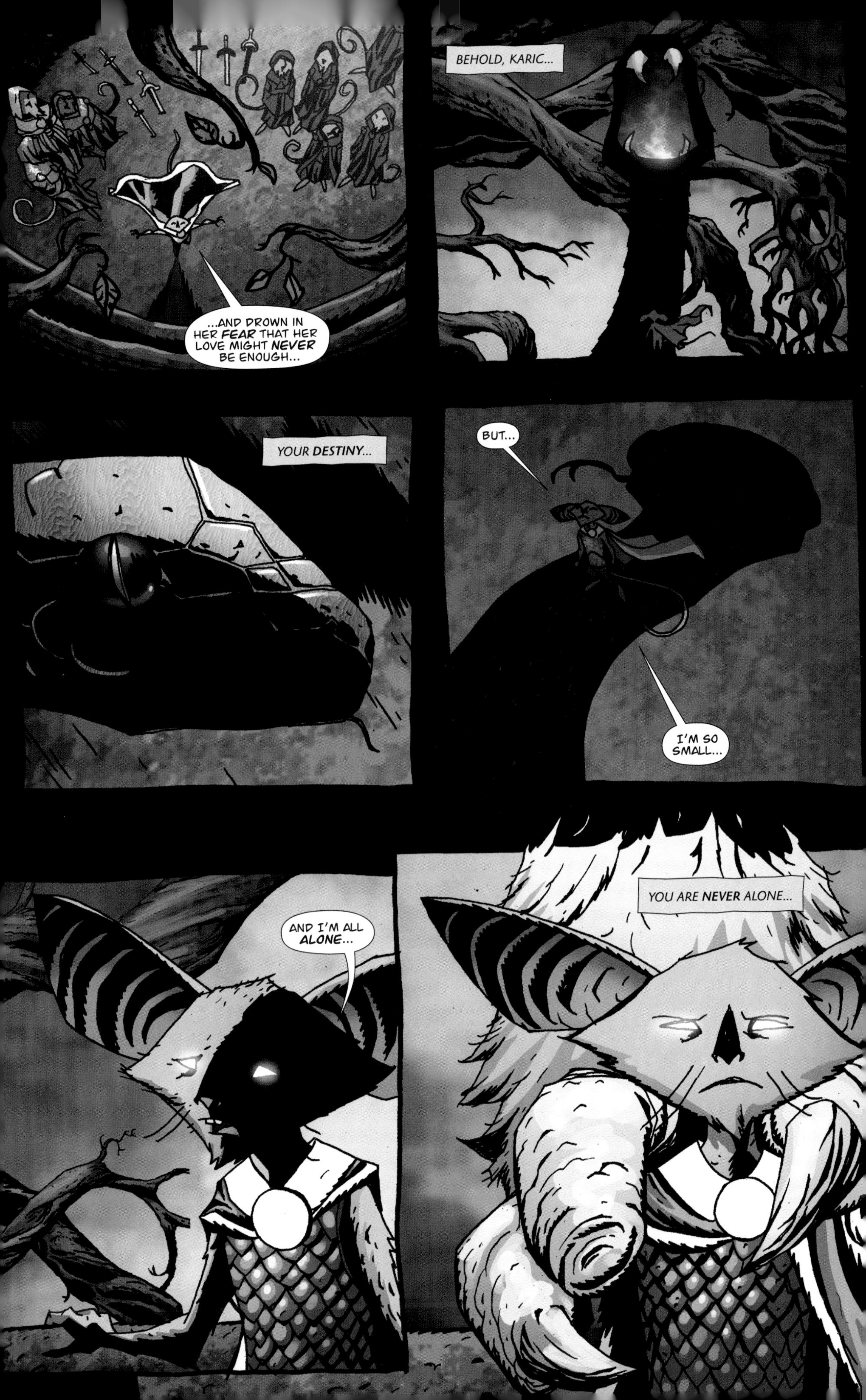
...AND DROWN IN HER FEAR THAT HER LOVE MIGHT NEVER BE ENOUGH...
BEHOLD, KARIC...
YOUR DESTINY...
BUT...
I'M SO SMALL...
AND I'M ALL ALONE...
YOU ARE NEVER ALONE...

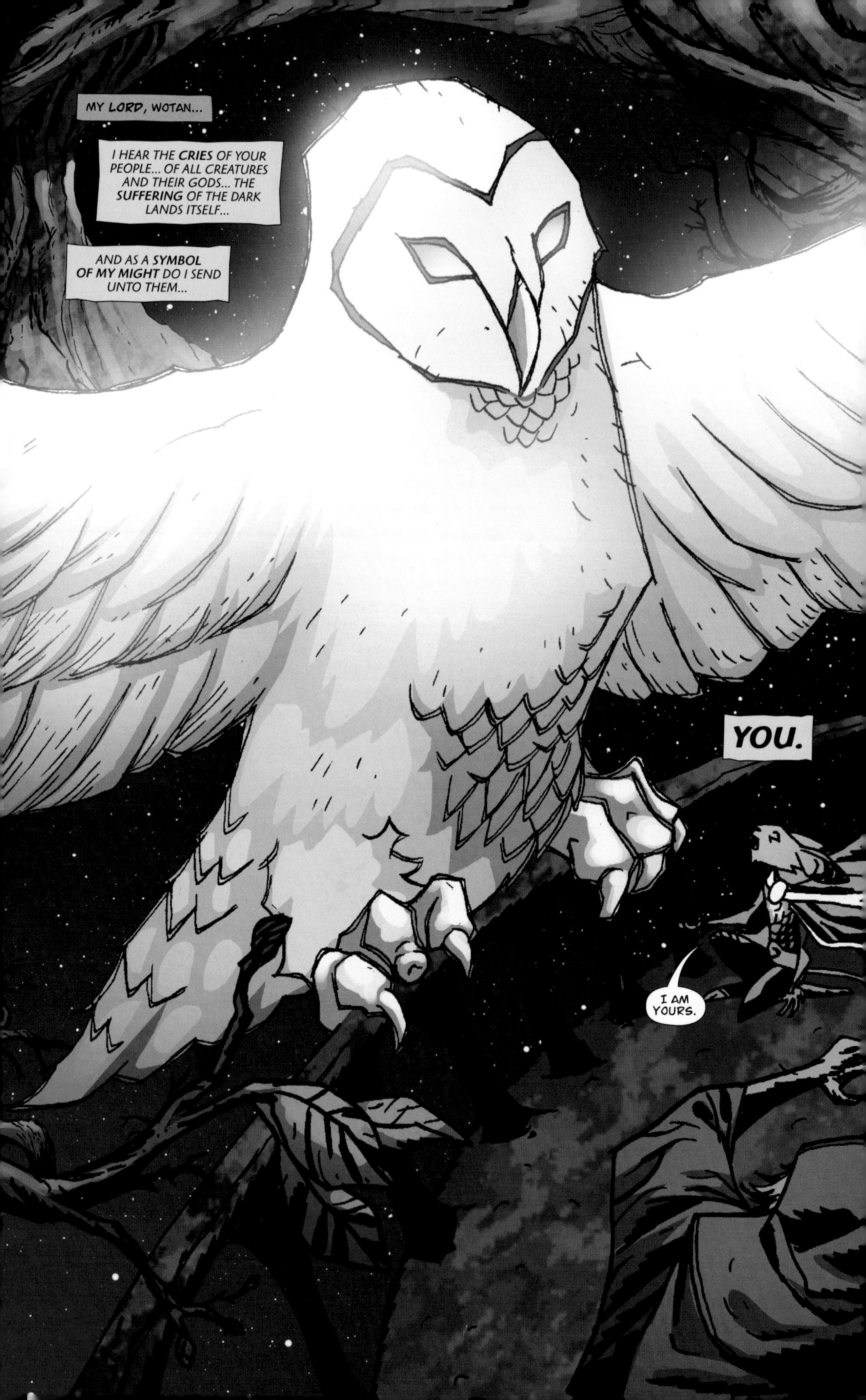
MY **LORD**, WOTAN...
I HEAR THE **CRIES** OF YOUR PEOPLE... OF ALL CREATURES AND THEIR GODS... THE **SUFFERING** OF THE DARK LANDS ITSELF...
AND AS A **SYMBOL OF MY MIGHT** DO I SEND UNTO THEM...
YOU.
I AM YOURS.

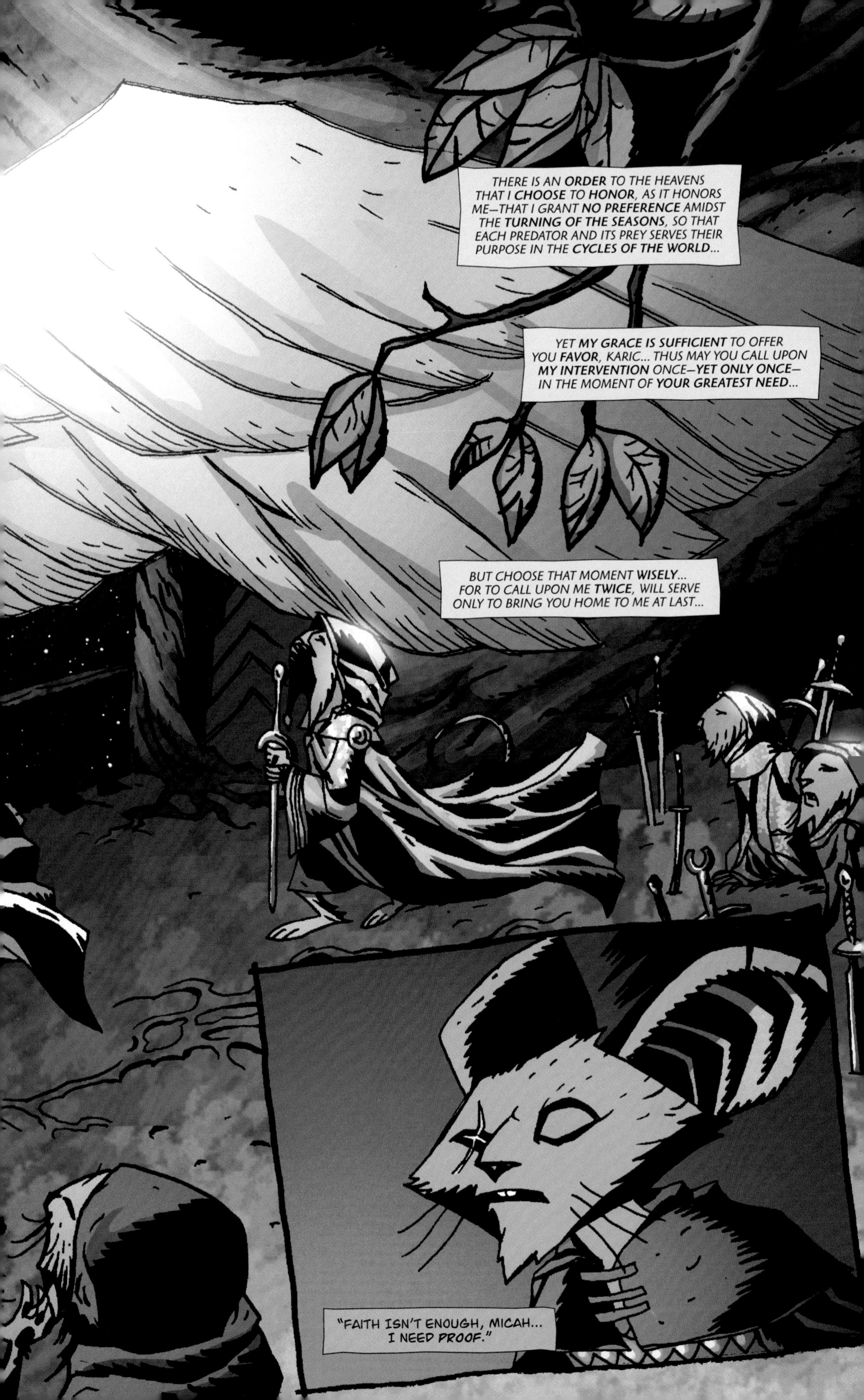
THERE IS AN ORDER TO THE HEAVENS THAT I CHOOSE TO HONOR, AS IT HONORS ME—THAT I GRANT NO PREFERENCE AMIDST THE TURNING OF THE SEASONS, SO THAT EACH PREDATOR AND ITS PREY SERVES THEIR PURPOSE IN THE CYCLES OF THE WORLD...
YET MY GRACE IS SUFFICIENT TO OFFER YOU FAVOR, KARIC... THUS MAY YOU CALL UPON MY INTERVENTION ONCE—YET ONLY ONCE—IN THE MOMENT OF YOUR GREATEST NEED...
BUT CHOOSE THAT MOMENT WISELY... FOR TO CALL UPON ME TWICE, WILL SERVE ONLY TO BRING YOU HOME TO ME AT LAST...
"FAITH ISN'T ENOUGH, MICAH... I NEED PROOF."

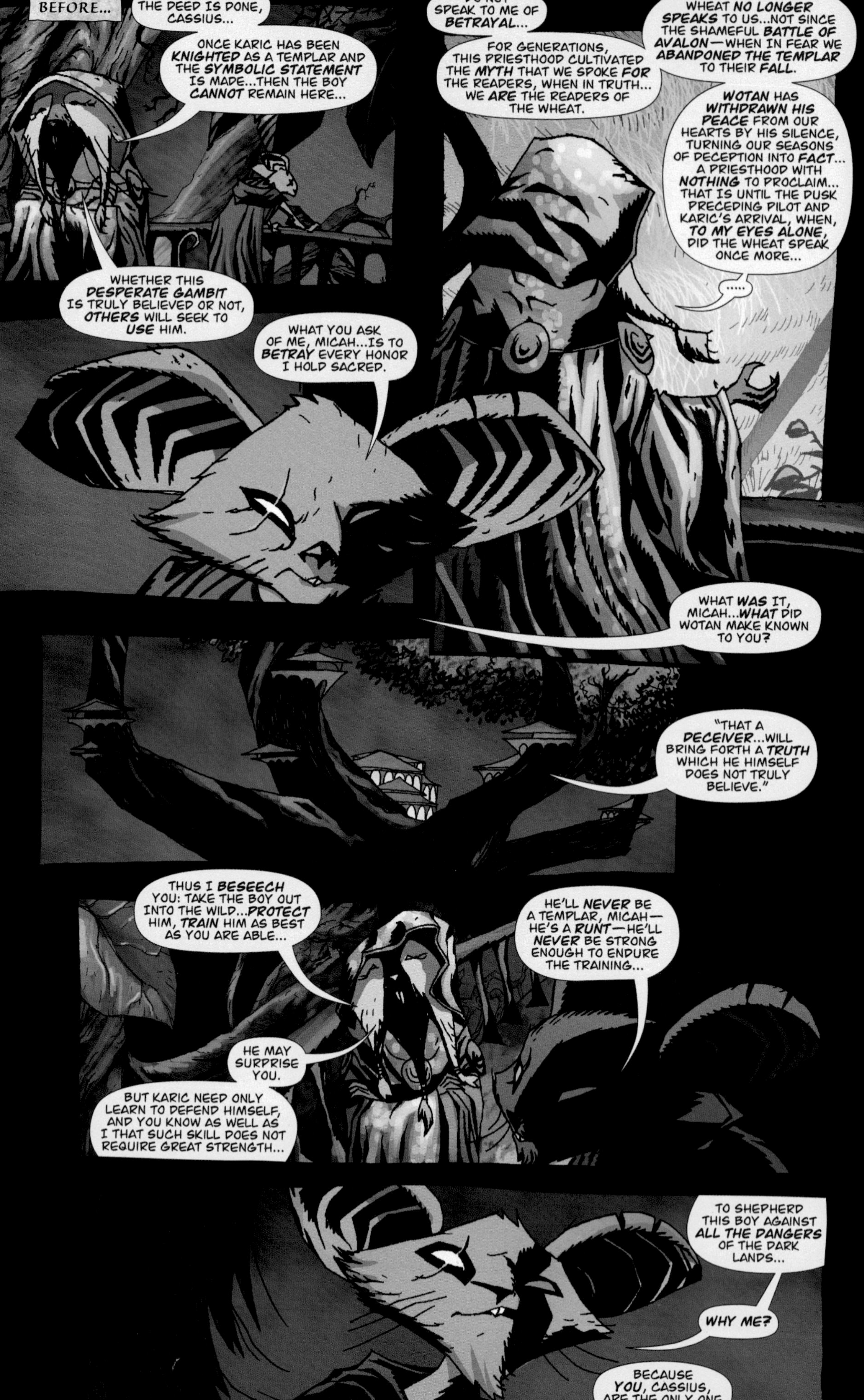
BEFORE...
BUT ONCE THE DEED IS DONE, CASSIUS...
ONCE KARIC HAS BEEN KNIGHTED AS A TEMPLAR AND THE SYMBOLIC STATEMENT IS MADE...THEN THE BOY CANNOT REMAIN HERE...
WHETHER THIS DESPERATE GAMBIT IS TRULY BELIEVED OR NOT, OTHERS WILL SEEK TO USE HIM.
WHAT YOU ASK OF ME, MICAH...IS TO BETRAY EVERY HONOR I HOLD SACRED.
DO NOT SPEAK TO ME OF BETRAYAL...
FOR GENERATIONS, THIS PRIESTHOOD CULTIVATED THE MYTH THAT WE SPOKE FOR THE READERS, WHEN IN TRUTH... WE ARE THE READERS OF THE WHEAT.
ONLY NOW...THE WHEAT NO LONGER SPEAKS TO US...NOT SINCE THE SHAMEFUL BATTLE OF AVALON—WHEN IN FEAR WE ABANDONED THE TEMPLAR TO THEIR FALL.
WOTAN HAS WITHDRAWN HIS PEACE FROM OUR HEARTS BY HIS SILENCE, TURNING OUR SEASONS OF DECEPTION INTO FACT... A PRIESTHOOD WITH NOTHING TO PROCLAIM... THAT IS UNTIL THE DUSK PRECEDING PILOT AND KARIC'S ARRIVAL, WHEN, TO MY EYES ALONE, DID THE WHEAT SPEAK ONCE MORE...
.....
WHAT WAS IT, MICAH...WHAT DID WOTAN MAKE KNOWN TO YOU?
"THAT A DECEIVER...WILL BRING FORTH A TRUTH WHICH HE HIMSELF DOES NOT TRULY BELIEVE."
THUS I BESEECH YOU: TAKE THE BOY OUT INTO THE WILD...PROTECT HIM, TRAIN HIM AS BEST AS YOU ARE ABLE...
HE'LL NEVER BE A TEMPLAR, MICAH— HE'S A RUNT—HE'LL NEVER BE STRONG ENOUGH TO ENDURE THE TRAINING...
HE MAY SURPRISE YOU.
BUT KARIC NEED ONLY LEARN TO DEFEND HIMSELF, AND YOU KNOW AS WELL AS I THAT SUCH SKILL DOES NOT REQUIRE GREAT STRENGTH...
TO SHEPHERD THIS BOY AGAINST ALL THE DANGERS OF THE DARK LANDS...
WHY ME?
BECAUSE YOU, CASSIUS, ARE THE ONLY ONE I TRUST.

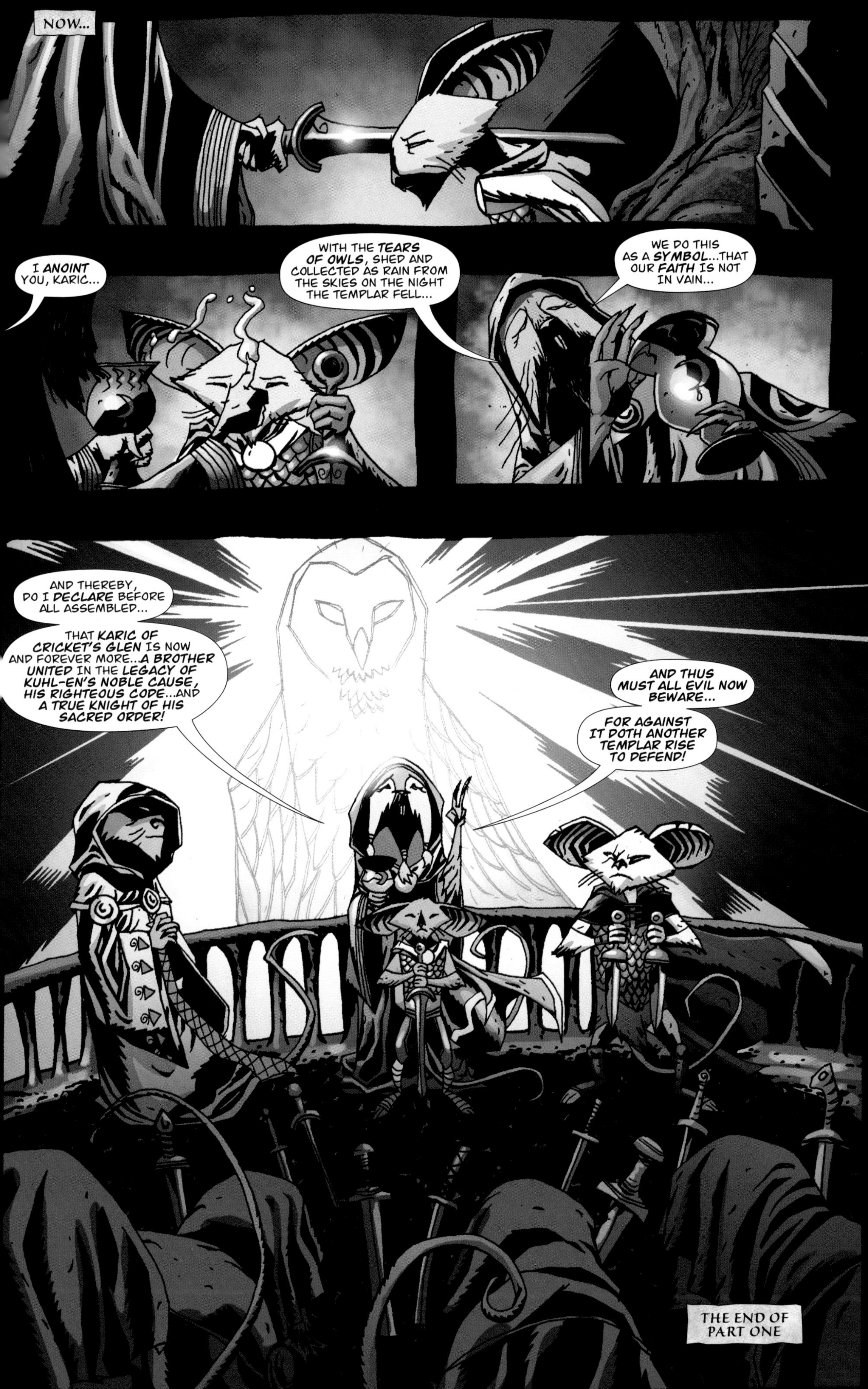
NOW...
I ANOINT YOU, KARIC...
WITH THE TEARS OF OWLS, SHED AND COLLECTED AS RAIN FROM THE SKIES ON THE NIGHT THE TEMPLAR FELL...
WE DO THIS AS A SYMBOL...THAT OUR FAITH IS NOT IN VAIN...
AND THEREBY, DO I DECLARE BEFORE ALL ASSEMBLED...
THAT KARIC OF CRICKET'S GLEN IS NOW AND FOREVER MORE...A BROTHER UNITED IN THE LEGACY OF KUHL-EN'S NOBLE CAUSE, HIS RIGHTEOUS CODE...AND A TRUE KNIGHT OF HIS SACRED ORDER!
AND THUS MUST ALL EVIL NOW BEWARE...
FOR AGAINST IT DOTH ANOTHER TEMPLAR RISE TO DEFEND!
THE END OF PART ONE

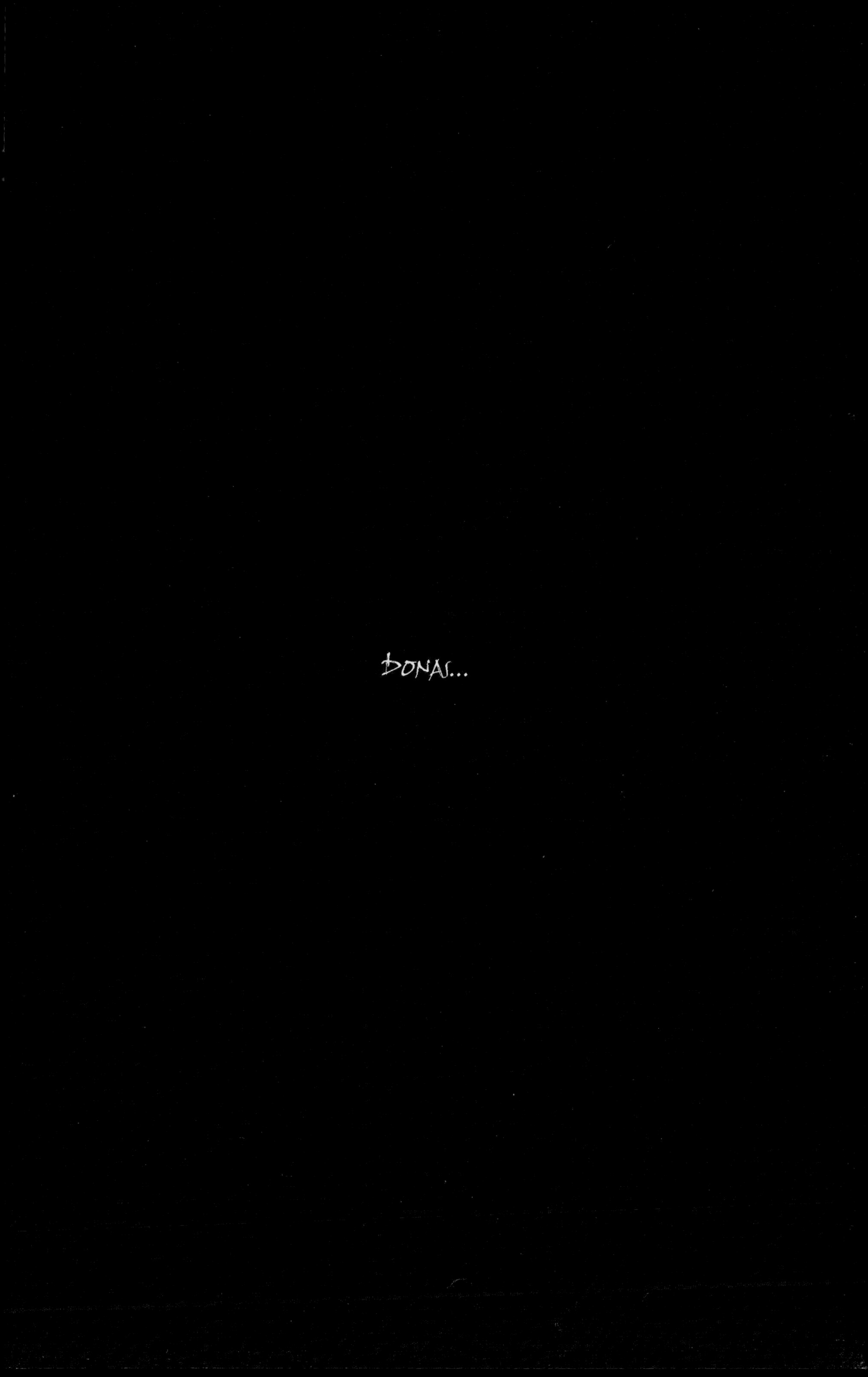
DONAS...

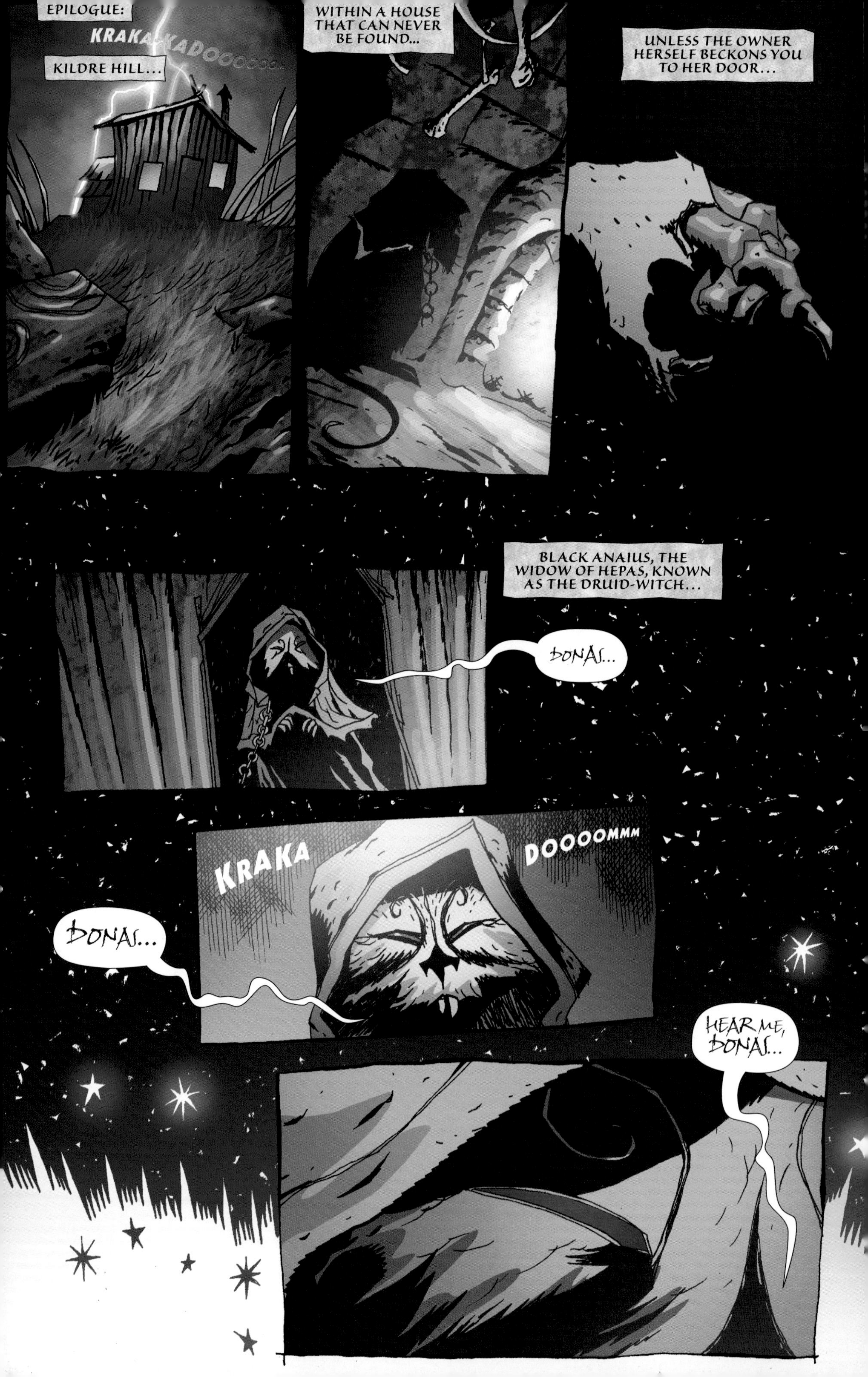

EPILOGUE:
KRAKA-KADOOOOOOO...
KILDRE HILL...
WITHIN A HOUSE THAT CAN NEVER BE FOUND...
UNLESS THE OWNER HERSELF BECKONS YOU TO HER DOOR...
BLACK ANAIUS, THE WIDOW OF HEPAS, KNOWN AS THE DRUID-WITCH...
DONAS...
KRAKA
DOOOOMMM
DONAS...
HEAR ME, DONAS...

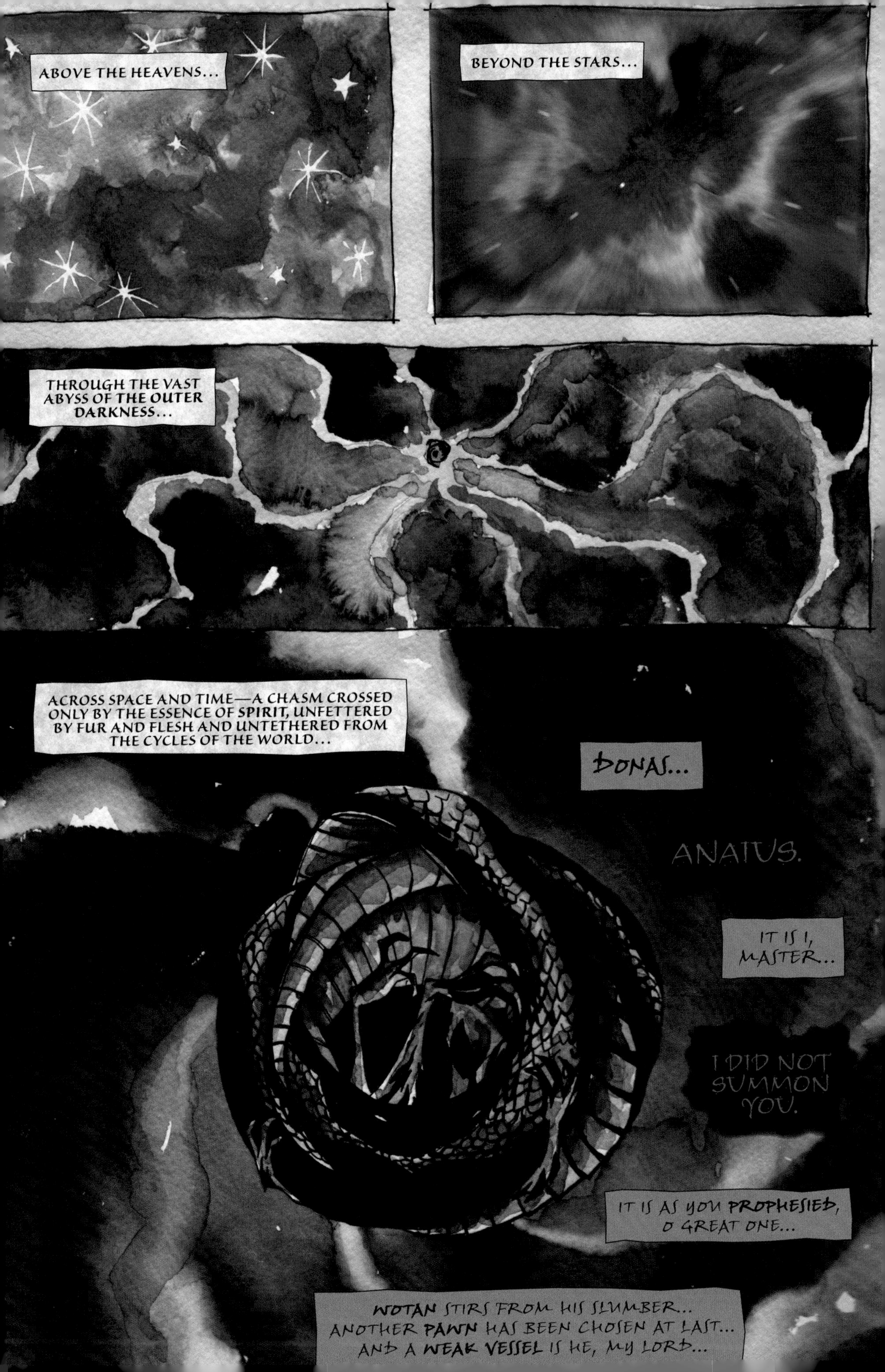
ABOVE THE HEAVENS...
BEYOND THE STARS...
THROUGH THE VAST ABYSS OF THE OUTER DARKNESS...
ACROSS SPACE AND TIME—A CHASM CROSSED ONLY BY THE ESSENCE OF SPIRIT, UNFETTERED BY FUR AND FLESH AND UNTETHERED FROM THE CYCLES OF THE WORLD...
DONAS...
ANAIUS.
IT IS I, MASTER...
I DID NOT SUMMON YOU.
IT IS AS YOU PROPHESIED, O GREAT ONE...
WOTAN STIRS FROM HIS SLUMBER... ANOTHER PAWN HAS BEEN CHOSEN AT LAST... AND A WEAK VESSEL IS HE, MY LORD...

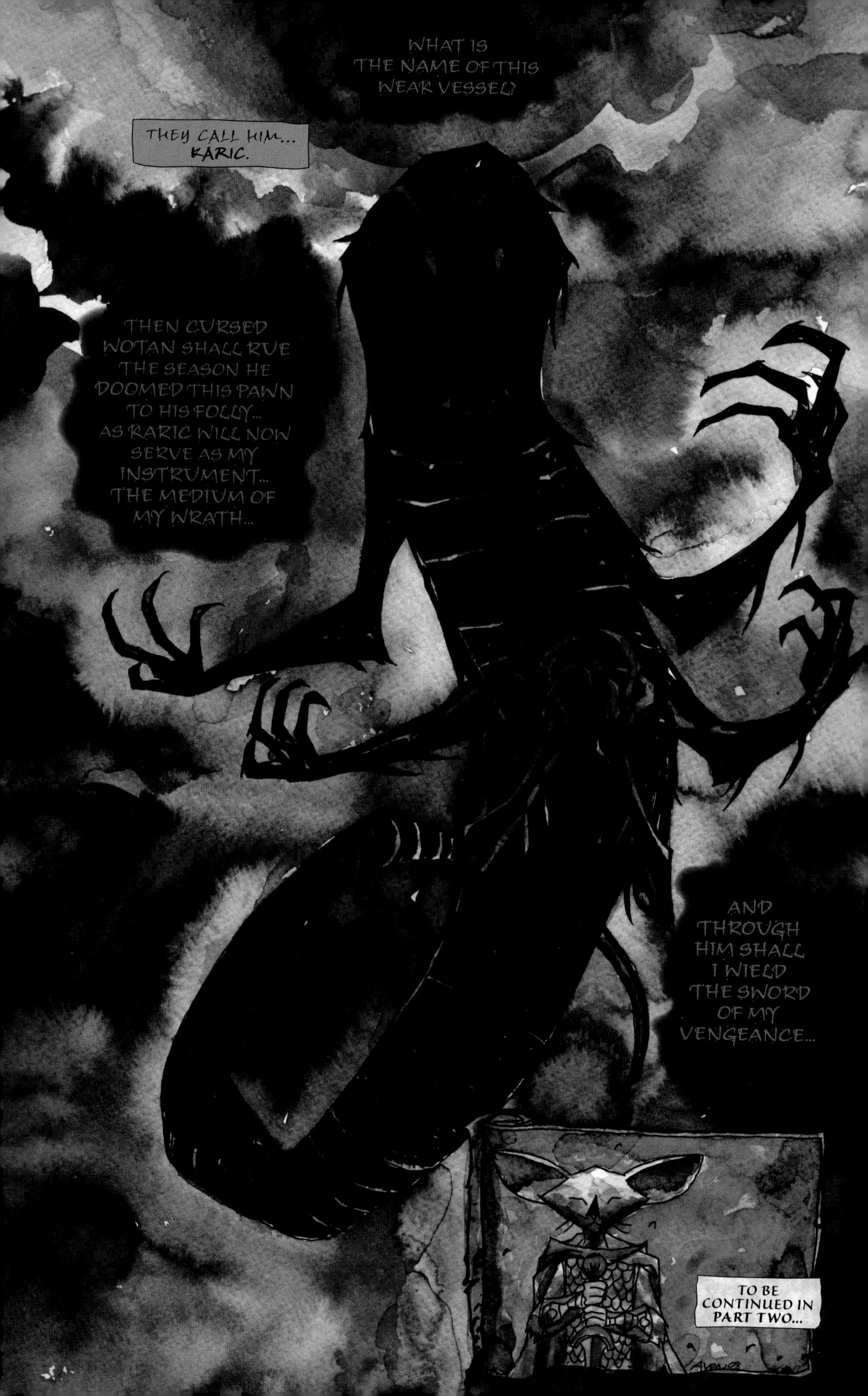
WHAT IS THE NAME OF THIS WEAK VESSEL?
THEY CALL HIM... KARIC.
THEN CURSED WOTAN SHALL RUE THE SEASON HE DOOMED THIS PAWN TO HIS FOLLY... AS KARIC WILL NOW SERVE AS MY INSTRUMENT... THE MEDIUM OF MY WRATH...
AND THROUGH HIM SHALL I WIELD THE SWORD OF MY VENGEANCE...
TO BE CONTINUED IN PART TWO...

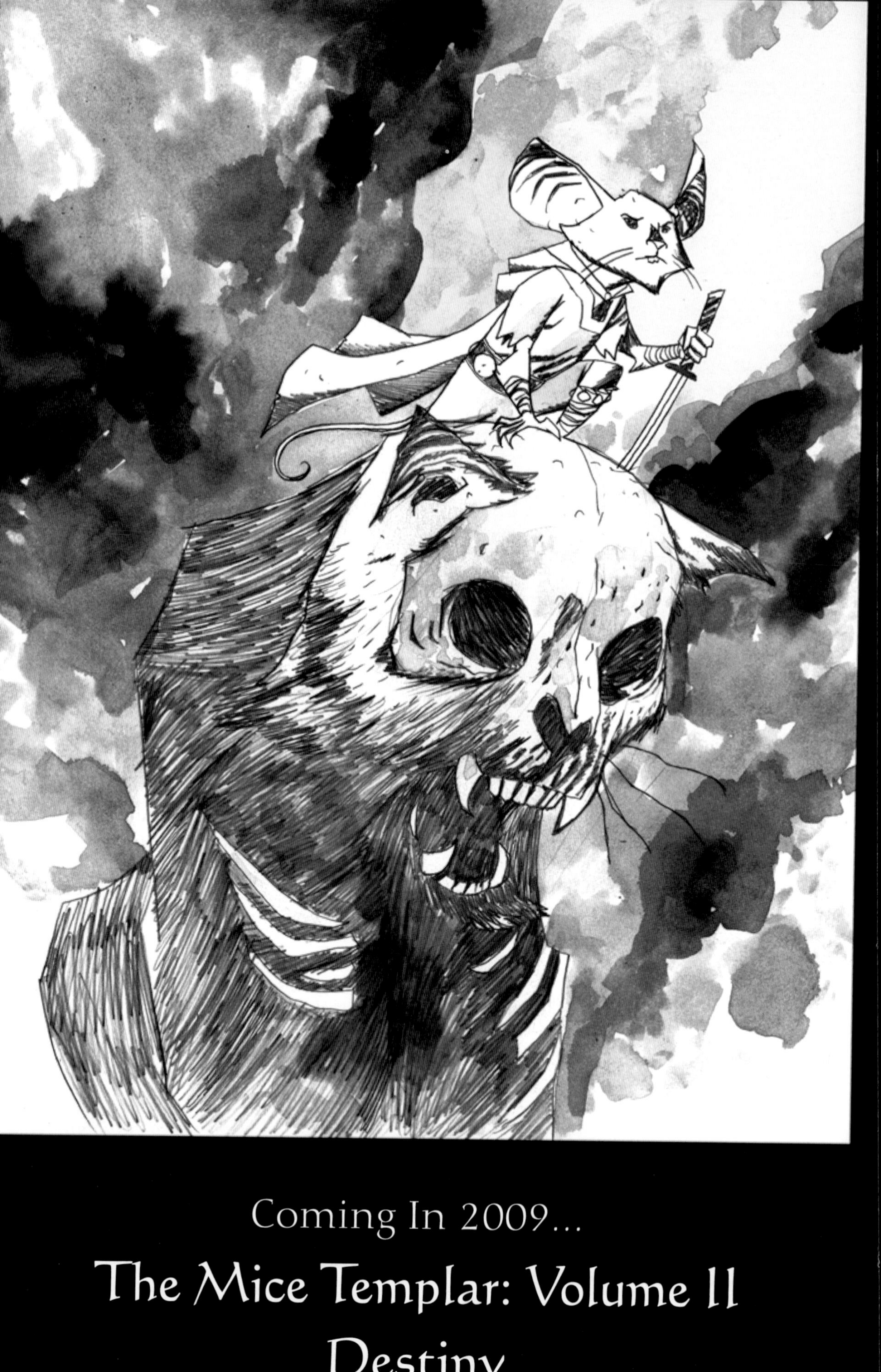

Coming In 2009...

The Mice Templar: Volume II

Destiny

Karic's adventure has only just begun, as he has traded his first mentor, the deceiver Pilot the Tall, for Cassius, a Templar exile who has no faith in Karic's divine calling. Together, their journey takes them from the supernatural terror of the Haunted Wood, to the underground Kingdom of the Mole Goblins, and then to the dangers and splendor of The Bright Realm. Cassius comes face-to-face with his bitter Templar rival Ronan—the mouse who stole his former love Llochloraine amidst the terrible Battle of Avalon where the Templar fell. The warrior sisterhood of Maeven string their bows, and Karic's heart is stirred by the young archer Aquila. In Dealrach Ard-Vale, King Icarus continues his planned ascendancy to godhood, as the plot of the rat druids and the schemes of Alexis are revealed. One-Arm Leito learns what it means to become leader of a lost cause, while Mornae struggles to never forsake hope. And the dark prophecy of Donas the Nathair leads all on a collision course with *destiny...*

Thus continues an extraordinary adventure of magic and wonder, of faith and valor, and of one small mouse whose destiny may change the entire world. Created by Bryan J.L. Glass (*Magician: Apprentice, Quixote*) & Michael Avon Oeming (*Powers, Rapture*).

An 8 issue mini-series event

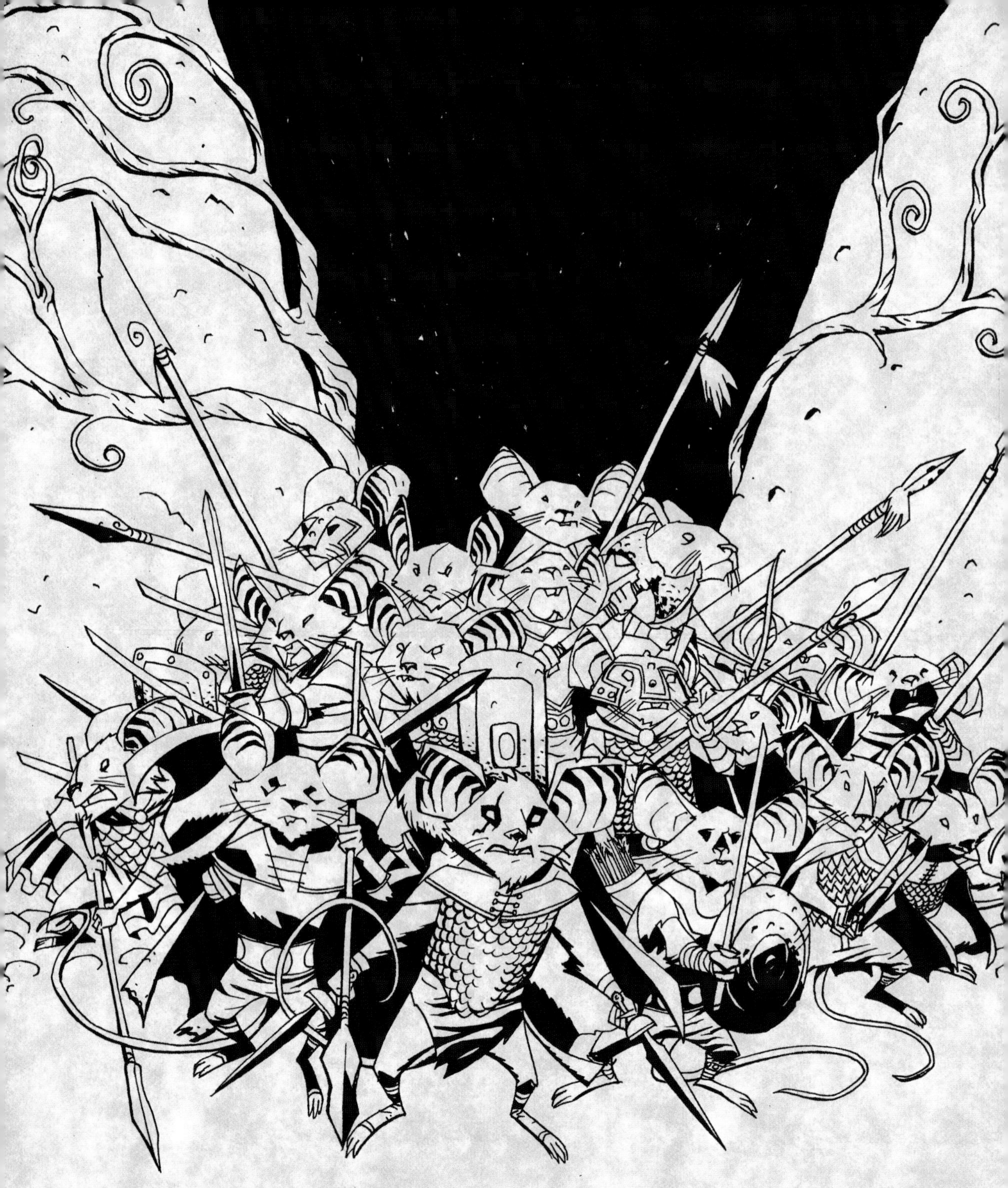

A TALE OF TWO MICE

An afterword from the creators

Wow, I can't believe I will be holding this collection in my hands in just a few short weeks from writing this. *Mice Templar's* origin is pre-*Powers*, possibly pre-*Hammer of the Gods*. It certainly spans back to shortly after Bryan and I completed *Ship of Fools*, when I was working as a security guard during my short retreat from comics in the late nineties. My twelve-year-old son was but a toddler then. Even more amazing is how much my life has changed since those days. It's been quite the journey, one which rivals what Karic has gone through in these very pages.

The earliest influences on the book are simple: *The Secret of NIMH* animated film ran endlessly on cable TV when I was a kid; so did *Watership Down*. Both films featured an anthropomorphic world that was dangerous, real and fantastic. Mythology has been a constant love in my life, stretching back even before my love of comics. Later, *The Lord of the Rings* entered my world, as did the mythic imagery of Led Zeppelin songs. Ironically, I was somewhat aware of the *Redwall* series of novels by Brian Jacques, but had never read them—until recently, just to make sure we weren't stepping on anyone's tail...*literally*.

So here we are now, thirty-something years of gestation come to life. These are my daydreams come alive with the penmanship of long-time friend and co-creator Bryan J.L. Glass. It's a living dream I believe will be part of our lives for many years to come. Just remember: *there are two paths you can go by, but in the long run...there's still time to change the road you're on.*

Mike Avon Oeming,
packing his bags out of Jersey...
October 2008

It's always been about *faith*...

For the mouse Karic, as well as for myself. And the completion of this volume is a testimony for both.

Our hero was taught a faith easy to believe in when playing with friends and loved by family, when meals were plentiful and a warm bed awaited the close of each day. But adulthood crashes upon him at breakneck speed. He loses the carefree security of his youth. Adrift and despairing, Karic finds a source of wisdom in Pilot the Tall, who casts a reasonable doubt upon his trust in things unseen. Yet Pilot has his own agenda. Their journey takes them to many dark places, and eventually to the Templar Priests, who pursue an agenda of their own. Each side casts suspicion upon the other, each trying to shape what Karic should believe, while the world around them continues its descent into chaos. Every strata of social order schemes for power and authority over others, be it King Icarus, his court, the Druid advisors, mice in captivity as well as those living in the luxury of the capital, the rat army and the weasel royal guards, Priests of the Great Ash Tree, and even between a pair of Templar exiles such as Pilot and Cassius. With so many forces competing for his loyalty, Karic must discern his own path amidst The Dark Lands. In his selfless desire to rescue those he loves, he uncovers the reality his faith is based upon, not through dogma and indoctrination, but through testing his faith, as the world around him tests his own belief in its truth. It is not Pilot nor the priests who determine the validity of Karic's trust, but a face-to-face encounter with Wotan himself, and accepting a destiny as yet unrevealed.

Such has been my own path to faith: raised to embrace the sacred, while needing answers that satisfied my own intense curiosity to make sense out of life's mysteries. The road to adulthood was ever a dark journey, filled with setbacks, despair, and crash-and-burning dreams. By trusting too readily, I learned that not everyone was to be trusted: many may exploit you if they see what you've done as an opportunity for themselves. On these terms, my faith offered the reassurance that my experience was the same for everyone living in these "Dark Lands." I came to embrace my faith, not in any quantifiable way or because it was something I was merely taught, but because it proved itself to me to be true in the dark times. All I've lacked is a face-to-face encounter with Wotan himself...but maybe I've even had that in those moments when I've been given the opportunity to help a stranger in need.

Much talk has been made of Mike Oeming's decade-plus journey to make *The Mice Templar* a reality. For myself, this deluxe, full-color hardcover edition is the result of a six-year adventure, and the fulfillment of a lifetime's dream. The Great Eye of Wotan has seen me through the darkness, and I prepare the pages for this edition with a pride and joy that extends far beyond its artwork and the mere words on a page. I believe in Karic. I believe in this book. I believe in my friend Mike. I believe in the journey I've taken to get here. And I believe in my Lord.

It's about faith.

Bryan J.L. Glass
October 2008

THE
MICE
TEMPLAR
BY
BRYAN J.L. GLASS
AND
MICHAEL AVON OEMING

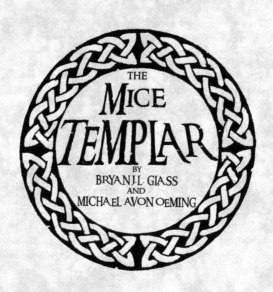

Send your letters for publication in *The Readers' Lore*:
TheMiceTemplar@aol.com

Visit *The Mice Templar* online:
hiddenrobot.com/MICETEMPLAR/

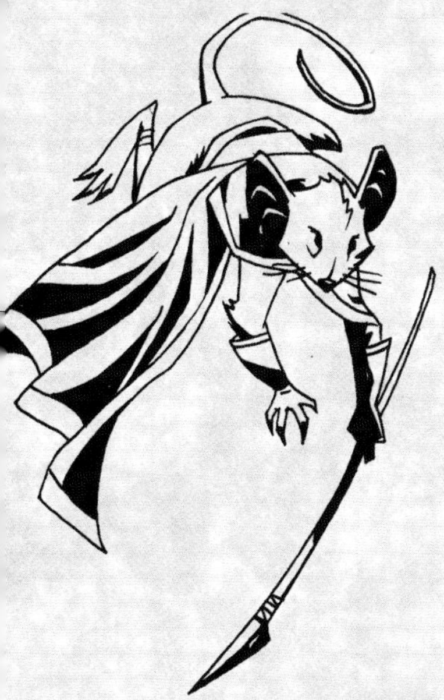

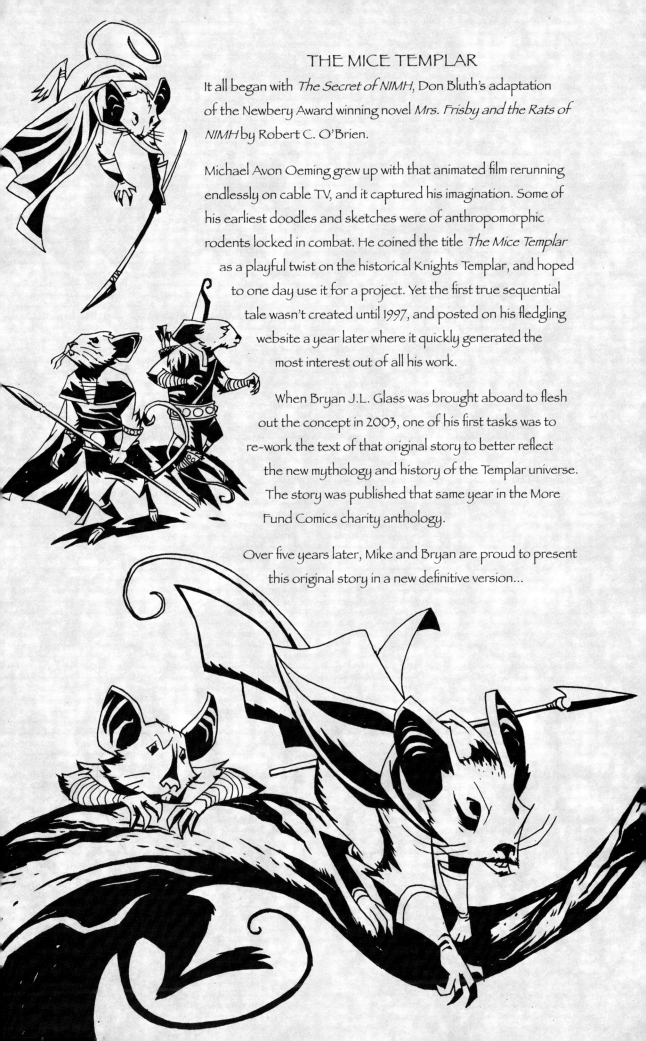

THE MICE TEMPLAR

It all began with *The Secret of NIMH*, Don Bluth's adaptation of the Newbery Award winning novel *Mrs. Frisby and the Rats of NIMH* by Robert C. O'Brien.

Michael Avon Oeming grew up with that animated film rerunning endlessly on cable TV, and it captured his imagination. Some of his earliest doodles and sketches were of anthropomorphic rodents locked in combat. He coined the title *The Mice Templar* as a playful twist on the historical Knights Templar, and hoped to one day use it for a project. Yet the first true sequential tale wasn't created until 1997, and posted on his fledgling website a year later where it quickly generated the most interest out of all his work.

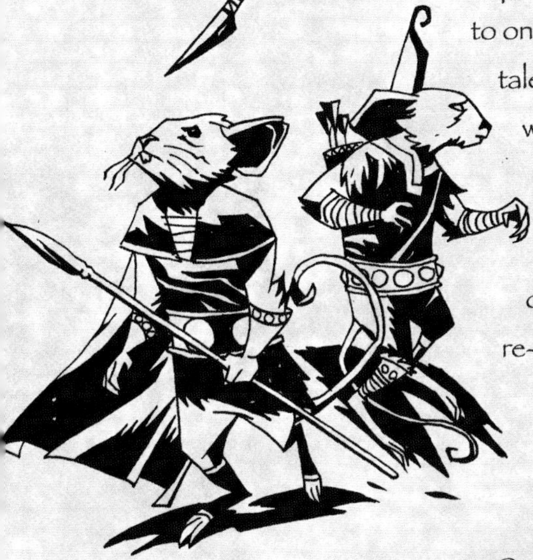

When Bryan J.L. Glass was brought aboard to flesh out the concept in 2003, one of his first tasks was to re-work the text of that original story to better reflect the new mythology and history of the Templar universe. The story was published that same year in the More Fund Comics charity anthology.

Over five years later, Mike and Bryan are proud to present this original story in a new definitive version...

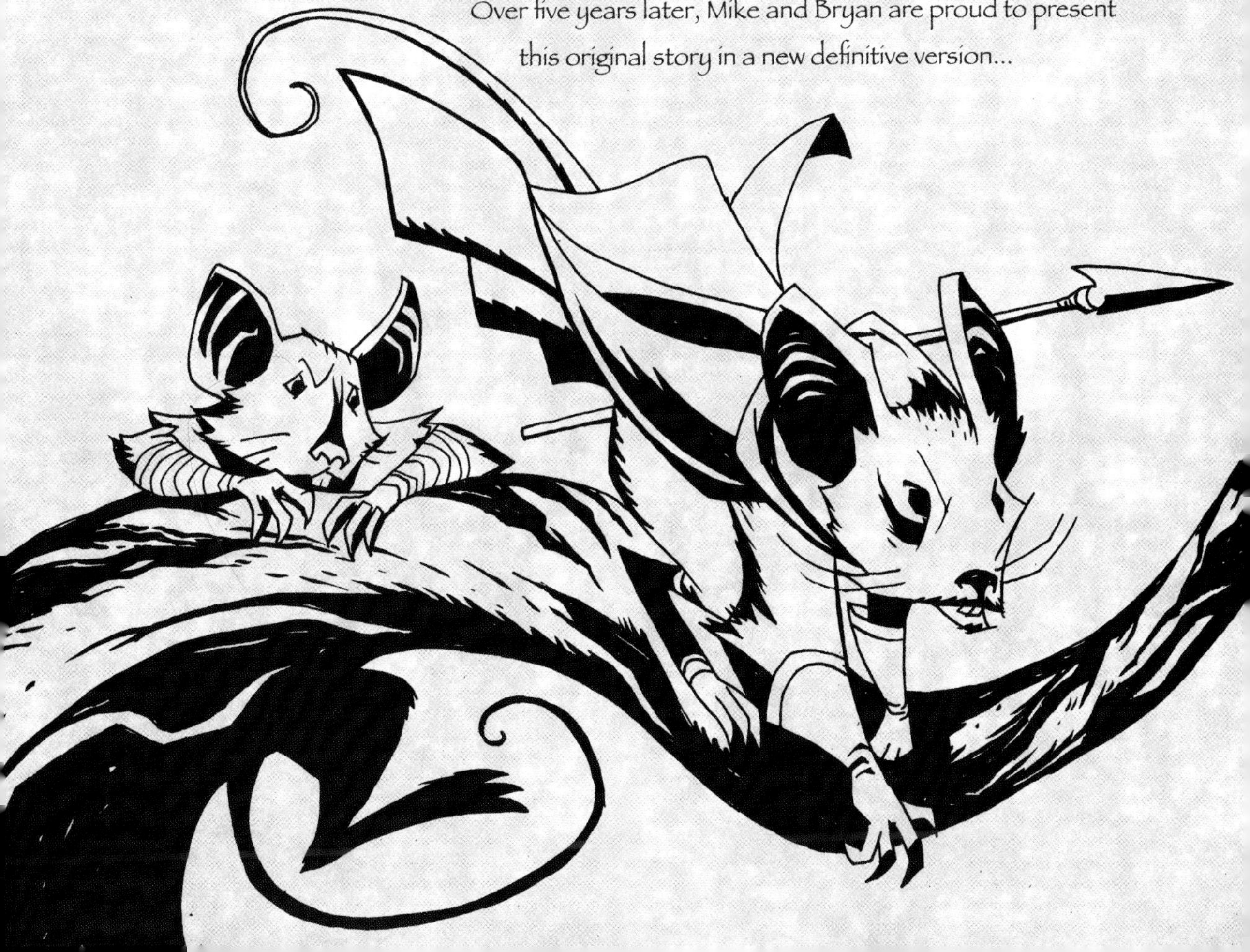

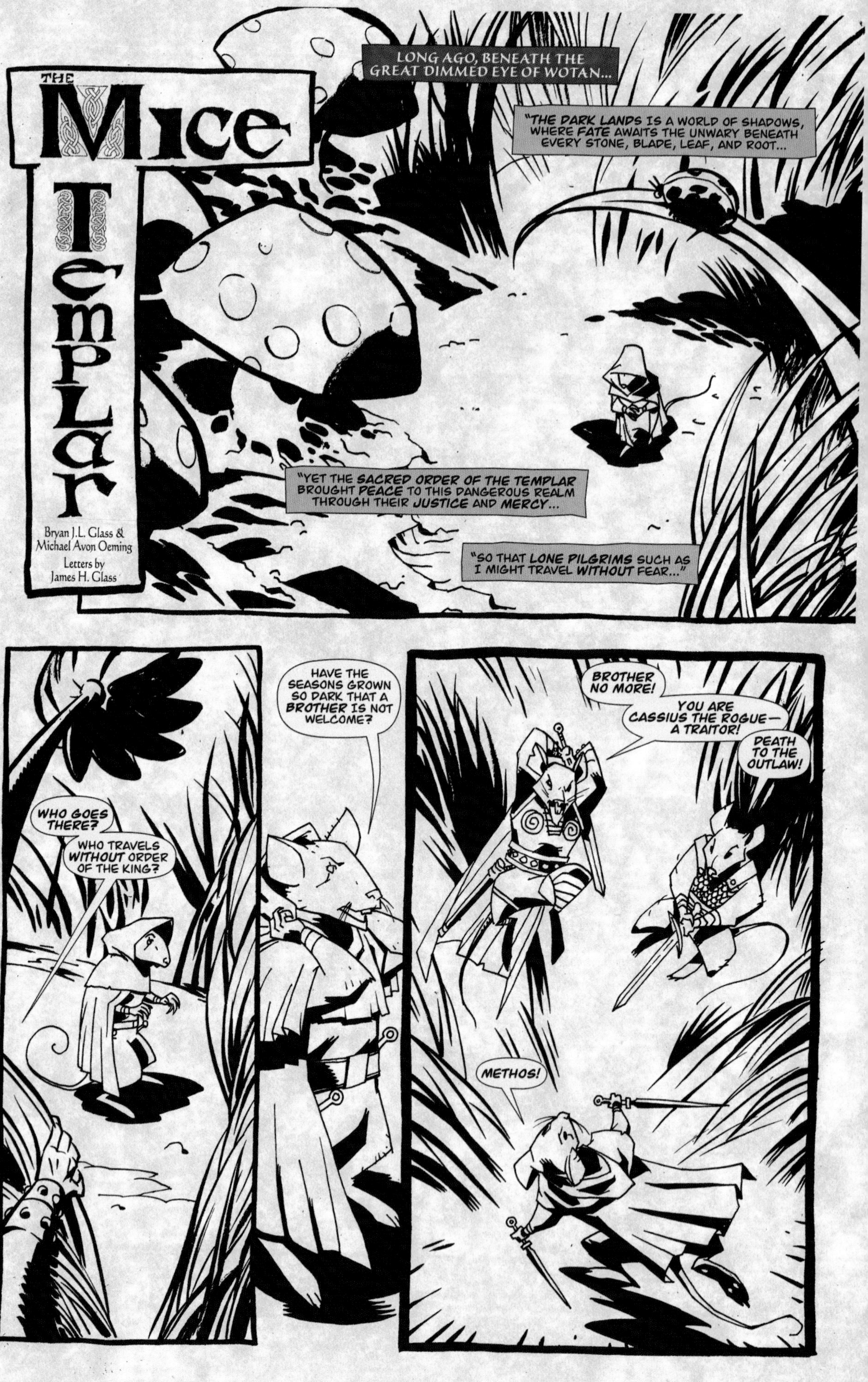

THE Mice Templar
Bryan J.L. Glass & Michael Avon Oeming
Letters by James H. Glass
LONG AGO, BENEATH THE GREAT DIMMED EYE OF WOTAN...
"THE DARK LANDS IS A WORLD OF SHADOWS, WHERE FATE AWAITS THE UNWARY BENEATH EVERY STONE, BLADE, LEAF, AND ROOT...
"YET THE SACRED ORDER OF THE TEMPLAR BROUGHT PEACE TO THIS DANGEROUS REALM THROUGH THEIR JUSTICE AND MERCY...
"SO THAT LONE PILGRIMS SUCH AS I MIGHT TRAVEL WITHOUT FEAR..."
WHO GOES THERE?
WHO TRAVELS WITHOUT ORDER OF THE KING?
HAVE THE SEASONS GROWN SO DARK THAT A BROTHER IS NOT WELCOME?
BROTHER NO MORE!
YOU ARE CASSIUS THE ROGUE— A TRAITOR!
DEATH TO THE OUTLAW!
METHOS!

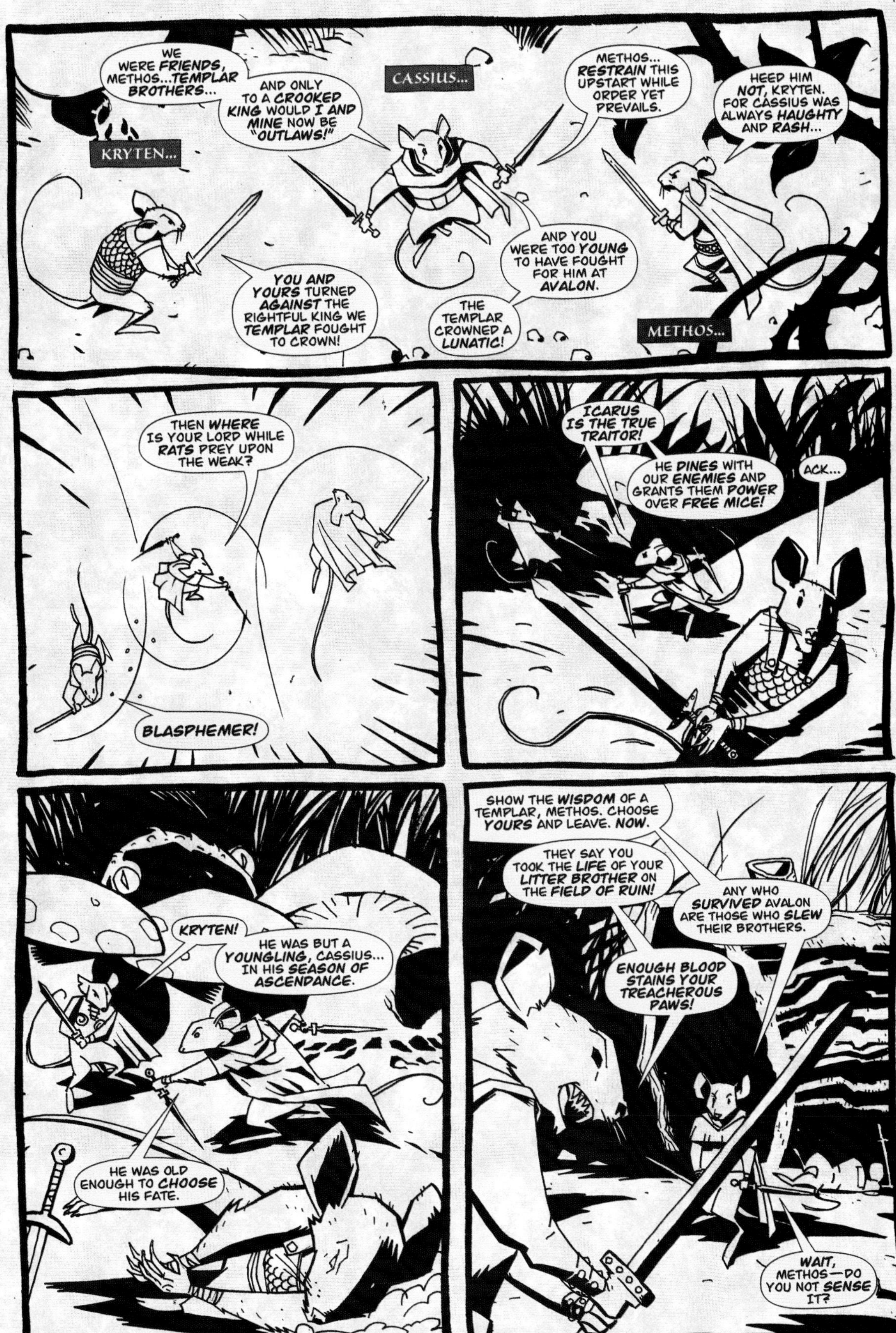
KRYTEN...
WE WERE FRIENDS, METHOS...TEMPLAR BROTHERS...
CASSIUS...
AND ONLY TO A CROOKED KING WOULD I AND MINE NOW BE "OUTLAWS!"
METHOS... RESTRAIN THIS UPSTART WHILE ORDER YET PREVAILS.
HEED HIM NOT, KRYTEN. FOR CASSIUS WAS ALWAYS HAUGHTY AND RASH...
YOU AND YOURS TURNED AGAINST THE RIGHTFUL KING WE TEMPLAR FOUGHT TO CROWN!
THE TEMPLAR CROWNED A LUNATIC!
AND YOU WERE TOO YOUNG TO HAVE FOUGHT FOR HIM AT AVALON.
METHOS...
THEN WHERE IS YOUR LORD WHILE RATS PREY UPON THE WEAK?
BLASPHEMER!
ICARUS IS THE TRUE TRAITOR!
HE DINES WITH OUR ENEMIES AND GRANTS THEM POWER OVER FREE MICE!
ACK...
KRYTEN!
HE WAS BUT A YOUNGLING, CASSIUS... IN HIS SEASON OF ASCENDANCE.
HE WAS OLD ENOUGH TO CHOOSE HIS FATE.
SHOW THE WISDOM OF A TEMPLAR, METHOS. CHOOSE YOURS AND LEAVE. NOW.
THEY SAY YOU TOOK THE LIFE OF YOUR LITTER BROTHER ON THE FIELD OF RUIN!
ANY WHO SURVIVED AVALON ARE THOSE WHO SLEW THEIR BROTHERS.
ENOUGH BLOOD STAINS YOUR TREACHEROUS PAWS!
WAIT, METHOS—DO YOU NOT SENSE IT?

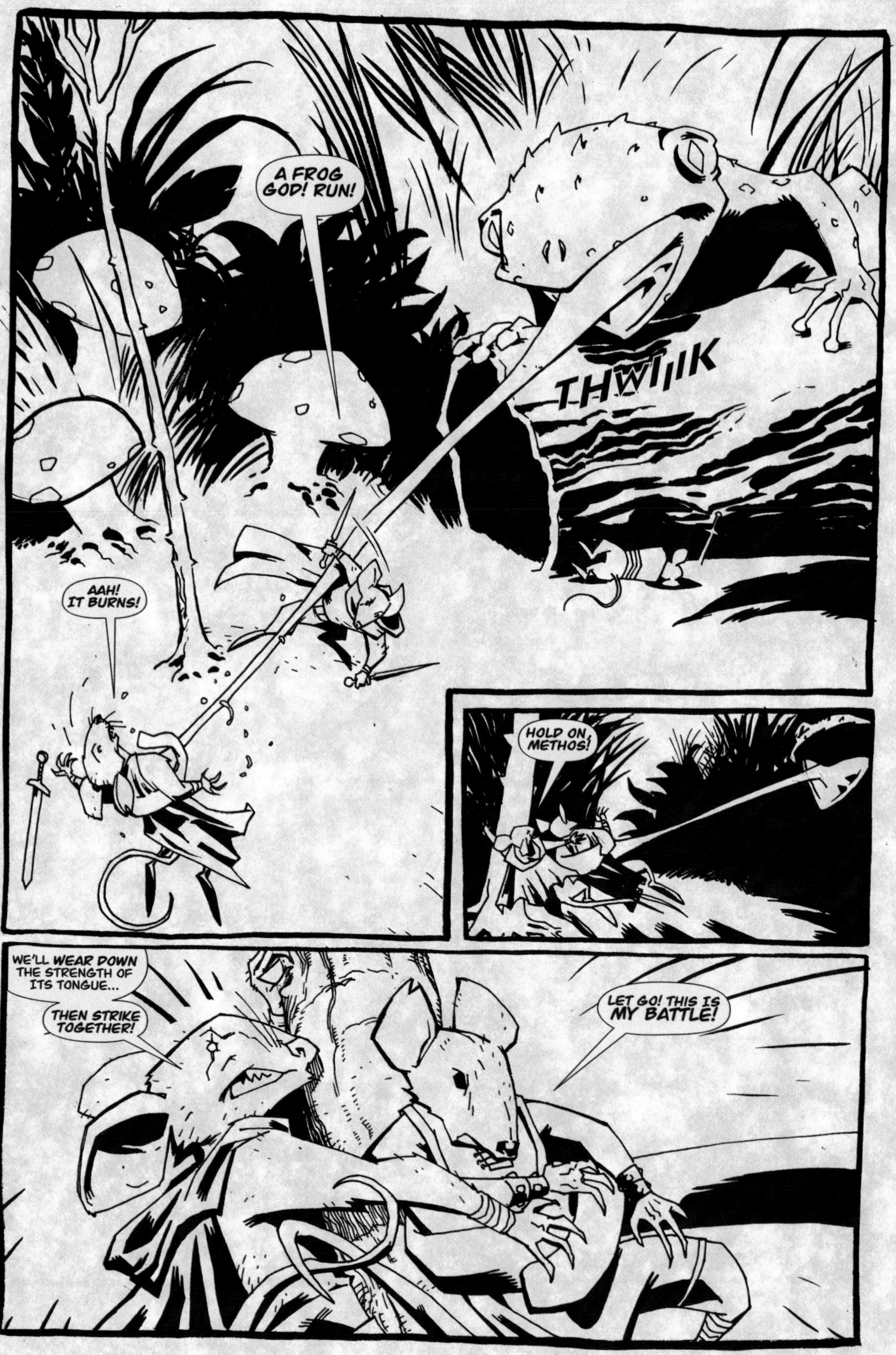
A FROG GOD! RUN!
THWIIIK
AAH! IT BURNS!
HOLD ON, METHOS!
WE'LL WEAR DOWN THE STRENGTH OF ITS TONGUE...
THEN STRIKE TOGETHER!
LET GO! THIS IS MY BATTLE!

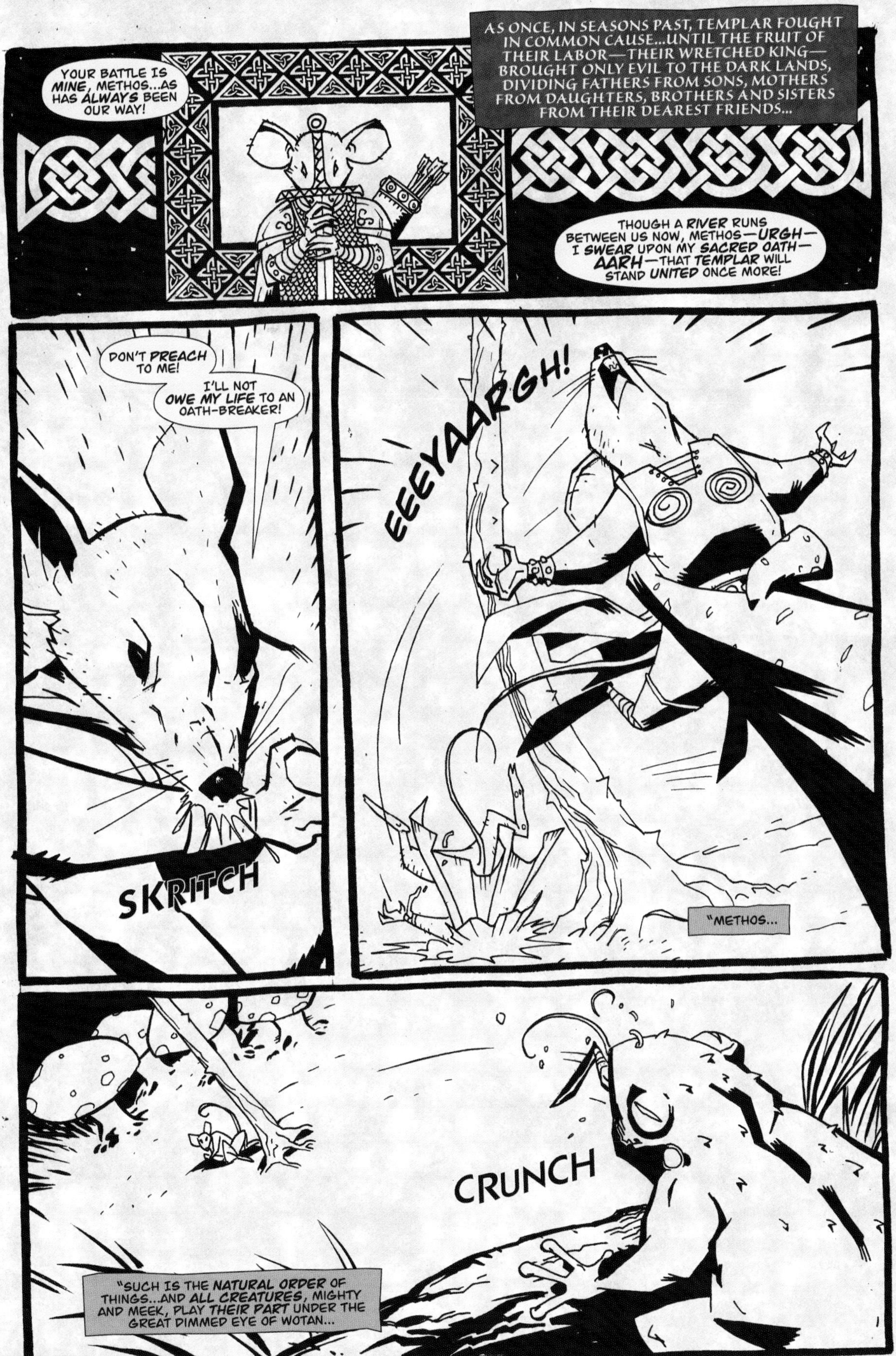

YOUR BATTLE IS MINE, METHOS...AS HAS ALWAYS BEEN OUR WAY!
AS ONCE, IN SEASONS PAST, TEMPLAR FOUGHT IN COMMON CAUSE...UNTIL THE FRUIT OF THEIR LABOR—THEIR WRETCHED KING—BROUGHT ONLY EVIL TO THE DARK LANDS, DIVIDING FATHERS FROM SONS, MOTHERS FROM DAUGHTERS, BROTHERS AND SISTERS FROM THEIR DEAREST FRIENDS...
THOUGH A RIVER RUNS BETWEEN US NOW, METHOS—URGH—I SWEAR UPON MY SACRED OATH—AARH—THAT TEMPLAR WILL STAND UNITED ONCE MORE!
DON'T PREACH TO ME!
I'LL NOT OWE MY LIFE TO AN OATH-BREAKER!
SKRITCH
EEEYAARGH!
"METHOS...
CRUNCH
"SUCH IS THE NATURAL ORDER OF THINGS...AND ALL CREATURES, MIGHTY AND MEEK, PLAY THEIR PART UNDER THE GREAT DIMMED EYE OF WOTAN...

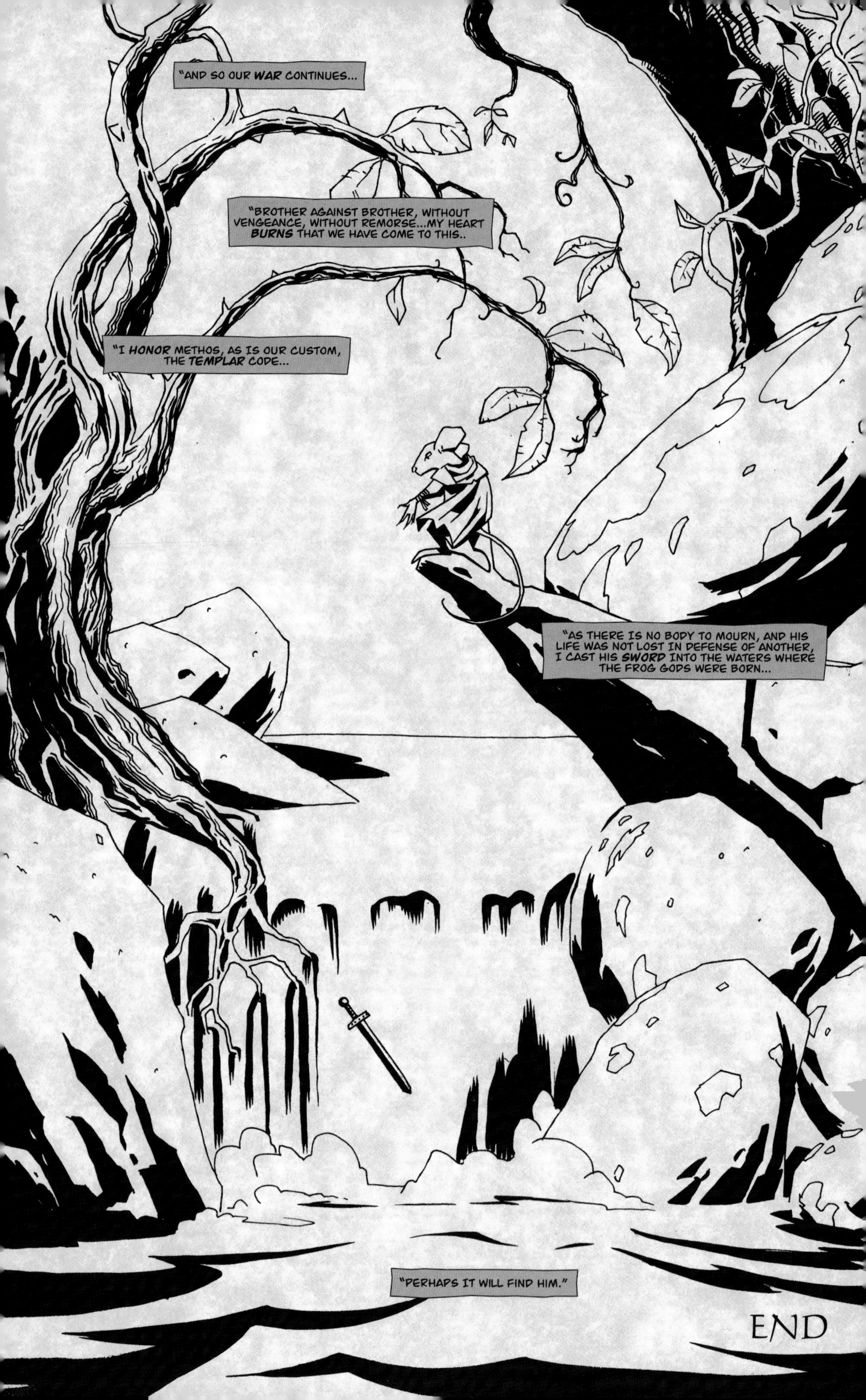
"AND SO OUR WAR CONTINUES...
"BROTHER AGAINST BROTHER, WITHOUT VENGEANCE, WITHOUT REMORSE...MY HEART BURNS THAT WE HAVE COME TO THIS..
"I HONOR METHOS, AS IS OUR CUSTOM, THE TEMPLAR CODE...
"AS THERE IS NO BODY TO MOURN, AND HIS LIFE WAS NOT LOST IN DEFENSE OF ANOTHER, I CAST HIS SWORD INTO THE WATERS WHERE THE FROG GODS WERE BORN...
"PERHAPS IT WILL FIND HIM."
END

a history of THE REALM

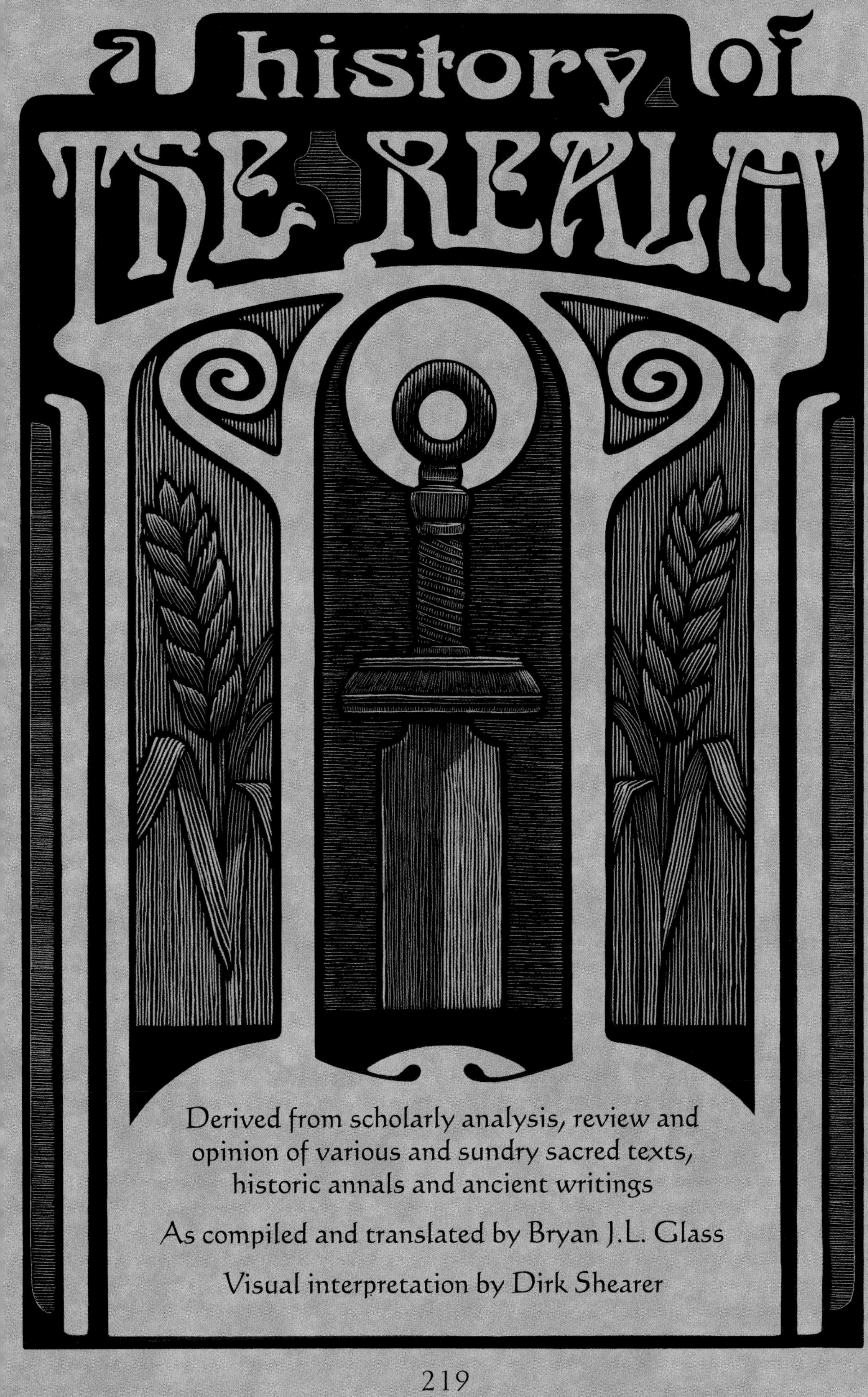

Derived from scholarly analysis, review and opinion of various and sundry sacred texts, historic annals and ancient writings

As compiled and translated by Bryan J.L. Glass

Visual interpretation by Dirk Shearer

The Great Eyes of Wotan

THE ORDER OF CREATION

I

In the beginning...

The Order of Creation brought about the origin of all things under the sky, when each creature was given its place and purpose under the stars. And the Creator of all things, **Wotan**, did divide his two Great Eyes, so that each might maintain separate watch upon the two halves of the day.

II

But amidst the waning seasons of **The Lost Days** — *that indeterminate period which followed the Order of Creation, when the two halves of the day were as one* — Chaos entered the world, and all creatures mighty and meek fought for dominance. Those who did not desire the **Eyes of Wotan** to bear witness to all their ways sought to end the all-seeing vision. Thus did the **Nathair**, first-born of all creatures, construct a massive catapult, *the Dubhlan*, so that both of Wotan's Great Eyes might be blotted out for all days to come. Only one strike did launch, yet for all its effort, a single Eye was but dimmed. And that sight diminished to but a pale watch upon that half of the day, which was thereafter known as **The Dark Lands**, where those who feared Wotan migrated to its shadow and continued in their evil.

Wotan cursed those creatures who had directly defied him, banishing the Nathair, along with their master **Donas**, beyond the stars to the **Outer Darkness**, to a realm of shadow without form. And it was there, bound within the very darkness they had so desired, that the Nathair nurtured their hatred and transformed themselves into **Diabhlan and Diabhul**, aspects of malice without substance. After which, it was only through the mystical possession of lesser creatures that they could again experience the physical world they had forsaken by their defiance.

III

Throughout **The Bright Realm**, the Falcon, Hawk, and Great Eagle each served the **Will of Wotan**, but across the Dark Lands, bats arose in a great multitude. By their wit, cunning, and dominance of the night sky, they presumed ownership over all that was under the stars. Bats basked in their own glory and subjugated all lesser creatures beneath their sway.

His Great Eye dimmed by the evil wrought by the Dark Lands' first inhabitants, Wotan called forth owls to be his servants, to be a thousand eyes in the darkness, and to usher souls back to their Creator. Thus it was that in the **Last Cycle of Chaos** — *The Nights of Shadow* — that bats and owls waged their final battle for dominance of Wotan's never-ending sky. Ultimately doomed by their pride and arrogance, bats were cast down from the heavens, to crawl upon their bellies into dark caves where they hung by their feet, heads downward, perched in defiance of natural order, twisting logic into riddle so that they could befuddle any other who sought their wisdom to follow in their ways.

IV

As night follows day, so the seasons cycled one upon

Catapult of Dubhlan

Donas the Nathair

another. The progenitors of each race declared themselves "gods," demanding worship from all who sprung from their loins. Yet the Will of Wotan is never diminished by the schemes of mortal creatures. Therefore, by his own wisdom, Wotan chose mice, no greater yet far less than nearly every other creature, to be his emissaries in the Dark Lands. He bestowed upon them two gifts: a *Code of Law*, that they might rule over all others with justice, as well as *Hearts of Compassion* so that judgment might ever be tempered with mercy. Wotan gave the Dark Lands to his chosen creatures, so that the peace brought by their order might reveal to the darkness that the **Light of Wotan** is imbued with many hues...

Thus was the calling of the **Templar**: to be guardians of justice, order and peace in the deep shadows of the Dark Lands.

THE FOUNDING OF THE TEMPLAR

I
The First Hero

In the ancient past, mice lived under the full gaze of Wotan's Great Eyes where they served as mere prey amid the primeval *Cycles of Chaos*.

Following the division of the day, the *First Great Season* began as Wotan blessed the mice with intelligence. Wotan inspired **Parthalon**, the first true hero of the mice, to lead his people into the *Dark Lands* where they would develop cunning to escape their enemies. But in time, even Parthalon's descendants scattered into disparate tribes, losing contact and kinship with one another, so that even fellow mice became enemies. Many warrior heroes rose and fell in the seasons that followed, yet their legends survived to inspire generations that followed them.

II
Sualtam

In the aftermath of the last Cycle—*the Nights of Shadow when bats were cast down from the sky*—the *Second Great Season* began with the rise of another mouse hero, **Sualtam**. He challenged his nomadic people to discover what larger role Wotan might have for them in the world, but that doing so required living in harmony with each other first, and then by extending that good will outward to all other creatures.

By doing so for the good of all, he believed that mice could impact the Dark Lands for all seasons to come. But the very mice he'd hoped to save betrayed Sualtam to his death, they who feared the future and felt threatened by any change to their simple lives.

III
Rise of Kuhl-En

Sualtam's son, the young mouse **Kuhl-En**, became a pariah of his people following his father's death. Cast out alone into the wilderness to die, Kuhl-En eventually climbed the highest peak of the **Kilmagenny Mountains, overlooking The Great Valley**, and railed at the sky, daring Wotan to claim him.

A Great Death Owl came for Kuhl-En's life, to return his spirit to Wotan, but the mouse fought back with a fury unseen in all the

Peak of Armagh

history of the Dark Lands. It is said that Kuhl-En battled the Death Owl for forty days, across an entire rotation of Wotan's gaze, and that storm clouds wreathed the mountain both day and night, with thunder and lightning fierce enough to terrorize all creatures in the Great Valley below.

Just as Kuhl-En could fight no more, he seemed to prevail over his foe. Yet as the mist around him parted, he saw he was surrounded by six Death Owls, any of whom could have claimed him amidst the struggle. His strength and fury spent, Kuhl-En then surrendered his adversary to the Owls and submitted himself to his presumed death. But at that moment, his adversary broke off one of his own talons and presented it to Kuhl-En, as a symbol of their struggle. The Owl then spoke, revealing that Wotan had felt his pain, but that his father's vision, however noble in intent, was not the way of Wotan, for mercy alone, untempered by justice, led only to anarchy. Sualtam's "peace" would have forever remained a false hope, never fulfilled, and brought only misery to the Dark Lands. Yet Kuhl-En himself could return to his people with the true path of Wotan: the **Code of the Templar**, offering valid justice tempered by genuine mercy, so that real peace might one day be known by every creature. Kuhl-En accepted the call on behalf of all his people, and for the sake of future generations of mice, that they might not live in fear.

Kuhl-En fashioned the talon into a sword, one

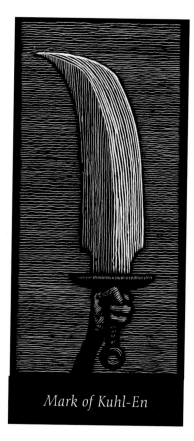

Mark of Kuhl-En

whose blade never dulled, a sacred blade in time dubbed by others as the **Mark of Kuhl-En**. And when wielded by a true servant of Wotan, the bearer carried the authority to speak for Wotan, and thereby gained the physical strength of his entire race, for his righteous deeds were truly being done for all.

IV
The Templar

Kuhl-En descended from the mountain he now called the **Peak of Armagh**, and sought to bring Wotan's **Templar Code** to the dispirited mice. He encountered many enemies from among the varied predators of the Dark Lands, as well as from amongst his own people. But as the seasons passed, he gained far more followers and supporters, whom he taught and trained.

Eventually, Kuhl-En took his twelve closest disciples to a vast field so that Wotan and all of the Dark Lands could bear witness, and there he knighted them into what he now called the **Order of the Templar**. It is said that owls of all breeds circled the field and perched upon the mighty branches of **Kros Cur Onnor Da**—*The Tree of Grace*—so that no predator would dare intrude upon the sacred ceremony.

It was on this same field that Kuhl-En later held the first gathering of the scattered tribes of mice, assembled in peace, to recognize each other as brothers. The field was named **Avalon** and considered a sacred site where, throughout mouse history, the Templar would gather whenever their business was something monumental enough that the Dark Lands themselves were symbolically summoned to bear witness.

V
Mice and Rats

In time, the struggle for dominance of the Dark Lands came down to mice and rats, cousins by their very nature, but together they came to epitomize the duality of all creatures. Rats embodied all that was base, loathsome, self-serving and ultimately destructive; while mice, when following the Templar Code, represented all that was noble and inspiring, self-sacrificing and benefiting the community and future generations. Thus were they two sides divided by their choices. Under these converse reflections, neither could live in harmony with the other, and Kuhl-En was ultimately forced to lead a mighty campaign to drive rats from the Great Valley.

The Templar campaign against the rats lasted generations, with many epic heroes made and lost on both sides.

In one season of the conflict, the mighty rat general, **Titus**—*the only rat to ever truly organize his race*—stole the sacred blade, the Mark of Kuhl-En, and Kuhl-En found himself without Wotan's direct guidance for the first time since accepting his divine commission. It was during this time that Kuhl-En was deceived by the devious schemes of bats, resulting in his edict that no mouse was to ever seek their counsel again.

VI
The Readers of the Wheat

With his sacred weapon in the paws of his enemy, Kuhl-En halted his campaign against the rats, and

Great Ash Tree

in the company of friends, advisors, and his twelve closest followers, he embarked on a controversial pilgrimage across the length of the Dark Lands to discern the Will of Wotan. Rats held all the land that led to the sacred Peak of Armagh, so Kuhl-En sought a new path to wisdom.

Kuhl-En discovered a mighty **Ash Tree** at the center of a vast and unruly field of wild wheat. Although portions of the tree's great trunk were hollow, it sat empty, for no creature of the Dark Lands would dare risk crossing such a vast wide open field in view of the Great Death Owls of Wotan who circled overhead. Only Kuhl-En was bold enough, for only he had ever survived an encounter with the Death Owls. Once within the safety of the ash tree, Kuhl-En and his followers fasted, meditated and prayed. It is said that one night, a firefly of the dusk awakened Kuhl-En, guiding him to the uppermost branches of the great tree, and directed his vision out across the broad field of grain blowing in the gentle winds. Only because his spirit was attuned, seeking the Will of Wotan, did he find he discerned messages in the shifting stalks. Kuhl-En then realized that the winds, both gentle and fierce, were created by the mighty beating of the owls' wings as they patrolled the field, and thus were the messages in the wheat the words of Wotan himself. The message conveyed that the burden of guiding the people was not Kuhl-En's alone. Moved by Wotan's great compassion, he thus appointed his twelve disciples to remain behind

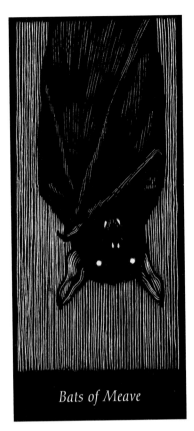

Bats of Meave

to continue to study and discern the Will of Wotan, and they became known as **The Readers of the Wheat**.

Kuhl-En also declared the firefly as sacred, a representative of Wotan's Light in the darkness, for any who were spiritually lost could find their way again by following their light.

As the seasons passed, the humble Readers considered themselves simply *priests* conveying the message of Wotan to the people. Inevitably, the legend grew that the Readers were actual mystical beings whom the Priests merely represented. Later generations of Readers deemed it wisdom to perpetuate this legend as truth, so that the priests themselves need never fear the consequences of their edicts.

In time, however, the Priesthood grew corrupted, distorting their readings of the Will of Wotan to suit their own agenda, often in pursuit of or even in exchange for political favors. When the Priesthood later refused to take a side in the tragic Templar **Civil War**, fearing the political consequences of supporting one view over another, it is said that Wotan withdrew his blessing and the messages of the wheat fell silent.

THE GREAT SEASONS OF HISTORY

Mice chart the passage of time as **Cycles**, each cycle containing four seasons: winter, spring, summer, fall, marking one full year.

On a larger scale, mice view their history through periods of time they call **Great Seasons**, periods of *social order* that have lasted as little as 20 cycles, the average lifetime of a mouse, or as long as a thousand cycles or more.

The Lost Days

Pre-Seasons: The indeterminate era before mice were blessed with intelligence. This time follows the *Order of Creation*, and is known as *The Lost Days*, which precede the *Cycles of Chaos*, that time when the *Nathair* constructed their catapult to put out the *Eyes of Wotan*, creating day and night, and were thus banished to the *Outer Darkness* and became *Diabhlan*.

The mice have only vague, primordial memories of these days, with various non-cohesive legends shared by numerous disparate tribes.

The First Great Season: Begins with Wotan blessing the mice with intelligence. It marks the rise of *Parthalon*, the first official hero who established his tribe in the *Dark Lands*—*becoming nocturnal*—so that they would no longer be such easy prey in the daylight. This period coincides with the *Last Cycle of Chaos* and the *Nights of Shadow* when bats ruled the night sky, until cast down by the owls of Wotan.

This Great Season is notable for mice forming their first spoken language, and beginning to use crude tools and weapons. Their society was still largely nomadic, and various warriors arose in turn to lead their respective tribes for a time. These were pre-Templar warriors, but many of these warrior/heroes established legends that were later grafted into Templar myths.

The Second Great Season: The generations that led directly to *Sualtam*, as well as his legendary son *Kuhl-En*, the founder of the *Templar Code* and *Templar Order*, unifier of the scattered tribes, establisher of the *Readers of*

Templar Warrior

the Wheat Priesthood, supreme commander of the first organized war against rats, and creator of the dusk/dawn barriers—*which separate the realms of night and day*—by his cursing of the insects.

This period features the first written language, refinement of tools, and the first mouse architecture, as well as the unifying of disparate tribes under a single governing system, establishing law and religion, as well as the first prolonged military campaign against an oppressor.

The Third Great Season: *The Golden Age* which follows the passing of Kuhl-En, when mouse society prospers under the Templar. Refinements of technology, culture, and the arts; true peace flourishes, as Templar Warriors readily suppress each threat as it arises. Marks the establishment of a female warrior class, the *Maeven*. This is an era in which each great crisis, natural, social or political, spawned a legendary Templar leader. The Maeven were granted the blessing of the Templar and thrived as an independent body.

The Fourth Great Season: This marks the beginning of what becomes known as *The Great Decline*, as the unity of mouse culture erodes. Political power plays increase, alongside scandals within the priesthood, both true and contrived. A perpetual state of war becomes the cultural norm as each conflict bleeds into the next, via border threats or from within due to various revolts and attempted secessions. Resentment festers as reluctant mice are pressed into military service to support the ongoing campaigns of various kings and generals.

This period is primarily recognized as the season when faith was questioned and challenged, Kuhl-En was declared mere legend, the deepest doctrines of the Templar were opened to ideological debate, and the perpetual skirmishes against rats transformed into outright suppression and systematic eradication of the rat species.

The Fifth Great Season: The rise of *Kobalt* and *Icarus* as political figures, exploitation of the ideological rift within the Templar by its enemies, leading to the crowning of Icarus as King. Civil War amongst the Templar leads to their climactic dissolution at the battle of Avalon, thus paving the way for subsequent rat dominance and the enslavement of mice.

This period sees the transition of rats from a tribal warlord society into a cohesive cultural, religious and military force, as their Templar suppressors collapse as a unified order.

The Sixth Great Season: Begins with the reign of King Icarus. Rats are granted unprecedented freedoms, while mouse culture is increasingly oppressed and restricted. The Templar Code and Order are outlawed, and the spiritual authority of the Priesthood/Readers is cast into doubt.

The mouse king Icarus, in league with rat druids, reigned unchallenged over what became known as The Dark Ages. In this Great Season, many settlements broke with the capital and king, fending off rat sieges from stronghold cities until conquered. Most mouse cities were either destroyed or abandoned, falling into utter ruin as the conquering rats preferred to dig into the

Reign of Icarus the Great

ground rather than build or settle into existing structures. Mouse population spread thin throughout the countryside, returning to their nomadic roots, ever on the run from rat encroachment. Templar survivors established scattered pockets of training to preserve the Order, yet each taught from the perspective of the side they had aligned with in the Civil War. ✺

This is the Season of our story: the rise of the hero *Karic,* whose leadership directly paves the way to the *Seventh Great Season.*

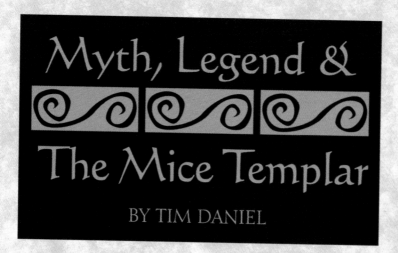

Myth, Legend & The Mice Templar

BY TIM DANIEL

The Salmon of Knowledge, Salmon of Wisdom, Bradán Feasa

The Salmon of Knowledge & Celtic Legend

The Salmon of Knowledge was a creature of Celtic legend, capable of granting the first man who tasted the fish's flesh all the knowledge or wisdom in the world. The salmon garnered this extraordinary power after ingesting nine hazel nuts fallen from the trees bordering the waters of the *Fountain of Wisdom*. From this fount, five rivers flowed, amongst them the rivers *Boyne*, long known as a rich salmon habitat, and *Shannon*, the longest such body of water in the Isle. Thus legend reasoned, that whomever should taste the flesh of the Salmon of Knowledge would then possess the power first bestowed upon the nine hazel nuts.

A young child named *Deimne*, later *Fionn mac Cumhaill*, was raised in the care of two Druid women, and at age ten was taken to *Slieve Bladhma*. There in the wood, he was trained in combat and tutored in the way of words, for to be both a skilled warrior and poet was the pinnacle of achievement for a Celtic warrior. Emboldened by the training, Deimne set forth across Ireland to seek his fortune. He soon came upon the poet *Finnegaes Eces* who had spent the last several years tracking the elusive red and white speckled Salmon of Knowledge.

With Deimne by his side, Finnegaes Eces's quest joyfully ended when he finally landed the Salmon of Knowledge upon a riverbank. Eager to test the legend's veracity, Finnegeas ordered Deimne to place the Salmon upon a spit over an open campfire, as it was custom for the young charge to prepare his master's meals. Finnegeas furthermore instructed the young man not to taste the readying meal, as doing so would invest the young man with the fish's knowledge.

Some time later, Deimne went to see if the Salmon was sufficiently cooked, and to test the firmness of the fish's roasting flesh, he placed a cautious thumb to the Salmon and was promptly burned. To ease his pain, Deimne brought his thumb to his mouth to cool the wound. Finnegeas looked upon the boy's face and saw the light of all knowledge shimmering in his eyes. Inadvertently, Deimne had tasted the Salmon by soothing his wound. The prized fish was no longer of use to Finnegeas and he asked his young charge his name. "It is Deimne," the boy responded. "No it is not," Finnegeas disagreed. "It was prophesied that someone named Finn would gain the knowledge from the Salmon, so your name must be Finn." Deimne was christened with the namesake of his master and a legend was born.

Fionn (Finn) mac Cumhaill, also known as *Finn MacCool*, eventually became one of Ireland's most celebrated heroes as the legendary leader of the *Fianna*, an elite band of warriors whose purpose it was to uphold order within Ireland.

Salmon of Knowledge & The Mice Templar Mythology

The Salmon of Knowledge appears in the mythos of *The Mice Templar* in a manner similar to the legend of Finn MacCool, though the fish is far from a simple meal bequeathing incredible knowledge. Instead, the Salmon, *Bradán Feasa*, swallows an unsuspecting and reluctant young mouse named *Karic*. In doing so, the fish spares his life and transports him to the awaiting *Fish Gods* who will impart to him the *Will of Wotan*.

Karic's first encounter with the Fish Gods comes while playing in *Cricket's Glen* with his older companion, *Leito*. Skipping along the branches of a tree, Karic snaps a frail limb, slips from Leito's frantic attempt to catch him, and plunges into the frigid waters of the pond below. Sinking unconscious into the pool, Karic is swallowed whole by an immense Salmon and awakens upon a small rocky shore in a dark cavern. Adorning the walls are a series of pictograms: a large salmon bearing a crown and hook-pierced lip, trailed by three smaller fish. This fish trio appears before Karic, hovering over the pool in a golden glow of light. They call his name, but he cannot heed their invitation because it is at this moment that Leito hauls Karic from the pool. Karic lies sputtering and confused upon the riverbank, convinced the fish were summoning him to fulfill a higher purpose, and to impart to him some greater understanding of his role in the world.

Karic would soon encounter the Salmon of Knowledge and Fish Gods once more during the melee of rats raiding Cricket's Glen. His house, aflame, topples into a nearby creek, and Karic is plunged once more into the water, trapped helplessly beneath the sinking debris. He blacks out and awakens on the shore of the cavern once again, deposited safely by the Salmon. As before, the fish trio hovers before Karic, telling him that he has been selected, like the legendary *Kuhl-En*, to become the liberator of *The Dark Lands*. To aid the young mouse, they bestow upon him a small pouch filled with water, the source of which will never run dry, and when needed, will freely flow with "all the waters of the world." Bradán Feasa emerges from the water, mouth gaping wide, fulfilling its duty of transporting Karic back to his now decimated village.

The Mythological Parallels

The Salmon of Knowledge connects the Mice Templar narrative to Celtic Mythology through the parallels established by the character of Karic and the legend of Finn MacCool. Both young and unsuspecting figures attain a higher purpose and understanding of their role as liberators and protectors compelled by a stronger will than their own. Through their interaction with Bradán Feasa, each figure emerges from their encounter transformed, imbued with a knowledge they could never have attained through natural means and even the most rigorous training. Finn MacCool would eventually become the leader of the Fianna, and should the Fish Gods' words prove true, Karic's journey might see the resurrection of the long dead Mice Templar order.

Other noteworthy parallels involving the Salmon of Knowledge is the association of water with knowledge or wisdom. While Celtic legend saw the Salmon of Knowledge attain its power through the Fountain Of Wisdom, the Fish Gods of Mice Templar mythology equip Karic with a bottomless source of water in the form of a small pouch. Like Finn MacCool, who could attain the world's knowledge simply by placing his finger to his mouth in a moment of need, Karic too may discover much needed solutions during his forthcoming journey by employing the water pouch. The correlation between MacCool's source of knowledge, the Fountain of Wisdom, and Karic's Water Pouch reinforces the mythological parallel.

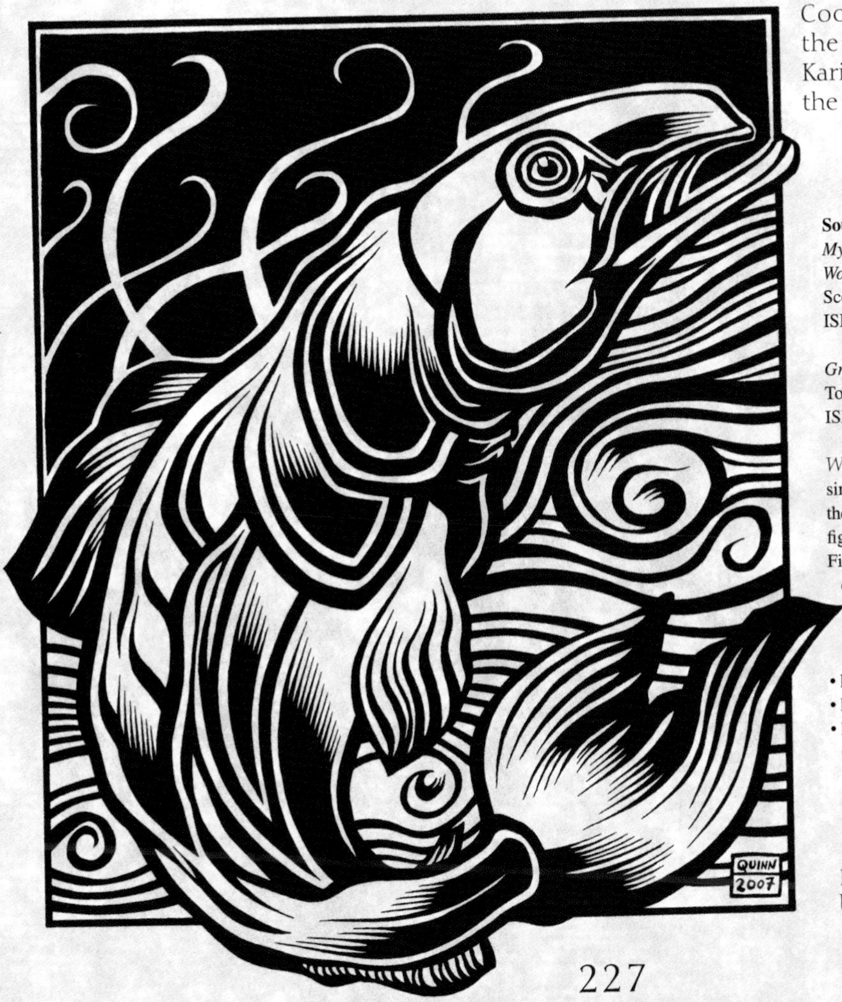

QUINN
2007

Sources:

Mythology: The Illustrated Anthology of World Myth and Storytelling, Ed., Scott Littleton, Pub., Duncan Baird, 2002, ISBN 1-904292-01-1

Great Heroes of Mythology, Ed., Tony Burgess, Pub., Petra Press, 1997, ISBN 1-56799-433-4

Wikipedia (the following pages where used simply as a basis for gaining an overview of the legends pertaining to the above described figures, legends and associated landmarks. Final content was derived from the source citations above).

- http://en.wikipedia.org/wiki/Salmon_of_Wisdom
- http://en.wikipedia.org/wiki/River_Boyne
- http://en.wikipedia.org/wiki/River_Shannon
- http://en.wikipedia.org/wiki/Fionn_mac_Cumhaill

Illustration by Brian Quinn
bcqillustrator.blogspot.com

Mice Templar: The Master & Apprentice

One of the fundamental motifs of mythology is the relationship between Master and Apprentice. On the surface, this relationship seems a simple enough exchange: the Master is typically ancient, wizened, hunched by time, bent by one too many adventures, while the Apprentice—youthful, vigorous, and naively idealistic—is woefully unprepared and often overwhelmed by the challenges his journey presents. The exchange between these two figures is one of wisdom for vigor, guidance for enthusiasm.

Outside of compensating for certain shortcomings in each other, the Master/Apprentice relationship is founded upon an agenda, usually the Master's driving impetus to seek and accept an Apprentice, or in some cases vice versa. Yet for all the mutual benefits this relationship yields, it is one often beset with sly deceit, half-truths, outright lies, deft manipulation, and a constant struggle to break free of limits while testing the boundaries of trust and ability.

A Duo Of Duos

Two of the more notable and popular Master/Apprentice relationships in mythology are those of Merlin to King Arthur and Obi Wan "Ben" Kenobi to Luke Skywalker in the *Star Wars* saga.

Merlin's presence as an integral figure to Arthur's ascendancy to the throne predates the young king's birth. Merlin casts the spell that enables Arthur's father, King Uther, to sleep with the Duchess Ygraine (Igrayne), thus begetting Arthur, in return for which Uther promises the child to Merlin. Merlin obviously has ulterior motives, a private agenda that sees Arthur as the fulfillment of the old man's desire for a King who would one day unite England: "I have walked my way since the beginning of time. Sometimes I give, sometimes I take. It is mine to know which and when!" After securing the infant, Merlin leaves Arthur in the care of Sir Ector, to rear him until such time as Merlin sees fit to reveal Arthur's true lineage and thus begin his rise to the throne under Merlin's tutelage.

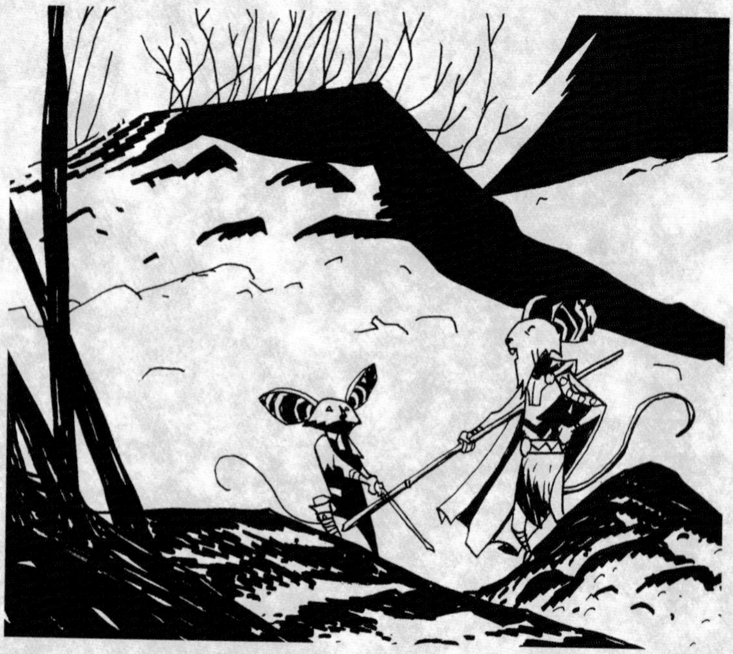

Likewise, Ben Kenobi's patronage of Luke Skywalker precedes the future Jedi's birth. Following the Clone Wars and subsequent Jedi slaughter at the hands of Darth Vader, Kenobi is charged with hiding Luke far away from the nefarious intentions of the Empire. Living a hermit's life in the sands of Tatooine, Kenobi entrusts him to the care of his aunt and uncle. From a distance, he vigilantly watches over the boy who, under his guidance, he believes will eventually topple the Empire and unite the galaxy. Thus would he also fulfill his own personal agenda he thought had failed many years before, when Luke's father, Anakin, rejected his supervision.

Just as Merlin timed the revelation of Arthur's parentage to deftly illuminate the way for Arthur's crowning, so too does Kenobi use this key piece of information to shield Luke from the burden that lies before him, allowing his protégé to focus on his training in the ancient Jedi arts. Skewing the truth of Vader's identity, then watching proudly as Skywalker learns to wield the very lightsaber Vader fashioned when he was Kenobi's pupil, the old Jedi informs Luke that he has taken the "first step into a larger world," a world no doubt shaped by Kenobi's decades-old agenda.

Karic & Pilot the Tall — Mice Templar

In Pilot the Tall, Karic has found a figure who certainly fits the mold of the Master living in exile. Pilot first appears mysteriously in Cricket's Glen just before a murderous raid by Captain Tosk's Rats. Wounded and left for dead, the old mouse is discovered by Karic amongst the rubble of his ruined village. His friends murdered, his family vanished, Karic has little recourse but to accept Pilot's friendship. Soon the old mouse is relaying a prophecy of "The Chosen One

MERLIN

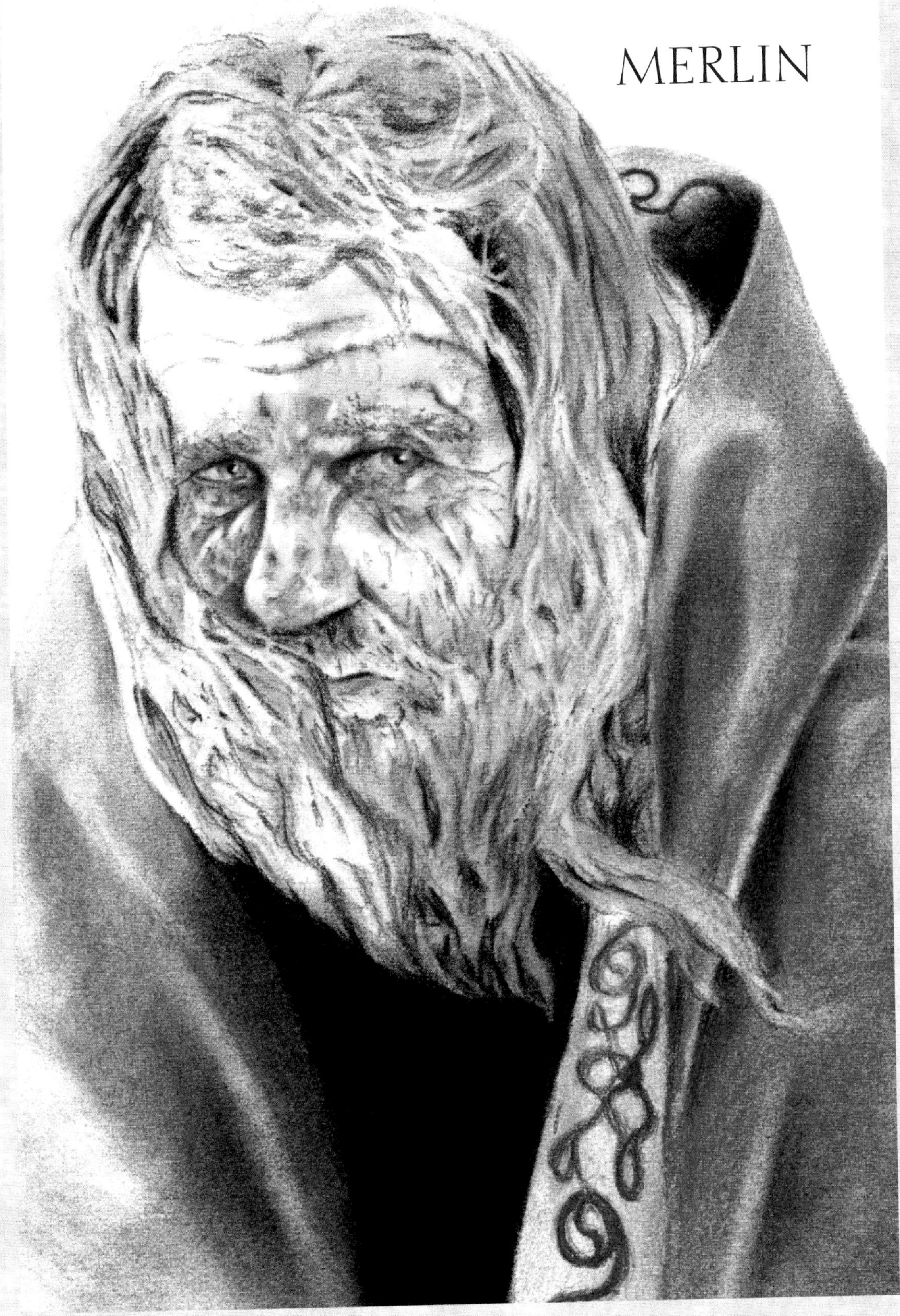

Painted by Taki Soma
www.takisoma.com

warning to take care with his sword when fighting The Many. Luke rushes out recklessly in the midst of his training to confront Vader on Bespin, despite Kenobi's prophetic warnings of the impending disaster awaiting him.

Such is the sometimes uneasy alliance formed between Master and Apprentice. Boundaries and rules are set and broken, then new ones established and broken yet again. Trust is found, lost, and regained. The Master's intentions are perpetually painted in blurry shades of grey while he attempts to prepare his protégé for the inevitable conflict and awesome burden that is sure to befall him, all the while keeping one eye upon the goal and another wary one upon the Apprentice.

But what happens when the Master reveals himself to be something other than altruistic? What happens when the Master's will ensures that the Apprentice fulfills a dark destiny fitting his own private agenda, one at odds with the hero's own journey? Luke's father learns the torturous outcome to these questions, served to him by the unforgiving blade of Kenobi's lightsaber. As Obi Wan later rebuffs a sarcastic space smuggler's skepticism, "Who's the more foolish—the fool, or the fool who follows him?". ༄

of Wotan" to his bewildered companion, an ancient doctrine which suggests that Wotan will choose one small mouse to recreate the mythical exploits of Kuhl-En and thereby bring salvation to all mice. Thus, with determined efficiency, Pilot begins to train Karic in the ways of the Templar.

The Mythological Parallels

Like Luke's wistful dreaming of one day joining the Academy, idly passing the hours scanning the stars and racing Beggar's Canyon, Karic too nurtures his fantasies of the Templar, role-playing with his friend Leito amongst the branches and underbrush of Cricket's Glen. Like Merlin and

Kenobi, Pilot uses his years of experience and knowledge of the larger conflict to begin to shape Karic's perceptions of Templar history as it relates to the young mouse's destiny. The old grey mouse challenges his every assumption, shattering Karic's cherished beliefs in the Templar, and Kuhl-En in particular. Under Pilot's tutelage, Karic gains a broader understanding of what awaits him outside the safe and familiar confines of Cricket's Glen.

The innocence of childhood stripped from them, Luke and Karic begin to test the limits set forth for them by their respective Masters. Karic bests Pilot during their training routines, and later disregards his

Sources:
Internet Movie Data Base www.imdb.com (keywords: Star Wars, Excalibur)

Star Wars.com www.starwars.com/databank/character/obiwankenobi/

The Hero with a Thousand Faces, Joseph Campbell, Pub., Princeton University Press, 1972, ISBN 0691017840

Great Heroes of Mythology, Ed., Tony Burgess, Pub., Petra Press, 1997, ISBN 1-56799-433-4

Mythology: The Illustrated Anthology of World Myth and Storytelling, Ed., Scott Littleton, Pub., Duncan Baird, 2002, ISBN 1-904292-01-1

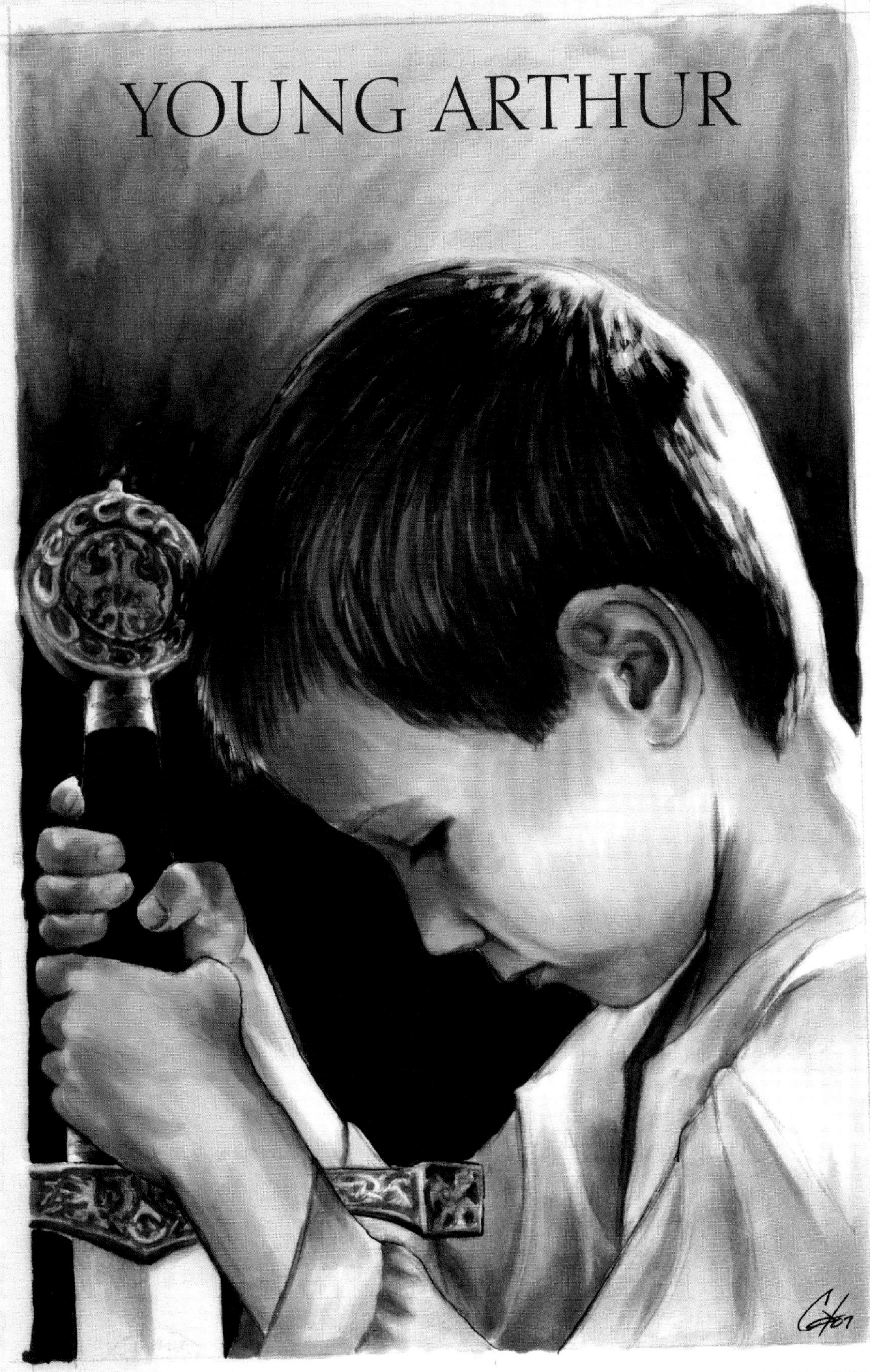
YOUNG ARTHUR

Painted by Cat Staggs
www.airbrushcat.com

Black Anaius: Enter the Bogeyman

A gnarled hand reaching from the well-black shadow under the stair. The unblinking crimson eye peering into your soul from an open closet's maw. The what-ever-it-is, that does what-ever-it-does, and somehow manages to wriggle itself between your mattress and floor, lying in wait each night for the telltale rustling of your covers as you slide under the sheets. The craggy old woman just around the bend—you know the one. She's always in the cottage through the wood, or down at the last corner house where the paved road ends and the twisted tendrils of nature are reclaiming the earth.

The bogeyman of myth and literature has always occupied the blurry fringes somewhere just outside reality, while clawing ever hungrily at the doorway of plausibility. Bogeymen are our waking nightmares cloaked in the ragged skin of our deepest fears, a terrifying form draped in the sulfurous stench of our temptations, its daggered fingers bloodied with the harsh justice it metes out mercilessly for our transgressions and sins.

The role of a great bogeyman has always been loosely defined, but usually serves as the delineation of our behavioral boundaries, reinforcing our societal mores through the focus of our fears. Storytellers throughout history have made use of the bogeyman as a means to instruct an impressionable audience about important values in the established paradigm of a particular era. In the introduction to *The Shining*, Stephen King writes, "We sometimes need to create...bogies to stand in for all the things we fear in our real lives." To be sure, the bogeyman is as much a mirror for our very real fears as it is a stake in the ground reminding us all what happens when good little boys and girls don't eat their greens or study their lessons, or stray too far from the straight and narrow. And what better way to maneuver the flock than by fears that the stray lamb won't just be lost, but mutilated, eviscerated, devoured alive.

What the Lamb Saw

And what exactly does that stray lamb see when it comes upon that stake beyond the far edges of reason and good judgment? A good bogey takes many shapes, reveals the nature of our many fears, and illuminates, even embodies, the form our punishment shall take.

The legend of Black Annis is murky and varied to say the least. For some, Black Annis was long of claw and yellow of fang—sharp as deadly knife points—with blue skin gleaming in the moonlight as she emerged from her cave, shape-shifting into the form of a child-eating cat demon. Some claimed to hear her unearthly howls from miles away. Her hideous face bore a single blazing eye, wild with the fire of an insatiable hunger for human flesh.

The children of Leicester, England, were warned against a terrifying presence prowling the surrounding hillsides that would claw them to death and suck their blood if she were to catch them. Parents described Annis as having grotesquely elongated arms. She could reach through open windows to snatch sleeping children, and then disappear into the night. The monstrous hag would hang her victims' skins from an oak tree outside her bower and scatter the bones about the glens of the Leicester countryside.

Others believed a much more benign story that she was once merely a nun, named Agnes Scott, a leader of a leper colony who dwelled in a cave in the Dane Hills on the western edge of the city of Leicestershire, until a poet gave birth to legend, and the woman was no more.

Still others believed she was a dark mystic, a "wise-woman" whom legend suggests foretold the death of King Richard III.

The Dark Witch

It is impossible to draw out a definitive legend of Black Annis from these varied accounts and descriptions, nor would we want to. Such revelation would only defame and unceremoniously rob our bogey of her mystique. Fortunately, while additional accounts can flesh out her portrait, they only seem to make her more inscrutable.

The Witch from the Brothers Grimm tale, *Hansel and Gretel*, lies in wait in her wooded bungalow, fattening Hansel with candy and other desserts in order to eat him. In Russian folklore there is Baba Yaga, a cannibalistic witch who dwells in the forest and flies about in a mortar, using the pestle as a rudder to help her steer.

Modern motion pictures have also made use of the mythic dark witch. 1982's *The Dark Crystal* presents a haggish character named Aughra, the keeper of secrets. Like Annis, this wrinkled, stooped hag possesses one eye,

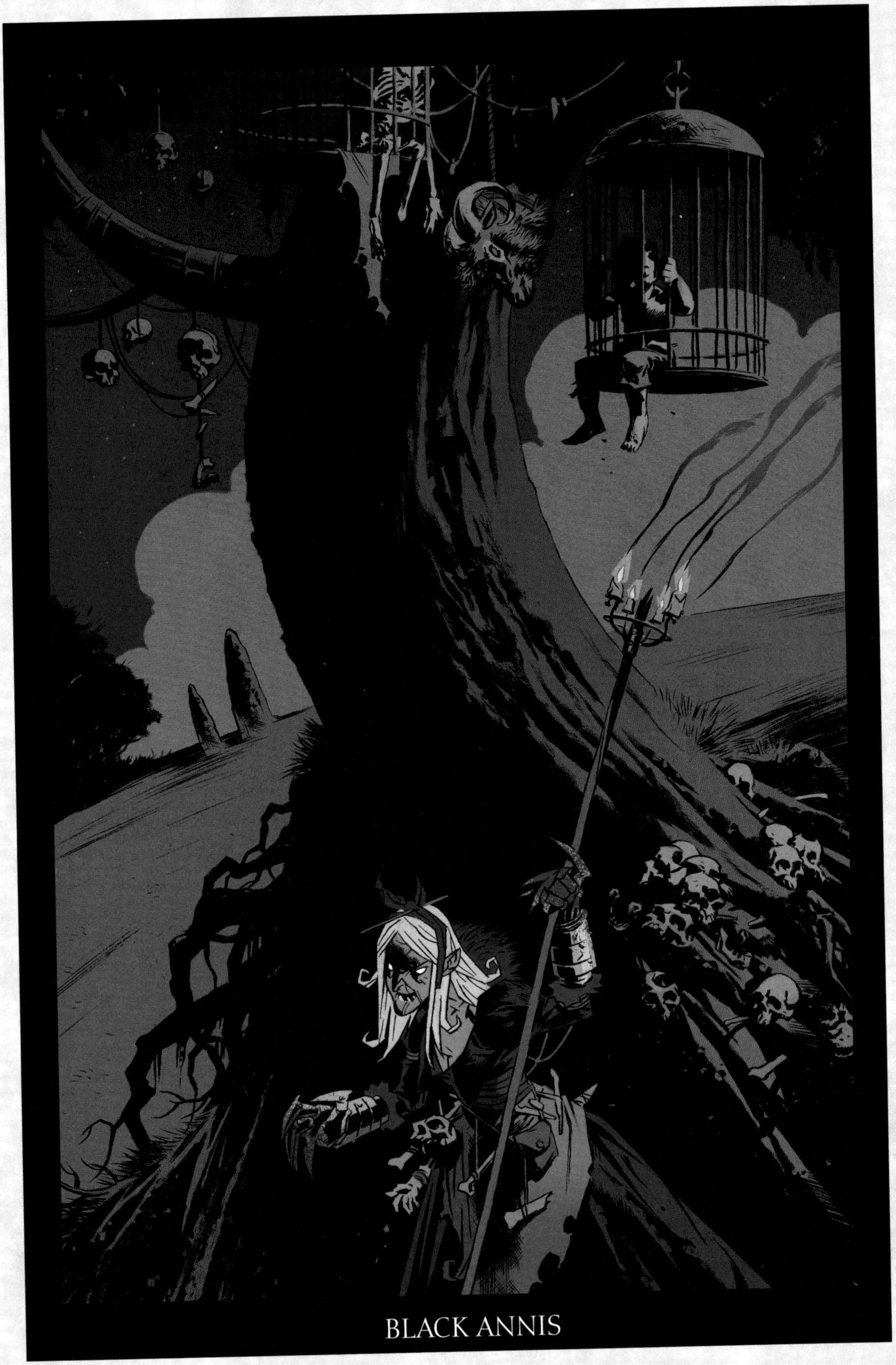

BLACK ANNIS

Nic Klein
www.nic-klein.com

and helps the protagonist fulfill an ages-old prophecy.

Absent an actual witch, M. Night Shyamalan's 2004 film *The Village* invoked a legend similar to the hillside-roaming Annis. Residents of the bucolic hamlet warned their restless children of a race of hooded, flesh-eating beasts in the adjacent forest that would devour them should they trespass beyond the boundary established as a line of truce, a literal stake in the ground swabbed with yellow paint.

What The Mouse Saw

"The storme will arise,
And trouble the skies;
This night, and more for
the wonder,
The ghost from the Tomb
Affrighted shall come,
Cal'd out by the clap of the
Thunder."
—*The Hag*, Robert Herrick, 1648

Black Anaius (note spelling difference from the English legend) of *The Mice Templar* lore appears as Pilot leads Karic to the base of Kildre Hill. There a very frightened Karic recounts the legend of Black Anaius, a dark figure who eats mice children. Pilot rebuffs his young charge, claiming the druid-witch is very real, but the rest is myth: "Anaius does not eat those she sacrifices." With a warning for Karic to stay close to the light of the fire with his sword close at hand, Pilot vanishes into the night, leaving Karic alone with the crackling fire and swirling sounds of the forest.

Just as in Herrick's poem, a storm builds overhead. A thunderclap heralds the arrival of rain, heavy enough to extinguish Karic's fire. Illuminated by lightning's glare, a rat-warrior's form reaches for Karic from the brush, its ghostly voice warning of "Doom."

Another flash reveals the rat as nothing more than branches and brambles. Is this a trick of the forest, or a witch's warning?

From the smoke of the doused campfire, the ghostly form of Karic's sister Gabrielle rises, beckoning him by name with a hollow-sounding call. From that same ashen plume, Karic then sees the smoke wend itself into the guise of his mother, frightening the young mouse enough to brandish his sword. Desperately, he impales the ghost and flees.

Following the path to the hill, Karic arrives at a small shack, the ghostly forms trailing closely behind. He enters the small dwelling and discovers a lone hooded figure seated before a fire. When he takes hold of the cloak, the figure dissolves into thin air, leaving him trembling and alone in the hut. In the open doorway, the impaled figure of his mother glides toward him, "You've come home to me my little one..." she calls.

On What Path, Karic?

Considering how the bogeymen in literature and Mice Templar act in many instances as a manifestation of fear or alternately as a guide for the protagonist, we must ask: is Black Anaius appearing before Karic as a punishment for his transgressions, is she steering him away from impending doom and back onto the path of safety, or is the Druid Witch of Kildre Hill operating as a broker for a far more powerful and sinister force?

After Karic has felled the familial manifestations she has put before him, and realized that the abandoned shack is yet another form of Black Anaius' dark power, the hag finally reveals her true physical form. Seeking the Wisdom of the Nathair, Pilot uses Death Magic to summon forth Anaius. Offering her a bloody

mouse skull housing the essence of a soul as a sacrifice, Anaius accepts Pilot's offering, severing and claiming one of his fingers in the process, leaving Karic's mentor with the esoteric answer of "Yes" to his unspecified riddle.

Pilot uses Anaius' answer as evidence that Karic is Wotan's Chosen One, a discovery that will redeem Pilot in the eyes of the Templar Priests, those few who survive, who alone are imbued with the power to so anoint Karic.

"YOUR ANSWER... IS YESSSSS..."

Anaius's connection to the Nathair, the race of creatures banished to the Outer Darkness for attempting to blind Wotan, is the key to understanding the Witch's role in the events conspiring to shape Karic's destiny. Being in league with the Nathair, her answer to Pilot is greatly biased by that association. Pilot, ever the manipulative opportunist, seizes upon Anaius' response as the means to validate his desire to see Karic deemed the Chosen One. Pilot, the "Old Deceiver," is so consumed with the notion of his own redemption that he fails to see how his presenting Karic to the Templar Priests as a false Chosen One may yet allow the Nathair to impact the physical worlds of the Bright Realm and the Shadow Time. ◎

Sources:

Black Annis
http://www.bbc.co.uk/dna/h2g2/A14129318
http://www.whitedragon.org.uk/articles/
blackann.htm
http://en.wikipedia.org/wiki/Black_Annis

Baba Yaga
http://en.wikipedia.org/wiki/Baba_Yaga

Hansel & Gretel
http://en.wikipedia.org/wiki/Hansel_and_Gretel

IMDB: http://imdb.com
keywords: Dark Crystal, The Village

The Great Ash Tree: The Root of All Myth

No doubt about it, trees have given humankind every manner of physical support and sustenance imaginable through the ages: fuel, food, shelter, and weaponry, and countless tools and technologies all derive from the tree. It is no wonder we have formed so many traditions, rituals, and cultural practices around their sturdy trunks and beneath the safety of their outstretched boughs.

Trees are the world's oldest—by some reckonings, 370 million years and counting—and largest living things. Their relationship with humans frequently transcends the mere physical. A select few varieties of the 80,000 known recorded species have found fertile ground in the soul of humankind, giving rise to a number of myths and traditions, from ensuring fertility to serving as a metaphor for organizing genealogies.

A Great Shadow Cast

The Rowan or Mountain Ash holds a unique legendary status, casting quite a long shadow across many cultures' myths. In Norse mythology in particular, the Ash was the tree designated as the "World Tree." Its wood was thought to possess healing powers and its mighty roots responsible for holding the universe together. One account tells how this same tree was believed to have saved the great god Thor from death by drowning.

Perhaps in tribute to this legend and the tree's other mythic associations, Ash trees were often planted near houses to ward off evil spirits, and travelers on Midsummer's Night were advised to carry a sprig of Rowan Ash for protection from overly zealous fairies on that mystical night.

YGGDRASIL

No myth factors more strongly in granting the Ash Tree its lofty status than that of the legend of Yggdrasil (pronounced *ihg-drah-sill*). This grand Tree bridges the nine worlds of Norse Cosmology, a mythical axis and center of the Universe connecting Asgard, the realm of Gods, Midgard, the place of mortals, and far below Niflheim, the Norse Underworld. The Norse God Odin was known to have hung upside-down for nine nights from one of its boughs in order to gain access to the Rune alphabet. Other tales tell how one could pluck out an eye in sacrifice to the spring beneath the tree, Mimir, in hopes of receiving wisdom.

Yggdrasil is guarded by the Dragon Nidhogg, stationed at the trunk's base eagerly awaiting the opportunity to consume trespassers who come too close. Other animals of mythic power also inhabit Yggdrasil: an Eagle resides at the tree's apex, and a squirrel, Ratatosk, lives among its branches and transports messages of great import among all the tree's residents.

In essence, Yggdrasil represents the eternal struggle of life, in the form of the mighty Eagle, and death, in the guise of Nidhogg and his serpent cohorts feasting endlessly upon rotted mortal flesh and Yggdrassil's roots. Scuttling back and forth between the opposing forces, little Ratatosk carries Nidhogg's lies and deceitful words along the taproot —thought to be the shaft of Thor's Hammer—back to the boughs high above where the great Eagle resides.

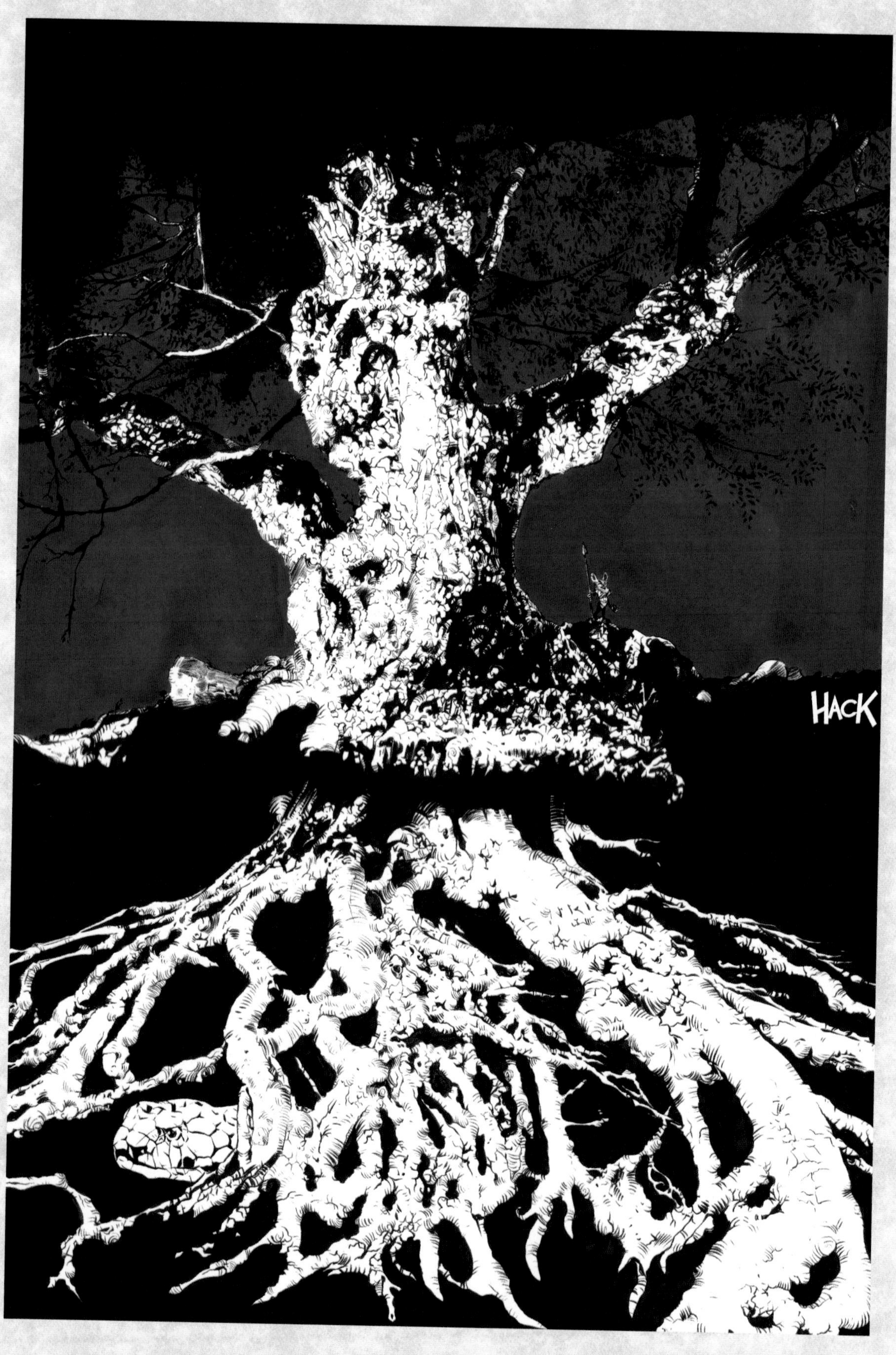
HACK

YGGDRASIL • THE GREAT ASH TREE

Robert Hack
www.roberthackstudios.com

As It Is Written

The ancient Great Ash Tree of Mice Templar lore is the sanctuary home of the mystical Readers of the Wheat, the surviving Templar Priesthood. Death Owls in flight overhead guard the Great Ash Tree and the seemingly endless Fields of Gold that surround it. From the height of its highest branches, the Readers discern the Will of Wotan from the patterns blown in the wheat by the great Owls' wings. While the majority of the tree is vibrant and healthy, substantial areas are dead wood and have been hollowed out as living quarters for the priests and guards.

A Pillar in the Gold

At the outskirts of the Fields of Gold, Pilot warns the newly knighted Karic that passage through the wheat to the Great Ash is virtually impossible. The ever-shifting wheat is hypnotic, and disoriented travelers, lost in the wheat's spell and stumbling through the vast field, are soon betrayed by the path they themselves create against the wheat's gentle, rhythmic sway. This visual aberration alerts the Great Death Owls, and the winged sentries easily pinpoint trespassers and snatch them into the heavens for a final meeting with the omnipotent Wotan.

Employing Death Magic once again, Pilot conjures a powerful spell to bend the stalks of wheat creating a path that leads straight to the Great Ash Tree. Along their hurried and desperate jaunt, Pilot tells Karic that the time has come to challenge the Priests' authority, giving new voice to the Readers' divinations, thereby reversing the years of chaos the Priests have wrought. The Priests, Pilot claims, have used their position to poison the minds of the Templar leaders, fracturing the Order and bringing ruin upon all mice.

As the Owls circle nearer, Pilot and Karic are ambushed by the fierce Cassius, who has been tracking them for some time, and the two former adversaries square off in a battle of cold accusations and blades. Cassius' bitter words reveal Pilot to be the deceitful traitor he is—a disgraced former Templar responsible for twisting the vision of Cassius' brother, and now apparently young Karic as well.

The Owl Comes

As the duel continues, spilling the blood of both combatants, the Templar Priests watch from high up in the Great Ash Tree, struggling to discern the origin of this clash and its possible portent. Down below, Karic, greatly influenced by the litany of Pilot's lies and half-truths, rushes to prevent Cassius from killing the defeated Pilot, and is impaled on Cassius's blade.

The stricken innocent descends into the darkness of unconsciousness where, upon the wings of a Great Death Owl, Karic communes with Wotan. He is granted a vision of events past: the founding and fracturing of the Templar Order, the fall of the capital city Dealrach Ard-Vale, the mad King Icarus, and finally the fate of his family and friends at the hands of the Rats.

"To save them all, Karic...what do you offer in exchange?" Wotan beckons. In return, without hesitation, Karic finds himself saying, "Everything..."

Across the Mythic Boughs

Should Pilot indeed be an emissary of the Nathair, a Ratatosk if you will, carrying with him the twisted lies of Donas (Nidhogg), then the confrontation between him and Cassius is aptly staged at the base of Great Ash, a sacred place connecting Wotan to the Readers of the Wheat, the Templar Priests, and finally to the race of Mice impacted by the will of their God.

The Mice Templar's Great Ash Tree serves as a fine corollary to the Norse myth of Yggdrasil, a mythic parallel in which deceit and death stage an eternal battle with truth and life, affecting the events of all those in between the worlds above and below, of Asgard and Niflheim, of Wotan and the Bright Realm. 〜∾

Sources:
The Tree – Wonder of the Natural World
Jenny Linford ISBN: 13: 978-0-7607-8534-8

Wikipedia
http://en.wikipedia.org/wiki/Ash_tree
http://en.wikipedia.org/wiki/Yggdrasil
http://en.wikipedia.org/wiki/World_Tree

The Templar: of Mice & Men

Legends derive from famous deeds or figures of history that may or may not be true. *Myths* are generally considered to be traditional stories whose importance lies in their significance to a particular people, society or culture. In common usage, "myth" usually but not always implies fantasy and does not necessarily find a basis in truth.

Then there is this very murky intersection where legend and myth *converge*, the result of a combination of factors not limited to the relevance, stature and enduring nature of the object, being or institution. It is within this morass that one finds the Knights Templar.

The Knights Templar: of Legend & Myth

Here is what one needs to know about the Knights Templar. Trust me when I say that these truths may well be based upon lies—or myths, if you will—because there are only two things I know for certain...*maybe*...about the Knights Templar: they existed, and they were referred to as the Knights Templar.

Theirs is a storied history, attributed with a wealth of heroic deeds and some of the world's most sacred artifacts. Following the First Crusade—led by European nobility and ending in 1099 with the Christian capture of Jerusalem—Hugues de Payens and Geoffrey de St. Omer arrived at the palace of King Baldwin II. Their express desire was to defend Christian pilgrims, who were traveling to the newly acquired Jerusalem, against the bands of infidels, robbers and all manner of geographic treachery they would encounter in the mountain passes to the Holy City.

From this meeting, the *Knights Templar* proper may have originated, but this is of course im-possible to verify. Contradictory research also suggests this Order might have been named *The Poor Fellow-Soldiers of Jesus Christ, the Order of the Temple*, or possibly the *Knights of the Temple of Solomon*. Their original number is also difficult to confirm—as few as seven or as many as nine, the latter being more commonly acknowledged. Regardless, these noble knights raised their blades in service to Christ and, after taking vows of poverty, chastity and obedience at the feet of the Patriarch of Jerusalem, formed a holy brotherhood and took up the charge to serve and protect the sojourners. Patterning their vows after Christian Monks, and adorned in flowing white robes emblazoned with an enormous red cross, the Knights Templar became exemplars of devotion and valor, gaining a vast reputation under de Payens, the Order's first Master.

Bernard of Clairvaux, the Cistercian abbot, thought so favorably of the Knights that he wrote a letter entitled, "In praise of the new knighthood." The Cistercians were a highly respected monastic order founded by St. Robert of Molesme in Cîteaux, France. Bernard's endorsement served to substantially boost interest amongst Christian nobility far and wide, and the Templar swelled in ranks, monies and land, all gifted to the Order by legions of newly enamored supporters. Lands were farmed by the Templar and the crops sold to raise additional revenue. This newly acquired wealth could not be enjoyed by the individual Knight, as private profit ran contrary to their vows, but was used shrewdly by the Order and their European financiers as the capital construct upon which an international banking system was pioneered.

Further fueling their wealth were the lands and possessions obtained in defense of the cross throughout the territories bordering the Eastern Mediterranean. Yet nine men, no matter how swift of sword and flowing of robe, cannot achieve and maintain such a level of wealth and military power by themselves. The Knights Templar used their considerable capital to stockpile arms and fortify armies. However, less than 100 years after their formation, circumstances arose for which the Order would desperately need these resources and more. Following their defeat in the First Crusade, the Mussalmen (Muslims) led by Saladin, the Syrian commander and Egyptian Vice-regal-Executive Officer, once again mustered their vast and powerful armies against the Christians occupying the Holy Lands. But the many threats aligning themselves against the Knights Templar would not only be confined to the external, as an economically deprived Europe began to cast its scrutinous eye upon the Order.

From Men to Mice

In this saga of rodent chivalry, it is easy to chart how, just like the Knights Templar under de Payens, the Mice Templar Order was created with noble intent by their founder Kuhl-En. That, like their human counterparts, the brave founding members of Mice were knighted with the express mission of protecting innocent beings, and that they were sworn to uphold a code, a set of vows in pursuit of peace, order and justice.

To be continued...

When Mice Templar Myth & Legend returns in the next arc, we'll continue to examine the Templar, both Knights and Mice. The second installment will detail the bloody Fall of each order, and if you're lucky we'll toss in a few Shrouds, Grails, Marks, Diabhlan and Diabhuls. ❧

Tim Daniel is the founder of Hidden Robot Media and webmaster to many of today's top comic industry professionals. www.HiddenRobot.com

Sources:
Knights Templar http://en.wikipedia.org/wiki/Knights_Templar
History Knights Templar: http://en.wikipedia.org/wiki/History_of_the_Knights_Templar
Templar History.com http://www.templarhistory.com/
Piers Paul Read, The Templars: The Dramatic History of the Knights Templar, the Most Powerful Military Order of the Crusades, Macmillan, 2000 (ISBN 0312266588)

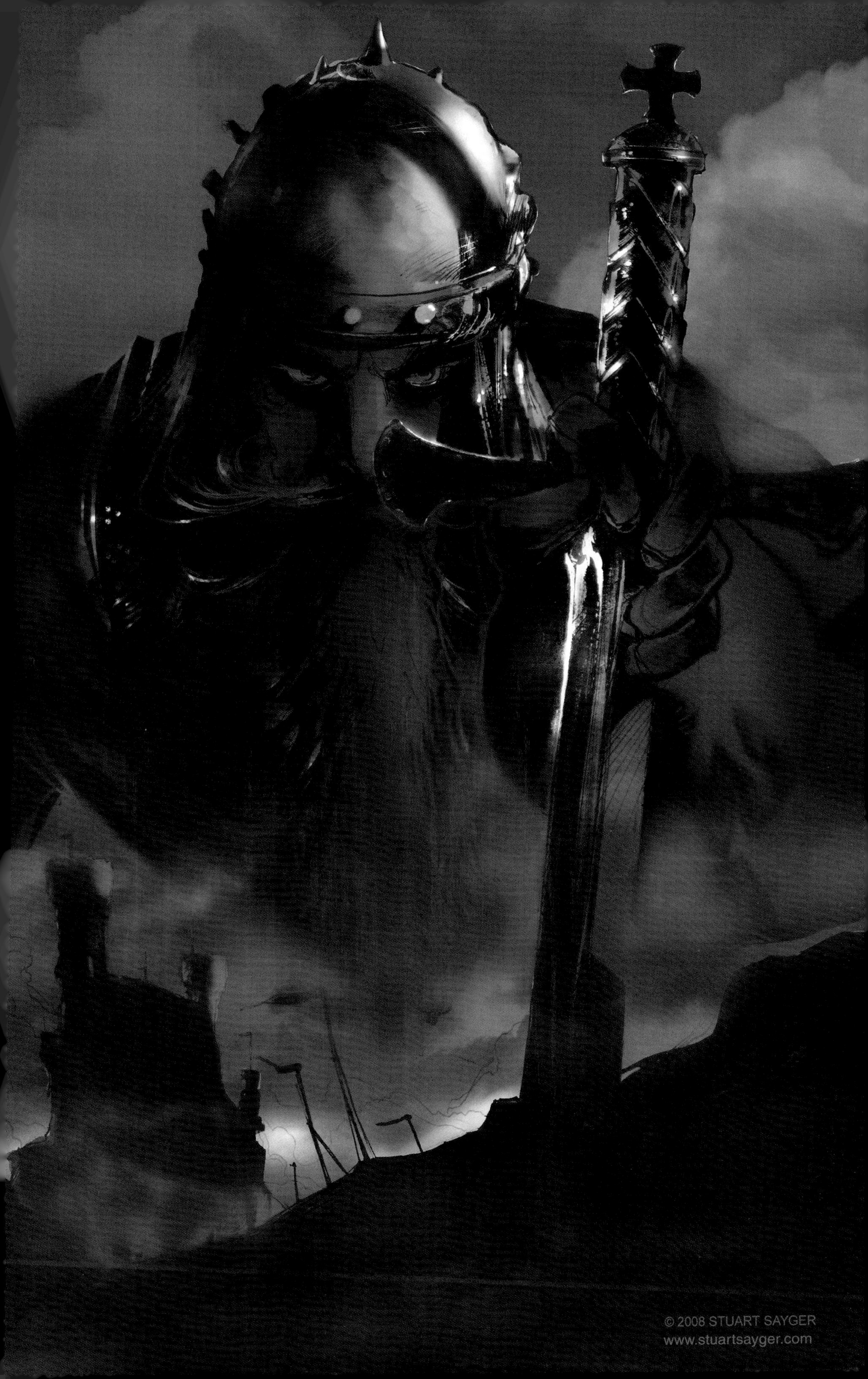

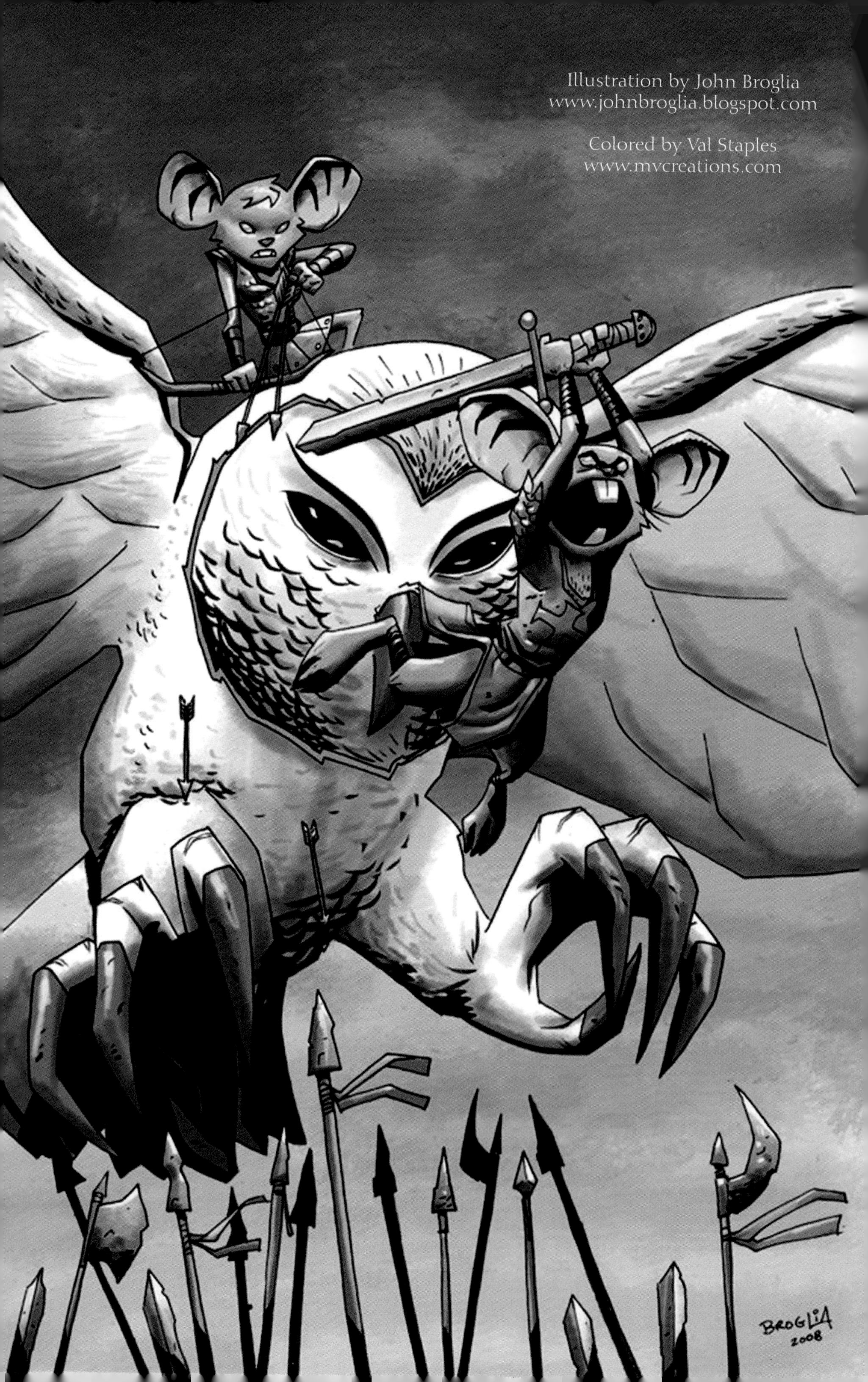
BROGLIA
2008

Illustration by John Broglia
www.johnbroglia.blogspot.com

Colored by Val Staples
www.mvcreations.com

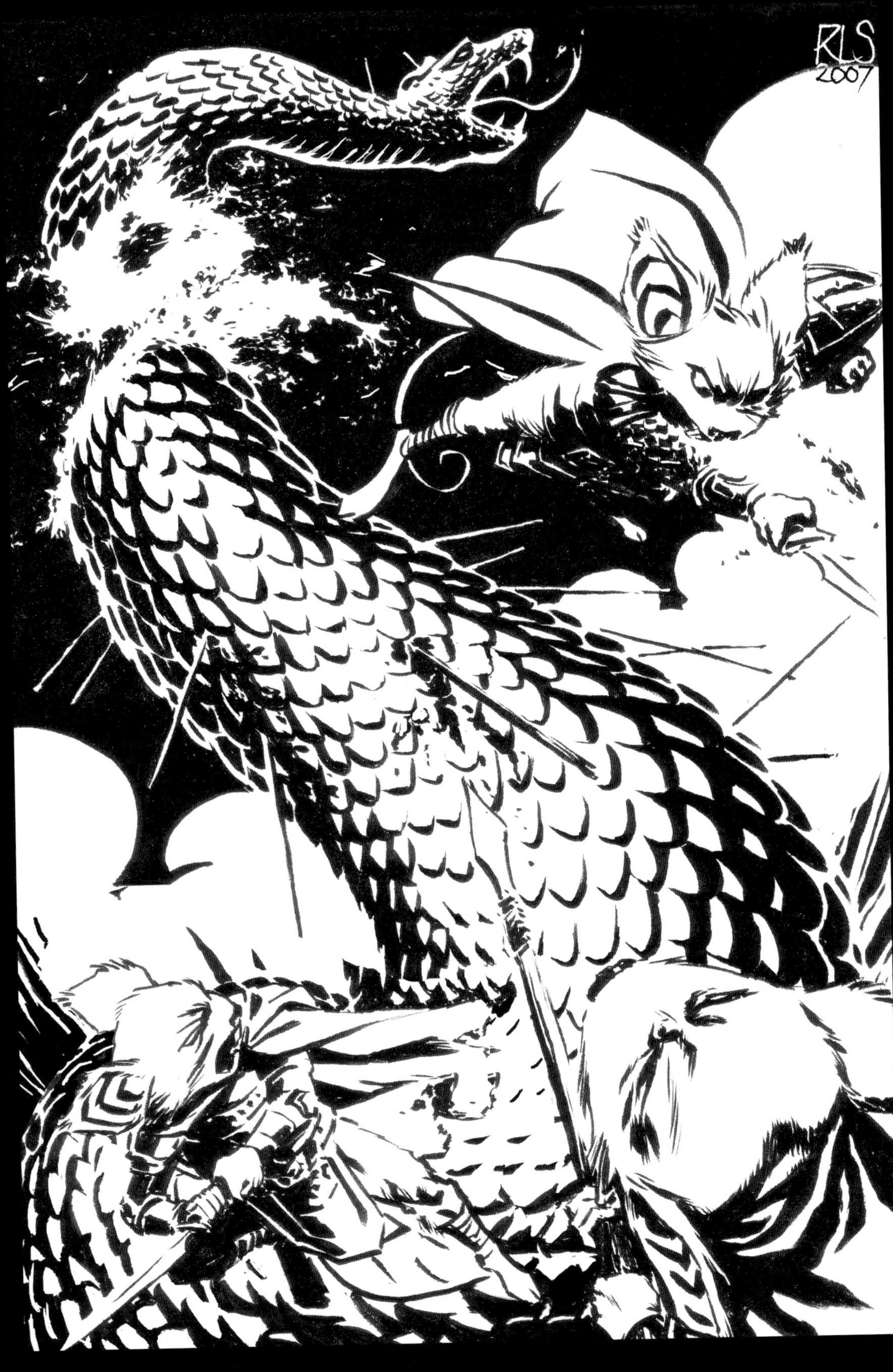
RLS
2007

Illustration by Ron Salas
www.zenwavearts.com

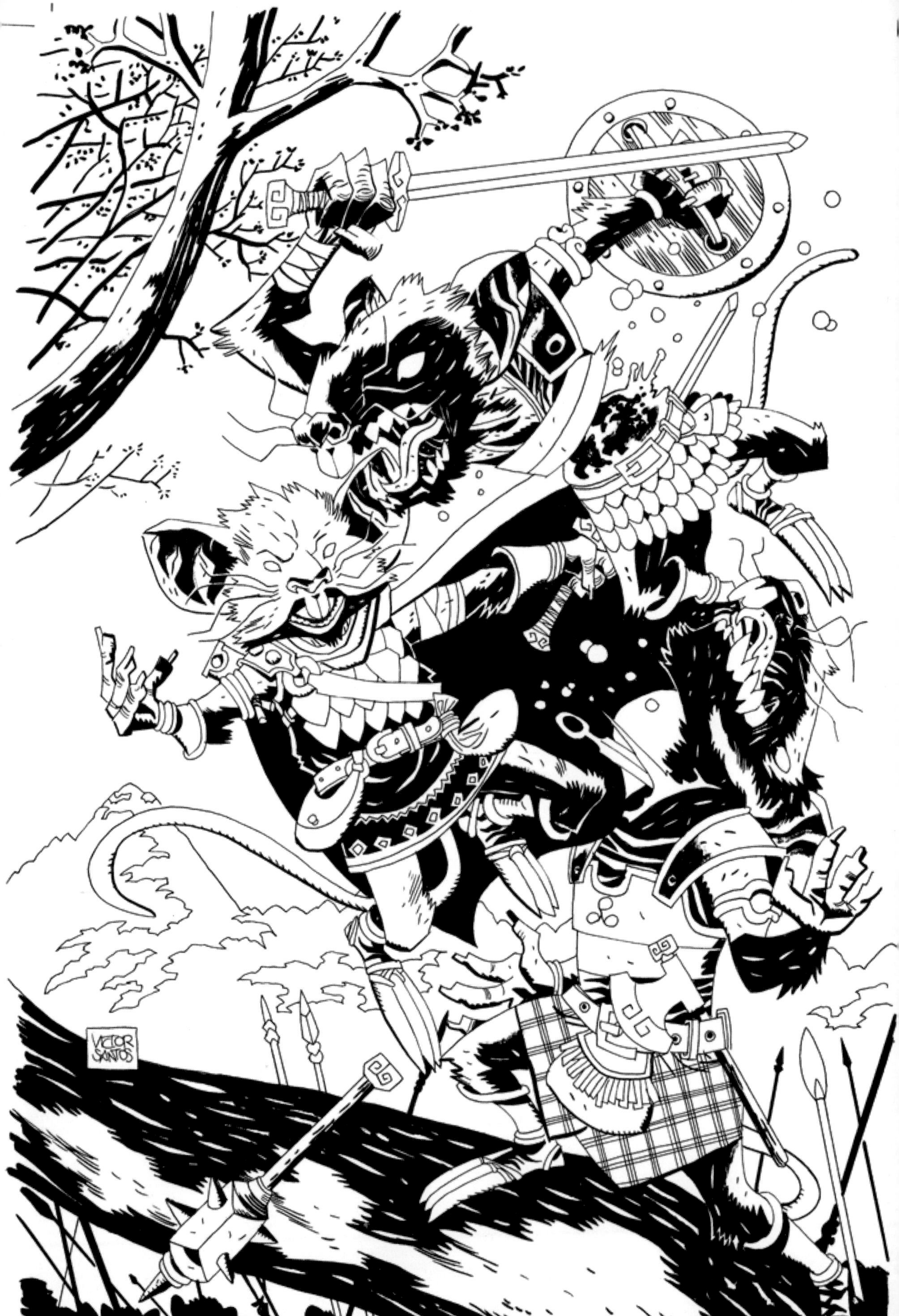
VICTOR SANTOS

MICE TEMPLAR PIN-UP

VICTOR SANTOS

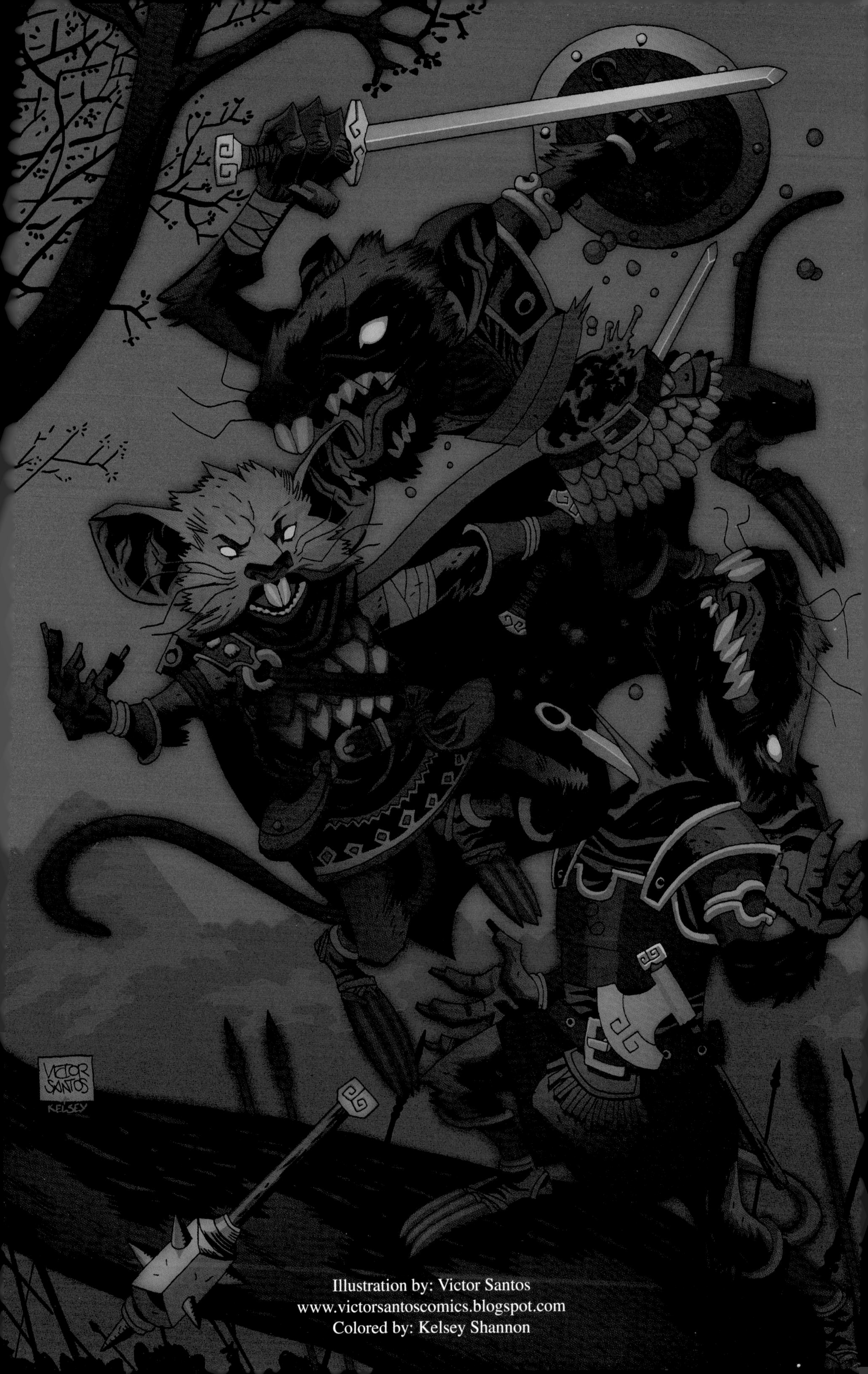
VICTOR SANTOS
KELSEY

Illustration by: Victor Santos
www.victorsantoscomics.blogspot.com
Colored by: Kelsey Shannon

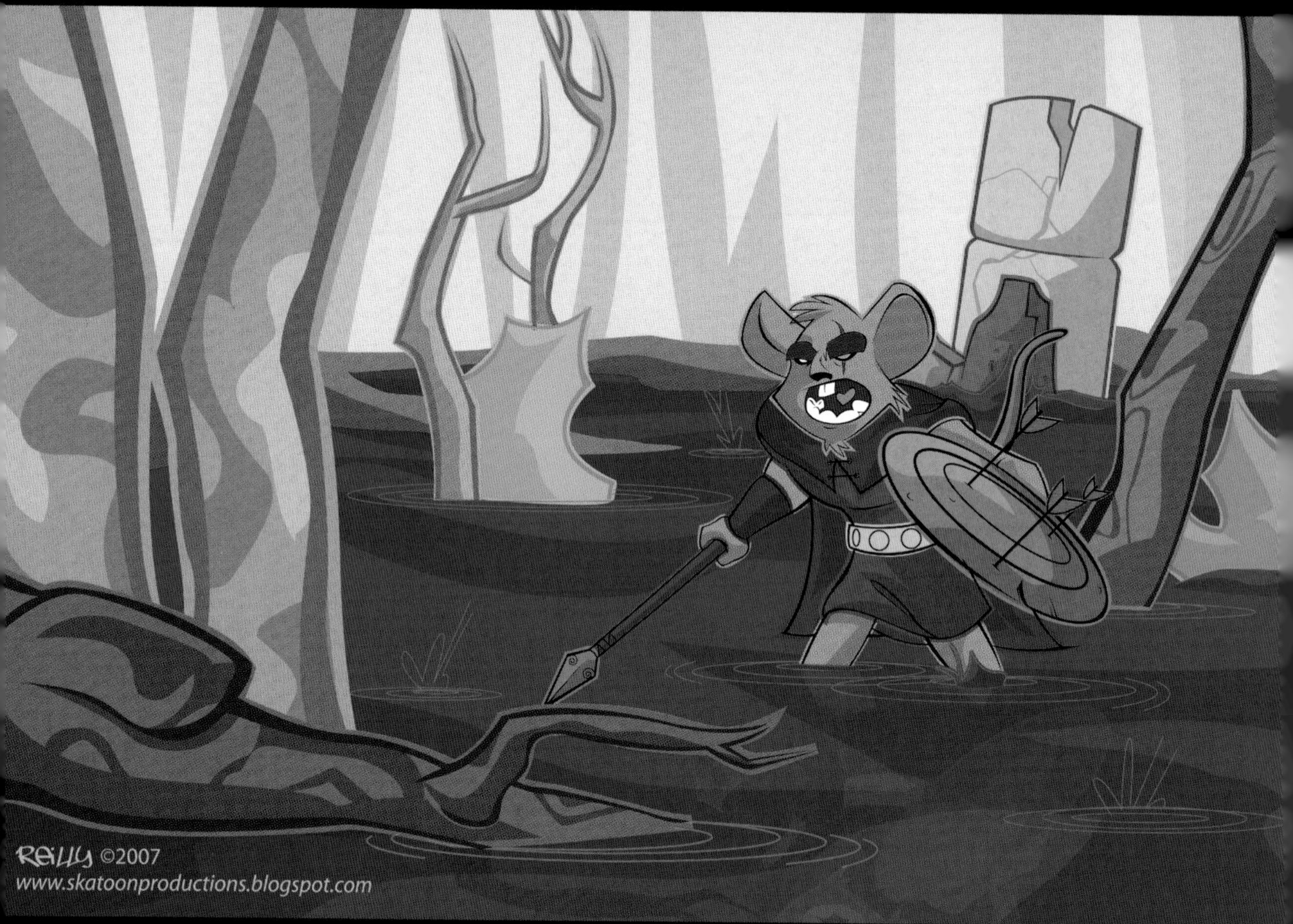
REILLY ©2007
www.skatoonproductions.blogspot.com

Illustration by Rob Reilly

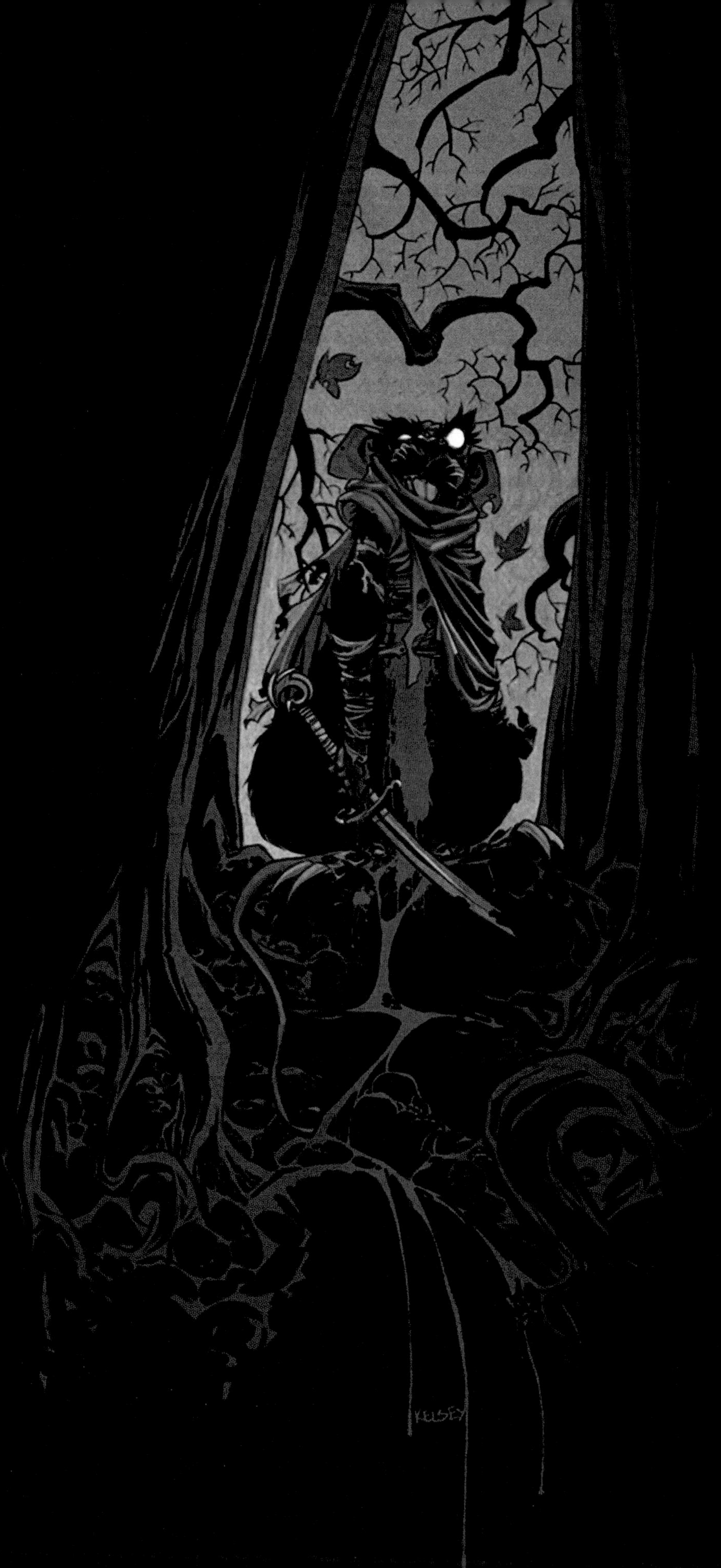
KELSEY

Illustration by Kelsey Shannon

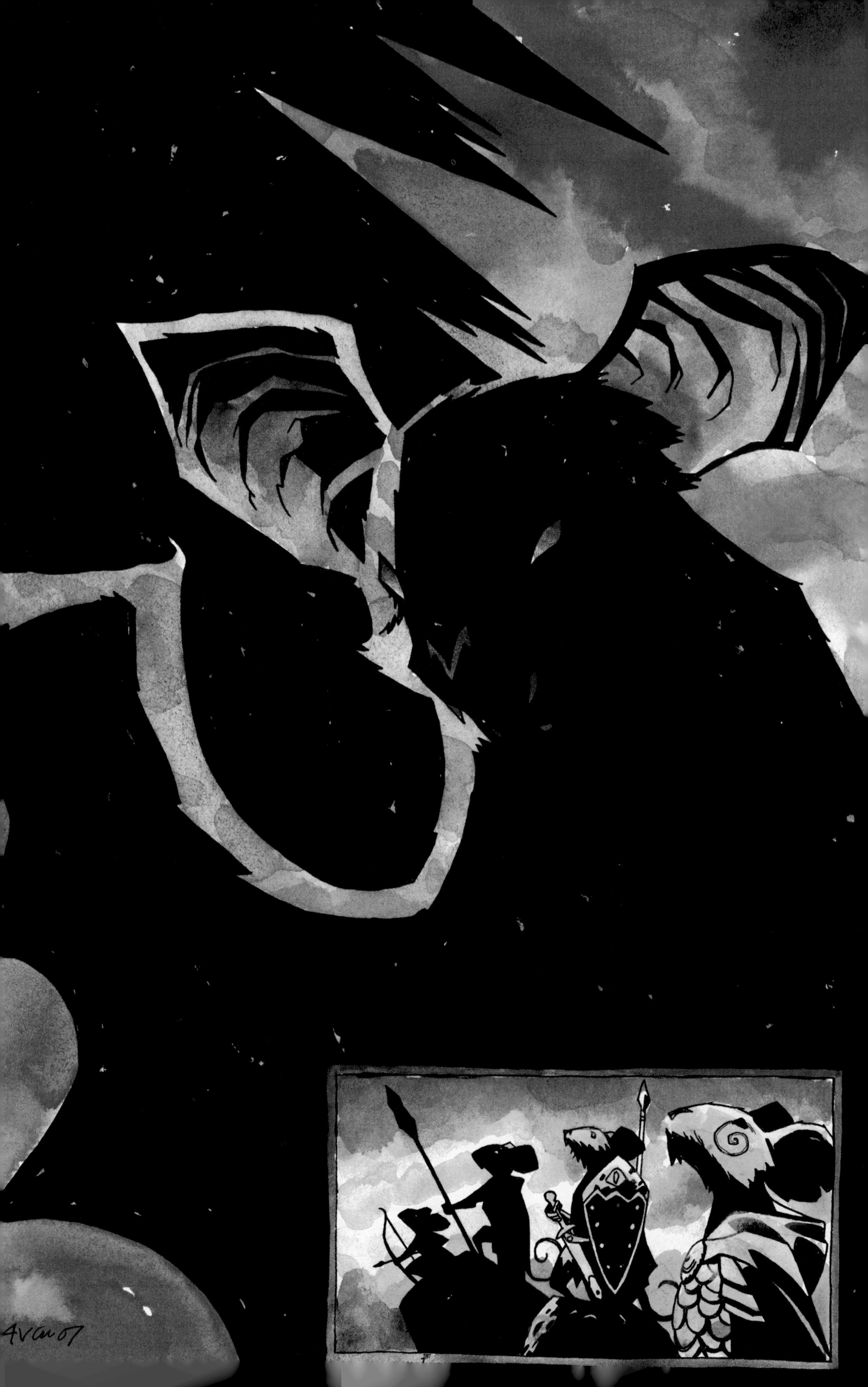

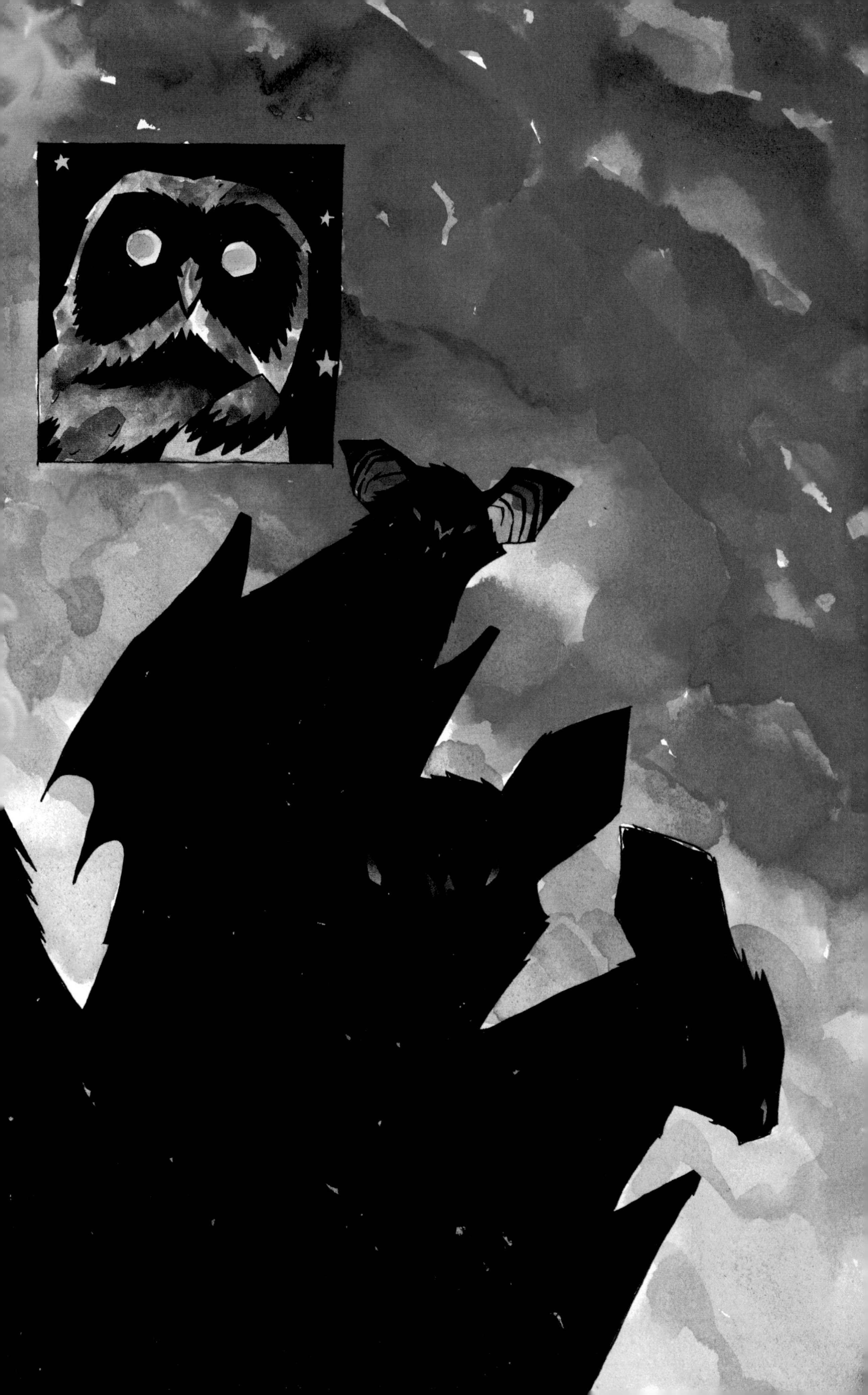

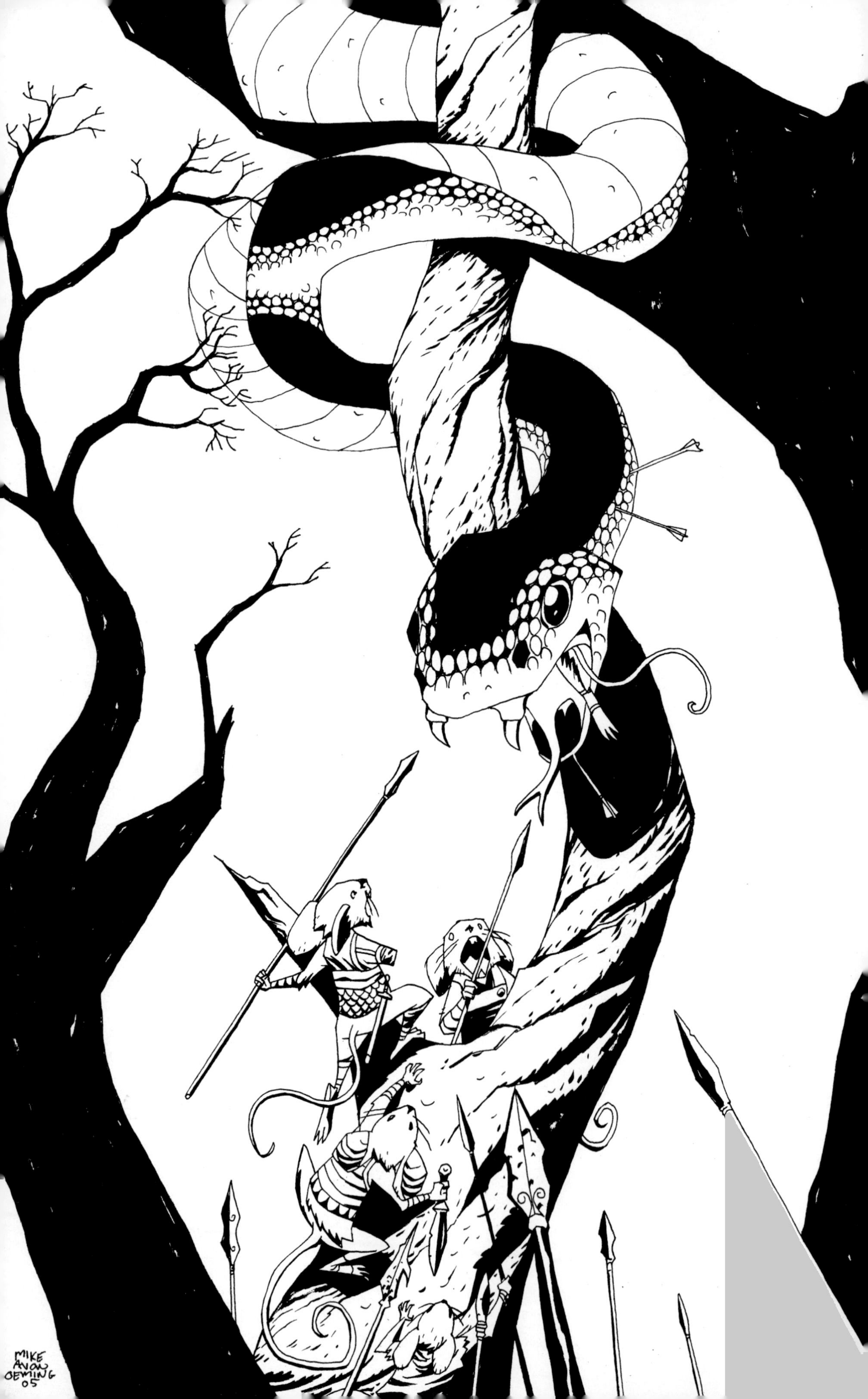
MIKE AVON OEMING 05

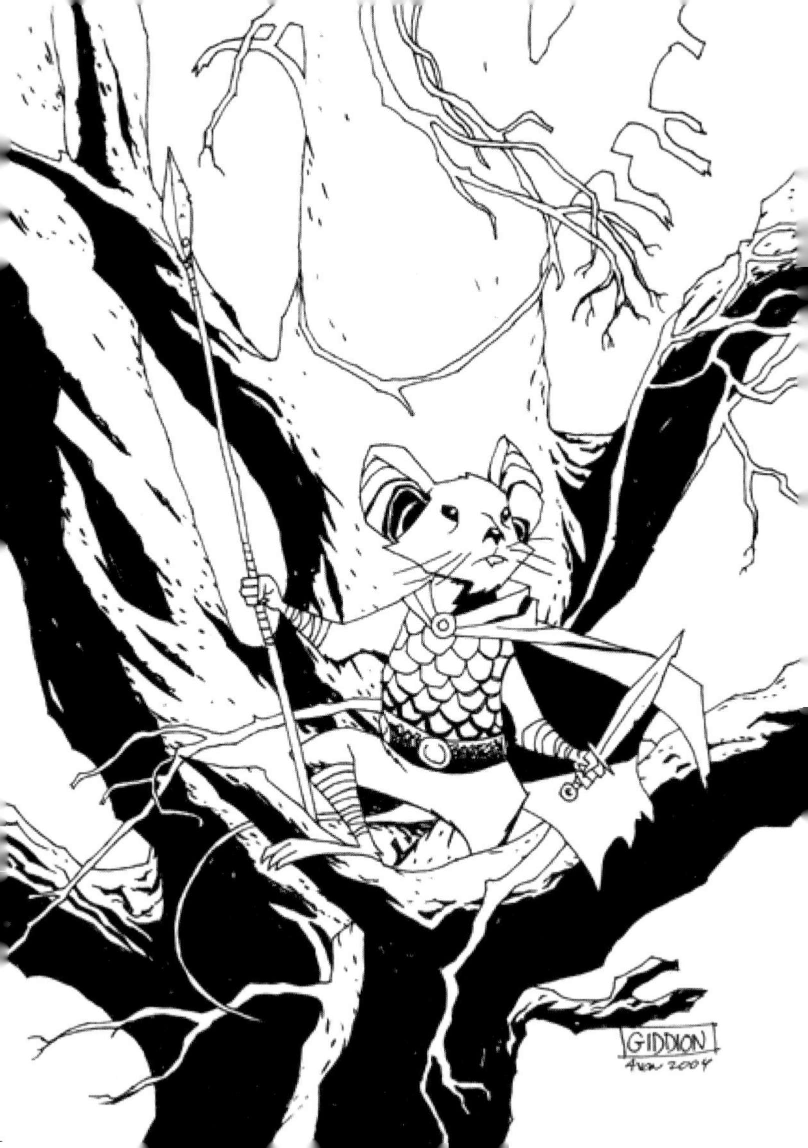
GIDDION
Aug 2004

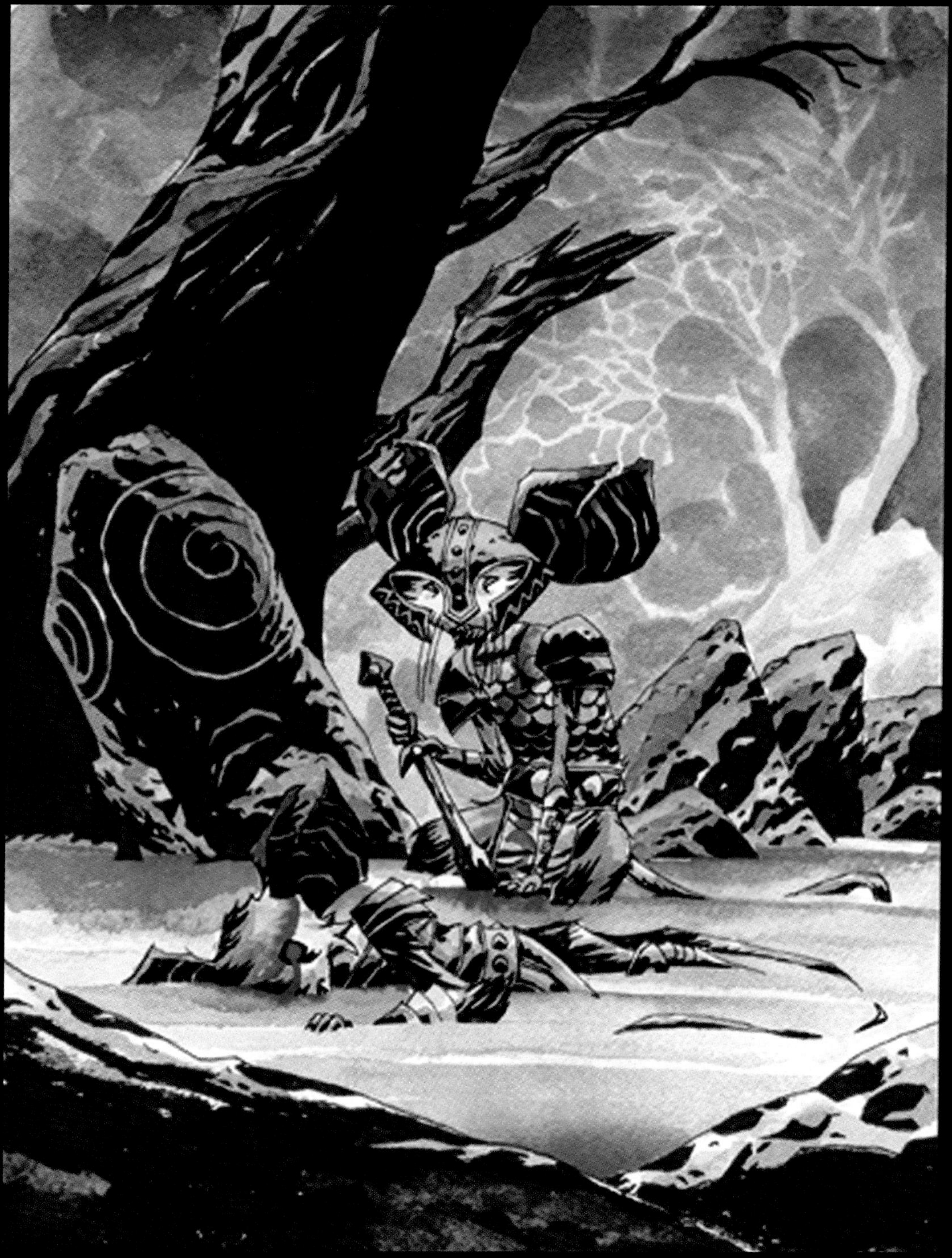

Painting by: Michael Avon Oeming
Commissioned for Heroes Initiative fundraiser
Dragon Con, 2007
heroinitiative.org

CREDITS & ACKNOWLEDGMENTS

THE MICE TEMPLAR
Created by Michael Avon Oeming & Bryan J.L. Glass

PRODUCTION TEAM
Wil Quintana • James H. Glass • Judy Glass • Will Swyer
Harry Lee • Tim Daniel

FOREWORD
Illustration: Mark Buckingham • buckycomics.blogspot.com
Illustration Colorist: D'Israeli • disraeli-demon.com/
Text: Bill Willingham • clockworkstorybook.net

MAP OF THE DARK LANDS
Brian Quinn • bcqillustrator.blogspot.com

"CASSIUS"
Glass & Oeming • James Glass

A HISTORY OF THE REALM
Bryan J.L. Glass & Dirk Shearer • myspace.com/projectdirk

MYTH, LEGENDS & THE MICE TEMPLAR
Tim Daniel • hiddenrobot.com
    Salmon of Knowledge: Brian Quinn • bcqillustrator.blogspot.com
    Merlin: Taki Soma • takisoma.com
    Young Arthur: Cat Staggs • airbrushcat.com
    Black Annis: Nic Klein • nic-klein.com
    Great Ash Tree: Robert Hack • roberthackstudios.com
    Knights Templar: Stuart Saygar • stuartsaygar.com

PIN-UP ILLUSTRATIONS
John Broglia • johnbroglia.blogspot.com
Val Staples • mvcreations.com
Ron Salas • zenwavearts.com
Victor Santos • victorsantoscomics.blogspot.com
Kelsey Shannon
Rob Reilly • skatoonproductions.blogspot.com
Kelsey Shannon
Michael Avon Oeming • hiddenrobot.com/MIKEOEMING/

SPECIAL THANKS
Kristyn Ferretti • Mike Freiheit (mikefreiheit.com) • Adam Levine • Marisol
Len O'Grady • Cris Peter • Image Comics: Branwyn Bigglestone, Drew Gill,
Allen Hui, Traci Hui, Joe Keatinge, Erik Larsen, Eric Stephenson, Jim Valentino

BRYAN J.L. GLASS

For as long as he can remember, Bryan has told stories. Expressing himself in a variety of media, all of his efforts inevitably returned him to the craft of storytelling. While originally pursuing a career in filmmaking, his first work in the comics industry was providing a photo-cover to Bill Willingham's *The Elementals* in 1983. That led to shooting another photo-cover for Matt Wagner's *Mage*, followed by a series of interior photos for Eliot R. Brown's *Punisher Armory* for Marvel Comics.

Exchanging his pursuit of film in the early '90s for the pursuit of writing, Bryan collaborated with his good friend Mike Oeming and created the indie comic series *Spandex Tights*, a humorous take on the superhero genre. When Mike's career soon took him away to work at the "Big Two," Bryan continued his series with artists P. Sky Owens, Bob Dix, Paul Bonanno and G.W. Fisher. Later, Bryan collaborated again with Mike Oeming on their dark humored sci-fi series *Ship of Fools*. But the comic industry itself seemed to collapse around them during this time, leading both partners to leave the field.

Mike's success on *Powers* enabled him to reunite with Bryan for the prose novel *Quixote*, in which he provided hundreds of spot illustrations. Their collaborations continued with *86 Voltz: The Dead Girl*, the comic adaptation of the Raymond E. Feist fantasy classic *Magician: Apprentice*, and *The Mice Templar*.

Outside of his comic work, Bryan founded the touring theatre troupe *mere*Breath Drama (mereBreath.com), alongside John J. McGready and Elliot Silver, where he served as producer, writer, director, and sometimes actor, in the original stage productions *Asylum*, *Perfect Justice*, *Edifice*, *Skit*, *The Eschaton*, and *The Inner Room*. Here is where he met Judy Hummel, his beloved wife—as well as his first and best editor.

Bryan appeared as the face of Eastern State Penitentiary's annual event, *Terror Behind the Walls*, as featured on the Travel Channel special, *America's Scariest Halloween Attractions*, where he can be seen having corn flakes applied to his face. He also achieved anonymous notoriety in 1997 as the infamous "Area 51 Caller" on the Art Bell *Coast-to-Coast* radio program—a call that can now be heard on the Tool album *Lateralus*: "Faaip de Oiad."

Bryan's three primary interests are books, movies, and music. J.R.R. Tolkien's *The Lord of the Rings*, Richard Adams's *Watership Down*, Stephen King's *The Shining*, Dan Simmons's *Hyperion*, and F. Paul Wilson's *The Keep* were all major influences in his life. *Casblanca* and *The Fisher King* are his favorite films. The film scores of John Williams, Jerry Goldsmith, Hans Zimmer, and Howard Shore typically accompany him as he writes. And he sings along to Kerry Livgren in each of his musical incarnations: Kansas, A.D., solo, and now reunited with his original band Proto-Kaw.

Bryan is currently developing a new sci-fi/horror series with illustrator Robert Hack. ◐

TheMiceTemplar@aol.com
hiddenrobot.com/BJLG/

Right: Oeming & Glass
East coast drink-n-draw
The Grey Lodge, Philly, 2007.

MICHAEL AVON OEMING

Mike began his comics career at the age of 14, breaking in as an inker. From inker to penciling/inking to writing, Mike has spread his creative wings in both indie and mainstream comics. Growing up in a small town, Mike found tutelage under Neil Vokes and Adam Hughes, while corresponding with *Nexus* creators Steve Rude and Mike Baron. Dedicated to his craft, Mike was eventually kicked out of high school for skipping class—to stay home and draw—and from his teens into his twenties, he languished in the indie field.

His first big break was as an inker on *Daredevil*, and shortly after as penciler/inker on DC's version of *Judge Dredd*, then *Foot Soldiers* at Dark Horse Comics. During the mid-'90s comics crash, Mike moved back into indie comics, starting on his path of creator-owned comics with *Ship of Fools*, co-created with Bryan J.L. Glass. While drawing *Ship of Fools*, Mike continued with other paying work, such as inking Neil Vokes on *Ninjack* and drawing *Bulletproof Monk*, which later became a John Woo film. Business was slow, so when Mike's first child was born, he got a "real job" working as a security guard—where he drew on the job, of course. This was when Mike experi-mented with a new, simpler style of drawing, and began developing several projects, including *The Mice Templar*, *Hammer of the Gods*, *Quixote*, and what would become *Powers* with Brian Michael Bendis, whom Mike had met several years earlier.

Powers became the dream project Mike and Brian had worked so hard for—a creator-owned project they could live on. *Powers* has been nominated for a Harvey Award and won an Eisner Award, and Mike himself was nominated for an Eisner for his work on the book. With *Powers* ongoing, Mike has since tackled several other projects, including *Hammer of the Gods*, *Bastard Samurai*, *Bluntman and Chronic*, *Parliament of Justice*, *Hellboy*, *Catwoman*, *86 Voltz: The Dead Girl*, *The Goon*, *Quixote*, *Blood River*, *Six*, *What If?*, *Magician: Apprentice* (with Bryan J.L. Glass) and has begun writing for Marvel Comics. His writing stint on the final run of *Thor* as well as on *Thor: Blood Oath* has been widely acclaimed. *Beta Ray Bill* and *Ares* are amongst his other writing credits, along with writing the monthly *Red Sonja* series.

Currently he is busy with *Powers*, *The Mice Templar* and the upcoming *Rapture* mini-series with creator Taki Soma... even as you read this. ◧

hiddenrobot.com/MIKEOEMING/

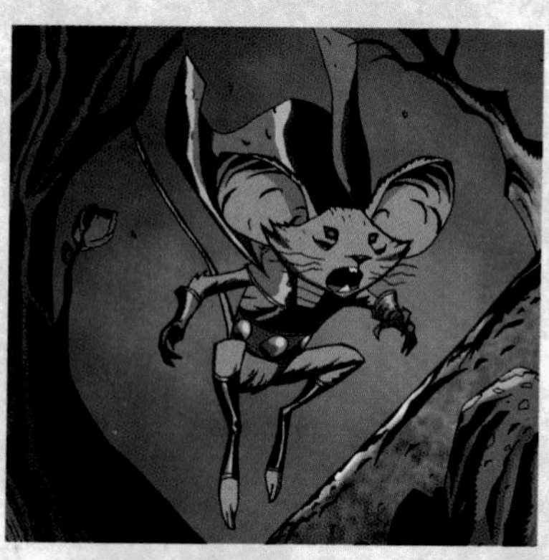

WIL QUINTANA
Wil first worked with Mike Oeming on the Marvel Comics graphic novel *Thor: Blood Oath* with art by Scott Kolins. His work in crafting natural tones is what inspired Mike to select him as the coloring artist to establish the look and color palette of the Mice Templar universe. Wil continues to apply his coloring artistry to a wide assortment of Marvel Comics titles.

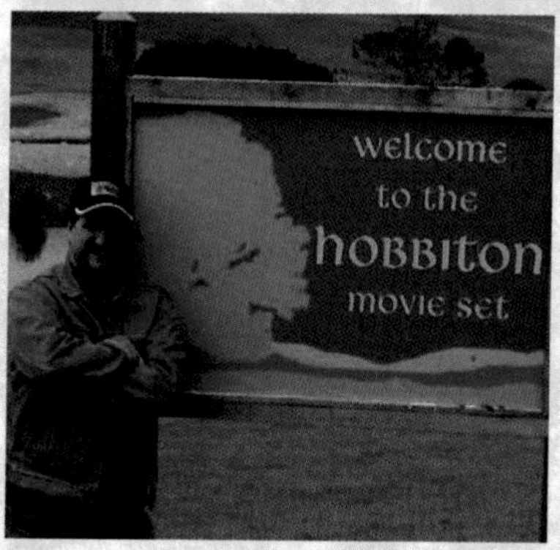
welcome
to the
hobbiton
movie set

JAMES H. GLASS
Despite his relationship to the author, there is absolutely no nepotism whatsoever responsible for securing Jim's distinquished position as *The Mice Templar* letterer. He has crafted a distinct voice for each race represented through his discerning use of font styles. Jim shares his love of great stories—fantasy, sci-fi, and sweeping historic narrative—with his brother Bryan, and is proud to be associated with the outstanding creative team responsible for this book.

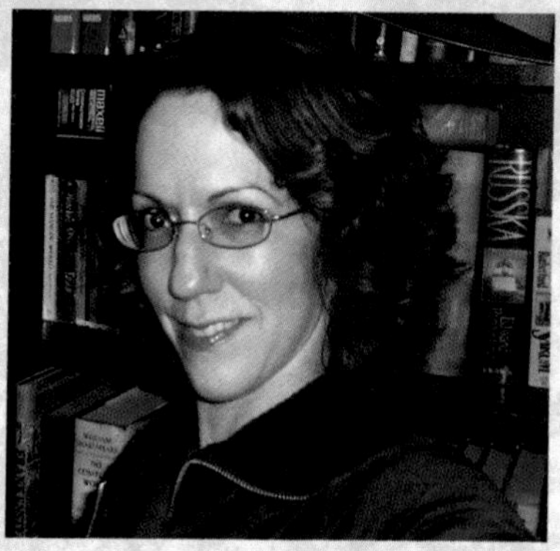

JUDY GLASS
Judy has always loved good books and stories, and from an early age aspired to write her own. While that hasn't yet materialized formally, she has nevertheless had a lifelong enjoyment and profound appreciation for the craft of writing and the art of a well-turned phrase, and has tended to gravitate to jobs and other venues that enable her to use these skills. As luck would have it, she met and married Bryan Glass, who has no lack of stories to tell and who proved a quick study on a few grammatical basics to hone and refine and thereby communicate the brilliant creative universes in his mind. Judy is privileged to be part of the team producing *The Mice Templar*.

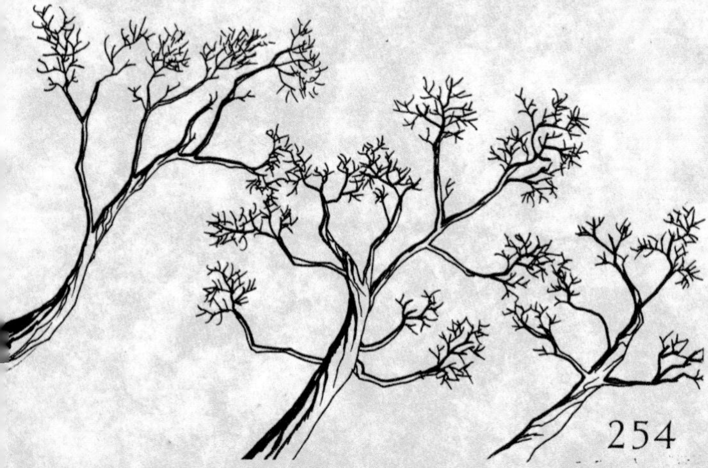

WILL SWYER

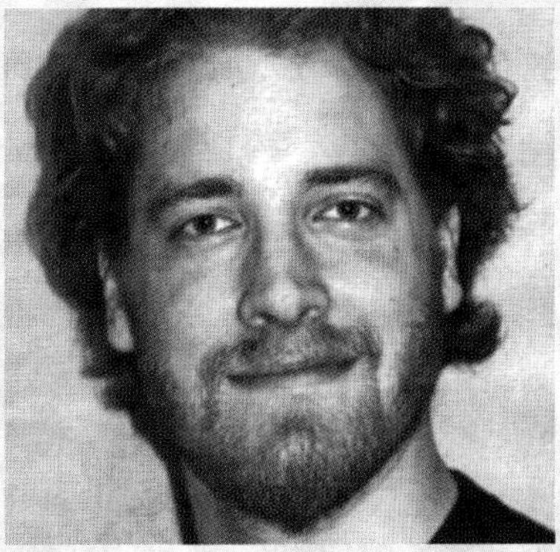

Will has worked previously with Bryan Glass in *mere*Breath Drama as producer, actor, and technical wizard. He is currently the Assistant Master Electrician at People's Light & Theatre. He writes and edits from his home in Philadelphia.

HARRY LEE

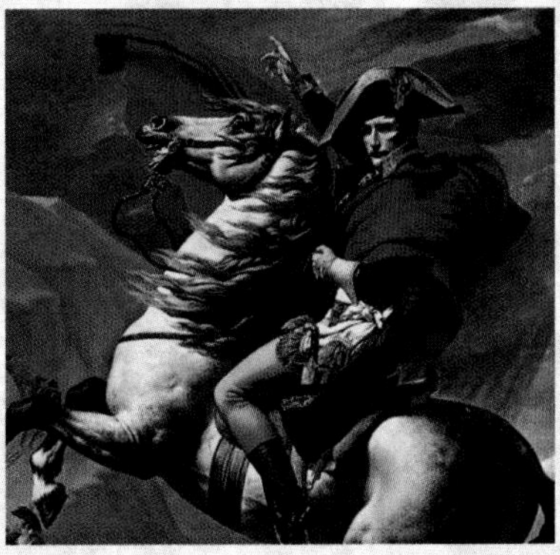

When not preoccupied conquering the world, or posing astride his mighty war horse to have his portrait painted, this mysterious and shadowy production hack loans his various and sundry talents to the care and feeding of small rodents. His basketball skills are legendary.

TIM DANIEL

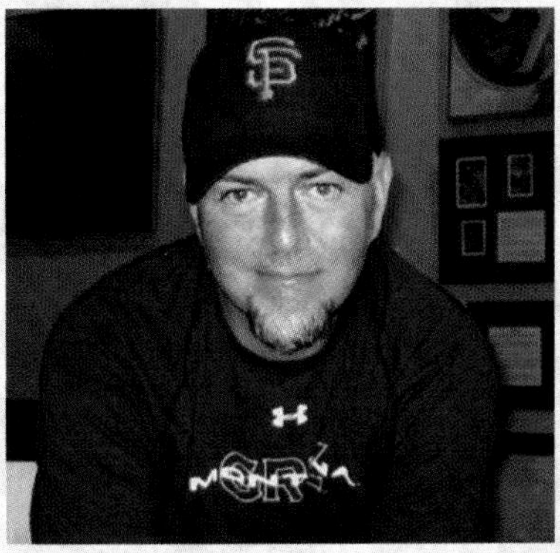
SF

Born in Philly, raised in Northern California, Tim discovered comics at about the time Jean Grey was sacrificing herself on a hidden moon base and saving humanity. In the process, she saved Tim too, opening the door to a lifelong love affair with comics. After earning a BA in English from Southern Oregon University in 1997, Tim fell in love with Erin, his now wife of 11 years, had a daughter (Elle), and has since gotten older but has never grown up. Tim has written for Image Comics' *Popgun Anthology* Vol. 2, the *Powers Encyclopedia*, and operates Hiddenrobot.com, host to some of the world's greatest comics' official websites and daily serial presentations!

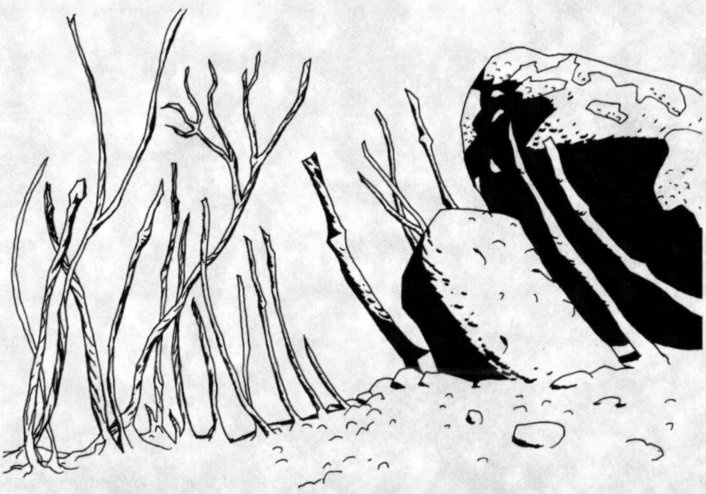

BY BRYAN J.L. GLASS

Magician: Apprentice
   Volumes 1 & 2
   Comic adaptation of the
   Raymond E. Feist novel

86 Volts: The Dead Girl
Quixote: A Novel
Ship of Fools
   Dante's Compass
   Death & Taxes

BY MICHAEL AVON OEMING

Powers
   Who Killed Retro Girl
   Roleplay
   Little Deaths
   Supergroup
   Anarchy
   Sellouts
   Forever
   Legends
   Psychotic
   Cosmic
   Secret Identity
   The 25 Coolest Dead Superheroes of All Time
Spider-Man/Red Sonja
Highlander Volume 1
Red Sonja: She-Devil with a Sword
   Volumes 1-5
Omega Flight: Alpha to Omega
Magician: Apprentice
   Volume 1 Comic Adaptation
The Cross Bronx
Thor: Blood Oath
Ares: God of War
Blood River
Wings of Anansi
Stormbreaker: The Saga of Beta Ray Bill

Doctor Cyborg
86 Voltz: The Dead Girl
Quixote: A Novel
Avengers: Disassembled—Thor
SIX
Parliament of Justice
Bastard Samurai
Hammer of the Gods
   Mortal Enemy
   Hammer Hits China
   Back From the Dead
Bluntman & Chronic
Bulletproof Monk
Ship of Fools
   Dante's Compass
   Death & Taxes
The Foot Soldiers

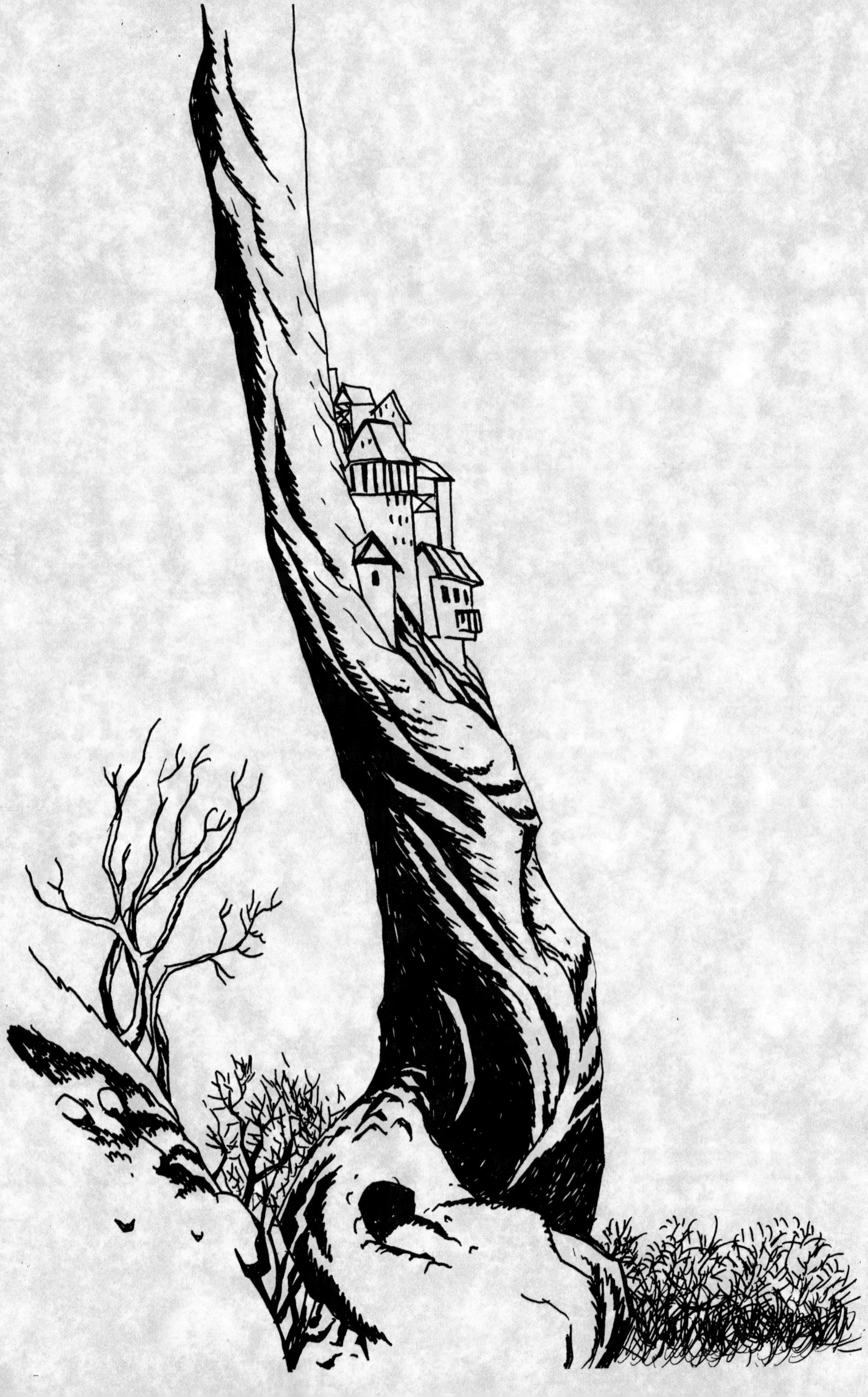